North Carolina Defender Manual

Julie Ramseur Lewis
John Rubin

Volume Two

Trial

Second Edition

2012

This manual is part of the North Carolina Indigent Defense Manual Series. Production of this series is made possible by funding from the North Carolina Office of Indigent Defense Services. John Rubin is series editor.

UNC
SCHOOL OF
GOVERNMENT

The School of Government at the University of North Carolina at Chapel Hill works to improve the lives of North Carolinians by engaging in practical scholarship that helps public officials and citizens understand and improve state and local government. Established in 1931 as the Institute of Government, the School provides educational, advisory, and research services for state and local governments. The School of Government is also home to a nationally ranked graduate program in public administration and specialized centers focused on information technology, environmental finance, and civic education for youth.

As the largest university-based local government training, advisory, and research organization in the United States, the School of Government offers up to 200 courses, seminars, and specialized conferences for more than 12,000 public officials each year. In addition, faculty members annually publish approximately fifty books, book chapters, bulletins, and other reference works related to state and local government. Each day that the General Assembly is in session, the School produces the *Daily Bulletin*, which reports on the day's activities for members of the legislature and others who need to follow the course of legislation.

The Master of Public Administration Program is a full-time, two-year program that serves up to sixty students annually. It consistently ranks among the best public administration graduate programs in the country, particularly in city management. With courses ranging from public policy analysis to ethics and management, the program educates leaders for local, state, and federal governments and nonprofit organizations.

Operating support for the School of Government's programs and activities comes from many sources, including state appropriations, local government membership dues, private contributions, publication sales, course fees, and service contracts. Visit www.sog.unc.edu or call 919.966.5381 for more information on the School's courses, publications, programs, and services.

Printed in the United States of America

21 20 19 18 17 2 3 4 5 6

ISBN 978-1-56011-688-2

Contents

Each chapter contains a detailed table of contents.

Preface to the Second Edition

I commandeered this preface so I could give proper credit to this manual's principal author, Julie Lewis. In 2002, after completing volume one of the Defender Manual on pretrial criminal procedure, we began working on volume two on trial procedure. During the next few years we released a few chapters—the "first edition"—but we were nowhere near completion. Then Julie Lewis joined the project. Julie and I assessed what the trial procedure volume should cover, and then she got down to the hard work of making the manual actually happen. She read and analyzed the ever-expanding body of cases on trial procedure as well as the broad array of pertinent statutes and rules, came up with a coherent approach for each chapter, and clearly, concisely, painstakingly, accurately, and insightfully laid out her legal analysis. I had the easy part, reviewing drafts, making suggestions, adding my ideas, and collaborating with Julie on each successive draft. I am proud to announce the release of this "second edition" of volume two of the Defender Manual. I have put quotation marks around "edition" because this is essentially a brand new resource for indigent defense attorneys. We also hope the manual will be useful to others who work in North Carolina's criminal courts. Although our principal aim was to create a manual for trial level criminal defense attorneys (and with that in mind incorporated numerous practice pointers), we recognize the importance of providing a full and accurate picture of the procedures that govern the trial of criminal cases.

Julie and I both want to express our gratitude to the organizations and people who supported this manual. Thanks go first to Kevin Tully, who heads the Office of the Public Defender for Mecklenburg County, and Staples Hughes, who heads the North Carolina Office of the Appellate Defender, for their willingness to share Julie's time for this project; in her spare moments Julie provides trial support to the attorneys in the Mecklenburg County Public Defender's Office and handles appeals for the Appellate Defender's Office. Thanks go as well to Tom Maher, who heads the North Carolina Office of Indigent Defense Services, for his continued support of this and other manuals in the North Carolina Indigent Defense Manual Series. Thanks also go to Janine Fodor and Jeanette Doran, who worked on earlier chapters of this volume of the manual; to legal editors Kathryn Burke and Paige C. Worsham, who scrutinized our research and tightened our analysis; to Katrina Hunt, Kevin Justice, and Dan Soileau at the School of Government and Susan Brooks at the Office of Indigent Defense Services, who helped with production of the manual; and to the print shops at the School of Government and the North Carolina Administrative Office of the Courts. In addition, I want to thank the indigent defense education team at the School of Government, Alyson Grine, Whitney Fairbanks, and Meredith Wales; without their talents and dedication, it would be impossible to juggle all of the education efforts we have going on at once. Last, Julie and I want to thank the many North Carolina attorneys who listened to our questions and shared their insights about the often challenging and sometimes puzzling practice of criminal law. Of course, any errors are our own.

This manual is current through February 2012. (We also could not resist adding two U.S. Supreme Court decisions from March 2012.) Comments and suggestions are welcome.

They may be sent to John Rubin at the UNC School of Government (rubin@sog.unc.edu or 919-962-2498) or Julie Lewis at the Mecklenburg County Public Defender's Office (julie.lewis@mecklenburgcountync.gov or 704-686-0956).

John Rubin
April 2012
Chapel Hill

About the North Carolina Indigent Defense Manual Series

The North Carolina Indigent Defense Manual Series is a collection of reference manuals addressing law and practice in areas in which indigent defendants and respondents are entitled to the representation of counsel at state expense. The series was created to address the need for comprehensive, up-to-date reference materials for public defenders and appointed counsel, who devote their time, skill, and effort to representing poor people. In addition to assisting indigent defenders with their responsibilities, the manuals also may be useful to others who work in the court system and who need a reference source on the law. In keeping with the School of Government's commitment to practical scholarship, the manuals are written by authors with subject-matter expertise in their respective fields, experience in developing effective educational materials, and knowledge of how things actually work in practice. The editor of the series is John Rubin, a member of the School of Government faculty who specializes in indigent defense education. For a current listing of manuals in the series, see www.sog.unc.edu/node/654. Production of the series is made possible by funding from the North Carolina Office of Indigent Defense Services, which is responsible for overseeing and enhancing the provision of indigent defense representation in North Carolina.

About the Authors of the North Carolina Defender Manual Volume 2, Trial (Second Edition)

Julie Ramseur Lewis has served as an assistant public defender in Charlotte since 1993. The majority of her practice is in the state appellate courts. She has also practiced in district and superior court and continues to provide trial support for the Office of the Mecklenburg County Public Defender. Before serving as an assistant public defender, Ms. Lewis clerked for Chief Judge R.A. Hedrick of the North Carolina Court of Appeals and thereafter was a staff attorney for the North Carolina Court of Appeals. She has also served as an adjunct professor of Legal Research and Writing at the University of North Carolina School of Law at Chapel Hill. Ms. Lewis earned a B.A. magna cum laude from Catawba College and a J.D. from the University of North Carolina at Chapel Hill.

John Rubin is a Professor of Public Law and Government at the School of Government. He joined the faculty in 1991 and specializes in criminal law and procedure and indigent defense education. In 2008, he received the Albert and Gladys Coates Term Award for Faculty Excellence. Before joining the School, he practiced law for nine years in Washington, D.C., and Los Angeles, California. He teaches, writes for, and consults with indigent defenders, judges, magistrates, and others who work in the court system. Mr. Rubin earned a B.A. from the University of California at Berkeley and a J.D. from the University of North Carolina at Chapel Hill.

Chapter 21
Personal Rights of Defendant

The Due Process Clause of the Fourteenth Amendment and the Fifth and Sixth Amendments to the U.S. Constitution, as well as article I, sections 19 and 23 of the N.C. Constitution, guarantee a defendant certain personal rights during his or her trial. North Carolina statutes supplement these rights. This chapter covers six personal rights of an accused:

- the right to be present at his or her trial,
- the right to confront witnesses in the courtroom,
- the right to choose whether to testify,
- the right to allocution,
- the right to appear for trial in civilian clothes, and
- the right to appear for trial free of physical restraints.

The scope of this chapter is limited to the above. It does not cover the right to counsel or the right to self-representation, which are covered in 1 NORTH CAROLINA DEFENDER MANUAL Ch. 12 (Right to Counsel) (Feb. 2004). Nor does it discuss the defendant's rights to expert assistance, addressed in 1 NORTH CAROLINA DEFENDER MANUAL Ch. 5 (Experts and Other Assistance) (May 1998). This chapter also does not fully address a defendant's confrontation rights during trial or the defendant's privilege against self-incrimination.

21.1 Right to Be Present

A. Basis of Right

Summary of law. A defendant's right to presence depends on several sources of law, and the cases occasionally combine and confuse them. This brief summary offers the authors' understanding of the basic legal principles.

Once the trial begins, a defendant has a right to be present at every stage of trial under the Confrontation Clause of the U.S. Constitution and its counterpart under the N.C. Constitution. The right to presence applies not only to stages of the trial in which the defendant is actually confronting witnesses but also to stages at which testimony is not being offered, such as jury selection. Under the state constitution, a capital defendant's right to presence at every stage of the trial cannot be waived.

Some matters that take place during trial may not be considered stages of the trial and so may not trigger a defendant's right to presence under the federal and state confrontation clauses. A defendant still may have a due process right to presence, which applies whenever the defendant's presence has a reasonably substantial relation to his or her opportunity to defend against the charges.

Before trial, a defendant's right to presence depends primarily on due process. The courts have recognized a defendant's right to presence at pretrial proceedings that implicate the defendant's confrontation rights—that is, proceedings at which witnesses are giving testimony or other evidence is being presented—or when the defendant's presence has a reasonably substantial relation to his or her opportunity to defend against the charges. The right is not absolute and depends on the particular proceedings at issue.

North Carolina statutes also may supplement the defendant's constitutional rights by guaranteeing the defendant a right to presence at particular proceedings, such as jury views (discussed in subsection C., below).

When the courts have found no violation of the right to presence, they sometimes hold specifically that a defendant does not have a right to presence at the proceeding—for example, at grand jury proceedings before trial. Often, however, they base a finding of no violation, at least in part, on a form of waiver—that is, the failure of the defendant or counsel to request that the defendant be present during the proceeding. The courts also have engaged in harmless error analysis without specifically deciding whether the defendant had a right to presence and the trial judge erred. This analysis makes it difficult to say in some instances whether the defendant does or does not have a right to be present.

Practice note: If a proceeding or other matter begins without the defendant being present, and you believe that the defendant has a right to be present or that at least it is in the defendant's interest to be present, you should specifically request the defendant's presence in reliance on the constitutional and statutory authorities discussed below.

Federal constitution. The Confrontation Clause of the Sixth Amendment to the U.S. Constitution guarantees a defendant the right to personal presence at ***every stage of trial.*** *See Illinois v. Allen*, 397 U.S. 337 (1970); *see generally* 6 WAYNE R. LAFAVE ET AL., CRIMINAL PROCEDURE § 24.2(a), at 309 (3d ed. 2007) (recognizing principle); ROBERT L. FARB, NORTH CAROLINA CAPITAL CASE LAW HANDBOOK 70 (UNC School of Government, 2d ed. 2004) (recognizing principle in capital cases). Some North Carolina cases have stated that the Sixth Amendment right to presence under the U.S. Constitution applies only to *critical* stages of trial, in contrast to the broader state constitutional right to presence, discussed next, at *every* stage of trial. *See State v. Huff*, 325 N.C. 1, 29 (1989) (citing *Rushen v. Spain*, 464 U.S. 114 (1983)), *vacated on other grounds*, 497 U.S. 1021 (1990); *State v. Buchanan*, 330 N.C. 202 (1991) (repeating statement from *Huff*). The statement of the federal standard in these North Carolina decisions appears to be incorrect. *See State v. Golphin*, 352 N.C. 364, 389 (2000) (relying on *Illinois v. Allen*, 397 U.S. 337 (1970), and recognizing the defendant's right to be present at every stage of trial under the Sixth Amendment Confrontation Clause). As a practical matter, however, federal cases may construe the federal right to presence more narrowly than North Carolina courts have interpreted the state constitutional right to presence. Application of the right to various proceedings is discussed further in the succeeding sections.

The Confrontation Clause also may give the defendant a right to presence at ***pretrial proceedings*** at which testimony or other evidence is presented. *See State v. Seaberry*, 97 N.C. App. 203, 210–11 (1990) (in addressing whether defendant had right to be present at hearing on pretrial motions, court states in reliance on *Illinois v. Allen*, 397 U.S. 337 (1970), that "[t]he Confrontation Clause of the Sixth Amendment made applicable to the states by the Fourteenth Amendment grants defendants the right to be present at any stage of the proceedings at which witnesses are to be questioned"). *But cf. Kentucky v. Stincer*, 482 U.S. 730, 740 (1987) (finding in child sex abuse case that defendant did not have right to presence at hearing to determine competency of child witnesses to testify).

The defendant also has a due process right under the Fourteenth Amendment to be present at a proceeding "whenever his presence has a relation, reasonably substantial, to the fullness of his opportunity to defend against the charge." *Snyder v. Massachusetts*, 291 U.S. 97, 105–06 (1934) (announcing test); *see also Kentucky v. Stincer*, 482 U.S. 730, 745 ("[A] defendant is guaranteed the right to be present at any stage of the criminal proceeding that is critical to its outcome if his presence would contribute to the fairness of the procedure."). This due process right gives the defendant the right to presence at various pretrial proceedings as well as at trial proceedings at which the right to confrontation may not apply. The right includes "situations where the defendant is not actually confronting witnesses or evidence against him." *United States v. Gagnon*, 470 U.S. 522, 526 (1985) (per curiam).

State constitution. A defendant's right to presence under the Confrontation Clause of the N.C. Constitution (N.C. CONST. art. I, § 23) is broader than the right to presence under the federal constitution in two respects. First, the North Carolina courts have held that the state constitutional right is broader than its federal counterpart in that it guarantees the defendant's right to be present at *every* stage of his or her trial. *See State v. Badgett*, 361 N.C. 234 (2007); *State v. Huff*, 325 N.C. 1 (1989), *vacated on other grounds*, 497 U.S. 1021 (1990). While the U.S. Constitution also guarantees the right to presence at *every* stage of trial (in light of the cases discussed above), the state constitutional protection may be broader as applied to different trial proceedings (discussed in subsection C., below). The state right "extends to all times during the trial when anything is said or done which materially affects defendant as to the charge against him." *State v. Chapman*, 342 N.C. 330, 337–38 (1995). Although the defendant's right to presence is typically discussed in the context of proceedings inside the courtroom, the right to be present also can attach to proceedings outside the courtroom during the trial, such as if a judge communicates to jurors in the jury room or to counsel in the court's chambers. *See State v. Hudson*, 331 N.C. 122 (1992) (recognizing this principle but finding that chance meeting between judge and juror in corridor might not constitute "stage" of trial and, if error, it was harmless beyond a reasonable doubt); *State v. Buchanan*, 330 N.C. 202 (1991) (providing wide range of examples of stages).

Second, the state constitution offers greater protection to capital defendants than the federal constitution because a capital defendant's right to presence cannot be waived and the trial judge has the duty to ensure the defendant's presence at trial. *See infra* § 21.1E, Waiver of Right.

The North Carolina courts have stated that in general the right to presence under the state constitution's confrontation clause does not guarantee the defendant's presence before the trial commences. *See, e.g., State v. Golphin*, 352 N.C. 364, 389 (2000) (finding no violation of state constitutional right to presence at pretrial discussions with judge about possible venues for trial; defendants were present at later hearing at which their counsel stipulated to the venue change); *cf.* ROBERT L. FARB, NORTH CAROLINA CAPITAL CASE LAW HANDBOOK 70 & n.4 (UNC School of Government, 2d ed. 2004) (noting cases in which capital defendants did not have the right to be present at the pretrial proceedings at issue, but observing that the N.C. Supreme Court "has not definitively decided whether or to what extent this unwaivable right exists at pretrial stages").

Practice note: Because the U.S. and N.C. Constitutions may provide different protections, be sure to ground any objection to a presence violation on both the federal and the state constitution.

B. Pretrial Proceedings

Generally, the defendant's right to be present at every stage of trial "does not arise prior to the commencement of trial." *State v. Chapman*, 342 N.C. 330, 338 (1995) (determining that a conference that took place before the jury panel was selected and sworn was not "a stage of the trial" and the defendant's right to be present at "every stage of his trial" was not implicated). However, if the subject matter of the hearing "implicates the defendant's confrontation rights, or is such that the defendant's presence would have a reasonably substantial relation to his opportunity to defend," then he or she has the right to be present. *See State v. Buchanan*, 330 N.C. 202, 223–24 (1991). For a further discussion of the applicable constitutional principles, see *supra* § 21.1A, Basis of Right.

Evidentiary hearings. Under the above principles, a defendant generally has the right to be present at hearings involving the examination of witnesses, such as suppression hearings, voir dire determinations, and other proceedings involving the presentation of evidence or determination of the admissibility of evidence at trial. *See State v. Seaberry*, 97 N.C. App. 203 (1990); *see also State v. Trapper*, 48 N.C. App. 481 (1980) (finding no prejudice from sequestration of defendants during testimony of witnesses during suppression hearing because their exclusion was for a short period of time and trial judge soon after reversed his sequestration order); *State v. Braswell*, 312 N.C. 553 (1985) (recognizing defendant's right to be present during mid-trial voir dire of witness, but finding that defendant waived right); *State v. Jones*, 89 N.C. App. 584 (1988) (recognizing defendant's right to be present at proceeding to determine competency of child witness in sexual abuse case, but finding that defendant's right was not violated because defendant could see and hear testimony via closed-circuit television and had adequate opportunity to communicate with his attorney). *But cf. Kentucky v. Stincer*, 482 U.S. 730, 740 (1987) (finding under U.S. Constitution that defendant could be excluded from voir dire hearing to determine competency of child witness in sexual abuse case even without an opportunity to see and hear proceedings). [For a further discussion of the use of closed-circuit television for certain witnesses, see *infra* § 29.4D, Child Witnesses (exclusion of defendant from competency hearing involving child witness) and § 29.8, Remote Testimony.]

Non-evidentiary proceedings. A number of cases have found no violation of the defendant's right to presence during certain non-evidentiary pretrial proceedings or communications. Many of these cases involved housekeeping or administrative matters that did not implicate the defendant's constitutional rights. In some that involved more substantive proceedings, the courts did not definitively resolve whether the defendant had a right to be present, finding no violation based, in part, on the defendant's failure through counsel to request that the defendant be present or on the absence of prejudice to the defendant. The cases finding no presence violation include ones involving:

- A Rule 24 hearing on whether a case was to be tried capitally. *State v. Chapman*, 342 N.C. 330 (1995) (finding no violation of capital defendant's unwaivable right to presence at trial because Rule 24 hearing is pretrial proceeding and not stage of trial). Notwithstanding *Chapman*, the defendant in a capital case is typically present at a Rule 24 hearing.
- A meeting between prosecutors, defense attorneys, and the judge to discuss possible change of venue sites or special venire locations where the defendants were present at a later hearing at which their counsel stipulated to the venue change. *State v. Golphin*, 352 N.C. 364 (2000).
- A pretrial conference on "housekeeping matters," including the trial's daily schedule, the basics of publicity, security in the courtroom, the jury selection procedure (which had previously been discussed), and the availability of a jury questionnaire, as well as a brief, nonbinding review of pending motions and a discussion of the possibility of a motion to continue. *State v. Buckner*, 342 N.C. 198 (1995).
- A hearing on a pretrial motion for discovery where defense counsel was present, consented to the defendant's absence, and the defendant could show no resulting prejudice. *State v. Davis*, 290 N.C. 511 (1976).
- An announcement of a ruling in open court by the trial judge regarding a decision to partially release the defendant's prison records to the State. *State v. Rich*, 346 N.C. 50, 56 (1997) (finding that "[a]lthough a better practice in this case may have been for the judge to have summoned defendant and defense counsel prior to announcing his final ruling," there was no error and defendant's presence would have served no purpose).
- A routine communication between the judge and the prosecutor concerning scheduling matters. *State v. Locklear*, 349 N.C. 118 (1998) (defendant had no right to be present when prosecutor requested that the judge schedule an arraignment hearing).
- A hearing with defense counsel present on motions for a special venire, consolidation of the cases, sequestration of witnesses, and change in venue where "at no time did counsel suggest the absence of defendants or note exceptions to their absence." *State v. Richards*, 21 N.C. App. 686, 690 (1974).
- An alleged in-chambers proceeding resulting in the trial judge changing the forensic psychiatrist assigned to evaluate the defendant. *State v. Davis*, 349 N.C. 1 (1998).
- The disinterment of the remains of the deceased. *State v. Bowman*, 80 N.C. 432 (1879).
- The grand jury's return of an indictment. *State v. Stanley*, 227 N.C. 650 (1947).

C. Trial Proceedings

Stages of a trial at which a defendant has a constitutional right to presence include, of course, any part of the trial involving the testimony of witnesses or other presentation of evidence. *See generally Illinois v. Allen*, 397 U.S. 337 (1970); *Snyder v. Massachusetts*, 291 U.S. 97 (1934); *Diaz v. United States*, 223 U.S. 442 (1912). The defendant also has a right to presence, as described below, at other aspects of the trial.

Jury selection. Once the defendant's case has been called for trial, the defendant's right to be present during the process of selecting and impaneling the jury attaches. *Diaz v. United States*, 223 U.S. 442, 455. A judge therefore may not have private, unrecorded communications with a prospective juror in order to determine whether or not the juror may be excused. *State v. Smith*, 326 N.C. 792, 794 (1990) ("The process of selecting and impaneling the jury is a stage of the trial at which the defendant has a right to be present."). Nor may a judge question jurors in the defendant's absence even if defense counsel is present and the proceedings are recorded. *State v. Payne*, 328 N.C. 377 (1991).

The defendant's right to be present during all stages of trial does not include the preliminary handling of jury venires before the defendant's case has been called. *State v. Workman*, 344 N.C. 482, 498 (1996) (defendant "had no right to be present when prospective jurors were preliminarily sworn, oriented and qualified for jury service in general, without regard to any particular case or trial"); *see also State v. Williams*, 363 N.C. 689, 710 (2009) (random splitting of jury pool for "defendant's proceeding and other matters being handled at the courthouse that day was a preliminary administrative matter at which defendant did not have a right to be present").

Nor is a defendant's right to presence violated by a judge's private communications with prospective jurors if the defendant's case has not yet been called for trial. *State v. Rannels*, 333 N.C. 644 (1993) (no error where trial judge held unrecorded side bar conferences with jurors before any case on calendar was called and before oath was administered to jury pool); *State v. Cole*, 331 N.C. 272 (1992) (no error where judge held unrecorded bench conferences and excused prospective jurors before defendant's case was called for trial, but it was error to do so after the defendant's trial commenced).

Jury view. In an early U.S. Supreme Court decision, before many constitutional protections were made applicable to state criminal proceedings by incorporation through the Due Process Clause (such as the right of a defendant not to testify), the Court held that the Due Process Clause did not require the defendant's presence at a jury view during trial unless a fair and just hearing would be thwarted by his or her absence. *See Snyder v. Massachusetts*, 291 U.S. 97, 107–08 (1934). Assuming this principle remains valid under the U.S. Constitution, a defendant in North Carolina nevertheless has a statutory and a state constitutional right to be present at that proceeding. *See* N.C. GEN. STAT. § 15A-1229(a) (hereinafter G.S.); *State v. Harris*, 333 N.C. 543 (1993) (recognizing state constitutional right to presence during jury view, but finding that right was not violated by permitting jurors to roam independently through the alleged crime scene during the jury view while the defendant was present).

In-chambers conferences with counsel. A defendant has the right to presence at an in-chambers conference during trial. *State v. Buchanan*, 330 N.C. 202 (1991) (finding that to the extent that federal courts do not treat in-chambers conferences as a "stage" of trial, the defendant's state constitutional right to presence is broader). It is error for a trial judge, during trial, to "conduct an in-chambers conference with the attorneys but without the defendant." *See State v. Exum*, 343 N.C. 291, 295 (1996) (characterizing an in-chambers conference as a "critical stage" of trial). *But cf. State v. Daniels*, 337 N.C. 243

(1994) (judge's telephone calls over the weekend to prosecutor and defense counsel after trial had commenced, in which trial judge merely informed them of the decision she had reached and heard no argument were not "such a stage" of the defendant's trial as to require the defendant's presence; judge announced ruling in open court the following day).

Although exclusion of the defendant is error, it will be found to be "harmless error" if nothing was done or said during the in-chambers conference that affects the defendant as to the charge against him or her "in any material respect." *See State v. Brogden*, 329 N.C. 534, 541–42 (1991) (finding harmless error where an informal meeting was held in chambers with only the attorneys to discuss the jury instructions before the formal charge conference held in open court); *see also State v. Boyd*, 343 N.C. 699 (1996) (harmless error found where a recorded in-chambers conference was held with the attorneys, outside the presence of defendant, to discuss proposed mitigating circumstances; defense counsel was given the opportunity to preserve on the record every objection to the trial judge's rulings and the reasons for their objections, and the substance of each of the defendant's requested mitigating circumstances discussed during the conference was later submitted to the jury).

Where the right to presence is not waived or is not waivable (*see infra* § 21.1E, Waiver of Right) and the subject matter of the in-chambers conference cannot be gleaned from the record, the State cannot meet its burden of showing that the error was harmless beyond a reasonable doubt and the defendant is entitled to a new trial. *See, e.g., State v. Meyer*, 345 N.C. 619 (1997) (granting new capital sentencing hearing where trial judge held an in-chambers discussion with attorneys during jury selection, the substance of which was not summarized on the record in open court or otherwise gleanable from the record); *Exum*, 343 N.C. 291 (capital defendant granted a new trial because the trial judge held a private in-chambers conference with the attorneys after a defense expert's testimony and the substance of the private discussions was not revealed in the record).

Bench conferences with counsel. The North Carolina courts have held that bench conferences are a stage of trial and that the defendant's state constitutional right to presence attaches; however, the defendant's rights are not necessarily violated if the defendant is not at the bench itself.

Generally, a defendant's constitutional right to be present is not violated "when, with defendant present in the courtroom, the trial court conducts bench conferences, even though unrecorded, with counsel for both parties." *See State v. Buchanan*, 330 N.C. 202, 223 (1991). Holding a bench conference without the defendant present is permissible if the subject of the bench conference is a point of law, a procedural matter, or an administrative matter, and the conference does not involve communication with the jury or testimony by a witness concerning the defendant's guilt. *See State v. Robinson*, 330 N.C. 1 (1991). "If, however, the subject matter of the conference implicates the defendant's confrontation rights, or is such that the defendant's presence would have a reasonably substantial relation to his opportunity to defend, the defendant would have a constitutional right to be present" at the bench conference itself. *Buchanan*, 330 N.C.

202, 223–24. The defendant bears the burden of showing the "usefulness" of his or her presence to prove a violation of the right to presence. "Once a violation of the right is apparent, the burden shifts to the State to show that it is harmless beyond a reasonable doubt." *Id.* at 224.

Although the defendant was not actually present at the bench with the attorneys in *Buchanan*, the N.C. Supreme Court reasoned that there was no constitutional violation of the right to presence since the defendant was personally present in the courtroom. By holding a bench conference with counsel for both sides, the trial judge did not "negate" the defendant's actual presence at all stages of the trial. *See Buchanan*, 330 N.C. 202, 223. According to the court, the defendant was able to observe the context of the conference and obtain first-hand knowledge of what transpired through his attorneys. Defense counsel was free to raise for the record any matters to which the defendant took exception. The court also found it relevant that conferences typically deal with nonprejudicial administrative matters or "legal matters with which an accused is likely unfamiliar and incapable of rendering meaningful assistance." *Id.*

Federal courts have generally interpreted the federal right to presence at bench conferences more narrowly than the state right is interpreted by North Carolina courts. Some federal cases, discussed in *Buchanan*, have found no right to presence on the ground that a bench conference is not a "stage" of the trial, but North Carolina courts have rejected that rationale in favor of the above approach.

Practice note: If the judge conducts a bench conference without the defendant present, and you believe that it implicates the defendant's confrontation rights or that the defendant's presence would have a reasonably substantial relation to his or her opportunity to defend against the charges, you should immediately object to the defendant's absence from the conference on state and federal constitutional grounds and assert for the record the reasons that the defendant's presence would be useful. Even in situations in which you do not object because you do not believe that the defendant's presence would be useful, you should ask afterward that the subject matter of the bench conference be placed on the record to ensure a complete record for appellate purposes.

Voir dire of witnesses. A defendant has the right to be present during a voir dire to determine the admissibility of evidence. *See supra* § 21.1B, Pretrial Proceedings (discussing right to presence at evidentiary hearings).

Summation. A defendant has the right to be present during closing arguments. *See Snyder v. Massachusetts*, 291 U.S. 97, 106 (1934) (assuming that defendants have a right under the Due Process Clause to be present at the "summing up of counsel, for it will be in his power, if present, to give advice or suggestion or even to supersede his lawyers altogether and conduct the trial himself"); *see also Larson v. Tansy*, 911 F.2d 392, 396 (10th Cir. 1990) (concluding that the defendant had a due process right to be present at the giving of jury instructions, closing statements, and rendering of the verdict; the denial of this right was not harmless error because there was "a reasonable possibility of prejudice to defendant in that his absence precluded him from providing any assistance to his attorney and from exerting any psychological influence on the jury"); *State v. Okumura*, 570 P.2d 848, 853 (Haw. 1977) (State failed to meet its burden of showing that defendant's absence from jury instructions, closing argument, and rendition of the verdict was harmless beyond a reasonable doubt; presence of defense counsel could not render error harmless per se because "'the presence of counsel is no substitute for the presence of the defendant himself'" (citation omitted)).

Charge conference. A defendant has a right to be present during the charge conference. *See State v. Brogden*, 329 N.C. 534 (1991) (error for judge to hold informal meeting to discuss jury instructions in chambers out of defendant's presence, but harmless because a formal charge conference was then held in open court where entire matter was entered into the record and counsel made legal arguments and took exceptions); *State v. Wise*, 326 N.C. 421 (1990) (holding that error, if any, in excluding defendant from the unrecorded charge conference was harmless where the trial judge subsequently announced the proposed instructions on the record and gave counsel an opportunity to be heard).

Judge instructions to or communications with jury. Once the defendant's case has been called for trial, the trial judge may not privately communicate with any member of the jury in the absence of the defendant. *See State v. Payne*, 320 N.C. 138 (1987) (right to presence violated where judge gave admonishments to the jury in the jury room); *State v. Buckom*, 100 N.C. App. 179 (1990) (reversible error occurred where judge engaged in ex parte communication with jury in jury room before the verdict and record did not disclose the content of the discussion); *cf. State v. Wilson*, 363 N.C. 478 (2009) (trial judge violated defendant's right to a unanimous verdict under N.C. Constitution article I, section 24 by holding unrecorded bench conferences with jury foreperson in which he gave instructions to that juror and not others; judge also told juror not to discuss those issues with the other jurors when he returned to the jury room); *State v. Ashe*, 314 N.C. 28, 36 (1985) (it is a violation of a defendant's right to a unanimous verdict under N.C. Constitution article I, section 24 for a judge to communicate instructions privately to "a jury foreman, another individual juror, or anyone else" regarding matters material to the case and then have that person relay the instructions to the full jury because all twelve jurors must be instructed consistently).

Bailiff communications with jury. Cases have held that where the bailiff enters the jury room to give clerical instructions, such as permitting the jury to take a break, there is not a presence violation. *See, e.g., State v. Gay*, 334 N.C. 467, 483 (1993) (finding no reversible error but acknowledging that trial judge's procedure in having the bailiff instruct the jury regarding breaks and reminding them to follow the judge's earlier instructions "may run the risk of violating defendant's right to be present"); *State v. May*, 334 N.C. 609 (1993) (no constitutional violation where judge instructed the bailiff to tell the jury to take a fifteen minute break); *State v. Coleman*, 161 N.C. App. 224 (2003) (no constitutional violation where trial judge had bailiff admonish a juror, outside the presence of the defendant, not to discuss the case with anyone).

Clerk communications with jury. There is not a presence violation when the court clerk, outside the presence of the defendant, speaks with the jury about administrative matters if the matters discussed are not substantive, they do not relate to the consideration of the defendant's guilt or innocence, and the defendant cannot show that his or her presence would have a reasonably substantial relation to his or her opportunity to defend. *See, e.g., State v. Golphin*, 352 N.C. 364 (2000) (no constitutional violation where judge had clerk perform administrative duties outside defendant's presence, including providing logistical information to newly selected jurors); *State v. Bacon*, 337 N.C. 66 (1994) (no constitutional violation where trial judge had clerk, outside defendant's presence, perform the administrative duties of calling the jury roll and explaining to the jurors what time they needed to arrive at court).

Verdict. A defendant has the right to be present at the return of the verdict. *Diaz v. United States*, 223 U.S. 442, 455 (1912) (recognizing right); *State v. Harris*, 27 N.C. App. 15, 20 (1975) (holding that although the non-capital defendant had a right to be present at the rendition of the verdict, he waived this right where there was nothing in the record "to indicate that the absence of defendant and his counsel was other than voluntary"); *see also State v. Webster*, 111 N.C. App. 72 (1993) (any error in the acceptance of the verdict against defendant in her absence was harmless because the judge had already explained to the jury that defendant was absent for good cause shown, defense counsel was present, and defendant's presence at that stage of the proceedings could not have made a difference to the outcome of the trial), *aff'd*, 337 N.C. 674 (1994).

Sentencing. A defendant has the right to be present "'when evidence is introduced for the purpose of determining the amount of punishment to be imposed'" or when sentence is actually imposed. *State v. Davis*, 186 N.C. App. 242, 249 (2007) (quoting *State v. Pope*, 257 N.C. 326, 330 (1962)); *see also State v. Crumbley*, 135 N.C. App. 59 (1999) (sentence vacated and the matter remanded for the entry of a new sentencing judgment where the trial judge, in the defendant's absence, substantively altered the original sentence when entering the written judgment to make the sentences run consecutively instead of concurrently); *State v. Midyette*, 87 N.C. App. 199 (1987) (after noting that a defendant is to be present when oral testimony concerning punishment is heard, the appellate court cautioned against in camera hearings such as the recorded one held here with attorneys and rape victim, but without the defendant, to permit the victim to express her views about appropriate punishment and without an opportunity for the defendant to rebut the information received by the court), *aff'd per curiam*, 322 N.C. 108 (1988).

The right of a defendant to be present at the time "sentence or judgment is pronounced is a common law right, separate and apart from the constitutional or statutory right to be present at the trial." *Pope*, 257 N.C. 326, 330; *see also Ball v. United States*, 140 U.S. 118, 129 (1891) ("At common law no judgment for corporal punishment could be pronounced against a man in his absence . . . .").

The right to presence at sentencing appears to apply to all felony and misdemeanor cases where a "corporal" sentence is imposed—i.e., one that includes a sentence of imprisonment, active or suspended. *See State v. Cherry*, 154 N.C. 624 (1911) (setting aside judgments sentencing defendants "to a term of 12 months on the roads" and remanding case for new sentencing hearing where defendants had voluntarily absented themselves from trial and sentencing after the first day); *State v. Beasley*, 118 N.C. App. 508 (1995) (remanding case for new sentencing hearing where, after the sentencing hearing and outside of defendant's presence, the trial judge added an aggravating factor to the judgment imposing a sentence of active imprisonment, among other errors). No constitutional violation appears to occur if the defendant is sentenced in absentia as long as he or she does not receive a sentence of imprisonment. *See State v. Ferebee*, 266 N.C. 606 (1966) (finding no constitutional error where judge pronounced judgment in defendant's absence imposing a fine and costs but no active or suspended sentence of imprisonment was imposed; defendant waived presence).

Not only does a defendant have a right to be present at sentencing if a sentence of imprisonment is imposed, he or she *must* be present unless the defendant expressly waives the right. No waiver of the right to be present at sentencing will be inferred even if the defendant is voluntarily absent from trial and sentencing. *See State v. Stockton*, 13 N.C. App. 287, 292 (1971) (trial judge erred in sentencing defendant in absentia to not less than two years nor more than five years in prison because "when a sentence involving corporal punishment is imposed upon a verdict, either on a capital felony charge, a felony charge less than capital, or a misdemeanor, the defendant must be present"); *see also infra* § 21.1E, Waiver of Right (discussing waiver further, including requirements for express waiver and that no waiver is inferred from a defendant's absence at sentencing).

Juvenile Proceedings. Juveniles have a state constitutional right to presence in delinquency hearings similar to that afforded to adult criminal defendants. *In re Lineberry*, 154 N.C. App. 246 (2002) (error, but harmless, for judge to hold an in-chambers discussion with defense counsel and prosecutor involving a conference call with the doctor who performed the court-ordered evaluation).

D. Post-Conviction Proceedings

The courts have found no constitutional right to presence on a motion for a new trial or similar motion. *See State v. Dry*, 152 N.C. 813 (1910) (so stating generally); *see also Barber v. United States*, 142 F.2d 805, 806 (4th Cir. 1944) (petitioner had no federal constitutional right to be present at a hearing of his motion for a new trial, filed six years after conviction, because "[s]uch a hearing is in no sense a part of the criminal trial at which the Constitution requires the presence of the accused"). A defendant has a statutory right under G.S. 15A-1420(c) to be present at an evidentiary hearing on a motion for appropriate relief (and perhaps a due process and confrontation right because of the nature of the proceeding).

The courts also have found no right to presence on appeal of asserted legal errors in the trial. *See State v. Jacobs*, 107 N.C. 772 (1890); *State v. Overton*, 77 N.C. 485 (1877); *see also Schwab v. Berggren*, 143 U.S. 442, 449 (1892) (neither reason nor public policy require that a defendant be personally present pending proceedings in an appellate court, especially where he or she has counsel to represent him in the court of review).

E. Waiver of Right

This discussion concerns the waiver of presence at trial following a *not guilty* plea. A defendant may enter a guilty plea, without being present, to relatively minor offenses, such as traffic offenses or misdemeanors for which the judge has accepted a written waiver of appearance. For a discussion of a defendant's entry of a guilty plea through counsel, see *infra* § 23.4I, Guilty Pleas through Counsel.

Capital cases. Under the N.C. Constitution, a capital defendant's right to presence cannot be waived and the trial judge has the duty to insure his or her presence at trial. *State v. Badgett*, 361 N.C. 234 (2007). A capital defendant need not object—and can even consent to being absent—without waiving appellate review of the issue of a violation of the right to presence. *State v. Williams*, 363 N.C. 689 (2009).

A defendant's presence at trial for a capital felony "is a matter of public as well as private concern. Public policy requires his attendance at such a trial." *State v. Moore*, 275 N.C. 198, 209 (1969) (citation omitted); *see also State v. Huff*, 325 N.C. 1 (1989) (error, but harmless, for trial judge to honor distraught capital defendant's request to allow the trial to proceed in his absence), *vacated on other grounds*, 497 U.S. 1021 (1990); *State v. Ferebee*, 266 N.C. 606, 609 (1966) (holding that not only does a capital defendant have "a right to be present; he must be present"); *compare infra* § 21.1F, Removal of Disruptive Defendant (discussing the removal of a disruptive defendant from the courtroom).

Non-capital cases. A non-capital defendant's right to be present at trial and related proceedings is a purely personal right and can be waived either expressly or by the failure to timely assert it. *State v. Richardson*, 330 N.C. 174 (1991); *State v. Braswell*, 312 N.C. 553 (1985). In non-capital felony cases, only the defendant may waive the right. In misdemeanor cases, the defendant may waive his or her right through counsel with the consent of the court. *Ferebee*, 266 N.C. 606, 609; *State v. Shackleford*, 59 N.C. App. 357 (1982). *But see State v. Piland*, 58 N.C. App. 95 (1982) (holding that the defense attorney representing the defendant in a non-capital *felony* case had the power to waive defendant's presence at a *pretrial* suppression hearing).

While it is the better practice for the trial judge to obtain an explicit waiver from the defendant before conducting any "important proceeding" in his or her absence, it is not necessarily error to fail to do so. *Braswell*, 312 N.C. 553, 559. Waiver of the right to presence may occur by the failure to assert it. *Id.*; *State v. Christian*, 150 N.C. App. 77, 81 (2002) (finding that the failure of defendant and his counsel to object to the removal of defendant from the courtroom during the judge's questioning of a juror who asked to be dismissed from the jury, followed by defense counsel's request to have that juror removed and replaced, amounted to a waiver of defendant's right to be present); *see also infra* "Waiver by failure to assert the right" in this subsection E.

Express waiver. A defendant charged with a misdemeanor or a non-capital felony may expressly waive the right to be present for the trial of his or her case by following the procedure set out in G.S. 15A-1011(d). Under this statute, if a defendant seeks to waive this right, he or she must execute a written waiver of appearance, plead not guilty, and designate legal counsel to appear on his or her behalf. The defendant also must agree in writing to

- waive the right to testify in person;
- waive the right to face his or her accusers in person; and
- be bound by the decision of the court and entry of judgment (subject to the right of appeal).

G.S. 15A-1011(d)(1).

The defendant also must submit the following in writing:

- an enumeration of circumstances justifying the request; and
- a request to proceed under this section.

G.S. 15A-1011(d)(2). The judge may allow the defendant to be absent from his or her trial "because of distance, infirmity or other good cause." G.S. 15A-1011(d)(3).

If the defendant's request to waive presence is granted, the trial will proceed as if he or she were actually present. The State will present its case, and the defense will be given the opportunity to cross-examine the witnesses against the defendant and to present its case if desired. *See* G.S. 15A-1011(e).

It is not an abuse of discretion for a trial judge to deny a defendant's motion to be allowed to waive his or her presence at trial if the defendant does not comply with the above procedures. *See State v. Forrest*, 168 N.C. App. 614 (2005) (no abuse of discretion by trial judge in denying defendant's *oral* motion to waive his right to appear at trial made after the judge ordered defendant to appear at trial strapped to a chair, handcuffed, and masked from the eyes down). *But see State v. Whitted*, ___ N.C. App. ___, 705 S.E.2d 787 (2011) (rejecting the defendant's argument that the trial judge violated G.S. 15A-1011 by accepting defense counsel's oral waiver of the defendant's right to be present for certain parts of the trial after the trial had commenced; according to the court of appeals, G.S. 15A-1011 applies only when the defendant wants to waive the right to be present for entry of plea, not when the defendant wants to waive the right to be present at other parts of trial; the court of appeals went on to hold that the defendant waived her right to be present by refusing to leave her jail cell and return to the courtroom after the trial had commenced). [The *Whitted* opinion's limitation of G.S. 15A-1011 to the entry of plea appears to be inconsistent with the statute and other opinions interpreting it; that portion of the opinion was unnecessary to the ultimate holding in *Whitted*, which is consistent with the line of cases finding a waiver of the right to presence based on the defendant's voluntary absence after the trial commences, discussed below.]

No absolute "right to absence" at trial. The N.C. Court of Appeals has held that there is no absolute "right to absence"—i.e., there is no absolute right to waive one's presence at trial. *See State v. Shaw*, ___ N.C. App. ___, 721 S.E.2d 363 (2012). The *Shaw* court found that the N.C. Supreme Court, in *State v. Kelly*, 97 N.C. 404 (1887), had "contemplated a trial court's power to require a defendant's presence at his trial, even despite that defendant's attempted absence." 721 S.E.2d at 365. The *Shaw* court rejected the defendant's argument that G.S. 15A-1011(d) provided support for his contention that he had an absolute right to waive his presence at trial. Citing *State v. Whitted*, ___ N.C. App. ___, 705 S.E.2d 787 (2011), the court stated that G.S. 15A-1011(d) applies only to a defendant's waiver of the right to be present for the entry of pleas and not to waivers of presence at trial. [As discussed under Express waiver, above, the *Whitted* opinion's limitation of G.S. 15A-1011 to the entry of pleas appears to be inconsistent with the statute and other opinions interpreting it; that portion of the opinion was unnecessary to the ultimate holding in *Whitted.*]

Practice note: Proceeding to trial without the defendant's presence is ordinarily not desirable since he or she will be unable to participate or assist in the defense. If the defendant indicates a desire to waive this right, you should strongly advise him or her not to do so except in extraordinary circumstances.

Voluntarily absent defendant. In a noncapital case, a defendant's voluntary and unexplained absence from court *after his or her trial begins* constitutes a waiver of the right to be present. *State v. Richardson*, 330 N.C. 174 (1991); *State v. Davis*, 186 N.C. App. 242 (2007); *State v. Mulwee*, 27 N.C. App. 366 (1975); *see also State v. Montgomery*, 33 N.C. App. 693, 695 (1977) (once a trial for a non-capital felony has begun in defendant's presence, he or she waives the right to presence and the trial can be validly completed in his or her absence if the defendant is on bail and is voluntarily absent or if he or she escapes from custody and flees). To hold otherwise would allow a defendant who is out on bond "'to break up a trial already commenced'" and "'to prevent any trial whatever until the accused person himself should be pleased to permit it.'" *Diaz v. United States*, 223 U.S. 442, 457 (1912) (citation omitted); *see also United States v. Taylor*, 414 U.S. 17 (1973) (defendant's voluntary absence from trial after lunch recess of first day of trial amounted to a waiver of the right to be present and continuation of trial in his absence was proper under Fed. R. Crim. P. 43).

Once trial has commenced, the defendant has the burden of explaining his or her absence to the satisfaction of the trial judge. *State v. Stockton*, 13 N.C. App. 287 (1971) (finding waiver where defendant voluntarily absented himself after the first day of trial and noting that defense counsel did not offer any explanation for defendant's absence). If this burden is not met, a waiver of the right to be present is inferable. *Richardson*, 330 N.C. 174 (defendant failed to meet burden of explaining his absence where explanation was uncorroborated, untimely, and initially offered by an unidentified friend of the defendant).

Where a defendant's absence is attributable to a lack of notice, his or her absence does not operate as a waiver. *See State v. Hayes*, 291 N.C. 293 (1976) (defendant did not waive his right to appear where defendant and counsel had been instructed by district attorney that they would receive one-half day's notice before the case would be called but received only two hours' notice).

While there are no North Carolina cases that deal specifically with *commencing* a trial in a defendant's absence, the implication from the above cases is that a case cannot be tried in absentia where the defendant was not present *when the trial began*. The implicit rationale of the cases discussed above is that a defendant who is present when trial commences has due notice of the time that the trial is to recommence and, by absenting himself or herself, voluntarily waives the right to presence. *See, e.g., Davis*, 186 N.C. App. 242; *Stockton*, 13 N.C. App. 287; *cf. Crosby v. United States*, 506 U.S. 255, 261–62 (1993) (holding that Fed. R. Crim. P. 43 "prohibits the trial *in absentia* of a defendant who is not present at the beginning of trial" and noting that there is a difference between flight before and flight during a trial because a defendant's initial presence at trial "serves to assure that any waiver is indeed knowing").

Practice note: If the defendant explicitly or implicitly waives his or her right to be present at trial, you should consider whether it would be helpful for the jury to be instructed that the defendant has the right to do so and that the defendant's absence should not be considered with regard to his or her guilt or innocence. *See, e.g., State v. Webster*, 111 N.C. App. 72 (1993) (judge informed jury that the defendant had been excused from the day's proceedings for good cause), *aff'd*, 337 N.C. 674 (1994). If you do not request such an instruction, the failure of the judge to instruct on this subordinate feature of the case will not be held to be error. *See State v. Turner*, 11 N.C. App. 670 (1971) (so holding). The pattern jury instructions do not contain an instruction on this issue. If you desire an instruction on the defendant's absence, you should draft one that fits the facts of your case and request that it be submitted to the jury. You should not leave it up to others to draft the instruction. *See, e.g., State v. McNeil*, ___ N.C. App. ___, 707 S.E.2d 674, 684 (2011) (judge "merely explained defendant's absence for the record" and did not err in instructing the jury that "[t]he defendant, for whatever reason and only known to him, has refused to return after the lunch recess. We have given him ample opportunity to show up. He has failed to do so.").

No waiver of right inferred from a defendant's absence at sentencing. In all felony and misdemeanor cases in which a defendant receives a sentence of imprisonment, active or suspended, a defendant may not be sentenced in his or her absence even if the absence is voluntary. *See State v. Cherry*, 154 N.C. 624, 627 (1911) (the defendant's presence, if voluntarily waived, is not necessary to a valid trial and conviction, but his or her presence at sentencing is essential if the sentence "involves and includes corporal punishment"); *State v. Stockton*, 13 N.C. App. 287, 292 (1971) (holding that even though the defendant waived his right to be present during trial and at rendition of the verdict by voluntarily absenting himself from trial after the first day, the trial judge erred in sentencing defendant in absentia to a sentence of imprisonment because "when a sentence involving corporal punishment is imposed upon a verdict, either on a capital felony charge, a felony charge less than capital, or a misdemeanor, the defendant must be present"); *see also supra* § 21.1C, Trial Proceedings (discussing right to presence at sentencing).

G.S. 15A-1011(d), discussed above under "Express waiver," allows a defendant to plead not guilty and waive the right to be present at trial in misdemeanor and non-capital felony cases in certain circumstances. This statute may override cases decided before the statute's enactment indicating that the defendant must be present if the court imposes a sentence of imprisonment. *See, e.g., State v. Ferebee*, 266 N.C. 606, 609 (1966) (in a misdemeanor case in which the defendant signed a written waiver of appearance and entered a guilty plea, court stated that a sentence imposing corporal punishment may not be pronounced against a defendant in his or her absence).

Waiver by failure to assert the right. In a non-capital case, a defendant's failure to assert his or her right to presence at certain proceedings may be treated as a waiver. For example, if a judge calls a juror to the bench, or conducts an in-chambers conference that the defendant knows about but does not ask to attend, the right to presence may be deemed waived. *See, e.g., State v. Watson*, 338 N.C. 168 (1994) (by failing to object to judge's directive to bailiff to instruct the jury to reduce its question to writing and then retrieve it, defendant waived his right to presence and could not assign as error the judge's alleged denial of the right); *State v. Pittman*, 332 N.C. 244 (1992) (finding waiver where defendant failed to request to be present at or object to his absence from bench and in-chambers conferences held by the judge with the attorneys); *State v. Braswell*, 312 N.C. 553 (1985) (defendant waived right to be present at a voir dire hearing on the admissibility of evidence where he knew or should have known about the hearing and failed to assert his right to attend).

F. Removal of Disruptive Defendant

Notwithstanding the constitutional right to presence, a non-capital defendant may "waive" this right and be removed from the courtroom if he or she becomes so disruptive that the trial cannot proceed in an orderly fashion. *See State v. Brown*, 19 N.C. App. 480 (1973); *see also Illinois v. Allen*, 397 U.S. 337, 344 (1970) (in order to maintain a proper courtroom atmosphere when the defendant is acting disruptively, the trial judge may constitutionally "(1) bind and gag him, thereby keeping him present; (2) cite him for contempt; [or] (3) take him out of the courtroom until he promises to conduct himself properly").

Practice note: Removal of the defendant is a drastic measure because it undermines the defendant's rights to effective assistance of counsel and to confront the witnesses and evidence against him or her. Counsel should ask for a recess first to give the client an opportunity to collect himself or herself. If the judge opts for physical restraints of a disruptive defendant instead of removal, the restraints should be unobtrusive and not viewable by the jury. *See generally State v. Woodard*, 102 N.C. App. 687 (1991) (trial judge did not err by refusing to remove the defendant where the defendant ceased to be disruptive once shackled). For a discussion of the use of physical restraints and potential interference with the defendant's rights, see *infra* § 21.6, Right to Appear Free of Physical Restraints.

Statutory authorization and procedure for removal of non-capital defendant. After warning a disruptive non-capital defendant, the trial judge may order the defendant removed from the trial if he or she continues to interrupt the proceedings. Unless impracticable, this warning and any subsequent order of removal must be made outside the presence of the jury. G.S. 15A-1032(a); *see also State v. Rowe*, 33 N.C. App. 611 (1977) (trial judge had no opportunity to warn defendant before removal where defendant violently threw counsel's table, shouted obscenities at the judge, and continued shouting after he was physically restrained by officers and dragged to a corner of courtroom).

The judge must set forth on the record the reasons for the defendant's removal and instruct the jury not to consider the defendant's removal from the proceedings when weighing the evidence or determining the issue of guilt. G.S. 15A-1032(b); *see also State v. Callahan*, 93 N.C. App. 579, 584 (1989) (trial judge did not err by instructing jury on defendant's "removal from the courtroom" rather than his "absence").

After removal, the defendant must be given the opportunity to learn of the proceedings through counsel and to confer with counsel at reasonable intervals as directed by the court. G.S 15A-1032(b); *see also State v. Brown*, 19 N.C. App. 480 (1973) (defendant removed to an adjoining room from which he could listen to proceedings by intercom and speak with counsel by telephone). He or she must be given the opportunity to return to the courtroom "upon assurance of his [or her] good behavior." G.S 15A-1032(b).

Removal of disruptive capital defendant constitutionally prohibited. It is a constitutional violation to remove a disruptive defendant from the courtroom during a capital trial if the trial is continued in his or her absence. *State v. Huff*, 325 N.C. 1 (1989), *vacated on other grounds*, 497 U.S. 1021 (1990). However, a new trial need not be granted for such a violation if the State can show that the error was harmless beyond a reasonable doubt. *State v. Cunningham*, 344 N.C. 341 (1996) (defendant's exclusions from the courtroom were harmless beyond a reasonable doubt where he was able to observe all proceedings through an audio-video hookup and upon his return to the courtroom was able to object to anything that occurred in his absence).

Practice note: If your client is removed from trial for being disruptive, you should specifically object to the removal on statutory and state and federal constitutional grounds or the issue will be waived on appeal. *See State v. Watson*, 338 N.C. 168 (1994) (defendant's failure to object to the alleged denial of his constitutional right to presence constituted a waiver of the right to argue the issue on appeal); *State v. Miller*, 146 N.C. App. 494 (2001) (same). You also should consider whether an instruction on the removal or absence would be helpful to your client's case or whether it would call more attention to his or her absence. If you determine that you do not want the judge to instruct on the removal pursuant to G.S. 15A-1032(b)(2), you should inform the judge that you wish to waive that instruction. *See State v. Ash*, 169 N.C. App. 715, 726 (2005) (defense counsel specifically waived the instruction required by G.S. 15A-1032(b)(2) because they felt "it will just call more attention to the fact that [defendant's] not here"). If you want the instruction to be given and the judge fails to give it, you must object to the failure to instruct or the error will be waived.

G. Standard of Review on Appeal

The right to be present at all critical stages of the prosecution is subject to harmless error analysis. If the defendant's constitutional right to presence is violated, the State bears the burden of showing that the error was harmless beyond a reasonable doubt. *See State v. Braswell*, 312 N.C. 553 (1985); *see also Rushen v. Spain*, 464 U.S. 114 (1983). "[T]he presence of overwhelming evidence of guilt may render error of constitutional dimension harmless beyond a reasonable doubt." *State v. Autry*, 321 N.C. 392, 400 (1988).

21.2 Right to Confront Witnesses

This section addresses the state and federal constitutional right to confront and cross-examine witnesses only. It does not discuss strategies or procedures relating to cross-examination. For a discussion of cross-examination, see *infra* § 29.6, Witness Examination.

A. Basis of Right

Federal constitution. The Sixth Amendment to the U.S. Constitution guarantees a defendant the right to confront the witnesses against him or her. *See Crawford v. Washington*, 541 U.S. 36 (2004); *California v. Green*, 399 U.S. 149 (1970). "The central concern of the Confrontation Clause is to ensure the reliability of the evidence against a criminal defendant by subjecting it to rigorous testing in the context of an adversary proceeding before the trier of fact." *Maryland v. Craig*, 497 U.S. 836, 845 (1990). A criminal defendant is provided two types of protection under the Confrontation Clause—"the right physically to face those who testify against him, and the right to conduct cross-examination." *Pennsylvania v. Ritchie*, 480 U.S. 39, 51 (1987); *see also Davis v. Alaska*, 415 U.S. 308 (1974). *But cf. infra* § 29.8, Remote Testimony (discussing permissibility of remote testimony by witnesses).

The Sixth Amendment right to confrontation is applicable to the states through the Fourteenth Amendment. This right is "'[o]ne of the fundamental guarantees of life and liberty,' and 'a right long deemed so essential for the due protection of life and liberty that it is guarded against legislative and judicial action by provisions in the Constitution of the United States and in the constitutions of most if not of all the States composing the Union.'" *Pointer v. Texas*, 380 U.S. 400, 404 (1965) (citation omitted).

State constitution. Article I, section 23 of the N.C. Constitution has a guarantee of the right to confront similar to that set out in the Sixth Amendment. *State v. Chandler*, 324 N.C. 172 (1989). This section secures to the defendant the right to have his or her witnesses in court and to examine them on his or her behalf. It also secures to the defendant a fair opportunity to prepare and present his or her defense. *See State v. Hackney*, 240 N.C. 230, 235 (1954) (discussing article I, section 11 of the N.C. Constitution of 1868, a precursor to article I, section 23 of the current version of the constitution).

The N.C. Supreme Court "has generally construed the right to confrontation under our state constitution consistent with the federal provision." *State v. Fowler*, 353 N.C. 599, 614–15 (2001). The court "has repeatedly held that the right to confront is an affirmance of the rule of the common law that in criminal trials by jury the witness must not only be present, but must be subject to cross-examination under oath." *State v. Perry*, 210 N.C. 796, 797 (1936).

B. Waiver

The right to confront is a personal privilege for the benefit of the defendant and, unlike the right to presence (discussed *supra* in § 21.1), is not a matter of public concern. Thus, the right to be confronted by witnesses may be waived, even in a capital case, by the defendant either by express consent or by a failure to assert the right in apt time. *State v. Braswell*, 312 N.C. 553 (1985); *State v. Moore*, 275 N.C. 198 (1969); *see also State v. Craven*, 312 N.C. 580 (1985) (by failing to request that a witness be recalled, defendant waived his right to confront her about her written note entered into evidence by the State after the witness had testified and left the courthouse).

This right may be waived by the defendant or by defense counsel acting on behalf of the defendant. *See State v. Splawn*, 23 N.C. App. 14 (1974) (right to confront waived by defense counsel's stipulation in open court that the SBI chemist's testimony could be taken, both on direct and cross-examination, on the day preceding the trial and then read to the jury at the trial by the court reporter).

C. Standard of Review on Appeal

The denial of a defendant's right to confront the witnesses against him or her is subject to harmless error analysis. *See State v. Braswell*, 312 N.C. 553 (1985). If the defendant's constitutional right to confrontation is violated, the State bears the burden of showing that the error was harmless beyond a reasonable doubt. *See State v. Morgan*, 359 N.C. 131 (2004).

Practice note: When making an objection based on the denial of the defendant's right to confrontation, be sure to object on both state and federal constitutional grounds. Also, when making an objection to hearsay, be sure to give both the constitutional and hearsay grounds. *See State v. Gainey*, 355 N.C. 73 (2002) (defendant's confrontation claim not properly before the court on appeal because defendant objected at trial only on hearsay grounds).

D. Additional Resources

For further discussion of the right to confrontation and cross-examination, see Jessica Smith, *Understanding the New Confrontation Clause Analysis:* Crawford, Davis, *and* Melendez-Diaz, ADMINISTRATION OF JUSTICE BULLETIN No. 2010/02 (UNC School of Government, Apr. 2010), *available at* http://sogpubs.unc.edu/electronicversions/pdfs/aojb1002.pdf.

21.3 Right to Testify

A. Right to Testify

Federal constitution. The defendant has a constitutional right to take the witness stand and to testify in his or her own defense. This right is applicable to the states through the Fourteenth Amendment. *Rock v. Arkansas*, 483 U.S. 44 (1987). Although not recognized at common law or specifically enumerated in the U.S. Constitution, this right is now accepted to be an inherent part of the Due Process Clause of the Fourteenth Amendment and the Compulsory Process Clause of the Sixth Amendment. *See id.*; *State v. Colson*, 186 N.C. App. 281 (2007).

Statutory authority. G.S. 8-54 provides that a criminal defendant is "at his own request, but not otherwise, a competent witness." If a defendant decides to testify, he or she will be treated as any other witness and thereby subjects himself or herself "'to all the disadvantages of that position.'" *State v. Auston*, 223 N.C. 203, 205 (1943) (citations omitted). The defendant is subject to cross-examination and impeachment as is any other witness. *See id.*; *State* v. *Weaver*, 3 N.C. App. 439 (1969); *see also* G.S. 8-54.

The decision whether to testify. Whether to testify "is an important tactical decision as well as a matter of constitutional right." *Brooks v. Tennessee*, 406 U.S. 605, 612 (1972). "[T]he decision whether to testify is a substantial right belonging to the defendant." *State v. Luker*, 65 N.C. App. 644, 649 (1983) (counsel can advise defendant not to testify, but the ultimate decision belongs to the defendant), *aff'd in part, rev'd in part on other grounds*, 311 N.C. 301 (1984); *see also* 1 NORTH CAROLINA DEFENDER MANUAL § 12.8A (Control and Direction of Case) (Feb. 2004) (discussing decision-making in the attorney-client relationship); Appendix A, *infra*, N.C. COMM'N ON INDIGENT DEFENSE SERVS., PERFORMANCE GUIDELINES FOR INDIGENT DEFENSE REPRESENTATION IN NON-CAPITAL CRIMINAL CASES AT THE TRIAL LEVEL, Guideline 7.6(b) Presenting the Defense Case (Nov. 2004) ("Counsel should discuss with the client all of the considerations relevant to the client's decision to testify, including but not limited to, the likelihood of cross-examination and impeachment concerning prior convictions and prior bad acts that affect credibility.").

If the defendant chooses to testify, the trial judge is not required to instruct the jury, on request or otherwise, that the defendant cannot be compelled to testify. *State v. Walden*, 311 N.C. 667, 677 (1984) (no error by trial judge in denying defendant's request for an instruction on his decision to testify, "the inference of which would be to insure that the jury look favorably upon his willingness to testify").

Waiver. A defendant may waive the constitutional right to testify as long as the waiver is knowing and voluntary. *State v. Luker*, 65 N.C. App. 644 (1983), *aff'd in part, rev'd in part on other grounds*, 311 N.C. 301 (1984). Unlike other waivers of constitutional rights, however, the trial judge is not required to inform a defendant of his or her right to testify or to make an inquiry on the record to determine whether his or her waiver is knowing and voluntary. *State v. Carroll*, 356 N.C. 526 (2002); *see also State v. Hayes*,

314 N.C. 460 (1985) (finding no denial of the right to testify because defendant did not indicate to the judge that he wished to testify).

Impermissible chilling of the defendant's right to testify. The trial judge, by his or her statements or conduct, should not impermissibly chill the defendant's right to testify. For example, a delay in ruling on, or the erroneous denial of, a motion in limine could have an unacceptable chilling effect on a defendant's right to testify. *Compare State v. Lamb*, 321 N.C. 633 (1988) (new trial granted where the bald denial of defendant's motion in limine to exclude inadmissible evidence implicating her in other killings impermissibly chilled the defendant's right to take the stand in her own defense), *with State v. Barber*, 120 N.C. App. 505 (1995) (no impermissible chilling of the right to testify where judge declined to rule on defendant's motion in limine to suppress evidence of underlying facts of prior convictions where the evidence did not clearly show that defendant's decision whether to testify rested solely on the judge's decision on the motion, and the judge did not erroneously deny the motion but deferred the decision until he had more facts and assured defendant that he would not admit impermissible evidence). Whether the denial of a defendant's motion in limine impermissibly chills his or her right to testify "depends on the peculiar facts of each case." *Lamb*, 321 N.C. 633, 648.

Likewise, if the trial judge undertakes to advise the defendant about the legal consequences of taking the stand, he or she may impermissibly chill the defendant's free exercise of that right by giving erroneous advice. *See State v. Autry*, 321 N.C. 392 (1988) (error found where trial judge gave a defendant an incorrect explanation about the scope of cross-examination to which the defendant could have been subjected). If the judge correctly advises the defendant in general on the consequences of testifying, there is not an impermissible chilling effect on a defendant's right to testify. *See State v. Davis*, 349 N.C. 1 (1998) (no error where trial judge did not attempt to give the defendant detailed instruction on the scope of cross-examination, and defendant had discussed the consequences of testifying with his attorneys); *see also State v. Davis*, 353 N.C. 1 (2000) (no error by failure to give more detailed instructions to defendant about cross-examination; instructions were not inaccurate).

B. Right Not to Take the Stand

Constitutional privilege against self-incrimination. A defendant has a right to refuse to testify under the Fifth Amendment to the U.S. Constitution, as incorporated by the Fourteenth Amendment, and also under article I, section 23 of the N.C. Constitution. A defendant's exercise of this right may not be used against him or her, and any reference by the State to a defendant's failure to testify violates the defendant's constitutional rights. *See Griffin v. California*, 380 U.S. 609 (1965); *State v. Mitchell*, 353 N.C. 309 (2001).

Statutory privilege against self-incrimination. G.S. 8-54 likewise recognizes that, although the defendant has the right to testify if he or she so chooses, nothing in that statute renders a criminal defendant "competent or compellable to give evidence against himself," nor does it "render any person compellable to answer any question tending to criminate himself."

Right not to be called as witness. The right of a defendant not to testify means not only that the defendant has the right not to take the stand but also that the court, the State, and a co-defendant in a joint trial may not call the defendant as a witness. *See Jones v. State*, 586 A.2d 55 (Md. Ct. Spec. App. 1991).

Comment on the exercise of the right not to testify. Prosecutors are strictly prohibited from making any reference to a defendant's failure to testify. *See State v. Reid*, 334 N.C. 551 (1993); *see also Baxter v. Palmigiano*, 425 U.S. 308, 319 (1976) (holding that the trial judge and prosecutor are prohibited from suggesting to the jury that it may treat a defendant's silence as substantive evidence of guilt); *State v. Baymon*, 336 N.C. 748 (1994) (new trial granted where prosecutor's argument directly referred to defendant's failure to testify and was intended to disparage defendant in the eyes of the jury); *State v. Reid*, 334 N.C. 551 (1993) (new trial granted where prosecutor argued that defendant had not testified, that he had that right, and that the jury was not to hold it against him); *see also infra* § 33.7C, Impermissible Content (discussing impermissible closing arguments by prosecution).

Judges likewise may not comment on the defendant's failure to testify except, if requested by the defendant, to instruct the jury on the right not to testify.

Defense counsel may refer to the defendant's right not to testify in closing argument by reading the Fifth Amendment and G.S. 8-54. The cases also indicate that defense counsel may use words to that effect and may paraphrase that right. *See State v. Banks*, 322 N.C. 753, 764 (1988) (defense counsel should have been permitted to read that clause of the Fifth Amendment pertinent to the defendant's right not to testify and "to say simply that because of this provision, the jury must not consider defendant's election not to testify adversely to him, or words to this effect"); *State v. Bovender*, 233 N.C. 683, 690 (1951) ("mere statement by defendants' counsel that the law says no man has to take the witness stand would seem to be unobjectionable"). Defense counsel is not allowed to comment on or explain further why the defendant did not testify. *Bovender*, 233 N.C. 683, 689–90 (so holding because permitting extended comment by defense counsel "would open the door for the prosecution and create a situation the statute was intended to prevent").

Defense counsel also has the right to inquire of jurors about their ability to follow the law, including the laws on the defendant's right not to testify. *See State v. Blankenship*, 337 N.C. 543, 554–55 (1994).

Instruction on the effect of the decision not to testify. If the defendant requests an instruction on his or her decision not to testify, the trial judge is required by the Fifth and Fourteenth Amendments to give one. *Carter v. Kentucky*, 450 U.S. 288, 305 (1981) (the failure to give the requested prophylactic instruction "exacts an impermissible toll on the full and free exercise of the privilege"); *see also State v. Sanders*, 288 N.C. 285 (1975) (there is no mandatory formula for instructing the jury on a defendant's decision not to testify but an instruction is sufficient if it makes clear to the jury that the defendant has the right to offer or to refrain from offering evidence as he or she sees fit and that the failure to testify should not raise any adverse inference).

Absent a request, it is discretionary with the trial judge whether to instruct the jury on the defendant's decision not to testify. The appellate courts have emphasized, however, that it is the "better practice" for a judge not to give such an instruction unless it is requested by the defendant. *See State v. Barbour*, 278 N.C. 449 (1971); *State v. Powell*, 11 N.C. App. 465 (1971).

Practice note: If you believe that an instruction on the defendant's decision not to testify would be helpful, you should specifically request that the judge instruct the jury that the defendant has not testified, that the law gives him or her that privilege, that the decision creates no presumption against him or her, and that the defendant's silence is not to influence their decision in any way. *See* N.C. Pattern Jury Instruction—Crim. 101.30 (May 2005); *see also Carter v. Kentucky*, 450 U.S. 288, 301 (stating that without an instruction on the defendant's decision not to testify, "the jury is left to roam at large with only its untutored instincts to guide it, to draw from the defendant's silence broad inferences of guilt").

The U.S. Supreme Court has held that the giving of a "no-inference" instruction, over the defendant's objection, does not violate the privilege against compulsory self-incrimination guaranteed by the Fifth and Fourteenth Amendments. *See Lakeside v. Oregon*, 435 U.S. 333 (1978). However, if the judge indicates that he or she intends to give a "no-inference" instruction and you do not want one, be sure to object so that any error will be preserved on appeal. *See State v. Bennett*, 308 N.C. 530 (1983) (where defendant failed to object to the trial judge's instruction on the defendant's failure to testify, the error would be reviewed for "plain error" only). Include as a basis for your objection the state constitutional right not to testify under article I, section 23 of the N.C. Constitution. *See also State v. Bryant*, 283 N.C. 227, 233 (1973) ("Some jurisdictions hold that unless the defendant so requests, such an instruction tends to accentuate the significance of his silence and thus impinges upon defendant's unfettered right to testify or not to testify at his option." (citing 18 A.L.R.3d 1335)).

Additional resources. For a checklist on the right of witnesses as well as criminal defendants not to give self-incriminating testimony, see John Rubin, *Basics of Right against Self-Incrimination* (UNC School of Government, June 2008), *available at* www.sog.unc.edu/sites/www.sog.unc.edu/files/BasicsofRightagainstSelfIncrimination.pdf.

21.4 Right to Allocution

A. Purpose

Allocution, or a defendant's right to make a statement on his or her own behalf before the pronouncement of a sentence, was a right granted to a defendant at common law. *State v.*

Miller, 137 N.C. App. 450, 460 (2000). The purpose of common law allocution was to give the defendant the opportunity "to present legal grounds why sentence ought not be pronounced." *State v. Green*, 336 N.C. 142, 191 (1994) (citing *State v. Johnson*, 67 N.C. 55 (1872)). The grounds included that the defendant "was not the person convicted, he had the benefit of clergy, he was insane, or, if a woman, she was pregnant." *Green*, 336 N.C. 142, 191. The purpose of modern-day allocution is "to afford defendant an opportunity to state any further information which the trial court might consider when determining the sentence to be imposed." *See State v. Rankins*, 133 N.C. App. 607, 613 (1999). For a thorough discussion of the purposes of allocution in modern times, see *State v. Chow*, 883 P.2d 663 (Haw. Ct. App. 1994).

B. Basis of Right

Federal constitution. The U.S. Supreme Court has not decided whether a defendant who affirmatively requests to speak at sentencing has the right to do so under the U.S. Constitution. *See McGautha v. California*, 402 U.S. 183, 219 n.22 (1971), *vacated on other grounds sub nom. Crampton v. Ohio*, 408 U.S. 941 (1972); *Hill v. United States*, 368 U.S. 424 (1962); *see also United States v. Barnette*, 211 F.3d 803 (4th Cir. 2000); *Green v. French*, 143 F.3d 865 (4th Cir. 1998).

Federal circuit courts are split on whether the federal constitution grants a defendant this right. *Compare, e.g., Boardman v. Estelle*, 957 F.2d 1523 (9th Cir. 1992) (recognizing a due process right to allocution at sentencing), *and Ashe v. North Carolina*, 586 F.2d 334, 336 (4th Cir. 1978) ("[W]hen a defendant effectively communicates his desire to the trial judge to speak prior to the imposition of sentence, it is a denial of due process not to grant the defendant's request."), *with United States v. Li*, 115 F.3d 125, 132 (2d Cir. 1997) (the right to allocution "is a matter of criminal procedure and not a constitutional right"), *and United States v. Fleming*, 849 F.2d 568, 569 (11th Cir. 1988) ("[T]he right to allocution is *not* constitutional." (emphasis in original)).

State constitution. The N.C. Supreme Court has held that capital defendants have no constitutional right to make unsworn statements of fact to the jury at the conclusion of a capital sentencing proceeding. *See State v. Moseley*, 338 N.C. 1 (1994); *State v. Green*, 336 N.C. 142 (1994). Additionally, no state constitutional right to allocution has been recognized in non-capital cases. The question has been raised in previous cases but not specifically decided by North Carolina's appellate courts. *See, e.g., State v. Miller*, 137 N.C. App. 450 (2000); *State v. Rankins*, 133 N.C. App. 607 (1999).

Statutory right to allocution in misdemeanor and non-capital felony cases. G.S. 15A-1334(b) codifies the common law right of allocution and expressly gives a defendant in misdemeanor and non-capital felony cases the right to "make a statement in his own behalf" at the sentencing hearing. *State v. Miller*, 137 N.C. App. 450 (2000). The defendant must request the opportunity to speak before the pronouncement of sentence or the right is lost. *See State v. Rankins*, 133 N.C. App. 607 (1999) (defendant was properly denied the opportunity to address the court where the request came after the jury had returned its verdict and the trial judge had already imposed sentence).

Neither the constitution nor G.S. 15A-1334 requires the trial judge to address the defendant personally and ask whether he or she wishes to make a statement. *See Hill v. United States*, 368 U.S. 424 (1962) (a defendant has no federal constitutional right to be asked if he or she wishes to address the court before sentencing); *State v. Poole*, 305 N.C. 308, 325 (1982) ("While it may be the better practice for the trial court specifically to inquire if the defendant wishes to speak prior to sentencing, our statute does not command this practice."); *cf.* FED. R. CRIM. P. 32(i)(4)(A)(ii) (before imposing sentence a federal sentencing judge must "address the defendant personally in order to permit the defendant to speak or present any information to mitigate the sentence"). However, if the defendant requests an opportunity to address the court before being sentenced and he or she is denied the right to allocute under G.S. 15A-1334(b), a new sentencing hearing must be ordered. *See Miller*, 137 N.C. App. 450.

Practice note: Counsel should discuss with the defendant the advantages and disadvantages of allocution. The U.S. Supreme Court has observed that even "[t]he most persuasive counsel may not be able to speak for a defendant as the defendant might, with halting eloquence, speak for himself." *See Green v. United States*, 365 U.S. 301, 304 (1961). On the other hand, a defendant may do harm to his or her cause and, should the case be reversed and a new trial granted, any admissions the defendant makes may be used against him or her. *See* Caren Myers, Note, *Encouraging Allocution at Capital Sentencing: A Proposal for Use Immunity*, 97 COLUM. L. REV. 787 (1997).

Allocution in capital cases. The N.C. Supreme Court has held that defendants in North Carolina have no common law or statutory right to make unsworn statements of fact to the jury at the conclusion of a capital sentencing proceeding. *See State v. Moseley*, 338 N.C. 1 (1994); *State v. Green*, 336 N.C. 142 (1994). The only remnant of the common law right of allocution in capital cases in North Carolina "is the right to present strictly legal arguments to the presiding judge as to why no judgment should be entered." *Green*, 336 N.C. 142, 192.

Since G.S. 15A-1334(b), by its own terms, is restricted to non-capital cases, it does not apply when the defendant is charged with a capital offense. *See Green*, 336 N.C. 142. The statute applicable to capital sentencing proceedings, G.S. 15A-2000(a)(4), has no provision for a defendant to make an unsworn statement of fact or to testify without being subject to cross-examination. It merely provides that a defendant or defense counsel has the right to "present argument for or against sentence of death." *See State v. Ray*, 137 N.C. App. 326, 331 (2000).

Although no absolute right of allocution in capital cases is recognized in North Carolina, the trial judge nevertheless may be willing to grant a defendant's request to make a statement. *See, e.g., Moseley*, 338 N.C. 1 (finding no error where trial judge failed to afford the capital defendant the opportunity to allocute even though defendant's motion for allocution had been granted before jury selection, because the defendant failed to remind the judge to allow him to speak at the appropriate time); *State v. Reeves*, 337 N.C. 700 (1994) (trial judge did not express an opinion on a fact to be proved when he allowed the capital defendant's request to allocute but required him to speak from a position that was a greater distance from the jury than the distance from which the attorneys argued).

Practice note: If you believe that it would be helpful for a capital jury to hear your client speak—for example, to express remorse or plead for leniency—you should make a motion to allow the defendant to address the jury. You should cite the Fifth, Sixth, and Fourteenth Amendments to the U.S. Constitution as well as article I, sections 19 and 23 of the N.C. Constitution and argue that it is important for the defendant to be allowed to speak for himself or herself to the jury because it is the jurors who must make the ultimate decision whether to impose the death penalty. You also can argue that the Criminal Justice Section of the American Bar Association has recommended that the "offender should be permitted the right of allocution" at the sentencing hearing. *See* ABA STANDARDS FOR CRIMINAL JUSTICE SENTENCING THIRD EDITION, Standard 18-5.17 (1994). A sample motion to permit allocution is available on the Office of Indigent Defense Services website, www.ncids.org, under the Training & Resources link, then under the Capital Trial Motions link, under the Beginning of Sentencing Phase heading (Motion to Allow Defendant to Address the Jury).

21.5 Right to Appear in Civilian Clothes

A. Basis of Right

Federal constitution. Trial of a defendant in prison garb has been recognized as an affront to the dignity of the proceedings and as jeopardizing a defendant's due process right to a fair trial; thus, the State may not compel a defendant to appear for trial before a jury in identifiable prison or jail clothing. The constant reminder of a defendant's condition implicit in prison attire may affect a juror's judgment and thereby endanger the presumption of innocence by creating an unacceptable risk that the jury will impermissibly consider that circumstance in rendering its verdict. Unlike the need to impose physical restraints on unruly defendants, "compelling an accused to wear jail clothing furthers no essential state policy." *Estelle v. Williams*, 425 U.S. 501, 505 (1976).

The U.S. Supreme Court in *Estelle* also recognized that defendants who are compelled to stand trial in prison garb are usually "only those who cannot post bail prior to trial" and to "impose the condition on one category of defendant, over objection, would be repugnant to the concept of equal justice embodied in the Fourteenth Amendment." *Id.* at 505–06.

Whether a defendant was prejudiced by being compelled to stand trial while wearing prison attire is subject to harmless error analysis on appeal. The State has the burden of showing that the error was harmless beyond a reasonable doubt. *Id.*

Statutory right to wear civilian clothes in superior court. To protect a defendant's right to be tried in clothing other than prison garb, North Carolina law prohibits any sheriff, jailer, or other officer from requiring a defendant to appear for trial in superior court dressed in the uniform of a prisoner or in any apparel other than ordinary civilian dress (or with a shaven head unless it was shaven while the defendant was serving a term of imprisonment for the commission of a crime). A violation of this prohibition is a Class 1 misdemeanor. G.S. 15-176. Since the statute applies only to trials, defendants are not entitled to wear civilian clothing at pretrial hearings.

While it is unlawful for an official to require a defendant to appear for trial in prison garb, it is not necessarily unlawful for a defendant to so appear. Where a defendant is given the opportunity to obtain alternate clothing but refuses to do so, he or she may stand trial in a prison uniform. *See State v. Westry*, 15 N.C. App. 1 (1972).

The N.C. Court of Appeals has held that although a defendant may not be required to wear the clothing of a prisoner or convict, G.S. 15-176 does not prohibit requiring the defendant to wear an unobtrusive form of identification, such as a wristband. *See State v. Johnson*, 128 N.C. App. 361 (1998).

Civilian clothes in district court. The above cases and statutes do not recognize a right for a defendant to wear civilian clothes in district court. The holding in *Estelle* applies only to trials "before a jury." *See Estelle*, 425 U.S. 501, 512. G.S. 15-176 applies only to trials in superior court.

Some of the reasons for not requiring a defendant to appear in jail clothing have been recognized, however, as potentially applicable to cases tried before a judge.

> There are considerations here other than possible bias. These considerations were undoubtedly overlooked in the press of immediate decision. One is equality before the law. A defendant who can afford bail appears for trial in the best array he can muster. He may be a veritable satyr clad like Hyperion himself. Imposition of jail clothing on a defendant who cannot afford bail subjects him to inferior treatment. He suffers a disadvantage as a result of his poverty. Our traditions do not brook such disadvantage. The second consideration is psychological. Some defendants may be callous; others confused and embarrassed by prison garb to the point where they may be handicapped in presenting or assisting their defense. Presumed to be innocent, the prisoner is entitled to as much dignity and respect as safety allows. As one court tersely put it: "The presumption of innocence requires the garb of innocence . . . ." (*Eaddy v. People*, 115 Colo. 488 [174 P.2d 717, 718].)

People v. Zapata, 220 Cal. App. 2d 903, 911 (1963) (footnote omitted) (holding that these considerations apply to a trial before a judge, but that the error did not cause a miscarriage of justice and did not require reversal); *see also State v. Billups*, 301 N.C. 607, 617 (1981) (Exum, J., dissenting) (dissenters observed in a case before a jury involving shackling [discussed *infra* in § 21.6] that "the presumption of innocence requires the garb of innocence, for 'regardless of the ultimate outcome, or of the evidence awaiting presentation, every defendant is entitled to be brought before the court with the appearance, dignity, and self-respect of a free and innocent man'" (citations omitted)).

Practice note: In light of the lack of authority guaranteeing a defendant the right to appear in civilian clothing in a nonjury trial, if you would like your client to appear in civilian clothing for trial before a district court judge, you should make that request to the judge before trial *and* show why requiring your client to appear in jail clothing would deny his or her due process right to a fair trial in that case. For example, in a case that turns on eyewitness identification, the defendant's appearance in jail clothing could influence the witnesses' testimony (in addition to implicating the more general concerns discussed above).

Statutory right for defense witnesses to appear in civilian clothes in superior court. G.S. 15-176 also provides that it is unlawful for any sheriff, jailer, or other officer to require *any prisoner* to appear in any court for trial while dressed in prison garb. Violations of this prohibition are Class 1 misdemeanors. G.S. 15-176; *see also State v. Knight*, 87 N.C. App. 125 (1987) (trial judge did not abuse discretion in denying defendant's motion for mistrial; the jailer wrongfully brought a defense witness into the courtroom in his jail uniform and handcuffed, but the appearance was brief and the judge immediately ordered the witness removed and declared a recess while the witness changed into civilian clothing).

Practice note: If you wish to have a defense witness testify while wearing civilian clothes, you should ensure that the witness has access to appropriate clothes and request that the jailer produce the witness for court in the civilian clothes. If the jailer does not comply, you must make a motion on the record for the witness to appear in civilian clothes or the error will be waived on appeal. *See State v. Abraham*, 338 N.C. 315 (1994) (no abuse of discretion found where defense counsel made no specific motion to permit three incarcerated defense witnesses to appear in civilian clothes and the trial judge required the witnesses to testify while in prison uniform and physically restrained).

B. Preservation of Issue for Appeal

Necessity for objection. The failure of a defendant to object to being tried in prison clothing "is sufficient to negate the presence of compulsion necessary to establish a constitutional violation." *Estelle v. Williams*, 425 U.S. 501, 512–13 (1976); *cf. State v. Tolley*, 290 N.C. 349, 371–72 (1976) (citing *Estelle* and finding that any error in shackling of defendant was waived because defense counsel made no objection). Counsel must specifically assert a constitutional and statutory basis for the objection to preserve the issue on both grounds on appeal. *See State v. Holmes*, 355 N.C. 719 (2002) (where defendant failed to object on constitutional grounds, review of the trial judge's decision to restrain was limited to statutory error pursuant to the abuse of discretion standard). The trial judge is not required to inquire of the defendant or defense counsel whether the defendant is deliberately going to trial in jail clothes. *Estelle*, 425 U.S. 501.

Record must affirmatively show that the defendant was in jail clothing. The nature of clothing worn by a defendant may make it unclear whether the attire is in fact a prison or jail uniform. Some jail uniforms are comprised of standard-issue trousers and shirts and are not readily associated with the attire of a prisoner. To preserve the issue for appeal, a defendant required to wear a uniform for trial should ensure that the record includes evidence of the type of clothing he or she is wearing and evidence that his or her apparel is in fact a jail uniform. *See, e.g., State v. Berry*, 51 N.C. App. 97 (1981) (insufficient showing that defendant appeared in prison garb where record showed defendant appeared in green pants, white socks, tennis shoes, and a white T-shirt); *cf. State v. Simpson*, 202 N.C. App. 586 (2010) (unpublished) (finding sufficient evidence that defendant's white pants, white T-shirt, and white tennis shoes were prison garb but holding that violation was not prejudicial and did not require reversal where defendant was on trial for assaulting a prison guard at the unit where he was housed and jury therefore knew that defendant was incarcerated).

21.6 Right to Appear Free of Physical Restraints

A. Constitutional Basis of Right

Federal constitution. The Fifth and Fourteenth Amendments to the U.S. Constitution prohibit the use of physical restraints visible to the jury unless the trial judge has determined, in the exercise of his or her discretion, that the restraints are justified by an essential state interest specific to a particular trial. *Deck v. Missouri*, 544 U.S. 622 (2005). Examples of essential state interests include physical security, escape prevention, and courtroom decorum. Courts can take into account factors traditionally relied on by courts in determining potential security problems and the risk of escape at trial.

The U.S. Supreme Court observed that the routine use of shackling would:

- undermine the presumption of innocence and the related fairness of the factfinding process;
- interfere with the defendant's ability to communicate with his or her lawyer and to participate in his or her own defense; and
- affront the dignity and decorum of judicial proceedings.

Id. at 630–32.

Where a trial judge, without adequate justification, orders a defendant to be visibly shackled during trial, the defendant need not demonstrate actual prejudice to make out a due process violation. Instead, the burden is on the State to prove beyond a reasonable doubt that the shackling error did not contribute to the verdict obtained against the defendant. *Id.* at 635.

State constitution. Before the decision in *Deck*, the N.C. Supreme Court had also held that a criminal defendant is entitled under the Due Process Clause of the federal constitution and the Law of the Land Clause in article I, section 19 of the state constitution to be tried "free from all bonds or shackles except in extraordinary instances." *See State v. Tolley*, 290 N.C. 349, 365 (1976). Unless there is a showing of necessity, compelling a defendant to stand trial while physically restrained is inherently prejudicial. *Id.*

While *Tolley* involved a superior court jury trial, it can also be argued that the state and federal constitutions likewise bar physical restraint of a defendant in a district court nonjury proceeding unless the judge finds that it is necessary to do so (see subsection B., below).

The court in *Tolley* set out circumstances appropriate for the trial judge to consider in determining whether restraints are necessary. These include but are not limited to:

- the seriousness of the charges,
- the defendant's temperament and character,
- the defendant's age and physical attributes,
- the defendant's past record,
- any past escapes or attempted escapes, and evidence of a present plan to escape,
- any threats to harm others or cause a disturbance,
- any self-destructive tendencies,
- the risk of mob violence or of attempted revenge by others,
- the possibility of rescue by other offenders still at large,
- the size and mood of the audience,
- the nature and physical security of the courtroom, and
- the adequacy and availability of alternative remedies.

Id. at 368–69 ("The propriety of physical restraints depends upon the particular facts of each case, and the test on appeal is whether, under all of the circumstances, the trial court abused its discretion.").

The appropriateness of the particular type of restraints also appears to depend on the circumstances of each case. *See State v. Forrest*, 168 N.C. App. 614 (2005) (no abuse of discretion by trial judge in requiring defendant to appear in court strapped to his chair, handcuffed and wearing a white mask covering his mouth and nose, Hannibal-Lecter-style, where defendant was on trial for brutally attacking his former attorney and biting a deputy during a previous trial).

B. Statutory Basis of Right

Restraint of adult defendants in superior court. G.S. 15A-1031 reflects the concerns about shackling expressed in *Tolley* and provides that a defendant may be physically restrained during his or her trial "when the judge finds the restraint to be reasonably necessary to maintain order, prevent the defendant's escape, or provide for the safety of persons." If the trial judge determines that a defendant should be restrained, he or she must:

- enter in the record out of the presence of the jury and in the presence of the person to be restrained and his or her counsel, if any, the reasons for the restraint;
- give the restrained person an opportunity to object; and
- unless the defendant or his or her attorney objects, instruct the jurors that the restraint is not to be considered in weighing evidence or determining the issue of guilt.

If the defendant objects to the stated reasons for the restraint, the judge must conduct a hearing and make findings of fact. *Id.* The judge may base his or her findings supporting the decision to use restraints on information, if reliable, that would not be admissible at trial. *State v. Paige*, 316 N.C. 630 (1986) (permissible to consider hearsay testimony from deputy that defendants had attempted to escape the week before trial). The judge must make a "meaningful record" evidencing the basis of his or her discretion and "provide the rationale for that discretion, via some finding substantiated in the record." *State v. Jackson*, 162 N.C. App. 695, 701 (2004).

Restraint of adult defendants in district court. While G.S. 15A-1031 discusses the procedures for the court to follow in a jury trial (for example, the judge must instruct the jury not to consider the restraints unless the defendant objects to the instruction), it is not expressly limited to jury trials. Its language and title allow for the argument that a district court judge is prohibited from trying a defendant while shackled. The statute is part of Subchapter X, General Trial Procedure, which is applicable both to superior and district court. Also, the reasons articulated by *Deck* and *Tolley*, discussed in subsection A., above, apply to bench trials as well as to jury trials (other than the potential impact on the presumption of innocence and the fairness of the factfinding process when a lay jury is the factfinder).

Practice note: If your district court client is shackled and you would like him or her to be tried free of restraints, you should make a motion to have them removed and assert that G.S. 15A-1031 requires that the shackles be removed. You should also assert that the denial of your motion without holding a hearing and making the findings described in *Tolley* violates your client's rights to due process under the state and federal constitutions. You can argue that even though one of the reasons that physical restraints are inherently prejudicial is not present when the proceeding is not in front a jury—i.e., the physical restraints may cause jury prejudice and affect the presumption of innocence—there are other reasons to restrict their use in district court. Shackles may:

- impair the defendant's mental faculties;
- impede communication between the defendant and his or her attorney;
- detract from the dignity and decorum of the judicial proceedings; and
- be painful to the defendant.

See State v. Russ, 709 N.W.2d 483, 491 (Wis. Ct. App. 2005) (Anderson, J., concurring) (quoting *Spain v. Rushen*, 883 F.2d 712, 721 (9th Cir. 1989)); *see also Illinois v. Allen*, 397 U.S. 337, 344 (1970) ("[N]o person should be tried while shackled and gagged except as a last resort").

You also can cite G.S. 7B-2402.1 (discussed below) in support of your motion and argue that by enacting this statute limiting the restraint of juveniles, the General Assembly recognized the importance of subjecting a person to physical restraint only after a judicial determination of need even in nonjury proceedings. *See also In re Staley*, 364 N.E.2d 72, 73–74 (Ill. 1977) (holding in juvenile delinquency case that "[t]he reasons for forbidding shackling are not limited to trials by jury" and that in the absence of a showing of clear necessity "an accused cannot be tried in shackles whether there is to be a bench trial or a trial by jury").

Restraint of juveniles. G.S. 7B-2402.1, enacted in 2007, provides that in a delinquency hearing, "the judge may subject a juvenile to physical restraint in the courtroom only when the judge finds the restraint to be reasonably necessary to maintain order, prevent the juvenile's escape, or provide for the safety of the courtroom." These restrictions are comparable to those in the statute on restraint of adult defendants, discussed above. Before ordering the use of restraints, the judge, whenever practical, must provide the juvenile and his or her attorney an opportunity to be heard to contest the use of restraints.

Restraint of witnesses during trial. G.S. 15A-1031 also grants the trial judge the authority to restrain witnesses. The procedures applicable to the restraint of the defendant, described above, also are applicable to the restraint of witnesses. Whether to restrain a witness is a discretionary decision and will not be disturbed absent an abuse of discretion. *See State v. Abraham*, 338 N.C. 315 (1994) (no abuse of discretion or expression of opinion on credibility shown where trial judge permitted incarcerated prosecuting witness to appear without shackles but required three incarcerated defense witnesses to be restrained while testifying).

C. Preservation of Issue for Appeal

Record must affirmatively show physical restraint. To preserve the right to appellate review, the record must show that the defendant was physically restrained. *See State v. Valentine*, 200 N.C. App. 436 (2009) (unpublished) (overruling assignment of error because defendant failed to demonstrate that he was in fact shackled at trial).

Necessity for objection. Appellate review is waived if counsel fails to object to the trial judge's order of restraint. *See State v. Paige*, 316 N.C. 630 (1986) (holding that the defendant's failure to object to the trial court's lack of instructions to the jury that restraints could not be considered in weighing evidence or determining guilt waived the right to review the lack of instructions); *State v. Tolley*, 290 N.C. 349 (1976) (holding that the defendant waived the right to appeal the lack of instructions concerning shackles and to shackling itself by failing to object); *State v. Thomas*, 134 N.C. App. 560 (1999) (holding that defendant waived the right to appeal shackling where no objection to shackling made). A constitutional and statutory basis for the objection must be given to preserve the issue on both grounds on appeal. *See State v. Holmes*, 355 N.C. 719 (2002) (where defendant failed to object on constitutional grounds, review of the trial judge's decision to restrain was limited to statutory error pursuant to the abuse of discretion standard).

Practice note: If the trial judge, over objection, orders the defendant or a defense witness to be physically restrained during trial, counsel should request that the jury's view of the restraints be obstructed and that the defendant or witness walk to and from the witness chair outside the presence of the jury. *See, e.g., State v. Wilson*, 354 N.C. 493 (2001) (defendant's leg braces were hidden underneath his clothing); *State v. Atkins*, 349 N.C. 62 (1998) (cloth was draped over defense table to conceal defendant's leg restraints from jury); *State v. Wright*, 82 N.C. App. 450 (1986) (oversized briefcase placed by defendant's chair to obstruct jurors' view of his shackles). If the restraints are not visible to the jury, the risk is reduced that the restraints will create prejudice in the minds of the jurors. *See Holmes*, 355 N.C. 719. However, the restraints may still impede the defendant's thought processes and ease of communication with counsel.

To preserve any error for appeal, make sure the record reflects that the defendant was in fact shackled during trial. Also identify the type of restraints used and the effect that the restraints had on the defendant and the proceedings.

Chapter 22
Duties and Conduct of Presiding Judge

This chapter addresses the duties of the judge presiding at trial and the restrictions on his or her conduct in the presence of the jury. Specifically, this chapter covers the trial judge's duty of impartiality, disqualification of the trial judge when his or her impartiality might reasonably be questioned, control of the proceedings, and maintaining order and security in the courtroom (including restraint and removal of the defendant and witnesses).

22.1 Impartiality

A. In General

Every person charged with a crime in North Carolina has a right to a fair trial before an impartial judge and an unprejudiced jury. *State v. Harris*, 308 N.C. 159 (1983); *State v. Carter*, 233 N.C. 581 (1951). The Due Process Clause of the U.S. Constitution imposes on the trial judge the duty of absolute impartiality, and he or she must supervise and control a defendant's trial to ensure fair and impartial justice for both parties. *See Tumey v. Ohio*, 273 U.S. 510 (1927); *State v. Fleming*, 350 N.C. 109 (1999); *Ponder v. Davis*, 233 N.C. 699 (1951).

B. Expression of Opinion Prohibited

A judge may not express an opinion, either explicitly or implicitly, on any question of fact to be determined by the jury. N.C. GEN. STAT. § 15A-1222 (hereinafter G.S.) [formerly G.S. 1-180]; *State v. Crummy*, 107 N.C. App. 305 (1992). G.S. 15A-1222 does not apply to comments made outside the presence of the jury. *Fleming*, 350 N.C. 109. G.S. 15A-1232 expressly prohibits a judge from expressing an opinion during the jury charge as to whether or not a fact has been proved.

The trial judge must abstain from conduct or language that tends to discredit or prejudice the defendant's case because the judge holds an exalted station and his or her opinion is greatly respected by the jury. *State v. Allen*, 353 N.C. 504 (2001). "The slightest intimation from a judge as to the strength of the evidence or as to the credibility of a witness will always have great weight with the jury. . . ." *Id.* at 510 (citation omitted).

Practice note: Although G.S. 15A-1222 and G.S. 15A-1232 do not apply when the conduct or remarks are made outside the presence of the jury, counsel should nevertheless object and make sure that the record reflects the conduct or remarks that indicate an opinion. On appeal, those statements or actions may be used to buttress a claim that the defendant did not receive a fair trial in front of an impartial judge in violation of due process.

What constitutes prejudicial error. Once the trial judge has expressed an opinion before the jury, the resulting prejudice to the defendant is "virtually impossible to cure." *State v. Clanton*, 20 N.C. App. 275, 277 (1973). However, not every indiscreet or improper remark by a trial judge will warrant relief. Whether the defendant was deprived of a fair trial by the trial judge's comments, questions, or actions "must be determined by what was said and its probable effect upon the jury in light of all attendant circumstances, the burden of showing prejudice being upon the appellant." *State v. Faircloth*, 297 N.C. 388, 392 (1979). A new trial will only be awarded if the remarks by the trial judge go to the "heart" of the case. *State v. Sidbury*, 64 N.C. App. 177, 179 (1983); *State v. Whitted*, 38 N.C. App. 603, 606 (1978).

Selected examples. Types of improper judicial remarks or actions that have been found to require relief include:

- Statements intimating the defendant's guilt. *See State v. Guffey*, 39 N.C. App. 359, 361 (1979) (new trial required where trial judge stated that defendant was "pretty busy that day" since the indictment reflected two different victims); *State v. Teasley*, 31 N.C. App. 729, 731–32 (1976) (even with a curative instruction, defendant was prejudiced by trial judge's question, "What is this, another case of somebody ripping off an insurance company?" when, during a break in the trial with the jury in the jury box, another case with similar charges was called for disposition by plea).
- Remarks tending to suggest facts to be found by the jury. *See State v. Blue*, 356 N.C. 79 (2002) (trial judge's remark that the front porch, where the offense allegedly took place, was not in defendant's home denied defendant the coverage of defense of habitation and necessitated a new trial); *State v. Grogan*, 40 N.C. App. 371 (1979) (new trial granted where trial judge's explanation of his ruling denying the jury access to photographs never admitted into evidence may have led the jury reasonably to conclude that the photographs were important evidence that they should see and that the judge would allow them to see but for defendant withholding consent).
- Comments tending to belittle or humiliate the defendant's cause or his or her counsel before the jury. *See State v. Lynch*, 279 N.C. 1 (1971) (trial judge's blanket instruction to the court reporter to overrule *any* objection made by defendant's counsel necessarily belittled both defendant's cause and his attorney in the eyes of the jury); *State v. Frazier*, 278 N.C. 458, 464 (1971) (awarding a new trial because a series of comments by the trial judge, when viewed cumulatively, portrayed such an antagonistic attitude toward the defense that they breached "the cold neutrality of the law . . . to the prejudice of this defendant"); *State v. Brinkley*, 159 N.C. App. 446, 450 (2003) (new trial ordered because the trial judge's harsh criticisms of defense counsel "may have (1) prejudiced the jury against defendant, and (2) given the jury the impression that defense counsel was not trustworthy or ethical").
- Expressions concerning the credibility of witnesses. *See State v. Hensley*, 120 N.C. App. 313, 323 (1995) (trial judge's refusal to recall a child witness because doing so would be "very traumatic" and "injurious" to the witness, amounted to an expression that the judge believed the witness).
- Conduct concerning the credibility of the defendant. *See State v. Jenkins*, 115 N.C. App. 520 (1994) (improper expression of opinion about defendant's credibility where trial judge turned his back to the jury for 45 minutes while defendant testified on direct examination).
- Warnings or admonitions to witnesses concerning the consequences of committing perjury. *See State v. Locklear*, 309 N.C. 428 (1983) (while carefully given warnings to a witness with reference to perjury are permitted outside the presence of the jury, trial judge's actions in admonishing the witness and threatening her with imprisonment and a fine invaded the province of the jury, probably caused the witness to change her testimony, and may have deprived defendant of a fair trial before an impartial judge).
- Statements concerning sentencing. *See State v. Griffin*, 44 N.C. App. 601 (1980) (trial judge improperly expressed an opinion on defendant's guilt where, prior to the return of a verdict, the foreman asked if the jury could explain its decision and the judge

made remarks about sentencing that assumed that the jury had reached a guilty verdict and left little doubt that he expected a guilty verdict).

It is not an impermissible expression of opinion for the trial judge:

- To refuse to grant a defendant's request that he or she be referred to by name and not as "the defendant." *State v. Brown*, 306 N.C. 151 (1982).
- To use the word "victim" when referring to the alleged victim of the crime. *State v. Gaines*, 345 N.C. 647 (1997); *State v. Hill*, 331 N.C. 387 (1992).
- To make ordinary rulings during the course of the trial. *State v. Weeks*, 322 N.C. 152 (1988); *State v. Welch*, 65 N.C. App. 390 (1983).
- To explain the role of the prosecutor and defense attorney to the jury. *State v. Hudson*, 54 N.C. App. 437 (1981).

Practice note: The provisions of G.S. 15A-1222 and G.S. 15A-1232 are mandatory; therefore, a defendant's failure to object to an alleged expression of opinion by the trial court in violation of those statutes does not result in waiver of the issue on appeal. *State v. Young*, 324 N.C. 489 (1989). However, counsel must still object to an expression of opinion by the trial judge on *constitutional* grounds in order to preserve that issue on appeal.

C. Questioning of Witnesses Allowed, within Limits

A trial judge may direct questions to a witness in order to clarify the witness's testimony and to promote a better understanding of it. *See State v. Whittington*, 318 N.C. 114 (1986); *State v. Alston*, 38 N.C. App. 219 (1978). N.C. Rule of Evidence 614(b) specifically allows the trial judge to "interrogate witnesses, whether called by itself or by a party."

However, a trial judge may not, by his or her questions, intimate an opinion regarding the guilt of the defendant, the witness's credibility, or whether any fact essential to the State's case has been proved. *See State v. Yellorday*, 297 N.C. 574 (1979); *State v. Lowe*, 60 N.C. App. 549 (1983). A judge must conduct his or her questioning carefully and in a manner that avoids prejudice to the parties. If the judge expresses an opinion by the tenor, frequency, or persistence of his or her questions, error has occurred in violation of G.S. 15A-1222. *State v. Rinck*, 303 N.C. 551 (1981); *State v. Currie*, 293 N.C. 523 (1977). If the expression of opinion might reasonably have had a prejudicial effect on the defendant's trial, the error will not be considered harmless and a new trial will be awarded. *State v. Gregory*, 340 N.C. 365 (1995); *see also supra* § 22.1B, Expression of Opinion Prohibited.

As with other remarks and conduct prohibited by G.S. 15A-1222, the prohibition against the trial judge expressing an opinion when questioning a witness applies only when the jury is present. *State v. Rogers*, 316 N.C. 203 (1986).

Practice note: N.C. Rule of Evidence 614(c) provides that no objection is necessary "to questions propounded to a witness by the court but it shall be deemed that proper objection has been made and overruled." Counsel must still specifically object to prejudicial questioning by the trial judge on *constitutional* grounds in order to preserve the issue on those grounds.

D. Absence of Trial Judge During Proceedings

Occasionally, some trial judges will absent themselves temporarily during the proceedings. To the extent this practice goes on, it occurs most often during jury selection and closing argument. *See, e.g., State v. Parker*, 119 N.C. App. 328 (1995) (finding no gross impropriety in the prosecutor's closing argument even though the prosecutor made an untrue representation where defendant neither objected to the argument nor to the trial judge's absence from the courtoom during portions of closing argument); *State v. Colbert*, 65 N.C. App. 762, 769 (1984) (Becton, J., dissenting) (noting that "[i]t is not uncommon for trial judges to be inattentive, or even absent themselves from the courtroom, during jury selection"), *rev'd*, 311 N.C. 283 (1984); *State v. Soloman*, 40 N.C. App. 600, 604 (1979) (defendant entitled to new trial where "not only was the judge not in the courtroom when the [prosecutor's objectionable closing] argument was made, he also refused to make an effort to ascertain [in violation of G.S. 15A-1241(c)] what had been argued so that he could fairly consider defendant's objection and motion for a mistrial").

Courts from other jurisdictions have found that the judge's absence during trial violates various constitutional rights, discussed in the practice note below. These cases also suggest a basis for finding a violation of the defendant's statutory rights under North Carolina law, also discussed in the practice note. There is a split of authority among these courts over whether a trial judge's absence from the bench is reversible error per se or whether it is subject to harmless error analysis. *See Riley v. Deeds*, 56 F.3d 1117 (9th Cir. 1995) (so noting and collecting cases). Some courts find that the error renders the verdict a nullity while others will reverse a conviction only if the defendant shows actual prejudice resulting from the judge's absence from the proceedings. Many courts place emphasis on whether the defendant explicitly or implicitly waived the right to the judge's presence. *See id.*; *see also Peri v. State*, 426 So. 2d 1021 (Fla. Dist. Ct. App. 1983) (although a judge's absence during jury voir dire, over a defendant's objection, constitutes reversible error per se, this error can be waived); *Stirone v. United States*, 341 F.2d 253 (3d Cir. 1965) (defense counsel implicitly assented to trial judge's absence during peremptory challenges to the jury where counsel made no objection and did not mention the absence during any part of the trial).

While the N.C. Supreme Court has not definitively addressed the issue of a trial judge's absence during trial, the Court has stated in dicta that "the absence of the judge from the proceedings will not constitute reversible error unless the record shows that something occurred which would harm the defendant." *State v. Arnold*, 314 N.C. 301, 308 (1985) (defendant's argument that the trial judge left the courtroom during closing arguments was not supported by the record so the issue was not properly before the court for review; apparently neither the State nor the defendant had requested that closing arguments be recorded); *see also State v. Smith*, 162 N.C. App. 46 (2004) (quoting *Arnold* but declining to address defendant's contention that the trial judge erred by leaving the courtroom during a portion of the prosecutor's closing argument because a new trial had been granted on other grounds). Although the *Arnold* court describes the review standard as "well established," the three cases it cites were from other jurisdictions and date back to 1907, 1915, and 1950.

The N.C. Court of Appeals addressed the issue in *State v. Levya*, 181 N.C. App. 491 (2007), but in the context of whether the trial judge violated his statutory duty under G.S 15A-1211(b) to decide all "questions concerning the competency of jurors." The judge in *Levya* absented himself from jury selection and left the parties to excuse jurors for cause by stipulation. "[S]ome potential jurors" were dismissed by stipulation in his absence. *Id.* at 494. The Court of Appeals found the judge had erred in excusing himself from the courtroom during jury selection but the defendant was not entitled to relief because he failed to show that he was prejudiced by the judge's absence.

Practice note: If the judge announces his or her intention to leave the courtroom during a portion of the trial, you should object immediately. If the judge leaves the courtroom during the proceedings without advance notice, object on the record at the next opportunity. As grounds for your objection, assert that the judge's absence violates your client's right to a trial before a fair and impartial jury under the Sixth Amendment to the U.S. Constitution and under article I, section 24 of the N.C. Constitution. *See Peri*, 426 So. 2d 1021, 1023 ("[t]he presence of the trial judge is at the very core of [the Sixth Amendment] constitutional guarantee" to a trial by an impartial jury); *United States v. Heflin*, 125 F.2d 700, 700 (5th Cir. 1942) ("In a trial by jury the judge is an essential actor, and he should be present during all the proceedings. If he has to leave the bench, the trial should be suspended."). You also should assert a violation of the defendant's right to a fair trial under the Due Process Clause of the Fourteenth Amendment to the U.S. Constitution and under article I, section 19 of the N.C. Constitution. *See Gay v. Graham*, 269 F.2d 482, 486 (10th Cir. 1959) (for a trial judge "to leave the courtroom or to be out of hearing so as to lose control of the trial so that the proceeding is, in effect, without a judge is a denial of due process").

If the judge's absence reflects adversely on the defendant's case—for example, he or she leaves during the defendant's closing argument—assert in addition to the above constitutional violations that the judge, by his or her absence, violated G.S. 15A-1222 by expressing an opinion to the jury that the defendant's argument was unimportant. *See, e.g., United States v. Mortimer*, 161 F.3d 240, 242 (3d Cir. 1998) (although court did not require defendant to show prejudice since it found the absence of the judge during defendant's closing argument to be structural error, it noted that "[p]rejudice to the defendant from the jury inferring that the defense was not worth listening to may have occurred").

Preserve the record by asking the court reporter to note the times that the judge left and returned to the bench. You should ask for complete recordation of the proceedings in all cases (*see infra* Appendix B, Preserving the Record on Appeal); but, if you failed to do so, you will need to make sure that you reconstruct the record to reflect accurately and completely any irregularities that occurred during the judge's absence.

E. Judicial Comment on the Verdict Prohibited

A trial judge is prohibited from commenting on the verdict in criminal cases in open court in the presence or hearing of any member of the jury panel. If he or she comments on the verdict, or praises or criticizes the jury on account of its verdict, any defendant whose case is calendared for that session of court is entitled to a continuance of his or her case to a time when all members of the jury panel are no longer serving. *See* G.S. 15A-1239; *see also* G.S. 1-180.1. The right to a continuance is waived by failing to move to continue before trial. *State v. Neal*, 60 N.C. App. 350 (1983). Under the provisions of G.S. 15A-1239 and G.S. 1-180.1, a continuance is the only remedy for a judicial comment on the verdict. *Id.*

22.2 Recusal of Trial Judge

A. Applicable Law

Due process requires the trial judge to be absolutely impartial. *See Caperton v. Massey Coal Co., Inc.*, 556 U.S. 868, 129 S. Ct. 2252, 2259 (2009) ("It is axiomatic that '[a] fair trial in a fair tribunal is a basic requirement of due process.'") (citation omitted); *Hope v. Charlotte-Mecklenburg Bd. of Educ.*, 110 N.C. App. 599, 602 (1993) ("One of the essential elements of due process is a fair hearing by a fair tribunal. In order to provide a fair hearing, due process demands an impartial decision maker."); *see also supra* § 22.1A, Impartiality: In General (discussing general obligation of impartiality). G.S. 15A-1223 and Canon 3 of the N.C. Code of Judicial Conduct both address the disqualification of a judge presiding over a criminal trial when a claim of partiality is raised.

Under G.S. 15A-1223(a), a judge may disqualify him or herself on his or her own motion. On motion of the State, or on the motion of the defendant, recusal is mandatory in a criminal case if the judge is:

- prejudiced against the moving party or in favor of the adverse party;
- closely related to the defendant by blood or marriage;
- for any other reason unable to perform the duties required of him or her in an impartial manner; or
- a witness for or against one of the parties in the case.

G.S. 15A-1223(b), (e).

Canon 3(C)(1)(a) of the N.C. Code of Judicial Conduct provides that on the motion of any party, a judge should disqualify himself or herself in a proceeding in which his or her impartiality may reasonably be questioned, including but not limited to instances where he or she has a personal bias or prejudice concerning a party. For other instances requiring disqualification, such as kinship or financial interest in the matter in controversy, see Canon 3(C)(1)(b)–(d).

B. Procedural Requirements

The motion to disqualify "must be in writing and must be accompanied by one or more affidavits setting forth facts relied upon to show the grounds for disqualification." G.S. 15A-1223(c). The motion must be filed no less than five days before the time the case is called for trial unless good cause is shown for failure to file within that time period. G.S. 15A-1223(d).

C. Burden on Moving Party

When a party moves for recusal, that party has the burden "'to demonstrate objectively that grounds for disqualification actually exist.'" *State v. Scott*, 343 N.C. 313, 325 (1996) (citations omitted). A mere allegation of bias or prejudice is not enough to compel recusal. *State v. Moffitt*, 185 N.C. App. 308 (2007). The party must show that substantial evidence exists that the judge has such a personal bias, prejudice, or interest that he or she would be unable to rule impartially. *Scott*, 343 N.C. 325. "The bias, prejudice, or interest which requires a trial judge to be recused from a trial has reference to the personal disposition or mental attitude of the trial judge, either favorable or unfavorable, toward a party to the action before him." *State v. Kennedy*, 110 N.C. App. 302, 305 (1993). If a reasonable person knowing all of the circumstances would have doubts about the judge's ability to rule on the motion to recuse in an impartial manner, then the judge should either recuse himself or herself or refer the matter to another judge to consider the motion. *State v. Poole*, 305 N.C. 308, 320 (1982). If the allegations in the motion to recuse are such that findings of fact are required, the trial judge should not rule on the motion but should refer the matter to another judge for hearing. *N.C. Nat'l Bank v. Gillespie*, 291 N.C. 303 (1976) (citing *Ponder v. Davis*, 233 N.C. 699 (1951)).

D. Additional Resources

For a collection of cases and further discussion of this topic, including a discussion of actual vs. perceived partiality on the part of the trial judge, see Michael Crowell, *Recusal*, ADMINISTRATION OF JUSTICE BULLETIN No. 2009/03 (UNC School of Government, Sept. 2009), *available at* http://sogpubs.unc.edu/electronicversions/pdfs/aojb0903.pdf. For case summaries addressing recusal motions, see 1 NORTH CAROLINA DEFENDER MANUAL § 13.4C (Motion to Recuse Trial Judge) (Mar. 2009).

22.3 Control of Proceedings

A. In General

It is the duty of the trial judge to regulate the conduct and the course of business during trial. *State v. Spaulding*, 288 N.C. 397 (1975), *vacated in part on other grounds*, 428 U.S.

904 (1976). "Generally, in the absence of controlling statutory provisions or established rules, all matters relating to the orderly conduct of the trial or which involve the proper administration of justice in the court, are within his [or her] discretion." *State v. Rhodes*, 290 N.C. 16, 23 (1976). Judges may take whatever legitimate steps are necessary to maintain proper decorum and an appropriate atmosphere in the courtroom during a trial. *State v. Dickerson*, 9 N.C. App. 387 (1970).

For a collection of cases addressing the measures taken by trial judges to preserve proper decorum in the courtroom, see 1 KENNETH S. BROUN, BRANDIS & BROUN ON NORTH CAROLINA EVIDENCE § 168, at 608 n.551 (7th ed. 2011).

B. Control of Examination of Witnesses

The trial judge has the power and duty to control the examination and cross-examination of the witnesses both for the purpose of conserving the time of the court and protecting the witness from prolonged, needless, or abusive examination. *See State v. Fleming*, 350 N.C. 109 (1999); *State v. Arnold*, 284 N.C. 41 (1973). He or she may ban unduly repetitious and argumentative questions as well as inquiry into matters of tenuous relevance. *State v. Satterfield*, 300 N.C. 621 (1980); *see also* 1 KENNETH S. BROUN, BRANDIS & BROUN ON NORTH CAROLINA EVIDENCE § 168, at 605–08 (7th ed. 2011) (discussing method of examination and order in the courtroom).

C. Control of Examination of Potential Jurors

The trial judge has the power to regulate and supervise jury selection so that the defendant and the State receive the benefit of a trial by a fair and impartial jury. *See State v. Brady*, 299 N.C. 547 (1980). Regulation of the manner and extent of the questions of a potential juror regarding his or her fitness rests in the trial judge's discretion and that decision will not be disturbed on appeal in the absence of a showing of an abuse of discretion and prejudice to the defendant. *State v. Johnston*, 344 N.C. 596 (1996); *State v. Hunt*, 37 N.C. App. 315 (1978). For a further discussion of jury selection, see *infra* Ch. 25, Selection of Jury.

D. Control of Witnesses and Spectators

A trial judge has the power and duty to control the conduct of witnesses and spectators in the courtroom. *See State v. Maness*, 363 N.C. 261, 282 (2009) (no abuse of discretion by trial judge in denying defendant's motion for mistrial based on the "troubling" conduct of three uniformed law enforcement officers who approached the jury box and stood very close to jurors when autopsy photographs of the victim, a slain officer, were passed to the jury); *State v. Braxton*, 344 N.C. 702 (1996) (trial judge properly denied motion for mistrial based on the spectators wearing buttons allegedly depicting a victim where defendant failed to show sufficient facts, including whether the jury even noticed the buttons); *State v. Higginbottom*, 312 N.C. 760 (1985) (judge did not improperly express opinion when, outside the presence of the jury, he admonished defendant's witnesses and warned them that their actions could result in their being jailed).

For a discussion of the trial judge's authority to remove witnesses or spectators from the courtroom, see *infra* § 22.4D, Removal of Disruptive Witnesses or Spectators. For a discussion of the constitutional implications of spectator conduct, focusing particularly on the wearing of buttons at criminal trials, see Scott Kitner, Note, *The Need and Means to Restrict Spectators From Wearing Buttons at Courtroom Trials*, 27 REV. LITIG. 733 (2008).

22.4 Maintaining Order and Security in the Courtroom

A. Controlling Access to the Courtroom

Generally. Article I, section 18 of the N.C. Constitution requires that "[a]ll courts shall be open," and section 24 provides that "[n]o person shall be convicted of any crime but by the unanimous verdict of a jury in open court." Additionally, the Sixth Amendment to the U.S. Constitution mandates that "[i]n all criminal prosecutions, the accused shall enjoy the right to a speedy and public trial." This right extends to the states through the Fourteenth Amendment. *See Presley v. Georgia*, ___ U.S. ___, 130 S. Ct. 721 (2010) (defendant's right to a public trial encompasses the jury selection phase). "The trial and disposition of criminal cases is the public's business and ought to be conducted in public in open court." *In re Edens*, 290 N.C. 299, 306 (1976).

"Although the right of access to criminal trials is of constitutional stature, it is not absolute." *Globe Newspaper Co. v. Superior Court*, 457 U.S. 596, 606 (1982). A trial judge may, "in the interest of the fair administration of justice, impose reasonable limitations on access to a trial." *Richmond Newspapers, Inc. v. Virginia*, 448 U.S. 555, 581 n.18 (1980). Under certain circumstances, a "reasonable limitation" may include closure of the courtroom to the public. *See Waller v. Georgia*, 467 U.S. 39 (1984). Reasons justifying closure include threats to participants and observers and attempts by the defendant to escape. *See State v. Murray*, 154 N.C. App. 631 (2002).

Procedural requirements for closing a courtroom. Before closing a courtroom to the public in a criminal case, the trial judge must:

- determine whether the party seeking closure has advanced an overriding interest that is likely to be prejudiced;
- order closure no broader than necessary to protect that interest;
- consider reasonable alternatives to closing the proceeding; and
- make findings adequate to support the closure.

State v. Jenkins, 115 N.C. App. 520, 525 (1994) (citing *Waller*, 467 U.S. 39, 48).

The trial judge should take care not to unduly restrict access to the courtroom. *State v. Moctezuma*, 141 N.C. App. 90 (2000) (new trial awarded where trial judge made no findings of fact before closing the courtroom not only to the general public, but to defendant and defense counsel as well). The trial judge may order the courtroom closed for the entire trial or for only a portion of the proceedings. *See, e.g.*, *State v. Clark*, 324 N.C. 146 (1989) (no impropriety found where trial judge limited public egress from the courtroom during closing arguments so as not to distract the jury).

Statutory authority for limiting access. Under G.S. 15A-1034(a), a judge "may impose reasonable limitations on access to the courtroom when necessary to ensure the orderliness of courtroom proceedings or the safety of persons present." G.S. 15-166 specifically provides that the trial judge may exclude bystanders in rape or sex offense trials during the taking of the testimony of the prosecutrix. *See State v. Register*, ___ N.C. App. ___, 698 S.E.2d 464 (2010) (no abuse of discretion by trial judge in child sex offense case in excluding, pursuant to G.S. 15A-166 and G.S. 15A-1034, all spectators from the courtroom during the alleged victim's testimony except for the alleged victim's mother and stepfather, an investigator for each side, and a high school class that was observing court proceedings).

Statutory authority for ordering search of persons in courtroom. G.S. 15A-1034(b) authorizes a trial judge to "order that all persons entering or any person present and choosing to remain in the courtroom be searched for weapons or devices that could be used to disrupt or impede the proceedings." The judge may also "require that belongings carried by persons entering the courtroom be inspected." If the judge orders a search pursuant to this subsection, he or she must enter it on the record.

Practice note: Although the denial of the right to a public trial is considered structural error necessitating a new trial, counsel must make a timely objection on state and federal *constitutional* grounds in order to preserve the issue on appeal. *See State v. Garcia*, 358 N.C. 382 (2004).

B. Controlling Access to Other Areas

In especially unusual circumstances, the trial judge may restrict activities not only in the courtroom itself, but also in areas around the courthouse. *See, e.g.*, *State v. Grant*, 19 N.C. App. 401, 414 (1973) (trial judge's prohibition of picketing, parading, and congregating in and around courthouse and requirement that spectators submit to a search for weapons before entering courtroom were proper where the case was "of a nature which would attract public attention" and "[i]t was necessary for the court to maintain discipline and decorum in the courtroom and its environs").

C. Removal of Disruptive Defendant

All criminal defendants have a constitutional right to be present at every stage of trial. This right can be waived by a non-capital defendant either expressly or by his or her disruptive behavior. When a defendant becomes disruptive, the trial judge has the authority to remove him or her from the courtroom, but strict procedures must be followed before doing so. For a detailed discussion of the defendant's right to be present, and the procedures that must be followed in order to remove a disruptive defendant, see *supra* § 21.1F, Removal of Disruptive Defendant (describing personal rights of defendant).

D. Removal of Disruptive Witnesses or Spectators

G.S. 15A-1033 authorizes a trial judge, in his or her discretion, to order any person other than a defendant removed from a courtroom when his or her actions disrupt the conduct of the trial. *See also State v. Dawson*, 281 N.C. 645, 656 (1972) (no prejudicial error by trial judge in ejecting two disruptive spectators from the courtroom "until they decided to behave themselves" because the action was necessary in order for the trial to continue "under circumstances of judicial decorum and fairness to all concerned"); *State v. Dean*, 196 N.C. App. 180 (2009) (no abuse of discretion by trial judge in removing four spectators from the courtroom during defendant's trial for an allegedly gang-related murder where one spectator was a co-defendant, jurors had expressed concerns for their safety as had jurors in defendant's first trial, and the spectators had violated pretrial orders concerning decorum in the courtroom). The judge is not required to make findings of fact to support his or her removal of disruptive spectators from the courtroom. *Dean*, 196 N.C. App. at 189 (while a trial judge is required by G.S. 15A-1032 to enter in the record the reasons for removing a disruptive defendant from the courtroom, G.S. 15A-1033 "imposes no such requirement").

E. Restraint of Defendant and Witnesses During Trial

Restraint of defendant allowed only under extraordinary circumstances. The Fifth and Fourteenth Amendments to the U.S. Constitution prohibit the use of physical restraints visible to the jury unless the trial court has determined, in its discretion, that the restraints are justified by an essential state interest specific to a particular trial. *Deck v. Missouri*, 544 U.S. 622 (2005); *see also State v. Tolley*, 290 N.C. 349 (1976) (the Due Process Clause of the U.S. Constitution and Article I, section 19 of the N.C. Constitution require the defendant to be tried free of all bonds or shackles except in extraordinary instances). G.S. 15A-1031 provides that a defendant may be physically restrained during his or her trial "when the judge finds the restraint is reasonably necessary to maintain order, prevent the defendant's escape, or provide for the safety of persons." For a detailed discussion of the defendant's right to appear at trial free from physical restraints and the procedures that must be followed before a defendant may be restrained, see *supra* § 21.6, Right to Appear Free of Physical Restraints (describing personal rights of defendant).

Restraint of witnesses during trial. In addition to allowing a defendant to be restrained under certain circumstances, G.S. 15A-1031 grants the trial judge the authority to restrain witnesses. The procedures applicable to the restraint of the defendant, described *supra* in § 21.6, are also applicable to the restraint of witnesses. Whether to restrain a witness is a discretionary decision and will not be disturbed absent an abuse of discretion. *See State v. Abraham*, 338 N.C. 315 (1994) (no abuse of discretion or expression of opinion on credibility shown where trial judge permitted incarcerated prosecuting witness to appear without shackles but required three incarcerated defense witnesses to be restrained while testifying).

Necessity for objection. Appellate review is waived if counsel fails to object to the trial judge's order of restraint. *See State v. Tolley*, 290 N.C. 349 (1976); *State v. Thomas*, 134 N.C. App. 560 (1999). Counsel must specifically assert a constitutional and statutory basis for the objection to preserve the issue on both grounds on appeal. *See State v. Holmes*, 355 N.C. 719 (2002) (where defendant failed to object on constitutional grounds, review of the trial judge's decision to restrain was limited to statutory error pursuant to the abuse of discretion standard). To preserve a challenge to the trial judge's failure to comply with the statutory requirements of G.S. 15A-1031, a defendant must object and specify the grounds on which the objection is based. *See State v. Paige*, 316 N.C. 630 (1986) (appellate review of the trial judge's failure to give instruction required by G.S. 15A-1031(3) was waived because defendant made no objection at trial).

Practice note: If the trial judge, over objection, orders the defendant or a defense witness to be physically restrained during trial, counsel should request that the jury's view of the restraints be obstructed and that the defendant or witness walk to and from the witness chair outside the presence of the jury. *See, e.g., State v. Wilson*, 354 N.C. 493 (2001) (defendant's leg braces were hidden underneath his clothing); *State v. Atkins*, 349 N.C. 62 (1998) (cloth was draped over defense table to conceal defendant's leg restraints from jury); *State v. Wright*, 82 N.C. App. 450 (1986) (oversized briefcase placed by defendant's chair to obstruct jurors' view of his shackles). If the restraints are not visible to the jury, the risk is reduced that the restraints will create prejudice in the minds of the jurors. *See Holmes*, 355 N.C. 719. However, the restraints may still impede the person's thought processes and ease of communication.

When a defendant or a defense witness is restrained, counsel also should consider whether an instruction to the jury regarding the restraints would be helpful or whether it would draw negative attention to the trial judge's determination to restrain that person during trial. If you do not want an instruction, you must object; otherwise, the trial judge is required by G.S. 15A-1031(3) to instruct the jurors "that the restraint is not to be considered in weighing evidence or determining the issue of guilt."

F. Contempt Powers

In addition to the use of the powers set out above, a presiding judge is authorized by G.S. 15A-1035 to maintain courtroom order through the use of his or her contempt powers as provided in G.S. Ch. 5A, Contempt, and through the use of other inherent powers of the court.

Chapter 23
Guilty Pleas

This chapter deals with issues involving guilty pleas and the procedures that must be followed when a defendant pleads guilty. Specifically, it addresses duties that counsel owe to their clients with regard to guilty pleas, the plea bargaining process, the plea colloquy, sentencing, and appeals. The chapter also includes a checklist for entering guilty pleas.

Statutes addressing plea procedures in superior court are primarily in Chapter 15A, Articles 57 (Pleas) and 58 (Procedures Relating to Guilty Pleas in Superior Court) of the North Carolina General Statutes (hereinafter G.S.). Although the procedures discussed in Article 58 do not apply explicitly to plea negotiations in district court, the expectation of the General Assembly in enacting the procedures was that the same general procedures would be used in district court, albeit in a "less formal" manner. *See* G.S. Ch. 15A, Art. 58 Official Commentary (located immediately before G.S. 15A-1021).

For an additional resource on guilty pleas, see Jessica Smith, *Pleas and Plea Negotiations in North Carolina Superior Court*, ADMINISTRATION OF JUSTICE BULLETIN No. 2005/03 (UNC School of Government, July 2005), *available at* http://sogpubs.unc.edu/electronicversions/pdfs/aojb0503.pdf.

23.1 In General

Prevalence of plea bargaining. Although the right to a trial by jury is considered one of the most fundamental rights afforded to criminal defendants under the U.S. Constitution, jury trials are actually the exception to the way in which most American criminal cases are resolved. Jacqueline E. Ross, *The Entrenched Position of Plea Bargaining in United States Legal Practice*, 54 AM. J. COMP. L. 717 (Supp. 2006). Guilty pleas are "the predominant method by which most criminal cases are resolved—approximately 93 percent of cases in the federal system and approximately 91 percent in the states." ABA STANDARDS FOR CRIMINAL JUSTICE: PLEAS OF GUILTY, at xi–xii (3d ed. 1999); *see also State v. Alexander*, 359 N.C. 824 (2005) (stating that 96% of criminal cases that survived dismissal in North Carolina during fiscal year 2002–03 resulted in guilty pleas).

The U.S. Supreme Court sanctioned plea agreements in *Santobello v. New York*, 404 U.S. 257, 260–61 (1971), stating:

> The disposition of criminal charges by agreement between the prosecutor and the accused, sometimes loosely called "plea bargaining," is an essential component of the administration of justice. Properly administered, it is to be encouraged. If every criminal charge were subjected to a full-scale trial, the States and the Federal Government would need to multiply by many times the number of judges and court facilities.
>
> Disposition of charges after plea discussions is not only an essential part of the process but a highly desirable part for many reasons. It leads to prompt and largely final disposition of most criminal cases; it

> avoids much of the corrosive impact of enforced idleness during pre-trial confinement for those who are denied release pending trial; it protects the public from those accused persons who are prone to continue criminal conduct even while on pretrial release; and, by shortening the time between charge and disposition, it enhances whatever may be the rehabilitative prospects of the guilty when they are ultimately imprisoned. *See Brady v. United States*, 397 U.S. 742, 751–752 (1970).

See also State v. Slade, 291 N.C. 275, 277 (1976) (noting that "'plea bargaining' has emerged as a major aspect in the administration of criminal justice"); ABA STANDARDS FOR CRIMINAL JUSTICE: PLEAS OF GUILTY, at xiii (3d ed. 1999) (noting that the allowance of negotiated guilty pleas "is an appropriate and beneficial part of the criminal justice system" and "is necessary to ensure the continued functioning of the system in those cases that go to trial").

Basic characteristics of plea bargains. "Generally, a plea arrangement or bargain is '[a] negotiated agreement between a prosecutor and a criminal defendant whereby the defendant pleads guilty to a lesser offense or to one of multiple charges in exchange for some concession by the prosecutor, usu[ally] a more lenient sentence or a dismissal of the other charges.'" *Alexander*, 359 N.C. 824, 830–31 (quoting BLACK'S LAW DICTIONARY 1173 (7th ed. 1999)). Plea bargaining is expressly permitted in North Carolina, and the trial judge is permitted to participate. *State v. Simmons*, 65 N.C. App. 294 (1983) (citing G.S. 15A-1021). However, there is no constitutional right to plea bargain—the prosecutor need not make any plea offer if he or she prefers to go to trial. *Weatherford v. Bursey*, 429 U.S. 545 (1977); *see also State v. Collins*, 44 N.C. App. 141 (1979), *aff'd*, 300 N.C. 142 (1980).

Pleading guilty to a crime waives a number of significant constitutional rights, including the right to a jury trial, the right to put the State to its proof, and most defenses to a crime. *Boykin v. Alabama*, 395 U.S. 238, 242–43 (1969); *State v. Ford*, 281 N.C. 62 (1972); *see also State v. Caldwell*, 269 N.C. 521 (1967) (by pleading guilty, the accused generally waives all defenses other than that the indictment charges no offense). Thus, as a matter of due process, under the Fifth and Fourteenth Amendments to the U.S. Constitution, the decision to plead guilty must be "knowing and voluntary." *See Boykin*, 395 U.S. 238; *Johnson v. Zerbst*, 304 U.S. 458 (1938); *State v. Bozeman*, 115 N.C. App. 658 (1994). This means that:

- the decision to plead guilty must be the client's;
- the client must be informed about his or her options and the consequences of pleading guilty; and
- the client may not be coerced by any party, including the court, to plead guilty.

See North Carolina v. Alford, 400 U.S. 25 (1970); *State v. Pait*, 81 N.C. App. 286 (1986). If a defendant's guilty plea is not made voluntarily and knowingly, "it has been obtained in violation of due process and is therefore void." *Boykin*, 395 U.S. 238, 243 n.5.

23.2 Basic Steps

As a practical matter, entering a guilty plea involves a four-step process. The ***first step*** is to negotiate and prepare the plea agreement and memorialize the agreement in a written transcript of plea. The N.C. Administrative Office of the Courts has created a "Transcript of Plea" form, AOC-CR-300, which is typically used as the written transcript of plea. The attorney should read the questions on this form to the client and record the client's answers before going to court.

The ***second step*** is the plea colloquy that occurs in open court. The trial judge must address the defendant directly to ensure that he or she is pleading guilty knowingly and voluntarily. The judge must be informed of the conditions of any plea agreement, and he or she has the responsibility to ensure that there is a sufficient factual basis for the plea. At the conclusion of the plea colloquy, the judge, if satisfied, accepts the plea.

The ***third step*** of the process is sentencing. A specific sentence may or may not be included in a plea agreement. If there is no sentencing agreement, or if the plea agreement permits a range of possible sentences, counsel will need to prepare for a sentencing hearing. Sentencing is not covered in this manual, but a few selected topics are included below.

Finally, the ***fourth step*** is to consider whether to file an appeal. The scope of a possible appeal is limited after entry of a guilty plea in superior court. Likewise, when a defendant pleads guilty to a felony in district court, the right to appeal is limited, and the appeal is to the court of appeals. In contrast, when a defendant pleads guilty to a misdemeanor in district court, the defendant has the right to appeal de novo to superior court.

Each of these four steps is discussed in more detail below. Also discussed are some related issues, including the admissibility of plea negotiations at trial, challenges to prior guilty pleas, and conceding guilt to a lesser offense during trial.

23.3 Preparing the Plea Agreement

A. Client's Right to Enter Plea

Generally. The recommended and required procedures for plea agreements come from several sources: North Carolina case law, statutes, and rules of professional conduct; performance guidelines adopted by the N.C. Commission on Indigent Defense Services (Appendix A of this manual); and the ABA STANDARDS FOR CRIMINAL JUSTICE: PROSECUTION FUNCTION AND DEFENSE FUNCTION (3d ed. 1993), *available at* www.americanbar.org/publications/criminal_justice_section_archive/crimjust_standards_dfunc_toc.html. These sources are cited throughout this chapter.

The decision as to what plea to enter is ultimately the client's. ABA STANDARDS FOR CRIMINAL JUSTICE: PROSECUTION FUNCTION AND DEFENSE FUNCTION, Standard 4-5.2

(quoted with approval in *State v. Ali*, 329 N.C. 394 (1991)); *see also* ABA STANDARDS FOR CRIMINAL JUSTICE: PLEAS OF GUILTY, Standard 14-3.2 (c) (3d ed. 1999) ("Defense counsel should conclude a plea agreement only with the consent of the defendant, and should ensure that the decision whether to enter a plea of guilty or nolo contendere is ultimately made by the defendant."), *available at* www.americanbar.org/publications/criminal_justice_section_archive/crimjust_standards_guiltypleas_toc.html.

Counsel's duties. An attorney has a duty to explore alternatives to trial, including the possibility of a plea bargain. The progress of negotiations and all plea offers ***must be communicated to the client.*** *See Missouri v. Frye*, ___ U.S. ___ (2012) (finding counsel ineffective for allowing a plea offer by prosecution to expire without advising defendant of offer or allowing him to consider it); *State v. Simmons*, 65 N.C. App. 294, 300 (1983) ("[A] failure to inform a client of a plea bargain offer constitutes ineffective assistance of counsel absent extenuating circumstances."); N.C. STATE BAR REV'D RULES OF PROF'L CONDUCT R. 1.4, Comment [2] (2003); Appendix A, *infra*, N.C. COMM'N ON INDIGENT DEFENSE SERVS., PERFORMANCE GUIDELINES FOR INDIGENT DEFENSE REPRESENTATION IN NON-CAPITAL CRIMINAL CASES AT THE TRIAL LEVEL, Guideline 6.1(b) The Plea Negotiation Process and the Duties of Counsel (Nov. 2004). The ABA's ethical guidelines require an attorney to investigate the facts of the case as well as controlling law before recommending any plea to his or her client. *See* ABA STANDARDS FOR CRIMINAL JUSTICE: PROSECUTION FUNCTION AND DEFENSE FUNCTION, Standard 4-6.1; ABA STANDARDS FOR CRIMINAL JUSTICE: PLEAS OF GUILTY, Standard 14-3.2(b). After receiving discovery, and adequately investigating the facts and any possible defenses, it is perfectly ethical and often appropriate for an attorney to attempt to persuade a client to accept a plea bargain that the attorney believes is in the client's best interest. Ultimately, however, it must be the client who makes the final decision. *See infra* Appendix A, N.C. COMM'N ON INDIGENT DEFENSE SERVS., PERFORMANCE GUIDELINES FOR INDIGENT DEFENSE REPRESENTATION IN NON-CAPITAL CRIMINAL CASES AT THE TRIAL LEVEL, Guideline 6.3(b) The Decision to Enter a Plea of Guilty (Nov. 2004). ***No plea offer should be accepted or rejected by counsel without the client's express authorization.***

Early pleas. Sometimes a client may wish to accept responsibility and plead guilty as charged early in the process, before discovery or your investigation. Often this is an unwise course, as the client is making a critically important decision without full information. The more serious the charge, the more risky an early plea may be. If the motivation for the early plea is to obtain release from jail, you may want to persuade your client to seek a bond reduction rather than plead early. If a client decides to enter an early guilty plea, and you have advised the client to wait until after discovery was complete to enter his or her plea, you may want to document the file to reflect your advice.

Defendants incapable of proceeding. A client who lacks the capacity to proceed under G.S. 15A-1001 cannot enter a knowing and voluntary plea. Incapacity means the client, for reason of mental illness or defect, is unable to:

- understand the nature of the proceedings against him or her;
- comprehend his or her own situation in reference to the proceedings; or

- rationally assist in his or her defense.

See G.S. 15A-1001(a); *see also State v. LeGrande*, 346 N.C. 718, 730 (1997) (the N.C. statutory test for competency to proceed is essentially the same as the constitutional test).

The standard for incapacity to plead is the same as the standard for incapacity to proceed to trial. *See Godinez v. Moran*, 509 U.S. 389 (1993) (competence to stand trial is same as competence to plead guilty). If you suspect that your client is incapable of proceeding, you should seek a mental health evaluation and a capacity hearing pursuant to G.S. 15A-1002. *See infra* Appendix A, N.C. COMM'N ON INDIGENT DEFENSE SERVS., PERFORMANCE GUIDELINES FOR INDIGENT DEFENSE REPRESENTATION IN NON-CAPITAL CRIMINAL CASES AT THE TRIAL LEVEL, Guideline 3.2 Client's Competence and Capacity to Proceed (Nov. 2004).

For a further discussion of incapacity to proceed, see 1 NORTH CAROLINA DEFENDER MANUAL Ch. 2 (Capacity to Proceed) (May 1998); *see also* Ripley Rand, *Guilty Pleas and Related Proceedings Involving Defendants with Mental Health Issues: Best Practices* (Superior Court Judges Conference, Fall 2008), *available at* www.sog.unc.edu/sites/www.sog.unc.edu/files/ 2_ripleyrand.pdf.

Mentally disabled defendants. A mentally impaired defendant, if not incapable of proceeding under G.S. 15A-1001, may enter a valid plea of guilty. North Carolina's Rules of Professional Conduct and the ABA Standards state that, to the extent possible, an attorney should seek to maintain a normal attorney-client relationship with a mentally impaired client and give him or her the same control over the case as a fully functional adult. *See* N.C. STATE BAR REV'D RULES OF PROF'L CONDUCT R. 1.14 (2003) (client under diminished capacity); *see generally* ABA STANDARDS FOR CRIMINAL JUSTICE: PROSECUTION FUNCTION AND DEFENSE FUNCTION, Standard 4-5.2 (3d ed. 1993) (control and direction of case). This means that a client with a mental illness or mental disability should be given the choice of how to plead. However, it is the attorney's responsibility to investigate all possible defenses to a crime before recommending a plea of guilty, including, of course, all defenses based on the client's mental state. *See generally* David A. Green, *"I'm Ok-You're Ok": Educating Lawyers to "Maintain a Normal Client-Lawyer Relationship" with a Client with a Mental Disability*, 28 J. LEGAL PROF. 65 (2003–04).

Mental impairments may create grounds for moving to suppress confessions or searches or may negate elements of the crime. They also may make it more difficult for a client to make a genuinely voluntary and informed choice to plead guilty.

If the attorney believes that a client is too impaired to make informed choices in his or her best interest, the attorney may move to have the client's capacity assessed or may seek the appointment of a guardian ad litem. *See* N.C. STATE BAR REV'D RULES OF PROF'L CONDUCT R. 1.14(b) (2003).

Counsel also may seek the appointment of a mental health expert to assist in communicating with the defendant and exploring possible defenses. Such motions may and should be made ex parte to the court in noncapital cases. *See State v. Ballard*, 333 N.C. 515 (1993) (motion for psychological expert may be made *ex parte*). If your client has been arrested for a felony but not yet indicted, and jurisdiction over the case lies in district court, the district court may hear motions for expert assistance. For a further discussion of obtaining experts, see 1 NORTH CAROLINA DEFENDER MANUAL Ch. 5 (Experts and Other Assistance) (May 1998).

Juvenile clients. Ethical guidelines provide that an attorney should seek to give a juvenile client the same control over his or her case as an adult. *See* N.C. STATE BAR REV'D RULES OF PROF'L CONDUCT R. 1.14 (2003); *see also infra* Appendix A, N.C. COMM'N ON INDIGENT DEFENSE SERVS., PERFORMANCE GUIDELINES FOR APPOINTED COUNSEL IN JUVENILE DELINQUENCY PROCEEDINGS AT THE TRIAL LEVEL, Guideline 2.1 Role of Defense Counsel (Dec. 2007). An attorney may not disclose confidential information regarding the juvenile's case to his or her parents without the client's consent. Such confidential information includes plea offers and the progress of plea negotiations. North Carolina State Bar, 98 Formal Ethics Opinion 18 (1999), *available at* www.ncbar.gov/ethics/.

For a discussion of representing juveniles in plea negotiations, see LOU A. NEWMAN, ALYSON GRINE & ERIC J. ZOGRY, NORTH CAROLINA JUVENILE DEFENDER MANUAL § 12.3 (UNC School of Government 2008), *available at* www.ncids.org/other%20manuals/JuvDefenderManual/Text.htm. For a discussion of juvenile clients who may be incapable of proceeding, see Chapter 7 of that manual.

B. Types of Pleas

A defendant may plead

- guilty;
- not guilty; or
- no contest (if the prosecutor and the judge consent).

G.S. 15A-1011(a), (b).

Guilty plea. "A valid guilty plea acts as a conviction of the offense charged [and] serves as an admission of all the facts alleged in the indictment or other criminal process." *State v. Thompson*, 314 N.C. 618, 623–24 (1985). A guilty plea "is more than a confession which admits that the accused did various acts; it is itself a conviction; nothing remains but to give judgment and determine punishment." *Boykin v. Alabama*, 395 U.S. 238, 242 (1969).

No contest plea. A "no contest" plea is a plea in which the defendant does not acknowledge guilt but agrees not to contest the charge. *See State v. Cooper*, 238 N.C. 241 (1953). "Implicit in a plea of no contest is the recognition that although the defendant is unwilling to expressly admit guilt, he is faced with 'grim alternatives' and is willing to waive his trial and accept the sentence." *State v. Chery*, 203 N.C. App. 310, 314 (2010). This type of plea may be entered only with the prosecutor's and court's permission. G.S. 15A-1011(b). When accepting a plea of no contest, the judge must advise the defendant that he or she will be treated as guilty whether or not guilt is admitted. G.S. 15A-1022(d).

For criminal law purposes, a conviction based on a "no contest" plea carries all of the consequences of a conviction based on a plea of guilty. *State v. Outlaw*, 326 N.C. 467 (1990) (witness may be impeached under N.C. Evidence Rule 609 on basis of "no contest" plea); *State v. Jackson*, 128 N.C. App. 626 (1998) ("no contest" plea entered after 1975 may be used as prior conviction under habitual felon statutes). *But cf. State v. Petty*, 100 N.C. App. 465 (1990) ("no contest" convictions entered before 1975 may not be used to adjudicate habitual felon status). The principal benefit of a "no contest" plea is that it does not constitute an admission of guilt in civil proceedings. *See* Michael G. Okun & John Rubin, *Employment Consequences of a Criminal Conviction in North Carolina*, POPULAR GOV'T, Winter 1998, at 13, *available at* http://sogpubs.unc.edu/electronicversions/pg/rubin.htm.

***Alford* plea.** In *North Carolina v. Alford*, 400 U.S. 25 (1970), the U.S. Supreme Court held that a defendant can factually maintain his innocence but at the same time plead guilty. The trial judge may accept a plea of guilty if there is sufficient evidence of guilt, even if the defendant does not admit guilt. *See State v. McClure*, 280 N.C. 288 (1972). Like a "no contest" plea, a conviction based on an *Alford* plea carries all of the consequences of a conviction based on a guilty plea. "'There is nothing inherent in the nature of an *Alford* plea that gives a defendant any rights, or promises any limitations, with respect to the punishment imposed after the conviction.'" *State v. Alston*, 139 N.C. App. 787, 793 (2000) (quoting *State ex rel. Warren v. Schwarz*, 579 N.W.2d 698, 707 (Wis. 1998) (citation omitted) (internal quotation marks omitted)) (defendant who entered *Alford* plea could still be required as a condition of probation to participate in sex offenders' rehabilitation program where program mandated him to acknowledge guilt). Although there is no statutory requirement that the prosecutor consent to an *Alford* plea, as a practical matter obtaining consent may be necessary as the prosecutor could withdraw the plea offer if dissatisfied with the defendant's unwillingness to concede guilt.

For further discussion of this topic, including whether an *Alford* plea constitutes an admission for later civil proceedings, see Jeff Welty, *Alford Pleas*, N.C. CRIM. L., UNC SCH. OF GOV'T BLOG (April 13, 2010), http://sogweb.sog.unc.edu/blogs/ncclaw/?p=1198.

Conditional plea. Under G.S. 15A-979(b), a defendant may plead guilty in superior court on the condition that he or she retains the right to appeal the denial of a suppression motion filed pursuant to G.S. 15A-974, whether based on a constitutional violation or substantial statutory violation. If the appeal is successful, the plea is vacated.

To preserve the right to appeal, the defendant must explicitly notify the State and the court of his or her intention to appeal before the plea is entered. *See State v. Brown*, 142 N.C. App. 491 (2001); *State v. McBride*, 120 N.C. App. 623 (1995), *aff'd per curiam*,

344 N.C. 623 (1996). Both the written transcript of plea and the verbatim transcript of the in-court plea colloquy should include an explicit statement that the defendant's right to appeal the denial of a suppression motion is preserved.

Giving notice of appeal ***after*** the plea has been entered is necessary to invoke appellate jurisdiction but, without a separate notice of intent to appeal before entry of the plea, it will not suffice to preserve the issue of the denial of the motion to suppress. *See State v. Tew*, 326 N.C. 732 (1990); *Brown*, 142 N.C. App. 491; *McBride*, 120 N.C. App. 623. For more on this procedure, see *infra* § 23.6B, Appeal from Superior Court. *See also* 1 NORTH CAROLINA DEFENDER MANUAL Ch. 14 (Suppression Motions) (July 2002).

While G.S. 15A-979 explicitly gives the defendant the right to appeal from the denial of a suppression motion, a defendant who has entered a plea of guilty otherwise has a very limited right to appellate review. *See State v. Pimental*, 153 N.C. App. 69, 73 (2002) ("[A] defendant who has entered a plea of guilty is not entitled to appellate review as a matter of right, unless the defendant is appealing sentencing issues or the denial of a motion to suppress, or the defendant has made an unsuccessful motion to withdraw the guilty plea."). If your client wants to appeal from a ruling on a pretrial motion other than a motion to suppress, you will have to try the case to completion to preserve that right. For further discussion of a defendant's limited right to appeal from a guilty plea in superior court, see *infra* § 35.1D, Defendant's Right to Appeal from Guilty Plea in Superior Court.

C. Plea Bargaining

"A prosecutor has broad discretion to decide whether to engage in plea negotiations with a defendant and what plea will be offered." Jessica Smith, *Pleas and Plea Negotiations in North Carolina Superior Court*, ADMINISTRATION OF JUSTICE BULLETIN No. 2005/03, at 5 (UNC School of Government, July 2005), *available at* http://sogpubs.unc.edu/electronicversions/pdfs/aojb0503.pdf. The exercise of this discretion will not be found to be unconstitutionally infirm unless the defendant can prove that the prosecutor's decision was "'deliberately based on an unjustifiable standard, such as race, religion, or other arbitrary classification.'" *Id.* (quoting *State v. Woodson*, 287 N.C. 578, 595 (1975), *rev'd on other grounds*, 428 U.S. 280 (1976) (citation omitted) (internal quotation marks omitted)).

A valid plea bargain may include:

- an agreement by the prosecutor to dismiss or reduce charges;
- an agreement by the prosecutor not to charge an additional or more serious crime;
- specific sentencing arrangements;
- an agreement by the prosecutor not to recommend a sentence within the aggravated range;
- an agreement by the prosecutor not to oppose probation or other community or intermediate sentence;
- an agreement by the defendant to pay restitution, including the agreement to pay for

rehabilitative treatment for the victim;
- an agreement by the defendant to testify truthfully for the prosecution against a co-defendant in a related case or in another case;
- an agreement by the defendant not to appeal or not to seek post-conviction relief (except that the defendant may not waive his or her right to assert prosecutorial misconduct or ineffective assistance of counsel as grounds for relief. North Carolina State Bar Ethics Opinion RPC 129 (1993), *available at* www.ncbar.gov/ethics/). *But cf.* Jessica Smith, *Pleas and Plea Negotiations in North Carolina Superior Court*, ADMINISTRATION OF JUSTICE BULLETIN No. 2005/03, at 5–6 (UNC School of Government, July 2005), *available at* http://sogpubs.unc.edu/electronicversions/pdfs/aojb0503.pdf (finding that the North Carolina appellate courts have not specifically dealt with the issue of waiving the right to appeal, that the federal Fourth Circuit Court of Appeals has allowed the procedure, and that other jurisdictions are split on the issue).

See generally G.S. 15A-1021; *see also* G.S. 15A-1054 (charge reductions and sentencing concessions permissible in exchange for truthful testimony).

Limitations on prosecutors. A prosecutor may not seek to induce a defendant to plead guilty or no contest by:

- charging or threatening to charge the defendant with a crime not supported by the facts believed by the prosecutor to be provable;
- charging or threatening to charge the defendant with a crime not ordinarily charged in the jurisdiction for the conduct allegedly engaged in by him; or
- threatening the defendant that if he pleads not guilty, his sentence may be more severe than that which is ordinarily imposed in the jurisdiction in similar cases on defendants who plead not guilty.

G.S. 15A-1021 Official Commentary. Additionally, a prosecutor may not use or threaten to use his or her statutory calendaring power to coerce a defendant to plead guilty. *See* North Carolina State Bar Ethics Opinion RPC 243 (1997) (unethical for prosecutor to threaten that if the defendant does not accept the plea bargain, the prosecutor will make the defendant sit in the courtroom all week and then place the defendant's case "on the calendar every Monday morning for weeks to come"), *available at* www.ncbar.gov/ethics/.

Plea bargains may not include payment provisions except for payment of attorney's fees and court costs, restitution to the victim, and fines. For example, the prosecutor may not offer more advantageous pleas to defendants willing to make charitable contributions to designated organizations. *See* N.C. State Bar Ethics Opinion RPC 204 (1995) (finding that prosecutors could not ethically offer special treatment to offenders who were charged with violating traffic laws or minor criminal offenses in exchange for their donation to the local school board), *available at* www.ncbar.gov/ethics/.

The prosecutor may not agree to refrain from disclosing the defendant's prior record. Although a defense attorney has no affirmative obligation to inform the court of the defendant's prior record, the parties may not agree to withhold the information from the court. G.S. 15A-1340.14(f) requires the prosecutor in felony cases to make all feasible efforts to obtain and present to the court the offender's full record. This statute implies that the prosecutor may not agree to withhold information about the defendant's record as a condition of a plea bargain. The statute only applies to felony sentencing. Arguably, Rule 3.3 of the N.C. State Bar Revised Rules of Professional Conduct, imposing the duty of candor toward the tribunal, would preclude a prosecutor in a misdemeanor case from concealing or misrepresenting information about the defendant's record, although the prosecutor would not have the duty to search for the defendant's record as in felony cases.

A plea bargain may not include conditions that are otherwise barred by law. For instance, a defendant may not plead guilty in exchange for concurrent sentences when the law requires that consecutive sentences be imposed. *See State v. Wall*, 348 N.C. 671 (1998). Where a plea agreement contains invalid conditions, the defendant must be allowed to withdraw the plea. *See, e.g., State v. White*, ___ N.C. App. ___, 711 S.E.2d 862 (2011) (defendant pled guilty pursuant to a plea arrangement that purported to preserve his right to appeal from the denial of his pretrial motion to dismiss; court held that the plea agreement violated the law and the plea must be vacated because defendant had no right to appeal from the denial of that motion); *Hamilton v. Freeman*, 147 N.C. App. 195 (2001) (Department of Correction may not unilaterally alter illegal sentencing agreement contained in plea bargain; proper remedy is for Department to notify court to vacate plea). *But cf. State v. Rico*, ___ N.C. App. ___, 720 S.E.2d 801 (2012) (upholding portion of plea agreement benefitting defendant while striking illegal condition benefitting State), *writ of supersedeas and motion for temporary stay allowed*, ___ N.C.___, 721 S.E.2d 229 (2012). For a further discussion of the *Rico* case, see *infra* § 35.5B, Applicability of G.S. 15A-1335 (reinstatement of and sentencing on greater offense following vacation of negotiated plea to lesser offense).

A defendant may not plead guilty to an offense that is not the same offense or a lesser included offense of the crime for which he or she was indicted. *See, e.g., State v. Craig*, 21 N.C. App. 51 (1974) (defendant charged with DUI could not plead to reckless driving as that was not a lesser included offense); *State v. Cassada*, 6 N.C. App. 629 (1969) (defendant indicted for larceny could not plead guilty to receiving stolen goods, where that offense was not lesser included offense of larceny); *see also In re Fuller*, 345 N.C. 157, 160–61 (1996) (district court judge erred by soliciting and accepting a guilty plea to exceeding a safe speed when defendant was charged with passing a stopped school bus because it is "not within the trial judge's province to negotiate a plea or enter judgment on a plea to a charge which is not a lesser included offense of the charge at issue").

If you want to construct a plea bargain that includes pleading guilty to a related but unindicted offense, the prosecutor should dismiss the indictment with prejudice and seek a superseding indictment or prepare an information. On an appeal from district court, the prosecutor must prepare an information. A defendant charged with a non-capital offense may waive indictment and proceed on an information. In district court, the prosecutor should file a statement of charges. *See* 1 NORTH CAROLINA DEFENDER MANUAL Ch. 8 (Criminal Pleadings) (July 2004).

Benefits to third parties. Benefits to third parties are not impermissible in plea bargains but should be scrutinized carefully by the court. *See United States v. Morrow*, 914 F.2d 608, 613 (4th Cir. 1990) (plea bargain involving leniency for third person can pose greater danger of inducing false or involuntary guilty plea because it "'skew[s] the assessment of the risks a defendant must consider'" (quoting *Bordenkircher v. Hayes*, 434 U.S. 357, 365 n.8 (1978))); *see also State v. Salvetti*, 202 N.C. App. 18 (2010) (holding that the prosecutor did not use improper pressure when he made the defendant's wife's plea deal contingent on the defendant's plea of guilty; implicitly holding that package plea deals are not involuntary per se in North Carolina); *State v. Summerford*, 65 N.C. App. 519 (1983) (plea offer in which prosecutor offered to dismiss charges against wife if husband pled guilty was proper).

Pleas of guilty in capital murder cases. Even where evidence of an aggravating circumstance exists, the State may agree not to seek the death penalty against a defendant in exchange for the defendant's plea of guilty to first-degree murder. G.S. 15A-2001(b).

Substantial assistance in drug cases. G.S. 90-95(h)(5), governing drug trafficking offenses, states that the court may reduce the minimum sentence for trafficking or impose a suspended sentence if the court finds that the defendant "provided substantial assistance in the identification, arrest, or conviction of any accomplices, accessories, co-conspirators, or principals." Case law interpreting this section gives trial judges discretion in determining what constitutes "substantial assistance." *See also State v. Wells*, 104 N.C. App. 274 (1991) (whether trial judge finds that defendant's aid amounts to "substantial assistance" is discretionary); *State v. Perkerol*, 77 N.C. App. 292 (1985) (defendant has no right to lesser sentence even if he provides what he considers to be substantial assistance in identification of accomplices); *State v. Myers*, 61 N.C. App. 554 (1983) (no abuse of discretion for failing to find "substantial assistance" where defendant's proffered information was not new and defendant did not assist in prosecution).

D. Informing Client of Consequences of Plea Bargain

Effective assistance of counsel. Advising a client whether to enter a guilty plea is generally subject to the two-part test for ineffective assistance of counsel from *Strickland v. Washington*, 466 U.S. 668 (1984). Under that test, counsel is ineffective if (1) the representation falls below an objective standard of reasonableness and (2) there is a reasonable probability that, but for counsel's errors, the result of the proceeding would have been different. Where a defendant shows that his or her attorney's ineffective advice led to the improvident acceptance of a guilty plea, the second part of the *Strickland* inquiry focuses on whether "there is a reasonable probability that, but for counsel's errors, [the defendant] would not have pleaded guilty and would have insisted on going to trial." *Hill v. Lockhart*, 474 U.S. 52, 59 (1985). Where a defendant shows that his or her attorney's ineffective advice led to the improvident rejection of a plea offer, the inquiry focuses on whether "there is a reasonable probability the plea offer would have been presented to the court . . ., that the court would have accepted its terms, and that the conviction or sentence, or both, under the offer's terms would have been less severe than under the judgment and sentence that in fact were imposed." *Lafler v. Cooper*, ___ U.S. ___ (2012) (remanding for determination of appropriate remedy).

Resolution of claims of ineffective-assistance of counsel are fact-specific and are beyond the scope of this manual. The discussion below focuses primarily on professional standards for advising clients about entering a guilty plea. In evaluating claims of ineffective assistance, the courts have recognized that "these standards may be valuable measures of the prevailing professional norms of effective representation." *Padilla v. Kentucky*, ___ U.S. ___, 130 S. Ct. 1473, 1482 (2010).

National standards. The Compendium of Standards for Indigent Defense Systems is a compilation of national and state guidelines on the defense function. Many of the listed guidelines provide that, where applicable, defense attorneys should discuss the following issues with their clients regarding guilty pleas:

- Nature of the charges. The client should understand the crime he or she is pleading guilty to having done.
- Rights that are waived by pleading guilty, including any waiver of appellate or post-conviction rights.
- Maximum sentence, including any habitual offender or other sentencing enhancements.
- Mandatory minimum sentence.
- Sex offender registration requirements.
- Possibility of forfeiture of assets.
- Whether a sentence for future offenses may be enhanced on the basis of the current conviction.
- Effects on immigration status (discussed further below).
- Whether the court may impose costs, including attorneys fees and court costs.
- Loss of, or restrictions on, drivers' license or professional license.

See 2 BUREAU OF JUSTICE ASSISTANCE, U.S. DEP'T OF JUSTICE, COMPENDIUM OF STANDARDS FOR INDIGENT DEFENSE SYSTEMS, Section H. Disposition Without Trial (2000), *available at* www.mynlada.org/defender/DOJ/standardsv2/welcome.html.

North Carolina guidelines. The guidelines for defense services adopted by the North Carolina Commission on Indigent Defense Services (Appendix A of this manual) contain similar provisions on advising clients about entering into a guilty plea. The principal difference is that the North Carolina guidelines divide the potential consequences of a plea into two categories.

For most of the consequences listed above (with the exception of immigration consequences), the North Carolina guidelines recommend that counsel "be fully aware of, and fully advise the client." Appendix A, *infra*, N.C. COMM'N ON INDIGENT DEFENSE

SERVS., PERFORMANCE GUIDELINES FOR INDIGENT DEFENSE REPRESENTATION IN NON-CAPITAL CRIMINAL CASES AT THE TRIAL LEVEL, Guideline 6.2(b) The Contents of the Negotiations (Nov. 2004) (also recommending that counsel advise the client about earned time credits and the availability of any diversion or rehabilitation programs).

For "other potential collateral consequences," the North Carolina guidelines take a more modest approach, recommending that counsel "discuss" them with the client. *Id.* The other consequences include:

- motor vehicle or other licensing;
- parental rights;
- possession of firearms;
- voting rights;
- employment;
- military and government service considerations; and
- potential for exposure to or impact on any federal charges.

Practice note: The North Carolina guidelines include immigration consequences in this second category of consequences. But, in light of the *Padilla* decision, discussed next, counsel ***must*** consult with noncitizen clients about the immigration consequences of a criminal conviction.

Advice about immigration and other significant "collateral" consequences. The courts have sometimes distinguished between direct and collateral consequences in assessing counsel's obligation to advise clients about the impact of a criminal conviction. *See, e.g., State v. Goforth*, 130 N.C. App. 603, 605 (1998) (noting that, "[g]enerally, an attorney is not required to advise his [or her] client of the myriad 'collateral consequences' of pleading guilty"). In *Padilla v. Kentucky*, ___ U.S. ___, 130 S. Ct. 1473, 1481–82 (2010), the U.S. Supreme Court refused to apply this distinction to advice about immigration consequences. Because of the importance of immigration consequences and their close connection to the criminal process, the Court concluded that defense counsel has an obligation to advise noncitizen clients about immigration consequences, whether characterized as direct or collateral.

The *Padilla* court described a two-step approach. One, if the immigration consequences are clear—as they were in *Padilla*, where the defendant was facing virtually mandatory deportation if convicted—counsel must advise a noncitizen client of the consequences of conviction. In that instance, the failure to advise, as well as the giving of incorrect advice, falls below expected professional norms. Two, if the immigration consequences of a guilty plea are unclear, counsel at least must advise a noncitizen client that a conviction may carry adverse immigration consequences. *Cf. State v. Alshaif*, ___ N.C. App. ___, ___ S.E.2d ___ (2012) (finding that *Padilla* did not apply retroactively to defendant's case and upholding denial of motion for appropriate relief).

Practice note: As a practical matter, the two-step approach adopted in *Padilla* requires that counsel investigate a noncitizen's circumstances to determine whether potential immigration consequences are clear or unclear. Only then will counsel have sufficient information to satisfy the obligation of appropriately advising a noncitizen client. For a detailed discussion of the immigration consequences of a conviction, see SEJAL ZOTA & JOHN RUBIN, IMMIGRATION CONSEQUENCES OF A CRIMINAL CONVICTION IN NORTH CAROLINA (UNC School of Government 2008), *available at* www.ncids.org/Other%20 Manuals/Immigration%20Manual/Text.htm. The immigration consequences manual is not a substitute, however, for independent research and consultation with an immigration expert as needed.

The approach taken in *Padilla* may apply to other significant consequences of a conviction, whether characterized as direct or collateral. Thus, effective assistance of counsel may require the giving of advice about sex offender registration and monitoring requirements as a result of a criminal conviction. *See Bauder v. Dep't of Corr.*, 619 F.3d 1272 (11th Cir. 2010) (relying on *Padilla* and finding counsel's performance deficient based on counsel's incorrect advice about the potential for civil commitment as a result of the defendant's guilty plea to stalking of a minor). The North Carolina courts have held that sex offender registration and monitoring requirements are collateral matters for purposes of evaluating the taking of a guilty plea by a judge (*see infra* § 23.4B), but they have not addressed counsel's obligation to advise clients about these restrictions, which may last for life.

Misadvice about "collateral" consequences. For less significant "collateral" consequences, attorneys still may be found ineffective for gross misadvice to a client about that consequence. *See State v. Goforth*, 130 N.C. App. 603 (1998) (advice of attorney who failed to accurately answer defendant's question about collateral consequence of plea was deficient).

E. Judge's Participation in Plea Discussions

Generally. G.S. 15A-1021(a) allows trial judges to participate in plea negotiations. If represented by counsel, the defendant does not have to be present during these negotiations. *Id.* The judge's participation can be advantageous, both as a means of persuading the defendant to accept a plea bargain and because the judge is going to have to approve any sentencing agreement reached.

Pre-plea approval. G.S. 15A-1021(c) authorizes parties who have reached an agreement as to sentence to advise the judge, before the entry of the plea and with the judge's permission, of the terms of that arrangement and the reasons that the arrangement was made. The judge may indicate to the parties whether he or she will concur in the proposed disposition. The judge may withdraw his or her concurrence if he or she later learns of information that is not consistent with the information given previously. G.S. 15A-1021(c).

No coercion permitted. Neither the judge nor the prosecutor may "bring improper pressure upon a defendant to induce a plea of guilty or no contest." G.S. 15A-1021(b);

see also Brady v. United States, 397 U.S. 742, 750 (1970) ("[T]he agents of the State may not produce a plea by actual or threatened physical harm or by mental coercion overbearing the will of the defendant."); *State v. Benfield*, 264 N.C. 75 (1965) (statements made by the judge during defendant's jury trial to the effect the jury would likely convict and, if so, the judge felt inclined to give defendant a long sentence rendered defendant's subsequent guilty plea involuntary); *State v. Pait*, 81 N.C. App. 286 (1986) (judge who told defendant he was tired of frivolous not-guilty pleas coerced defendant into pleading guilty).

Judge's role in sentencing on plea bargain. The judge's role in acting on a plea bargain differs significantly depending on whether the plea bargain does or does not contain an agreed-on sentence. If the parties have agreed on a sentence as part of a plea bargain, the judge must approve the sentence to accept the plea. If the judge does not approve the sentence, he or she is not required to accept the plea. G.S. 15A-1023(b). If a plea agreement contains no sentence provision, the judge must accept the plea upon determining that it is an informed choice of the defendant and there is a factual basis for the plea. G.S. 15A-1023(c). The sentence for the agreed-on offense is then within the judge's discretion.

For a further discussion of the judge's role based on the presence or absence of a sentencing provision in a plea agreement, see *infra* § 23.4D, Judge's Sentencing Discretion.

23.4 The Plea Procedure

Once the parties have reached a negotiated plea settlement, the defendant must tender his or her plea of guilty (or no contest) in open court. G.S. 15A-1011(a). Before accepting the plea, the trial judge must be convinced of two things. First, the judge must be convinced that the plea is the informed choice of the defendant and, in so doing, must be aware of the conditions of any plea agreement. Second, the judge must ensure that there is a factual basis for the plea.

If the plea arrangement includes a sentencing recommendation, the trial judge must decide whether he or she will approve the recommendation before accepting the defendant's plea. The trial judge's responsibilities in accepting a plea are discussed below.

A. Recordation Requirement

A verbatim transcript must be made of any proceeding in which a defendant enters a guilty or no contest plea in superior court. The record of the proceeding must include the judge's statutorily required inquiries to the defendant, defense counsel, and the prosecutor, as well as all responses. If there is a written transcript of plea, this transcript must be made part of the record. If not, the terms of any plea bargain must be set forth orally on the record. G.S. 15A-1026.

If a defendant pleads guilty or no contest to an H or I felony in district court pursuant to G.S. 7A-272, this proceeding also must be recorded. G.S. 7A-191.1.

B. Judge's Duty to Ensure Informed Choice

Constitutional requirements. For a plea of guilty to be valid under the Fourteenth Amendment, the record must affirmatively show that the plea was the "knowing and voluntary" choice of the defendant. *Boykin v. Alabama*, 395 U.S. 238, 242–43 (1969).

A plea is "knowing and voluntary" only if the defendant is made fully aware of the direct consequences of pleading guilty, including the actual value of any sentencing commitments. *Brady v. United States*, 397 U.S. 742 (1970); *State v. Bozeman*, 115 N.C. App. 658 (1994) (quoting *Brady*). Direct consequences are those that have a "'definite, immediate and largely automatic effect on the range of the defendant's punishment.'" *Bozeman*, 115 N.C. App. 658, 661 (quoting *Cuthrell v. Director, Patuxent Inst.*, 475 F.2d 1364, 1366 (4th Cir. 1973)). *Bozeman* held that a mandatory minimum sentence is a "direct consequence" that must be revealed to the defendant. Additional periods of imprisonment that result from a defendant's guilty plea to habitual offender status are also considered "direct consequences." *State v. McNeil*, 158 N.C. App. 96 (2003).

North Carolina courts have held that a defendant's parole eligibility is not a "direct consequence" of a guilty plea. *State v. Daniels*, 114 N.C. App. 501 (1994). Likewise, North Carolina courts have held that satellite-based monitoring is a "collateral consequence," not a "direct consequence," of a plea to an offense resulting in that consequence. *State v. Bare*, 197 N.C. App. 461 (2009).

Under this approach, the failure of the judge to advise the defendant of indirect or collateral consequences does not render a guilty plea invalid; however, the failure of defense counsel to advise the defendant of significant consequences, even those traditionally considered collateral, may constitute ineffective assistance of counsel. *See Padilla v. Kentucky*, ___ U.S. ___, 130 S. Ct. 1473 (2010) (requiring that counsel advise noncitizen clients about immigration consequences); *Hill v. Lockhart*, 474 U.S. 52, 60 (1985) (declining to decide whether counsel's erroneous advice about parole eligibility may be considered constitutionally ineffective; erroneous advice was not prejudicial); *see also supra* § 23.3D (discussing counsel's obligations to advise clients about the consequences of a guilty plea).

Statutory colloquy with defendant. Before accepting a plea of guilty, the trial judge has a statutory obligation to personally address the defendant and inform him or her of the following:

- the right to remain silent;
- the right to plead not guilty;
- that the defendant is waiving his or her right to a jury trial and right to confront witnesses;
- the maximum sentence the defendant may receive and any mandatory minimum

sentence; and
- the possibility of deportation if he or she is not a citizen of the United States.

G.S. 15A-1022(a). In addition, the judge must

- determine that the defendant understands the nature of the charges; and
- ensure the defendant is satisfied with counsel.

Id. The judge must address the defendant in person and not only through counsel. *State v. Williams*, 65 N.C. App. 472 (1983) (error but harmless on unusual facts of case for judge to fail to address defendant in person; case put onus on defense counsel to object).

Unless the defendant makes a specific inquiry or indicates that he or she does not understand the charges, the judge does not have to list the elements of the offense or explain the different theories of an offense. *Compare State v. Barts*, 321 N.C. 170 (1987) (where defendant stated he did not understand the two theories of murder to which he was pleading guilty, judge adequately explained them to him, including the elements of premeditated and deliberate murder and felony murder) *with State v. Smith*, 352 N.C. 531 (2000) (plea colloquy adequate despite judge's failure to explain theories of first-degree murder where defendant indicated he understood the nature of the charges and their elements).

Colloquy with counsel. In addition to the requirements of G.S. 15A-1022(a), the trial judge must inquire personally of the defendant, the prosecutor, and defense counsel regarding whether:

- the plea of guilty is the product of a plea bargain and, if so, what the conditions of the bargain are;
- there were any prior plea discussions;
- the defendant is entering the plea of his or her own free will; and
- anyone has promised or threatened the defendant to cause him or her to enter the plea.

See G.S. 15A-1022(b). "The judge may not accept a plea of guilty or no contest from a defendant without first determining that the plea is a product of informed choice." *Id.*; *see also State v. Salvetti*, 202 N.C. App. 18 (2010) (trial judge correctly determined that defendant was fully informed of the consequences of his choice to enter an *Alford* plea; no violation of G.S. 15A-1022(b)).

Requirement that full agreement be disclosed on record. Both parties to a plea agreement have an ethical obligation to disclose all material elements of the plea bargain to the court. North Carolina State Bar Ethics Opinion RPC 152 (1993) (prosecutor may not knowingly conceal fact that he withdrew charge as part of plea agreement), *available at* www.ncbar.gov/ethics/.

Transcript of plea. The N.C. Administrative Office of the Courts has prepared a form for use in cases where the defendant is pleading guilty or no contest. *See* AOC Form AOC-

CR-300, "Transcript of Plea" (Mar. 2010), *available at* www.nccourts.org/Forms/Documents/839.pdf.

C. Factual Basis for Plea

Generally. Once the judge has determined that a plea is a voluntary and knowing decision by the defendant, he or she must find that there is a sufficient factual basis for the plea of guilty or no contest. The following information may be relied on in finding a factual basis:

- a statement of the facts by the prosecutor;
- a defendant's written statement;
- a presentence report;
- sworn testimony, including reliable hearsay; and
- a statement of the facts by defense counsel.

G.S. 15A-1022(c). The judge may rely on any of the above sources. *See State v. Atkins*, 349 N.C. 62 (1998) (not all of above sources required in every case; the trial judge may consider any information properly brought to his or her attention in determining whether there is a factual basis for a plea of guilty or no contest); *see also Santobello v. New York*, 404 U.S. 257, 261 (1971) (under federal rules of criminal procedure, the factual basis for a guilty plea must appear "on the record").

Under G.S. 15A-1022(c), there must be an independent judicial determination that a sufficient factual basis exists before a trial judge can accept a guilty plea. *State v. Agnew*, 361 N.C. 333, 337 (2007) (finding that the trial judge erred in accepting defendant's plea where the judge relied solely on the indictment, the transcript of plea, and defense counsel's stipulation that there was a factual basis for the plea; taken together these "did not contain enough information for an independent judicial determination of defendant's actual guilt"). The statute "contemplate[s] that some substantive material independent of the plea itself appear of record which tends to show that defendant is, in fact, guilty." *State v. Sinclair*, 301 N.C. 193, 199 (1980) (holding that a transcript of plea, standing alone, cannot provide the factual basis for a plea). While the standard for finding a factual basis for a guilty plea is fairly lenient, the record must positively show the factual basis. *See State v. Weathers*, 339 N.C. 441 (1994) (factual basis for failure to appear charge not present when the only witness at the plea colloquy testified that defendant was present when case was called); *State v. Flint*, 199 N.C. App. 709 (2009) (guilty plea set aside where the record showed a factual basis for only forty-seven of the sixty-eight felony charges to which defendant pled guilty).

Practice note: In preparing to negotiate a plea bargain with the prosecutor, you should consider developing a factual basis for lesser included offenses. In a murder case, for instance, you may have to convince the prosecutor and the court that there is a legitimate factual basis for a manslaughter plea.

Multiple counts of same offense. Use care when considering whether your client should plead guilty to multiple counts of the same offense, such as multiple larcenies or multiple conspiracies—the evidence may support only one such offense. *See, e.g., State v. Jaynes*, 342 N.C. 249 (1995) (larceny or robbery of different objects from same person constitutes one larceny or robbery). In *State v. Kimble*, 141 N.C. App. 144 (2000), the defendant pled guilty to eight counts of soliciting a murder, but on appeal argued the State's factual showing proved one solicitation only. The appellate court upheld the defendant's convictions because the defense attorney did not object during the plea hearing to the State's summary of the factual basis, did not argue before the trial court that the factual basis supported only one count of solicitation, and did not move to withdraw the defendant's plea on the grounds of the inadequacy of the factual basis. Note that a defendant usually waives any double jeopardy claim, including an objection to multiple punishment, by pleading guilty. *See State v. Hughes*, 136 N.C. App. 92 (1999) (defendant who pled guilty to offenses of accessing computers and obtaining property by false pretense waived multiple punishment defense and had no right to arrest of judgment on one offense); *see also* 1 NORTH CAROLINA DEFENDER MANUAL § 13.4B (Motion to Dismiss on Double Jeopardy Grounds) (Mar. 2009) (discussing waiver of double jeopardy claims).

Admission of facts resulting in "collateral" consequences. In some instances, the collateral consequences of a criminal conviction may depend on facts underlying the conviction, not the bare conviction itself. For example, for immigration purposes, a fraud or deceit offense involving a loss of more than $10,000 is treated as an aggravated felony, triggering the most severe immigration consequences. If the defendant admits those facts in pleading guilty or fails to contest the factual basis offered by the prosecutor in support of the plea, the entity responsible for administering the consequence may consider the fact as established.

Practice note: If during a plea colloquy in superior court, the prosecutor's factual proffer includes allegations that are broader than needed to establish the basis for the plea and that are disputed by the client, defense counsel should consider contesting them. If the prosecutor proffers the disputed allegations as part of the factual basis for the offense, counsel can state his or her disagreement with the particular allegations when asked by the judge to stipulate to the prosecutor's recitation of facts. Counsel does not necessarily need to present evidence or call witnesses. Defense counsel may need to discuss the matter with the prosecutor before the taking of the plea to be sure the prosecutor is willing to enter into the plea bargain under those circumstances. (In district court, plea proceedings are generally not recorded so it is not as critical for counsel to state the defendant's position.) Depending on the applicable law, the authority responsible for administering the collateral consequence may be able to go outside the record of the criminal proceedings to determine the circumstances of the offense; but, because the record of the criminal proceedings would indicate that the circumstances were disputed, the criminal case record should not be conclusive against the client. *See generally* SEJAL ZOTA & JOHN RUBIN, IMMIGRATION CONSEQUENCES OF A CRIMINAL CONVICTION IN NORTH CAROLINA § 6.1C, at 70–71 (UNC School of Government 2008), *available at* www.ncids.org/Other%20Manuals/Immigration%20Manual/Chapter%206.pdf. To determine the best course for the client in plea proceedings, counsel will need to determine the collateral consequences of greatest significance to the client and determine the convictions and any related circumstances that trigger the consequences.

D. Judge's Sentencing Discretion

Sentencing provisions in plea agreements. Where the parties have agreed on a particular sentence as part of a plea agreement, the judge must be informed of the sentencing arrangement at the time that the plea is taken. G.S. 15A-1023(a). The judge must advise the parties whether he or she will approve the arrangement and sentence the defendant accordingly. G.S. 15A-1023(b). A plea bargain that has a sentencing recommendation by the State must be approved by the judge before it is enforceable. *See State v. Wallace*, 345 N.C. 462 (1997) (trial judge permitted to reject plea agreement to second-degree murder that included specific sentencing recommendation); *State v. Hudson*, 331 N.C. 122 (1992) (a prosecutor has no authority to bind the State to a particular sentence in a defendant's case until the trial judge has approved the proposed sentence); *State v. Santiago*, 148 N.C. App. 62 (2001) (a lack of judicial approval of a plea arrangement with a sentence recommendation renders the proposed agreement null and void). *But see infra* § 23.4F (explaining that a defendant may enforce a plea agreement before a judge has accepted it if there has been detrimental reliance).

Sentencing recommendation rejected. If the judge does not approve the sentencing arrangement, he or she must

- inform the parties that he or she rejects the plea arrangement;
- refuse to accept the defendant's plea of guilty or no contest;
- advise the defendant personally that neither party is bound by the rejected plea arrangement;
- advise the parties of the reasons the arrangement was rejected; and
- give the parties an opportunity to modify the agreement accordingly.

G.S. 15A-1023(b). The judge's rejection must be noted on the plea transcript and made part of the record. *Id.*; *see also* G.S. 15A-1026.

When a plea arrangement is rejected, the defendant is entitled to a continuance until the next session of court. G.S. 15A-1023(b); *State v. Tyndall*, 55 N.C. App. 57 (1981); *see also State v. Martin*, 77 N.C. App. 61 (1985) (defendant must affirmatively ask for continuance). A defendant does not have the right to appeal from a trial judge's rejection of a plea arrangement with a sentence recommendation. G.S. 15A-1023(b); *see also Santiago*, 148 N.C. App. 62.

Even if the agreement had been previously disclosed to the judge and received his or her preliminary approval, the judge may change his or her mind and refuse to accept the agreement upon learning of information that is inconsistent with the prior representations. G.S. 15A-1021(c).

Sentencing recommendation initially approved, later rejected. Sometimes a judge will accept a plea entered pursuant to a plea arrangement containing a sentence recommendation and then, at the time of sentencing, change his or her mind and decide to impose a sentence different from that specified in the plea arrangement. If this occurs, the judge must inform the defendant of that fact and give the defendant an opportunity to withdraw the plea of guilty. If the defendant decides to withdraw the guilty plea, he or she is entitled to a continuance until the next session of court. G.S. 15A-1024; *see also State v. Puckett*, 299 N.C. 727 (1980) (once the trial judge determined that he would not consolidate the defendant's five charges and run them concurrently with defendant's other sentences as contemplated by the plea arrangement, he should have followed the provisions of 15A-1024 and given defendant the opportunity to withdraw his plea).

The mandates of G.S. 15A-1024 must be followed by the trial judge even if he or she intends to give a defendant a less severe sentence than was agreed to in the plea arrangement. *State v. Wall*, 167 N.C. App. 312, 316 (2004) ("[T]he Official Commentary accompanying [G.S. 15A-1024] actually indicates that a legislative committee considered and rejected the phrase 'more severe than' and instead amended the statute 'to apply if there is *any change at all* concerning the substance.'" (emphasis in original)).

Plea arrangements with no sentencing recommendation. If the parties reach a plea arrangement that does not involve the prosecutor's recommendation of a particular sentence, the judge must accept the plea when:

- it is the informed choice of the defendant; and
- there is a factual basis for the plea.

G.S. 15A-1023(c). For example, if the prosecutor agrees to accept a plea to a lesser offense than the one charged, and there is no sentencing provision included in the agreement, the judge must accept the plea when the above conditions apply. *See, e.g., State v. Melton*, 307 N.C. 370, 377 (1983) (after determining that the defendant's guilty plea had been made voluntarily and that there was a factual basis for the plea, the trial judge was required by G.S. 15A-1023(c) to accept the plea to the lesser included offense of second degree murder; "however, the plea bargain did not limit the judge's opportunity to exercise his discretion in determining an appropriate sentence for the defendant").

E. Defendant's Right to Withdraw Plea

Before entry of plea. A defendant has the right to withdraw from a plea agreement at any time before he or she enters the plea. *See State v. Collins*, 300 N.C. 142, 148–49 (1980) (stating that defendants "are always free to withdraw from plea agreements prior to entry of their guilty plea regardless of any prejudice to the prosecution that may result from a breach" (citation omitted) (internal quotation marks omitted)); *see also* Jessica Smith, *Pleas and Plea Negotiations in North Carolina Superior Court*, ADMINISTRATION OF JUSTICE BULLETIN No. 2005/03, at 7–8 (UNC School of Government, July 2005) (reaching same conclusion), *available at* http://sogpubs.unc.edu/electronicversions/pdfs/aojb0503.pdf. If the defendant has pled guilty but moves to withdraw his or her plea before being sentenced, he or she should be permitted to do so for any "fair and just" reason. *State v. Handy*, 326 N.C. 532, 539 (1990) (defendant permitted to withdraw plea of guilty to murder, before sentencing hearing, where he stated that he had felt "pressured" to plead guilty); *State v. Deal*, 99 N.C. App. 456 (1990) (defendant with limited intelligence who misunderstood his plea bargain permitted to withdraw plea before sentencing). Although there is no absolute right to the withdrawal of a guilty plea, a motion to withdraw the plea that is made before a defendant is sentenced "should be granted with liberality." *Handy*, 326 N.C. 532, 537.

Factors that favor permitting the defendant to withdraw a guilty plea include:

- the defendant's assertion of innocence;
- weakness in the State's evidence;
- a short length of time between the entry of the guilty plea and the desire to change it;
- lack of competent counsel at all relevant times;
- the defendant's misunderstanding of the consequences of a guilty plea;
- hasty entry of the guilty plea; and
- confusion or coercion.

See State v. Meyer, 330 N.C. 738, 743 (1992) (relying on *Handy*, 326 N.C. 532, 539); *see also State v. Graham*, 122 N.C. App. 635, 637 (1996) (defendant who moved to withdraw guilty plea five weeks after entry and who made no "concrete assertion of innocence" not permitted to withdraw guilty plea). No one of the above factors is determinative, and the list is not exclusive. *State v. Chery*, 203 N.C. App. 310 (2010).

If the defendant establishes a fair and just reason for withdrawal of his or her plea, the State may refute the defendant's showing "by evidence of concrete prejudice to its case by reason of the withdrawal of the plea." *Handy*, 326 N.C. 532, 539. However, a lack of prejudice to the State without other grounds for withdrawal of a plea does not necessarily constitute a "fair and just reason" for withdrawal. *See Meyer*, 330 N.C. 738 (finding that *Handy* did not support the defendant's argument that because the State failed to show concrete evidence of prejudice to its case, the motion to withdraw the plea should have been granted).

After sentencing. After sentence is imposed, a defendant may withdraw his or her plea of guilty only "'to avoid manifest injustice.'" *Handy*, 326 N.C. 532, 536 (quoting *State v. Olish*, 266 S.E.2d 134, 136 (W. Va. 1980)); *State v. Suites*, 109 N.C. App. 373 (1993). The courts have stated that the stricter standard that is applied to postsentence motions to withdraw "is warranted by the likelihood that, after sentencing, the defendant will view the plea bargain as a tactical mistake or that other portions of the plea bargain agreement already will have been performed by the prosecutor, such as the dismissal of additional charges." *Suites*, 109 N.C. App. 373, 376. The courts also have stated that this standard is warranted "by 'the settled policy of giving finality to criminal sentences which result from a voluntary and properly counseled guilty plea.'" *Id.* (citations omitted) (internal quotation marks omitted).

A motion to withdraw a plea that is made after sentencing is considered a motion for appropriate relief. *State v. Salvetti*, 202 N.C. App. 18 (2010). For a further discussion of motions for appropriate relief, see *infra* § 35.3, Motions for Appropriate Relief.

Additional resources. For further discussion of the withdrawal of guilty pleas, including a collection of cases applying the "fair and just" standard, see Jessica Smith, *Pleas and Plea Negotiations in North Carolina Superior Court*, ADMINISTRATION OF JUSTICE BULLETIN No. 2005/03, at 16–18 (UNC School of Government, July 2005), *available at* http://sogpubs.unc.edu/electronicversions/pdfs/aojb0503.pdf.

F. State's Right to Rescind Plea Agreement

Right to rescind before acceptance of plea. A prosecutor may withdraw from a plea agreement at any time until:

- entry of the plea by the defendant—that is, when the judge accepts the plea in open court; or
- there is an act of detrimental reliance by the defendant on the plea arrangement.

State v. Collins, 300 N.C. 142 (1980); *see also State v. Marlow*, 334 N.C. 273 (1993) (where two joined co-defendants were each offered a plea, the State was permitted to rescind offer when trial judge rejected plea agreement with one defendant and State considered pleas a "package deal"; taking polygraph not "detrimental reliance").

No right to rescind after acceptance of plea. Once a defendant's guilty plea is accepted by the court, the defendant has a constitutional right to enforcement of the plea's provisions. *Santobello v. New York*, 404 U.S. 257 (1971); *see also State v. Johnson*, 95 N.C. App. 757 (1989) (State obligated to abide by plea agreement when prosecutor did not move to vacate plea until after judge had accepted defendant's plea of guilty). If the prosecution fails to comply with the plea agreement, the defendant is entitled to either: (i) the opportunity to withdraw his or her guilty plea (i.e., to rescind it); or (ii) specific performance of the plea agreement, depending on the circumstances. *Santobello*, 404 U.S. 257; *see also State v. King*, ___ N.C. App. ___, 721 S.E.2d 327 (2012) (holding that State must comply with a condition of the plea agreement that required it to return funds seized from defendant even though it was later discovered that the funds had been turned over to the Drug Enforcement Administration; because money is fungible and it was within the State's power to return funds equal to the amount seized, the trial judge erred in finding that specific performance was not possible and in ordering rescission); *State v. Tyson*, 189 N.C. App. 408 (2008) (case remanded to trial court to determine whether defendant's guilty plea was induced by misrepresentations by the State; if so, defendant was entitled to specific performance of the plea agreement in accordance with defendant's reasonable interpretation of that agreement or rescission of the guilty plea); *State v. Isom*, 119 N.C. App. 225 (1995) (holding that defendant was entitled to withdraw his guilty plea); *State v. Rodriguez*, 111 N.C. App. 141 (1993) (ordering specific performance).

The factors that either an appellate or trial court may consider in deciding between rescission and specific performance are:

- who broke the bargain;
- whether the violation was deliberate;
- the wishes of the defendant; and
- any change of circumstances or new information between the plea and the violation.

State v. Blackwell, 135 N.C. App. 729, 731 (1999) (stating that "due process mandates strict adherence to any plea agreement" and remanding to trial court for determination of appropriate remedy), *remanded on other grounds*, 353 N.C. 259 (2000).

G. Defendant's Right to Plead to Other Crimes

On entry of a guilty plea, or after conviction on a plea of not guilty, a defendant may request permission of the court to enter pleas of guilty to any outstanding charges in the prosecutorial district. A defendant also may enter guilty pleas to outstanding charges in other districts with the written permission of the prosecutor from the other district. G.S. 15A-1011(c). The foreign prosecutor or his or her representative may appear in person or file an affidavit as to the nature of the evidence that proves the charges. A defendant's plea under this statute waives venue. *Id.*

The superior court has jurisdiction to accept pleas to some misdemeanors under G.S. 15A-1011(c). The misdemeanors must be before the superior court on an information or indictment, which means that the misdemeanors must have been transactionally related to a felony. *See id.*; *see also* G.S. 7A-271. The district court may not accept pleas to felonies except in cases within the concurrent jurisdiction of the district and superior court—that is, Class H and I felonies with the judge's, prosecutor's, and defendant's consent. G.S. 15A-1011(c); *see also* G.S. 7A-272(c).

H. Guilty Pleas to Class H or I Felonies in District Court

A district court judge has jurisdiction to accept a guilty (or no contest) plea to a Class H or I felony with the defendant's and prosecutor's consent. G.S. 7A-272(c). The State may proceed by information filed in district court pursuant to G.S. 15A-644.1. Or, if the defendant has been indicted and the case has been transferred to superior court, a superior court judge may transfer the case back to district court, with the defendant's, prosecutor's, and presiding district court judge's consent, to allow the defendant to plead guilty. G.S. 15A-1029.1(a); G.S. 7A-272(c). If the district court judge accepts a guilty plea to a Class H or I felony, the procedures set out in Chapter 15A, Article 58 apply in the same manner as if the plea were entered in superior court. G.S. 7A-272(d); G.S. 15A-1029.1. Appeals are to the appellate division, not to the superior court for a trial de novo as with guilty pleas to misdemeanors in district court. *See infra* § 23.6A, Appeal from District Court.

I. Guilty Pleas through Counsel

A defendant, through counsel and without making a personal appearance, may plead guilty to relatively minor offenses to the extent provided in G.S. 15A-1011(a). Appointed counsel rarely will be involved in such cases. G.S. 15A-1011(a)(3) allows a defendant to submit a written waiver of appearance and guilty plea with the approval of the presiding judge. G.S. 15A-1011(a)(4) allows written appearances and pleas of guilty to traffic, hunting, alcoholic beverage control (ABC), and other minor offenses on the "waiver" list. The list, created by the chief district court judges of North Carolina, authorizes defendants to submit written guilty pleas to magistrates and clerks of court. *See* G.S. 7A-148(a) [added by S.L. 1992-900, sec 118, in place of G.S. 7A-146(8), which was repealed but is still referenced in G.S. 15A-1011(a)(4)].

23.5 Felony Sentencing

Structured sentencing is not considered in this manual, but a few issues specific to guilty pleas are discussed below.

A. Aggravated Sentences

G.S. 15A-1022.1 provides that before accepting a guilty or no contest plea to a felony, the judge must determine whether the State intends to seek a sentence in the aggravated range and, if so, which factors the State seeks to establish. The judge also must determine whether the State seeks a finding that a prior record level point should be found under G.S. 15A-1340.14(b)(7) (whether the defendant committed the new offense while on probation, parole, or post-release supervision, while serving a sentence of imprisonment, or while on escape from a correctional facility). If the State is seeking to aggravate a sentence based on these factors, the judge also must determine whether the State has given notice to the defendant as required by G.S. 15A-1340.16(a6) or whether the defendant has waived his or her right to such notice. G.S. 15A-1022.1(a).

If the State has alleged one or more aggravating factors, but the defendant contests the existence of the factor or factors, a jury must be impaneled to determine whether the aggravating factor or factors exist (unless the alleged factor or factors are ones that a judge is permitted to find under G.S. 15A-1340.16(12a) or (18a)). G.S. 15A-1340.16(a3). Likewise, where the state alleges and the defendant contests the existence of a prior record level point under G.S. 15A-1340.14(b)(7), a jury must be impaneled to decide whether the defendant committed the new offense while on probation, parole, or post-release supervision, while serving a sentence of imprisonment, or while on escape from a correctional facility. G.S. 15A-1340.16(a5).

If the defendant admits the existence of the alleged aggravating factors or the G.S. 15A-1340.16(a5) prior record level points, a jury trial is unnecessary. In accepting the defendant's admission to aggravating factors or points, the judge must engage in the colloquy for accepting a guilty plea under G.S. 15A-1022(a) and must follow the procedures in G.S. 15A-1022.1, including advising the defendant of his or her rights, determining that there is a factual basis for the factors and points admitted by the defendant, and determining that the decision to admit is the informed choice of the defendant. *See* G.S. 15A-1022.1(b); G.S. 15A-1340.16(a1).

Practice note: If your client enters into a plea agreement in which the negotiated sentence is in the aggravated range of the sentencing chart, the State still must offer a factual basis for the aggravating factors. Likewise, if your client enters into a plea agreement in which the negotiated sentence is in the mitigated range of the sentencing chart, you must present evidence in support of a mitigating factor or factors because the trial judge is required to make sentencing findings that support the mitigated sentence. *See* G.S. 15A-1340.16(b), (c). The judge is not required to make findings if he or she accepts a negotiated sentence in the presumptive range. *See, e.g., State v. Caldwell*, 125 N.C. App. 161 (1997).

B. Aggravating Factors Based on Elements of a Dismissed Offense

Before the U.S. Supreme Court's decision in *Blakely v. Washington*, 542 U.S. 296 (2004), and the enactment of North Carolina's "*Blakely* bill," (S.L. 2005-145), North Carolina appellate courts held that the trial judge could find, as an aggravating factor, an element of an offense that is dismissed as part of a plea bargain. For example, in *State v. Melton*, 307 N.C. 370 (1983), the defendant had been charged with first-degree murder and pled guilty to second degree murder. The trial judge was permitted to find premeditation and deliberation as an aggravating factor. *Melton* held that, "[a]s long as they are not elements essential to the establishment of the offense to which the defendant pled guilty, all circumstances which are transactionally related to the admitted offense and which are reasonably related to the purposes of sentencing must be considered during sentencing." *Id.* at 378.

After the passage of North Carolina's *Blakely* bill, it appears that if the State seeks to establish as an aggravating factor an element of a dismissed offense, the State must, as with other aggravating factors not specifically listed in G.S. 15A-1340.16(d), include the allegation in an indictment or other charging instrument as specified in G.S. 15A-924 and, unless admitted by the defendant, prove its existence to the jury beyond a reasonable doubt. G.S. 15A-1340.16(a), (a4).

C. Use of Testimony from Prior Trial

Defendant's prior testimony. If the defendant testifies against a co-defendant at a trial held before the defendant's sentencing hearing, that testimony may be used as evidence against the defendant at his or her sentencing hearing. *See State v. O'Neal*, 116 N.C. App. 390 (1994) (sentencing judge could incorporate by reference, and consider as evidence of premeditation and deliberation, defendant O'Neal's own testimony from a co-defendant's trial).

Other witness's testimony at co-defendant's trial. Evidence other than the defendant's testimony that was developed from the trials of co-defendants connected with the same offense may not be used to support a finding of an aggravating factor. *See State v. Thompson*, 314 N.C. 618 (1985); *State v. Benbow*, 309 N.C. 538 (1983). The parties may avoid this limitation by stipulating to evidentiary facts developed at related trials as long as the stipulations are not too extensive. "Even with . . . a stipulation[,] reliance exclusively on . . . record evidence from other trials (in which the defendant being sentenced had no opportunity to examine the witness) as a basis for a finding of an aggravating circumstance may constitute prejudicial error." *Benbow*, 309 N.C. 538, 549. "The policy behind this ruling is that the focus at the previous trial is on the culpability of others and not the defendant being [presently] sentenced . . . ." *O'Neal*, 116 N.C. App. 390, 394.

D. Restitution Orders and Recommendations

Restitution or reparation may be made part of a plea arrangement. *See* G.S. 15A-1021(d). Any order or recommendation for restitution must be supported by evidence presented at the sentencing hearing. *See, e.g., State v. Burkhead*, 85 N.C. App. 535 (1987) (vacating restitution order for $5,000 when evidence showed unpaid medical expenses of about $450). A prosecutor's unsworn statement is not sufficient to support a restitution award. *State v. Smith*, ___ N.C. App. ___, 707 S.E.2d 779 (2011); *State v. Buchanan*, 108 N.C. App. 338 (1992). A restitution worksheet, unsupported by testimony or documentation, is likewise insufficient to support an order of restitution. *Smith*, 707 S.E.2d 779; *State v. Mauer*, 202 N.C. App. 546 (2010). A defendant's silence or lack of objection does not constitute a stipulation as to the amount of restitution. *State v. Mumford*, 364 N.C. 394 (2010); *Mauer*, 202 N.C. App. 546.

There is no explicit burden of proof established in the restitution statutes. However, the N.C. Court of Appeals has analogized the North Carolina restitution statutes to the federal restitution provision, 18 U.S.C. § 3664(e), which requires the attorney for the government to establish the amount of loss suffered by the victim, and the defendant to show lack of financial resources and the existence of financial needs of any dependents. *See State v. Tate*, 187 N.C. App. 593 (2007); *see also State v. Riley*, 167 N.C. App. 346, 349 (2004) (allocating burden of showing that she would not be able to make the required restitution payments to the defendant).

For further discussion of the requirements of the restitution statutes, see Jamie Markham, *Restitution*, UNC Sch. of Gov't (April 2009), www.sog.unc.edu/sites/www.sog.unc.edu/files/Restitution.pdf.

23.6 Appeal from Guilty Pleas

A. Appeal from District Court

Misdemeanor pleas. Except to the extent it is permissible for a defendant to waive his or her right to appeal as part of a plea agreement (*see supra* § 23.3C), a defendant who enters a plea of guilty to a misdemeanor in district court has the right to appeal for trial de novo in superior court. G.S. 15A-1431; *State v. Fox*, 34 N.C. App. 576 (1977). A trial de novo returns a defendant to his or her position before the plea in district court. *State v. Sparrow*, 276 N.C. 499 (1970) (in trial de novo, judgment below is completely annulled and not available for any purpose); *Fox*, 34 N.C. App. 576. Any charges dismissed as part of the plea bargain in district court may be reinstated, and the superior court has jurisdiction over those charges. G.S. 15A-1431. Also, the trial judge in superior court may sentence the defendant to a longer sentence than that imposed in the district court as long as the sentence is statutorily permissible. *Sparrow*, 276 N.C. 499; *State v. Meadows*, 234 N.C. 657 (1951). The State may not reinstate charges in superior court that were dismissed independently of the plea bargain as a way of penalizing the defendant for filing an appeal. For a discussion of vindictive prosecution, see 1 NORTH CAROLINA DEFENDER MANUAL § 13.4D (Motion to Dismiss for Vindictive or Selective Prosecution) (Mar. 2009).

For further discussion of the defendant's right to appeal from a district court judgment in misdemeanor cases, see *infra* § 35.1B, Defendant's Right to Appeal from District Court Judgment.

Felony pleas in district court. Where a defendant pleads guilty or no contest to a Class H or I felony in district court pursuant to G.S. 15A-1029.1(a) and G.S. 7A-272(c), the defendant's appeal is to the court of appeals. G.S. 7A-272(d); G.S. 15A-1029.1(b); *see also State v. Goforth*, 130 N.C. App. 603 (1998) (attorney erroneously advised defendant that she could appeal sentence to superior court after felony guilty plea in district court).

B. Appeal from Superior Court

Generally. A criminal defendant who enters a plea of guilty or no contest in superior court has a limited right of appeal. A defendant can appeal as a matter of right the following issues:

1. Whether the prior record level was properly calculated. G.S. 15A-1444(a2)(1).
2. Whether the sentence disposition was a type that was authorized for the defendant's class of offense and prior record level—e.g., the defendant received an active or intermediate sentence when only an intermediate or community sentence was authorized. G.S. 15A-1444(a2)(2).
3. Whether the lengths of the minimum and maximum sentences are outside those set by statute for the defendant's class of offense and prior record level. G.S. 15A-1444(a2)(3).
4. If the defendant was sentenced outside of the presumptive range, whether there were improper findings of aggravating circumstances or improper failures to find mitigating circumstances. *See* G.S. 15A-1444(a1); *see also State v. Davis*, ___ N.C. App. ___, 696 S.E.2d 917 (2010); *State v. Rogers*, 157 N.C. App. 127 (2003). The N.C. Court of Appeals has interpreted the governing statutory provision to mean that a defendant is entitled to an appeal when his or her sentence falls within the aggravated range *or* within the mitigated range. *See State v. Mabry*, ___ N.C. App. ___, 720 S.E.2d 697 (2011) (holding that "a defendant receiving a mitigated sentence

must, under the plain language of the statute, have a right to appeal the sufficiency of the evidence supporting his or her sentence").

5. Whether a motion to withdraw the plea of guilty or no contest was improperly denied. G.S. 15A-1444(e); *see also State v. Handy*, 326 N.C. 532 (1990) (defendant entitled to an appeal as of right after the trial judge denied his motion to withdraw his plea of guilty; death sentence vacated because denial of the presentence motion was improper).
6. Whether there were evidentiary and procedural issues in a sentencing hearing before a jury on the existence of aggravating circumstances or sentence enhancements. *See, e.g., State v. Hurt*, 361 N.C. 325 (2007) (granting new sentencing hearing where trial judge's *Blakely* error in failing to submit an aggravating factor to the jury was not harmless beyond a reasonable doubt).
7. Whether a motion to suppress evidence based on constitutional grounds or on a substantial violation of Chapter 15A was improperly denied. G.S. 15A-979(b); G.S. 15A-1444(e); *see also State v. Smith*, 193 N.C. App. 739 (2008).

A defendant who pleads guilty has no right of appeal from any other issue. *See, e.g., State v. Parks*, 146 N.C. App. 568 (2001) (no right to appeal denial of motion to dismiss habitual felon indictment following entry of guilty plea to charge of being habitual felon); *State v. Waters*, 122 N.C. App. 504 (1996) (no right to appeal ineffective assistance of counsel claim).

For an in-depth discussion of the defendant's limited right to appeal from a guilty plea in superior court, see *infra* § 35.1D, Defendant's Right to Appeal from Guilty Plea in Superior Court. For a discussion of possible alternative remedies following a guilty plea, see subsection C., below.

Waiver of right to appeal. If a defendant enters into a plea bargain that contains any type of sentencing provisions, the defendant may waive, or partially waive, the right to appeal his or her sentence. For example, in *State v. Hamby*, 129 N.C. App. 366 (1998), the court found that the defendant waived her right to appeal her sentence under G.S. 15A-1444(a2) by admitting in her plea agreement that her prior record level was II and that the judge was authorized to sentence her to a minimum of 29 months and a maximum of 44 months and by agreeing that her sentence could be intermediate or active in the trial judge's discretion.

Although the N.C. Court of Appeals has followed *Hamby* in some cases, another line of cases in that court has held that while a defendant's stipulation to his or her prior convictions and prior record level may be sufficient to prove the existence of those convictions and the record level, the trial judge's assignment of a prior record level is a conclusion of law that is reviewable de novo on appeal. *See, e.g., State v. Wright*, ___ N.C. App. ___, 708 S.E.2d 112 (2011) (although defendant stipulated to having two out-of-state convictions, the calculation of his prior record level was a conclusion of law reviewable de novo on appeal; whether the offenses were substantially similar to an offense under the North Carolina statutes was also a question of law); *State v. Fair*, 205 N.C. App. 315 (2010) (defendant's stipulation to his prior convictions and his record level bound him as to the existence of the convictions but whether the convictions could be counted toward sentencing points for determination of his prior record level was fully reviewable on appeal; trial judge erred in finding defendant to be Level IV rather than Level III because two of the felony convictions occurred on the same day in superior court); *State v. Fraley*, 182 N.C. App. 683, 691 (2007) ("Although defendant's stipulation as to prior record level is sufficient evidence for sentencing at that level . . ., the trial court's assignment of level IV to defendant was an improper conclusion of law, which we review *de novo*"; remanding for resentencing because two of convictions were obtained on the same day in superior court).

Preserving right to appeal from denial of suppression motion. Where a defendant intends to enter a guilty plea but wants to preserve his or her right to appeal the denial of a suppression motion, the defendant bears the burden of creating a record that clearly states the defendant's intention to appeal. The defendant must inform the judge and the prosecutor of his or her intent to appeal before the plea is entered. *State v. McBride*, 120 N.C. App. 623 (1995), *aff'd per curiam*, 344 N.C. 623 (1996). In *State v. Brown*, 142 N.C. App. 491 (2001), the Court of Appeals held that a stipulation in the appellate record that the defendant intended to appeal the denial of a suppression motion was not sufficient to preserve the issue—the trial record itself had to demonstrate the defendant's intention.

Practice note: To ensure the right is preserved, counsel should advise the State during plea negotiations of the defendant's intent to appeal from the denial of the suppression motion and should file a written "notice of intent to appeal" before entry of the plea. Additionally, both the written transcript of plea and the record from the in-court plea colloquy should include a statement that the defendant intends to appeal the denial of a suppression motion under G.S. 15A-979. The last step is to enter an oral or written "notice of appeal" from the judgment itself (not from the denial of the motion to suppress) *after* entry of final judgment in order to confer jurisdiction on the appellate court. *See State v. Miller*, 205 N.C. App. 724 (2010) (appeal dismissed because, although defendant properly gave notice of his intention to file an appeal before he pled guilty, his written notice of appeal entered after final judgment was "from the denial of Defendant's motion to suppress[,]" not from his judgment of conviction); N.C. R. APP. P. 4; *see also* 1 NORTH CAROLINA DEFENDER MANUAL § 14.7 (Appeal of Suppression Motions) (July 2002).

C. Alternative Remedies

Writs of certiorari. G.S. 15A-1444(e) provides that a defendant who has entered a plea of guilty or no contest and has no right to appeal may file a petition for writ of certiorari to the appellate division and request discretionary review. However, writs of certiorari are generally allowed by the N.C. Rules of Appellate Procedure in only three instances:

1. where the party lost the right to appeal by failing to take timely action;
2. where the order appealed from is interlocutory and there is no right of appeal; or

3. to review a trial judge's denial of a motion for appropriate relief.

See N.C. R. APP. P. 21(a)(1).

Faced with these conflicting provisions, the N.C. appellate courts have reached the conclusion that, other than in the three instances set out above and the one exception discussed below, they do not have the authority to issue a writ of certiorari. *See State v. White*, ___ N.C. App. ___, 711 S.E.2d 862 (2011) (defendant pled guilty after reserving his right to appeal from the denials of his motion to suppress and his motion to dismiss based on constitutional grounds; court found that defendant had a statutory right to appellate review of the denial of the motion to suppress but that the court had no jurisdiction to review, either by statute or by certiorari, the denial of the motion to dismiss); *State v. Pimental*, 153 N.C. App. 69 (2002) (although G.S. 15A-1444(e) allows a defendant to petition for a writ of certiorari after pleading guilty, the appellate court is still limited to granting certiorari under the three circumstances set out in Appellate Rule 21; appellate rules prevail over the general statutes when there is a conflict).

Although Appellate Rule 21 has been interpreted as limiting the authority of the appellate courts to grant a writ of certiorari to the three instances discussed above, the N.C. Supreme Court has specifically allowed petitions for writs of certiorari to challenge guilty plea procedures. *See State v. Bolinger*, 320 N.C. 596 (1987) (court acknowledged that defendant could not appeal as a matter of right the issue of whether his plea was accepted in violation of G.S. 15A-1022 but held that defendant could have sought review by writ of certiorari pursuant to G.S. 15A-1444(e)); *see also State v. Demaio*, ___ N.C. App. ___, 716 S.E.2d 863 (2011) (relying on *Bolinger*, the court granted defendant's petition for writ of certiorari and reviewed defendant's contention that the trial judge erred in accepting his plea because it was not based on an informed choice); *State v. Rhodes*, 163 N.C. App. 191 (2004) (treating defendant's appeal as a petition for writ of certiorari and reviewing the procedures employed in accepting the plea; error for judge to change mind and impose a sentence other than that specified in the plea arrangement without giving defendant an opportunity to withdraw his plea).

For further discussion of the circumstances under which an appellate court may grant a petition for writ of certiorari to review challenges to the procedures employed by the trial judge in accepting a defendant's guilty plea, see *infra* § 35.1D, Defendant's Right to Appeal from Guilty Plea in Superior Court. *See also infra* § 35.7D, Certiorari of Trial Court Orders and Judgments (discussing writs of certiorari generally).

Motions for appropriate relief. Although a defendant may not be entitled to an appeal of right after pleading guilty, he or she may be able to pursue a motion for appropriate relief under G.S. 15A-1414 and G.S. 15A-1415. *See infra* § 35.3, Motions for Appropriate Relief. Generally, a defendant who enters a guilty plea waives all errors in the proceeding, including constitutional violations that occurred before entry of the plea. One exception to this rule is that the defendant may challenge the power of the State to bring him or her into court. *See Blackledge v. Perry*, 417 U.S. 21, 30 (1974); *State v. Reynolds*, 298 N.C. 380 (1979) (discussing *Blackledge*). For example, a defendant who pled guilty may use a motion for appropriate relief to challenge a conviction based on a fatally defective indictment, which constitutes a jurisdictional defect under North Carolina law.

A defendant also may challenge whether his or her guilty plea was voluntary and intelligent and whether he or she received effective assistance of counsel in entering the plea. *See State v. Waters*, 122 N.C. App. 504 (1996) (proper remedy for defendant who pled guilty and alleged ineffective assistance of counsel was MAR in trial division); *State v. Mercer*, 84 N.C. App. 623 (1987) (finding that defendant's MAR should have been granted if he had been improperly induced to plead guilty; remanded for the entry of a new order supported by proper and sufficient findings of fact and conclusions of law); *see also Blackledge v. Allison*, 431 U.S. 63 (1977) (affirming Fourth Circuit's reversal of the summary dismissal of defendant's claim for habeas corpus relief based on allegation that defendant had been improperly induced to plead guilty).

Additionally, a defendant may file a motion for appropriate relief seeking relief from a guilty plea if it was entered under the mistaken impression that he or she could preserve the right to appeal from the denial of pretrial motions (other than a motion to suppress from which there is a right to appeal). *See State v. Rinehart*, 195 N.C. App. 774, 777 (2009) (dismissing defendant's appeal for lack of appellate jurisdiction "without prejudice to defendant's right to file a motion for appropriate relief").

For a further discussion of possible grounds for motions for appropriate relief after a guilty plea, see Jessica Smith, *Two Issues in MAR Procedure: Hearings and Showing Required to Succeed on a MAR*, ADMINISTRATION OF JUSTICE BULLETIN No. 2001/04 (UNC School of Government, Oct. 2001), *available at* www.sog.unc.edu/sites/www.sog.unc.edu/files/aoj200104.pdf.

Caution: Generally, when a case has been set aside after appeal or collateral attack, G.S. 15A-1335 bars the imposition of a greater sentence at the second sentencing hearing. The statute appears to preclude a court from imposing a more severe sentence for a conviction that has been set aside, whether the sentence was part of a negotiated plea or an open plea and whether the defendant reenters a guilty plea or is found guilty after trial. However, if a defendant is successful in having a guilty plea set aside on direct review or through an MAR, any charges that had been dismissed by the State as part of the negotiated plea agreement could be reinstated; the defendant may be sentenced on those reinstated charges and as a result receive a more severe sentence than he originally received pursuant to his or her plea bargain. For a further discussion of the risk of receiving a greater sentence after having a guilty plea set aside, see *infra* § 35.5B, Applicability of G.S. 15A-1335.

Due process also protects the defendant to some extent from the reinstatement of charges or the imposition of a more severe sentence to punish the defendant for challenging a plea bargain. *See North Carolina v. Pearce*, 395 U.S. 711 (1969) (punishing exercise of rights is vindictive and violates due process). However, unlike a successful appeal following a trial, no presumption of vindictiveness arises for due process purposes if the second sentence after a trial is more severe than a first sentence after a guilty plea; the defendant must prove actual vindictiveness. *Alabama v. Smith*, 490 U.S. 794 (1989); *see also infra* § 35.5A, Resentencing after Successful Appellate or Post-Conviction Review: In General (discussing constitutional limits on resentencing after successful appellate or post-conviction review).

23.7 Other Issues

A. Inadmissibility of Plea Negotiations at Trial

G.S. 15A-1025 states: "The fact that the defendant or his counsel and the prosecutor engaged in plea discussions or made a plea arrangement may not be received in evidence against or in favor of the defendant in any criminal . . . action . . . ." If plea negotiations fall apart, and the case goes to trial, neither side may introduce evidence about the prior plea negotiations. *State v. Bostic*, 121 N.C. App. 90 (1995) (G.S. 15A-1025 clearly prohibited introduction of evidence that defendant refused a plea bargain because he refused to admit guilt); *see also* N.C. R. EVID. 410 (Inadmissibility of pleas, plea discussions, and related statements).

G.S. 15A-1025 "was designed to facilitate plea discussions and agreements by protecting both defendants and prosecuting officials from being 'penalized for engaging in practices which are consistent with the objectives of the criminal justice system.'" *State v. Wooten*, 86 N.C. App. 481, 482 (1987) (citation omitted). A defendant is entitled to a new trial if he or she can show prejudice from the prosecutor's introduction of evidence obtained during plea negotiations. *See State v. Walker*, 167 N.C. App. 110 (2004) (admission of incriminating letters from defendant to the prosecutor discussing defendant's regret and his willingness to confess and "help in any way in order to get probation" constituted a plea discussion; admission was highly prejudicial and potentially influenced the jury's decision), *vacated in part on other grounds*, 361 N.C. 160 (2006); *Wooten*, 86 N.C. App. 481, 481 (testimony by officer that defendant spoke with him after arrest and said that "[defendant's] lawyer wanted to plead him to six years to the offense and he wanted to know what he should do"; this testimony referred to a plea bargain negotiated by defense counsel and prosecutor and therefore was expressly prohibited by G.S. 15A-1025). *But cf. State v. Flowers*, 347 N.C. 1 (1997) (letter from defendant to prosecutor, in which defendant admitted guilt, requested that codefendants not be tried for murder, requested that his counsel be removed, and mentioned possibility of a plea bargain without any specifics, was not barred by G.S. 15A-1025; prosecutor did not respond to defendant's letter, did not engage in plea discussions with defendant, and did not enter into plea arrangement with defendant).

The limitations set out in G.S. 15A-1025 apply only to evidence of communications related to plea bargaining between the prosecutor and the defense. Plea negotiations with a third party, including a law enforcement officer, may be admissible against the defendant. *See Bostic*, 121 N.C. App. 90, 102 (statement made by defendant to inmate that he hoped to get a plea was admissible because the statement "did not in any way indicate that 'defendant or his counsel and the prosecutor engaged in plea discussions'");

State v. Lewis, 32 N.C. App. 298 (1977) (finding discussion between arresting officer and defendant admissible and declining to expand G.S. 15A-1025 beyond its explicit parameters).

B. Challenging Former Guilty Pleas

Where a defendant challenges the validity of a guilty plea through an appeal or a petition for writ of certiorari filed contemporaneously with an appeal, the record must affirmatively show that the guilty plea was made knowingly and voluntarily; otherwise, the plea is invalid. *Boykin v. Alabama*, 395 U.S. 238 (1969). However, at the end of a direct appeal, or when the time for appeal has expired, a "presumption of regularity" applies to a guilty plea. *Parke v. Raley*, 506 U.S. 20 (1992). The "presumption of regularity" shifts the burden to the defendant to show that his or her plea was involuntary. This can be a difficult burden to carry. *See State v. Bass*, 133 N.C. App. 646 (1999) (defendant unsuccessful in overturning prior uncounseled guilty plea that became basis of capital aggravating circumstance).

North Carolina courts also have held that the proper procedure for challenging a prior guilty plea on *Boykin* grounds is to file a motion for appropriate relief in the original cause. A defendant may not raise the issue of the voluntariness of a plea that is being used as a sentencing enhancer, or as the basis for a habitual felon charge, at the sentencing hearing or during a habitual felon trial. *See State v. Creason*, 123 N.C. App. 495 (1996) (collateral attack on prior conviction used as basis of habitual felon charge improper; proper procedure for adjudicating *Boykin* claim was motion for appropriate relief in the original cause), *aff'd per curiam*, 346 N.C. 165 (1997); *State v. Stafford*, 114 N.C. App. 101 (1994) (claim that prior pleas of guilty used to support habitual impaired driving charge were received in violation of *Boykin* could not be raised in habitual impaired driving case; defendant must file MAR in original cause); *State v. Noles*, 12 N.C. App. 676 (1971) (defendant could not collaterally attack voluntariness of underlying guilty plea on appeal of revocation of probation; proper procedure is to file MAR in original cause). *Cf. Custis v. United States*, 511 U.S. 485 (1994) (if conviction is obtained in violation of right to counsel, defendant may collaterally attack conviction in case in which conviction is proposed to be used); *see also* G.S. 15A-980 (allowing motion to suppress prior conviction for violation of right to counsel).

For further discussion of this topic, see Robert L. Farb, Boykin v. Alabama *and Use of Invalid Guilty Pleas*, UNC SCH. OF GOV'T (Feb. 1, 2010), www.sog.unc.edu/sites/www.sog.unc.edu/files/boykin.pdf, and Jessica Smith, *Pleas and Plea Negotiations in North Carolina Superior Court*, ADMINISTRATION OF JUSTICE BULLETIN No. 2005/03, at 18–20 (UNC School of Government, July 2005), *available at* http://sogpubs.unc.edu/electronicversions/pdfs/aojb0503.pdf.

C. Concessions of Guilt during Trial

There may be situations in which conceding your client's guilt to a lesser-included offense is your best strategy. Concessions of guilt have the same practical effect as guilty pleas because they deprive the defendant of his or her right against self-incrimination, the right of confrontation, and the right to trial by jury. *State v. Harbison*, 315 N.C. 175 (1985). A defense attorney may not concede guilt without his or her client's explicit consent, and that consent must be given knowingly and voluntarily. *Id.*

For an in-depth discussion of admissions of the defendant's guilt, see *infra* § 28.6, Admissions of Guilt During Opening Statement, and § 33.6, Admissions of Guilt During Closing Argument.

Appendix 23-1
Checklist for Guilty Pleas

The following checklist may be useful in checking the validity of a guilty plea.

I. Preparing the Plea Agreement (§ 23.3)

✓ The offenses covered by the plea agreement are within the scope of the indictment (or warrant in district court).

✓ If the plea is outside the scope of the initial indictment, the indictment has been dismissed with prejudice and a superseding information filed. In district court, the prosecutor should file a statement of charges.

✓ The plea agreement contains no conditions that are barred by law.

✓ The judge has agreed to any explicit sentencing provisions in the agreement.

✓ If the plea is "no contest," both the prosecutor and judge have agreed to accept this form of plea. Although not required by statute, it is the better practice to inform the prosecutor and court that you intend to enter an *Alford* plea.

✓ The intent to appeal from the denial of any suppression motions is explicitly preserved on the face of the plea agreement.

✓ The defendant understands the nature of the charges and the direct consequences of the plea, including the maximum possible sentence and any mandatory minimum sentence.

✓ The defendant understands the major collateral consequences of the plea, including the risk of deportation for non-citizens.

✓ The defendant understands his or her obligations under the plea agreement, including any obligation to make restitution, to participate in treatment programs, or to testify for the State.

✓ The defendant understands his or her right to withdraw the plea of guilty for any good reason until the sentence is imposed, after which the right to withdraw from the plea is very limited.

✓ The defendant understands the limits on his or her right to appeal from a plea bargain.

✓ The defendant understands that the consequences of withdrawing from a plea agreement, or successfully appealing a plea, may be a trial in which a more severe sentence is imposed.

II. The Plea Procedure (§ 23.4)

✓ There is a factual basis for the plea presented on the record.

✓ The judge personally addresses the defendant, in accordance with G.S. 15A-1022(a), to ensure that the defendant is pleading voluntarily and understands the consequences of the plea.

- ✓ The judge questions counsel about the voluntariness of the plea in accordance with G.S. 15A-1022(b).
- ✓ The full plea agreement is disclosed to the court.
- ✓ If the defendant intends to appeal the denial of a suppression motion, the court and prosecutor are informed of this intent before the entry of the plea.
- ✓ The defendant is given the opportunity to plead to any other outstanding charges pursuant to G.S. 15A-1011(c).

III. Sentencing (§ 23.5)

- ✓ If a sentence is not a negotiated part of the plea agreement, counsel must be prepared for a full sentencing hearing, in which the State may present evidence of the defendant's prior record and any aggravating factors and the defendant has the burden of proving mitigating factors.
- ✓ If a negotiated sentence falls within the aggravated range in the sentencing chart, the defendant must admit the existence of the aggravating factors and the judge must question him or her in accordance with the procedures set out in G.S. 15A-1022 and G.S. 15A-1022.1. If the negotiated sentence falls within the mitigated range, the defendant must present evidence to support a mitigating factor or factors and the judge must make findings to support the sentence.

IV. Appeal From Guilty Pleas (§ 23.6)

- ✓ A defendant who enters a plea of guilty on a misdemeanor in district court may appeal for a trial de novo in superior court.
- ✓ A defendant who enters a plea of guilty on a felony in superior court generally may appeal only: (i) the legality of his or her sentence; (ii) the judge's denial of a motion to withdraw a plea; or (iii) the denial of a suppression motion if properly preserved.
- ✓ Certain other issues, such as the voluntariness of the plea, ineffective assistance of counsel, or capacity to plead guilty, may be raised either through a petition for writ of certiorari in the appellate court or a motion for appropriate relief in the trial division, depending on the issue.

V. Related Issues (§ 23.7)

- ✓ If plea negotiations fall apart and the case goes to trial, evidence of the negotiations is inadmissible.
- ✓ If the State intends to use a prior guilty plea as a sentencing enhancement, the proper procedure for challenging the former plea on *Boykin* grounds (plea not knowing and voluntary) is to file a motion for appropriate relief in the original cause.
- ✓ A lawyer may not concede his or her client's guilt to a lesser included offense during a trial without the client's informed consent.

Chapter 24
Right to Jury

This is the first of four chapters on issues relating to the right to jury trial. This chapter addresses the scope of the jury trial right under the Sixth Amendment to the U.S. Constitution and Article I, § 24 of the N.C. Constitution. Issues discussed include the types of crimes for which a defendant is entitled to a jury trial, the number of jurors required, and jury unanimity. Chapter 25 covers jury selection issues; chapter 26 addresses juror misconduct and remedies for the misconduct; chapter 27 addresses miscellaneous jury procedures. *See also infra* Chapter 32 (jury instructions); Chapter 34 (deliberations and verdict).

24.1 Right to Jury Trial under Sixth Amendment

The Sixth Amendment to the U.S. Constitution, as interpreted by the U.S. Supreme Court, establishes a defendant's basic right to a jury trial. In discussing the right to a jury, the Court has stated:

> [T]he primary purpose of the jury is to prevent the possibility of oppression by the Government; the jury interposes between the accused and his accuser the judgment of laymen who are less tutored perhaps than a judge or panel of judges, but who, at the same time, are less likely to function or appear as but another arm of the Government that has proceeded against him.

Baldwin v. New York, 399 U.S. 66, 72 (1970); *see also Duncan v. Louisiana*, 391 U.S. 145, 156 (1968) (explaining that framers of our state and federal constitutions provided defendants with the right to a jury trial to give them "an inestimable safeguard against the corrupt or overzealous prosecutor and against the compliant, biased, or eccentric judge").

The most important recent developments under the Sixth Amendment's jury trial provision involve limitations on a judge's ability to make sentencing findings. The current law, discussed further below, is that any fact, other than a prior conviction, that increases the penalty for a crime beyond the statutory maximum must be submitted to a jury and proven beyond a reasonable doubt. *See Blakely v. Washington*, 542 U.S. 296 (2004); *Apprendi v. New Jersey*, 530 U.S. 466 (2000); *see also Ring v. Arizona*, 536 U.S. 584 (2002) (application to capital sentencing); *cf.* 1 NORTH CAROLINA DEFENDER MANUAL § 8.8 (Potential *Apprendi* and *Blakely* Issues) (July 2004) (discussing pleading requirements in light of *Apprendi* and *Blakely*). These cases brought about a sea change in how sentences are to be determined and necessitated a change in North Carolina structured sentencing. *See infra* § 24.1E, Right to Jury Verdict on Every Element of Offense, including "Sentencing" Factors.

A. Application to States

The Sixth Amendment states "[i]n all criminal prosecutions, the accused shall enjoy the right to a speedy and public trial, by an impartial jury of the State and district wherein the crime shall have been committed." The right to a trial by jury has been incorporated into the Fourteenth Amendment and applies to state prosecutions. *See Duncan v. Louisiana*, 391 U.S. 145 (1968).

B. Scope of Sixth Amendment Right

The Sixth Amendment guarantees the right to a jury trial for all "serious offenses." There is no federal constitutional right to a jury trial for "petty" offenses. An offense is presumptively "petty" if it carries a maximum prison term of six months or less. *See Blanton v. City of North Las Vegas*, 489 U.S. 538, 543 (1989). However, a defendant charged with an offense for which the maximum penalty is six months imprisonment or less is entitled to a jury trial under the Sixth Amendment if he or she "can demonstrate that any additional statutory penalties, viewed in conjunction with the maximum authorized period of incarceration, are so severe that they clearly reflect a legislative determination that the offense in question is a 'serious' one." *Id.* at 543.

A defendant charged with multiple misdemeanor offenses, none of which individually carry a penalty of more than six months imprisonment, has no Sixth Amendment right to a jury trial. *See Lewis v. United States*, 518 U.S. 322 (1996). *But see Codispoti v. Pennsylvania*, 418 U.S. 506 (1974) (defendant entitled to jury trial where charged with multiple counts of criminal contempt based on conduct during course of trial and aggregate punishment exceeded six months).

The right to a jury trial does not extend to proceedings in juvenile court. *McKeiver v.*

Pennsylvania, 403 U.S. 528 (1971) (trial by jury in adjudicative stage of juvenile court delinquency proceeding is not constitutionally required). Nor does the right extend to hearings on probation violations. *See Minnesota v. Murphy*, 465 U.S. 420, 435 n.7 (1984) (noting in dicta that "there is no right to a jury trial before probation may be revoked. . . .").

North Carolina law is broader. A defendant has a jury trial right for all felonies in superior court and also for all misdemeanors appealed to or initiated in superior court. *See infra* § 24.2A, Scope of Right.

C. Number of Jurors

The Sixth Amendment requires that juries in criminal cases be composed of at least six people. *See Ballew v. Georgia*, 435 U.S. 223, 228 (1978) (concluding that five jurors is too few); *Williams v. Florida*, 399 U.S. 78, 89–90, 103 (1970) (finding state's decision to provide six jurors acceptable and explaining that the twelve-person jury required by common law was "a historical accident, unrelated to the great purposes which gave rise to the jury in the first place"). North Carolina law requires a jury of twelve. *See infra* § 24.2C, Number of Jurors.

D. Jury Unanimity

In *Apodaca v. Oregon*, 406 U.S. 404 (1972), the U.S. Supreme Court found that the Sixth Amendment, applicable to the states through the Fourteenth Amendment, does not require that the decision of a jury of twelve in a state criminal prosecution be unanimous. *See also Johnson v. Louisiana*, 406 U.S. 356, 362 (1972) (holding that nine jurors out of twelve majority sufficient in state court to support verdict). However, if a jury is comprised of only six members, the verdict must be unanimous. *See Burch v. Louisiana*, 441 U.S. 130 (1979) (leaving open the question whether verdicts of juries composed of more than six but fewer than twelve members must be unanimous).

Unanimity is required under North Carolina law. *See infra* § 24.2D, Jury Unanimity. Unanimity also is required in federal criminal trials as mandated by Rule 31(a) of the Federal Rules of Criminal Procedure.

E. Right to Jury Verdict on Every Element of Offense, Including "Sentencing" Factors

Generally. If a defendant has a right to a jury trial, he or she has a right to a jury verdict on every element of the offense. *See, e.g., Jones v. United States*, 526 U.S. 227, 251-52 (1999) (construing a federal statute as establishing separate offenses, "each of which must be charged by indictment, proven beyond a reasonable doubt, and submitted to a jury for its verdict"); *Apprendi v. New Jersey*, 530 U.S. 466, 476 (2000) (confirming principle expressed in *Jones* and applying it to a state statute); *compare Schad v. Arizona*, 501 U.S. 624 (1991) (jury unanimity not required as to whether defendant committed felony murder or premeditated murder because either means of commission satisfied the element of mens rea; jury does not have to be unanimous on theory of crime). For a discussion of disjunctive jury instructions, see *infra* § 24.2D, Jury Unanimity.

Definition of "element of offense." In *Jones* and *Apprendi*, the U.S. Supreme Court distinguished "elements" from "sentencing factors," defining an element as "any fact (other than prior conviction) that increases the maximum penalty for a crime . . . ." *Jones*, 526 U.S. 227, 243 n.6 ("serious bodily injury" was element of carjacking offense that had to be found by jury); *Apprendi*, 530 U.S. 466, 474 (hate crime enhancer was element and had to be submitted to jury); *see also Ring v. Arizona*, 536 U.S. 584, 609 (2002) (aggravating factors in capital sentencing must be found by jury). This broad definition of "element" includes traditional sentencing factors, including the defendant's course of conduct, motivations for the crime, or the particular vulnerability of the victim. *See Blakely v. Washington*, 542 U.S. 296, 303-04 (2004) (that defendant acted with "deliberate cruelty" is an element that must be found by a jury). The U.S. Supreme Court has continued to permit judges to find the fact of a prior conviction as a sentencing factor and has not required that this fact be treated as an "element" that must be found by a jury. *See Almendarez-Torres v. United States*, 523 U.S. 224, 247 (1998) (refusing to treat recidivism as an element of the offense). *But cf. infra* § 24.1G, Prior Conviction as Element of Offense (reviewing North Carolina statutes that make prior convictions an element of the offense, which must be submitted to the jury).

The U.S. Supreme Court has permitted the imposition of an enhanced mandatory *minimum* sentence on the basis of a judicial finding that a firearm was brandished. *See Harris v. United States*, 536 U.S. 545, 568 (2002) (reaffirming *McMillan v. Pennsylvania*, 477 U.S. 79 (1986), and upholding constitutionality of firearm enhancement statute that required imposition of mandatory minimum sentence if sentencing judge found that firearm was brandished). It is unclear whether *Harris* can be reconciled with *Blakely*, and the *McMillan* line of cases may be reconsidered at some point by the Court. *Cf. United States v. O'Brien*, ___ U.S. ___, 130 S. Ct. 2169 (2010) (majority found that whether the defendants had used a machine gun in furtherance of a crime of violence was an element of the offense that must be alleged in an indictment and proved to the jury beyond a reasonable doubt; in concurring opinions, Justices Stevens and Thomas noted the similarity between that element and the brandishing of a firearm found to be a sentencing factor in *Harris* and argued that *McMillan* and *Harris* should be overruled).

Aggravating factors under felony structured sentencing. In *Blakely v. Washington*, 542 U.S. 296 (2004), the U.S. Supreme Court defined "statutory maximum" as "the maximum sentence a judge may impose *solely on the basis of the facts reflected in the jury verdict or admitted by the defendant.*" *Blakely*, 542 U.S. at 303 (emphasis in original). Thus, a judge violates the Sixth Amendment if he or she imposes an enhanced sentence based on his or her own findings of aggravating factors (unless those factors relate solely to the defendant's recidivism or to the fact of a prior conviction). If the defendant does not admit the existence of the alleged aggravating factors, a jury must be impaneled to determine beyond a reasonable doubt whether the factors exist.

In *State v. Allen*, 359 N.C. 425 (2005), *opinion withdrawn on other grounds*, 360 N.C.

569 (2006), the court recognized that North Carolina's structured sentencing scheme violated these Sixth Amendment requirements because the scheme allowed a judge to impose an aggravated sentence, beyond the presumptive sentence range prescribed for the offense, based on judicial findings of aggravating factors. The *Allen* Court limited its holdings to those cases "in which the defendants have not been indicted as of the certification date of this opinion [July 21, 2005] and to cases that are now pending on direct review or are not yet final." *Id.* at 427; *see also State v. Coleman*, 181 N.C. App. 568 (2007) (holding that defendant was not entitled to *Blakely* review of his sentence because his case was final when the *Blakely* decision was rendered on June 24, 2004); *State v. Simpson*, 176 N.C. App. 719, 722 (2006) (denying defendant relief for *Blakely* error because defendant's conviction was "already final when *Allen* was certified on 21 July 2005").

Effective for offenses committed on or after June 30, 2005, the General Assembly revised North Carolina's structured sentencing statutes and established a new procedure for determining aggravating factors. *See* 2005 N.C. Sess. Laws Ch. 145; 2008 N.C. Sess. Laws Ch. 129. In brief, the revised statutes provide as follows:

- Unless admitted by the defendant, the jury must determine beyond a reasonable doubt any aggravating factors *other than* the aggravating factor in Section 15A-1340.16(d)(12a) of the North Carolina General Statutes (hereinafter G.S.) (defendant during the previous 10-year period has been found to be in willful violation of the conditions of probation, parole, or post-release supervision) [effective December 1, 2008], or the aggravating factor in G.S. 15A-1340.16(d)(18a) (defendant previously adjudicated delinquent of offense that would be Class A through E felony if committed by adult). The statutes provide that these aggravating factors continue to be decided by a judge. *See* G.S. 15A-1340.16(a3), (b). The N.C. Court of Appeals has issued conflicting opinions, however, on whether a judge may decide the juvenile adjudication factor. *Compare State v. Yarrell*, 172 N.C. App. 135, 141–42 (2005) (holding that judge may not find this factor), *with State v. Boyce*, 175 N.C. App. 663, 669 (2006) (treating juvenile delinquency adjudication as conviction and holding, without discussing *Yarrell*, that judge could find prior adjudication as aggravating factor), *aff'd*, 361 N.C. 670 (2007).
- A judge has the discretion to bifurcate the proceedings and allow a jury to determine guilt or innocence first and then the existence of aggravating factors. *See* G.S. 15A-1340.16(a1).
- The State does not need to allege aggravating factors in the indictment except for aggravating factor G.S. 15A-1340.16(d)(20) (catchall aggravator); however, the State must give notice of any aggravating factors at least 30 days before trial or a plea of guilty or no contest unless the defendant waives notice. *See* G.S. 15A-1340.16(a4), (a6).
- If aggravating factors are found by the jury or admitted by the defendant, the judge finds any mitigators and balances the aggravators and mitigators. *See* G.S. 15A-1340.16(b).

Practice note: If your client is being tried for an offense that occurred before the effective date of the above legislation, June 30, 2005, you must make sure that the trial judge complies with *Blakely* by submitting aggravating factors to the jury via the common law special verdict procedure. The judge must instruct the jury to use the "beyond a reasonable doubt" standard and require the jury to apply the law to the facts. *See State v. Blackwell*, 361 N.C. 41 (2006) (although structured sentencing statutes then in effect did not contain procedure for submitting aggravating factors to jury, trial judge could submit aggravating factors via a special verdict in cases subject to those statutes); *State v. Wilson*, 181 N.C. 540, 544-45 (2007) (trial judge "followed the clear edict from the United States Supreme Court in *Blakely* and properly submitted the alleged aggravating factors to the jury through the use of a special verdict").

Points for prior convictions (in-state and out-of-state) and other conduct. Under structured sentencing, a defendant may be assigned prior record level "points," primarily for prior convictions but also for other conduct. The statutes provide for different procedures for different types of points.

- The judge determines the points assigned to each of the defendant's prior convictions. *See* G.S. 15A-1340.14(a).
- The judge also determines whether an out-of-state conviction is substantially similar to a North Carolina offense in determining the prior record level points to assign to the conviction. G.S. 15A-1340.14(e); *see also State v. Hanton*, 175 N.C. App. 250, 254 (2006) (concluding that "whether an out-of-state offense is substantially similar to a North Carolina offense is a question of law that must be determined by the trial court, not the jury"). A stipulation of "substantial similarity" is not sufficient to support the assessment of points; the judge must make the determination. *See, e.g., State v. Lee*, 193 N.C. App. 748 (2008).
- A point is assigned for the commission of an offense that includes all the elements of a prior offense for which the defendant was convicted (repeat offender point). *See* G.S. 15A-1340.14(b)(6). Under the sentencing statutes, the defendant is not entitled to a jury determination of this point. *See State v. Poore*, 172 N.C. App. 839, 843 (2005) (finding that the trial judge's assessment of a prior record point for being a repeat offender "is not something that increases the 'statutory maximum' within the meaning of *Blakely* or *Allen*").
- A point is assigned if the defendant committed the present offense while on probation, parole, or post-release supervision, while serving a sentence, or while on escape from a correctional facility. *See* G.S. 15A-1340.14(b)(7). For offenses committed on or after June 30, 2005, the revised structured sentencing statutes establish jury trial procedures for finding the prior record point under this statute. *See* G.S. 15A-1340.16(a5), (a6).

Waiving right to jury sentencing. *Blakely* held that defendants may waive their right to a jury determination of aggravating factors by pleading guilty and either stipulating to certain facts or expressly consenting to judicial fact-finding. *Blakely*, 542 U.S. 296, 310.

Consenting to judicial fact-finding is not permissible under North Carolina's revised structured sentencing statutes. *See also infra* § 24.2B, Unwaivable Nature of Right (discussing nonwaivable state constitutional right to jury). A defendant may waive his or her right to a jury determination, however, by admitting properly alleged aggravating factors or the prior record level point in G.S. 15A-1340.14(b)(7). In accepting the defendant's admission to aggravating factors or points, the judge must engage in the colloquy for accepting a guilty plea under G.S. 15A-1022(a) and must follow the procedures in G.S. 15A-1022.1, including advising the defendant of his or her rights, determining that there is a factual basis for the factors and points admitted by the defendant, and determining that the decision to admit is the informed choice of the defendant. *See* G.S. 15A-1022.1(b), (c); 15A-1340.16(a1).

Other sentencing enhancements. North Carolina's firearms enhancement statute, unlike the mandatory minimum statute in question in *McMillan* and *Harris* (discussed above under "Definition of element of offense"), increases the *maximum* sentence a defendant may serve by 60 months. *See* G.S. 15A-1340.16A. This statute requires that the firearm enhancement be alleged in the indictment or information. G.S. 15A-1340.16A(d); *see also State v. Lucas*, 353 N.C. 568 (2001) (holding that previous version of G.S. 15A-1340.16A was unconstitutional because it did not require that the firearm enhancement be submitted to the jury), *overruled on other grounds*, *State v. Allen*, 359 N.C. 425 (2005), *opinion withdrawn on other grounds*, 360 N.C. 569 (2006). The defendant is entitled to a jury determination on the enhancement issues unless he or she waives that right and pleads guilty or no contest to those issues. If the defendant contests the existence of the enhancement issues, the state must prove their existence to the jury beyond a reasonable doubt. G.S. 15A-1340.16A(e).

Other statutes imposing sentencing enhancements likewise recognize the defendant's entitlement to a jury determination of enhancements. *See* G.S. 15A-1340.16B (authorizing sex offender recidivist enhancement); G.S. 15A-1340.16C (authorizing bullet-proof vest enhancement); and G.S. 15A-1340.16D (authorizing methamphetamine enhancement); *see generally* JOHN RUBIN, BEN F. LOEB, JR., & JAMES C. DRENNAN, PUNISHMENTS FOR NORTH CAROLINA CRIMES AND MOTOR VEHICLE OFFENSES 8–9 & n.11 (UNC School of Government, 3d ed. 2005) (discussing these statutes).

In 2008, the General Assembly added the offenses of rape and sexual offense by an adult involving a child under age 13. *See* G.S. 14-27.2A, 14-27.4A. These statutes establish a mandatory sentence of 300 months but allow a judge, on determining "egregious aggravation," to impose a sentence of up to life without parole. This procedure likely violates *Blakely*. *See* John Rubin, *2008 Legislation Affecting Criminal Law and Procedure*, ADMINISTRATION OF JUSTICE BULLETIN No. 2008/06, at 2–4 (UNC School of Government, Nov. 2008), *available at* http://sogpubs.unc.edu/electronicversions/pdfs/aojb0806.pdf.

Indictments. North Carolina courts have continued to uphold short-form indictments—that is, indictments that fail to list every element of an offense—notwithstanding the *Jones*, *Apprendi*, and *Blakely* decisions. *See, e.g.*, *State v. Morgan*, 359 N.C. 131, 147 (2004) (holding that "the short-form indictment is sufficient to charge first-degree capital murder without the inclusion of aggravating circumstances"); *see also Allen v. Lee*, 366 F.3d 319, 323–24 (4th Cir. 2004) (en banc) (holding that North Carolina's "short-form" first-degree murder indictment is constitutionally adequate).

F. Impaired Driving and Other Implied-Consent Offenses

In *State v. Speight*, 359 N.C. 602 (2005), *vacated on other grounds*, 548 U.S. 923 (2006), the court addressed the application of *Blakely* to misdemeanor impaired driving and held that, for impaired driving offenses tried in superior court (either when the offense is the subject of a misdemeanor appeal or is joined with a felony for trial initially in superior court), aggravating factors other than prior convictions must be found by a jury beyond a reasonable doubt or admitted by the defendant.

The General Assembly thereafter enacted legislation to address aggravating factors in impaired driving cases tried in district and superior court:

> After *Blakely*, the General Assembly amended G.S. 20-179 to require that aggravating factors in impaired driving cases, which increase the maximum sentence a defendant may receive, be proved beyond a reasonable doubt and, in superior court, to require that the state provide notice of its intent to prove such factors and that the jury determine whether the factors exist. In effect, aggravating factors are now treated as elements of the offense of impaired driving.

Shea Denning, *What's Blakely got to do with it? Sentencing in Impaired Driving Cases after Melendez-Diaz*, N.C. CRIM. L., UNC SCH. OF GOV'T BLOG (July 24, 2009), http://sogweb.sog.unc.edu/blogs/ncclaw/?p=567.

The provisions of G.S. 20-179 also apply to other implied consent offenses. *See* G.S. 20-179(a) (statute applicable to impaired driving in a commercial vehicle; second or subsequent violations for operating a commercial vehicle after consuming alcohol; or second or subsequent violations for operating a school bus, school activity bus, or child care vehicle after consuming alcohol). The defendant may waive the right to a jury determination and admit the existence of an aggravating factor or factors. G.S. 20-179(a1)(2). G.S 20-179(a1) and (a2) set out the jury procedures related to the finding of aggravating factors in superior court.

G. Prior Conviction as Element of Offense

The U.S. Supreme Court has not required the submission of prior convictions to the jury when the convictions enhance a defendant's sentence for an offense. *See, e.g., Apprendi v. New Jersey*, 530 U.S. 466, 490 (2000). Some North Carolina statutes, however, treat a defendant's prior conviction as an element of the offense being tried. In these circumstances, the jury must decide the prior conviction in determining the defendant's guilt or innocence of the offense.

Some statutes, such as the habitual felon, violent habitual felon, and habitual breaking and entering statutes, require a bifurcated procedure for the jury to determine whether the defendant has the required prior convictions. *See* G.S. 14-7.5 (habitual felon); G.S. 14-7.11 (violent habitual felon); G.S. 14-7.30 (habitual breaking and entering).

Other recidivist statutes, such as the habitual impaired driving statute (G.S. 20-138.5), habitual misdemeanor assault statute (G.S. 14-33.2), and shoplifting statute (G.S. 14-72.1(e)), are subject to G.S. 15A-928, which requires the jury to determine a defendant's prior conviction when the prior conviction "raises an offense of lower grade to one of higher grade and thereby becomes an element of the latter . . . ." *Id.* This statute allows the jury, during the principal trial, to determine those convictions that are elements of the offense if the defendant does not admit the convictions.

H. Fairness and Impartiality

Under both the Sixth Amendment and the Due Process Clause of the Fourteenth Amendment of the U.S. Constitution, whenever the defendant has a right to a jury trial, he or she has a concomitant right to the selection of a fair and impartial jury. *See Morgan v. Illinois*, 504 U.S. 719 (1992); *Irvin v. Dowd*, 366 U.S. 717 (1961); *see also Parker v. Gladden*, 385 U.S. 363 (1966). The Sixth Amendment and the Due Process Clause establish two requirements for the selection of juries. First, the venire from which petit juries are chosen must represent a "fair cross section of the community." *See Taylor v. Louisiana*, 419 U.S. 522, 535–36 (1975) (systematic exclusion of women violated fair cross-section requirement); *accord Duren v. Missouri*, 439 U.S. 357 (1979). Second, jurors with prior knowledge or other bias that would prevent them from deciding the case on the basis of the evidence presented and the law must be excused. *See Mu'Min v. Virginia*, 500 U.S. 415 (1991) (defendant has right to jurors who are not prejudiced against him by exposure to pretrial publicity); *Irvin*, 366 U.S. 717, 720–21 (defendant has right to change of venue if fair and impartial jury cannot be selected in district where offense occurred).

Other constitutional provisions also come into play in guaranteeing the fairness of juries. The Equal Protection Clause of the Fourteenth Amendment precludes the State or defendant from exercising peremptory challenges in a discriminatory manner. *See Batson v. Kentucky*, 476 U.S. 79, 89 (1986) (prosecutor may not exercise peremptories in discriminatory manner); *Georgia v. McCollum*, 505 U.S. 42, 59 (1992) (*Batson* rule applies to defendants); *see also Powers v. Ohio*, 499 U.S. 400, 415 (1991) (Equal Protection Clause prohibits use of peremptory challenges to discriminate based on race even where the defendant is not the same race as the excluded jurors).

The Sixth Amendment and the Fourteenth Amendment permit capital defendants to voir dire potential jurors about racial biases. *See Turner v. Murray*, 476 U.S. 28 (1986); *see also Ham v. South Carolina*, 409 U.S. 524, 526–27 (1973) (defendant had due process right under circumstances to voir dire jurors about racial attitudes in non-capital trial).

The above requirements are discussed in more detail in Chapter 25. The right to a fair and impartial jury as it relates to juror misconduct is discussed in Chapter 26.

24.2 Right to Jury Trial under North Carolina Constitution

Article I, § 24 of the N.C. Constitution states: "No person shall be convicted of any crime but by the unanimous verdict of a jury in open court. The General Assembly may, however, provide for other means of trial for misdemeanors, with the right to appeal for trial de novo." This right is also addressed in G.S. 15A-1201, which states that "[i]n all criminal cases the defendant has the right to be tried by a jury of 12 whose verdict must be unanimous."

Our state constitutional right to a jury trial is broader in several respects than the federal constitutional right to a jury trial. Our state constitutional right should always be cited, along with the federal constitutional right, in objecting to an infringement of the right to a jury trial.

A. Scope of Right

Our state constitution confers a right to a jury trial for *all* crimes, not just serious ones. There are two exceptions to the jury trial right.

First, the General Assembly has provided for the initial trial of misdemeanors without a jury in district court. People tried without a jury must be afforded the right to appeal for a trial de novo before a jury. *See* N.C. CONST. art. I, § 24; G.S. 15A-1201; G.S. 15A-1431(b); *State v. Hudson*, 280 N.C. 74 (1971); *accord State v. Reaves*, 142 N.C. App. 629, 634 (2001); *see also Ludwig v. Massachusetts*, 427 U.S. 618, 625–26 (1976) (two-tier system of adjudication not constitutionally infirm where defendant afforded an absolute right to a jury trial in the second tier).

Second, it appears that a judge may hold a defendant in criminal contempt, without affording him or her a jury trial, as long as the punishment is six months or less. *See Blue Jeans Corp. v. Amalgamated Clothing Workers*, 275 N.C. 503, 511 (1969) (court stated general six-month rule but on facts presented held only that defendant was not entitled to jury trial where he was charged with criminal contempt punishable by thirty days or less); *Reaves*, 142 N.C. App. 629, 635 (noting that *Blue Jeans* court only addressed criminal contempt punishable by thirty days or less); *see also Codispoti v. Pennsylvania*, 418 U.S. 506, 516–17 (1974) (holding that defendant entitled to jury trial under U.S. Constitution where charged with multiple counts of criminal contempt based on conduct during trial and aggregate punishment exceeded six months).

B. Unwaivable Nature of Right

Under Article I, § 24 of the N.C. Constitution, the right to a trial by jury in superior court is unwaivable, except by pleading guilty. *See State v. Hudson*, 280 N.C. 74 (1971); *State v. Bunch*, 196 N.C. App. 438, 440 (2009), *aff'd*, 363 N.C. 841 (2010); *see also State v. Muse*, 219 N.C. 226 (1941) (per curiam) (defendant who pled not guilty could not consent to judicial determination of facts in criminal case); *State v. Rogers*, 162 N.C. 656 (1913) (where defendant asked to proceed with eleven jurors after twelfth juror fell ill, conviction was nullity). Note that the Sixth Amendment right to a jury trial is waivable. *See Adams v. United States ex rel. McCann*, 317 U.S. 269, 279–80 (1942) (defendant may waive right to jury trial and be tried by judge); *Bunch*, 196 N.C. App. 438, 440 ("Unlike the right to a jury trial established by the Sixth Amendment of the U.S. Constitution, the right to a jury trial pursuant to Article I, Section 24, cannot be waived.").

C. Number of Jurors

Generally. North Carolina juries must be composed of twelve people. "It is elementary that the jury provided by law for the trial of indictments is composed of twelve persons; a less number is not a jury." *State v. Hudson*, 280 N.C. 74, 79 (1971) (notwithstanding defendant's consent, a jury of eleven could not return valid verdict); *see also State v. Poindexter*, 353 N.C. 440, 443 (2001) ("Article I, Section 24 of the North Carolina Constitution . . . contemplates no more or no less than a jury of twelve persons"; where juror was disqualified after guilt-innocence phase for misconduct during guilt-innocence phase, verdict violated defendant's constitutional right to jury of twelve qualified jurors); *State v. Bindyke*, 288 N.C. 608, 623 (1975) (finding alternate juror's presence in jury room during deliberations violated constitutional right to jury of twelve).

Substituting alternate during deliberations. Once the jury has begun its deliberations, an alternate may not be substituted without violating the defendant's constitutional right to a jury of twelve. *See State v. Bunning*, 346 N.C. 253 (1997); *State v. Hardin*, 161 N.C. App. 530 (2003). *Bunning* reasoned that a substitution during deliberations results in a verdict of eleven jurors plus two jurors who each participate partially. Such a verdict is unconstitutional.

Instructions to less than all the jurors. Article I, § 24 of the N.C. Constitution requires that a trial judge instruct all twelve jurors simultaneously. *See State v. Ashe*, 314 N.C. 28 (1985) (trial judge erred in speaking only with foreperson about exhibits the jury wished to see; all the elements of a trial should be viewed and heard simultaneously by all twelve jurors); *see also* G.S. 15A-1233 (if jury requests review of testimony or other evidence after deliberations have begun, all jurors must be conducted to the courtroom); *State v. Wilson*, 363 N.C. 478, 487–88 (2009) (State failed to show harmless error where trial judge gave instructions to a single juror in violation of defendant's right to a unanimous jury verdict under Article I, § 24).

For further discussion of the trial judge's responsibilities in giving additional instructions to the jury after it retires for deliberations, see *infra* § 32.5, Additional Instructions after Jury Retires. For further discussion of the trial judge's responsibilities when the jury requests a review of exhibits or testimony, see *infra* § 34.2, Requests to Review Testimony and Exhibits During Deliberations.

D. Jury Unanimity

Generally. All jury verdicts in North Carolina must be unanimous. *See* N.C. CONST. art. I, § 24; G.S. 15A-1237(b); *State v. Baldwin*, 330 N.C. 446, 453–54 (1992). The jury must unanimously agree that the State has proven every element of an offense. *See State v. Jordan*, 305 N.C. 274 (1982); *see also State v. Lewis*, 274 N.C. 438, 442 (1968) (defendant entitled to jury verdict on every essential element of the crime charged); N.C. Pattern Jury Instruction—Crim. 101.35 (June 2011) ("All twelve of you must agree to your verdict. You cannot reach a verdict by majority vote.").

Disjunctive jury instructions. The most common problem with jury unanimity occurs when jury instructions are given in the disjunctive—that is, when the instructions allow jurors to find that the defendant committed one act *or* another. Disjunctive jury instructions violate the defendant's state constitutional right to a unanimous jury verdict if the disjunctive alternatives state separate offenses. *See, e.g., State v. Lyons*, 330 N.C. 298 (1991) (disjunctive instructions are fatally ambiguous if the alternatives constitute separate offenses for which the defendant could be separately punished; instruction that permitted jury to find that defendant assaulted one person or another person violated jury unanimity requirement); *State v. Diaz*, 317 N.C. 545, 554 (1986) (instruction that permitted jury to find that defendant possessed *or* transported marijuana was fatally defective because possession and transportation are separate offenses).

Jury instructions that disjunctively list alternative ways of committing the same offense are not erroneous; the jury need not be unanimous on the method of committing a single element. *See, e.g., State v. Bell*, 359 N.C. 1, 30 (2004) (disjunctive instructions on first-degree kidnapping were not fatally ambiguous even though jury did not have to agree on the particular purpose for which the victim was restrained, removed, or confined; alternative purposes offered were "numerous routes" by which defendant could be convicted of one particular offense); *State v. Bradley*, 181 N.C. App. 557, 562 (2007) (no error by trial judge in submitting a verdict sheet to the jury that did not differentiate between the two statutory definitions of the offense of impaired driving; defendant was convicted of "a single wrong that could be established alternatively through either of its elements"); *State v. Petty*, 132 N.C. App. 453, 462–63 (1999) (in first-degree sex offense case, disjunctive instructions on whether sex act was cunnilingus or penetration by object not error because offense could be committed in either of two ways); *see also Schad v. Arizona*, 501 U.S. 624 (1991) (jury unanimity not required as to whether defendant committed felony murder or premeditated murder; jury does not have to be unanimous on theory of crime). However, reversal on appeal may still be required if the judge instructs the jury on alternative ways of committing the offense, there is insufficient evidence to support one of those theories, and the record does not indicate on which theory the jury relied. *See, e.g., State v. Pakulski*, 319 N.C. 562, 574 (1987) (insufficient evidence to support one of two felonies submitted to jury in support of felony murder); *State v. Moore*, 315 N.C. 738, 749 (1986) (insufficient evidence to support one of three purposes submitted to jury in support of first-degree kidnapping); *State v. Johnson*, 183 N.C. App. 576, 584–85 (2007) (insufficient evidence to support one of two purposes submitted to jury in support of second-degree kidnapping).

In determining whether two alternatives constitute separate offenses or merely different ways of committing one offense, the court considers legislative intent. *See, e.g., State v. Creason*, 313 N.C. 122, 129–31 (1985) (General Assembly's intent in making it unlawful to possess a controlled substance with the intent to sell *or* deliver was to prevent the transfer of controlled substances from one person to another; requirement of jury unanimity was met even if six jurors found that defendant intended to "sell" the LSD and six jurors found that defendant intended to "deliver" the LSD because it was one crime).

For a collection of cases that discuss the use of disjunctive language in jury instructions and the unanimity of jury verdicts, see Robert L. Farb, *The "Or" Issue in Criminal Pleadings, Jury Instructions, and Verdicts; Unanimity of Jury Verdict*, UNC SCH. OF GOV'T (Feb. 2010), www.sog.unc.edu/sites/www.sog.unc.edu/files/verdict.pdf.

Jury unanimity in capital sentencing. The unanimity requirement applies to certain jury sentencing decisions in capital cases. *See State v. McCarver*, 341 N.C. 364, 388–94 (1995). *McCarver* held that the jury must be unanimous on every "outcome determinative" issue in the sentencing decision. Outcome determinative issues are Issues I (existence of aggravating circumstances), III (mitigating circumstances do not outweigh aggravating circumstances), and IV (appropriateness of death as punishment). Jurors do not have to be unanimous on Issue II, the existence of mitigating circumstances. *See McKoy v. North Carolina*, 494 U.S. 433, 442–43 (1990) (Eighth Amendment requires that individual jurors be allowed to make their own findings with respect to the existence of reasons not to impose sentence of death).

Chapter 25
Selection of Jury

This chapter discusses issues that arise during jury selection. The chapter is divided into five sections. Section 25.1 addresses the fairness of the jury pool, the meaning of the requirement that jury selection be random, and the procedures for procuring regular and supplemental jurors. Section 25.2 discusses the process of preliminarily excusing jurors who do not meet statutory qualifications. Section 25.3 addresses the practice of voir dire—that is, the questioning of the jury panel by the attorneys for both sides. Sections 25.4 and 25.5 discuss the law on excusing jurors for cause and by peremptory challenges.

Practice note: Except in capital cases, jury selection is not recorded by the court reporter unless the defendant specifically requests it. There are numerous errors that can occur during jury selection. Defense counsel ***always*** should request that it be recorded. If requested, the trial judge must order complete recordation. *See* N.C. GEN. STAT. § 15A-1241(b) (hereinafter G.S.).

25.1 The Jury Pool

A. Fair Cross-Section Requirement

Test for fair cross-section violation. The Sixth Amendment to the U.S. Constitution, as well as Article I, sections 24 and 26 of the N.C. Constitution, require that petit juries be drawn from a "fair cross-section" of the community. *See Taylor v. Louisiana*, 419 U.S. 522 (1975); *State v. McNeill*, 326 N.C. 712 (1990); *see also Duren v. Missouri*, 439 U.S. 357 (1979) (Sixth Amendment's jury trial provision is applicable to the states through the Fourteenth Amendment; violation found where Missouri's jury-selection process systematically excluded women from the jury pool); *State v. Bowman*, 349 N.C. 459 (1998) (state constitution guarantees that members of defendant's race may not be systematically and arbitrarily excluded from the jury pool). The U.S. Supreme Court in *Taylor* accepted the fair cross-section requirement as a fundamental part of the jury trial guarantee of the Sixth Amendment, stating:

> The purpose of a jury is to guard against the exercise of arbitrary power—to make available the commonsense judgment of the community as a hedge against the overzealous or mistaken prosecutor and in preference to the professional or perhaps overconditioned or biased response of a judge. This prophylactic vehicle is not provided if the jury pool is made up of only special segments of the populace or if large, distinctive groups are excluded from the pool. Community participation in the administration of the criminal law, moreover, is not only consistent with our democratic heritage but is also critical to public confidence in the fairness of the criminal justice system. Restricting jury service to only special groups or excluding identifiable segments playing major roles in the community cannot be squared with the constitutional concept of jury trial. "Trial by jury presupposes a jury drawn from a pool broadly representative of the community as well as impartial in a specific case. . . . [T]he broad representative character of the jury should be maintained, partly as assurance of a

> diffused impartiality and partly because sharing in the administration of justice is a phase of civic responsibility."

419 U.S. 522, 530–31 (citations omitted).

To establish a "fair cross-section" violation in the selection of the jury pool, a defendant must show three things:

1. the group alleged to be excluded or underrepresented is a "distinctive" group (racial minorities and women are examples of "distinctive" groups);
2. the representation of this group in the jury pool or venire is not fair and reasonable in relation to the number of people within the group in the community; and
3. the underrepresentation is due to systematic exclusion of the group in the jury-selection process.

See Duren, 439 U.S. 357, 364; *State v. Williams*, 355 N.C. 501, 549 (2002). If the defendant makes a prima facie showing of a violation of his or her Sixth Amendment right to a jury drawn from a fair cross-section of the community, the government bears the burden of justifying the systematic exclusion "by showing attainment of a fair cross section to be incompatible with a significant state interest." *Duren*, 439 U.S. at 368.

There is no set percentage of underrepresentation that satisfies the second prong of this test. Our courts have said that the question of disproportionate representation is determined on a case-by-case basis. *State v. Golphin*, 352 N.C. 364, 393 (2000) (no prima facie case of systemic underrepresentation shown where population was 32% black and jury pool was 17.5% black); *see also Williams*, 355 N.C. 501, 549 (12.13% disparity not unreasonable); *Bowman*, 349 N.C. 459 (disparity of 16.17% not unreasonable). *But see Duren*, 439 U.S. 357 (systematic exclusion of women violated the fair cross-section requirement where women made up 54% of the jury-eligible population but accounted for less than 15% of jury venires); *Turner v. Fouche*, 396 U.S. 346 (1970) (23% disparity was unreasonable); *Jones v. Georgia*, 389 U.S. 24 (1967) (prima facie violation of fair cross-section requirement shown where blacks constituted 20% of community and only 5% of jury pool); 6 WAYNE R. LAFAVE ET AL., CRIMINAL PROCEDURE § 22.2(d), at 60 (3d ed. 2007) (observing that while disagreement exists, an absolute disparity of 10% between the group's representation on the panel and among those eligible for jury service is typically sufficient to show underrepresentation).

In *Berghuis v. Smith*, ___ U.S. ___, 130 S. Ct. 1382 (2010), the defendant argued that the fair cross-section requirement of the Sixth Amendment was violated because only three of the sixty to one-hundred prospective jurors in his jury pool were African-American. The U.S. Supreme Court reversed the Sixth Circuit Court of Appeals' finding that African-Americans were underrepresented in the defendant's jury pool as a result of systematic exclusion. After reviewing the statistical methods by which the defendant had measured the disparity, the Court declined to adopt any particular method for measuring underrepresentation. The Court noted that each of the three methods used by lower federal courts was imperfect.

Intentional discrimination not required. To show "systematic exclusion" of a protected group, the defendant does not have to show that any party acted with discriminatory motive or intent. Underrepresentation is "systematic" if it was an "inherent" product of the jury selection mechanism that was used or if it resulted from a rule or practice over which the state actor had control. *Duren v. Missouri*, 439 U.S. 357, 366 (1979). Examples of inherently problematic jury selection mechanisms might be "redlining" neighborhoods from which jurors are drawn or automatically excluding all homemakers on the presumption that they have child care responsibilities. If the discrimination was intentional, there also may be a violation of equal protection. *See infra* § 25.1B, Application of Equal Protection Clause to Jury Pool.

Standing. A defendant does not have to be a member of the excluded group to have standing to raise a Sixth Amendment fair cross-section challenge. *Taylor v. Louisiana*, 419 U.S. 522 (1975) (male could challenge systematic exclusion of females); *Holland v. Illinois*, 493 U.S. 474 (1990) (white person has standing to challenge exclusion of African-Americans).

No right to proportional representation on petit jury. The Sixth Amendment fair cross-section rule applies only to the jury pool and not to the final jury of twelve. In other words, a defendant has no right to proportional representation of racial minorities or other protected groups on his or her petit jury. *Holland v. Illinois*, 493 U.S. 474 (1990) (fair cross section does not apply to petit jury); *accord Lockhart v. McCree*, 476 U.S. 162 (1986) (exclusion of *Witherspoon* jurors—that is, those who would not vote for death penalty under any circumstances—not violation of fair cross-section requirement). The constitutional provision that protects against discrimination during the selection of the petit jury is the Equal Protection Clause of the Fourteenth Amendment. *See Batson v. Kentucky*, 476 U.S. 79 (1986). The application of that clause to the selection of the petit jury is discussed *infra* in § 25.5C, Equal Protection Limitation on Peremptory Challenges: *Batson* and Its Progeny.

Statistical evidence. Generally, to demonstrate a fair cross-section violation, the defendant will need to use statistical evidence to show that a distinctive group has been systematically excluded. *See Berghuis v. Smith*, __ U.S. ___, 130 S. Ct. 1382 (2010) (discussing methods used in lower federal courts to measure underrepresentation of distinctive groups in jury pools, including absolute disparity, comparative disparity, and standard deviation). It is not sufficient for the defendant simply to state that the percentage of the excluded population is larger in the county than in the current jury venire. *See State v. Jackson*, ___ N.C. App. ___, 716 S.E.2d 61 (2011) (fact that only three out of sixty potential Orange County jurors were African-Americans was insufficient, standing alone, to support the second and third prongs required by the *Duren* test to establish a prima facie violation for disproportionate representation in a jury venire; defense counsel's statement that the African-American population was "certainly greater than . . . five percent" was insufficient where no demographic data was presented to the court to show the racial composition of the county). The defendant must show the percentage of the distinctive group in the jury pool *and* in the community. Information regarding the percentage of distinctive groups in the community may be available in the most recent report for the county from the U.S. Census Bureau.

Usually, the defendant also will need to show the percentage of the group in question in past jury pools because, to satisfy the third prong of the *Duren* test, the defendant must show that the cause of the distinctive group's underrepresentation is systematic. *See Duren v. Missouri*, 439 U.S. 357 (1979) (defendant successfully showed that women were underrepresented as a result of Missouri's automatic exemption of women from jury service); *State v. Bowman*, 349 N.C. 459 (1998) (statistics concerning one jury pool, standing alone, were insufficient to show a systematic exclusion of a distinctive group); *State v. McNeill*, 326 N.C. 712, 717–18 (1990) (assuming that the defendant met his burden with regard to the first and second prongs of the *Duren* test, he failed to prove that the procedure establishing the jury pool was not racially neutral or that there was a history of relatively few blacks serving on Harnett County juries; statistics regarding his jury pool alone were not sufficient to establish a systematic exclusion of blacks from the jury pool); *see also* 3 DAVID S. RUDSTEIN ET AL., CRIMINAL CONSTITUTIONAL LAW § 14.07 (2011); 6 WAYNE R. LAFAVE ET AL., CRIMINAL PROCEDURE § 22.2(d), at 63 (3d ed. 2007).

Expert assistance. Because of the statistics needed to satisfy the *Duren* test, an indigent defendant may have grounds to request funds to hire a statistician. *Compare State v Moore*, 100 N.C. App. 217 (1990) (initial motion for statistical expert to analyze race discrimination in grand and petit juries granted; motion for funds for additional study denied), *rev'd on other grounds*, 329 N.C. 245 (1991), *with State v. Massey*, 316 N.C. 558 (1986) (finding that the defendant did not make an adequate showing to warrant funds for a statistician). In noncapital cases, requests for funds for expert assistance go to the court; in capital cases, they go to the Office of Indigent Defense Services. For a further discussion of requesting funds for expert assistance, see 1 NORTH CAROLINA DEFENDER MANUAL Ch. 5 (Experts and Other Assistance) (May 1998).

Practice note: To raise a fair cross-section violation claim about selection of the petit jury, counsel should move to discharge the venire before the start of the jury selection process. You must strictly comply with the requirements set out in G.S. 15A-1211(c). *See infra* § 25.1G, Preserving Denial of Challenges to the Panel. You should specifically state the grounds for your challenge.

Be sure the record reveals the race of each juror by using a juror questionnaire or by asking each member of the jury to state his or her personal information, including race. The record also must show the race of the defendant and of the alleged victim.

B. Application of Equal Protection Clause to Jury Pool

The Equal Protection Clause of the Fourteenth Amendment to the U.S. Constitution prevents the state or any state actor, including the court, from intentionally discriminating against a distinctive group in selecting the jury pool. *Castaneda v. Partida*, 430 U.S. 482 (1977); *State v. Hough*, 299 N.C. 245 (1980). To establish a violation of equal protection, the defendant must demonstrate a prima facie case of discrimination by showing statistical underrepresentation of the distinctive group. The burden then shifts to the state actor to explain the discrepancy in a non-discriminatory manner. *Castaneda*, 430 U.S. at 494–95. Because intentional discrimination is harder to show than a fair cross-section violation, the Equal Protection Clause is rarely invoked by defendants challenging the jury pool. However, the Equal Protection Clause also applies to the selection of the petit jury from the jury pool and provides a basis for challenging a prosecutor's use of peremptory challenges. *See infra* § 25.5C, Equal Protection Limitation on Peremptory Challenges: *Batson* and Its Progeny.

C. Random Selection Requirement

Statutory and constitutional basis. North Carolina law provides that the selection of jurors from the jury pool for questioning must be random. G.S. 15A-1214(a) states: "The clerk, under the supervision of the presiding judge, must call jurors from the panel by a system of random selection *which precludes advance knowledge of the identity of the next juror to be called*" (emphasis added). The fair cross-section cases, *Taylor* and *Duren*, strongly imply that a randomly selected jury pool and random selection from the pool is required by both the Sixth Amendment and the Equal Protection Clause of the Fourteenth Amendment. *See Holland v. Illinois*, 493 U.S. 474, 512 n.10 (1990) (Stevens, J., dissenting) (the logical, and desirable, way to impanel an impartial and representative jury . . . is to put together a complete list of eligible jurors and select randomly from it" (citation omitted)); *see also Truesdale v. Moore*, 142 F.3d 749 (4th Cir. 1998) (random procedure for selecting jurors satisfies Sixth and Fourteenth Amendments). For example, a jury selection process in which all the men in the pool were called into the box for questioning before any women were called would very likely be found unconstitutional.

Practice note: Because randomness is almost certainly a constitutional requirement, always constitutionalize any objection to a randomness violation in addition to making your objection on statutory grounds. State on the record that the nonrandom selection process violates the Sixth and Fourteenth Amendments to the U.S. Constitution as well as article I, sections 19 and 24 of the N.C. Constitution.

Organizing of jury pool into panels. The statutory randomness requirement is violated when a large jury pool is broken down into smaller panels and each panel is exhausted before any member of the next panel is called. At the tail end of each panel—when there is only one member of the panel left—the identity of the next juror to be called is known. *See, e.g., State v. Wiley*, 355 N.C. 592, 606–07 (2002) (defendant argued that dividing the jury pool into panels violated jury randomness; court did not review merits of the argument, finding that defendant failed to properly preserve the issue for appellate review); *accord State v. Cummings*, 353 N.C. 281 (2001) (breaking jury into panels and then proceeding while some jurors were not present was violation of randomness). To avoid a violation of randomness, the last member or last few members of each panel have to be combined with the next panel. This procedure creates the problem that a few unlucky individuals may have to sit through panel after panel of jury selection without being called. Under G.S. 15A-1211(c), a defendant may waive any objection to dividing the pool into panels by declining to enter an objection in writing before jury selection begins. *See Wiley*, 355 N.C. at 607; *State v. Golphin*, 352 N.C. 364, 411–12 (2000); *see also State v. Tirado*, 358 N.C. 551 (2004) (defendants waived review of randomness issue based on trial judge's division of the jury pool into smaller panels because defendants failed to challenge the jury panel using the statutory procedure mandated by G.S. 15A-1211(c)).

Practice note: Although you may decide to waive any objection to randomly selected small panels, you should lodge an objection if these smaller jury panels are created in a nonrandom manner. For example, if the judge puts all people who have transportation problems in a late panel, or groups teachers together into a late panel so that they can all attend the last day of school, the selection procedure is nonrandom, and you should object in writing before jury selection begins or as soon as the error occurs. *See* G.S. 15A-1211 (setting forth procedure defendants must follow to preserve issue for appellate review); *see also Golphin*, 352 N.C. 364, 413 (trial judge grouped in last panel all people who filed unsuccessful written requests to be excused, which minimized chance that these people would be selected for jury).

Demonstrating prejudice from randomness violation. This topic is discussed *infra* in § 25.1G, Preserving Denial of Challenges to the Panel.

D. Statutory Requirements for Preparation of Jury Lists

G.S. 9-1 through 9-7 describe the statutory requirements for preparing lists of prospective jurors for trial (petit) and grand juries. *See also* G.S. 9-10 (describing procedure for summoning prospective jurors from jury list). As a general rule, prospective jurors are drawn from a list of registered voters and people with driver's license records in the county, although a jury commission may use another source of names if it deems that source to be reliable. *See* G.S. 9-2(b).

While mere "technical and insubstantial violations of the statutes regulating jury selection procedure" are not "sufficient to vitiate a jury list or afford a challenge to the array" (*State v. Massey*, 316 N.C. 558, 570 (1986)), a defendant is entitled to have a bill of indictment quashed if he or she can show that:

1. the jury list was compiled with a corrupt intent;
2. there was systematic discrimination in the compilation of the list; or
3. irregularities in the compilation of the list affected the actions of the jurors actually drawn and summoned,

State v. Johnson, 317 N.C. 343, 379 (1986).

For a further discussion of the procedures used in preparing jury lists and in drawing panels, see JAMES C. DRENNAN & MIRIAM S. SAXON, A MANUAL FOR NORTH CAROLINA JURY COMMISSIONERS (UNC School of Government, 4th ed. 2007). *See also* 1 NORTH CAROLINA DEFENDER MANUAL § 9.1 (Composition of Grand Jury) (Jan. 2009).

E. Supplemental Jurors

Generally. Sometimes an original jury venire summoned in accordance with G.S. 9-10 will be insufficient to meet the needs of the court. To facilitate the business of the court, G.S. 9-11(b) permits a trial judge, in his or her discretion, at any time before or during a court session, to direct that supplemental jurors or a special venire be selected from the jury list in the same manner as regular jurors. These jurors may be discharged at any time during the session by the judge and they are subject to the same challenges as regular jurors. *Id.* This statute "neither explicitly nor impliedly requires the judge to wait a certain amount of time so that a particular number of summonses can be served." *State v. Mebane*, 106 N.C. App. 516, 524 (1992) (finding no abuse of discretion by trial judge in continuing with jury selection after the original panel had been depleted even though only four of the fifty supplemental jurors selected from the jury list had been served and reported for jury duty).

Under G.S. 9-11, trial judges also are permitted, without using the jury list, to "order the sheriff to summon from day to day additional jurors to supplement the original venire." Supplemental jurors summoned by the sheriff must have the same qualifications as jurors selected for the regular jury list and are subject to the same challenges. G.S. 9-11(a). This type of juror is "selected infrequently and only to provide a source from which to fill the unexpected needs of the court." *State v. White*, 6 N.C. App. 425, 428 (1969).

Historically, supplemental jurors were known as "talesmen" or "tales jurors" and were selected from the bystanders in or about the courtroom to serve as jurors when the original panel had become deficient. *See* Thomas L. Fowler, *Filling The Box: Responding to Jury Duty Avoidance*, 23 N.C. CENT. L.J. 1 (1997/1998) [hereinafter Fowler]; *see also State v. Benton*, 19 N.C. 196 (1836); BLACK'S LAW DICTIONARY 1592 (9th ed. 2009). This practice is authorized in North Carolina by G.S. 9-11, although the sheriff is no longer restricted to selecting bystanders found "in and about the court-house." Fowler at 4. A sheriff now "appears to be free to locate appropriate jurors 'from the body of the county,' whether in or near the courthouse, at the mall, or elsewhere." *Id.* (footnotes omitted); *see also Sheriff Apologizes for Searching for Jurors at Wal-Mart*, S.F. CHRON., Dec. 4, 2003 (discussing North Carolina judge's order to Wayne County sheriff to send deputies to a public place to search for jurors the day before Thanksgiving and ensuing confrontations between deputies and Goldsboro Wal-mart shoppers looking for Christmas gifts), *available at* www.sfgate.com/cgi-bin/article.cgi?f=/g/a/2003/12/04/MNjurorhunt.DTL.

Potential for discrimination. There is no set method prescribed by the statute or case law by which supplemental jurors must be selected. *See White*, 6 N.C. App. 425. The sheriff may use his or her discretion in determining the method of selection of the supplemental jurors; however, he or she "must act with entire impartiality." *Id.* at 428 (citation omitted); *see also State v. Nolen*, 144 N.C. App. 172, 180 (2001) (finding that G.S. 9-11, on its face, was not violative of the right to an impartial jury, and finding no error where sheriff selected supplemental jurors by contacting people in the county that he and his senior staff members "knew that [jury duty] wouldn't cause a financial hardship for").

But see Russell v. Wyrick, 736 F.2d 462 (8th Cir. 1984) (noting that several dangers are present when sheriffs are permitted to select jurors, including the chance that the sheriff will choose people who are favorable to the prosecution, the likelihood of which is heightened if the sheriff or deputies were involved in investigating the case or if they choose only people that they know).

As noted by the court in *White*, it obviously "would be possible for a sheriff, sent out to execute . . . an order of the court [to summon supplemental jurors], to discriminate in the selection of persons to be summoned." *White*, 6 N.C. App. 425, 427 (citation omitted). Challenges to the selection of the supplemental jurors are sustainable if "there is partiality or misconduct in the Sheriff, or some irregularity in making the list." *State v. Dixon*, 215 N.C. 438, 440 (1939) (citation omitted); *see also Bass v. State*, 368 So. 2d 447, 449 (Fla. Dist. Ct. App. 1979) (reversing defendant's conviction and stating that "[t]he choice of a special venire from an all-Caucasian church body, or from one's Caucasian friends, is a systematic, if unintended, exclusion of blacks"; the selection of supplemental jurors "must be administered in such a way as not to exclude identifiable segments of the populace systematically").

Practice note: If the supplemental jurors selected by the sheriff do not represent a fair cross-section of the community, you should consider moving to discharge the jurors. You likely will need a recess or a continuance to get the statistical information you need to support your claim of a fair cross-section violation. *See supra* "Statistical evidence" and "Expert assistance" in § 25.1A, Fair Cross-Section Requirement. If your motion is denied, you also will need to take the necessary steps to preserve the issue for appellate review. *See infra* § 25.1G, Preserving Denial of Challenges to the Panel; *see also State v. Wilson*, 313 N.C. 516 (1985) (defendant could not complain about the judge's order requiring the sheriff to recruit supplemental jurors, allegedly in excess of the judge's statutory authority, because the defendant failed to exhaust his last peremptory challenge to remove the twelfth juror who was one of the supplemental jurors); *State v. Shaw*, 284 N.C. 366, 369 (1973) (no error in trial judge's denial of defendant's motion to allow defense counsel or his representative to be present during the summoning of the jury by the sheriff; defendant failed to challenge array or "offer any proof that the Sheriff violated the trust placed in him as an elected official").

Potential conflict of interest. A special venire is not necessarily rendered invalid because the sheriff who summoned it (or his or her deputy) is a witness for the State. *State v. Wiggins*, 272 N.C. 147 (1967). In discussing this issue in *State v. Yancey*, 58 N.C. App. 52 (1982), the Court of Appeals found that although sheriffs and deputy sheriffs testify in many cases, it was not the intent of the General Assembly to disqualify sheriffs from summoning extra jurors in all of those cases. If it were, the General Assembly "would have designated some other official to summon extra jurors." *Id.* at 60; *see also State v. Barnard*, 346 N.C. 95 (1997). However, if the judge finds that the sheriff is not suitable to select additional jurors because of a direct or indirect interest in the action to be tried, the judge can appoint some other suitable person to summon the supplemental jurors. G.S. 9-11(a).

F. Supplemental Jurors from Outside the County

A special venire of jurors from outside the county or the district where the case is being tried may be summoned for jury duty by the judge if he or she determines that it is necessary for a fair trial. The defendant or the State may move for "outside" jurors, or the judge can order them summoned on his or her own motion. G.S. 9-12(a); G.S. 15A-958. This motion can be made as an alternative to a motion for a change of venue. *See, e.g., State v. Moore*, 319 N.C. 645 (1987) (defendant moved for a change of venue or for a special venire due to extensive inflammatory media coverage of the case, pervasive county-wide discussion of it, and the social prominence of the alleged victim and her family).

If the judge determines that "outside" jurors are needed, he or she can order them to be brought to court from any county or counties in the district or set of districts in which the county of trial is located or in any adjoining district or set of districts as defined in G.S. 7A-41.1(a). *See* G.S. 9-12(a). These jurors are selected and serve in the same manner as supplemental jurors selected from jury lists. They also are subject to the same challenges as other jurors with the exception of a challenge for non-residency in the county of trial. *Id.*

In ruling on a defendant's motion for a special venire, as with a motion for a change of venue, the trial judge must determine whether there is a reasonable likelihood that the defendant will not receive a fair trial. *See Moore*, 319 N.C. 645. In other words, a defendant's motion should be granted if he or she can show "that it is reasonably likely that prospective jurors would base their decision in the case upon pretrial information rather than the evidence presented at trial and would be unable to remove from their minds any preconceived impressions they might have formed." *Id.* at 650 (citations omitted) (granting defendant a new trial where the trial judge applied an incorrect standard when ruling on defendant's motion for a change of venue or for a special venire and defendant had presented substantial affirmative evidence tending to show that he could not receive a fair trial because jurors would be reasonably likely to base verdict on outside influences). The burden of proof is on the defendant. *See State v. Jaynes*, 342 N.C. 249, 264 (1995). A decision on a motion for a special venire from outside the county lies within the discretion of the trial judge and will not be disturbed on appeal absent an abuse of that discretion. *See State v. Walters*, 357 N.C. 68 (2003); *State v. Edwards*, 286 N.C. 140 (1974).

For a discussion of motions to change venue, see 1 NORTH CAROLINA DEFENDER MANUAL § 11.3 (Change of Venue) (Nov. 2008).

G. Preserving Denial of Challenges to the Panel

If a challenge to the jury panel is sustained, the trial judge is required to discharge the panel. G.S. 15A-1211(c). However, if a challenge is denied, the issue must be properly preserved or the appellate court may find waiver. To obtain relief on appeal for some violations, the defendant also may need to show prejudice by exhausting all of his or her peremptory challenges. The cases do not always distinguish clearly between the requirements for preserving error and for showing prejudice.

Constitutional challenges. To preserve a challenge to the jury panel based on the right to a fair and impartial jury under the state and federal constitutions, you must object and state the constitutional basis for the objection. Failure to challenge the jury panel on constitutional grounds at the trial level will waive review of the constitutional issue on appeal. *See State v. Tirado*, 358 N.C. 551, 571 (2004); *State v. Wiley*, 355 N.C. 592, 606 (2005).

Statutory challenges. To preserve a statutory challenge to a jury panel for appellate review, including challenges to the method in which individual jurors are called and selected, counsel must follow the mandates of G.S. 15A-1211(c). *See State v. Johnson*, 161 N.C. App. 68 (2003). This statute requires that challenges to the panel:

1. be made on the grounds that the jurors were not lawfully selected or drawn;
2. be in writing;
3. specify the facts supporting the grounds for the challenge; and
4. be made and decided before the examination of any juror.

G.S. 15A-1211(c). *See State v. Smith*, 359 N.C. 199 (2005) (defendant failed to preserve his challenge to the randomness of the jury where he did not comply with G.S. 15A-1211(c)); *Johnson*, 161 N.C. App. 68, 75 (although a trial judge's failure to follow a statutory mandate usually preserves an error without an objection, the defendant waived appellate review because he failed to follow the procedures outlined in G.S. 15A-1211(c) for challenging a jury panel).

If you consent to the jury procedures used by the trial judge, appellate review of the issue will be waived. *See, e.g., State v. Meyer*, 353 N.C. 92 (2000) (not only did defendant never object to the jury selection process or follow the statutory procedures for challenging the jury panel, he expressly approved of the reassignment of a prospective juror; court concluded that defendant failed to preserve the issue for appellate review).

Counsel also should be wary of expressing satisfaction with the jury once jury selection has concluded. *See State v. Bell*, 359 N.C. 1 (2004) (denying appellate review where defendant failed to follow the procedures set out in G.S. 15A-1211(c) and noting that defendant answered in the affirmative when asked if he approved of the panel).

Demonstrating prejudice from randomness violation. The N.C. Supreme Court has held that a defendant must show prejudice from a randomness violation occurring from a deviation from the procedures mandated by G.S. 15A-1214(a). *State v. Thompson*, 359 N.C. 77 (2004). It is hard to know exactly what it would take to demonstrate prejudice. In *State v. Golphin*, 352 N.C. 364 (2000), the N.C. Supreme Court found that even if a violation of the statutory requirement of randomness occurred, the defendants failed to show prejudice because they did not exhaust their peremptory challenges, which the court considered to be evidence of the defendants' satisfaction with the seated jury. *See also*

State v. Tirado, 358 N.C. 551 (2004) (even assuming that G.S. 15A-1214(a) was violated by the placing of a hearing-impaired prospective juror into the last panel, defendants could show no prejudice when they did not show that they were forced to accept an undesirable juror and, in fact, consented to her excusal). In light of these cases, trial counsel will have to exhaust peremptories to show prejudice and may need to object to the last seated juror (which counsel should do outside the presence of the jury). *See* "Recommended approach," below. Counsel also should try to explain on the record how the violation will affect the jury and prejudice the defendant. For example, in *Golphin*, reluctant jurors (who were put in the last panel by the judge) may have been more favorable jurors from a defense standpoint.

Recommended approach. To ensure preservation of jury panel selection errors and to show prejudice from any deviation from procedure, trial counsel should take the following steps:

1. Object to the erroneous procedure on the applicable statutory and constitutional grounds. This is a basic principle of preserving error for appeal.
2. Strictly follow the mandates of G.S. 15A-1211(c). These requirements may apply to statutory violations only but, to minimize the risk of waiver, counsel should follow the steps for constitutional violations as well.
3. Exhaust peremptory challenges. This step may not be required for constitutional violations such as fair cross-section violations. Among other things, the exercise of peremptories would do little to give the defendant a meaningful opportunity to select a representative jury from a jury pool that is constitutionally unrepresentative; therefore, it would be a fiction to suggest that the failure to exhaust peremptories shows the defendant's satisfaction with the seated jury. *See generally State v. Golphin*, 352 N.C. 364, 392–95, 410–14 (2000) (court based rejection of randomness claim, in part, on defendants' failure to exhaust their peremptories, but court did not mention that reason in rejecting defendants' fair cross-section claim).
4. Out of the presence of the jury and on the record, state that the defendant objects to the last seated juror, ask for an additional peremptory, and state that if the defendant had another peremptory, he or she would use it on the last seated juror. This action reinforces that the defendant was not satisfied with the seated jury and therefore was prejudiced, but it may no longer be legally required. *Compare infra* § 25.4C, Preserving Denial of Cause Challenges (Official Commentary to G.S. 15A-1214, which governs preservation of denial of cause challenges, states that this step is not required; however, some cases have continued to suggest that this step is required).
5. If you want to express satisfaction with the jury in front of the jury, do so in a qualified way, such as "conditioned on what we stated earlier regarding the selection process, Your Honor, defendant is satisfied with the jury." If you unqualifiedly express satisfaction with the jury, you may undo your efforts to show prejudice.

25.2 Qualifying the Jury

A. Statutory Qualifications

Generally. "[T]he law not only guarantees the right of trial by jury, but also the right of trial by a proper jury; that is to say, a jury possessing the qualifications contemplated by law." *Hinton v. Hinton*, 196 N.C. 341, 343 (1928). In giving effect to this constitutional guarantee, the General Assembly's purpose was to ensure "that all those and only those citizens who possess the proper qualifications of character and intelligence should be selected to serve on the juries." *State v. Ingram*, 237 N.C. 197, 204 (1953).

The qualifications for prospective jurors are set forth in G.S. 9-3. People are qualified to serve as jurors if they:

- are citizens of the state (a North Carolina citizen is one who is a citizen of the United States and a resident of North Carolina);
- are residents of the county;
- have not served as jurors in the previous two years;
- are 18 years of age or older;
- are physically and mentally competent;
- are able to understand English;
- have not been convicted of a felony or pled guilty or no contest to an indictment charging a felony, unless citizenship rights have been restored; and
- have not been adjudged non compos mentis (not of sound mind).

Calculation of two-year requirement. People who have served on federal juries as well as those who have served on state juries are disqualified from serving within two years. *State v. Golphin*, 352 N.C. 364, 424–25 (2000) (no error in judge's excusal of potential juror; two years had not passed from the time of her service on a federal jury until the time jury selection in defendant's case commenced). The two-year exclusion is triggered only if the juror is sworn—merely receiving a jury summons is not enough. *State v. Berry*, 35 N.C. App. 128 (1978). The date for determining the end of the two-year period is the date on which jurors are first sworn at the beginning of jury selection. *Golphin*, 352 N.C. 364, 425 (two-year limit could not be avoided by moving juror to a later panel so that she would not be questioned until after two-year exclusionary period had run).

Senior citizen status. There is no maximum age for jury service. People who are 72 years old or older may request to be excused from the jury in writing (rather than by personally appearing in court). The signed statement of the grounds for the request for excusal must be filed with the chief district court judge or his or her designee at least five business days before the date the person is summoned to appear. *See* G.S. 9-6.1(a). "The judge has the option of allowing or denying the request." *State v. Rogers*, 355 N.C. 420, 447 (2002).

Once the older person is in the venire in the courtroom, he or she may request to be excused on the basis of age. The request may be granted if he or she is unfit to serve, if there are reasons of compelling personal hardship, or if his or her service would be contrary to the public welfare, health or safety. *See* G.S. 9-3, 9-6(a); *Rogers*, 355 N.C. 420, 447–49 (also finding no violation of fair cross-section requirement of Sixth Amendment or Equal Protection Clause by statutory scheme for excusal of jurors in light of age). A trial judge may not adopt a blanket policy of excusing all senior citizens who request to be excused, however. Rather, "excusing prospective jurors present in the courtroom who are over the age of sixty-five [now seventy-two] must reflect a genuine exercise of judicial discretion." *Rogers*, 355 N.C. at 448; *see also State v. Elliott*, 360 N.C. 400 (2006) (trial judge did not abuse his discretion in refusing to excuse an elderly prospective juror where the record revealed that she had no hardship other than advanced age; four elderly prospective jurors that were excused each had a compelling personal hardship). For a discussion of a similar issue involving grand jurors, see 1 NORTH CAROLINA DEFENDER MANUAL § 9.1B (Qualifications of Individual Grand Jurors) (Jan. 2009).

English language capability. In *State v. Smith*, 352 N.C. 531 (2000), the N.C. Supreme Court upheld the constitutionality of the requirement that jurors speak and understand English. Also, the inquiry into whether a juror is an English speaker should be in English. *Id.* at 546–47 (error but no prejudice where prosecutor asked defendant in Spanish whether he understood English well enough to participate).

Physical and mental competence, disabilities, and hearing. The trial judge has broad discretion to determine whether a person is physically competent to serve as a juror. *See, e.g., State v. Neal*, 346 N.C. 608 (1997) (no error in excusing juror with history of medical problems and Valium addiction); *State v. Carter*, 338 N.C. 569 (1994) (no error in excusing juror who was eight months pregnant); *State v. King*, 311 N.C. 603 (1984) (no error in declining to excuse juror who suffered from hearing impairment but stated he could hear and understand lawyer's voir dire); *see also* G.S. 9-3 (effective July 1, 2011, statute requires that prospective jurors be able to understand English language but no longer requires that they be able to hear English language). A person summoned as a juror who has a disability may request to be excused from the jury in writing (rather than personally appearing in court); a signed statement of the grounds for the request for excusal, including a brief description of the disability, must be filed with the chief district court judge or his or her designee at least five business days before the date the person is summoned to appear. *See* G.S. 9-6.1(b).

Trial judges are not limited to excusing jurors who are disqualified under G.S. 9-3 and may excuse any person for whom jury service would constitute a "compelling personal hardship." G.S. 9-6; *see also infra* § 25.2B, Hardship Excuses. The N.C. Supreme Court has suggested that the reason the trial judge gives for excusing a juror as disqualified or for hardship should not be pretextual. *State v. Alston*, 341 N.C. 198 (1995) (rejecting defendant's contention that trial judge's actual reason for excusing juror with medical problems was her position on death penalty).

Restoration of citizenship rights for convicted felons. A convicted felon's citizenship rights are automatically restored on unconditional discharge from the Department of Correction. G.S. 13-1(1). A person with a prior felony conviction who is no longer on parole or probation is eligible for jury service. *Id.* Likewise, a person convicted of a federal crime or a crime in another state may serve on the jury if he or she has been unconditionally discharged by the agency having jurisdiction of him or her. G.S. 13-1(4), (5).

People with pending felony charges are excusable for cause under G.S. 15A-1212(7).

B. Hardship Excuses

Generally. The General Assembly has declared the public policy of the state to be that jury service is a solemn obligation of all qualified citizens and that people qualified for jury service should be excused or deferred only for reasons of "compelling personal hardship" or because service would be "contrary to the public welfare, health, or safety." G.S. 9-6(a), (c). Hardship excuses are heard and determined in district court, by a district court judge or trial court administrator. G.S. 9-6(b). The presiding judge in superior court also may excuse or defer prospective jurors for hardship. G.S. 9-6(f). The judge has broad discretion in determining what constitutes hardship. *E.g.*, *State v. Hedgepeth*, 350 N.C. 776 (1999) (no error in failing to excuse juror who had inoperable brain tumor where trial judge was convinced that juror's memory impairment was insufficient to disqualify juror); *State v. Norwood*, 344 N.C. 511 (1996) (no error in excusing last remaining African-American female venireperson where she had five children and was in community college); *State v. Fisher*, 336 N.C. 684 (1994) (no error in excusing juror who was apprehensive about leaving child in day care to perform jury service). Nevertheless, the judge's power to excuse jurors must be exercised within constitutional constraints. *See. e.g.*, *State v. Cole*, 331 N.C. 272 (1992) (violation of capital defendant's constitutional right to presence found where after the trial had commenced, the trial judge deferred service for some jurors at a bench conference outside defendant's presence).

Scope of district court's authority to excuse jurors. The district court should excuse prospective jurors only for hardship, pursuant to G.S. 9-6, and not because of bias, opinion about the death penalty, or other grounds that might constitute the basis for a cause challenge under G.S. 15A-1212. *State v. Murdock*, 325 N.C. 522 (1989) (proper practice is for district court judges to excuse jurors only on grounds set forth in G.S. 9-6). If the district court excuses jurors on too broad of a basis, the defendant may have grounds to move to dismiss the venire. A defendant who moves to dismiss the venire because of improper conduct by the district court must show evidence of corrupt intent, systematic discrimination, or other irregularities affecting the actions of the jurors actually drawn and summoned. *Murdock*, 325 N.C. at 526; *accord State v. Leary*, 344 N.C. 109 (1996) (reaffirming *Murdock*); *see also State v. Hyde*, 352 N.C. 37 (2000) (evidence that district court judge excused jurors on basis of "religious scruples" [presumably, about death penalty] did not entitle defendant to new trial; defendant failed to show corrupt intent or that he was prejudiced by jury that was impaneled).

No right to presence when district court excuses jurors. The North Carolina courts have held that a defendant's right to be present at all critical stages of his or her trial applies only after the defendant's trial is called in superior court. A defendant has no right to be present during the preliminary qualification of jurors by the district court because this occurs before the defendant's trial begins. *State v. McCarver*, 341 N.C. 364 (1995); *State v. Cole*, 331 N.C. 272 (1992).

Right to presence when superior court excuses jurors. A defendant has a constitutional right to be present after his or her case is called, when jurors are being selected for his or her case. Once a defendant's case is called for trial, a superior court judge may not excuse jurors for hardship in unrecorded bench conferences; he or she must conduct all jury selection proceedings on the record and in the presence of the defendant. *State v. Cole*, 331 N.C. 272 (1992); *State v. Smith*, 326 N.C. 792 (1990). If a defendant is not present during any part of jury selection, there is reversible error. *Smith*, 326 N.C. at 794. For further discussion of a defendant's right to be present during jury selection, see *supra* § 21.1C, Trial Proceedings (discussing right to presence at different proceedings).

25.3 Voir Dire

A. Preliminary Procedures

Before the jurors are selected, the judge is required to identify the parties and their attorneys. He or she also must briefly inform the prospective jurors of:

- the charges of each defendant,
- the dates of the alleged offenses,
- the name of any alleged victim, and
- the defendant's plea.

G.S. 15A-1213; G.S. 15A-1221(a)(2).

G.S. 15A-1213 also states that the trial judge must inform the prospective jurors of any affirmative defense of which the defendant has given pretrial notice. Amendments to G.S. 15A-905(c)(1) enacted in 2004, however, require the defendant, as part of reciprocal discovery, to give notice of all potential defenses identified in the statute. In recognition that the defendant may decide before trial not to pursue a particular defense, G.S. 15A-905(c)(1) states that "[n]otice of defense as described in this subdivision is inadmissible against the defendant." In light of this provision, if the defendant advises the trial judge that he or she does not intend to pursue a defense for which he or she has given notice as part of discovery, the trial judge would appear to be prohibited from informing the jury of the defense.

The judge also is prohibited from reading the indictment to the jury. G.S. 15A-1213; *see also* G.S. 15A-1221(b). The purpose of G.S. 15A-1213 "when read contextually and considered with the Official Commentary to the statute is to avoid giving jurors a distorted view of a case because of the stilted language of most indictments." *State v.*

Elkerson, 304 N.C. 658, 663 (1982) (citation omitted); *see also* G.S. 15A-1213 Official Commentary (stating that the "procedure is designed to orient the prospective jurors as to the case").

B. Purposes of Voir Dire

Jury voir dire serves two basic purposes:

1. helping counsel determine whether a basis for a challenge for cause exists, and
2. assisting counsel in intelligently exercising peremptory challenges.

State v. Wiley, 355 N.C. 592 (2002); *State v. Anderson*, 350 N.C. 152 (1999); *State v. Brown*, 39 N.C. App. 548 (1979); *see also Mu'Min v. Virginia*, 500 U.S. 415, 431 (1991) ("Voir dire examination serves the dual purposes of enabling the court to select an impartial jury and assisting counsel in exercising peremptory challenges."). The N.C. Supreme Court also has stated that the purpose of voir dire examination and the exercise of challenges, both peremptory and for cause, "is to eliminate extremes of partiality and to assure both the defendant and the State that the persons chosen to decide the guilt or innocence of the accused will reach that decision solely upon the evidence produced at trial." *State v. Conner*, 335 N.C. 618, 629 (1994).

Practice note: A proposed voir dire question is legitimate if the question is necessary to determine whether a juror is excludable for cause or to assist you in intelligently exercising your peremptory challenges. If the State objects to a particular line of questioning, you may defend your proposed questions by linking them to the purposes of voir dire.

C. Constitutional Entitlement to Voir Dire

Generally. Criminal defendants have a constitutional right under the Sixth and Fourteenth Amendments to voir dire jurors adequately. "[P]art of the guarantee of a defendant's right to an impartial jury is an adequate voir dire to identify unqualified jurors." *Morgan v. Illinois*, 504 U.S. 719, 729–30 (1992) (holding that capital defendant constitutionally entitled to ask specific "life qualifying" questions to the jury); *see also Rosales-Lopez v. United States*, 451 U.S. 182, 188 (1981) (plurality opinion) ("Without an adequate voir dire the trial judge's responsibility to remove prospective jurors who will not be able impartially to follow the court's instructions and evaluate the evidence cannot be fulfilled."). *But cf. Mu'Min v. Virginia*, 500 U.S. 415, 425 (1991) (emphasizing extent of trial judge's discretion in controlling voir dire and holding that voir dire questions about the content of pretrial publicity to which jurors might have been exposed are not constitutionally required).

Voir dire on racial prejudices of jurors. *Ham v. South Carolina*, 409 U.S. 524 (1973), held that an African-American defendant, who was a civil rights activist and whose defense was that he was selectively prosecuted for marijuana possession because of his civil rights activity, was entitled to voir dire jurors about racial bias. *Ham* was later limited by *Ristaino v. Ross*, 424 U.S. 589 (1976), which held that the Due Process Clause creates no general right in non-capital cases to voir dire jurors about racial prejudice. Such questions are constitutionally mandated under "special circumstances," such as those presented in *Ham. Turner v. Murray*, 476 U.S. 28 (1986), held that defendants in capital cases have a right under the Eighth Amendment to voir dire jurors about racial biases. In situations in which the defendant is entitled to question jurors about racial attitudes, the trial judge has the discretion to determine how extensive the voir dire on race will be. *See State v. Robinson*, 330 N.C. 1, 12–13 (1991) (trial judge allowed defendant to question prospective jurors about whether racial prejudice would affect their ability to be fair and impartial and allowed defendant to ask questions of prospective white jurors about their associations with blacks; trial judge did not err in sustaining prosecutor's objection to other questions, such as "Do you belong to any social club or political organization or church in which there are no black members?" and "Do you feel like the presence of blacks in your neighborhood has lowered the value of your property . . . ?").

Practice note: Considerations of race can be critical in capital and noncapital cases, and voir dire on such matters, whether or not constitutionally guaranteed, is often appropriate and permissible to determine potential bias that may make a juror unsuitable to hear the case. *See generally* G.S. 15A-1212(9) (challenge for cause may be made by any party on ground that juror is unable to render a fair and impartial verdict). Counsel should be prepared to show how questions concerning racial attitudes are relevant to the defendant's theory of defense. If the inquiry is particularly sensitive, counsel may request individual voir dire. A sample motion can be found on the Office of Indigent Defense Services website, www.ncids.org. Highlight "Training & Resources," click on "Motions Bank, Non-Capital" and then "Trial Motions (Non-Capital)," scroll down to "Juries," and click on "Motion for Individual Voir Dire on Sensitive Subjects."

D. Statutory Law Governing Voir Dire

Generally. Two sets of North Carolina statutes govern jury voir dire, G.S. 9-14 and 9-15, and G.S. 15A-1211 through 15A-1217. These statutes grant the trial judge broad discretion to determine the extent and manner of voir dire. *See, e.g., State v. Fisher*, 336 N.C. 684 (1994) (extent and manner of voir dire subject to close supervision of trial judge and subject to reversal only on showing of abuse of discretion).

Parties' entitlement to question jurors. Counsel for both parties are statutorily entitled to question jurors and are primarily responsible for conducting voir dire. G.S. 15A-1214(c); *see also* G.S. 9-15(a). The trial judge "may briefly question prospective jurors individually or as a group concerning general fitness and competency . . . ." G.S. 15A-1214(b). However, both parties are statutorily entitled to repeat the judge's questions. G.S. 15A-1214(c) (prosecution and defense not foreclosed from asking question merely because judge has previously asked same question); *State v. Jones*, 336 N.C. 490 (1994) (trial judge violated statute governing jury voir dire when, at outset of jury selection process, he indicated that he would not permit counsel for either side to ask any question of prospective juror that had been asked previously and had been answered).

To expedite voir dire, the trial judge may require the parties to direct certain questions to the panel as a whole. *State v. Campbell*, 340 N.C. 612 (1995) (no error where counsel allowed to question jurors individually if group question produced no response); *State v. Phillips*, 300 N.C. 678 (1980). However, a blanket ban prohibiting parties from questioning jurors individually would violate G.S. 15A-1214. *Phillips*, 300 N.C. 678; *see also infra* § 25.3G, Right to Individual Voir Dire.

Order of questioning. G.S. 15A-1214(d) requires that the prosecutor question prospective jurors first. When the prosecutor is satisfied with a panel of twelve, he or she passes the panel to the defense. The N.C. Supreme Court has upheld this statute against constitutional challenge. *State v. Anderson*, 355 N.C. 136, 147 (2002) (finding it "within the province of the legislature to prescribe the method by which jurors are selected, challenged, impaneled, and seated"). Failure to comply with the statute is error, but the courts may not necessarily find the error to be prejudicial. *E.g.*, *State v. Thompson*, 359 N.C. 77 (2004) (no error where defendant consented to out of order voir dire of two replacement jurors); *State v. Jaynes*, 353 N.C. 534 (2001) (defendant ended up conducting voir dire of jurors before State was required to pass on them; violation of statute but no prejudicial error); *State v. Lawrence*, 352 N.C. 1 (2000) (where State passed panel of ten, not twelve, jurors to defense, violation of statute but defendant failed to show prejudicial error where he failed to object, questioned and passed the one new prospective juror, failed to exhaust his peremptory challenges, and did not request removal of juror for cause).

Order of questioning in cases involving co-defendants. After the State is satisfied with a panel, the panel should be passed to each co-defendant consecutively and then back to the State to fill any vacancies. *See* G.S. 15A-1214(e), (f); *State v. Rogers*, 316 N.C. 203 (1986) (finding no merit to defendant's argument that her rights to examine a full jury panel were infringed because her examination of potential jurors came after the State and the co-defendant had examined them; procedure used by judge followed the provisions of G.S. 15A-1214).

Practice note: In a trial involving co-defendants, it would be inappropriate under G.S. 15A-1214 for the trial judge to pass the jury back to the State after Defendant 1 exercises his or her peremptory challenges and not pass the jury to Defendant 2 until both the State and Defendant 1 have exhausted their peremptories or expressed satisfaction with twelve jurors. This method of selection would appear prejudicial to Defendant 1—effectively, the State and Defendant 2 would pick the jury after Defendant 1 has no further opportunity for input. If faced with this situation, inform the trial judge that the provisions of G.S. 15A-1214 are mandatory and, if the judge nevertheless uses this method, put an objection and explanation of the prejudice on the record.

To preserve the error and/or demonstrate prejudice regarding the order of questioning, the defendant also may need to exhaust his or her peremptory challenges. *See generally supra* § 25.1G, Preserving Denial of Challenges to the Panel and *infra* § 25.4C Preserving Denial of Cause Challenges.

Challenging a juror. G.S. 9-15(a) states that making "direct oral inquiry" of a juror—that is, questioning a juror—does not itself constitute a challenge to the juror. A trial judge is not to consider a juror challenged by a party until that party formally states that the juror is challenged for cause or peremptorily. *Id.* If a juror is challenged for cause, the party should state the grounds for the challenge so that the trial judge can make his or her ruling. Generally, no grounds need be stated when a party exercises a peremptory challenge. *But see infra* § 25.5C, Equal Protection Limitation on Peremptory Challenges: *Batson* and Its Progeny (*Batson* line of cases requires a party to state reason for peremptory challenge if opposing party establishes a prima facie case of discrimination).

E. Scope of Permitted Questioning

Generally. The scope of permitted voir dire is largely a matter of trial court discretion. *E.g.*, *State v. Knight*, 340 N.C. 531 (1995) (trial judge properly sustained State's objection to question about victim's HIV status); *State v. Lee*, 335 N.C. 244 (1994) (judge properly sustained State's objection to questions about whether jurors believed death penalty had deterrent effect); *State v. Brown*, 327 N.C. 1 (1990) (no abuse of discretion shown when trial judge sustained objections to defendant's questions to prospective jurors about whether they would be comfortable with the defense questioning police procedure during trial); *see generally State v. Phillips*, 300 N.C. 678 (1980) (explaining boundaries on voir dire—questions should not be overly repetitious or attempt to indoctrinate jurors or "stake them out").

Certain topics constitutionally guaranteed. Criminal defendants are constitutionally entitled to explore certain topics in voir dire, including:

- A juror's ability to consider a life sentence as a possible punishment. *See Morgan v. Illinois*, 504 U.S. 719 (1992).
- Jurors' racial prejudices in capital cases, or, in non-capital cases, where "special circumstances" require it. *See Turner v. Murray*, 476 U.S. 28 (1986); *Rosales-Lopez v. United States*, 451 U.S. 182 (1981) (plurality opinion).

See supra § 25.3C, Constitutional Entitlement to Voir Dire.

Voir dire on parole eligibility. One topic that the North Carolina courts consistently have prohibited the parties from covering in voir dire is the defendant's parole eligibility. *E.g.*, *State v. Powell*, 340 N.C. 674 (1995); *State v. Price*, 337 N.C. 756 (1994). However, in *Simmons v. South Carolina*, 512 U.S. 154 (1994), the U.S. Supreme Court held that where life imprisonment without parole is the statutory alternative punishment to death, a capital sentencing jury must be informed of that fact. Since 1999, life without parole has been the statutory alternative punishment to death for first-degree murder in North Carolina. G.S. 15A-2002 requires trial judges to instruct capital sentencing juries that life imprisonment means life without parole. In light of *Simmons* and G.S. 15A-2002, defense counsel should be able to voir dire jurors in capital cases as to whether they could understand and follow an instruction that life imprisonment means life without parole. *E.g.*, *State v. Hedgepeth*, 66 N.C. App. 390 (1984) (defendant entitled to ask jurors about their ability to follow law on limited relevance of defendant's prior record). *But see State v. Williams*, 355 N.C. 501 (2002) (court continued to adhere to rule that voir dire about parole is impermissible); *accord State v. Jones*, 358 N.C. 330 (2004).

In lieu of voir dire by the attorneys, counsel can ask the court to give the G.S. 15A-2002 instruction and then ask the jurors whether they can follow that instruction. A sample motion requesting pre-selection instructions to potential jurors (including informing them that life imprisonment is an alternative to capital punishment) can be found on the Office of Indigent Defense Services website, www.ncids.org. Highlight "Training & Resources," click on "Capital Trial Motions," scroll down to "Guilt Phase," and click on "Motion for Pre-Selection Instructions to Potential Jurors."

"Staking out." Parties are not permitted to use voir dire to "stake out" jurors. Staking out jurors means asking jurors what their decision would be under a specific factual scenario. Jurors should not be asked to "pledge" themselves to a future course of action before hearing the evidence and receiving instructions on the law. *E.g.*, *State v. Fletcher*, 354 N.C. 455 (2001); *State v. Vinson*, 287 N.C. 326 (1975) (explaining "staking out" doctrine), *vacated in part on other grounds*, 428 U.S. 902 (1976). As the following cases illustrate, applying this rule consistently has proved difficult.

The N.C. Supreme Court has found the questions in the following cases to be improper "stake out" questions:

- *State v. Maness*, 363 N.C. 261 (2009) (defense counsel improperly attempted to stake out capital juror by asking whether the juror could, if convinced that life imprisonment was the appropriate penalty, return such a verdict even if the other jurors were of a different opinion).
- *State v. Wiley*, 355 N.C. 592, 610–13 (2002) (question posed by defense counsel, "Have you ever heard of a case where you thought that life without the possibility of parole should be the punishment?" was improper stake out question).
- *State v. Jaynes*, 353 N.C. 534 (2001) (question posed by defense counsel regarding which specific circumstances would cause jurors to consider life sentence was improper stake out question).
- *State v. Richmond*, 347 N.C. 412 (1998) (defense counsel's inquiry as to whether jurors could return life sentence knowing that defendant had prior conviction for first-degree murder was improper stake-out question).

The N.C. Supreme Court and Court of Appeals have found the questions in the following cases were not improper "stake out" questions:

- *State v. Bond*, 345 N.C. 1 (1996) (question posed by prosecutor as to whether jurors could return a death sentence knowing that the defendant was an accessory, and not present at the scene of the shooting, not improper).
- *State v. Green*, 336 N.C. 142 (1994) (prosecutor's inquiry into whether any juror could conceive of any first-degree murder case where the death penalty would be the right punishment not a stake out question).

- *State v. McKoy*, 323 N.C. 1 (1988) (question posed by prosecutor as to whether jurors would be sympathetic toward a defendant who was intoxicated at the time of the offense not improper), *vacated on other grounds*, 494 U.S. 433 (1990).
- *State v. Johnson*, 164 N.C. App. 1 (2004) (permissible for prosecutor to ask jurors whether they would consider accomplice's testimony where accomplice was testifying pursuant to plea bargain).
- *State v. Henderson*, 155 N.C. App. 719 (2003) (prosecutor's question as to whether jurors would expect the State to provide medical evidence that the crime occurred permissible).
- *State v. Roberts*, 135 N.C. App. 690 (1999) (question posed by prosecutor as to whether jurors would believe eyewitness identification not stake out question).

Practice note: There are two arguments you can make at trial in defending a proposed inquiry against an objection by the State that it is a "stake out" question. First, if a question is necessary to determine the jurors' fitness to serve, it should be allowed. If a particular answer to the proposed question would render the juror excludable for cause, then the question is required to ensure the impartiality of the jury. *See Bond*, 345 N.C. 1 (juror who claimed he could not give an accessory a death sentence properly excused for cause; thus, State entitled to ask jurors whether they could sentence an accessory to death); *accord Henderson*, 155 N.C. App. 719 (questions about importance to jurors of medical testimony were necessary to secure an impartial jury). Second, you are permitted to explain aspects of the law to jurors to ensure that they can follow the law. *See State v. Hedgepeth*, 66 N.C. App. 390 (1984) (defendant entitled to ask jurors about their ability to follow law on limited relevance of defendant's prior record).

As with most jury selection issues, if the trial judge sustains the State's objection to a line of questioning on voir dire, the defendant must exhaust his or her peremptory challenges to preserve the error for appellate review and to show prejudice from the trial judge's ruling. *E.g.*, *State v. Billings*, 348 N.C. 169 (1998); *State v. McCarver*, 341 N.C. 364 (1995); *State v. Avery*, 315 N.C. 1 (1985). *See also supra* § 25.1G, Preserving Denial of Challenges to the Panel, and *infra* § 25.4C, Preserving Denial of Cause Challenge.

Permissible and impermissible questions. This chapter does not review in detail the many possible questions that may be asked during jury selection. For papers reviewing permissible and impermissible questions in capital and noncapital cases, and possible approaches to voir dire in different kinds of cases, see *infra* § 25.3I, Additional Resources.

F. Reopening Voir Dire

After a juror has been accepted by one or both parties, if the trial judge discovers that a juror has made a misrepresentation during voir dire or for other "good reason," the judge may reopen voir dire of the juror. The trial judge may question the juror or permit the parties to do so, and he or she may excuse the juror for cause. G.S. 15A-1214(g) (permitting reopening voir dire before jury is impaneled); *see also State v. Holden*, 346 N.C. 404 (1997) (trial judge has discretion to reopen examination of juror after jury is impaneled); *accord State v. Waddell*, 289 N.C. 19 (1975), *vacated in part on other grounds*, 428 U.S. 904 (1976). Where a juror appears to have changed his or her mind since being examined by the State, or where the juror's answers to defense questions appear inconsistent with his or her answers to the State's inquiries, there may be "good cause" for reopening voir dire. *State v. Womble*, 343 N.C. 667, 678 (1996) (trial judge had "good reason" to reopen voir dire of juror whose answers to questions posed by defense counsel indicated that he might be unable to return sentence of death); *State v. Bond*, 345 N.C. 1 (1996) (same). If the trial judge reopens examination of a juror, each party has the right to exercise any remaining peremptory challenges to excuse the juror. G.S. 15A-1214(g)(3); *Womble*, 343 N.C. 667; *State v. Hammonds*, ___ N.C. App. ___, 720 S.E.2d 820 (2012); *State v. Thomas*, 195 N.C. App. 593 (2009).

In *State v. Boggess*, 358 N.C. 676 (2004), a seated juror returned to court after an overnight recess and informed the judge that she had learned that one of her close friends was a friend of the victim's mother. The judge then questioned the juror but declined to state that he was "reopening voir dire" and declined to permit the defendant to exercise a peremptory against the juror. The N.C. Supreme Court found reversible error and held that before impaneling the jury the judge should resolve any doubts in favor of reopening voir dire.

G. Right to Individual Voir Dire

Capital cases. In capital cases, the trial judge may permit individual voir dire of jurors. G.S. 15A-1214(j). The North Carolina courts have held that a defendant does not have an absolute right to individual voir dire and that the decision to permit it is within the trial judge's discretion. *E.g.*, *State v. Nicholson*, 355 N.C. 1 (2002); *State v. Bonnett*, 348 N.C. 417 (1998). It is a common practice for a trial judge to permit partial individual voir dire on death qualification, exposure to pretrial publicity, or other sensitive topics. The N.C. Supreme Court has approved this practice. *E.g.*, *State v. Jaynes*, 353 N.C. 534 (2001) (noted with approval in *Nicholson*); *State v. Hunt*, 323 N.C. 407 (1988) (no error in denying motion for complete individual voir dire where judge allowed selective partial individual voir dire), *vacated on other grounds*, 494 U.S. 1022 (1990).

Non-capital cases. Although there is little case law on the issue, the trial judge's duty to oversee jury selection almost certainly implies that the judge has the authority to order individual voir dire (or partial individual voir dire) in a non-capital case if necessary to select an impartial jury. *See State v. Watson*, 310 N.C. 384, 395 (1984) ("The trial judge has broad discretion in the manner and method of jury voir dire in order to assure that a fair and impartial jury is impaneled . . . ." (citation omitted)); *State v. Ysaguire*, 309 N.C. 780, 784 (1983) (stating that whether to allow individual voir dire is within trial judge's discretion); *see also* Jeff Welty, *Individual Voir Dire*, N.C. CRIM. L., UNC SCH. OF GOV'T BLOG (Nov. 28, 2011), http://sogweb.sog.unc.edu/blogs/ncclaw/?p=3086. The need for individual voir dire may be particularly compelling on sensitive issues. *See State v. Roache*, 358 N.C. 243, 274 (2004) (discussing individual voir dire procedures in capital cases but noting that "nothing in [the court's discussion of capital cases] should be interpreted to infringe upon the trial court's inherent authority to permit individual voir dire as to specific sensitive issues in any given case").

H. Voir Dire in Capital Cases

No right to bifurcated jury. The U.S. Supreme Court has held that there is no Sixth Amendment or other constitutional violation where the same jury determines guilt and innocence and decides the defendant's sentence. *Lockhart v. McCree*, 476 U.S. 162 (1986) (removal of *Witherspoon* excludables from guilt phase jury did not violate Sixth Amendment); *accord State v. Berry*, 356 N.C. 490 (2002); *State v. Bondurant*, 309 N.C. 674 (1983). North Carolina law provides that the same jury should be used for both guilt/innocence and sentencing phases of a capital trial, unless the trial jury is unable to reconvene for sentencing. G.S. 15A-2000(a)(2).

While a bifurcated jury is not an entitlement, defense counsel may still request it. An argument in favor of bifurcation is efficiency. If there is a real chance that the case will not go to a sentencing phase because the defendant will be acquitted, or found guilty of a non-capital offense, then a significant amount of court time can be saved by bifurcating. Selecting a death qualified jury, where individual voir dire may be necessary and cause challenges will be much more numerous, is a tedious and time-consuming process that may be avoided by bifurcation.

Death qualification. Jurors whose personal or religious opposition to the death penalty would preclude them from ever returning a sentence of death are excludable for cause. *Witherspoon v. Illinois*, 391 U.S. 510 (1968). The trial judge may not exclude jurors on any broader of a basis than *Witherspoon* allows. *Adams v. Texas*, 448 U.S. 38 (1980) (*Witherspoon* limits the state's power to exclude jurors—only those jurors who are not able to follow the law may be excused for cause). The test for determining whether a juror is excludable is whether the juror's views on the death penalty would prevent or substantially impair the performance of his or her duties as a juror in accordance with his or her instructions and oath. *Wainwright v. Witt*, 469 U.S. 412 (1985) (reaffirming the standard set out in *Adams v. Texas*). Jurors are qualified to serve on a capital jury even if they are personally opposed to the death penalty as long as they are capable of setting aside their personal opinions in deference to the law. *Lockhart v. McCree*, 476 U.S. 162 (1986); *cf. State v. Benson*, 323 N.C. 318 (1988) (excusal of juror was proper where her responses to the trial judge's questions about the death penalty, while ambivalent, clearly indicated that she was unwilling or unable to follow the law and her oath as a juror).

Life qualification. Jurors whose personal or religious beliefs would preclude them from considering a sentence of life imprisonment are also excludable for cause. *Morgan v. Illinois*, 504 U.S. 719 (1992). A defendant is constitutionally entitled to "life qualify" the jury by questioning jurors about their beliefs on capital punishment. *State v. Powell*, 340 N.C. 674 (1995) (defendant in murder prosecution may use voir dire to determine whether prospective jurors would automatically vote for death sentence). The N.C. Supreme Court has specifically approved life qualification questions, such as:

- Is your support for the death penalty such that you would find it difficult to consider

voting for life imprisonment for a person convicted of first-degree murder?
- Would your belief in the death penalty make it difficult for you to follow the law and consider life imprisonment for first-degree murder?

State v. Conner, 335 N.C. 618 (1994) (reversible error not to permit defendant to ask certain life qualification questions).

Life qualification questions that ask jurors if they could consider particular types of mitigating evidence, or whether they could consider a life sentence in light of certain aggravating facts, often have been struck down as improper "stake out" questions. *E.g.*, *State v. Jaynes*, 353 N.C. 534 (2001) (question posed by defense counsel regarding which specific circumstances would cause jurors to consider life sentence was an improper stake out question); *State v. Elliott*, 344 N.C. 242 (1996) (asking prospective juror whether he could think of any situation where he could vote to impose a sentence other than death for first-degree murder was an impermissible attempt to stake him out); *State v. Robinson*, 339 N.C. 263 (1994) (inquiry as to whether juror could return life sentence where defendant had prior murder conviction was a stake out question). *But see State v. Bond*, 345 N.C. 1 (1996) (question posed by prosecutor as to whether jurors could return death sentence knowing that defendant was an accessory and not present at scene of shooting, not improper). The defense should be entitled to ask whether jurors understand the concept of mitigation and can follow the law by giving consideration to mitigating evidence. *See State v. Hedgepeth*, 66 N.C. App. 390 (1984) (defendant entitled to ask jurors about their ability to follow law on limited relevance of defendant's prior record).

Right to rehabilitate jurors. If a juror is equivocal in his or her responses to death qualification questions posed by the State, the defendant is entitled to question the juror and attempt to demonstrate that the juror is competent. *State v. Brogden*, 334 N.C. 39 (1993); *accord State v. Rouse*, 339 N.C. 59 (1994). The defendant has no right to attempt to rehabilitate jurors whose inability to impose a sentence of death is unequivocal. *State v. Kemmerlin*, 356 N.C. 446, 469 (2002) (no error in judge's denial of defendant's request to rehabilitate two jurors because although both were initially equivocal, ultimately both "explicitly told the court that their views on the death penalty would prevent or substantially impair the performance of their duties as a juror"); *State v. Johnson*, 317 N.C. 343, 376 (1986) ("[W]hen a potential juror has expressed a clear and unequivocal refusal to impose the death penalty under all the circumstances, any additional cross-examination by defense counsel . . . would be a purposeless waste of valuable court time." (citation omitted)). The trial judge must exercise his or her discretion in determining whether to permit rehabilitation of particular jurors. *See Brogden*, 334 N.C. 39 (error for judge to issue a blanket rule prohibiting rehabilitation).

I. Additional Resources

For a detailed review of permissible and impermissible questions in capital and noncapital cases, see Steve Freedman and Mike Howell, *Jury Selection Questions* (North Carolina Defender Trial School, June 2006), *available at* www.ncids.org/Defender%20 Training/2011DefenderTrialSchool/JurySelectionQuestions.pdf. For a discussion of possible approaches to voir dire in different cases, see Ira Mickenberg, *Voir Dire and Jury Selection* (North Carolina Defender Trial School, July 2011), *available at* www.ncids.org/Defender%20Training/2011DefenderTrialSchool/VoirDire.pdf.

25.4 Excusing Jurors for Cause

A. Constitutional Basis

Under the Sixth Amendment and the Fourteenth Amendment Due Process Clause of the U.S. Constitution, jurors who are biased against the defendant and cannot decide the case based on the trial evidence and the law must be excused. *Irvin v. Dowd*, 366 U.S. 717 (1961). A defendant does not have a right to any particular juror, but he or she is entitled to twelve jurors who are competent and qualified to serve. *E.g.*, *State v. McKenna*, 289 N.C. 668 (1976), *vacated in part on other grounds*, 429 U.S. 912 (1976).

The Sixth and Fourteenth Amendments also are violated when the trial judge erroneously excludes a *qualified* juror in response to a cause challenge by the State. *See Witherspoon v. Illinois*, 391 U.S. 510 (1968) (only those jurors who cannot follow the law may be excused); *Gray v. Mississippi*, 481 U.S. 648 (1987) (excusing a qualified juror is reversible error per se even if State does not exhaust peremptory challenges); *accord State v. Brogden*, 334 N.C. 39 (1993); *see also infra* § 25.4D, Excusing a Qualified Juror.

Practice note: Be sure to constitutionalize any objection to an improper denial or the improper granting of a cause challenge. Remind the trial judge that either error violates the defendant's right to an impartial jury.

B. Statutory Law on Excusing Jurors for Cause

Grounds for cause challenge. G.S. 15A-1212 sets out statutory grounds for challenging a juror for cause. These grounds include that the prospective juror:

- is not qualified under G.S. 9-3 (*see supra* § 25.2A, Statutory Qualifications);
- is incapable of rendering jury service due to mental or physical infirmity;
- is, or has been previously, involved in the case against the defendant as a party, a witness, a grand juror, or a trial juror;
- has sued the defendant or been sued by him or her in a civil action;
- has complained against or been accused by the defendant in a criminal prosecution;
- is related to the defendant or alleged victim of the crime by blood or marriage within the sixth degree;[1]

1. G.S. 15A-1212 states that jurors should not be related to the defendant or alleged victim of the crime within the sixth degree. Degrees of kinship are explained in G.S. 104A-1. To calculate your degree of kinship to another person, you ascend up from yourself through the generations until you reach a common ancestor and then descend down to the other person. The count excludes yourself. For example, you are related in the second degree to your siblings and the fourth degree to your first cousins.

- has formed or expressed an opinion on the guilt or innocence of the defendant;
- stands charged with a felony;
- as a matter of conscience is unable to render a verdict in accordance with the law; or
- for any other reason is unable to render a fair and impartial verdict.

The above statute leaves the trial judge with considerable discretion. *See, e.g., State v. Jaynes*, 353 N.C. 534 (2001) (whether to grant a challenge for cause under G.S. 15A-1212 is a matter left to the sound discretion of the trial court); *State v. Dickens*, 346 N.C. 26, 42 (1997) ("The trial court has the opportunity to see and hear a juror and has the discretion, based on its observations and sound judgment, to determine whether a juror can be fair and impartial."). The judge's decision will be upheld on appeal unless there is an abuse of discretion. *See State v. Kennedy*, 320 N.C. 20 (1987).

Prior knowledge of case not sufficient by itself to support cause challenge. The North Carolina courts have consistently held that a juror is not disqualified simply because he or she has prior knowledge of the case. To be excused for cause, the prior knowledge or connection to the case must prevent the juror from rendering an impartial verdict. *See Mu'min v. Virginia*, 500 U.S. 415, 430 (1991) (relevant inquiry regarding pretrial publicity is not whether jurors remember facts about case, but whether they have fixed opinions regarding defendant's guilt); *State v. Jaynes*, 353 N.C. 534 (2001) (juror who knew of defendant's prior sentence of death not disqualified; she stated she could set her knowledge aside and base her sentencing decision on evidence presented in court); *State v. Yelverton*, 334 N.C. 532 (1993) (prior knowledge about case not sufficient to require granting of cause challenge); *State v. Hunt*, 37 N.C. App. 315, 320 (1978) (no error in denial of defendant's challenge for cause of prospective juror employed as a police officer who had heard defendant's case discussed by other officers; "the prospective juror clearly indicated that he could base his determination solely upon the evidence and the law *without being swayed by anything else*" (emphasis added)). *But cf. Irvin v. Dowd*, 366 U.S. 717, 728 (1961) (due process violation found where trial judge refused to change venue in a case with extensive pretrial publicity; two-thirds of the jurors admitted to having already formed an opinion that the defendant was guilty; jurors' statements asserting their own ability to be impartial could "be given little weight" under the circumstances of that case).

Jurors' opinion on own impartiality not dispositive. A juror's subjective or expressed belief that he or she can set aside prior information and decide the case on the basis of the evidence presented does not necessarily render the juror qualified. "[J]urors could in all truth and candor respond affirmatively [to a question about their fairness or impartiality], personally confident that [their biased] views are fair and impartial . . . ." *Morgan v. Illinois*, 504 U.S. 719, 735 (1992). The trial judge must make an independent, objective evaluation of the juror's impartiality. *See State v. Brogden*, 334 N.C. 39, 53 (1993) (Frye, J., concurring) ("While the potential juror should be asked questions regarding his [impartiality], whether he is or is not a qualified juror is a question of law to be decided by the court.").

Inability to follow law. Jurors who are unable to follow certain provisions of law must be excused for cause. *E.g.*, *State v. Cunningham*, 333 N.C. 744 (1993) (error to fail to excuse juror who could not afford defendant presumption of innocence); *State v. Hightower*, 331 N.C. 636 (1992) (error to fail to excuse juror who expected defendant to testify); *State v. Leonard*, 296 N.C. 58 (1978) (error to fail to excuse three jurors who stated they would not acquit even if defendant proved insanity defense); *compare State v. McKinnon*, 328 N.C. 668 (1991) (no error where trial judge refused to excuse juror who initially stated that she would want defendant to present evidence on his behalf; juror later agreed to abide by proper burden of proof).

Other sources of bias. The following selected cases deal with other possible sources of juror bias. The key inquiry is always whether the juror can be impartial.

<u>Error to fail to excuse juror for cause</u>:

State v. Lee, 292 N.C. 617 (1977) (juror's husband was police officer and juror stated her connection with police would bias her)

State v. Allred, 275 N.C. 554 (1969) (juror was related to accomplice witnesses and said he would likely believe these witnesses)

<u>No error in failing to remove juror for cause</u>:

State v. Jaynes, 353 N.C. 534 (2001) (juror had business relationship with homicide victim and had visited victim at home)

State v. House, 340 N.C. 187 (1995) (juror had a friend who had been murdered but juror stated she could separate facts of defendant's case from friend's case)

State v. Benson, 323 N.C. 318 (1988) (juror's mere acquaintance with four police officers who were prospective witnesses for the State was insufficient to require removal)

State v. Whitfield, 310 N.C. 608 (1984) (first juror challenged was father of an assistant district attorney who was not participating in defendant's trial; second juror challenged was a member of the police department but the officers who handled the case and testified were sheriff's deputies)

State v. Simmons, 205 N.C. App. 509 (2010) (juror was employed with a university police department as a traffic officer; although he worked closely with the prosecutor's office and had never testified for the defense, the court rejected the notion that a juror must be excused solely on the grounds of a close relationship with law enforcement)

State v. McNeil, 99 N.C. App. 235 (1990) (juror's job as assistant attorney general did not automatically disqualify him from service)

State v. Hunt, 37 N.C. App. 315, 319 (1978) (being a police officer who had heard the case discussed by other officers was not sufficient grounds to require removal of juror;

court declined "to hold that any individual must be excused for cause *solely* by virtue of the nature of his employment" (emphasis in original))

C. Preserving Denial of Cause Challenges

Importance of exhausting peremptories. If the defendant challenges a juror for cause and the trial judge declines to remove the juror, the defendant must follow precise steps to preserve the error for appellate review. The steps are set out in G.S. 15A-1214(h). To preserve the denial of a cause challenge the defendant must:

1. remove the challenged juror by a peremptory challenge (if the defendant has peremptories left);
2. exhaust his or her peremptory challenges;
3. renew his or her motion for cause against the juror at the end of jury selection as described in G.S. 15A-1214(i); and
4. have the renewed motion denied.

See State v. Cunningham, 333 N.C. 744 (1993) (reviewing procedure and ordering new trial where defendant followed procedure to preserve issue; juror should have been excused for cause where she stated that she believed that the defendant would need to prove his innocence).

Regarding the third step—renewing a motion for cause—a party who has exhausted his or her peremptory challenges may move orally or in writing to renew a previously denied challenge for cause if he or she:

- had peremptorily challenged the juror; or
- states in the motion that he or she would have challenged that juror if his or her peremptory challenges had not already been exhausted.

G.S. 15A-1214(i); *see also State v. Johnson*, 317 N.C. 417 (1986) (making it clear that G.S. 15A-1214(h) and (i), read together, require a defendant who has peremptory challenges available at the time that a challenge for cause is denied to exercise a peremptory to remove the unwanted juror).

Any deviation from the procedures set out in G.S. 15A-1214 will likely result in a waiver of appellate review. *E.g.*, *State v. Roseboro*, 351 N.C. 536 (2000) (defendant who exhausted peremptories and moved unsuccessfully for additional peremptory challenges still waived review of denial of cause challenge because he failed to renew challenge for cause at the end of jury selection); *State v. Ball*, 344 N.C. 290 (1996) (same); *State v. McNeil*, 324 N.C. 33 (1989) (defendant failed to exhaust all peremptory challenges), *vacated on other grounds*, 494 U.S. 1050 (1990).

The defendant no longer appears to be required to challenge another juror after his or her peremptories are exhausted in order to preserve the right to appeal. *See* G.S. 15A-1214 Official Commentary (noting that this requirement was undesirable since, in most cases, the juror attempted to be challenged remained on the jury); *see also State v. Sanders*, 317 N.C. 602 (1986) (common law rule for preserving error in denial of challenges for cause, which required a defendant to exhaust all peremptories and then challenge another juror to show his or her dissatisfaction with the jury, has been replaced by G.S. 15A-1214; common law rule does not offer an alternative method of preserving the error for appeal).

Notwithstanding the specific statutory requirements, some cases have restated the common rule that the defendant must challenge an additional juror after exhausting his or her peremptories. *E.g.*, *State v. Hartman*, 344 N.C. 445, 459–60 (1996) (stating this principle in dicta, but then finding that the defendant's compliance with G.S. 15A-1214 preserved for appeal the denial of defendant's challenge of a juror for cause). In light of this ambiguity, in addition to complying with G.S. 15A-1214(h), defense counsel may want to state that the defendant objects to the last seated juror, ask for an additional peremptory, and state that if the defendant had another peremptory, he or she would use it on the last seated juror. Defense counsel should do so out of the presence of the jury.

Some cases also suggest that to be able to argue prejudice from the trial judge's failure to excuse a juror for cause, the defendant must not have expressed satisfaction with the seated jury. *E.g.*, *Hartman*, 344 N.C. 445, 459–60 (exhausting peremptories not sufficient to demonstrate prejudice; defendant must show he or she was forced to seat an unsatisfactory juror). If you want to express satisfaction with the jury in front of the jury, do so in a qualified way, such as "conditioned on my renewed motion for cause, Your Honor, defendant is satisfied with the jury."

When alternates are selected. G.S. 15A-1217(c) provides that for each alternate selected, each defendant receives an additional peremptory, and the State receives an equal number. Thus, in a noncapital prosecution where the judge decides to seat one alternate, each defendant effectively has seven peremptory challenges. To properly exhaust your challenges, it is important to use up your first six challenges in selecting the first twelve jurors. If you use two of your seven challenges in choosing the alternate, the appellate courts may find that you failed to exhaust your peremptories, especially if the alternate ends up not participating in deliberations.

D. Excusing a Qualified Juror

Just as it is error for the trial judge to decline to excuse an unqualified juror, it is also erroneous for the judge to exclude a juror who is qualified to serve. *Witherspoon v. Illinois*, 391 U.S. 510 (1968) (only those jurors who cannot follow the law may be excused). If the trial judge excuses a qualified juror, the error is reversible per se on appeal, even if the State does not exhaust its peremptories. *Gray v. Mississippi*, 481 U.S. 648 (1987) (improperly excusing qualified juror under *Witherspoon* reversible error per se).

Practice note: Make sure you enter an objection to the dismissal for cause of any juror whom you believe was improperly excused. Be sure to constitutionalize your objection. *See supra* § 25.4A, Constitutional Basis. You also can request to rehabilitate, or ask the judge to question any juror challenged by the State, to try to establish that the juror is impartial and can follow the law. *See State v. Brogden*, 334 N.C. 39 (1993) (defendant has right to attempt to rehabilitate equivocal juror).

E. Additional Resources

For practical considerations in challenging a juror for cause, see Mike Howell, *Jury Selection: Challenges for Cause* (North Carolina Defender Trial School, July 2010) , *available at* www.ncids.org/Defender%20Training/2011DefenderTrialSchool/ChallengesForCause.pdf.

25.5 Peremptory Challenges

A. In General

In her concurrence in *J.E.B. v. Alabama ex rel. T.B.*, 511 U.S. 127 (1994), Justice Sandra Day O'Connor described peremptory challenges as follows:

> The peremptory challenge is "a practice of ancient origin" and is "part of our common law heritage." The principal value of the peremptory is that it helps produce fair and impartial juries. "Peremptory challenges, by enabling each side to exclude those jurors it believes will be most partial toward the other side, are a means of eliminating extremes of partiality on both sides, thereby assuring the selection of a qualified and unbiased jury." The peremptory's importance is confirmed by its persistence: It was well established at the time of Blackstone and continues to endure in all the States.

Id. at 147 (citations omitted).

Peremptory challenges allow the parties to excuse jurors on the basis of the party's own criteria, generally without inquiry or required explanation. *State v. Jenkins*, 311 N.C. 194 (1984) (any reason except race is an acceptable reason for peremptory challenge) (case decided before *Batson*); *accord State v. Smith*, 291 N.C. 505 (1977); *see also Swain v. Alabama*, 380 U.S. 202, 220 (1965) ("The essential nature of the peremptory challenge is that it is one exercised without a reason stated, without inquiry and without being subject to the court's control."(citation omitted)); *State v. Wooten*, 344 N.C. 316 (1996) (permissible for prosecutor to strike juror because of juror's hesitancy about death penalty). The only limit on the exercise of peremptories is that neither side may exercise a peremptory challenge because of the juror's race, gender, or other constitutionally protected characteristic. These limitations are discussed in detail *infra* in § 25.5C, Equal Protection Limitation on Peremptory Challenges: *Batson* and Its Progeny.

B. Statutory Right to Peremptory Challenges

The right to peremptory challenges is statutory. *See* G.S. 15A-1217 (entitling both State and defendant to peremptory challenges in criminal case). There is no constitutional right to peremptory challenges. *See Rivera v. Illinois*, 556 U.S. 148, 157 (2009) (peremptory challenges are "creature[s] of statute" and states "may decline to offer them at all"); *United States v. Martinez-Salazar*, 528 U.S. 304, 311 (2000) (peremptory challenges reinforce a defendant's right to trial by an impartial jury but the challenges are "auxiliary," not constitutional); *Ross v. Oklahoma*, 487 U.S. 81, 88 (1988) ("peremptory challenges are not of constitutional dimension").

Number of peremptory challenges. Peremptory challenges are allotted to the parties based on the number of defendants, not on the number of charges lodged against any one defendant. *State v. Boyd*, 287 N.C. 131 (1975). The State and each defendant in a non-capital case are entitled to six peremptory challenges. If there are co-defendants, the State gets six additional peremptory challenges per co-defendant. G.S. 15A-1217(b). In a capital case, each party is entitled to fourteen peremptories. If there are co-defendants, the State gets fourteen additional peremptory challenges per co-defendant. G.S. 15A-1217(a). Parties are entitled to one additional peremptory challenge for every alternate selected in capital or non-capital cases. G.S. 15A-1217(c).

The N.C. Supreme Court has said that the trial judge has no authority to grant additional peremptory challenges. *State v. Hunt*, 325 N.C. 187, 198 (1989). The court has found no error, however, where the trial judge granted each defendant an additional peremptory challenge because one juror who had been accepted by all parties was dismissed because of a family emergency. *State v. Barnes*, 345 N.C. 184, 208 (1997); *see also State v. Banks*, 125 N.C. App. 681 (as sanction for failure to preserve evidence, trial judge stripped State of two peremptory challenges), *aff'd per curiam*, 347 N.C. 390 (1997).

C. Equal Protection Limitation on Peremptory Challenges: *Batson* and Its Progeny

Generally. The U.S. Supreme Court has held that racial discrimination in the exercise of peremptory challenges violates the Equal Protection Clause of the Fourteenth Amendment. *Batson v. Kentucky*, 476 U.S. 79 (1986). Discrimination in jury selection also violates article I, section 26 of the N.C. Constitution, which states that no person may be excluded from jury service on account of sex, race, color, religion, or national origin. *See State v. White*, 349 N.C. 535 (1998) (racial discrimination in jury selection violates both state and federal constitution).

Three-prong *Batson* test. *Batson v. Kentucky*, 476 U.S. 79 (1986), established the following three-part test for demonstrating an equal protection violation in the exercise of peremptory challenges.

First, a defendant making a *Batson* challenge must establish a prima facie case of discrimination. *E.g.*, *State v. Golphin*, 352 N.C. 364 (2000) (citing *Hernandez v. New York*, 500 U.S. 352, 358–59 (1991)). The trial judge must consider all relevant circumstances, including the defendant's race, the victim's race, the race of key witnesses, discriminatory questions or statements made by the prosecutor, a pattern of strikes against minority jurors, or the relative acceptance rate of whites and blacks. *See Golphin*, 352 N.C. at 426; *White*, 349 N.C. 535, 548; *see also State v. Smith*, 328 N.C. 99, 121 (1991) (one of the most important considerations for whether a prima facie case is established is whether prosecutor uses a disproportionate number of peremptory challenges to strike African-American jurors).

"Step one of the *Batson* analysis, a prima facie showing of racial discrimination, is not intended to be a high hurdle for defendants to cross." *State v. Hoffman*, 348 N.C. 548, 553 (1998). *Hoffman* found that the trial judge erred in failing to find that the defendant had made out a prima facie case where the defendant was black, the victim white, and the prosecutor had filled eleven seats with white jurors and struck the three black prospective jurors not excused for cause. The case was remanded so that the prosecutor could place his or her reasons for the strikes on the record. *See also State v. Green*, 324 N.C. 238 (1989) (remanding for *Batson* hearing after trial judge erroneously failed to find prima facie case); *accord State v. McCord*, 140 N.C. App. 634 (2000). For a further discussion of this first step, see *infra* "U.S. Supreme Court decisions after *Batson*" in this subsection C. (discussing *Johnson v. California*).

Second, if the defendant is successful in establishing a prima facie showing of discrimination, the burden shifts to the State to proffer a race-neutral reason for the strike. *Purkett v. Elem*, 514 U.S. 765 (1995); *Hernandez v. New York*, 500 U.S. 352 (1991). "The [State's] explanation must be clear and reasonably specific, but 'need not rise to the level justifying exercise of a challenge for cause.'" *State v. Bonnett*, 348 N.C. 417, 433 (1998) (citations omitted). In *Purkett*, the U.S. Supreme Court held that at step two the proffered race-neutral explanation does not have to be persuasive or even plausible as long as it is facially non-discriminatory. *Purkett*, 514 U.S. at 768 (but recognizing that implausible reason probably will fail step three); *see also State v. Fletcher*, 348 N.C. 292 (1998) (following *Purkett*); *Bonnett*, 348 N.C. at 433 ("[U]nless a discriminatory intent is inherent in the prosecutor's explanation, the reason offered will be deemed race neutral." (citation omitted)).

When the State proffers explanations for its challenges, the defendant is entitled to an opportunity to rebut the proffered reason for excusing the juror. *E.g.*, *State v. Gaines*, 345 N.C. 647, 668 (1997); *State v. Peterson*, 344 N.C. 172 (1996). The defendant does not have the right to call as a witness and examine the prosecutor in the effort to show that his or her proffered explanations are a pretext. *State v. Porter*, 326 N.C. 489, 497 (1990); *State v. Jackson*, 322 N.C. 251 (1988).

Third, the trial judge assesses the State's proffered reason and determines whether the defendant has proved purposeful discrimination. If the judge finds that the prosecutor's proffered reasons are disingenuous, or "pretextual," and the real reason for the strike is discriminatory, then he or she must find a violation of the Equal Protection Clause. *Hernandez*, 500 U.S. 352, 359; *Gaines*, 345 N.C. 647, 668. "At [this] stage, implausible or fantastic justifications may (and probably will) be found to be pretexts for purposeful discrimination." *Purkett*, 514 U.S. 765, 768; *Garrett v. Morris*, 815 F.2d 509, 511 (8th Cir. 1987) (trial court "has a duty to satisfy itself that the prosecutor's challenges were based on constitutionally permissible trial-related considerations, and that the proffered reasons are genuine ones, and not merely a pretext for discrimination"). Factors the judge should consider in determining whether a proffered explanation is pretextual include:

- The susceptibility of the particular case to racial discrimination. The race of the defendant, the victims, and the key witnesses is relevant to this determination.
- The prosecutor's demeanor.
- The credibility of the explanation itself. The evaluation of the explanation involves objective and subjective criteria, such as whether similarly situated white venirepersons were passed by the State and whether the State's justification is relevant to this case. The prosecutor's explanation also should be evaluated "'in light of the explanations offered for the prosecutor's other peremptory strikes' and 'the strength of the prima facie case.'"

State v. Porter, 326 N.C. 489, 498–99 (1990) (citation omitted).

***Practice note*:** Because it is relatively easy for the State to proffer a race-neutral reason for a strike and meet the second prong of the *Batson* test, defense counsel needs to focus on the third step—convincing the trial judge that the State's proffered explanations for strikes are not credible. Implausible reasons unrelated to the juror's fitness to serve, such as hairstyle, gum chewing, or a remote connection to a minor State witness, may well be pretextual. Try to identify and bring to the judge's attention white jurors with characteristics similar to the characteristic identified by the State as its reason for striking a juror. For example, if the prosecutor claims he struck a black juror because he or she was young, list for the judge the young white jurors passed by the prosecutor. If the reason proffered is simply false—if, for example, the prosecutor asserts that a perfectly forthright juror was "hesitant," or "seemed defiant"—inform the trial judge that you noticed no hesitation or defiance.

For a further discussion of this step, see *infra* "U.S. Supreme Court decisions after *Batson*" (discussing *Miller-El v. Dretke*) and "Suspect reasons for strikes" (discussing reasons found unacceptable by some courts) in this subsection C.

Importance of getting jurors' race on record. To preserve a *Batson* challenge for appellate review, the record must be clear as to the race of the jurors peremptorily challenged by the State as well as the race of the other members of the jury panel (prospective and selected); otherwise, the appellate court will find insufficient evidence in the record to support the defendant's claim. *See State v. Brogden*, 329 N.C. 534 (1991) (defendant failed to carry his burden of establishing an adequate record for appellate review because he did not elicit the race of the jurors by means of questioning or other proper evidence); *State v. Payne*, 327 N.C. 194 (1990) (affidavit submitted by defense counsel containing counsel's perceptions concerning the races of the excused potential jurors was not adequate to support defendant's claim of improper use of peremptory challenges under *Batson*); *State v. Mitchell*, 321 N.C. 650, 654 (1988) (statements of counsel, standing alone, are not sufficient to support a finding that peremptory challenges were used discriminatorily).

Practice note: Before jury selection begins, counsel should request that the trial judge have each prospective juror state his or her race for the record during the judge's initial questioning. *See Brogden*, 329 N.C. 534 (notations by the court reporter of defense counsel's subjective impressions concerning race were not acceptable); *Payne*, 327 N.C. 194 (no error in trial judge's denial of the defendant's motion for the clerk to record the race of the prospective jurors made after they had been excused and the jury had been selected; clerk's perception of a particular person's race is inappropriate); *Mitchell*, 321 N.C. 650, 656 (inappropriate for court reporter to note the race of the jurors based on his or her perception; "if there is any question as to the prospective juror's race, this issue should be resolved by the trial court based upon questioning of the juror or other proper evidence").

U.S. Supreme Court decisions after *Batson*. In 2005, the U.S. Supreme Court issued two opinions applying *Batson v. Kentucky*. The first, *Miller-El v. Dretke*, 545 U.S. 231 (2005), addressed the issue of what sort of evidence a defendant can rely on to show intentional discrimination in the exercise of a peremptory strike. The opinion is most useful with respect to step three, explained above, where the defendant is trying to rebut proffered "race neutral" reasons for a strike articulated by a prosecutor.

One important kind of rebuttal evidence is side-by-side comparisons between black and white panelists. If a prosecutor accepts a white juror with certain characteristics, and then uses those characteristics to strike a black juror, discrimination can be inferred. For example, in *Miller-El*, the prosecutor stated that he struck a black venireman who expressed the opinion that he would vote against the death penalty if he believed the defendant could be rehabilitated. That was not a race neutral reason, the Court found, where the prosecutor accepted white jurors with comparable views. *Miller-El* also found an explanation for a strike to be pretextual where the prosecutor did not fully inquire into the issue. Where a black juror was struck ostensibly because his brother had prior convictions, but the prosecutor did not ask about the juror's relationship with his brother, the Court found the prosecutor's reason unconvincing.

Practice note: It is improper for the reviewing judge to substitute a better reason than the prosecutor offers. If you find that the trial judge is doing this—"saving" the prosecutor's explanations—you should object and make a record of the difference between the reason advanced by the prosecutor and the reason accepted by the judge.

In another part of the opinion, *Miller-El* holds that intentional discrimination can be shown by patterns of questioning or other conduct. If a prosecutor starts asking questions of black jurors that he or she is not asking of white jurors, such as whether they think the criminal justice system is fair, then discrimination is more likely to be present. In *Miller-El*, the Court found discrimination where the prosecutor described the death penalty vividly and explicitly to black jurors but very blandly to white jurors.

Texas, where *Miller-El* originates, allowed any party to "shuffle" the venire cards during jury selection. The U.S. Supreme Court criticized the prosecutor's practice of shuffling the cards when there were several black jurors in the next group of jurors to be called into the box. The effect of the shuffling was often to move those jurors back in line. A North Carolina equivalent might occur where jurors are divided into panels. If at the end of a panel there are two black venirepersons left and no whites, and the prosecutor chooses that moment to suggest merging the remaining members of the panel with the next panel, this would tend to show discrimination. *See supra* § 25.1C, Random Selection Requirement.

A final part of the decision emphasizes patterns of discrimination shown by the district attorney's office over time. This part of the decision reinforces the need for the defense bar to keep track of patterns in particular offices or with respect to particular prosecutors.

In *Johnson v. California*, 545 U.S. 162 (2005), the Court addressed the standard of proof needed to meet step one in *Batson*—establishing a prima facie case of discrimination. *Johnson* makes clear that at step one, the party alleging discrimination does not carry a burden of proof but merely a burden of production. To establish a prima facie case of discrimination and require the State to proceed to step two, a defendant need only produce sufficient evidence to permit the trial judge to draw an inference of discrimination. The defendant does not have to show a "strong likelihood" of discrimination or even that it is more likely than not that the prosecutor is acting in a racially discriminatory manner. The defendant does carry the burden of proof at step three. *Johnson* can be cited both at the trial court level to encourage the judge to ask the prosecutor to place his or her reasons for strikes on the record, and on appeal to request a *Batson* remand, where a trial judge erroneously failed to find a prima facie case of discrimination.

In 2008, the U.S. Supreme Court decided *Snyder v. Louisiana*, 552 U.S. 472 (2008), in which it reiterated that it is unconstitutional to strike even a single prospective juror based on a discriminatory purpose. In *Snyder*, the Court found that the trial judge committed clear error in overruling the defendant's *Batson* objection to the State's use of a peremptory challenge to remove a prospective black juror. The State had offered two race-neutral explanations for striking the juror: (1) the juror looked very nervous during the questioning; and (2) the juror was a student teacher and was concerned about missing class. As a result of the juror's concerns, the prosecutor asserted that he felt that the juror might agree to a lesser verdict in order to bypass the penalty phase and finish quickly. The Court declined to rule based on the first proffered explanation since the record did not show that the trial judge actually made a determination regarding the juror's demeanor. The Court noted in dicta, however, that great deference is due a trial judge's ruling on demeanor since "determinations of credibility and demeanor lie 'peculiarly within a trial judge's province.'" *Id.* at 477 (citation omitted); *see also Thaler v. Haynes*, ___ U.S. ___, 130 S. Ct. 1171 (2010) (per curiam) (holding that although a judge must take into account, among other things, his or her observations of a juror's demeanor when a challenge is based thereon, neither *Batson* nor *Snyder* require that a demeanor-based explanation be rejected if the judge did not observe or cannot recall the juror's demeanor).

The Court then found the prosecutor's second explanation implausible and highly speculative because the prospective juror had not seemed overly concerned about the student-teaching situation once his dean was contacted and gave assurances that the class time could be made up. The Court compared the testimony of the juror who was struck with that of two white jurors who also were concerned about conflicting obligations. Although one of those jurors had asked to be excused based on a hardship and related obligations that seemed "substantially more pressing" than the struck juror's concerns, the prosecutor did not strike him. *Snyder*, 552 U.S. at 484. A second white prospective juror also expressed concern about serving, stating that he would "'have to cancel too many things,' including an urgent appointment at which his presence was essential." *Id.* Despite these concerns, the prosecutor nevertheless failed to strike this juror. Based on these circumstances, the Court held that discriminatory intent was a substantial or motivating factor in the actions taken by the prosecutor and reversed the lower court's decision upholding the validity of the peremptory strike.

Other groups cognizable under *Batson*. In addition to prohibiting racial discrimination in the exercise of peremptory strikes, the Equal Protection Clause of the Fourteenth Amendment prohibits gender discrimination in the exercise of peremptories. *See J.E.B. v. Alabama ex rel. T.B.*, 511 U.S. 127, 129 (1994) (holding that "gender, like race, is an unconstitutional proxy for juror competence and impartiality"); *accord State v. Gaines*, 345 N.C. 647 (1997); *State v. Bates*, 343 N.C. 564 (1996). The N.C. Constitution likewise prohibits discrimination in jury selection based on gender. *See State v. Maness*, 363 N.C. 261 (2009) (gender discrimination prohibited by article I, section 26 of N.C. Constitution). The procedure for establishing gender discrimination, and the factors the court should consider in evaluating a defendant's prima facie showing and deciding the ultimate question of whether there is intentional discrimination, are the same as under *Batson. See Gaines*, 345 N.C. 647; *Bates*, 343 N.C. 564.

Article I, section 26 of the N.C. Constitution explicitly prohibits discrimination against jurors on the basis of religion (as well as prohibiting race and gender discrimination). In *State v. Eason*, 336 N.C. 730 (1994), the defendant contended that the prosecutor had violated article I, section 26 by striking a juror because the juror was a Jehovah's Witness. While recognizing the potential legitimacy of the claim, the court held that the particular juror was struck because of her beliefs about the death penalty. The legitimacy of a federal constitutional claim of discrimination based on religion has not been determined by the U.S. Supreme Court. In *Davis v. Minnesota*, 511 U.S. 1115 (1994), the U.S. Supreme Court refused to grant certiorari to review the propriety of the use of peremptory challenges to exclude a Jehovah's Witness from jury service on the ground that the members of that religion are reluctant to exercise authority over other human beings. Justice Thomas dissented from the denial of certiorari, stating that after the Court's decision in *J.E.B.* extending *Batson* to cover gender-based discrimination, "no principled reason immediately appears for declining to apply *Batson* to any strike based on a classification that is accorded heightened scrutiny under the Equal Protection Clause." *Id.* at 1115.

Native Americans are recognized as "a racial group cognizable for *Batson* purposes." *State v. Locklear*, 349 N.C. 118, 136 (1998) (quoting *State v. Porter*, 326 N.C. 489, 499 (1990)); *see also United States v. Iron Moccasin*, 878 F.2d 226 (8th Cir. 1989); *United States v. Chalan*, 812 F.2d 1302 (10th Cir. 1987).

Subgroups. The U.S. Supreme Court has not decided whether subgroups, such as African-American women, are a cognizable group under *Batson.* If the only African-Americans being passed by the State are men, arguably there is a *Batson/J.E.B.* violation. In *State v. Best*, 342 N.C. 502 (1996), the defendant argued that the prosecutor had discriminated against African-American women, but the court found the claim had not been preserved and did not reach it.

Suspect reasons for strikes. North Carolina appellate courts have been extraordinarily deferential in reviewing *Batson* issues. Other states have regularly found certain types of reasons for strikes unacceptable. These reasons include:

- Age. *See, e.g., Richmond v. State*, 590 So. 2d 384, 385 (Ala. Crim. App. 1991) (age as reason for peremptory strikes is "'highly suspect because of its inherent susceptibility to abuse'" (citation omitted)); *Washington v. Commonwealth*, 34 S.W.3d 376, 379 (Ky. 2000) ("[c]ertainly age was not a sufficient reason to strike a 43-year-old man"). *But see State v. Caporasso*, 128 N.C. App. 236, 244 (1998) (no error by trial judge in allowing the prosecutor to peremptorily challenge a black juror based on the prosecutor's explanation that the juror was excused based on his "young age and lack of maturity"; the prosecution is allowed to "seek jurors who are stable and mature").
- Facial expressions or other non-verbal behaviors. *Bernard v. State*, 659 So. 2d 1346 (Fla. Dist. Ct. App. 1995) (that juror made facial expression during another juror's comment insufficient reason for strike where expression not observed by trial judge and not confirmed by judge in record); *Somerville v. State*, 792 S.W.2d 265 (Tex. Ct. App. 1990) (reversing conviction where State inappropriately struck juror who prosecutor thought had muttered under his breath, showing disrespect for judge, and who was member of NAACP); *Avery v. State*, 545 So. 2d 123 (Ala. Crim. App. 1988) (reasons such as looks, body language, and negative attitude are susceptible to abuse and must be closely scrutinized by courts).
- Clothing or jewelry. *See Rector v. State*, 444 S.E.2d 862 (Ga. Ct. App. 1994) (case reversed where prosecutor struck juror because she had gold tooth); *People v. Bennett*, 206 A.D.2d 382, 383 (N.Y. App. Div. 1994) (prosecutor struck an African-American juror who was wearing a headscarf because it showed "a certain disrespect for the proceedings"; pretextual basis found and conviction reversed); *Roundtree v. State*, 546 So.2d 1042, 1044–45 (Fla. 1989) (prosecutor's reasons for striking two African-American jurors were an "obvious pretext" where prosecutor asserted that he struck the jurors based on their clothing, "specifically commenting that the first juror was wearing maroon socks and 'pointy New York shoes'").

Challenges by white defendant of strikes against African-Americans. In *Powers v. Ohio*, 499 U.S. 400 (1991), the U.S. Supreme Court held that the defendant does not have to be of the same race as the improperly excluded jurors to raise a *Batson* challenge. Any defendant has standing to assert the equal protection rights of jurors. *See also State v. Locklear*, 349 N.C. 118 (1998) (explaining *Powers*); *State v. Williams*, 343 N.C. 345 (1996) (same).

Improper strike of one juror sufficient. If even one juror is struck for racial reasons, there is constitutional error in the jury selection. *State v. Robbins*, 319 N.C. 465, 491 (1987) ("Even a single act of invidious discrimination may form the basis for an equal protection violation."); *see also Snyder v. Louisiana*, 552 U.S. 472, 478 (2008) ("'[T]he Constitution forbids striking even a single prospective juror for a discriminatory purpose.'"(citation omitted)).

Review of failure to find prima facie case of discrimination. Under U.S. Supreme Court law, once the prosecutor puts his or her reasons for strikes against minority jurors on the record, the issue of whether there is a prima facie case of discrimination becomes moot. The only issue before either the trial judge or the reviewing court is whether the proffered reasons are acceptable or discriminatory. *Hernandez v. New York*, 500 U.S. 352, 359 (1991). The N.C. Supreme Court has not fully followed *Hernandez*. The court has held that when a trial judge explicitly rules that a defendant failed to make out a prima facie case, even where the prosecutor's reasons for strikes are on the record, appellate review is limited to the question of whether the trial judge's finding of no prima facie case was erroneous. *E.g.*, *State v. Fletcher*, 348 N.C. 292 (1998); *State v. Smith*, 347 N.C. 453 (1998). Only when the trial judge does not explicitly rule on whether the defendant made a prima facie case, or when the judge makes an explicit ruling but before doing so the State articulates explanations for its challenges, does the question of whether the defendant established a prima facie case become moot. *State v. Golphin*, 352 N.C. 364, 426 (2000); *State v. Williams*, 343 N.C. 345 (1996). This approach appears to be contrary to *Hernandez*. The constitutional requirement is that whenever there is a record of the prosecutor's reasons for striking jurors, the question of whether there is a prima facie case of discrimination is moot. This point should be pressed on appeal and may ultimately be remedied by a federal habeas court.

Remedy for *Batson* violation. *Batson* itself does not specify the proper trial remedy for a violation. In *Foster v. State*, 111 P.3d 1083 (Nev. 2005), the Nevada Supreme Court observed:

> In implementing *Batson*, the states have generally followed one of three different approaches. Some jurisdictions require the trial courts to disallow a peremptory strike made in violation of *Batson* or to reseat the improperly stricken juror. Other jurisdictions require the trial courts to discharge the venire and commence jury selection anew from an entirely new venire. "The majority of courts, however, have delegated to the discretion of the trial judge the determination of the appropriate remedy for a *Batson* violation."

Id. at 1089 (footnotes omitted).

In *State v. McCollum*, 334 N.C. 208 (1993), the N.C. Supreme Court held that if the trial judge finds that the State has violated *Batson*, the venire should be dismissed and jury selection should begin again. However, the court has not been absolutely consistent on this approach. In *State v. Fletcher*, 348 N.C. 292 (1998), the prosecutor initially struck a juror because the juror was a member of the NAACP. When the trial judge found the prosecutor's reason to be discriminatory, the prosecutor withdrew his strike and passed the juror. The trial judge then found no *Batson* violation, and the N.C. Supreme Court affirmed. Chief Justice Mitchell, dissenting in *Fletcher*, would have ordered a new trial, emphasizing that dismissing the venire is the better practice where the prosecutor makes an invalid strike.

Application of *Batson* to defendants. The *Batson* rule applies to defendants as well as to the State. The Equal Protection Clause prohibits criminal defendants from exercising peremptory strikes in a manner that discriminates on the basis of race, gender, or other suspect characteristic. *Georgia v. McCollum*, 505 U.S. 42 (1992); *accord State v. Locklear*, 349 N.C. 118 (1998) (citing *McCollum*); *State v. Cofield*, 129 N.C. App. 268 (1998) (same).

A reverse *Batson* claim is established just like a *Batson* claim. First, the State must show a prima facie case of discrimination. The burden then shifts to the defendant to explain his or her strikes in a race neutral manner.

Practice note: In defending against a prima facie case of discrimination, be sure to note for the record how many African-American or other minority jurors are being passed to you for questioning. It may be that you are exercising 90% of your strikes against white jurors, but that 95% of the jurors being passed to the defense are white because most of the black or other minority jurors have been excused for cause or struck by the State.

Reverse *Batson* claims have rarely been made in North Carolina, possibly as a result of a fear by prosecutors that if the trial judge is deemed to have erred in disallowing a defendant's peremptory challenge, the appellate court will find structural error and grant the defendant a new trial. *See* Jeff Welty, *Rivera v. Illinois and "Reverse Batson,"* N.C. CRIM. L., UNC SCH. OF GOV'T BLOG (Apr. 7, 2009), http://sogweb.sog.unc.edu/blogs/ncclaw/?p=226.

Although the question of the remedy available for improperly denied challenges has not been directly answered, the U.S. Supreme Court discussed it in *Rivera v. Illinois*, 556 U.S. 148 (2009). In *Rivera*, the judge, based on his own concerns about discrimination, required the defendant to explain his peremptory challenge of a black female juror. After hearing the explanation, the judge denied the defendant's peremptory challenge and required that the juror be seated on the jury. That juror later became the jury foreperson. On appeal, the defendant argued that the trial judge's error in denying his peremptory challenge violated his rights under the Due Process Clause and amounted to structural error—that is, the defendant was entitled to a new trial without having to show prejudice. The Illinois Supreme Court found that the defendant was deprived of his state right to exercise his peremptory challenges but determined that the error was harmless beyond a reasonable doubt in light of the overwhelming evidence against him.

The U.S. Supreme Court affirmed the decision of the lower court, holding that "the loss of a peremptory challenge due to a state court's good-faith error is not a matter of federal constitutional concern. Rather, it is a matter for the State to address under its own laws." *Id.* at 157. The Court noted that structural errors requiring automatic reversal are typically reserved for the type of error that "'necessarily renders a criminal trial fundamentally unfair or an unreliable vehicle for determining guilt or innocence.'" *Id.* at 160 (citations omitted). The Court held that the mistaken denial of a state-provided peremptory challenge, under the circumstances presented in *Rivera*, did not constitute an error of that magnitude.

No North Carolina decision has addressed the issue.

Additional resources. A collection of materials on dealing with race in jury voir dire can be found on the Office of Indigent Defense Services website, www.ncids.org. Highlight "Training & Resources," click on "Training Materials" and then on "Training Materials—Indexed by Subject," and scroll down to "Juries." For a comprehensive article on litigating *Batson* claims, see the article within those materials entitled *Litigating Race in Voir Dire* by Susan Jackson Balliet and Bruce Hackett. Although written for attorneys who represent indigent clients in Kentucky, the article offers a wealth of practical information and advice.

Chapter 26
Jury Misconduct

This chapter deals with issues related to jurors who engage in inappropriate conduct and possible remedies. Miscellaneous jury procedures are discussed *infra* in Chapter 27, issues dealing with jury instructions are covered *infra* in Chapter 32, and issues related to jury deliberations are covered *infra* in Chapter 34.

26.1 Right to a Fair and Impartial Jury

A. Trial Judge's Constitutional Responsibilities

Under the Sixth and Fourteenth Amendments to the U.S. Constitution, every defendant in a criminal action who is entitled to a jury trial is entitled to a trial before a neutral and impartial jury. *See Morgan v. Illinois*, 504 U.S. 719 (1992); *Duncan v. Louisiana*, 391 U.S. 145 (1968). This right is also guaranteed by article I, section 24 of the N.C. Constitution. *State v. Garcell*, 363 N.C. 10 (2009). "It is the duty and responsibility of the trial judge to insure that the jurors remain impartial . . . ." *State v. Rutherford*, 70 N.C. App. 674, 677 (1984). Thus, it is the trial judge's responsibility to conduct investigations into apparent juror misconduct, "including examination of jurors when warranted, to determine whether any misconduct has occurred and has prejudiced the defendant." *State v. Barnes*, 345 N.C. 184, 226 (1997). An examination is generally required only where some prejudicial content is reported. *State v. Harrington*, 335 N.C. 105, 115 (1993).

B. Statutory Admonitions

Section 15A-1236(a) of the North Carolina General Statutes (hereinafter G.S.) requires the trial judge at appropriate times to admonish the jurors that it is their duty:

- not to talk among themselves about the case except in the jury room after their deliberations have begun;
- not to talk to anyone else or to allow anyone else to talk with them or in their presence about the case, and to report to the judge immediately the attempt of anyone to communicate with them about the case;
- not to form an opinion about the guilt or innocence of the defendant or express any opinion about the case until they begin their deliberations;
- to avoid reading, watching, or listening to accounts of the trial; and
- not to talk during trial to parties, witnesses, or counsel.

Under this statute, the judge may also admonish the jurors about other matters that he or she considers appropriate. The defendant must object to any failure to properly admonish the jury and must show prejudice resulting therefrom. *State v. Harris*, 315 N.C. 556 (1986).

C. Remedies for Misconduct

In the event that prejudicial juror misconduct has occurred, the trial judge can take "any appropriate action." *State v. Drake*, 31 N.C. App. 187, 191 (1976). The most common remedies are:

- Issuing a contempt citation. *See* G.S. 15A-1035 (a presiding judge may maintain courtroom order through the use of his or her contempt powers as provided in G.S. Chapter 5A, Contempt).
- Giving an appropriate instruction. *See State v. Hines*, 131 N.C. App. 457 (1998) (holding that appropriate instructions may cure even constitutional errors).
- Discharging the juror and substituting an alternate juror. G.S. 15A-1215(a) authorizes a trial judge to replace a juror with an alternate juror if any juror becomes incapacitated or disqualified at any time before final submission of the case to the jury. The exercise of this power rests in the sound discretion of the trial judge and is not reversible error absent a showing of an abuse of discretion. *State v. Nelson*, 298 N.C. 573 (1979). G.S. 15A-2000(a)(2) authorizes the substitution of an alternate juror during a capital sentencing hearing if any juror dies, becomes incapacitated or disqualified, or is discharged for any reason prior to the start of deliberations.
- Granting a motion for mistrial for misconduct discovered prior to the verdict. *See* G.S. 15A-1061 ("[T]he judge must declare a mistrial upon the defendant's motion if there occurs during the trial an error or legal defect in the proceedings, or conduct inside or outside the courtroom, resulting in substantial and irreparable prejudice to

the defendant's case."). Misconduct on the part of a jury member may result in a mistrial if it would render a fair and impartial trial impossible under the law. Whether a motion for mistrial should be granted is a matter that rests in the sound discretion of the trial judge, and this decision is not reversible absent a showing of an abuse of that discretion. *State v. McCarver*, 341 N.C. 364 (1995).

- Granting a motion for a new trial for misconduct discovered after the verdict. Like a motion for mistrial, a motion for a new trial is addressed to the sound discretion of the trial judge, and unless his or her ruling is clearly erroneous or an abuse of discretion, it will not be disturbed. *State v. Johnson*, 295 N.C. 227 (1978); *State v. Sneeden*, 274 N.C. 498 (1968).

Practice note: If misconduct occurs, counsel should immediately bring it to the attention of the trial judge. Mere conclusory statements by defense counsel alleging juror misconduct will rarely be found to be sufficient to show improper conduct. Counsel should, whenever possible, substantiate assertions of misconduct by presenting witness testimony or affidavits. Counsel should also specifically request inquiry by the court, including juror examination, so that there is a sufficient basis for appellate review in the event that the motion for relief is denied.

26.2 Exposure to Extraneous Information

Juror misconduct encompasses a wide range of improper activities. Misconduct is determined by the facts and circumstances in each case. Exposure to extraneous information has occupied the courts' attention in numerous cases and is discussed here. Other common types of misconduct are discussed *infra* in § 26.3.

A. Discovered Before Verdict

A fundamental aspect of a criminal defendant's constitutional right to confront witnesses and evidence against him or her is that a jury's verdict must be based on evidence produced at trial, not on extrinsic evidence that has escaped the rules of evidence, supervision of the court, and other procedural safeguards of a fair trial. *See, e.g., Parker v. Gladden*, 385 U.S. 363 (1966); *Turner v. Louisiana*, 379 U.S. 466 (1965). "'[W]hen there is a *substantial reason to fear* that the jury has become aware of improper and prejudicial matters, the trial court must question the jury as to whether such exposure has occurred and, if so, whether the exposure was prejudicial.'" *State v. Campbell*, 340 N.C. 612, 634 (1995) (emphasis added) (citation omitted); *see also State v. Hines*, 131 N.C. App. 457 (1998) (defendants' right to confrontation violated and motion for mistrial should have been granted where prosecutor's notes and typewritten list of statements defendants made, including hearsay statements, were mistakenly published to the jury without being admitted into evidence).

When information or evidence that would not be admissible at trial reaches the jury, the trial judge must weigh all the circumstances and determine in his or her discretion whether or not a defendant's right to a fair trial has been violated. *State v. Jones*, 50 N.C.

App. 263, 268 (1981). The denial of a motion for a mistrial based on alleged misconduct affecting the jury is equivalent to a finding by the trial judge that prejudicial misconduct has not been shown, and the decision will be reversed only on a clear showing that the trial judge abused his or her discretion. *State v. Bonney*, 329 N.C. 61 (1991); *State v. Degree*, 114 N.C. App. 385, 392 (1994).

B. Discovered After Verdict

Generally. As a general rule, once a verdict is rendered, it may not be impeached—that is, a juror may not testify nor may evidence be received as to matters occurring during deliberations or calling into question the reasons on which the verdict was based. *See State v. Cherry*, 298 N.C. 86 (1979). "However, harsh injustice has sometimes resulted from the view that jury verdicts are beyond challenge. Thus, as an 'accommodation between policies designed to safeguard the institution of trial by jury and policies designed to insure a just result in [an] individual case,' certain exceptions to the rule have been carved out." *State v. Lyles*, 94 N.C. App. 240, 244 (1989) (citation omitted). G.S. 15A-1240 and N.C. Rule of Evidence 606(b) provide limited exceptions to the anti-impeachment rule.

Application of statute. G.S. 15A-1240(c)(1) allows impeachment of a verdict only in a criminal case and only when matters not in evidence came to the attention of one or more jurors under circumstances that would violate the defendant's constitutional right to confront the witnesses against him or her. If the challenged evidence does not implicate the defendant's right to confront, G.S. 15A-1240(c)(1) does not apply. *State v. Rosier*, 322 N.C. 826, 832 (1988) (defendant's right to confront not violated where jury foreman watched a program on child abuse contrary to the trial judge's instructions and foreman told other jurors about a young friend of his who had been raped; jurors' affidavits concerning these events should not have been considered by the court because "[p]arties do not have the right to cross examine jurors as to the arguments they make during deliberation as the foreman did in this case"). Under subsection (c)(2) of G.S. 15A-1240, a verdict may also be impeached after the jury has been dispersed when there is evidence of bribery, intimidation, or attempted bribery or intimidation of a juror.

Application of rule. N.C. Rule of Evidence 606(b), which applies in both criminal and civil cases, provides that a juror is competent to testify when the validity of a verdict is challenged, but only on the question (1) whether extraneous prejudicial information was improperly brought to the jury's attention or (2) whether any outside influence was improperly brought to bear upon any juror. Extraneous information under Rule 606(b) has been interpreted to mean information that reaches a juror without being introduced into evidence and that deals specifically "with the defendant or the case which is being tried." *Rosier*, 322 N.C. 826, 832 (judge's consideration of jurors' affidavits found improper where the affidavits related that jury foreman watched a program on child abuse contrary to the trial judge's instructions and told jurors about a young friend of his who had been raped because that information was not "extraneous information" within the meaning of Rule 606 since it did not deal with defendant or the case being tried). General information that a juror has gained in his or her day-to-day experiences does not constitute "extraneous information." *Compare State v. Heatwole*, 344 N.C. 1 (1996) (juror's exchange with his professor about violent tendencies of paranoid schizophrenics was not "extraneous information" because it did not deal with defendant or with the case being tried), *with State v. Lyles*, 94 N.C. App. 240 (1989) (testimony by jurors was proper under both Rule 606 and G.S. 15A-1240(c)(1) where a juror peeled paper from the bottom of an exhibit during deliberations and uncovered information that implied that defendant had prior criminal involvement and that directly contradicted the defendant's alibi witnesses; jurors' exposure to the information was found to entitle the defendant to a new trial). *See also* 1 KENNETH S. BROUN, BRANDIS & BROUN ON NORTH CAROLINA EVIDENCE § 148, at 535–39 (7th ed. 2011) (discussing the anti-impeachment rule).

Steps to resolve allegation of juror exposure to improper information. Where a defendant claims that he or she is entitled to relief under G.S. 15A-1240(c) or Rule 606(b), the judge first must determine whether the type of misconduct alleged falls within the purview of the statute or evidence rule (as discussed above). If the judge finds that the verdict may be impeached within the terms of the statute or rule, then the judge must decide whether the exposure to the information violated the defendant's right of confrontation. If a constitutional violation is found, the error is presumed prejudicial and the burden is on the State to show that the jury's exposure to the improper information was harmless beyond a reasonable doubt. *See State v. Lyles*, 94 N.C. App. 240 (1989).

C. Selected Examples

Dictionaries/reference materials. The N.C. Supreme Court has stated that "'[i]t generally is ground for reversal that the jury obtained and took into the jury room a dictionary which they consulted to determine the meaning of legal or other terms, which they do not understand.'" *In re Will of Hall*, 252 N.C. 70, 87 (1960) (citation omitted); *see also State v. McLain*, 10 N.C. App. 146, 148 (1970) ("It was improper for the jury to obtain and read a dictionary definition of one of the offenses charged in the bill of indictment."). However, in *Lindsey v. Boddie-Noell Enterprises, Inc.*, 355 N.C. 487 (2002), the N.C. Supreme Court reversed per curiam the decision of the N.C. Court of Appeals, 147 N.C. App. 166 (2001), and adopted the reasoning of the dissenting opinion, which held that the dictionary definitions at issue were not "extraneous information" within the meaning of N.C. Rule of Evidence 606(b) because the definitions of the words "willful" and "wanton" did not specifically concern the defendant or the evidence presented in the case. These definitions were simply matters of common knowledge that jurors were supposed to possess. The court then held that even if the dictionary definitions were "extraneous information" within the meaning of Rule 606(b), there was no actual prejudice to the defendant in that case due to the trial judge's sufficient instructions.

In a later case, *State v. Bauberger*, 176 N.C. App. 465 (2006), the court of appeals majority held that even though dictionary definitions appear to fall within the extraneous information exception of N.C. Rule of Evidence 606(b), the court was bound to find otherwise based on the supreme court's decision in *Lindsey*. The majority also held that juror affidavits concerning dictionary use could not be used to impeach the jury's verdict under G.S. 15A-1240 because the dictionary definitions considered by the jury "concerned legal terminology" and did not discredit the defendant's testimony or witnesses; thus, the defendant's Sixth Amendment rights were not implicated. Judge Geer dissented, stating that she would hold in accordance with the universal rule adopted by the rest of the country that a jury's unauthorized consultation of a dictionary constitutes consideration of extraneous information. She further stated that the jury's consultation of a dictionary violates a defendant's constitutional rights under the Sixth and Fourteenth Amendments to be present at every stage of his or her trial and to a trial by fair and impartial jurors. The N.C. Supreme Court affirmed the decision of the court of appeals in *State v. Bauberger*, 361 N.C. 105 (2006). The court, however, was evenly split, three to three, leaving the court of appeals' decision undisturbed and without precedential value. Thus, it appears that the law with regard to the jury's use of dictionaries may not be completely settled, and it is still worthwhile to move for a mistrial or to set aside the verdict based on the jury's consultation of reference materials during trial.

Bibles. With regard to a jury's consideration of the Bible during deliberations, the questions before the trial judge will be whether the Bible falls within the definition of extraneous information under N.C. Rule of Evidence 606(b) and whether the jury's consultation of the Bible violates the defendant's constitutional rights. These questions have not been squarely decided by the North Carolina appellate courts. *Cf. State v. Barnes*, 345 N.C. 184, 228 (1997) (finding no abuse of discretion in the trial judge's failure to inquire of the jury regarding defense counsel's unsubstantiated assertion that the jury consulted a Bible prior to deliberations "[a]s there is no evidence that the alleged Bible reading was in any way directed to the facts or governing law at issue in the case").

For a case discussing jurisdictions that have held that a Bible in the jury room is an "external influence on the jury's deliberations," see *Oliver v. Quarterman*, 541 F.3d 329, 338 n.10 (11th Cir. 2008). *See also* Amanda C. Shoffel, *The Theocratic Jury Room:* Oliver v. Quarterman *and the Burgeoning Circuit Split on Biblical Reference and Influence in Capital Sentencing*, 36 NEW ENG. J. ON CRIM. & CIV. CONFINEMENT 113 (2010) (arguing that the physical presence of a Bible in a jury room during the sentencing phase in a capital case should create an irrebuttable presumption of prejudice under the Sixth Amendment).

Media reports. The courts have recognized that the exposure of jurors to news media reports during trial has been a "very real problem for a long time." *State v. Jones*, 50 N.C. App. 263, 268 (1981). When there is a *substantial reason to fear* that the jury has become aware of improper and prejudicial matters such as media reports, inquiry by the trial judge is required. *See State v. Barts*, 316 N.C. 666, 683 (1986) (no abuse of discretion in denying motion for mistrial where defendant made no showing that jury had been exposed to highly prejudicial newspaper article about defendant and inquiry revealed no violation of the judge's instruction to avoid exposure to the news media); *State v. McVay*, 279 N.C. 428 (1971) (holding that while inquiry was not required because there was no evidence that the jury was actually exposed to the newspaper article, it is the better practice for the judge to inquire of the jurors to see if they had been exposed or influenced by it).

If a jury has been exposed to media coverage, the trial judge may still properly deny a motion for mistrial if the coverage was merely an objective account of what has occurred at trial and was not prejudicial to the defendant. *See State v. Woods*, 293 N.C. 58 (1977). However, where the jurors have been exposed to prejudicial matters and the error is not cured by a subsequent instruction by the court, a new trial is warranted. *See State v. Reid*, 53 N.C. App. 130 (1981).

Practice note: If the jury is exposed to extraneous material, counsel should immediately bring it to the attention of the trial judge. Counsel should not merely assert that the exposure occurred but should also substantiate the claim, if possible, by presenting affidavits or testimony. *See State v. Barnes*, 345 N.C. 184 (1997) (in reviewing defendant's argument that the trial judge erred in failing to conduct an investigation into alleged Bible-reading by a juror in the jury room, court noted that counsel had failed to substantiate the claim).

Failure to object to extraneous material being taken into the jury room may also result in the waiver of appellate review of the issue. *See, e.g., State v. Jones*, 339 N.C. 114 (1994) (defendant's assent to allowing the jury to use a dictionary during its deliberations waived any error by the trial judge in giving the jury the dictionary definition of "mitigate"); *State v. Poole*, 154 N.C. App. 419 (2002) (defendant waived right to argue on appeal that the trial judge erred in reading a definition from dictionary and allowing jury to use dictionary during its deliberations where defendant stated no objections to the jury's use of the dictionary when asked by the trial judge).

26.3 Other Common Types of Misconduct

A. Third Party Communication

It is misconduct for a juror during the trial to discuss the matter outside the court or to receive any information related to the case except in open court and in the manner provided by law. Thus, any pertinent communication between jurors and third parties including victims, defendants, counsel, courtroom personnel, witnesses, relatives, friends, etc., is prohibited. If allegedly improper contact with a juror is discovered, or if a prejudicial statement is inadvertently overheard by a juror, the trial judge must determine whether such contact resulted in substantial and irreparable prejudice to the defendant. It is within the discretion of the trial judge as to what inquiry to make. *State v. Burke*, 343 N.C. 129, 149 (1996) (citing *Remmer v. United States*, 347 U.S. 227 (1954)); *State v. Jacobs*, 172 N.C. App. 220 (2005).

If outside contacts are improperly brought to bear against a juror and are intended to influence the verdict, the trial judge abuses his or her discretion in denying a motion for a mistrial or new trial. *See State v. Lewis*, 188 N.C. App. 308 (2008) (granting defendant a new trial where the lead detective made comments during a break to a deputy sheriff serving as a juror that were intended to influence the verdict). "'[B]rief, public, and nonprejudicial conversations between jurors and parties or their relatives will not vitiate the verdict or require that the jury be discharged . . . .'" *O'Berry v. Perry*, 266 N.C. 77, 81 (1965) (citation omitted).

B. Intoxicated/Impaired Jurors

"The law requires that jurors, while in the discharge of their duties, shall be temperate, and in such condition of mind as to enable them to discharge those duties honestly, intelligently, and free from the influence and dominion of" impairing substances. *State v. Jenkins*, 116 N.C. 972, 974 (1895). If a juror, while hearing the evidence, argument of counsel, or charge, or while deliberating as to verdict, is so incapacitated by reason of intoxicants or otherwise as to be physically or mentally incapable of functioning as a competent, qualified juror, the trial judge may order a mistrial. *State v. Tyson*, 138 N.C. 627 (1905) (mistrial was proper where a juror was found to be intoxicated and unfit for duty during the trial). However, use of impairing substances *outside* the courtroom does not justify granting a mistrial unless it is found that the juror is unfit to serve while present in court. *See State v. Crocker*, 239 N.C. 446 (1954) (although several jurors became intoxicated during an overnight recess, a mistrial was not warranted where there was no evidence or finding that any of those jurors were impaired upon the reconvening of the court on the following morning). Under G.S. 15A-1215, if a juror becomes incapacitated for any reason, an alternate may be substituted. *See infra* § 27.3, Substitution of Alternates.

C. Failure to Disclose Information During Voir Dire

If a juror fails to disclose or misrepresents potentially important information during jury selection, the party moving for a new trial must show:

- the juror concealed material information during voir dire;
- the moving party exercised due diligence during voir dire to uncover the information; and
- the juror demonstrated actual bias or bias implied as a matter of law that prejudiced the moving party.

State v. Maske, 358 N.C. 40, 48 (2004). If the party meets this burden, the trial judge must grant the motion. For a discussion of the meaning of bias implied as a matter of law, see *State v. Buckom*, 126 N.C. App. 368, 382 (1997).

If it is discovered prior to the jury being impaneled that a juror made an incorrect statement during voir dire:

- The judge may examine, or permit counsel to examine, the juror to determine whether there is a basis for a challenge for cause.
- If the judge determines there is a basis for a challenge for cause, he or she must excuse the juror or sustain any challenge for cause that has been made.
- If the judge determines there is no basis for a challenge for cause, any party who has

not exhausted his or her peremptory challenges may challenge the juror.

G.S. 15A-1214(g).

D. Sleeping/Inattentive Juror

In superior court, a defendant has the right to be convicted by a jury of twelve. N.C. CONST. art. I, § 24; G.S. 15A-1201; *State v. Hudson*, 280 N.C. 74 (1971). If a juror is sleeping during the trial or otherwise inattentive (working crossword puzzles, etc.), the defendant can move to substitute the juror or for a mistrial. The defendant must show by competent evidence that the juror was inattentive or sleeping and also that the defendant was prejudiced thereby. *State v. Lovin*, 339 N.C. 695 (1995) (no abuse of discretion in denial of defendant's motion to substitute a juror because the evidence was sufficient to support the conclusion that the juror, although inattentive to parts of the case, could nevertheless perform his duties); *State v. Williams*, 33 N.C. App. 397 (1977) (no error in trial judge's failure to grant a mistrial ex mero motu based on a sleeping juror because defendant did not show any prejudice). The misconduct should be brought to the attention of the trial judge immediately and supported by witness testimony or affidavits if possible. *See State v. Engle*, 5 N.C. App. 101 (1969) (court of appeals would not consider affidavits regarding a sleeping juror when presented for the first time on appeal).

E. Unauthorized Jury View of Crime Scene

Unless authorized by the trial judge (*see infra* § 27.2A, View of the Crime Scene), a view of the crime scene by a juror is considered misconduct. *State v. Perry*, 121 N.C. 533 (1897). However, the fact that a juror makes an unauthorized visit to the place of the crime is not grounds for a new trial unless it appears that some prejudice resulted to the defendant. *State v. Boggan*, 133 N.C. 761 (1903) (no undue influence shown where jurors passed through crime scene during their stay at a hotel pending the trial); *State v. Hawkins*, 59 N.C. App. 190 (1982) (although jurors used information about the lighting at the crime scene provided by a juror who visited scene, there was no constitutional violation because there was considerable testimony by an officer as to the lighting conditions); *State v. Smith*, 13 N.C. App. 583 (1972) (noting that courts in other jurisdictions have suggested that possible prejudice from unauthorized viewing by one juror can be removed by having the entire jury view the scene). Whether to grant relief is in the trial judge's discretion. *State v. Farris*, 13 N.C. App. 143 (1971).

F. Presence of Unauthorized Persons in Jury Room During Deliberations

Alternate jurors. The presence of an alternate juror in the jury room *during deliberations* violates a statutory mandate and the defendant's right to a jury trial as contemplated by article I, section 24 of the N.C. Constitution. *See* G.S. 15A-1215(a) (alternate jurors must be discharged on final submission of a case to the jury); *State v. Bindyke*, 288 N.C. 608 (1975) (new trial granted based on constitutional violation where alternate was present in the jury room for three to four minutes during deliberations).

The presence of an alternate in the jury room at any time *after deliberations begin* is reversible error per se. However, if the alternate's presence is inadvertent and momentary, and it occurs under circumstances from which it can clearly be determined that the jury has not begun its function, then the alternate's presence will not void the trial. If the trial judge believes it is probable that deliberations had not yet begun when the alternate was in the jury room, the trial judge may recall the jury and the alternate and make limited inquiry as to whether there has been any discussion of the case or comment as to what the verdict should be. If the answer is yes, the judge must declare a mistrial. If the answer is no, the alternate will be excused and the jury returned to deliberate. *Bindyke*, 288 N.C. 608; *State v. Jernigan*, 118 N.C. App. 240 (1995) (no mistrial warranted where alternate was present in jury room during selection of a foreman because this did not amount to "deliberation"); *see also State v. Locklear*, 180 N.C. App. 115 (2006) (no prejudicial error occurred where alternate spoke with trial jurors after deliberations had begun because the conversations did not take place in the deliberations room and the alternate did not express her feelings about the case to the other jurors).

The right to a jury trial by twelve cannot be waived by the defendant. *State v. Rowe*, 30 N.C. App. 115 (1976) (even though defendant refused trial judge's offer of mistrial, a new trial was granted because an alternate was in the jury room for ten minutes and deliberations had begun).

Other nonjurors. The presence of a "stranger" in the jury room is improper, but it does not automatically invalidate a verdict. If the trial judge finds facts showing that neither the deliberations nor the verdict were in any manner influenced by the misconceived entrance of an outsider and that there was no communication between the outsider and any juror, it may refuse to set aside the verdict. *State v. Hill*, 225 N.C. 74 (1945) (affirming the denial of defendant's motion to set aside the verdict based on the presence of two reporters in the jury room for several minutes where inquiry showed that neither the deliberations nor the verdict were in any manner influenced by their unauthorized presence); *see also State v. Battle*, 271 N.C. 594 (1967) (no error in the denial of defendant's motion to set aside the verdict where a juror from a different case mistakenly went into the jury room for a short time with defendant's jury); *State v. Riera*, 6 N.C. App. 381 (1969) (no error in the denial of defendant's motion for mistrial where record revealed that the jury became silent and said nothing when an unauthorized female mistakenly entered the jury room during deliberations), *rev'd on other grounds*, 276 N.C. 361 (1970).

Although older cases such as *Hill* and *Battle* state that a trial judge's refusal to set aside the verdict or grant a mistrial is not reviewable on appeal, later cases utilize an abuse of discretion standard of review. *See State v. Billups*, 301 N.C. 607 (1981) (finding no abuse of discretion by trial judge in denial of defendant's motion for mistrial where prosecuting witness entered the jury room during a recess at the conclusion of trial, but prior to the charge of the court, to use the bathroom and did not communicate with any of the jurors); *State v. Washington*, 141 N.C. App. 354 (2000) (finding no abuse of discretion in trial judge's failure to declare a mistrial sua sponte where bailiff entered the jury room during deliberations to retrieve some magazines and did not communicate with any of the jurors nor did he hear any deliberations); *State v. Phillips*, 87 N.C. App. 246 (1987) (no abuse of discretion by trial court in failing to set aside the verdicts where the victim's wife was in the jury room before the opening of court one day and the sheriff took coffee cups to the jury in the jury room).

Chapter 27
Miscellaneous Jury Procedures

This chapter deals with miscellaneous procedural issues related to jurors. Issues dealing with jury misconduct are covered *supra* in Chapter 26, jury instructions are covered *infra* in Chapter 32, and issues related to deliberations and verdict are covered *infra* in Chapter 34.

27.1 Note Taking by the Jury

Jurors may make notes and take them into the jury room unless the trial judge, on his or her own motion or the motion of any party, directs otherwise. N.C. GEN. STAT. § 15A-1228 (hereinafter G.S.). Whether jurors are allowed to take notes is within the trial judge's discretion, and that decision will not be reversed absent an abuse of that discretion. *State v. Crawford*, 163 N.C. App. 122 (2004).

Practice note: If the trial judge allows the jury to take notes during the trial, counsel may request an instruction in accordance with N.C. Pattern Jury Instruction—Crim. 100.30 (June 2008), which directs the jurors to use their notes to help refresh their recollection but not give them undue significance.

27.2 Authorized Jury View

A. View of the Crime Scene

Under G.S. 15A-1229, a trial judge may permit a jury view. This decision is a discretionary one and will not be disturbed absent an abuse of that discretion. *State v. Fleming*, 350 N.C. 109 (1999). If a view is ordered pursuant to G.S. 15A-1229(a):

- an officer must accompany the jury to the location;
- no person is permitted to communicate with the jury on any subject connected to the trial;
- the judge, prosecutor, and defense counsel must be present; and
- the defendant is entitled to be present.

A witness may testify at the site of the view and point out objects and physical characteristics material to his or her testimony if permitted by the court. This testimony must be recorded. G.S. 15A-1229(b).

The press is allowed to be present at a jury view because criminal trials in North Carolina are open to the press and to the public. N.C. CONST. art. I, § 24; *State v. Davis*, 86 N.C. App. 25 (1987) (no prejudice shown from allowing press to attend the jury view where judge kept press quiet and gave adequate instructions to the jury concerning the publicity surrounding the trial).

Unless authorized by the trial judge, a view of the crime scene by a juror is considered misconduct. *See supra* § 26.3E, Unauthorized Jury View of Crime Scene.

B. View of the Defendant

Generally. The State may require a defendant to stand or otherwise exhibit himself or herself before the jury as long as the act is not of a testimonial or communicative nature. Such an exhibition does not offend the Due Process Clause of the Fourteenth Amendment, nor does it violate the Fifth Amendment's protection against self-incrimination. Both federal and state courts have usually held that the privilege against self-incrimination "offers no protection against compulsion to submit to fingerprinting, photographing, or measurements, to write or speak for identification, to appear in court, to stand, to assume a stance, to walk, or to make a particular gesture." *Schmerber v. California*, 384 U.S. 757, 764 (1966); *see also* 1 KENNETH S. BROUN, BRANDIS & BROUN ON NORTH CAROLINA EVIDENCE § 126 (7th ed. 2011) (discussing the privilege against self-incrimination).

Selected examples. Courts have found no constitutional violation where the defendant was required to:

- Stand before the jury and place a stocking mask over his head and face in the manner described by the robbery victim. *State v. Perry*, 291 N.C. 284 (1976).

- Remove his shirt and show scars on cross-examination to impeach or corroborate his testimony that the victim cut him with a razor. *State v. Sanders*, 280 N.C. 67 (1971).
- Speak a word or phrase for purposes of voice identification in court. *State v. Locklear*, 117 N.C. App. 255 (1994).
- Display his teeth to the jury. *State v. Summers*, 105 N.C. App. 420 (1992).
- Exhibit himself to the jury for the purpose of allowing a witness to identify certain physical characteristics on his person. *State v. McNeil*, 47 N.C. App. 30 (1980).
- Give a signature sample in court to compare with a signature on a motel registration card. *State v. Valentine*, 20 N.C. App. 727 (1974).

27.3 Substitution of Alternates

G.S. 15A-1215(a) authorizes a trial judge to replace a juror with an alternate juror if any juror dies, becomes incapacitated or disqualified, or is discharged for any reason at any time before final submission of the case to the jury. The exercise of this power rests in the sound discretion of the trial judge and is not reversible error absent a showing of an abuse of discretion. *State v. Nelson*, 298 N.C. 573 (1979).

An alternate must be discharged on final submission of the case to the jury and cannot be substituted for a juror after the jury has begun its deliberations. *See* G.S. 15A-1215(a); *State v. Bunning*, 346 N.C. 253 (1997) (substitution of an alternate juror for an incapacitated juror after jury deliberations had started violated the defendant's right to a trial by a jury of twelve as guaranteed by article I, section 24 of the N.C. Constitution because it resulted in a verdict rendered by eleven jurors plus two jurors who each participated partially).

If a juror is replaced by an alternate after deliberations have begun, trial counsel need not object to preserve the issue for appeal because "[a] trial by a jury which is improperly constituted is so fundamentally flawed that the verdict cannot stand." *Bunning*, 346 N.C. 253, 257. A violation of a defendant's constitutional right to have the verdict determined by twelve jurors constitutes error per se. *Id.*

G.S. 15A-2000(a)(2) authorizes a trial judge to replace a juror with an alternate juror if any juror dies, becomes incapacitated or disqualified, or is discharged for any reason before the beginning of deliberations at a capital sentencing hearing.

27.4 Questioning of Witnesses by the Jury

A trial judge, in his or her discretion, may allow a juror to question a testifying witness. *State v. Kendall*, 143 N.C. 659 (1907). However, in *State v. Howard*, 320 N.C. 718, 726 (1987), the N.C. Supreme Court recognized that possible prejudice may arise if counsel is put in "the untenable position of having to choose between not objecting to an incompetent or prejudicial question, thus letting the testimony in, or objecting to the question with the potential result of offending a juror." To alleviate this concern, the court stated that the better practice is:

- for the juror to submit written questions to the judge;
- for the judge to hold a bench conference to rule on any objections outside the presence of the jury; and
- for the judge to read the jurors' questions to the witness.

The trial judge should exercise due care to see that the jurors' questions are limited to ones that clarify the testimony. *Id.* The judge's decision whether to allow juror questioning will not be reversed absent an abuse of discretion. *See State v. Jones*, 158 N.C. App. 465 (2003).

Practice note: Although cases indicate that it is not necessary for counsel to object to the jurors' questions when actually asked at trial in order to preserve the issue for appeal (*see, e.g., Howard*, 320 N.C. 718, 726), counsel should always object at a bench conference if one is held before the questions are asked or at the next available opportunity when the jury is not present.

27.5 Sequestration of Jurors During Trial

Jurors may be sequestered during trial if so directed by the trial judge in his or her discretion. G.S. 15A-1236(b). This statute authorizes either complete sequestration, which includes separate lodging facilities at night, or partial sequestration during lunch or while in the vicinity of the courthouse. *See* G.S. 15A-1236 Official Commentary. When sequestration is ordered in a criminal case, the State must pay for all accommodations of jurors. G.S. 9-17.

A defendant does not have a federal constitutional right to have the jurors sequestered during trial. Sequestration is a matter of state procedural law and does not reach constitutional proportions. *Baldwin v. Blackledge*, 330 F. Supp. 183 (E.D.N.C. 1971).

If sequestration is ordered during deliberations in a capital case, the alternate jurors must be sequestered in the same manner as the trial jurors. The alternates must also be sequestered from the trial jury. G.S. 15A-1215(b).

27.6 Polling of the Jury

A. In General

"To poll the jury means to ascertain by questions addressed to the jurors, individually, whether each juror assented and still assents to the verdict tendered to the court." *State v.*

Boger, 202 N.C. 702, 704 (1932). The right to poll the jury in criminal cases is firmly established by article I, section 24 of the N.C. Constitution and by statute. *See, e.g., State v. Lackey*, 204 N.C. App. 153 (2010).

By polling the jury, the judge gives each juror an opportunity, before the verdict is recorded, to declare in open court his or her assent to the verdict that the foreman has returned and thus enables the judge and the parties "to ascertain *with certainty* that a unanimous verdict has been in fact reached and that no juror has been coerced or induced to agree to a verdict to which he [or she] has not fully assented." *Davis v. State*, 273 N.C. 533, 541 (1968) (emphasis in original); *see also State v. Black*, 328 N.C. 191, 198 (1991) ("The purpose of polling the jury is to ensure that the jurors unanimously agree with and consent to the verdict at the time it is rendered."); *State v. Young*, 77 N.C. 498, 499 (1877) (the right to poll the jury "is surely one of the best safeguards for the protection of the accused" since it is the mode of "ascertaining the *fact* that it is the verdict of the whole jury") (emphasis in original).

In both capital and non-capital cases, the poll must be conducted individually. *See* G.S. 15A-1238; G.S. 15A-2000(b). It is error for the trial judge to ask the jury collectively if they assented to and still assent to the verdict. *See State v. Boger*, 202 N.C. 702 (1932) (trial judge erred by requesting the jury to "stand up" if they assented to the verdict of manslaughter); *State v. Holadia*, 149 N.C. App. 248 (2002) (error to question the jury collectively and have them respond collectively by raising their hands).

The appellate courts have approved of three questions to be asked of individual jurors at the time of polling:

1. Was this your verdict?
2. Is this now your verdict?
3. Do you still agree and assent thereto?

See, e.g., State v. Asbury, 291 N.C. 164 (1976); *State v. Norris*, 284 N.C. 103 (1973). The first question is asked to ensure that no improper influence or coercion took place in the jury room during deliberations and the latter two are asked to confirm that the juror still assents in open court to the jury verdict. *See Asbury*, 291 N.C. 164.

Although jurors must be polled individually, they do not necessarily have to be questioned about each conviction separately. For example, if the jury returns verdicts against a defendant finding him or her guilty of kidnapping and second-degree murder, G.S. 15A-1238 has been interpreted as not requiring that the jurors be polled about the kidnapping and then polled separately about the murder. Instead, the judge may direct the clerk to recite all of the verdicts and ask each juror if they were his or her verdicts and whether he or she still assents. *State v. Ramseur*, 338 N.C. 502 (1994); *State v. Hunt*, 198 N.C. App. 488 (2009); *State v. Sutton*, 53 N.C. App. 281 (1981).

Practice note: If you would like the jurors to be polled separately as to each individual conviction, you should specifically request the judge to do so during your motion to poll and offer reasons why it is important in your particular case. Be sure your request and, if denied, the judge's ruling are both on the record.

B. Noncapital Cases

Need for motion. The jury must be polled on the motion of any party or on the trial judge's own motion. G.S. 15A-1238. Pursuant to this statute:

- The poll must be conducted after verdict but before the jury has been dispersed.
- The poll may be conducted by the judge or by the clerk by asking each juror individually whether the verdict announced is his or her verdict.
- If the poll reveals that there is not unanimous concurrence, the jury must be directed to retire for further deliberations.

Waiver. A defendant waives his or her right to request a polling of the jury pursuant to G.S. 15A-1238 where he or she does not make the request before the jury's discharge. *State v. Baynard*, 79 N.C. App. 559 (1986). The rationale behind requiring that the polling occur before dispersal of the jury is to ensure that nothing extraneous to the jury's deliberations can cause any of the jurors to change their minds. *See State v. Black*, 328 N.C. 191, 198 (1991) (defendant's motion to poll came too late where it was made after the jury had entered its verdict and was given a thirty-minute recess during which it was free to leave the courtroom and go into the streets); *see also State v. Ballew*, 113 N.C. App. 674 (1994) (defendant waived right to poll jury where request was made after the jury had been released to the jury room and had been told that they could discuss the case with anyone if they wished), *aff'd per curiam*, 339 N.C. 733 (1995); *State v. Froneberger*, 55 N.C. App. 148 (1981) (defendant waived right to poll jury where motion was not made until after the jury was discharged and court had recessed for lunch).

Practice note: Counsel should *always* request that the jury be polled after a defendant is convicted in a noncapital case. A juror who was struggling with the verdict or feeling pressured by the other jurors may welcome the opportunity to say so in open court. It is especially important to timely request polling because, as a general rule, once a verdict has been rendered and received in open court, it may not later be impeached—that is, a juror may not testify nor may evidence be received as to matters occurring during deliberations or calling into question the reasons on which the verdict was based. *See, e.g., State v. Martin*, 315 N.C. 667 (1986). For a discussion of the anti-impeachment rule and its limited exceptions, see *supra* § 26.2B, Exposure to Extraneous Information Discovered After Verdict.

C. Capital Cases

After delivery of the sentence recommendation by the foreman of the jury in a capital case, the jury must be individually polled to establish whether each juror concurs and agrees to the sentence recommendation returned. G.S. 15A-2000(b). Since the right to a jury poll in a capital case is statutorily mandated, it is not dependent on a defendant's request for polling. *State v. Buchanan*, 330 N.C. 202 (1991). The trial judge's error in failing to properly poll a capital jury is not waived by the defendant's failure to object. *Id.*

D. Equivocation by Juror During Polling

If, during polling in a non-capital case, there is not unanimous concurrence by all jurors, the judge must direct the jury to retire for further deliberations. G.S. 15A-1238; *see also* G.S. 15A-1235(c) (if the jury has been unable to agree on a verdict, "the judge may require the jury to continue its deliberations and may give or repeat the instructions provided in subsections (a) and (b)"). G.S. 15A-2000(b) is silent as to what the judge must do when the polling reveals a nonunanimous sentencing recommendation in a capital case; however, the N.C. Supreme Court has held that when "an inconsistency arises between the verdict and the responses of jurors during the polling process, the trial court must nevertheless allow the jury a reasonable opportunity to attempt to reach a unanimous sentence recommendation." *State v. Maness*, 363 N.C. 261, 288 (2009). If the judge concludes under G.S. 15A-2000(b) that "the jury cannot, within a reasonable time, unanimously agree to its sentence recommendation," he or she is authorized to impose a life sentence. *Id.*

For a collection of cases that consider or decide whether the declaration of a mistrial or the granting of a new trial is warranted where a juror who has assented to a verdict of guilty in a criminal case equivocates upon being polled after verdict, see M. J. Greene, Annotation, *Juror's Reluctant, Equivocal, or Conditional Assent to Verdict, on Polling, as Ground for Mistrial or New Trial in Criminal Case*, 25 A.L.R.3d 1149 (1969 & Supp. 2010).

Chapter 28
Opening Statements

The opening statement is a critical part of the defendant's case. Although the jury may have obtained some sense of the defendant's side of the case during jury voir dire, opening statement is counsel's first main opportunity to communicate the theory of defense to the jury.

An opening statement is factual. It is a condensed version of the story of your case, giving the jurors the pertinent facts necessary for them to understand your client's story of innocence or reduced culpability. *See* Ira Mickenberg, *Improve Your Opening Statements* (North Carolina Defender Trial School, July 2011), *available at* www.ncids.org/Defender%20Training/2011 DefenderTrialSchool/OpeningStatements.pdf. This chapter does not discuss in detail the different techniques for delivering opening statements. It focuses instead on the procedural rules relating to opening statements as well as limitations on their scope.

28.1 Right to Opening Statement

Section 15A-1221(a)(4) of the North Carolina General Statutes (hereinafter G.S.) grants the defendant the right to give an opening statement before the introduction of evidence. Rule 9 of the General Rules of Practice for the Superior and District Courts also provides that counsel for each party, at any time before the presentation of evidence, may make an opening statement setting forth the grounds for his or her claim or defense. The defendant has the right to make an opening statement regardless of whether he or she intends to present evidence. *State v. Paige*, 316 N.C. 630, 648 (1986) ("Even if the defendant does not intend to offer evidence, he may in his opening statement point out to the jury facts which he reasonably expects to bring out on cross-examination.")

Although North Carolina law gives the defendant the right to make an opening statement before the guilt-innocence phase of the case, it does not give a defendant the right to give an opening statement before the sentencing phase of a capital trial. *State v. Call*, 349 N.C. 382 (1998) (trial judge did not abuse his discretion in forbidding opening statement before sentencing phase of capital case; supreme court found no authority that defendant is entitled to opening statement before sentencing phase of capital case). In practice, however, trial courts will often grant the defendant's request to make an opening statement before sentencing in a capital case, and counsel should take advantage of this additional opportunity to address the jury.

Unlike the right to make a closing argument, the right to make an opening statement is not guaranteed by the U.S. Constitution. *See Herring v. New York*, 422 U.S. 853 (1975); *United States v. Salovitz*, 701 F.2d 17 (2d Cir. 1983); *United States v. Ciancaglini*, 945 F. Supp. 813 (E.D. Pa. 1996).

28.2 Purpose and Scope

A. In General

"The purpose of an opening statement is to permit the parties to present to the judge and jury the issues involved in the case and to allow them to give a general forecast of what the evidence will be." *See State v. Gladden*, 315 N.C. 398, 417 (1986); *see also State v. Elliott*, 69 N.C. App. 89, 93 (1984) ("[T]he proper function of an opening statement is to allow the party to inform the court and jury of the nature of his case and the evidence he plans to offer in support of it."). Counsel is permitted "something more than just a limited preview" of his or her evidence and should be allowed to state his or her legal claim or defense in basic terms. *State v. Freeman*, 93 N.C. App. 380, 389 (1989). The purpose of an opening statement is not, however, to argue the case, instruct on the law, or contradict the other party's witnesses. *State v. Mash*, 328 N.C. 61 (1991).

Whether to limit the scope of an opening statement rests largely within the trial judge's discretion. *State v. Paige*, 316 N.C. 630 (1986); *see also* N.C. GEN. R. PRAC. SUPER. & DIST. CT. 9 ("Opening statements shall be subject to such time and scope limitations as may be imposed by the court."). Generally, however, counsel is "'afforded wide latitude in the scope of the opening statement.'" *Freeman*, 93 N.C. App. 380, 389 (quoting *State v. Gladden*, 315 N.C. 398, 417 (1986)).

B. Permissible Content

During opening statement, the defendant is allowed to:

- Preview the evidence he or she intends to present. *Gladden*, 315 N.C. 398.
- Set forth the grounds for his or her defense, i.e., state the evidence on which the claim or defense is based. *Paige*, 316 N.C. 630.
- Point out facts that the defendant reasonably expects to bring out in cross-examination even if the defendant does not intend to present evidence. *Id.*

Defense counsel also may make the following general observations in an opening statement, although as a practical matter such observations do little to articulate the defendant's theory of defense to the jury. Counsel may:

- Tell the jury that it should give attention to all of the witnesses. *Mash*, 328 N.C. 61.
- Ask the jury to consider each piece of evidence carefully. *Freeman*, 93 N.C. App. 380.
- Inform the jury that the defendant intends to rely on the presumption of innocence and that the State has the burden of proof beyond a reasonable doubt. *Paige*, 316 N.C. 630, 648.

For additional considerations and objectives in making an opening statement, see *infra* Appendix 28-1, Guideline 7.4 Opening Statement from N.C. COMM'N ON INDIGENT DEFENSE SERVS., PERFORMANCE GUIDELINES FOR INDIGENT DEFENSE REPRESENTATION IN NON-CAPITAL CRIMINAL CASES AT THE TRIAL LEVEL (Nov. 2004). For the complete guidelines, see *infra* Appendix A of this manual.

C. Impermissible Content

Counsel is generally given wide latitude in opening statements, but it is improper for counsel to engage in argument. The line between a permissible opening statement and an impermissible argument is not always easy to apply. *See Freeman*, 93 N.C. App. 380, 389 ("The scope and extent of an opening statement are admittedly vague."). Relying on a treatise on trial practice, the court in *Freeman* observed that counsel should not:

- refer to inadmissible evidence;
- exaggerate or overstate the evidence; or
- discuss evidence he or she expects the other party to introduce.

Id. at 389. These principles do not appear to preclude the defense from responding to assertions made by the prosecutor in his or her opening statement, including promises of proof made by the prosecutor.

Freeman also observed that it is improper to ask the jurors to resolve disputes, make inferences, or interpret facts favorable to the speaker—in other words, to argue the evidence as opposed to describing or highlighting it in a way that supports the defendant's theory of defense. *Id.* at 389; *see also* STEVEN LUBET, MODERN TRIAL ADVOCACY: ANALYSIS AND PRACTICE 374–76 (4th ed. 2009) (describing the rule against argument and the techniques counsel may nonetheless use in an opening statement).

D. Time Limits

The length of opening statements is a matter within the sound discretion of the trial judge. *See State v. Call*, 349 N.C. 382 (1998); N.C. GEN. R. PRAC. SUPER. & DIST. CT. 9. The N.C. Supreme Court has upheld a trial judge's decision limiting the defendant's opening statement to five minutes. *See Call*, 349 N.C. 382; *see also State v. Fie*, 80 N.C. App. 577 (1986) (finding that trial judge acted within his discretion in limiting each defense counsel's opening statement to fifteen minutes), *rev'd on other grounds*, 320 N.C. 626 (1987). Trial judges are generally not so restrictive, however.

Practice note: Regardless of whether the trial judge sets a time limit, counsel will want to focus the opening statement on the aspects of the case most important to the defendant's theory of defense. If, however, the judge intends to set a time limit that does not allow you to apprise the jury adequately of the pertinent evidence to be presented in the case, be prepared to explain to the judge why the circumstances of the case require additional time.

28.3 Reserving or Waiving Opening Statement

A. Reserving

If the defendant will be offering evidence, he or she has the right to reserve opening statement and give it after the State's case-in-chief. G.S. 15A-1221(a)(6). It is the rare case, however, in which it is beneficial to the defense to reserve opening until after the jury has heard the State's entire case.

Opening statements afford counsel an opportunity at the outset to draw the jury's attention to evidence that the parties expect to be introduced as well as to gaps in the evidence. By reserving opening statement, the defense allows the State's evidence to be viewed without direction from defense counsel and without benefit of a forecast of the defense's theory of the case. Some behavioral scientists have reached the conclusion that up to "80 to 90 percent of all jurors come to a decision during or immediately after the opening statements." Dr. Donald E. Vinson, *Excerpts from National Institute on Litigating "Rule of Reason" Cases: Jury Psychology and Antitrust Trial Strategy*, 55 ANTITRUST L.J. 591, 591 (1986).

The supposed advantages of reserving opening statement—such as waiting to hear the State's evidence before revealing the defendant's theory of defense—are generally outweighed by the advantages of communicating to the jury early in the case. Ordinarily, counsel should have sufficient information through discovery, particularly under the broader discovery rules now in effect in North Carolina, to know the evidence that the State will present and to develop the theory of defense that the defendant will advance. There may be strategic reasons not to reveal particular information in an opening statement—for example, problems with the anticipated testimony of a State's witness, which you hope to draw out on cross-examination, or evidence that you aren't certain will be admissible. Even a brief opening statement, however, will communicate to the jury the broad outlines of your theory of defense and convey an alternative way to view the evidence.

B. Waiving

Either party may elect to waive opening statements. N.C. GEN. R. PRAC. SUPER. & DIST. CT. 9. Waiver can be express or implied. A defendant's failure to request the opportunity to make an opening statement amounts to a waiver of this right. *State v. McDowell*, 301 N.C. 279 (1980).

As with the reservation of opening statement, it is the rare case in which defense counsel should consider waiving opening statement. By waiving opening statement, the defense allows the State's evidence to be viewed without direction from defense counsel and without benefit of a forecast of the defense's theory of the case. Accordingly, waiver of opening statement is generally ill-advised.

C. Giving an Opening Statement in District Court Cases

Defense counsel often do not request the opportunity to make an opening statement in cases tried in district court, thus waiving the right. Although district court judges may be resistant to taking up court time for opening statements, the same reasons for giving an opening statement in jury trials apply to bench trials—to give the fact finder an alternative view of the case at the outset. To alleviate the judge's concerns about moving the docket along, counsel may want to give a summary opening statement rather than a detailed review of the evidence—for example, in an assault case, counsel may limit the opening to alerting the judge that the case involves self-defense. Such a statement may help the judge keep that perspective in mind during the State's presentation of its case.

28.4 Variance between Opening Statement and Proof

A. Importance of Keeping Promises

Counsel should not promise to present witnesses or evidence unless he or she is sure of being able to follow through with that promise. The failure to keep a promise to the jury made during opening statement impairs personal credibility, and the jury may view unsupported claims as an outright attempt at misrepresentation. *See* 2 PATRICK L. MCCLOSKEY & RONALD L. SCHOENBERG, CRIMINAL LAW DESK BOOK § 15.06[3], at 15–18 (2008).

As the N.C. Supreme Court has noted, "[a] cardinal tenet of successful advocacy is that the advocate be unquestionably credible. If the fact finder loses confidence in the credibility of the advocate, it loses confidence in the credibility of the advocate's cause." *State v. Moorman*, 320 N.C. 387, 400, 401 (1987) (defense counsel's failure to present evidence of a complete defense to rape as promised in his opening statement "severely undercut the credibility of the actual evidence offered at trial, including defendant's own testimony").

B. Failure to Keep Promises and Ineffective Assistance of Counsel

It is not improper for the prosecutor, during closing argument, to highlight the defendant's failure to introduce evidence that was promised during opening statement. *State v. Harris*, 338 N.C. 211 (1994); *State v. Anderson*, 200 N.C. App. 216 (2009). Defense counsel likewise may take advantage of the prosecutor's failure to follow through on promised proof.

Counsel may render ineffective assistance of counsel if he or she fails to keep promises made during opening statement about central aspects of the case. *See, e.g., State v. Campbell*, 359 N.C. 644 (2005) (defense counsel was possibly ineffective by promising that the jury would hear evidence and instructions on self-defense and intoxication when he knew that the State might not introduce the defendant's confession supporting these claims and the confession was subsequently not introduced); *Moorman*, 320 N.C. 387 (defense counsel was ineffective because, among other things, he failed to present promised evidence of a complete defense to rape); *State v. Duncan*, 188 N.C. App. 508, 515–16 (2008) (ineffective assistance found where, among other things, defense counsel promised in his opening statement to "offer evidence as to Defendant's state of mind, but he failed to do so, undercutting any possible defense that Defendant could offer to the serious charges against him"), *rev'd on other grounds*, 362 N.C. 665 (2008).

Practice note: If you are unsure of the admissibility of evidence you intend to offer during trial, ask the trial judge for a pretrial ruling on the record so that you will know whether you can deliver the evidence before describing it in your opening statement. When the course of a trial leads you to decide not to present evidence or call witnesses promised during your opening statement, you should acknowledge the change during your closing argument and explain to the jury the reasons for your deviation.

28.5 Opening the Door to Otherwise Inadmissible Evidence

The N.C. Supreme Court has held that opening statements are ***not*** evidence. *See State v. Faison*, 330 N.C. 347 (1991). Nevertheless, some North Carolina appellate decisions have found no error where a trial judge allowed arguably inadmissible evidence to be introduced by the State to rebut a defendant's contentions made during opening statement. The defendants in those cases were found to have "opened the door" during their opening statements to the introduction of the otherwise inadmissible evidence. *See, e.g., State v. Murillo*, 349 N.C. 573 (1998) (character evidence relating to the victim's performance as a school teacher was properly admitted where defense counsel, during opening statement, contended that the victim was a violent, abusive alcoholic); *State v. Jones*, 342 N.C. 457 (1996) (where the defendant's attorney contended in opening statement that the defendant's former girlfriend had reported him for murder in order to get away from him and to get reward money, the State was entitled to introduce evidence that the three-year delay in reporting was actually due to her fear of the defendant based on a separate assault she knew he had committed); *State v. Peterson*, 179 N.C. App. 437 (2006) (State properly introduced evidence of the defendant's bisexuality where defense counsel had asserted in opening statement that the defendant and the victim had an idyllic marital relationship), *aff'd on other grounds*, 361 N.C. 587 (2007).

In a recent case, however, the N.C. Court of Appeals reiterated that statements made by counsel during opening statement are not evidence and therefore do not "open the door" to the State's admission of otherwise inadmissible evidence during its case-in-chief. In *State v. Buie*, 194 N.C. App. 725 (2009), the defendant argued on appeal that the State should not have been permitted to introduce testimony of the alleged victim's good character under N.C. Rule of Evidence 404(a)(2) when the defendant had not presented any evidence to the contrary. The State asserted that the defendant had "opened the door" to the Rule 404(a)(2) evidence when defense counsel called the alleged victim's character into question during opening statement. The *Buie* court cited the N.C. Supreme Court's decision in *Faison*, 330 N.C. 347, for the proposition that opening statements are not evidence and then held that "the State should not have been allowed to introduce evidence in its case-in-chief about the female's good character merely because the Defendant forecast the introduction of evidence of the female's bad character [during the defendant's opening statement]." 194 N.C. App. 725, 729. The *Buie* court further held that since the defendant had offered no evidence of the alleged victim's character during his case-in-chief, the admission of the State's character evidence was erroneous (although not prejudicial in light of the other evidence introduced by the State against the defendant). *See also United States v. Green*, 648 F.2d 587, 595 (9th Cir. 1981) ("An opening statement, . . . having no evidentiary value, cannot operate to place an issue in controversy."); *United States v. Tomaiolo*, 249 F.2d 683, 689 (2d Cir. 1957) (holding that the opening statement of defense counsel "could not have put the defendant's character in issue" because it had "no evidentiary value, and therefore does not call for or justify cross-examination or rebuttal evidence"; also stating that "[a]n instruction from the Court or argument of counsel is sufficient correction, not the introduction of otherwise inadmissible evidence."); *State v. Anastasia*, 813 A.2d 601, 606 (N.J. Super. Ct. App. Div. 2003) ("Opening statements are not evidential and should not be responded to by 'rebuttal' evidence. If improper remarks are made by counsel, the remedy lies in a curative instruction to the jury or, if absolutely necessary, a mistrial."); *Bynum v. Commonwealth*, 506 S.E.2d 30, 34 (Va. Ct. App. 1998) ("[S]tatements made during an opening statement are not evidence; therefore, opening statements may not 'open the door' to otherwise inadmissible evidence.").

Assuming that a defendant's opening statement does not open the door to inadmissible evidence, it still could affect the trial judge's consideration of the admissibility of evidence proffered by the State. In *State v. Britt*, ___ N.C. App. ___, 718 S.E.2d 725 (2011), the trial judge initially granted the defendant's motion in limine precluding the State's expert witnesses from testifying that the bullets at issue were fired from the same gun. Thereafter, in opening statement the defendant told the jury that his experts would testify that the bullets at issue could not be matched. In light of the defendant's opening statement and forecast of the evidence, the trial judge reversed his ruling and allowed the State's experts to give their opinion that the bullets matched. The Court of Appeals upheld the trial judge's ruling on the ground that the State's expert testimony was admissible and that the trial judge had the discretion to allow it.

For a discussion of the split of authority elsewhere on the "opening the door" theory of admissibility as it relates to statements made during opening statement, see *Commonwealth v. Cepeda*, 2009 MP 15 (N. Mar. I. 2009), *available at* www.cnmilaw.org/pdf/supreme_court/2009-MP-15.pdf.

Practice note: If the State attempts to introduce inadmissible evidence during its case-in-chief and asserts that your forecast of evidence during your opening statement "opened the door" to its admission, you should object and cite *Buie* and *Faison* for the proposition that opening statements made by attorneys are not evidence. Although there are some inconsistencies in the appellate court rulings in this area of the law, you can argue that *Buie* and *Faison* are the two decisions that specifically address whether assertions made in opening statements are evidence and are the more thoroughly reasoned opinions. You can point out that the State has other remedies to address an improper opening statement, including objecting to the opening statement and commenting in closing on promises made but not kept. *See supra* § 28.4B, Failure to Keep Promises and Ineffective Assistance of Counsel. Further, the State may introduce evidence in rebuttal if the defendant introduces evidence that makes the State's evidence relevant and admissible.

28.6 Admissions of Guilt During Opening Statement

A. Defendant's Consent Required Prior to Admission of Guilt

If trial counsel concludes that the best trial strategy is to concede a defendant's guilt to a criminal charge in order to secure a conviction for a less serious offense (or a sentence of life instead of death), counsel must obtain the defendant's informed consent before making such a concession. *See State v. Harbison*, 315 N.C. 175 (1985). The decision to consent "must be made exclusively by the defendant," and it must be "made knowingly and voluntarily . . . after full appraisal of the consequences." *Id.* at 180; *see also State v. Thomas*, 327 N.C. 630 (1990) (remanding case to superior court for an evidentiary hearing to determine whether defendant knowingly consented to concessions of guilt made by trial counsel during closing argument); *State v. Perez*, 135 N.C. App. 543 (1999) (due process requires that a defendant's consent to concede guilt be made knowingly and voluntarily after full appraisal of the consequences).

Generally, if counsel admits the defendant's guilt without first obtaining consent, it is per se ineffective assistance of counsel because counsel's admission deprives the defendant of the right to have his or her guilt or innocence determined by the jury. *See Harbison*, 315 N.C. 175, 180 ("When counsel admits his client's guilt without first obtaining the client's consent, the client's rights to a fair trial and to put the State to the burden of proof are completely swept away."); *State v. Wiley*, 355 N.C. 592, 619 (2002) (interpreting *Harbison* as based on Sixth Amendment of U.S. Constitution and article 1, section 19 (law of the land) and section 23 (rights of the accused) of N.C. Constitution); *see also* N.C. CONST. art. I, section 24 (right to unanimous verdict by jury).

In *Florida v. Nixon*, 543 U.S. 175 (2004), the U.S. Supreme Court held on the facts of the case that, under the U.S. Constitution, counsel's admission of the defendant's guilt during opening statement without the defendant's express consent was not per se ineffective assistance of counsel but was subject to the prejudice analysis of *Strickland v. Washington*, 466 U.S. 668 (1984). The Court reasoned, "[I]n a capital case, counsel must consider in conjunction both the guilt and penalty phases in determining how best to proceed. When counsel informs the defendant of the strategy counsel believes to be in the defendant's best interest and the defendant is unresponsive, counsel's strategic choice is not impeded by any blanket rule demanding the defendant's explicit consent." *Nixon*, 543 U.S. 175, 192. Although the N.C. Supreme Court has had opportunities to do so, it has not disavowed the *Harbison* rule in light of the narrow ruling in *Nixon. See State v. Goss*, 361 N.C. 610 (2007); *State v. Campbell*, 359 N.C. 644 (2005); *see also State v. Maready*, 205 N.C. App. 1 (2010) (discussing *Nixon* and holding that North Carolina continues to adhere to the *Harbison* rule).

The rule prohibiting defense counsel from admitting a defendant's guilt to the jury without the defendant's consent applies only to the guilt/innocence phase of a trial. *State v. Boyd*, 343 N.C. 699 (1996); *State v. Walls*, 342 N.C. 1 (1995).

Practice note: *Boyd* and *Walls*, cited above, were decided before the line of U.S. Supreme Court cases culminating in *Blakely v. Washington*, 542 U.S. 296 (2004), in which the Court recognized that circumstances that increase a defendant's sentence beyond the maximum authorized for an offense are the functional equivalent of an element of a greater offense. *See also Ring v. Arizona*, 536 U.S. 584 (2002) (holding that factors that authorize imposition of the death penalty are subject to the same analysis). The N.C. appellate courts have not specifically considered the impact of *Blakely* and like cases on the application of *Harbison* to what previously were characterized as purely sentencing matters, such as the determination of aggravating factors. *Cf. State v. Harris*, 175 N.C. App. 360 (2006) (observing that North Carolina cases finding that defense counsel's concession of aggravating factors were a sufficient admission by the defendant were not applicable after *Blakely*, which requires a valid waiver by the defendant of the right to a jury trial; the court cites *Harbison* in support of the requirement of a valid waiver), *vacated on other grounds*, 361 N.C. 154 (2006) (remanding for determination whether the failure to submit aggravating factors to the jury was harmless beyond a reasonable doubt). *But cf. State v. Womack*, ___ N.C. App. ___, 712 S.E.2d 193 (2011) (relying on prior cases and rejecting the argument that defense counsel violated *Harbison* by conceding the defendant's prior convictions at the habitual felon phase of the case without the defendant's consent because, among other things, *Harbison* does not apply to proceedings to determine whether the defendant's sentence should be enhanced). Regardless of how the N.C. appellate courts resolve this issue, as a practical matter defense counsel should ***not*** admit in jury argument a matter that increases the defendant's sentence beyond the statutory maximum for the underlying offense without the client's consent.

B. What Constitutes Admission of Guilt

Admission must be express. There must be an actual admission of guilt for error to occur. It is not impermissible under *Harbison* to argue that the defendant is not guilty, but if he or she is found guilty of any crime, it should be of a lesser included offense or of a lesser crime for which he or she has not been charged. *See State v. Gainey*, 355 N.C. 73, 93 (2002) (defense counsel did not admit guilt to murder but only that "if he's guilty of anything, he's guilty of accessory after the fact"); *State v. Greene*, 332 N.C. 565, 572 (1992) (no admission of guilt where defense counsel argued that the defendant was innocent of all charges, but if found guilty of any charge it should be of the lesser crime of involuntary manslaughter "because the evidence came closer to proving that crime than any of the other crimes charged"); *see also State v. Hinson*, 341 N.C. 66 (1995) (defense counsel's statements regarding the guilt of a co-defendant did not amount to an admission that the defendant himself had committed any crime).

Admissions of facts or elements. Merely admitting the existence of a fact or an element of an offense is not the equivalent of an admission of guilt. *See State v. Wiley*, 355 N.C. 592 (2002) (placed in context, defense counsel's remarks that there may be some physical evidence linking the defendant to the murder victim's car did not constitute an admission); *State v. Strickland*, 346 N.C. 443 (1997) (statements by defense counsel during jury voir dire that the uncontroverted evidence showed that the defendant was holding a gun when the victim was killed did not amount to a concession of guilt to which defendant had not agreed); *State v. Fisher*, 318 N.C. 512 (1986) (defense counsel's admission of the existence of malice was not an admission of guilt so it was not per se ineffective assistance of counsel); *State v. Maniego*, 163 N.C. App. 676 (2004) (defense counsel's admission of the fact that the defendant was present at the scene of the crime was not an admission of guilt and was consistent with the theory of defense).

Assertion of defense. Some defenses may constitute an admission of guilt, at least of a lesser offense, and require the defendant's consent. *See State v. Johnson*, 161 N.C. App. 68 (2003) (defense counsel in opening statement stated that defendant was unable to premeditate and deliberate killings because of his intoxication and jury should return verdict of lesser offense; trial judge's inquiry of defendant was adequate to show consent); *see also State v. Berry*, 356 N.C. 490 (2002) (trial judge conducted *Harbison* inquiry to determine whether defendant consented to insanity defense, which necessitated admission of critical aspects of charged offense).

C. Procedural Requirements

Although there is no particular procedure that the trial judge "must invariably follow when confronted with a defendant's concession," (*Berry*, 356 N.C. 490, 514), an on-the-record exchange between the trial judge and the defendant is the preferred method of determining whether the defendant knowingly and voluntarily consented to an admission of guilt. *See State v. McDowell*, 329 N.C. 363 (1991); *see also State v. Matthews*, 358 N.C. 102 (2004) (holding that *Harbison* requires more than implicit consent based on an overall trial strategy and the defendant's intelligence). A clear record of consent is required, but the trial judge need not engage in the formal colloquy that is required for a guilty plea under G.S. 15A-1022(a). *State v. Perez*, 135 N.C. App. 543 (1999). Appellate courts will not presume the defendant's lack of consent from a silent record. *State v. Boyd*, 343 N.C. 699 (1996).

Practice note: If you decide that a concession of guilt is the best strategy in a particular case, fully discuss the concession and its value with the defendant. Before admitting guilt to the charge or to a lesser included offense during opening statement (or closing argument), present the defendant's written consent (if you have obtained one) to the trial judge or ask the judge to inquire of the defendant and obtain his or her express consent on the record. *See State v. House*, 340 N.C. 187, 197 (1995) (urging both the bar and the trial bench to be diligent in making a full record of a defendant's consent when a *Harbison* issue arises at trial).

28.7 Preservation of Issues for Appellate Review

A. Necessity for Objection

If the prosecutor makes improper and prejudicial statements during opening statement, defense counsel must object in a timely manner to preserve the issue for appeal. *See State v. Smith*, 96 N.C. App. 352 (1989). The standard of review on appeal is rigorous even if a timely objection is made. The trial judge's discretion in permitting the statements "will not be reviewed unless counsel's remarks are extreme and are clearly calculated to prejudice the jury in its deliberations." *See State v. Burmeister*, 131 N.C. App. 190, 196 (1998) (citing *State v. Taylor*, 289 N.C. 223 (1976)).

B. Waiver

If no timely objection is made to the prosecutor's opening statement in a capital case, review is limited to an examination of whether the remarks were so "grossly improper" that the trial judge abused his or her discretion in failing to intervene ex mero motu. *See State v. Gladden*, 315 N.C. 398, 417 (1986). It appears that this standard will also be utilized in non-capital cases although it has never been specifically addressed in a published opinion.

C. Complete Recordation

Requirement for and timing of motion. Pursuant to G.S. 15A-1241(a)(2), trial judges are not required to order the court reporter to record opening statements and closing arguments. However, on the motion of any party (or on the judge's own motion), these proceedings ***must*** be recorded. G.S. 15A-1241(b). "The motion for recordation of jury arguments must be made before the commencement of any argument and if one argument is recorded all must be." *Id.*

If a party suggests that an improper statement has been made during an unrecorded argument, the judge has the discretion to require that the rest of the argument be recorded. G.S. 15A-1241(b).

A sample Motion for Complete Recordation appears in the non-capital trial motions bank (under the Training & Resources link) at www.ncids.org. This motion covers not only jury arguments but also pretrial hearings, jury selection in non-capital cases, motions hearings, and bench conferences since those proceedings are also exempt from mandatory recordation under G.S. 15A-1241(a) unless a request for recordation is made.

Reconstruction of record. If an objection is made to an unrecorded statement or other conduct in the presence of the jury, on motion of either party, the trial judge "must reconstruct for the record, as accurately as possible, the matter to which objection was made." G.S. 15A-1241(c). It is defense counsel's responsibility to ensure that the record is reconstructed with regard to improper statements made by the prosecutor, and the appellate courts will decline review if the record is incomplete. *See, e.g., State v. Spellman*, 167 N.C. App. 374 (2004); *State v. Ussery*, 106 N.C. App. 371 (1992).

Practice note: The appellate courts have never held that it is ineffective assistance of counsel per se for defense counsel to fail to request complete recordation. *See, e.g., State v. Hardison*, 326 N.C. 646 (1990) (defendant cannot show ineffective assistance of counsel where there are no specific allegations of prejudice and no attempt to reconstruct the record); *State v. Verrier*, 173 N.C. App. 123, 130 (2005) (denying defendant's request to adopt "a per se rule granting a new trial where counsel neither requests nor the trial court requires that the entire trial, jury selection, arguments of counsel and bench conferences" be recorded). ***Still, there is no good reason not to make the request!*** Opening statements and closing arguments are often fertile ground for appellate issues. You must protect the rights of your client even if it means irritating the judge or court reporter, who may not feel that complete recordation is necessary. Complete recordation will obviate the need for reconstruction of the transcript in the event that improper statements are made and will greatly facilitate appellate review. It may also inhibit prosecutors from "push[ing] the envelope" during closing argument. *See State v. Jones*,

355 N.C. 117, 127 (2002). If, however, you have failed to request complete recordation and an issue arises regarding an improper statement made by the prosecutor, you must take steps immediately to ensure that the record is accurately reconstructed.

Appendix 28-1
Guideline 7.4 Opening Statement*

(a) Prior to delivering an opening statement, counsel should consider whether to ask for sequestration of witnesses.

(b) Counsel should be familiar with North Carolina law and the individual trial judge's practices regarding the permissible content of an opening statement. Counsel should consider the need to, and if appropriate, ask the court to instruct the prosecution not to mention in opening statement contested evidence for which the court has not determined admissibility.

(c) Counsel should consider the strategic advantages and disadvantages of disclosure of particular information during opening statement.

(d) Counsel's objectives in making an opening statement may include the following:

(1) to introduce the theory of the defense case;
(2) to provide an overview of the defense case;
(3) to identify the weaknesses of the prosecution's case;
(4) to emphasize the prosecution's burden of proof;
(5) to summarize the anticipated testimony of witnesses, and the role of each in relationship to the entire case;
(6) to describe the exhibits that will be introduced and the role of each in relationship to the entire case;
(7) to clarify the jurors' responsibilities;
(8) to state the ultimate inferences counsel wants the jury to draw;
(9) to personalize the client and counsel for the jury; and
(10) to prepare the jury for the client's testimony or decision not to testify.

(e) Counsel should consider incorporating the promises of proof the prosecutor makes to the jury during opening statement into the defense opening statement and summation.

(f) Whenever the prosecutor oversteps the bounds of a proper opening statement, counsel should consider objecting, requesting a mistrial, or seeking cautionary instructions, unless sound tactical considerations weigh against any such objections or requests. Such tactical considerations may include, but are not limited to:

(1) the significance of the prosecutor's error; and
(2) the possibility that an objection might enhance the significance of the information in the jurors' minds, or otherwise negatively affect the jury.

---

*Reprinted from N.C. COMM'N ON INDIGENT DEFENSE SERVS., PERFORMANCE GUIDELINES FOR INDIGENT DEFENSE REPRESENTATION IN NON-CAPITAL CRIMINAL CASES AT THE TRIAL LEVEL (Nov. 2004). For the complete guidelines, see *infra* Appendix A of this manual.

Chapter 29
Witnesses

This chapter discusses selected topics dealing with witnesses, including securing the attendance of witnesses and the production of documents at trial though the use of subpoenas. Subpoenas and other mechanisms for obtaining records before trial are also addressed in the chapter on discovery in Volume 1 of this manual. *See* 1 NORTH CAROLINA DEFENDER MANUAL § 4.7A (Evidence in Possession of Third Parties) and § 4.8 (Subpoenas) (May 1998). Also covered in this chapter are the sequestration of witnesses, competency of adult and child witnesses to testify, general rules governing the examination of witnesses, use of remote testimony, and oaths and affirmations. The chapter does not address the requirements for the admission of expert testimony.

29.1 Securing the Attendance of Witnesses by Subpoena and Other Process

A writ issued under the authority of the court to compel the personal attendance of a witness is called a subpoena ad testificandum (also called a witness subpoena). *See Vaughan v. Broadfoot*, 267 N.C. 691 (1966). Generally, a jurisdiction's subpoena procedure is a statutory method of implementing a defendant's Sixth Amendment right to present a defense, which includes the right to compulsory process to obtain witnesses and documents for his or her defense. *See generally United States v. Echeles*, 222 F.2d 144, 152 (7th Cir. 1955) (observing that federal criminal procedure rules implement the right to compulsory process in federal cases).

Among the steps counsel should consider in preparing for trial are subpoenaing potentially helpful witnesses and examining and subpoenaing potentially helpful physical or documentary evidence. *See infra* Appendix A, N.C. COMM'N ON INDIGENT DEFENSE SERVS., PERFORMANCE GUIDELINES FOR INDIGENT DEFENSE REPRESENTATION IN NON-CAPITAL CRIMINAL CASES AT THE TRIAL LEVEL, Guideline 7.1(c)(1), (2) General Trial Preparation (Nov. 2004); *see also* 1 KENNETH S. BROUN, BRANDIS & BROUN ON NORTH CAROLINA EVIDENCE § 12, at 39 (7th ed. 2011) ("[I]f the defendant desires the testimony of . . . witnesses he or his counsel must call them."). If a witness has not been subpoenaed to appear, the witness is not required to be present, and the court has no authority to punish his or her failure to appear. *State v. Wells*, 290 N.C. 485 (1976).

For a discussion of subpoenas from the perspective of the recipient, see John Rubin & Aimee Wall, *Responding to Subpoenas for Health Department Records*, HEALTH LAW BULLETIN No. 82 (UNC School of Government, Sept. 2005), *available at* http://sogpubs.unc.edu/electronicversions/pdfs/hlb82.pdf. Although the bulletin focuses on health department records, it discusses requirements and procedures applicable to all subpoenas.

A. Constitutional Basis of Right to Compulsory Process

The Sixth Amendment to the U.S. Constitution guarantees that "[i]n all criminal prosecutions the accused shall enjoy the right . . . to have compulsory process for obtaining witnesses in his favor . . . ." This federal constitutional right is applicable to the states through the Due Process Clause of the Fourteenth Amendment to the U.S. Constitution. *Washington v. Texas*, 388 U.S. 14, 19 (1967) ("[t]he right to offer the testimony of witnesses, and to compel their attendance, if necessary, is in plain terms the right to present a defense," which is "a fundamental element of due process of law" and thus incorporated into the Fourteenth Amendment and applicable to state proceedings); *accord State v. Melvin*, 326 N.C. 173, 184 (1990); *see also infra* § 29.2F, Constitutional Right to Obtain Evidence in Possession of Third Parties (discussing Due Process right to favorable, material evidence). The right to confront one's accusers and witnesses with other testimony is also guaranteed by article I, section 23 of the N.C. Constitution. *State v. Cradle*, 281 N.C. 198 (1972).

The right to compulsory process is not absolute. The court may require a defendant who requests such process at state expense to establish some "colorable need" for the person to be summoned, "lest the right be abused by those who would make frivolous requests." *State v. House*, 295 N.C. 189, 206 (1978) (quoting *Hoskins v. Wainwright*, 440 F.2d 69, 71 (5th Cir. 1971)); *see also United States v. Valenzuela-Bernal*, 458 U.S. 858, 867 (1982) (holding that the defendant could not establish a violation of his constitutional right to compulsory process merely by showing that the deportation of potential witnesses deprived him of their testimony; he had to make "some plausible showing" of how their testimony would have been material and favorable to his defense); *Washington v. Texas*, 388 U.S. 14, 23 (finding a violation of the defendant's right to compulsory process where state statutes prohibiting alleged accomplices from testifying for one another prevented the defendant from putting "on the stand a witness who was physically and mentally capable of testifying to events that he had personally observed, and whose testimony would have been relevant and material to the defense").

Under North Carolina's subpoena procedures, discussed in subsection B., below, the defendant does not have to make any showing to obtain a subpoena. Nor is it likely in the typical case for the need for a witness subpoena to be questioned before the witness is scheduled to appear because the significance of a witness's testimony is difficult to determine before the witness actually testifies. *See* 6 WAYNE R. LAFAVE ET AL., CRIMINAL PROCEDURE § 24.3(f), at 390–91 (3d ed. 2007) (contrasting witness and document subpoenas). *But see State v. Carroll*, 17 N.C. App. 691 (1973) (upholding the trial judge's denial of the defendant's request that the State subpoena inmate-witnesses in a prosecution of the defendant for escape where the witnesses had no knowledge of the facts of the alleged escape and could offer no testimony relevant and material to the defense); KELLA W. HATCHER, JANET MASON & JOHN RUBIN, ABUSE, NEGLECT, DEPENDENCY, AND TERMINATION OF PARENTAL RIGHTS PROCEEDINGS IN NORTH CAROLINA § 11.2.A.5, at 300–01 (UNC School of Government 2011) (noting cases in which trial courts quashed the respondents' subpoenas for children in abuse, neglect, dependency, and termination of parental rights proceedings), *available at* www.sog.unc.edu/sites/www.sog.unc.edu/files/Evidence_Chapter11.pdf.

The defendant may have to make a showing of "need" for a witness's testimony if the witness challenges a subpoena on the ground that the sought-after testimony is privileged. *See infra* § 29.1I, Motions to Modify or Quash Witness Subpoenas. The question of "need" for a witness's testimony also may arise when the defendant requests a continuance of the trial because the witness has failed to comply with the defendant's subpoena. *See, e.g., State v. Beck*, 346 N.C. 750 (1997) (upholding the denial of a continuance where the likelihood of the witness's availability was de minimus—the record did not contain a copy of a subpoena for the witness, defense counsel was uncertain whether the witness had been served, and law enforcement had been unable to locate the witness despite five outstanding warrants—and where counsel's asserted need for the witness consisted of his unsworn statements about the witness's potential testimony regarding events that occurred after the offense).

Although there are no time limits set by the Constitution within which to exercise the right to compulsory process, this right can be lost by the defendant's delay in subpoenaing witnesses. Thus, in the following cases, the defendants did not subpoena the witnesses until after the trial had started and failed to explain why they had not issued a subpoena for the witnesses earlier. *See State v. House*, 295 N.C. 189 (1978) (no error in trial judge's refusal to issue subpoenas for defense witnesses where the request was made after the State had rested its case and the testimony sought to be introduced did not appear to be material); *State v. Wells*, 290 N.C. 485 (1976) (finding no constitutional violation where trial judge did not issue subpoenas for defense witnesses mid-trial where defendant failed to subpoena his witnesses prior to trial when he had ample opportunity to do so); *State v. Cyrus*, 60 N.C. App. 774 (1983) (no constitutional or statutory violation by trial judge in denying defendant's motion to secure the attendance of a material out-of-state witness made on the first day of trial where the defense had knowledge well before the case was calendared that the witness had issues that might prevent him from coming back to North Carolina). *But cf. State v. Rankin*, 312 N.C. 592 (1985) (defendant's right to compulsory process was denied where trial judge denied his motion to compel the attendance of prisoners to testify at trial without giving defense counsel an opportunity to show "good cause" or to explain why the motion was not filed until the day before the trial was to start).

Practice note: You should prepare and serve your subpoenas far enough in advance of trial to give the witnesses a reasonable time to make arrangements to appear. If you wait until the last minute to serve a subpoena (without good reason for doing so) and the witness does not appear, the trial judge may have grounds to deny a motion to compel a witness's attendance or for a continuance. If you plan to use your county's sheriff's department to serve the subpoenas, you need to check with them to determine their policies and requirements. For example, in Mecklenburg County, a local order states that defendants who want the sheriff to serve a subpoena on a law enforcement officer must submit the subpoena to the sheriff no less than fourteen days before the scheduled court appearance.

B. Securing the Attendance of In-State Witnesses

Witnesses who are present in North Carolina must come to court to testify in a criminal proceeding if they are properly served with a subpoena ad testificandum. The subpoena must be issued and served in accordance with the provisions of N.C. Rule of Civil Procedure 45. This rule governs subpoenas in criminal proceedings, with certain exceptions discussed below. *See* N.C. GEN. STAT. § 15A-801 (hereinafter G.S.) (so stating for criminal cases); G.S. 8-59 (so stating for all causes in the trial divisions of the North Carolina courts).

A subpoena to obtain the testimony of a witness in a pending cause may be issued by

- the clerk,
- any district or superior court judge or magistrate, or
- any attorney for a party.

N.C. R. CIV. P. 45(a)(4) (clerk, district court judge, superior court judge, magistrate, or attorney); G.S. 7A-103(1) (powers of clerk of superior court); G.S. 7A-292(4) (powers of magistrate). An unrepresented party may not issue a subpoena but may request the clerk to issue a subpoena, signed but otherwise blank, which the party then fills out. N.C. R. CIV. P. 45(a)(4).

Mandatory contents of subpoena. N.C. Rule of Civil Procedure 45(a)(1) requires that every subpoena state the following:

- the title of the action;
- the name of the court in which the action is pending;
- the name of the party who is responsible for summoning the witness;
- a command to the person to whom it is directed to attend and testify [including the place, date, and time that appearance is required];
- the protections of persons subject to subpoenas as stated in Rule 45(c); and
- the duties of persons in responding to subpoenas as stated in Rule 45(d).

The form subpoena issued by the Administrative Office of the Courts (AOC-G-100, "Subpoena" (Dec. 2009), *available at* www.nccourts.org/Forms/Documents/556.pdf), contains space for the issuing party to fill in the specific case information as well as the form language required in all cases.

Manner of service. A subpoena may be served by

- the sheriff,
- a sheriff's deputy,
- a coroner, or
- any person who is not a party and is not less than 18 years of age.

N.C. R. CIV. P. 45(b)(1).

Service on the party named in the subpoena may be made by

- personally delivering a copy of the subpoena to that person;
- registered or certified mail, return receipt requested; or
- telephone communication with the person to be subpoenaed if service is made by a sheriff, his or her designee who is not less than 18 years old and not a party, or a coroner. (This last form of service may be used for subpoenas to testify, not for subpoenas to produce documents, discussed *infra* in § 29.2B.)

Id. G.S. 8-59 states that a subpoena also may be served by telephone communication by any employee of a law enforcement agency; however, when a person is served by telephone under that statute, neither a show cause order nor an order for the person's arrest may be issued for a violation of the subpoena until the person is personally served with the written subpoena. Although not expressly stated in Rule 45(b)(1), this limitation also may apply to subpoenas served by telephone by a sheriff, designee, or coroner under the above-cited rule of civil procedure.

Practice note: Because the court may not be able to issue a show cause order re contempt (with an order for arrest) to enforce a subpoena served by telephone communication, and because disputes may arise about whether a person named in a subpoena signed for and received a subpoena served by mail, counsel should consider serving all subpoenas by personal delivery on the person whose attendance is sought.

Service exception in criminal cases. In civil cases, a copy of the subpoena also must be served on other parties to the case, but G.S. 15A-801 exempts criminal cases from that requirement. The subpoenaing party in a criminal case need only serve the person or entity being subpoenaed in accordance with the above requirements.

Attendance required until discharge; consequences of failure to comply. Every witness who has been summoned in a criminal prosecution must appear and continue to attend from day to day and session to session until discharged by the court or by the party who summoned him or her to appear. G.S. 8-63. The statute also states that the prosecutor may discharge a witness from a subpoena, but presumably this authority applies only to witnesses summoned by the prosecutor.

A person who fails to obey a properly served subpoena without adequate excuse may be held in contempt of court for violating a court order (that is, the subpoena directing attendance, whether signed by an attorney or a judicial official). N.C. R. CIV. P. 45(e)(1); *see also* G.S. 5A-11(a)(3) (criminal contempt for willful disobedience of a court's lawful process or order); G.S. 5A-21 (civil contempt for continuing failure to comply with order of a court). A court may issue an order for arrest along with an order to show cause re contempt if the court has probable cause to believe the person named in the show cause order will not appear in response to the show cause order. G.S. 5A-16(b).

G.S. 8-63 also provides that if a witness does not comply with a subpoena, he or she may be required to pay a financial penalty.

Avoidance of undue burden or expense. N.C. Rule of Civil Procedure 45(c)(1) provides that the party or attorney responsible for issuing a subpoena "shall take reasonable steps to avoid imposing an undue burden or expense on a person subject to the subpoena." Failure to do so may result in sanctions. The sanctions may include compensating the person unduly burdened for his or her lost earnings and for reasonable attorney's fees. *See infra* subsection I. of § 29.1, Motions to Modify or Quash Witness Subpoenas.

Compensation and expenses. Witnesses under subpoena, other than salaried law enforcement officers, are entitled to be compensated in the amount of $5.00 per day. G.S. 7A-314(a) (amount of compensation). A witness also may be entitled to receive reimbursement for travel expenses. *See* G.S. 7A-314(b). Witnesses are not entitled to receive their fees in advance. G.S. 6-51. Rather, the witness must apply to the clerk after attendance for payment. *See* G.S. 6-53 (witness to prove attendance by oath or affirmation); G.S. 7A-316 (to same effect); AOC-CR-235, "Witness Attendance Certificate" (Mar. 2010), *available at* www.nccourts.org/Forms/Documents/76.pdf. A judge decides, in his or her discretion, what compensation and allowances to authorize for a witness who appears in the capacity of an expert witness. *See* G.S. 7A-314(d). (This statute does not govern requests by the defense for funds for expert assistance, discussed in 1 NORTH CAROLINA DEFENDER MANUAL Ch. 5 (Experts and Other Assistance) (May 1998).)

C. Material Witness Orders

Statutory authorization. To assure the attendance of an uncooperative witness, the State or the defendant may seek a material witness order asserting that there are reasonable grounds to believe that a witness in a pending criminal proceeding has information material to the determination of the proceeding and may not come to court to testify even after being served with a subpoena. *See* G.S. 15A-803(a); *see also State v. Jacobs*, 128 N.C. App. 559 (1998).

G.S. 15A-803(g) authorizes the court to assure the attendance of a material witness by issuing a subpoena or an order for arrest. Since the purpose of a material witness order is to assure the attendance of a material witness who may not be responsive to a subpoena, it is not clear when a subpoena alone would be an effective device for the court to use. If arrested, the witness may be incarcerated or released on bond pending the proceeding where his or her testimony is required. *See* G.S. 15A-803(e).

Applicable to in-state witnesses only. G.S. 15A-803 should be used to secure the attendance of uncooperative in-state witnesses. For witnesses located outside North Carolina, the procedures outlined in G.S. 15A-813 (Uniform Act to Secure Attendance of Witnesses from Without a State in Criminal Proceedings) should be followed. *See State v. Tindall*, 294 N.C. 689 (1978). For a discussion of that procedure, see *infra* § 29.1E, Securing the Attendance of Nonresident Witnesses.

Mandatory procedure. To obtain a material witness order, the State or the defendant must file a motion supported by an affidavit showing cause for its issuance. The witness must be given

- reasonable notice;
- an opportunity to be heard and present evidence; and
- the right to representation by counsel at a hearing on the motion.

G.S. 15A-803(d). The witness is entitled to the appointment of counsel in accordance with rules adopted by the Office of Indigent Defense Services. *Id.*

Issuance of order. A material witness order may be issued by a district court judge at the time that a defendant is bound over to superior court at a probable cause hearing or by a superior court judge at any time after the criminal proceeding is initiated. G.S. 15A-803(b). The judge must make findings of fact that support the issuance of the material witness order. G.S. 15A-803(d).

Length of effectiveness. A witness may be incarcerated pursuant to a material witness order for up to twenty days. This order may be renewed one or more times by a superior court judge, in his or her discretion, for periods not longer than five days each. The material witness order remains in effect for the period stated in the order unless modified or vacated earlier by a superior court judge. G.S. 15A-803(c).

Modification or vacation. A superior court judge may modify or vacate a material witness order if the witness, the State, or any defendant shows new or changed facts or circumstances. G.S. 15A-803(f).

Compliance with the Sixth Amendment. The use of the term "may" in G.S 15A-803 suggests that the decision whether to grant a motion for a material witness order lies within the discretion of the judge; however, the judge must exercise his or her discretion in a way that does not violate the guarantee of the Sixth Amendment to the U.S. Constitution that a criminal defendant be afforded compulsory process for obtaining witnesses in his or her favor. *State v. Tindall*, 294 N.C. 689 (1978); *see also State v. Jacobs*, 128 N.C. App. 559 (1998) (no abuse of discretion in denying defendant's motion for a material witness order because the testimony of the witness who was the subject of the motion would have been merely cumulative and was therefore not material to the determination of guilt or innocence).

It appears that it would be an abuse of discretion and a violation of the Sixth Amendment if a trial judge denied a motion for a material witness order where the defendant:

- has shown reasonable grounds to believe that the witness possesses material information;
- complies with the requirements of G.S. 15A-803; and
- has not been dilatory in securing the attendance of the witness.

Cf. State v. Love, 131 N.C. App. 350 (1998), *aff'd per curiam*, 350 N.C. 586 (1999); *Jacobs*, 128 N.C. App. 559; *State v. Coen*, 78 N.C. App. 778 (1986).

Practice note: You should file a motion for a material witness order as soon as you have reasonable cause to believe that a witness might not appear for the proceeding. If you have reason to know that the witness is not cooperating but wait until the last minute to file the motion, the trial judge's denial of your motion may be upheld for lack of diligence. *See Coen*, 78 N.C. App. 778 (finding no abuse of discretion under G.S. 15A-803 and no violation of the Sixth Amendment in trial judge's denial of defendant's motion for a material witness order made right before the defense rested where the defense knew on the first day of trial that the witness was not cooperating with service of the subpoena, which the defense did not issue until the first day of trial); *State v. Poindexter*, 69 N.C. App. 691, 700 (1984) (no merit to pro se defendant's argument that the trial judge failed to assist him in locating and subpoenaing witnesses where defendant failed "to make the necessary motions and applications to secure the presence of any unwilling or confined witnesses" despite having the opportunity to do so, the defendant made his request after the close of the State's case-in-chief, and the judge directed police officers to try to locate defendant's witnesses).

D. Voluntary Protective Custody for Material Witnesses

If a witness wishes, he or she can ask a superior court judge to place him or her in protective custody. If the judge determines that the witness is material, the judge may order that the witness be:

- confined;
- placed in custody in a non-penal institution;
- released to the custody of a law enforcement officer or other person; or
- made subject to any other provisions appropriate to the circumstances.

G.S. 15A-804(a). A superior court judge can modify or vacate the order on request by the witness or on the judge's own motion. G.S. 15A-804(d). A voluntary protective custody order may be issued even if there is also a material witness order in effect for the witness and vice versa. G.S. 15A-804(c).

The custodian of a witness under a voluntary protective custody order may not release the witness without the witnesses's consent "unless directed to do so by a superior court judge, or unless the order so provides." G.S. 15A-804(b). The Official Commentary to this statute states that "[a]lthough it may seem farfetched in North Carolina, the basis for this section sprang from the fear that members of organized crime might attempt to obtain the release of a witness who would prefer to remain in custody."

E. Securing the Attendance of Nonresident Witnesses

Necessity of interstate cooperation. In 1902, the U.S. Supreme Court recognized that state legislatures did not have the power to make any provision that would result in the compulsory attendance of an out-of-state witness in a proceeding held in the home state's court. *See Minder v. Georgia*, 183 U.S. 559 (1902). After that decision, states began adopting the Uniform Act to Secure the Attendance of Witnesses from Without a State in Criminal Proceedings. This Act was written "to provide a means for state courts to compel the attendance of out-of-state witnesses at criminal proceedings." Jay M. Zitter, Annotation, *Availability under Uniform Act to Secure the Attendance of Witnesses from Without a State in Criminal Proceedings of Subpoena Duces Tecum*, 7 A.L.R.4th 836, 837 (1981). The N.C. General Assembly adopted this Act in 1937, currently codified at G.S. 15A-811 through 15A-816. *See Preston v. Blackledge*, 332 F. Supp. 681 (E.D.N.C. 1971). The Act has been enacted in all fifty states and the District of Columbia and has been found to be constitutional by the U.S. Supreme Court. *See New York v. O'Neill*, 359 U.S. 1 (1959); Rhonda Wasserman, *The Subpoena Power:* Pennoyer's *Last Vestige*, 74 MINN. L. REV. 37 (1989).

Required procedures and orders. If the State or the defendant wants to secure the presence of a person located in another state (as defined in G.S. 15A-811) to be a witness in a criminal proceeding in North Carolina, the party first must apply for a certificate and order under seal from the North Carolina court in which the criminal proceeding is pending. The moving party then must seek an order from the other state's courts requiring the person to attend court proceedings in North Carolina. G.S. 15A-813; *see also State v. Tindall*, 294 N.C. 689, 699–700 (1978).

Practice note: The AOC has issued a form certificate for use by parties seeking to require the attendance of out-of-state witnesses. *See* AOC-CR-901M, "Certificate for Attendance of

Out-of-State Witness" (June 1997), *available at* www.nccourts.org/Forms/Documents/162.pdf.

Witness must be material. In applying to a North Carolina court for a certificate and order of attendance for an out-of-state witness, the applicant must show that the person requested to be a witness "is a material witness" in a proceeding that is pending in a court of record in this state. G.S. 15A-813. For a discussion on what constitutes materiality, see Jay M. Zitter, Annotation, *Sufficiency of Evidence to Support or Require Finding that Out-of-State Witness in Criminal Case Is "Material Witness" Justifying Certificate to Secure Attendance Under Uniform Act to Secure the Attendance of Witnesses from Without a State in Criminal Proceedings*, 12 A.L.R.4th 742 (1982 & Supp. 2010).

***Practice note*:** Always support your application with affidavits or other testimony to meet your burden of materiality. Bare allegations may be insufficient. *See* 81 AM. JUR. 2D *Witnesses* § 45 (2004). Also, as with a motion for a material witness order, discussed *supra* in § 29.1C, you should file your application as soon as you know that the witness will be needed. *See State v. Cyrus*, 60 N.C. App. 774 (1983) (no constitutional or statutory violation by trial judge in denying defendant's motion to secure the attendance of a material out-of-state witness made on the first day of trial where the defense had knowledge well before the case was calendared that the witness had issues that might prevent him from coming back to North Carolina).

Specific location must be given. In addition to making an adequate showing that the testimony of the prospective witnesses is material, the applicant must adequately designate the location where the witness can be found. *See State v. Tindall*, 294 N.C. 689, 700 (1978).

Issuance of certificate. If the judge finds that the applicant has made a sufficient showing to secure the witness's presence, he or she may issue a certificate under seal that sets out the facts and specifies the number of days the witness will be required to attend. G.S. 15A-813. The certificate and order must be "presented to a judge of a court of record in the county [of the other state] in which the witness is found," and it may include a recommendation that the witness be immediately taken into custody and delivered to an officer of this state to assure his or her attendance. G.S. 15A-813.

The judge in the witness's home state then may have the witness appear before him or her to determine whether to issue an order. *See* 81 AM. JUR. 2D *Witnesses* § 48 (2004); *cf.* G.S. 15A-812 (witness in North Carolina may be summoned to another state to testify if found to be a material and necessary witness and no undue hardship will result). If the home state judge finds that the witness is material and necessary, will suffer no undue hardship, and will be protected from arrest and service of process by the trial state, he or she may issue an order directing the witness's attendance in North Carolina. *See Preston v. Blackledge*, 332 F. Supp. 681 (E.D.N.C. 1971); *Tindall*, 294 N.C. 689; Rhonda Wasserman, *The Subpoena Power:* Pennoyer's *Last Vestige*, 74 MINN. L. REV. 37 (1989).

Practice note: To obtain an order from another state requiring the attendance of a witness, North Carolina counsel will need to arrange for the matter to be presented to the court of the other state. The AOC form certificate states that it and the bill of indictment (or presumably an information if indictment has been waived) are to be transmitted to the presiding judge of the court of the other state, but counsel still needs to ensure that the matter is properly presented and argued. Typically, North Carolina counsel will associate counsel in the other state to appear before that state's court. A public defender's office in the other state, if there is one for the county where the witness is located, may be willing to handle the matter as a courtesy. Failing that, North Carolina counsel should request funds from the court to obtain counsel to appear in the other state. Counsel also may be able arrange to appear pro hac vice in the other state (that is, be permitted to appear in the other jurisdiction although not admitted to practice in the other jurisdiction).

Compensation. The out-of-state witness is entitled to compensation for mileage and $5.00 for each day that he or she is required to travel and attend as a witness. If the witness is required to appear for more than one day, he or she also is entitled to reimbursement of actual expenses incurred for lodging and meals in the same manner as state employees who are authorized to travel within the state. G.S. 7A-314(c); G.S. 15A-813; AOC-CR-235, "Witness Attendance Certificate" Side Two (Mar. 2010), *available at* www.nccourts.org/Forms/Documents/76.pdf.

Failure to comply. If a witness fails to comply with an order directing him or her to attend a North Carolina proceeding, the witness may be punished by the home state court in the same manner as if the failure had been to attend a trial in the home state. *See Preston*, 332 F. Supp. 681; *cf.* G.S. 15A-812 (providing this remedy when North Carolina witness fails to comply with order to attend out-of-state proceeding). Additionally, if a witness comes to this state and then fails without good cause to attend and testify as directed by the order, he or she may be punished as any other witness who disobeys an order issued from a North Carolina court of record. G.S. 15A-813.

Exemption from arrest and service of process. If a nonresident witness comes to North Carolina in obedience to an order directing him or her to attend and testify, the witness may not be arrested or served with criminal or civil process in connection with matters that arose before he or she entered this state under the order. G.S. 15A-814.

Compliance with Sixth Amendment. Use of the term "may" in G.S. 15A-813 indicates that the judge has discretion whether to grant a motion to procure the attendance of an out-of-state witness. Nevertheless, the trial judge may not exercise his or her discretion in a manner inconsistent with the Sixth Amendment's right to compulsory process. *See Preston*, 332 F. Supp. 681 (finding an abuse of discretion in the trial judge's denial of the defendants' request to secure the attendance of nonresident witnesses whose testimony was vital to the defendants' right to receive a fair trial); *State v. Brady*, 594 P.2d 94 (Ariz. 1979) (trial court abused its discretion and violated defendant's due process rights by denying her motion to compel the attendance of an out-of-state witness whose testimony went to the heart of the defense; written interrogatories admitted at trial were not a sufficient substitute for live testimony under the Sixth Amendment); *People v. Trice*, 476 N.Y.S.2d 402 (App. Div. 1984) (abuse of discretion found where trial judge denied defendant's motion to secure the attendance of a nonresident witness who signed an affidavit stating that he saw the victim alive two days after the defendant had allegedly killed her).

F. Securing the Attendance of Witnesses in Custody Within the State

Criminal Procedure Act. At common law, anyone who had been convicted of a crime was disqualified from testifying as a witness. The legislature removed this disqualification by enacting G.S. 8-49, which provides that no person shall be excluded from giving testimony "by reason of incapacity from interest or crime." *See* 1 KENNETH S. BROUN, BRANDIS & BROUN ON NORTH CAROLINA EVIDENCE § 131, at 492 n.5 (7th ed. 2011). Pursuant to G.S. 15A-805(a), the State or the defendant in a pending criminal proceeding may move to require that a North Carolina prisoner "be produced and compelled to attend as a witness in the action or proceeding." If the movant shows good cause, the judge of the court in which a criminal proceeding is pending must order the person be produced as a witness. G.S. 15A-805(a).

G.S. 15A-805 does not require that the motion be in writing, that it be accompanied by an affidavit, or that it be made within a certain time (although see the practice note below). The statute does not specify any particular method by which the movant show the "good cause" necessary to the production of the witness. *See State v. Rankin*, 312 N.C. 592 (1985) (so noting and holding that the defendant's right to compulsory process was denied where trial judge denied defendant's motion to compel the attendance of prisoner to testify at defendant's trial without giving defense counsel an opportunity to show "good cause" or to explain why the motion was not filed until the day before the trial was to start).

Practice note: Although not required, you should file a written motion detailing the reasons why the witness's presence is necessary. Support the motion with an affidavit showing good cause for the production of the prisoner. File the motion as soon as practicable so that the logistics of transporting a prisoner will not delay the trial and potentially provide grounds for denial of the motion. In addition to citing the statute in your motion, you should cite the Sixth Amendment to the U.S. Constitution and article I, sections 19 and 23 of the N.C. Constitution to reinforce your right to production of the witness as well as preserve the constitutional issue for appellate review if your motion is denied.

If the prisoner has pending criminal proceedings and the judge determines that the order of production would unreasonably interfere with those prior proceedings, G.S. 15A-805(b) provides that he or she may deny the motion. That statute also appears to provide that if an order of production is obtained for a prisoner with pending criminal proceedings, the prisoner (that is, that defendant) or the prosecutor in the other district may apply to a judge or justice in the appellate division and request that the order of production be vacated for good cause shown. G.S. 15A-805(b). Presumably, these provisions for denial or cancellation of an order of production would have to yield to the constitutional rights of the defendant then on trial to obtain necessary witnesses for his or her defense.

Habeas corpus ad testificandum. Independently of G.S. 15A-805, G.S. 17-41 to 17-46 set out a "much more complicated" procedure for obtaining the presence of a prisoner at a proceeding to testify. *Rankin*, 312 N.C. 592, 597. According to the Official Commentary to

G.S. 15A-805, the provisions of G.S. 15A-805 "replace[d] the old 'habeas corpus ad testificandum' with a simple motion and order for the production of a prisoner (or other person confined in an institution)." Nevertheless, G.S. 17-41 et seq. still provide an alternative method of securing the attendance of a prisoner housed in North Carolina. *See also* AOC-G-112, "Application and Writ of Habeas Corpus Ad Testificandum" (Mar. 2007), *available at* www.nccourts.org/Forms/Documents/567.pdf.

The difference between a writ of habeas corpus ad testificandum and a subpoena ad testificandum is that a subpoena directs the witness to appear at the proceeding while the writ of habeas corpus directs the custodian of the witness to bring him or her to court. *Mabe v. Wythe County Dep't of Soc. Servs.*, 671 S.E.2d 425 (Va. Ct. App. 2009).

G.S. 17-41 authorizes "[e]very court of record," on application of any party to a pending civil or criminal proceeding, to issue a writ of habeas corpus to bring a prisoner in any jail or prison in North Carolina before the court to testify for the applicant. The writ also may be issued by a magistrate or clerk of superior court if the prisoner is confined in an institution within that county.

This statute allows judges to issue the writ for any incarcerated person except for a prisoner who has been sentenced to death. This exception does not apply to the State of North Carolina—a judge may issue a writ of habeas corpus to bring a condemned prisoner to court to testify on behalf of the State. *See State v. Jones*, 176 N.C. 702 (1918) (holding that the statute stating that a writ of habeas corpus ad testificandum could not be issued for a prisoner who had been sentenced to death did not apply to the State); *cf. State v. Adair*, 68 N.C. 68, 70 (1873) (a prohibition against writs ordering prisoners sentenced for a felony to testify "applies only to parties strictly so called, and not to the State"). There is not a comparable restriction in G.S. 15A-805, discussed above, on the defendant's right to secure the attendance and testimony of a prisoner.

The application for the writ must:

- be made by the party to the proceeding or by his or her agent or attorney;
- be verified by the applicant;
- state "[t]he title and nature of the suit or proceeding in regard to which the testimony of such prisoner is desired"; and
- state that the prisoner's testimony is "material and necessary to such party on the trial or hearing of such suit or proceeding, as he is advised by counsel and verily believes."

G.S. 17-42. For other miscellaneous statutory requirements regarding the writ of habeas corpus ad testificandum, see G.S. 17-43 et seq.

G. Securing the Attendance of Witnesses in Custody Outside the State

If a prisoner (other than a person confined due to mental illness) who is confined in another state is needed as a witness in a criminal proceeding in North Carolina, the State or the defendant may apply to the court where the action is pending for a certificate securing the attendance of the prisoner. G.S. 15A-822. The judge may issue the certificate if

- there is reasonable cause to believe that the prisoner possesses material information; and
- the state in which the prisoner is confined has a statute that is equivalent to G.S. 15A-821 (permitting prisoners in North Carolina to testify in proceedings in other states).

Id. The certificate, if issued, must

- be under the seal of that court;
- certify that the prisoner is a material witness in a pending criminal proceeding; and
- specify the number of days that the prisoner's attendance is required.

G.S. 15A-822(a)(4). After the certificate is issued, the judge "may cause it to be delivered to a court of such other state which is authorized to initiate or undertake action for the delivery of such prisoners to this State as witnesses." G.S. 15A-822(c).

H. Securing the Attendance of Witnesses in Federal Custody

The State or the defendant may secure the attendance of a witness who is confined in a federal institution by making application in the court where the defendant's criminal proceeding is pending. The applicant must show that there is "reasonable cause" to believe that the witness "possesses information material" to the pending proceeding. G.S. 15A-823.

Upon application, the judge may issue a certificate (known as a writ of habeas corpus ad testificandum) addressed to the Attorney General of the United States certifying that there is reasonable cause to believe that the prisoner possesses material information and requesting the Attorney General to have the prisoner brought to court "for a specified number of days under custody of a federal public servant." G.S. 15A-823(a)(3).

The judge, after issuing the certificate, "may cause it to be delivered to the Attorney General of the United States" or to his or her authorized representative. G.S. 15A-823(c). It is the policy of the U.S. Bureau of Prisons to allow federal prisoners to testify in state court criminal proceedings pursuant to a writ of habeas corpus ad testificandum issued by a state court. *Barber v. Page*, 390 U.S. 719 (1968).

I. Motions to Modify or Quash Witness Subpoenas

A person commanded by a subpoena to appear at trial may file a motion to quash or modify the subpoena in the county in which the trial is to occur. The motion must be made within ten days after service of the subpoena or before the time specified for compliance if the time is less than ten days after service. N.C. R. CIV. P. 45(c)(5).

The judge may modify or quash a subpoena if the subpoenaed person shows that it

- fails to allow reasonable time for compliance;
- requires disclosure of privileged or protected matter and there is no applicable exception

or waiver;

- subjects the person subpoenaed to an undue burden;
- is unreasonable or oppressive; or
- is procedurally defective.

N.C. R. CIV. P. 45(c)(3), (c)(5); *see, e.g., In re Will of Johnston*, 157 N.C. App. 258 (2003), *aff'd per curiam*, 357 N.C. 569 (2003) (propounder of will filed a motion to quash subpoena of deceased's attorney based on attorney-client privilege); *State v. Pallas*, 144 N.C. App. 277 (2001) (judge properly granted State's motion to quash subpoena of assistant district attorney who had prosecuted the co-defendant because his testimony may have been privileged work product [under former discovery statute] and lacked materiality); *State v. McRae*, 58 N.C. App. 225 (1982) (no error in trial judge's denial of defendant's motion to quash the State's subpoenas for two young children because there is no age below which one is considered incompetent as a matter of law to testify in North Carolina); *see also supra* § 29.1A, Constitutional Basis of Right to Compulsory Process (discussing defendants' constitutional right to compulsory process to secure the testimony of witnesses for their defense).

If the judge enters an order to quash or modify a subpoena, he or she may order the party who issued the subpoena to pay all or part of the reasonable expenses and attorney's fees of the subpoenaed person. N.C. R. CIV. P. 45(c)(8). This provision appears to have greater applicability to parties in civil cases than to either the State or defendant (particularly an indigent defendant) in a criminal case.

Practice note: If the judge quashes a subpoena or refuses to enforce a subpoena against a witness who fails to comply, you must make an offer of proof showing "the essential content or substance of the witness's testimony" in order for the appellate court to ascertain whether prejudicial error occurred. *See State v. Simpson*, 314 N.C. 359, 370 (1985); *see also* N.C. R. EVID. 103(a)(2); *Pallas*, 144 N.C. App. 277 (defendant waived appellate review of trial judge's decision not to enforce the subpoena of a co-defendant as a witness because the defendant made no offer of proof as to what the co-defendant would say and its significance was not obvious from the record).

J. Defense Depositions in Criminal Actions

G.S. 8-74 provides a procedure for a criminal defendant in limited circumstances to take a witness's deposition before a proceeding. The defendant may take a deposition if he or she files an affidavit with the clerk of superior court where the action is pending stating that:

- the testimony of the named witness is important for the defense; and
- the witness's attendance cannot be procured for the proceeding because the witness is infirm, or otherwise physically incapacitated, or is a nonresident of North Carolina.

Once the affidavit is filed, the clerk must appoint "some responsible person" to take the witness's deposition. The district attorney must be given ten days' notice of the taking of the deposition and may appear (or send a representative) to cross-examine the witness. The deposition may be read during the criminal proceeding in the same manner as depositions in civil cases.

29.2 Securing the Production of Documents or Physical Evidence by Subpoena

A subpoena duces tecum (also called a document subpoena) is used to compel a witness to produce papers or other tangible objects needed at trial. It is a useful tool for obtaining records that are not subject to discovery because they are not in the possession, custody, or control of the State. *See State v. Burr*, 341 N.C. 263 (1995). This ancient writ was recognized at common law, and its use is now authorized and governed by several statutes discussed below. *See Vaughan v. Broadfoot*, 267 N.C. 691 (1966) (in-depth discussion of subpoenas duces tecum); 1 KENNETH S. BROUN, BRANDIS & BROUN ON NORTH CAROLINA EVIDENCE § 13, at 42 (7th ed. 2011); *see also Wilson v. United States*, 221 U.S. 361 (1911) (discussing the origins of the subpoena duces tecum).

For a discussion of subpoenas from the perspective of the recipient, see John Rubin & Aimee Wall, *Responding to Subpoenas for Health Department Records*, HEALTH LAW BULLETIN No. 82 (UNC School of Government, Sept. 2005), *available at* http://sogpubs.unc.edu/electronicversions/pdfs/hlb82.pdf. Although the bulletin focuses on health department records, it discusses requirements and procedures applicable to all subpoenas.

A. Statutory Authorization

The production of records, books, papers, documents, or tangible things in a criminal proceeding may be obtained by a subpoena properly issued and served as provided in Rule 45 of the N.C. Rules of Civil Procedure, which is applicable to criminal proceedings in most respects. G.S. 15A-802 (so stating); *see also* G.S. 8-61 ("Subpoenas for the production of records, books, papers, documents, or tangible things may be issued in criminal actions in the same manner as provided for civil actions in Rule 45 of the Rules of Civil Procedure.").

Generally, a criminal action must actually have been commenced for a party to issue a subpoena under G.S. 15A-802. *See In re Superior Court Order Dated April 8, 1983*, 70 N.C. App. 63 (1984), *rev'd on other grounds*, 315 N.C. 378 (1986); *see also* N.C. R. CIV. P. 45(a)(1)a. (every subpoena must state the name of the court in which the action is pending); *cf.* John Rubin & Aimee Wall, *Responding to Subpoenas for Health Department Records*, HEALTH LAW BULLETIN No. 82, at 3 & n.4 (UNC School of Government, Sept. 2005) (discussing circumstances in which a party may obtain a subpoena or its equivalent before the filing of a case), *available at* http://sogpubs.unc.edu/electronicversions/pdfs/hlb82.pdf.

Technically, the person named in the subpoena is not being compelled to testify but rather to produce and authenticate the specified records. If the party also needs the person to testify, he or she also needs to subpoena the person for that purpose. *See State v. Richardson*, 59 N.C. App. 558 (1982), *rev'd in part on other grounds*, 308 N.C. 470 (1983); *see supra* § 29.1, Securing the Attendance of Witnesses by Subpoena and Other Process (discussing subpoenas to testify). A subpoena to produce evidence may be issued separately or joined with a subpoena to appear and testify. N.C. R. CIV. P. 45(a)(2). The AOC form subpoena, AOC-G-100, may be used for both purposes; it contains boxes for the subpoenaing party to indicate whether the recipient is being asked to testify, to produce documents, or both. *See* AOC-G-100, "Subpoena" (Dec. 2009), *available at* www.nccourts.org/Forms/Documents/556.pdf.

The items sought by a subpoena duces tecum must be material to the inquiry. The subpoena "must specify with as much precision as fair and feasible the particular items desired." *State v. Newell*, 82 N.C. App. 707, 708 (1986). It must describe the items sought "with such definiteness that the witness can identify them without prolonged or extensive search." *Vaughan v. Broadfoot*, 267 N.C. 691, 696 (1966). Discovery is not a proper purpose for a subpoena duces tecum. Parties are not entitled to have a mass of records and other documents brought into court to search through them for evidence. *Id.* (disapproving of "fishing or ransacking" expeditions). A defendant is not limited, however, to using a subpoena duces tecum to require production of documents at trial; a subpoena duces tecum is an appropriate device for a defendant to obtain documents before trial that are potentially material and favorable to his or her defense, which is not for improper discovery but rather is considered a part of a defendant's right to a fair trial. *See infra* § 29.2F, Constitutional Right to Obtain Evidence in Possession of Third Parties. For a further discussion of the right to obtain documents before trial, see 1 NORTH CAROLINA DEFENDER MANUAL § 4.7A (Evidence in Possession of Third Parties), § 4.8 (Subpoenas) (May 1998).

If the documents sought are not material to the issue or are protected by a privilege, the witness may contest their production. *See infra* § 29.2E, Motions to Modify or Quash a Subpoena Duces Tecum.

B. Statutory Requirements

The required contents of a subpoena duces tecum and its manner of service are similar to those for a subpoena ad testificandum under N.C. Rule of Civil Procedure 45(a) and (b). *See supra* § 29.1B, Securing the Attendance of In-State Witnesses. No affidavit showing materiality or necessity is required. *See Vaughan*, 267 N.C. 691. The admissibility of the items will be determined at trial unless the subpoena is quashed before trial. *Id.*

Mandatory contents of subpoena duces tecum. Rule 45(a)(1) requires that every subpoena state all of the following:

- the title of the action;
- the name of the court in which the action is pending;
- the name of the party who is responsible for summoning the witness;
- a command to the person to whom it is directed to produce and permit inspection and copying of designated records, books, papers, documents, or tangible things in the possession, custody, or control of that person;
- the protections for recipients of subpoenas as stated in Rule 45(c); and
- the duties of recipients in responding to subpoenas as stated in Rule 45(d).

The AOC form subpoena, AOC-G-100, includes space for the issuing party to fill in the specific case information as well as the form language required in all cases. *See* AOC-G-100, "Subpoena" (Dec. 2009), *available at* www.nccourts.org/Forms/Documents/556.pdf.

Manner of service. Under Rule 45(b)(1), a subpoena duces tecum may be served by

- the sheriff;
- a sheriff's deputy;
- a coroner; or
- any person who is not a party and is not less than 18 years of age.

Service on the party named in the subpoena duces tecum may be made by

- personally delivering a copy of the subpoena to that person; or
- registered or certified mail, return receipt requested.

Unlike a subpoena ad testificandum (discussed *supra* in § 29.1B), a subpoena duces tecum may not be served by telephone communication. *See* N.C. R. CIV. P. 45(b)(1).

In civil cases, a copy of a subpoena duces tecum also must be served on other parties to the case, but G.S. 15A-802 exempts criminal cases from that requirement. The subpoenaing party in a criminal case need only serve the person or entity being subpoenaed in accordance with the above requirements.

Form of compliance. To comply with a subpoena duces tecum, the person must produce the requested items as kept in the usual course of business, or the documents must be organized and labeled to correspond with the categories stated in the request. N.C. R. CIV. P. 45(d)(1).

Place of production. Typically, a subpoena duces tecum requires production at some sort of proceeding in the case to which the recipient is subpoenaed, such as a pretrial hearing, deposition (rare in criminal cases but common in civil cases), or trial. In 2003, the General Assembly amended Rule 45 of the N.C. Rules of Civil Procedure to modify this requirement for subpoenas for documents (but not subpoenas to testify). Thus, before the amendment, a party in a civil case would have to schedule a deposition, to which the party would subpoena the records custodian, even if the party merely wanted to inspect records in the custodian's possession and did not want to take any testimony. Under the revised rule, a party may use a subpoena in a pending case to direct the recipient to produce documents at a designated time and place, such as the issuing party's office, even though no deposition or other proceeding is scheduled for that time and place. Because G.S. 15A-802 makes Rule 45 applicable to criminal cases, this use of a subpoena appears to be permissible in a criminal case.

The change in Rule 45 authorizing an "office" subpoena may not be readily apparent. It is reflected in the following italicized portion of revised Rule 45(a)(2): "A command to produce evidence may be joined with a command to appear at trial or hearing or at a deposition, *or any subpoena may be issued separately.*" *See* North Carolina State Bar,

2008 Formal Ethics Opinion 4 (2008) (so interpreting quoted language), *available at* www.ncbar.gov/ethics/; Bill Analysis, H.B. 785: Rules of Civil Proc/Rewrite Rule 45 (S.L. 2003-276), from Trina Griffin, Research. Div., N. C. General Assembly (June 27, 2003) (same); Memorandum to Superior Court Judges et al. re: Subpoena Form Revised (AOC-G-100) & S.L. 2003-276 (HB 785), from Pamela Weaver Best, Assoc. Counsel, Div. of Legal & Legislative Servs., N.C. Admin. Office of the Courts (Sept. 29, 2003) (same). The latter two memos are available from the authors of this manual. The revised language is comparable to Rule 45(a)(1) of the Federal Rules of Civil Procedure, which has authorized a similar procedure in federal cases. *See* 9 JAMES WM. MOORE ET AL., MOORE'S FEDERAL PRACTICE § 45.02[3], at 45-21 (3d ed. 2011).

Practice note: When seeking sensitive records, defense counsel may not want to use an "office" subpoena. The subpoenaed party often will contest the subpoena, necessitating a court hearing in any event. Further, if a records custodian who is subpoenaed discloses confidential information to defense counsel without proper authorization (typically, consent by the subject of the records or a court order, not just a subpoena), defense counsel may be subject to sanctions. *See* North Carolina State Bar Ethics Opinion RPC 252 (1997) (attorneys should refrain from reviewing confidential materials inadvertently sent to them by opposing party), *available at* www.ncbar.gov/ethics/; *Susan S. v. Israels*, 67 Cal. Rptr. 2d 42 (Cal. Ct. App. 1997) (attorney read and disseminated patient's confidential mental health records that treatment facility mistakenly sent directly to him in response to subpoena; court allowed patient's suit against attorney for violation of state constitutional right of privacy).

Notice of receipt and opportunity to inspect; potential applicability to criminal cases. Rule 45(d1) of the N.C. Rules of Civil Procedure states that within five business days of receipt of materials produced in compliance with a subpoena duces tecum, the party who was responsible for issuing the subpoena must serve all other parties with notice of receipt. On request, the party receiving the material must provide all the other parties a reasonable opportunity to copy and inspect such material at the inspecting party's expense.

The applicability of this requirement to criminal cases, particularly when the defendant is the subpoenaing party, is not entirely clear. In 2007, the General Assembly revised Rule 45 to add the notice and inspection requirements in subsection (d1) of Rule 45. This change appears to have been prompted by concerns from civil practitioners after the 2003 changes to Rule 45. Those earlier changes, discussed above, allowed a party to issue a subpoena for the production of documents without also scheduling a deposition, at which the opposing party would be present and would have an opportunity to review and obtain copies of the subpoenaed records.

Criminal cases are not specifically exempted from the notice and inspection requirements enacted in 2007, although somewhat paradoxically the subpoenaing party in a criminal case is not required to give notice of the service of a subpoena (discussed under "Manner of service," above). The new subpoena provisions also are in tension with G.S. 15A-905 and 15A-906, which essentially provide that a criminal defendant is only obligated to disclose to the State evidence that he or she intends to use at trial.

If the notice and inspection requirements in Rule 45(d1) apply to criminal cases, a party may have grounds to seek a protective order under G.S. 15A-908 to withhold records from disclosure. Alternatively, instead of using a subpoena, a party may move for a court order for production of records, which is not governed by Rule 45. For a discussion of motions for a court order requiring production of records, see 1 NORTH CAROLINA DEFENDER MANUAL § 4.7A (Evidence in Possession of Third Parties) (May 1998).

C. Production of Public Records and Hospital Medical Records

If a custodian of public records or hospital medical records (as defined in G.S. 8-44.1) has been subpoenaed to appear for the sole purpose of producing records in his or her custody and not also to testify, the custodian may elect to tender the records to the court in which the action is pending instead of making a personal appearance. The custodian may tender the records to the court by registered or certified mail or by personal delivery on or before the time specified in the subpoena. The custodian must certify by affidavit that the records are true and correct copies and that the records were made and kept in the regular course of business or, if no such records were kept, an affidavit to that effect. N.C. R. CIV. P. 45(c)(2).

Rule 45(c)(2) states that if records are delivered under this subsection, the records are admissible in the proceeding without further authentication or certification unless they are otherwise objectionable. The rule also states that if the records are hospital medical records, they are not open to inspection except by the parties and their attorneys until ordered published by the trial judge and nothing in Rule 45(c)(2) shall be construed as waiving the physician-patient privilege or requiring any privileged communication to be disclosed. *Id.* The meaning of this provision is not entirely clear. On the one hand, it appears to allow the parties to review the records without further order of the court; on the other hand, it appears to restrict disclosure of confidential information.

Practice note: As a practical matter, hospital records that have been mailed to the court will not be available for review, and should not be reviewed, by the parties unless the court so orders. Hospital records custodians typically will seal and mark as confidential mailed-in records; and clerks of court who receive the records will not make them available for review by the parties unless the court so orders. Further, counsel is at risk by reviewing confidential records mailed to the court if the court has not ordered disclosure. *See Bass v. Sides*, 120 N.C. App. 485 (1995) (before obtaining judge's permission, plaintiff's attorney reviewed confidential medical records of defendant that records custodian had sealed and provided to clerk of court in response to subpoena; judge ordered plaintiff's attorney to pay defendant's attorney fees, totaling approximately $7,000, and prohibited plaintiff from using the records at trial).

D. Objections to a Subpoena Duces Tecum

A person who has been served with a subpoena to produce records may object to the subpoena. The objection must be in writing and must be served on the party or the attorney designated in the subpoena within ten days of service of the subpoena or before the time set for compliance if the time is less than ten days after service. A person may object on the grounds that the subpoena

- does not allow reasonable time for compliance;
- requires disclosure of privileged or protected matter and there is no applicable exception or waiver;
- imposes an undue burden on the party subpoenaed;
- is unreasonable or oppressive; or
- is procedurally defective.

N.C. R. CIV. P. 45(c)(3).

If the person objects to the subpoena because he or she believes that the information sought by the subpoena is privileged or otherwise protected from disclosure, he or she must object "with specificity" and support the objection by sufficiently describing the nature of the communications, records, books, papers, documents, or other tangible things not produced. N.C. R. CIV. P. 45(d)(2).

Court order required to override objection. If an objection is made, the party serving the subpoena is not entitled to inspect or copy the designated materials unless the court enters an order permitting him or her to do so. N.C. R. CIV. P. 45(c)(4). In some instances, the subpoenaed party will appear in court at the time designated in the subpoena and make an objection to disclosure. If this procedure is followed, the defendant will have an opportunity to obtain a ruling from the court then and there. In other instances, the subpoenaed party will object before the scheduled proceeding. The subpoenaing party then will have to file a motion to compel production, with notice to the subpoenaed person, in the court of the county where the production is to occur. *Id.*

Practice note: If the judge refuses to require that the documents be turned over, counsel should move to have the documents sealed and included in the record in the event of appeal. *See State v. Hardy*, 293 N.C. 105 (1977); *see also State v. Burr*, 341 N.C. 263 (1995) (court states that it could not review trial judge's denial of motion to require production of witness's medical records because defendant failed to make documents part of record). If the judge refuses to require production of the documents for inclusion in the record, make an offer of proof about the anticipated contents of the documents.

Subpoenaed person may be compensated for expenses of production. If following an objection (or motion to modify or quash, discussed next) a judge enters an order compelling the production of records, books, papers, documents, or other tangible things, he or she may protect any person who is not a party or a party's agent from "significant" expense from complying with the subpoena. The judge may order the subpoenaed person to be "reasonably compensated" for the cost of producing the designated material. N.C. R. CIV. P. 45(c)(6).

Practice note: Typically, judges do not order the payment of document production expenses because compliance with a subpoena is an ordinary, not significant, expense of responding to court proceedings. In a case involving extraordinary production expenses, if a judge orders payment, defense counsel for an indigent defendant may request the court to authorize payment from state funds as a necessary expense of representation. *See* G.S. 7A-450(b); G.S. 7A-454.

E. Motions to Modify or Quash a Subpoena Duces Tecum

A person commanded by a subpoena duces tecum to produce items may test the relevancy and materiality (but not the admissibility) of the designated items by filing a motion to quash or modify the subpoena in the county where the items are to be produced. N.C. R. CIV. P. 45(c)(5); *Vaughan v. Broadfoot*, 267 N.C. 691 (1966). The motion must be made within ten days after service of the subpoena or before the time specified for compliance if the time is less than ten days after service. N.C. R. CIV. P. 45(c)(5).

The judge may modify or quash a subpoena duces tecum if the subpoenaed person shows that it

- does not allow reasonable time for compliance;
- requires disclosure of privileged or protected matter and there is no applicable exception or waiver;
- imposes an undue burden on the party subpoenaed;
- is unreasonable or oppressive; or
- is procedurally defective.

See N.C. R. CIV. P. 45(c)(3), (c)(5). If the judge enters an order to quash or modify a subpoena, he or she may order the party who issued the subpoena to pay all or part of the reasonable expenses and attorney's fees of the subpoenaed person. N.C. R. CIV. P. 45(c)(8).

Although it has been held that the decision whether to quash or modify the subpoena is within the discretion of the trial judge and is not subject to review absent an abuse of that discretion, the judge must be guided by sound legal principles when making the decision. *See Vaughan*, 267 N.C. 691. In exercising his or her discretion, "the trial judge should consider the relevancy and materiality of the items called for [by the subpoena], the right of the subpoenaed person to withhold production on other grounds, such as privilege, and also the policy against 'fishing expeditions.'" *State v. Newell*, 82 N.C. App. 707, 709 (1986). The ruling also must be measured against the defendant's constitutional right to obtain material, favorable evidence in the possession of third parties, discussed in subsection F., below. *See also Love v. Johnson*, 57 F.3d 1305 (4th Cir. 1995) (finding that state trial judge violated defendant's due process rights by quashing subpoena on overbreadth grounds without requiring that records be produced for review by court after defendant made a plausible showing that information material and favorable to his defense existed within the records), *reviewing on habeas sub nom. State v. Love*, 100 N.C. App. 226 (1990).

Subject to constitutional limitations, a judge may quash or modify a subpoena if it is overly broad or not served in a timely manner. *See, e.g., Newell*, 82 N.C. App. 707, 709 (no abuse of discretion by trial judge in quashing overbroad subpoena where only a "tiny fraction" of the materials requested were "even arguably material to the inquiry") [decided before *Pennsylvania v. Ritchie*, discussed in subsection F., below] ; *see also Vaughan*, 267 N.C. 691, 699 (subpoena for production of documents on first day of trial properly quashed where it was a "fishing or ransacking expedition"); *Ward v. Taylor*, 68 N.C. App. 74 (1984) (no abuse of discretion by trial judge in quashing subpoena as unreasonable and oppressive since plaintiffs waited until the last minute to serve an extremely broad subpoena for all time cards and records of all work over an eight-year period when they had known of the importance of the records for at least two weeks); *State v. Richardson*, 59 N.C. App. 558 (1982) (recognizing trial court's authority to modify subpoena to limit it), *aff'd in part and rev'd in part on other grounds*, 308 N.C. 470 (1983).

Practice note: If the judge quashes a subpoena requiring the production of documents, counsel should move to have the documents sealed and included in the record in the event of appeal. *See State v. Hardy*, 293 N.C. 105 (1977); *see also State v. Burr*, 341 N.C. 263 (1995) (court states that it could not review trial judge's denial of motion to require production of witness's medical records because defendant failed to make documents part of record). If the judge refuses to require production of the documents for inclusion in the record, make an offer of proof about the anticipated contents of the documents.

F. Constitutional Right to Obtain Evidence in Possession of Third Parties

A defendant's constitutional right to compulsory process, discussed *supra* in § 29.1A, includes the right to compel witnesses to produce records or other evidence. *See generally* 6 WAYNE R. LAFAVE ET AL., CRIMINAL PROCEDURE § 24.3(f), at 392 (3d ed. 2007). A defendant also is entitled under the Due Process Clause of the Fourteenth Amendment to the U.S. Constitution to obtain records from third parties that contain favorable, material evidence even if the records are confidential under state or federal law. This right is an offshoot of the right to favorable, material evidence in the possession of the prosecution. *See Pennsylvania v. Ritchie*, 480 U.S. 39 (1987) (records in possession of child protective agency). An attorney in a criminal case may apply directly to a judge for an order of production of records rather than issuing a subpoena duces tecum. Such an application is known as a *Ritchie* motion. For a discussion of the procedure to obtain a court order for the production of records, see 1 NORTH CAROLINA DEFENDER MANUAL § 4.7A (Evidence in Possession of Third Parties) (May 1998).

G. Failure to Comply with a Subpoena Duces Tecum

A person who fails to obey a properly served subpoena duces tecum without adequate cause may be held in contempt of court. *See* N.C. R. CIV. P. 45(e)(1); *see also* G.S. 5A-11 (criminal contempt); G.S. 5A-21 (civil contempt).

H. Obtaining Documents or Other Items Located Outside North Carolina

A defendant can secure the production of documents or other tangible items located outside of North Carolina by subpoenaing them through the Uniform Act to Secure the Attendance of Witnesses from Without a State in Criminal Proceedings. *See* G.S. 15A-813 (witness from another state summoned to testify in this state), discussed *supra* in § 29.1E. Several states have found that "in view of the remedial purpose of the Act and also in view of the broad construction placed on the term 'subpoena' in similar statutes, it is clear that the Act authorizes the issuance of a subpoena duces tecum." Jay M. Zitter, Annotation, *Availability under Uniform Act to Secure the Attendance of Witnesses from Without a State in Criminal Proceedings of Subpoena Duces Tecum*, 7 A.L.R.4th 836, 837 (1981). Counsel may not use an ordinary Rule 45 subpoena duces tecum to compel an out-of-state witness to produce records. *See* North Carolina State Bar, 2010 Formal Ethics Opinion 2 (2010) (also stating that attorney may not use records improperly obtained from out-of-state health care provider), *available at* www.ncbar.gov/ethics.

29.3 Sequestration of Witnesses

The practice of separating witnesses and excluding them from the courtroom until they are called to testify "is a long-established and well-recognized measure designed to increase the likelihood that testimony will be candid." *Bell v. Duckworth*, 861 F.2d 169, 170 (7th Cir. 1988). The value of sequestration has been extolled by courts and commentators. As early as 1917, the N.C. Supreme Court noted that "[n]o harm can come from separation of the witnesses, and much injury might result if it is not done when it is made to appear to the presiding judge that there may be collusion among the witnesses, tracking each other's testimony, like sheep jumping over a fence." *Lee v. Thornton*, 174 N.C. 288, 289 (1917); *see also* Gregory M. Taube, *The Rule of Sequestration in Alabama: A Proposal for Application Beyond the Courtroom*, 47 ALA. L. REV. 177, 179 (1995) (discussing the origins of sequestration and noting that it has been used without change for "perhaps longer than any other truth-seeking device"); Sarah Chapman Carter, Comment, *Exclusion of Justice: The Need for a Consistent Application of Witness Sequestration Under Federal Rule of Evidence 615*, 30 U. DAYTON L. REV. 63 (2004) ("Separation of witnesses during a trial has been deemed 'one of the greatest engines that the skill of man has ever invented for the detection of liars in a court of justice.'" (citation omitted)); *Geders v. United States*, 425 U.S. 80, 87 (1976) (noting that "the practice of sequestration of witnesses 'already had in English practice an independent and continuous existence, even in the time of those earlier modes of trial which preceded the jury and were a part of our inheritance of the common Germanic law'" (quoting 6 J. WIGMORE, EVIDENCE § 1837, at 348 (3d ed., 1940))).

A. Purpose of Sequestration

There are two purposes for sequestering witnesses at trial. First, sequestration prevents a later witness from tailoring his or her testimony to that of a previous witness and, second, it aids the factfinder in detecting testimony that is less than candid. *State v. Harrell*, 67 N.C. App. 57, 64 (1984) (citing *Geders v. United States*, 425 U.S. 80 (1976)). The idea of keeping the witnesses from interacting with each other is not to *prevent* the fabrication of false stories before they testify but to *detect* fabrications by separate cross-examinations. *State v. Jackson*, 309 N.C. 26 (1983).

B. Statutory Authorization

A judge's authority to exclude witnesses has been codified in two separate provisions. G.S. 15A-1225 authorizes, on motion of a party, the exclusion of some or all of the witnesses from the courtroom until they are called to testify. N.C. Rule of Evidence 615 (enacted after G.S. 15A-1225) also authorizes the exclusion of witnesses from the courtroom so they cannot hear the testimony of other witnesses. Under Rule 615, a trial judge may order sequestration on motion of either party or on his or her own motion.

Exceptions to the rule. Rule 615 sets out the following four exceptions to the general rule allowing the exclusion of witnesses from the courtroom until called to testify:

1. A party who is a natural person may not be excluded. To exclude parties would "raise serious problems of confrontation and due process." N.C. R. EVID. 615 Official Commentary; *see also Perry v. Leeke*, 488 U.S. 272, 282 (1989) ("The defendant's constitutional right to confront the witnesses against him immunizes him from . . . physical sequestration."). An alleged crime victim is not considered a "party" in a criminal action and has no statutory right that guarantees him or her the right to be present at all times during the trial. *Cf.* G.S. 15A-832(e) ("When the victim is to be called as a witness . . ., the court shall make every effort to permit the fullest attendance possible by the victim . . ."; however, "[t]his subsection shall not be construed to interfere with the defendant's right to a fair trial.").
2. An officer or employee of a party that is not a natural person is entitled to have its designated representative present. The exception would allow a police officer who has been in charge of an investigation to remain in the courtroom during testimony even though he or she will be a witness. N.C. R. EVID. 615 Official Commentary; *see also State v. Stanley*, 310 N.C. 353, 356–57 (1984) (in case involving charge of first-degree rape of child under twelve, no abuse of discretion shown where trial judge allowed two State's witnesses—a DSS worker and a juvenile court officer—to remain in the courtroom at the State's request during the victim's testimony because, as the trial judge explained, they "were instrumental in the preparation of the case and . . . necessary to the handling of the examination of" the witness).
3. A person whose presence is shown by a party to be essential to the presentation of his or her cause may not be excluded. This category includes an expert who needs to listen to other testimony in order to testify in his or her capacity as an expert. *See* N.C. R. EVID. R. 615 Official Commentary. It also has been used to allow a law enforcement officer in charge of an investigation to remain in the courtroom while other witnesses were sequestered. *See State v. Jones*, 337 N.C. 198 (1994) (no abuse of discretion by trial judge in allowing the lead officer to remain in the courtroom as a person essential to the presentation of the State's case; ruling did not amount to an endorsement of the officer's veracity at a critical point in the trial).
4. A person whose presence is determined by the judge to be "in the interest of justice" may be present during others' testimony. This exception would apply, for example, to a case in which a minor child is testifying and the judge determines that it is in the interest of justice for the child's parent or guardian to be in the courtroom even though the parent or guardian may be called subsequently to testify. *See* N.C. R. EVID. 615 Official

Commentary. If the judge relies on this exception, he or she should state the reasons for determining that the presence of the person is in the interest of justice. *Id.* G.S. 15A-1225 also specifically allows (but does not mandate) the presence of the parent or guardian of a minor child who is called as a witness. *See State v. Weaver*, 117 N.C. App. 434, 436 (1994) (finding no error under G.S. 15A-1225 in the exclusion of the mother of two child witnesses from the courtroom; "[t]hat a parent *may* be present while a child is testifying does not mean that such presence is required" (emphasis in original)).

Sequestration not a matter of right but favored. The judge's ruling on a motion to sequester witnesses under either N.C. Rule of Evidence 615 or G.S. 15A-1225 is discretionary and will be reversed only on a showing of abuse of discretion. *See State v. Fullwood*, 323 N.C. 371 (1988), *vacated on other grounds*, 494 U.S. 1022 (1990); *State v. Harrell*, 67 N.C. App. 57 (1984). The Official Commentary to N.C. Rule of Evidence 615 notes that the rule is similar to Federal Rule of Evidence 615; however, the federal rule makes sequestration a matter of right on request. Still, in discussing the difference between the two rules, Judge (now Justice) Edmunds, in a concurring opinion, emphasized the importance of granting sequestration requests:

> Those with experience in state and federal trials cannot fail to have observed the impact of these different rules. Testimony provided by witnesses who hear each other testify often converges. This effect, while not necessarily sinister, appears to be a reflection of human nature; it can lead irresolute witnesses, consciously or not, to conform their testimony to what they have heard before, undermining a jury's ability to evaluate the evidence provided by each witness. Particularly in cases as consequential as the capital murder case at bar, trial courts should be mindful of the words of the Commentary to North Carolina Rule of Evidence 615: "[T]he practice should be to sequester witnesses on request of either party unless some reason exists not to."

State v. Wilds, 133 N.C. App. 195, 209–10 (1999); *see also State v. Anthony*, 354 N.C. 372, 396 (2001) (acknowledging the recommendation of the Official Commentary to N.C. Rule of Evidence 615 that witnesses should ordinarily be sequestered if requested and cautioning judges to give sequestration motions "thoughtful consideration," particularly in capital cases).

Scope of sequestration. G.S. 15A-1225 and N.C. Rule of Evidence 615 provide for the exclusion of witnesses from the courtroom itself. But, the cases indicate that, if requested, the judge may order further that witnesses not interact with each other before trial, outside the courtroom, or during recesses. *See Geders v. United States*, 425 U.S. 80 (1976) (trial judge had broad power to sequester witnesses before, during, and after their testimony); *State v. Stanley*, 310 N.C. 353, 357 (1984) (trial judge's power to control the progress of a trial "has long included the broad power to sequester witnesses before, during, and after their testimony"); *State v. Jackson*, 309 N.C. 26 (1983) (for good reason and at his discretion, the trial judge could have ordered the separation before trial of two inmate-witnesses who were incarcerated in the same cell); *State v. Washington*, 141 N.C. App. 354

(2000) (no error in judge's failure to prohibit two State's witnesses from travelling to court together while under a sequestration order because the order only precluded the witnesses from being present while the other testified in court, and defendant had made no specific request in his written motion to prevent contact outside the courtroom).

Grounds and timing. The sequestration statutes do not require that a motion to exclude witnesses be in writing or that it be made at a certain time. *See State v. Mason*, 295 N.C. 584, 590 (1978) (motions to sequester are not required to be made at or before arraignment under G.S. 15A-952(b), and no law prohibits them from being "made after the jury panel is called into open court and just prior to the State's calling its first witness"). However, when practical, a written motion to sequester should be filed before trial and should set out with specificity the reasons that it should be granted.

Practice note: Some appellate decisions have upheld a trial judge's denial of a motion to sequester when the motion was not timely or defense counsel failed to state specific reasons for believing that the State's witnesses would tailor their testimony to the testimony of previous witnesses. *See, e.g., State v. Conaway*, 339 N.C. 487 (1995) (denial of sequestration motion upheld where defendant had only a general concern that the co-defendant witnesses who were testifying for the State would tailor their testimony because they each had a stake in the outcome of the case); *State v. Pittman*, 332 N.C. 244 (1992) (no abuse of discretion by trial judge in denying defendant's motion for sequestration where defendant gave no reason for suspecting the State's witnesses would tailor their testimony); *State v. Patino*, ___ N.C. App. ___, 699 S.E.2d 678, 682 (2010) (upholding denial of defendant's motion to sequester the State's witnesses where defense counsel did not give specific reasons to suspect that witnesses might tailor their testimony; counsel's assertions that there were a "number" of State's witnesses and "they might have forgotten in the time since the incident occurred" were not "typical reason[s] for sequestering witnesses"); *State v. Lindsey*, 25 N.C. App. 343 (1975) (sequestration motion properly denied where it was made after the State had begun to present its case and defendant gave no explanation for seeking sequestration); *State v. Jones*, 21 N.C. App. 666 (1974) (to same effect).

It may be difficult to articulate specific reasons for suspecting that the State's witnesses will use a previous witness's testimony as their own. To penalize a defendant for not being able to do so, however, appears to conflict with the recommendation of the Official Commentary to N.C. Rule of Evidence 615 that sequestration should be granted liberally "unless some reason exists not to." If you do not have a particular reason to suspect that the State's witnesses will tailor their testimony but still want them sequestered, you should emphasize the purpose of the rule, citing *State v. Anthony*, 354 N.C. 372, 396 (2001) (taking note of the commentary to Rule 615 and cautioning judges, particularly in capital cases, to give such motions "thoughtful consideration"), and *State v. Van Cross*, 293 N.C. 296, 299 (1977) ("It is the general practice in North Carolina in both civil and criminal cases to separate the witnesses and send them out of the hearing of the court when requested . . . .").

For a sample sequestration motion, see the N.C. Office of Indigent Defense Services website, www.ncids.org, under Training & Resources and then Non-Capital Motions Bank (indexed under the Witnesses heading).

Logistical issues in sequestering witnesses. If the logistics of separating witnesses in the courthouse is a problem, a motion to sequester should offer recommendations on how to implement the sequestration order. If no realistic solutions are offered, the trial judge's decision to deny the motion may be upheld on this ground. *See State v. Call*, 349 N.C. 382, 400 (1998) (no abuse of discretion by trial judge in denying defendant's motion to sequester because "the courthouse could not accommodate sequestration of the witnesses"); *see also State v. Bumgarner*, 299 N.C. 113, 117 (1980) (trial judge did not abuse his discretion by denying defendant's sequestration motion "on the grounds that no notice had been given, that there was no reason appearing from the statement of counsel to sequester, and that the number of witnesses involved was too great for the limited area in the courthouse").

Sequestration at pretrial hearings. Although sequestration of witnesses at pretrial hearings is not specifically addressed by statute, the discretionary power of judges to sequester witnesses includes the power to exclude witnesses at proceedings that occur before trial. *See State v. Hyde*, 352 N.C. 37 (2000) (pretrial motions hearing); *State v. Byrd*, 67 N.C. App. 168 (1984) (probable cause hearing); *State v. Trapper*, 48 N.C. App. 481 (1980) (suppression hearing); *State v. Accor*, 13 N.C. App. 10 (1971) (preliminary hearing), *aff'd*, 281 N.C. 287 (1972).

C. Constitutional Considerations

The U.S. Supreme Court has never held that a failure to sequester witnesses can violate a defendant's constitutional right to due process. *Larson v. Palmateer*, 515 F.3d 1057 (9th Cir. 2008) (stating that the decision whether to sequester witnesses at common law was a discretionary one and there is no indication that Fed. R. Evid. 615 has a constitutional basis); *see also Bell v. Duckworth*, 861 F.2d 169 (7th Cir. 1988) (holding that a refusal to separate witnesses until they testify is not a denial of due process). Likewise, the N.C. Court of Appeals has held that "[d]ue process does not automatically require separation of witnesses who are to testify to the same set of facts." *State v. Harrell*, 67 N.C. App. 57, 64 (1984) (finding that although defendant's arguments in favor of sequestration were persuasive, there was no abuse of discretion by the trial judge and there was no violation of defendant's right to due process or his right to confront and cross-examine witnesses).

Even though due process may not "automatically" require sequestration, there may be instances where it is appropriate to argue a constitutional basis in addition to a statutory one. *See, e.g., Commonwealth v. Fant*, 391 A.2d 1040, 1043–44 (Pa. 1978) (holding that the trial judge's denial of defendant's motion to sequester witnesses who identified defendant as the perpetrator of the crimes was an abuse of discretion and led to a denial of due process where the witnesses identified defendant for the first time "in the highly suggestive setting of open court"; the suggestive identification occurred nine months after the alleged murders; the witnesses, depending on when they testified, heard anywhere from one to sixteen other witnesses testify that the defendant was the perpetrator; and neither the prosecutor nor the judge offered any reason for the denial of the motion to sequester); *Commonwealth v. Lavelle*, 419 A.2d 1269 (Pa. Super. Ct. 1980) (applying *Fant* and finding an abuse of discretion and a denial of due process based on the trial judge's failure to sequester witnesses who identified defendant as the perpetrator of the alleged crimes).

D. Response to Violations of Sequestration Orders

Although not specifically addressed by the sequestration statutes, a trial judge has the discretion to impose a variety of sanctions in the event that a witness violates a sequestration order. These include:

- Sanctioning the witness. If a witness intentionally violates a sequestration order, he or she could be held in contempt. *See Holder v. United States*, 150 U.S. 91 (1893). The problem with this sanction is that it does not remedy any unfairness to the parties that may have resulted from the violation. *See Lee v. Thornton*, 174 N.C. 288 (1917).
- Instructing the jury to consider the violation in assessing the credibility of the witness. *See Holder*, 150 U.S. 91.
- Permitting cross-examination of the witness regarding the violation. *See, e.g., State v. Wilson*, 322 N.C. 117 (1988) (where defendant's mother remained in the courtroom during testimony by the State's witnesses, including that of an alleged accomplice, and then testified and directly contradicted that testimony, it was appropriate for the State to impeach her credibility by cross-examining her about her presence during parts of the trial and her knowledge of the existence of the sequestration order).
- Declaring a mistrial. *See, e.g., State v. Howell*, 343 N.C. 229, 237 (1996) (no evidence that the inadvertent violation of a sequestration order by a State's witness "so prejudiced defendant as to render the denial of a mistrial an abuse of discretion").
- Excluding the testimony of the witness who violated the order (*see Holder*, 150 U.S. 91) or striking the testimony once the violation becomes known. *See State v. McGraw*, 137 N.C. App. 726 (2000). Like the declaration of a mistrial, this is a harsh remedy and may be appropriate only when the party offering the testimony (or his or her attorney) is at fault and the opposing party will suffer prejudice if the testimony is not excluded. *See, e.g., United States v. Blasco*, 702 F.2d 1315 (11th Cir. 1983). The exclusion of testimony by a defense witness may be constitutionally limited, as discussed below.

For further discussion of this topic, see J.A. Bock, Annotation, *Effect of Witness' Violation of Order of Exclusion*, 14 A.L.R.3d 16 (1967 & Supp. 2011).

Exclusion of defense witness testimony. If the trial judge excludes the testimony of a material defense witness as a result of a sequestration order violation, "in the absence of connivance by the defendant or counsel (and possibly despite such connivance)," it "may well be an abuse of discretion or a denial of the defendant's constitutional right to present evidence." 1 KENNETH S. BROUN, BRANDIS & BROUN ON NORTH CAROLINA EVIDENCE § 174, at 649 (7th ed. 2011); *see also United States v. Cropp*, 127 F.3d 354, 363 (4th Cir. 1997) (finding that the trial judge who excluded a defense witness's testimony "would have been well advised to employ a lesser sanction to punish the violation because to do so would have preserved both the purpose of the sequestration rule and the defendant's right to present a defense").

Even though the defendant's right to present a defense may be impinged by the exclusion of the testimony of his or her witness, North Carolina appellate courts have upheld decisions by trial judges that have precluded a defense witness from testifying in some circumstances.

See, e.g., *State v. Williamson*, 122 N.C. App. 229 (1996) (no abuse of discretion in excluding the testimony of defendant's girlfriend because she was not on the potential witness list, she had been present in the courtroom for a portion of the State's evidence, she had discussed other testimony with the defendant's sister who had been present for the entire trial, and the defendant was the party who had moved for an order sequestering the witnesses); *State v. Williamson*, 110 N.C. App. 626, 632 (1993) (no abuse of discretion in the exclusion of a defense witness's testimony where he had been present during defendant's testimony in violation of a sequestration order, there was the "distinct possibility of collusive testimony," and it was unlikely that the witness's testimony could have "effectively controverted any of the State's case"); *State v. Sings*, 35 N.C. App. 1 (1978) (where defendant failed to show that his father's excluded testimony would have been material or that he suffered any prejudice as a result of the exclusion, the trial judge's refusal to permit the witness to testify after violating a sequestration order was upheld). *But see State v. Hare*, 74 N.C. 591 (1876) (error to exclude a defense witness from testifying who was not aware of the sequestration order and had come into the courtroom during the examination of a prior witness but did not hear that testimony).

Practice note: If the judge is considering excluding the testimony of your witness because of a sequestration violation, you should argue that exclusion would violate your client's right to present a defense as guaranteed by the Sixth and Fourteenth Amendments to the U.S. Constitution and article I, sections 19 and 23 of the N.C. Constitution. Where appropriate, you should assert that the violation was unintentional, that it occurred without the fault of the defendant or yourself, and that the witness is material to the defense. Also explain how the defense will be prejudiced by the exclusion and make an offer of proof of materiality by asking that the witness be sworn and allowed to testify outside the presence of the jury. If the judge refuses to allow you to make your offer of proof, state with specificity what the witness would have testified to and in what way it would have been material. It is not enough for you simply to tell the judge that the witness's testimony is material. *See State v. Hodge*, 142 N.C. 676 (1906) (no error in the exclusion of a defense witness where counsel asserted that the testimony was material but did not make it known to the judge what that testimony would have been and how it would have been material).

E. Additional Resources

For additional discussion of sequestration of witnesses, see 1 KENNETH S. BROUN, BRANDIS & BROUN ON NORTH CAROLINA EVIDENCE § 174 (7th ed. 2011), and WALKER JAMESON BLAKEY, DEAN P. LOVEN & GLEN WEISSENBERGER, NORTH CAROLINA EVIDENCE: 2011 COURTROOM MANUAL Ch. 615, at 231–33 (2011).

29.4 Competency of Witnesses

This section deals with the competency of witnesses to testify at trial. For a discussion of a defendant's capacity, or competency, to proceed to trial, see 1 NORTH CAROLINA DEFENDER MANUAL Ch. 2 (Capacity to Proceed) (May 1998).

A. General Rule

In order to testify, a witness must be competent. 81 AM. JUR. 2D *Witnesses* § 160 (2004). Before adoption of the N.C. Rules of Evidence, a witness was considered competent if he or she understood the obligations of an oath or affirmation and had sufficient capacity to understand and relate facts that would assist the fact finder. *See State v. Gordon*, 316 N.C. 497, 502 (1986). This standard is comparable to the competency standard under the N.C. Rules of Evidence, which has governed competency determinations since 1984. *Id.* (so noting). The common law imposed a variety of other grounds for disqualifying witnesses from testifying. Most of these disabilities have been removed by the rules of evidence, which allow anyone to be a witness who meets the standard of competency. *See* 1 KENNETH S. BROUN, BRANDIS & BROUN ON NORTH CAROLINA EVIDENCE § 131, at 492–93 (7th ed. 2011).

N.C. Rule of Evidence 601(a) provides that, unless disqualified by the Rules of Evidence, "[e]very person is competent to be a witness." A person is only disqualified as a witness if the person is incapable of (1) expressing himself or herself so as to be understood (either directly or through an interpreter) or (2) understanding the duty of a witness to tell the truth. N.C. R. EVID. 601(b). This rule "does not ask how bright, how young, or how old a witness is." *State v. Davis*, 106 N.C. App. 596, 605 (1992). The only question is: "does the witness have the capacity to understand the difference between telling the truth and lying?" *Id.*; *see also State v. Hicks*, 319 N.C. 84 (1987) (to be found competent, a witness is not required to understand his or her obligation to tell the truth from a religious point of view; it is sufficient if the witness knows the difference between the truth and a lie, has the capacity to understand and relate facts, recognizes the obligation to tell the truth, and expresses the intention to tell the truth).

The competency standards set out in Rule 601(a) and (b) "are very nearly the lowest requirements that it is logically possible to imagine." WALKER JAMESON BLAKEY, DEAN P. LOVEN & GLEN WEISSENBERGER, NORTH CAROLINA EVIDENCE: 2011 COURTROOM MANUAL Ch. 601, at 166 (2011). The witness need only "have some ability to communicate and some understanding of the duty to tell the truth." *Id.*

Whether a person is competent to testify is a decision within the discretion of the trial judge, and his or her determination will not be disturbed on appeal absent a showing of an abuse of discretion. *State v. Gordon*, 316 N.C. 497 (1986).

B. Procedures for Determining Competency

Generally. The trial judge must determine the competency of a witness when the issue is raised by a party or by the circumstances. *State v. Eason*, 328 N.C. 409 (1991). Competency is a preliminary question; therefore, the Rules of Evidence (other than those governing privileges) do not apply. *See* N.C. R. EVID. 104(a); *State v. Fearing*, 315 N.C. 167 (1985) (recognizing applicability of Rule 104 to competency determination). In determining competency, the judge may consider any relevant and reliable information even if that information would not be technically admissible in evidence at trial. *See, e.g., In re Will of*

Leonard, 82 N.C. App. 646 (1986) (proper for trial judge to consider court records of the witness's involuntary commitment proceedings even if they were hearsay and not properly authenticated, identified, or received in evidence at the voir dire hearing).

Burden on party contesting competency. In jurisdictions such as North Carolina where every person is considered competent to testify unless shown otherwise, the party challenging a witness's competence has the burden of establishing incompetence. *See* JOHN E.B. MYERS, MYERS ON EVIDENCE OF INTERPERSONAL VIOLENCE: CHILD MALTREATMENT, INTIMATE PARTNER VIOLENCE, RAPE, STALKING, AND ELDER ABUSE § 2.13[B], at 165 (5th ed. 2011).

Inquiry should be made before witness testifies. No particular procedure is required for determining competency but, if a party objects to a witness testifying based on competency grounds, a voir dire of the witness is typically conducted before he or she testifies. *See Fearing*, 315 N.C. 167; *see also State v. Reynolds*, 93 N.C. App. 552, 556–57 (1989) (stating that the better practice is to determine competency before a witness begins to testify in order to avoid having to strike prejudicial testimony or to grant a mistrial). The trial judge must make sufficient inquiry to satisfy himself or herself that the witness "is or is not competent to testify." *Leonard*, 82 N.C. App. 646, 649. "The form and manner of that inquiry rests in the discretion of the trial judge." *Id.* An adequate inquiry generally includes personal observation of the witness. *Fearing*, 315 N.C. 167. The judge also may hear testimony from witnesses who are familiar with the witness, but such testimony is not required. *See State v. Roberts*, 18 N.C. App. 388 (1973). If the competency of a State's witness is at issue, the defendant should have the opportunity to examine the witness, but the denial of that opportunity may not always violate the defendant's confrontation rights. *See State v. Beane*, 146 N.C. App. 220 (2001) (finding in circumstances of case that the trial judge's decision not to allow defense counsel to cross-examine a child witness at a competency hearing was harmless error and that the defendant's cross-examination of the witness at trial cured any prejudice).

The failure of the trial judge to hold a voir dire hearing or to make findings of fact or conclusions of law in support of his or her decision does not automatically entitle the defendant to a new trial. *See State v. Spaugh*, 321 N.C. 550 (1988); *State v. Huntley*, 104 N.C. App. 732 (1991).

Judge has no authority to order evaluation of witness. There is no statutory authority for a trial judge to order a witness to undergo a psychiatric or psychological evaluation to determine the witness's competency. *See State v. Phillips*, 328 N.C. 1 (1991); *State v. Fletcher*, 322 N.C. 415 (1988).

C. Unavailability Distinguished

The standard of incompetency under N.C. Rule of Evidence 601 is not the same as unavailability under North Carolina's hearsay rules. A person may be found unavailable for the purpose of admitting a hearsay statement by that person if he or she is unable to be present or to testify because of a then existing physical or mental illness or infirmity. *See*

N.C. R. EVID. 804(a)(4). An illness or infirmity does not necessarily mean that a person is incompetent to testify. Only if the person's illness or infirmity renders the person incapable of expressing himself or herself or understanding the obligation to tell the truth will the person be found incompetent to testify. *See In re Faircloth*, 137 N.C. App. 311 (2000) (explaining the difference between competency and unavailability and holding that the trial court erred in relying on the unavailability standard in disqualifying children from testifying). On the other hand, if a person is found incompetent to testify under Rule 601, then he or she also is "unavailable" within the meaning Rule 804. *See In re Clapp*, 137 N.C. App. 14, 20 (2000). Further discussion of this issue as it relates to child witnesses can be found immediately below.

D. Child Witnesses

No set age limit. There is no fixed age under which a person is considered too young to testify. *State v. Eason*, 328 N.C. 409 (1991). Children as young as four years old have been permitted to testify in North Carolina. *See, e.g., State v. Kivett*, 321 N.C. 404, 414 (1988) (no abuse of discretion by the trial judge in finding a four-year-old witness to be competent where the voir dire record revealed that the witness testified that "he knew what it meant to tell the truth, that it was good to tell the truth and not good to tell a lie, that he knew that he was there to tell the truth, and that he was going to tell the truth"); *State v. Robinson*, 310 N.C. 530 (1984) (four-year-old found competent to testify as to events that allegedly occurred when she was three years old even though her answers on voir dire examination were sometimes vague and nonsensical); *State v. Ward*, 118 N.C. App. 389 (1995) (four-year-old found competent and allowed to testify as to offenses that allegedly occurred when she was two years old); *see also Wheeler v. United States*, 159 U.S. 523, 524 (1895) (stating that "[w]hile no one would think of calling as a witness an infant only two or three years old, there is no precise age which determines the question of competency"; competency depends on the capacity and intelligence of the child, his or her appreciation of the difference between truth and falsehood as well as of his or her duty to tell the truth). That a child may have told a lie in the past and is uncertain as to dates and times does not disqualify him or her from being a competent witness. *See State v. Fletcher*, 322 N.C. 415 (1988).

North Carolina cases finding a child incompetent to testify are: *State v. Wagoner*, 131 N.C. App. 285, 286–87 (1998) (four-year-old child found incompetent to testify to events that allegedly occurred when she was two years old because at trial "she could not then remember the events . . . , could not express herself in court, and did not understand the obligation of the oath or the duty to tell the truth"); *State v. Jones*, 89 N.C. App. 584 (1988) (four-year-old alleged victim found incompetent to testify).

Adequate inquiry required. As with determining the competency of any witness, the judge must make adequate inquiry. This generally includes a personal examination or observation of the child on voir dire. *See State v. Fearing*, 315 N.C. 167, 174 (1985) ("[I]n exercising . . . discretion in ruling on the competency of a child witness to testify, a trial judge must rely on his [or her] personal observation of the child's demeanor and responses to inquiry on . . . examination."). A stipulation by the parties as to the competency of a child witness is not sufficient. *Id.* (finding "no informed exercise of discretion" where trial judge merely adopted the stipulations of counsel that a child was not competent to testify); *State v. Pugh*, 138 N.C. App. 60 (2000) (judge disqualified four-year-old from testifying without making adequate inquiry; judge's brief questions were insufficient to determine competency of the witness).

Instead of personally observing the child on voir dire, the judge may choose to observe the child while he or she testifies. *See State v. Spaugh*, 321 N.C. 550 (1988) (court states that primary concern in *Fearing* was that trial judge exercise independent discretion in deciding competency after observation of child and not particular procedure used by trial judge in conducting the observation; trial judge's observation of witness while she testified was adequate without separate voir dire). However, if the judge waits until the child begins testifying and then finds the child incompetent, the child's preceding testimony may need to be stricken and the jury instructed to disregard it. *See generally State v. Reynolds*, 93 N.C. App. 552 (1989) (stating that better practice is to determine competency before witness begins to testify to avoid prejudice); JOHN E.B. MYERS, MYERS ON EVIDENCE IN CHILD, DOMESTIC AND ELDER ABUSE CASES § 2.13[C], at 166–67 (5th ed. 2011) (if during a child's testimony the judge determines that the child is incompetent, the judge may order the child's testimony stricken).

Reconsideration of ruling. The party challenging competency may move for reconsideration if the child was found competent before testifying at trial but then it becomes apparent during the child's trial testimony that he or she is not competent. *See, e.g.*, *State in Interest of R.R.*, 398 A.2d 76 (N.J. 1979) (at close of State's case, defense attorney moved that the four-year-old witness be declared incompetent on basis of actual testimony given by the child).

Exclusion of defendant from competency hearing. Cases have upheld the trial judge's decision to exclude a defendant from the voir dire examination of a child to determine competency; however, exclusion may implicate the defendant's right to confront witnesses and right to be present under the Confrontation Clause of the Sixth Amendment to the U.S. Constitution, the Due Process Clause of the Fourteenth Amendment to the U.S. Constitution, and article I, section 23 of the N.C. Constitution.

In *Kentucky v. Stincer*, 482 U.S. 730 (1987), the U.S. Supreme Court held that the defendant's Confrontation Clause rights were not violated by being excluded from a voir dire hearing to determine a child's competency where the questions asked were unrelated to the basic issues at trial, the judge found the children competent, and the defendant thereafter had the opportunity fully to cross-examine the children at trial. In *State v. Jones*, 89 N.C. App. 584 (1988), the court found no Confrontation Clause violation by the defendant's sequestration in the judge's chambers during the child victim's competency hearing. The court ruled that the defendant had the opportunity for effective cross-examination because he watched the hearing on closed circuit television and was able to hear all the testimony, interact freely with his attorney, and confront the victim through his attorney. Both decisions were issued before the U.S. Supreme Court's decisions in *Maryland v. Craig*, 497 U.S. 836 (1990), which set constitutional limits on remote testimony, and *Crawford v. Washington*, 541 U.S. 36 (2004), which drastically modified Confrontation Clause analysis. For a further discussion of the impact of *Crawford*, including a post-*Crawford* decision by the N.C. Court of Appeals upholding the constitutionality of remote testimony by a child at trial, see *infra* § 29.8A, Constitutional Implications.

Stincer also found no due process violation in the circumstances of the case. In *Stincer*, the U.S. Supreme Court held that exclusion did not violate the defendant's federal constitutional right to presence at all critical stages of a criminal proceeding, finding first that the competency hearing was limited in scope and did not involve substantive testimony that might bear a substantial relationship to the defendant's opportunity to defend himself at trial. The Court noted, however, that if a competency hearing bears a substantial relationship to the defendant's opportunity to defend, the trial judge must balance the defendant's role in assisting his defense and substantial, identifiable injury to the specific child witness. *Stincer*, 482 U.S. at 746 n.20. The Court found next that the defendant provided no indication that his presence at the competency hearing would have been useful in ensuring a more reliable determination of the witness's competency. *Id.* at 747 (finding that the defendant presented "no evidence that his relationship with the children, or his knowledge of facts regarding their background, could have assisted either his counsel or the judge in asking questions that would have resulted in a more assured determination of competency").

Jones found no violation of the defendant's state constitutional right to be present in light of the remote testimony procedures used in that case. The charges were noncapital so the court did not discuss whether exclusion would violate a capital defendant's unwaivable right to presence under the N.C. Constitution. *See* Jessica Smith, *Evidence Issues in Criminal Cases Involving Child Victims and Child Witnesses*, ADMINISTRATION OF JUSTICE BULLETIN No. 2008/07, at 5 (UNC School of Government, Dec. 2008) ("[E]xcluding a defendant from a voir dire presents a special problem in a capital case, given the capital defendant's unwaivable right to be present at all stages of a capital trial."), *available at* http://sogpubs.unc.edu/electronicversions/pdfs/aojb0807.pdf.

For a further discussion of testimony by children outside the defendant's presence during trial, see *infra* § 29.8, Remote Testimony. For a further discussion of a defendant's right to presence, see *supra* § 21.1, Right to Be Present.

Incompetent child is "unavailable." As with any other witness, if a child witness is found incompetent, he or she would be considered unavailable to testify for purposes of the hearsay rules. *See In re Clapp*, 137 N.C. App. 14, 20 (2000). Whether the child's out-of-court statements would be admissible would depend on whether their admission would violate the defendant's right to confrontation (*see Crawford v. Washington*, 541 U.S. 36 (2004)), and whether the statements satisfy the requirements for admission of hearsay. *Compare State v. Wagoner*, 131 N.C. App. 285 (1998) (child's incompetence to testify satisfied unavailability requirement but did not render out-of-court statements too untrustworthy to be admitted under residual hearsay exception), *with State v. Stutts*, 105 N.C. App. 557 (1992) (court found child unavailable as witness on ground that child could not tell truth from fantasy and ruled that child's statements were inadmissible under residual hearsay exception).

Appellate review of competency. Appellate decisions have generally upheld a trial judge's finding that a child witness was competent to testify. *See State v. Fearing*, 315 N.C. 167, 172–73 (1985) ("By far, the vast majority of cases in which a child witness's competency has been addressed have resulted in the finding, pursuant to an informal *voir dire* examination of the child before the trial judge, that the child was competent to testify.").

Additional resources. For a discussion of issues involving children as witnesses, including competency and examination issues, see Jessica Smith, *Evidence Issues in Criminal Cases Involving Child Victims and Child Witnesses*, ADMINISTRATION OF JUSTICE BULLETIN No. 2008/07 (UNC School of Government, Dec. 2008), *available at* http://sogpubs.unc.edu/electronicversions/pdfs/aojb0807.pdf; KELLA W. HATCHER, JANET MASON & JOHN RUBIN, ABUSE, NEGLECT, DEPENDENCY, AND TERMINATION OF PARENTAL RIGHTS PROCEEDINGS IN NORTH CAROLINA Ch. 11 (UNC School of Government, 2011), *available at* www.sog.unc.edu/sites/www.sog.unc.edu/files/Evidence_Chapter11.pdf.

E. Common Competency Issues

Elderly witnesses. Witnesses are not automatically disqualified from testifying due to their advanced age. As long as they meet the qualifications of Rule 601, they are competent to testify. *See State v. Forte*, ___ N.C. App. ___, 698 S.E.2d 745, 752 (2010) (no abuse of discretion by trial judge in finding the prosecuting witness who was 88 or 98 years old to be competent because "at certain points in his testimony" he showed an understanding of the difference between truth and falsehood and the importance of the truth; that some of his answers were vague and ambiguous and that he was unable to answer some questions was not determinative because "it would not be unusual for an elderly individual to have some difficulty in responding coherently to all of the questions asked during *voir dire*").

Hearing and speech impaired witnesses. People who cannot hear or speak are not incompetent as witnesses merely because of their disability. *State v. Galloway*, 304 N.C. 485 (1981). If the impaired person is capable of expressing himself or herself concerning the matter in a way that can be understood, and is capable of understanding the duty of a witness to tell the truth, the person is competent to testify. *See* N.C. EVID. R. 601(b). Testimony presented through an interpreter utilizing American Sign Language is "proper in every respect" and "[a]ny confusion arising from the use of sign language to communicate with a deaf and [mute] witness goes to the weight, and not the admissibility, of the evidence." *Galloway*, 304 N.C. 485, 494; *cf. State v. Felton*, 330 N.C. 619 (1992) (although defendant's girlfriend had no formal training in sign language, sufficient evidence established her as a competent witness capable of understanding and recounting the deaf mute defendant's communications to her).

Mentally or physically disabled witnesses. A person who is mentally or physically disabled is not disqualified from testifying merely because of the disability. As long as the disability does not cause the witness to be incapable of expressing himself or herself in a way that can be understood, or incapable of understanding the duty of a witness to tell the truth, the person is competent to testify. *See State v. Oliver*, 85 N.C. App. 1 (1987) (no abuse of discretion by trial judge in finding a 16-year-old witness competent even though she was mentally retarded, functioned at an 8-year-old level, and was unable to answer some questions); *see also State v. Hyatt*, 355 N.C. 642 (2002) (no abuse of discretion in finding witness competent even though witness suffered from viral encephalitis, a disease affecting his speech, and he had to repeat himself many times so the court reporter could understand him); *State v. DeLeonardo*, 315 N.C. 762, 767 (1986) (mildly mentally retarded witness was properly not disqualified as a witness even though his I.Q. was between 55 and 64; his answers to voir dire questions demonstrated that he had "a sufficient level of intelligence to express himself concerning the matter involved" and "an understanding of the importance of telling the truth"); *State v. Davis*, 106 N.C. App. 596 (1992) ("intellectually limited" children were competent where they testified that they knew the difference between truth and falsehood and they swore to tell the truth). *But see State v. Washington*, 131 N.C. App. 156 (1998) (where mentally retarded witness with cerebral palsy was incapable of effectively communicating at trial because of her disabilities and her inability to speak in a manner that was easily understood, trial judge did not abuse his discretion in ruling that she was incompetent to testify).

Mentally ill witnesses. "[U]nsoundness of mind is not *per se* grounds for ruling a witness incompetent under Rule 601." *In re Will of Leonard*, 82 N.C. App. 646, 649–50 (1986); *see also DeLeonardo*, 315 N.C. 762, 766 (the general rule is that "a lunatic or weak-minded person" may testify if he or she has sufficient understanding to apprehend the obligation of an oath and is capable of giving a correct account of the matters that he or she has seen or heard with respect to the questions at issue) (citing *State v. Benton*, 276 N.C. 641, 650 (1970), decided before enactment of the rules of evidence)).

Unless a person who is suffering from a mental illness meets the standards for disqualification of a witness set out in Rule 601(b), he or she is competent to testify. *See State v. Liles*, 324 N.C. 529 (1989) (trial judge properly found witness with a past history of mental illness to be competent where finding was based on the judge's personal observation and on a report by Dorothea Dix Hospital that the witness had the capacity to proceed as a defendant); *State v. Liner*, 98 N.C. App. 600, 607 (1990) (even though the witness was paranoid schizophrenic and a "walking drug store," trial judge properly found him competent to testify based on the evidence presented during voir dire and on judge's "opportunity to view the witness and listen to his answers to the questions"). *But see Leonard*, 82 N.C. App. 646 (trial judge properly found witness to be incompetent, not based solely on the witness's diagnosis of schizophrenia, but on personal observation and on the witness's answers to voir dire questions in which she denied ever having been involuntarily committed even though court records directly contradicted that testimony).

Use of drugs or alcohol. A witness is not incompetent to testify on the basis of drug or alcohol abuse alone. The use of impairing substances is only relevant insofar as it affects the user's ability to be understood or to respect the importance of veracity. *See State v. Fields*, 315 N.C. 191, 203 (1985) (that witnesses were abusers of alcohol and hallucinogenic and psychotropic drugs and were actually impaired on the night in question did not render them "inherently incredible" so as to be incompetent to testify); *State v. Edwards*, 37 N.C. App. 47 (1978) (no abuse of discretion in ruling that accomplice was competent to testify where there was no evidence that the witness was under the influence of drugs at the time of testifying nor was there any showing that he was unable to see or remember the events to which he testified).

Credibility distinguished. Where mental instability or drug or alcohol use is concerned, the question is more properly one of the witness's credibility, not his or her competence. *See Fields*, 315 N.C. 191; *State v. Williams*, 330 N.C. 711 (1992). "As such, it is in the jury's province to weigh his [or her] evidence, not in the court's to bar it." *Fields*, 315 N.C. at 204. A witness with a mental impairment or substance abuse problem may be cross-examined about that matter if it affects his or her ability to observe, remember, or narrate. *See State v. Newman*, 308 N.C. 231 (1983). Past mental problems, including chronic substance abuse, likewise may be a proper subject of cross-examination if they bear on the credibility of the witness's testimony about the relevant events in the case. *Williams*, 330 N.C. 711 (evidence of a key witness's past drug use, his suicide attempts, and his psychiatric history was proper and admissible for purposes of impeachment under Rule 611).

If a proper subject of impeachment, extrinsic evidence—that is, testimony of other witnesses as well as supporting documentation—may be used to impeach the witness's credibility. *Id.* at 719 (noting that "while specific instances of drug use or mental instability are not directly probative of truthfulness," if they cast doubt on the capacity of a witness to observe, recollect, and recount, they are properly the subject not only of cross-examination but of extrinsic evidence as well (quoting 3 DAVID LOUISELL & CHRISTOPHER B. MUELLER, FEDERAL EVIDENCE § 305, at 236 (1979)).

Practice note: If a witness has been impeached based on his or her mental illness or substance abuse, you should consider whether a jury instruction regarding the credibility of that witness would be helpful. If you decide that one would be helpful, you should draft one based on the specific impairments of that witness and submit it in writing to the trial judge at or before the charge conference. Since this is a subordinate feature of a case, the trial judge is not required to instruct on it unless a specific request has been made. For a discussion of instructions on subordinate features of the case, see *infra* § 32.3, Explanation of the Law.

Additional resources. For a further discussion of impeachment of witnesses based on mental or physical impairments, see 1 KENNETH S. BROUN, BRANDIS & BROUN ON NORTH CAROLINA EVIDENCE § 156 (7th ed. 2011).

F. Preservation of Competency Issues for Appellate Review

Objection required to finding of competency. If the defendant fails to object to a judge's ruling that a witness is competent, he or she waives the right to appellate review of the issue. *See State v. Gordon*, 316 N.C. 497 (1986). If the defendant objects to the trial judge's finding of competency, he or she may assert as error on appeal the subsequent admission of evidence from that witness even though the defendant did not object to or move to strike the testimony on the ground of incompetency at the time the testimony was offered at trial. G.S. 15A-1446(d)(9). If there are other grounds for objection to the testimony (e.g., hearsay), counsel must make a specific objection on that additional ground when the objectionable question is asked to preserve the issue for appeal.

Practice note: If you believe that the trial judge erroneously found a witness to be competent to testify, always object on the record to the judge's finding, whether the judge explicitly finds the witness competent or implicitly so finds by allowing the witness to testify. *See Gordon*, 316 N.C. 497 (after voir dire hearing on a witness's competency, trial judge's action in allowing witness to testify was an implicit ruling of competency and defendant was required to object in order to preserve the issue for appellate review).

Offer of proof required if finding of incompetency. If a judge finds that a witness is incompetent to testify, the party seeking to call the witness must make an offer of proof in order to preserve the issue for appellate review. *See, e.g., In re M.G.T.-B.*, 177 N.C. App. 771 (2006) (based on telephone conversation with child's therapist and without observing or examining child, trial judge found child incompetent and quashed subpoena for child; appellate court declined to address propriety of trial judge's determination of incompetency, finding that respondent made no offer of proof and therefore failed to preserve for appellate review the exclusion of the child's testimony).

G. Additional Resources

For additional information on the competency of witnesses, see 1 KENNETH S. BROUN, BRANDIS & BROUN ON NORTH CAROLINA EVIDENCE §§ 131–135 (7th ed. 2011) (also includes discussion of the competency of an accused and of spouses), and WALKER JAMESON BLAKEY, DEAN P. LOVEN & GLEN WEISSENBERGER, NORTH CAROLINA EVIDENCE: 2011 COURTROOM MANUAL Ch. 601, at 165–71 (2011) (listing additional authorities and collecting cases).

29.5 Presentation of the Evidence

A. Order of Proceedings

The order in which a criminal jury trial proceeds is governed by G.S. 15A-1221. After a jury is empanelled and an opportunity for opening statements is given, the State must present evidence of the defendant's guilt, that is, its "case-in-chief." *See* G.S. 15A-1221(a)(5). The State goes first because it has the burden of proof. *See State v. Temple*, 302 N.C. 1 (1981) (party with the burden of proof generally is the first to put on evidence).

After the State has rested, the defendant, if he or she desires, may present evidence, that is, his or her "case-in-chief." *See* G.S. 15A-1221(a)(6); *see also State v. Fair*, 354 N.C. 131, 149 (2001) ("The right to present evidence in one's own defense is protected under both the United States and North Carolina Constitutions.").

Thereafter, the State and the defendant may offer successive rebuttals concerning matters elicited in the evidence in chief of the other party. *See* G.S. 15A-1221(a)(7); G.S. 15A-1226. The defendant's rebuttal evidence is sometimes referred to as "surrebuttal."

G.S. 15A-1221 sets the usual order of presentation of evidence, but the Official

Commentary to this section notes that this "does not preclude a differing order if authorized by the common law or other applicable statutes or rules of court." *See also* N.C. R. EVID. 611(a) ("The court shall exercise reasonable control over the mode and order of interrogating witnesses and presenting evidence so as to . . . make the interrogation and presentation effective for the ascertainment of the truth . . . ."). For example, in *State v. Britt*, 291 N.C. 528 (1977), the court found no gross abuse of discretion by the trial judge in varying the order of proof by allowing the State's witnesses to testify as rebuttal witnesses when their testimony did not rebut the defendant's evidence but would have been admissible during the State's case-in-chief.

B. Rebuttal

Statutory authorization. The introduction of rebuttal evidence is governed by G.S. 15A-1226(a), which provides:

> Each party has the right to introduce rebuttal evidence concerning matters elicited in the evidence in chief of another party. The judge may permit a party to offer new evidence during rebuttal which could have been offered in the party's case in chief or during a previous rebuttal, but if new evidence is allowed, the other party must be permitted further rebuttal.

Scope of State's rebuttal. During the State's rebuttal of the defendant's evidence (if presented), it may offer evidence "to impeach defendant's witnesses or to explain, modify or contradict defendant's evidence." 1 KENNETH S. BROUN, BRANDIS & BROUN ON NORTH CAROLINA EVIDENCE § 166, at 598 (7th ed. 2011); *see also State v. Anthony*, 354 N.C. 372 (2001) (questions posed by prosecutor to rebuttal witnesses were properly formulated to rebut matters presented during defendant's case-in-chief and as such did not exceed the scope of rebuttal).

Scope of defendant's surrebuttal. After the State presents its rebuttal evidence, the defense then may be entitled to offer evidence on surrebuttal. "[I]n determining whether a defendant is entitled to present surrebuttal evidence, the dispositive issue is whether the state presented new evidence on rebuttal." *State v. Clark*, 128 N.C. App. 87, 98 (1997) (defendant had no right to surrebuttal where the State's rebuttal witness presented no new evidence regarding the State's version of the case); *see also State v. Yancy*, 58 N.C. App. 52 (1982) (defendant did not have the right to put on surrebuttal evidence where the State's evidence on rebuttal did not add primarily to its original case but only impeached the defendant's testimony and corroborated the earlier testimony of a State's witness).

Admission of new evidence during rebuttal or surrebuttal. Although the scope of rebuttal and surrebuttal is generally limited, G.S. 15A-1226(a) allows a trial judge, in his or her discretion, to permit a party to offer new evidence during rebuttal that could have been offered during the party's case-in-chief. *See Anthony*, 354 N.C. 372; *see also State v. Lowery*, 318 N.C. 54 (1986) (double jeopardy principles are not applicable at the rebuttal phase of a trial, and due process rights are not violated when the State is allowed to introduce new evidence during the rebuttal phase as long as the defendant is given the opportunity to rebut the new evidence offered by the State); *State v. Boykin*, 298 N.C. 687 (1979) (State's witness properly allowed to testify as to new evidence during rebuttal; order of proof is within the trial judge's discretion).

If the judge allows the introduction of new evidence during the rebuttal phase, the other party must be permitted further rebuttal. G.S. 15A-1226(a); *see also State v. Quick*, 323 N.C. 675 (1989); *Clark*, 128 N.C. App. 87.

Practice note: If the State presents new evidence during its rebuttal, object on the grounds that the evidence exceeds the scope of rebuttal. If the judge exercises his or her discretion and allows the testimony, you are entitled to further rebuttal. Assert in support of further rebuttal the defendant's statutory rights under G.S 15A-1226(a) and his or her due process rights to present a defense under the state and federal constitutions. If the judge denies further rebuttal, be sure to put the statutory and constitutional grounds for your request on the record and make an offer of proof of the evidence you intended to present.

C. Reopening the Case to Present Additional Evidence

Statutory authority. G.S. 15A-1226(b) authorizes a trial judge, in his or her discretion, to permit any party to introduce additional evidence at any time before verdict. *See also State v. Quick*, 323 N.C. 675, 681 (1989). Under this statute, a judge may allow a party to reopen its case to present new evidence at any stage of the trial, even after the jury has begun its deliberations. *See State v. Riggins*, 321 N.C. 107 (1987); *State v. Goldman*, 311 N.C. 338 (1984); *State v. Allen*, 19 N.C. App. 660 (1973). Once the verdict has been entered, however, the trial judge does not have the discretion to allow a party to reopen its case to introduce additional evidence. *State v. Murray*, 154 N.C. App. 631, 637 (2002) ("[T]he applicable statute and case law are clear that any additional evidence must be introduced prior to entry of the verdict.").

Essential elements of the crime. It appears that the trial judge has the discretionary authority to allow the State to reopen its evidence to introduce evidence of an essential element of the crime charged that was omitted during its case-in-chief. *See State v. Wise*, 178 N.C. App. 154 (2006) (no abuse of discretion by trial judge in allowing State to reopen its case to produce evidence of defendant's release date from prison to show defendant was required to register as a sex offender under G.S. 14-208.11); *see also State v. Miles*, 193 N.C. App. 611 (2008) (unpublished) (finding no abuse of discretion by trial judge in allowing "the State to reopen its case for the purpose of showing ownership of the property alleged to have been stolen"; court rejected defendant's argument that if allowed to reopen its case, the State is limited to introducing additional evidence that "clears up a misunderstanding or corroborates evidence already presented" and may not introduce evidence that is used to establish an element of the offense).

Significant factors. While the appellate courts of North Carolina have not specifically described the factors that are significant in ruling on a party's motion to reopen the evidence, other jurisdictions have. Factors that have been considered important by the

Fourth Circuit Court of Appeals in reviewing rulings on motions to reopen include:

1. whether the party moving to reopen provided a reasonable explanation for failing to present the evidence in its case-in-chief;
2. whether the evidence was relevant, admissible, or helpful to the jury; and
3. whether reopening the case would have infused the evidence with distorted importance, prejudiced the opposing party's case, or precluded the opposing party from meeting the evidence.

See United States v. Abbas, 74 F.3d 506, 510–11 (4th Cir. 1996); *see also United States v. Crawford*, 533 F.3d 133 (2d Cir. 2008) (expressing approval of 4th Circuit's approach and finding that the trial judge erred in reopening the evidence during jury deliberations to allow the government to introduce a trace report); *People v. Newton*, 87 Cal. Rptr. 394, 409–10 (Cal. Ct. App. 1970) (factors to consider in reviewing decisions on motions to reopen include the stage of the proceedings that had been reached when the motion was made, the diligence shown by the moving party in discovering the new evidence, the prospect that the jury would accord the evidence undue emphasis, and the significance of the evidence).

Illustrative cases. A review of North Carolina cases that address rulings on motions to reopen reveals that our appellate courts implicitly consider factors similar to the ones described above. For example, the granting of a motion to reopen was upheld in the following cases:

- The State did not know of the evidence before the parties rested their cases, the timing of the introduction did not appear to be prejudicial to the defendants, and the defendants were not denied the opportunity to offer testimony in rebuttal if they had so desired. *State v. Perry*, 231 N.C. 467 (1950).
- The judge allowed the State, after resting its case but before the defendant presented evidence, to introduce stipulated evidence concerning the results of a medical examination of the rape victim because the defendant could not have been surprised by its admission. *State v. Revelle*, 301 N.C. 153 (1980).
- The additional evidence was presented in response to a question by the jury regarding the date of a pretrial identification procedure; the defendant did not object to the State's recalling of the officer to the stand; and the question concerned an incidental aspect of the case and did not involve a necessary element or feature of the State's case-in-chief or that of the defendant. *State v. Riggins*, 321 N.C. 107, 109 (1987); *see also State v. Jackson*, 306 N.C. 642, 645 (1982) (finding that trial judge's ruling allowing State to reopen its case was not prejudicial to defendant because evidence did not relate to essential element of the case).

The denial of a motion to reopen was upheld in the following cases:

- The party seeking to reopen the case was at fault. *See, e.g., State v. Davis*, 317 N.C. 315 (1986) (no abuse of discretion in denying defendant's motion to reopen to allow the playing of a tape recording made after defendant rested his case where defense counsel had more than adequate opportunity to timely produce equipment to play the tape and substantially the same evidence was presented to the jury through a transcription); *State v. Mutakbbic*, 317 N.C. 264 (1986) (defendant's motion to reopen during jury deliberations in order to admit a DSS report properly denied where defendant knew about the report and chose not to introduce it during trial); *State v. Perkins*, 57 N.C. App. 516 (1982) (defendant's motion to reopen after judge had concluded his charge to the jury because the defendant decided he wanted to testify was properly denied because defendant had the opportunity to present evidence and could have testified then); *see also United States v. Bayer*, 331 U.S. 532 (1947) (no reversible error for judge to refuse defendants' request to reopen their case after four hours of jury deliberations to admit corroborating evidence where no excuse was offered for the untimeliness of the offer of the evidence, the existence and importance of which should have been well-known to defendants, and the evidence was easily obtainable before trial).

- The evidence was merely cumulative. *See, e.g., State v. Hoover*, 174 N.C. App. 596 (2005) (no abuse of discretion in refusing to allow defendant to reopen his case to admit testimony from a witness about driving defendant to and from work because testimony about defendant's work schedule had already been admitted); *State v. Phillips*, 171 N.C. App. 622 (2005) (defense counsel was not dilatory in immediately moving to reopen to introduce newly discovered evidence, but no abuse of discretion in denial of motion because the evidence would have been merely cumulative of other evidence that had already been presented by defendant).

Special consideration of defendant's motion to reopen. If a trial judge denies a defendant's motion to reopen to present evidence that is crucial to his or her defense, the appellate courts may find an abuse of discretion. *See, e.g., State v. Allen*, 19 N.C. App. 660, 662–63 (1973) (trial judge abused discretion in denying defendant's motion to reopen to present an alibi witness's testimony that was newly discovered after jury deliberations had begun where the possibility of mistaken identification was obviously present under the identification procedures followed in the case); *see also State v. Lang*, 301 N.C. 508, 511–12 (1980) (although ruling on other grounds, court noted its "particular concern" about the trial judge's denial of defendant's motion to reopen to present a time card because the time card corroborated the "crucial testimony" of defendant's alibi witness).

Although not discussed in either of the above cases, there were also constitutional implications in the denial of the motions. The rights of a defendant charged with a crime to make a defense by confronting the evidence against him or her, presenting his or her own witnesses, and placing before the jury his or her own version of the facts are fundamental elements of due process of law as guaranteed by the Sixth and Fourteenth Amendments to the federal constitution and by article I, sections 19 and 23 of the state constitution. *See, e.g., Faretta v. California*, 422 U.S. 806 (1975); *Washington v. Texas*, 388 U.S. 14 (1967); *State v. Locklear*, 309 N.C. 428 (1983). These constitutional grounds may apply to a motion to reopen along with the statutory grounds authorized by G.S. 15A-1226. *See State v. Carter*, 636 A.2d 821 (Conn. 1994) (trial judge abused his discretion in a murder case when he denied defendant's motion to reopen to introduce the victim's criminal record to show the victim's character for violence; the exclusion deprived defendant of his Sixth Amendment right to present his version of the facts, including his defense of self-defense; error not harmless beyond a reasonable doubt because the evidence was highly relevant and might well have influenced the jury's decision); *see also Blaikie v. Callahan*, 691 F.2d 64, 68 (1st Cir. 1982) (for a trial judge's adverse ruling on a defendant's motion to reopen to violate the Sixth Amendment "it must be shown that the proffered evidence was of such importance to the achievement of a just result that the need for admitting it overrides the presumption favoring enforcement of the state's usual trial procedures").

Although there are North Carolina cases stating that "there is no constitutional right to have one's case reopened" (*State v. Hoover*, 174 N.C. App. 596, 599 (2005); *see also State v. Perkins*, 57 N.C. App. 516, 520 (1982)), this is not exactly true. *Hoover* and *Perkins* both cite *State v. Shelton*, 53 N.C. App. 632 (1981), as support for the above assertion; however, *Shelton* did not hold that a constitutional right could *never* be the basis of a motion to reopen. In *Shelton*, the defendant argued that the trial judge's denial of his motion to reopen to present the testimony of a co-defendant who had pled guilty mid-trial violated his state and federal constitutional rights to due process and to fairly present one's evidence. The Court of Appeals held that "*under the facts and circumstances of this particular case*," the defendant did not have a constitutional right to have his case reopened. *Id.* at 647 (emphasis added). The court reasoned that the defendant had "ample opportunity" to present evidence in his defense and the witness in question had been available and could have been called as a witness at any time before the defendant rested.

Practice note: If you move to reopen the evidence pursuant to G.S 15A-1226(b) because you mistakenly failed to introduce evidence or you discovered new evidence that was unavailable before resting your case, you should be prepared to offer an explanation for the untimeliness of the evidence. Tell the judge exactly what the evidence entails, why it is admissible, and the reasons why it is material or significant to the defendant's case. Also explain why the reopening of the evidence will not unduly delay the trial and why the State will not be unduly prejudiced by its late admission. Cite both the statutory and constitutional grounds for your motion, discussed above. If your motion is denied, make an offer of proof so that the denial of your motion can be properly reviewed on appeal.

If the State moves to reopen to introduce further evidence, object and assert (where applicable) that

- the State's failure to offer the evidence earlier was the result of a lack of due diligence;
- the evidence is merely cumulative;
- the evidence unfairly surprised the defendant; and
- due to the timing of the offer, the jury may give the evidence undue weight.

Base your objection on statutory grounds and, if the admission of the additional evidence would violate the defendant's constitutional rights to due process and to confront witnesses, state that those bases as well. *Cf. United States v. Nunez*, 432 F.3d 573, 580–81 (4th Cir. 2005) (finding an abuse of discretion based on Confrontation Clause concerns where trial judge allowed the government to reopen its case and (1) the government offered no "reasonable explanation" for its failure to timely introduce the report in question; (2) the defendants were not permitted to cross-examine witnesses about the report; and (3) the late introduction "infused the evidence with distorted importance," prejudiced the defendants' case, and denied them a fair opportunity to respond).

Right to present additional evidence if State is permitted to reopen its case. If the judge grants the State's motion to reopen its case, a judge's refusal to grant the defendant's request to present additional evidence in response may be reversible error. *See State v. Thompson*, 19 N.C. App. 693, 696 (1973) (stating that the judge's refusal to allow defendant to present material evidence in rebuttal after State was allowed to reopen its case to present further testimony "cannot be considered harmless error"); *see also United States v. Peay*, 972 F.2d 71 (4th Cir. 1992) (trial judge committed reversible error by allowing government to reopen its case to present new testimony of a witness who had testified for the defense while denying defendant the opportunity to impeach the witness with testimony of a new witness). If permission to offer further evidence is denied, the defendant must make an offer of proof to preserve the issue for appellate review.

Effect of sequestration orders on request to reopen. The trial judge has the discretion to grant a motion to reopen a party's evidence to recall a witness even if a sequestration order was in effect during the trial and that witness remained in the courtroom after his or her initial testimony. *See State v. Noblett*, 47 N.C. 418 (1855) (finding that a judge has the discretion to permit witnesses who already have been examined to be called again at any time before a verdict is rendered even though the witnesses had been sequestered before their first examination and had since had an opportunity to speak with each other).

Practice note: If the State is allowed to reopen its case to recall a witness who was originally subject to a sequestration order and who remained in the courtroom after testifying, you should consider requesting an instruction to the jury that the witness's presence in the courtroom during the testimony of other witnesses can be considered by the jury in determining his or her credibility. *See Gresham v. State*, 420 S.E.2d 71 (Ga. Ct. App. 1992).

29.6 Witness Examination

This section discusses the legal principles governing direct and cross examinations. It does not address how to fashion and deliver an effective direct or cross. There are many good practical guides on these advocacy skills. *See, e.g.*, STEVEN LUBET, MODERN TRIAL ADVOCACY: ANALYSIS AND PRACTICE (4th ed. 2009). The website of the N.C. Office of Indigent Defense Services also has a collection of materials on direct and cross-examination by various authors, which may be accessed at www.ncids.org. Highlight "Training & Resources" and click on the "Training Materials" link and then on "Training Materials—Indexed by Subject." The materials are located under the topic "Trial Practice." For additional considerations and recommendations with respect to preparing for direct and cross-examination, see *infra* Appendix A, N.C. COMM'N ON INDIGENT DEFENSE SERVS., PERFORMANCE GUIDELINES FOR INDIGENT DEFENSE REPRESENTATION

IN NON-CAPITAL CRIMINAL CASES AT THE TRIAL LEVEL, Guideline 7.5 Confronting the Prosecution's Case and Guideline 7.6 Presenting the Defense Case (Nov. 2004).

A. General Limits

The parties have considerable latitude in examining witnesses, but the trial judge has the ultimate authority to control the examination and cross-examination of witnesses. Pursuant to N.C. Rule of Evidence 611(a), the judge may exercise reasonable control over the mode and order of interrogating witnesses and presenting evidence so as to

1. make the interrogation and presentation effective for the ascertainment of the truth;
2. avoid needless consumption of time; and
3. protect witnesses from harassment or undue embarrassment.

See also State v. Fleming, 350 N.C. 109 (1999); *State v. Satterfield*, 300 N.C. 621 (1980); *State v. Arnold*, 284 N.C. 41 (1973).

In North Carolina, the examination of witnesses must be conducted from a seated position behind counsel table. If counsel wishes to approach the witness in order to present, inquire about, or examine him or her about an exhibit, document, or diagram, counsel must request permission from the trial judge. *See* N.C. GEN. R. PRAC. SUPER. & DIST. CT. 12; *see also State v. Bass*, 5 N.C. App. 429 (1969).

B. Direct Examination

Although sometimes paid less attention by defense counsel than other aspects of the case, direct examination is an important part of the entire trial process. Direct examination can be "a powerful tool . . . to tell the jury a compelling and convincing story, to convey to the jury the utter trustworthiness of the witness and the advocate, and to severely limit and frustrate the ability of the opposing party to cross-examine the witness." H. Mitchell Caldwell et al., *Primacy, Recency, Ethos, and Pathos: Integrating Principles of Communication into the Direct Examination*, 76 NOTRE DAME L. REV. 423, 516 (2001).

Scope and form. The scope of direct examination is limited only by relevancy. The use of open-ended questions is generally advised, and leading questions are usually prohibited. *See* N.C. R. EVID. 611(c) ("Leading questions should not be used on the direct examination of a witness except as may be necessary to develop his testimony."). Leading questions are disapproved on direct examination because the witness usually favors the calling party's case, and he or she "may readily accede to the version of the events stated in the examiner's question rather than describing the [events] as he or she actually remembers" them. WALKER JAMESON BLAKEY, DEAN P. LOVEN & GLEN WEISSENBERGER, NORTH CAROLINA EVIDENCE: 2011 COURTROOM MANUAL Ch. 611, at 210 (2011). For a detailed discussion of the use of leading questions on direct and cross-examination, see *infra* § 29.6F, Leading Questions During Direct or Cross-Examination.

C. Redirect Examination

Purpose and scope. Redirect examination of a witness after cross-examination is much narrower in scope than direct examination. The general purpose of redirect examination is "to clarify testimony which has been cast into doubt upon cross-examination, to clarify new matter brought out on cross-examination or to refute testimony elicited on cross-examination." *State v. Franks*, 300 N.C. 1, 12 (1980); *State v. Davis*, 68 N.C. App. 238, 242 (1984) (quoting *Franks*); *see also State v. Calloway*, 305 N.C. 747, 755 (1982) (noting that "after a witness has been cross-examined the party calling him may reexamine the witness so as to clarify the new matter elicited on cross-examination").

Counsel may not use redirect examination to introduce new matters (*State v. Weeks*, 322 N.C. 152 (1988)), or to have the witness merely repeat testimony from his or her direct examination. *State v. Stitt*, 147 N.C. App. 77 (2001). However, the trial judge has the discretion to expand the scope of redirect examination to allow testimony that exceeds the scope of direct and cross-examination as long as the testimony is relevant and otherwise admissible. *See State v. Barton*, 335 N.C. 696 (1994); *Davis*, 68 N.C. App. 238; *see also* N.C. R. EVID. 611(a).

Practice note: If the State is permitted to introduce new matters during redirect examination of a witness, you are entitled to recross-examine the witness about those matters. *See infra* § 29.6E, Recross Examination. If you are surprised by the new matters and need additional time to prepare for recross-examination, you should request a recess or continuance.

Opening the door. If a witness is impeached on cross-examination, the witness may be allowed to explain or clarify the matter on redirect examination even though the testimony would not have been admissible during the calling party's case-in-chief. *See, e.g., State v. Johnson*, 344 N.C. 596, 606 (1996) (victim's girlfriend permitted to testify on redirect regarding the victim's character for peacefulness where defendant opened the door to this line of testimony on cross-examination by suggesting that the victim was "looking for a fight" on the night he was killed); *State v. Patterson*, 284 N.C. 190 (1973) (murder victim's daughter properly allowed to testify on redirect that one of the reasons she did not like defendant was that he had raped her; defendant had asked the witness on cross-examination about her dislike of defendant and her ill will against him); *see also* 1 KENNETH S. BROUN, BRANDIS & BROUN ON NORTH CAROLINA EVIDENCE § 171, at 632 n.606 (7th ed. 2011) (collecting cases).

D. Cross-Examination

Generally. "Cross-examination is the principal means by which the believability of a witness and the truth of his testimony are tested." *Davis v. Alaska*, 415 U.S. 308, 316 (1974). It has been described as the "'greatest legal engine ever invented for the discovery of truth.'" *California v. Green*, 399 U.S. 149, 158 (1970) (citation omitted). It is also "'[o]ne of the most jealously guarded rights in the administration of justice.'" *State v. Harrill*, 289 N.C. 186, 191 (1976) (quoting 1 STANSBURY'S NORTH CAROLINA EVIDENCE § 35, at 100 (Brandis Rev. 1973)), *vacated in part on other grounds*, 428 U.S. 904 (1976); *Barnes v. N.C. State*

Highway Comm'n, 250 N.C. 378, 394 (1959) (citation omitted). "The right to have an opportunity for a fair and full cross-examination of a witness upon every phase of his examination in chief, is an absolute right and not a mere privilege." *Riverview Milling Co. v. State Highway Comm'n*, 190 N.C. 692, 696 (1925).

Constitutional bases. The Sixth Amendment to the U.S. Constitution guarantees the right of an accused in a criminal prosecution "to be confronted with the witnesses against him." *See also Chambers v. Mississippi*, 410 U.S. 284, 295 (1973) (the right of cross-examination is not just a desirable rule of trial procedure but "is implicit in the constitutional right of confrontation, and helps assure the 'accuracy of the truth-determining process'" (citation omitted)). This right of confrontation is secured for defendants in state as well as federal criminal proceedings. *Pointer v. Texas*, 380 U.S. 400 (1965); *see also* U.S. CONST. amend. XIV. The right to confront "means more than being allowed to confront the witness physically." *Davis*, 415 U.S. 308, 315. Its main and essential purpose is *"'to secure for the opponent the opportunity of cross-examination.'"* *Id.* at 315–16 (emphasis in original) (quoting 5 J. WIGMORE, EVIDENCE § 1395, at 123 (3d ed. 1940)). Article I, section 23 of the N.C. Constitution likewise guarantees a defendant the right to cross-examine adverse witnesses. *State v. Thorne*, 173 N.C. App. 393 (2005).

The right of confrontation "'ensure[s] the reliability of the evidence against a criminal defendant by subjecting it to rigorous testing in the context of an adversary proceeding before the trier of fact.'" *State v. Brewington*, 352 N.C. 489, 507 (2000) (quoting *Maryland v. Craig*, 497 U.S. 836, 845 (1990)). A defendant has the right "to expose to the jury the facts from which jurors, as the sole triers of facts and credibility, could appropriately draw inferences relating to the reliability of the witness." *Davis*, 415 U.S. 308, 318.

Purposes. Cross-examination serves three general purposes:

1. to elicit further details of the story related on direct examination, in the hope of presenting a complete picture that will be less unfavorable to the cross-examiner's case;
2. to bring out new and different facts relevant to the whole case; and
3. to impeach the witness or cast doubt on his or her credibility.

Barnes v. N.C. State Highway Comm'n, 250 N.C. 378, 394 (1959).

Scope. The scope of permissible cross-examination is generally limited only by the trial judge's discretion and the requirement that the questions be asked in good faith. *State v. Locklear*, 349 N.C. 118 (1998); *State v. Bates*, 343 N.C. 564 (1996). Cross-examination ordinarily may extend to any matter relevant to the issues in the case, including credibility. *See* N.C. R. EVID. 611(b); *State v. Stanfield*, 292 N.C. 357 (1977); *see also* 1 KENNETH S. BROUN, BRANDIS & BROUN ON NORTH CAROLINA EVIDENCE § 150, at 542–43 (7th ed. 2011) ("[T]he range of facts that may be inquired into [on cross-examination] is virtually unlimited except by the general requirement of relevancy and the discretionary power of the trial judge to keep the examination within reasonable bounds.").

Because the scope of inquiry in North Carolina is not confined to matters testified to on direct examination, it is called "wide-open" cross-examination. *See State v. Burgin*, 313 N.C. 404 (1985); *State v. Penley*, 277 N.C. 704 (1971). "Wide-open" cross-examination does not mean, however, "that all decisions on cross-examination are left to the cross-examiner." *Stanfield*, 292 N.C. 357, 362. Rule of Evidence 611(b) allows cross-examination on any relevant matter, but it "neither stands alone nor preempts other rules of evidence." *State v. Lynch*, 334 N.C. 402, 410 (1993). Cross-examination questions remain subject to the limitations of other rules on relevancy and impeachment, including N.C. Rules of Evidence 402 (relevancy), 403 (prejudice, confusion, and waste of time), 404 (character evidence to prove conduct), 608 (character and conduct to impeach), and 609 (prior convictions). *Lynch*, 334 N.C. at 411; *see also State v. Wilson*, 118 N.C. App. 616 (1995). For example, during cross-examination, the trial judge should:

- Rule out immaterial, irrelevant, and incompetent matters. *Lynch*, 334 N.C. 402; *State v. Jones*, 98 N.C. App. 342 (1990);
- Disallow cross-examination on a matter if the probative value of the evidence is substantially outweighed by the danger of unfair prejudice, confusion of the issues, or misleading the jury, or by considerations of undue delay, waste of time, or needless presentation of cumulative evidence under Rule 403. *State v. Whaley*, 362 N.C. 156, 159–60 (2008);
- "'[B]an unduly repetitious and argumentative questions, as well as inquiry into matters of tenuous relevance.'" *State v. Hatcher*, 136 N.C. App. 524, 526 (2000) (citation omitted).
- Prohibit cross-examination that is intended to harass, annoy, or humiliate a witness. *State v. Mason*, 315 N.C. 724, 730 (1986); *State v. Pharr*, 110 N.C. App. 430 (1993).

A judge's ruling on the cross-examination of a witness will not be reversed unless the verdict was improperly influenced by that ruling. *State v. Woods*, 345 N.C. 294 (1997). However, if the trial judge violates a defendant's constitutional right to confrontation by improperly limiting his or her right to cross-examination, the State must show that the erroneous ruling was harmless beyond a reasonable doubt. *See State v. McNeil*, 350 N.C. 657 (1999); *State v. Hoffman*, 349 N.C. 167 (1998); *see also Delaware v. Van Arsdall*, 475 U.S. 673 (1986).

Practice note: When objecting to a trial judge's ruling on the cross-examination of a witness, be sure to constitutionalize your objection; otherwise, the constitutional issue will be waived on appeal. *See State v. Greene*, 351 N.C. 562 (2000). Also, if the judge limits or prohibits your cross-examination of a witness on a particular subject, you must make an offer of proof to preserve the issue for appellate review. *See State v. Williams*, 355 N.C. 501 (2002) (appellate review of trial judge's rulings sustaining the State's objections to questions propounded by defense counsel during cross-examination was waived because defendant made no offer or proof as to the answers to the questions); *State v. Braxton*, 352 N.C. 158 (2000) (same).

Treatment of cross-examination testimony. Any testimony elicited during cross-examination is generally considered as coming from the party calling the witness, not from the cross-examiner. This is true "'even though its only relevance is its tendency to support the cross-examiner's case.'" *State v. Shuler*, 135 N.C. App. 449, 452 (1999) (quoting 1 KENNETH S. BROUN, BRANDIS & BROUN ON NORTH CAROLINA EVIDENCE § 170, at 559 (5th ed. 1998)) [now, 7th ed. 2011, § 170 at 626]. Leading questions asked on cross-examination "to which the witness is *expected* to answer 'yes' or 'no,' also become part of the testimony of the witness." *State v. Baize*, 71 N.C. App. 521, 526 (1984) (emphasis in original).

However, in certain situations, it may be determined that the defendant "introduced" evidence during his or her cross-examination of a State's witness. If the defendant is found to have "introduced" evidence within the meaning of Rule 10 of the N.C. General Rules of Practice for the Superior and District Courts, his or her right to final argument may be lost. *See supra* § 33.5B, What Constitutes "Introduction" of Evidence.

Additional resources. For further discussion of cross-examination in general, including the right to confrontation, see 1 KENNETH S. BROUN, BRANDIS & BROUN ON NORTH CAROLINA EVIDENCE § 170 (7th ed. 2011).

E. Recross-Examination

General rule. Once a witness has been cross-examined and re-examined (redirect), a party does not have the right to a second cross-examination (recross) unless the redirect examination included new matters. *See State v. Thompson*, 139 N.C. App. 299 (2000); *State v. Moorman*, 82 N.C. App. 594 (1986), *rev'd on other grounds*, 320 N.C. 387 (1987). If no new matter is brought forth during redirect examination, it is within the trial judge's discretion to permit or refuse recross-examination. *Moorman*, 82 N.C. 594; *see also* 1 KENNETH S. BROUN, BRANDIS & BROUN ON NORTH CAROLINA EVIDENCE § 171, at 634 (7th ed. 2011).

Multiple defendants. In cases involving multiple defendants, a defendant is entitled to recross-examine a witness if new matters are brought out by another party during its cross-examination even if there has technically been no redirect examination by the calling party. In *State v. Hamad*, 92 N.C. App. 282 (1988), *aff'd per curiam*, 325 N.C. 544 (1989), defendant Wells and defendant Hamad were tried together for trafficking in cocaine. Defendant Wells testified and was cross-examined by defendant Hamad's attorney. The State then cross-examined defendant Wells and brought out new matters that incriminated defendant Hamad. Defendant Hamad sought a second cross-examination of defendant Wells to address the new matters brought up by the State. Defendant Wells objected to further cross-examination, and the trial judge sustained the objection. On appeal, the State argued that the trial judge's ruling was correct because defendant Wells' attorney had not tendered any questions on redirect; therefore, defendant Hamad was not entitled to recross-examination.

The court of appeals reversed the judge's ruling and found "that the semantic designation of the examination of defendant Wells by the State as cross-examination and the absence of redirect examination by Wells' counsel should not operate to abridge defendant Hamad's constitutional right to confront witnesses against him." 92 N.C. App. at 286. Although the label attached to the State's examination of defendant Wells was "cross-examination," it had the "same practical import of a redirect examination" and since new matters were elicited, the trial judge's decision to permit or refuse defendant's recross-examination was not a discretionary one. *Id.* at 287.

F. Leading Questions During Direct or Cross-Examination

Definition. A leading question has been defined as one that suggests a desired answer. Questions that may be answered with a "yes" or a "no" have sometimes been regarded as leading. *State v. Young*, 291 N.C. 562 (1977); *see also State v. Williams*, 304 N.C. 394 (1981). However, that a question may be answered "yes" or "no" does not make it leading—the question also must suggest the answer. *See State v. Thompson*, 306 N.C. 526 (1982). Further, a question is not leading simply because the examiner directs attention to the subject matter at hand without suggesting answers. *See State v. White*, 349 N.C. 535, 557 (1998) ("A question is not leading where it directs the witness toward a specific matter . . . without suggesting an answer."); *State v. Smith*, 135 N.C. App. 649, 655 (1999) (challenged questions "were not so much 'leading' as they were 'bridges'"—that is, they directed the witness's attention to a certain topic in the long and complicated case). "Whether a question is leading 'depends not only on the form of the question but also on the context in which it is put.'" *State v. Howard*, 320 N.C. 718, 721–22 (1987) (quoting *Thompson*, 306 N.C. at 529).

Use of leading questions on direct or redirect examination. Ordinarily, counsel may not ask leading questions during the direct or redirect examination of his or her own witness. *See State v. Royal*, 300 N.C. 515 (1980); *see also* N.C. R. EVID. 611(c) ("Leading questions should not be used on the direct examination of a witness except as may be necessary to develop his testimony."). The purpose of this general prohibition is to prevent counsel from putting a desired response into the mouth of a witness that he or she has called to testify. *State v. Tate*, 307 N.C. 242, 246 (1982). The rule is not based on a technical distinction between direct and cross-examination, but on the alleged friendliness of the witness to the calling party's case. 1 KENNETH S. BROUN, BRANDIS & BROUN ON NORTH CAROLINA EVIDENCE § 169, at 611 (7th ed. 2011); *see also State v. Hosey*, 318 N.C. 330, 338 (1986) (noting concerns that this relationship "'would allow the examiner to provide a false memory to the witness by suggesting the desired reply to his [or her] question'" (citation omitted)).

Notwithstanding the general rule precluding the use of leading questions on direct examination, a trial judge has the discretion to allow counsel to ask leading questions of his or her own witness and, in the absence of abuse, the exercise of that discretion will not be disturbed on appeal. *Tate*, 307 N.C. 242, 246; *see also State v. Bass*, 280 N.C. 435 (1972). The trial judge should consider the true relationship between counsel and the witness in ruling on the propriety of leading questions on direct (or cross-examination) of the witness. *Hosey*, 318 N.C. 330. Where the relationship between the questioner and the witness belies the rationale of the general prohibition against leading questions on direct examination, the trial judge may be more inclined to permit counsel to lead the witness.

The trial judge's discretion to permit leading questions on direct examination is aided by certain guidelines that have evolved over the years. Generally, counsel may be allowed to lead a witness where:

- The witness is hostile, is an adverse party or is identified with an adverse party, or is unwilling to testify. *See* N.C. R. EVID. 611(c); *State v. Dickens*, 346 N.C. 26 (1997); *State v. Maddox*, 159 N.C. App. 127 (2003); *see also Hosey*, 318 N.C. 330.
- The witness has difficulty in understanding the question because of immaturity, advanced age, infirmity, or ignorance. 1 KENNETH S. BROUN, BRANDIS & BROUN ON NORTH CAROLINA EVIDENCE § 169, at 613 (7th ed. 2011); *see also State v. Cox*, 344 N.C. 184 (1996) (low mentality); *State v. Riddick*, 315 N.C. 749 (1986) (young age); *State v. Smith*, 307 N.C. 516 (1983) (elderly).
- The inquiry is into a subject of a delicate nature such as sexual matters. *State v. Chandler*, 324 N.C. 172 (1989); *State v. Pearson*, 258 N.C. 188 (1962); *State v. Dalton*, 96 N.C. App. 65 (1989).
- The witness is called to contradict the testimony of prior witnesses. *State v. Greene*, 285 N.C. 482 (1974); *Gunter v. Watson*, 49 N.C. 455 (1857).
- The examiner seeks to aid the witness's recollection or refresh his or her memory when the witness has exhausted his or her memory without stating the particular matters required. *State v. Young*, 291 N.C. 562 (1977); *State v. Lesane*, 137 N.C. App. 234 (2000).
- The questions are asked for securing preliminary or introductory testimony. *State v. Corbett*, 307 N.C. 169 (1982); *State v. Williams*, 304 N.C. 394 (1981); *see also* WALKER JAMESON BLAKEY, DEAN P. LOVEN & GLEN WEISSENBERGER, NORTH CAROLINA EVIDENCE: 2011 COURTROOM MANUAL Ch. 611, at 210 (2011) (leading questions may be allowed on direct examination when used to elicit preliminary matters that are usually undisputed).
- "[T]he mode of questioning is best calculated to elicit the truth." *State v. Greene*, 285 N.C. 482, 492–93 (1974); *see also State v. Hood*, 294 N.C. 30 (1978).

Practice note: If the prosecutor improperly uses leading questions during direct or redirect examination of his or her witness, you must object to preserve the issue for appellate review. *See State v. Williams*, 304 N.C. 394 (1981). If the answer the witness gives is objectionable on additional grounds, counsel must move to strike the answer on those additional grounds to preserve the issue for review. *See State v. Proctor*, 62 N.C. App. 233 (1983); *State v. Wooten*, 20 N.C. App. 499 (1974).

Use of leading questions during cross or recross-examination. Rule 611(c) provides that leading questions ordinarily should be allowed on cross-examination. This rule follows the traditional view that counsel may use leading questions as a matter of right during cross-examination. *State v. Mitchell*, 317 N.C. 661 (1986). However, use of the qualifier "ordinarily" means that this right is not absolute. *See State v. Hosey*, 318 N.C. 330 (1986). As stated in the above discussion on leading questions on direct and redirect, the trial judge should consider the true relationship between counsel and the witness in ruling on the propriety of leading questions during cross-examination.

If the witness is "friendly" to the non-calling party and cross-examination is cross-examination in form only and not in fact, the trial judge has the discretionary power to deny the use of leading questions. *Id.* The denial is justified in a "friendly witness" situation to prevent counsel "from providing 'a false memory to the witness by suggesting the desired reply to his question' inadvertently or otherwise." *Id.* at 339 (citation omitted).

No formal requirements for finding a witness to be "hostile" or "friendly." A trial judge may make a determination that a witness is friendly or hostile without conducting a voir dire hearing. Although not required, the better practice is for the judge first to make findings of fact and conclusions of law and then formally declare that the witness is friendly or hostile before allowing or disallowing leading questions. *Hosey*, 318 N.C. 330.

General limitations on the use of leading questions. When examining a witness, counsel may not use leading questions to:

- Inject his or her own knowledge, beliefs, and personal opinions that are not supported by the evidence. *State v. Sanderson*, 336 N.C. 1 (1994); *State v. Britt*, 288 N.C. 699 (1975); *State v. Phillips*, 240 N.C. 516 (1954).
- "[D]istort the witness' testimony by purposely misconstruing answers and cross-examining the witness on the basis of the misconstruction." *Sanderson*, 336 N.C. 1, 14; *see also Berger v. United States*, 295 U.S. 78 (1935); N.C. GEN. R. PRAC. SUPER. & DIST. CT. 12 ("Counsel shall not knowingly misinterpret . . . the testimony of a witness . . . .").
- Testify himself or herself. *See State v. Walls*, 342 N.C. 1 (1995) (counsel asked the witness whether she had told counsel that she did not remember making a particular statement to the sheriff; trial judge permitted counsel to rephrase the question and ask about the same matter). [Although generally disfavored, testimony by counsel may be unavoidable in some instances. *See* N.C. STATE BAR REV'D RULES OF PROF'L CONDUCT R. 3.7(a) (2003) (prohibiting counsel from acting as witness in a case in which he or she is an advocate but recognizing limited exceptions); *State v. Elam,* 56 N.C. App. 590 (1982) (the parties stipulated for the jury to what counsel would have testified if called as a witness; whether to allow defense counsel to testify on a collateral matter, impeachment of a witness, was within the trial judge's discretion); *Town of Mebane v. Iowa Mut. Ins. Co.*, 28 N.C. App. 27 (1975) (observing that in most instances counsel who acts as a witness has surrendered the right to participate in the litigation but that counsel is not incompetent to testify). To avoid this dilemma, counsel should have an investigator or other person present when interviewing a witness so, if necessary, counsel may cross-examine the witness about statements to the other person as well as call the other person to testify to those statements.]

Additional resources. For additional discussion of leading questions, see 1 KENNETH S. BROUN, BRANDIS & BROUN ON NORTH CAROLINA EVIDENCE § 169 (7th ed. 2011), and WALKER JAMESON BLAKEY, DEAN P. LOVEN & GLEN WEISSENBERGER, NORTH CAROLINA EVIDENCE: 2011 COURTROOM MANUAL Ch. 611, at 209–18 (2011).

G. Witness Examination in Joint Representation Cases

Rule 11 of the General Rules of Practice for the Superior and District Courts states:

> When several counsel are employed by the same party, the examination or cross-examination of each witness for such party shall be conducted by one counsel, but the counsel may change with each successive witness or, with leave of the court, in a prolonged examination of a single witness.

Under this rule, it is within the trial judge's discretion whether to allow a change of counsel if an examination is to be lengthy. *State v. Houston*, 19 N.C. App. 542 (1973) (defendant failed to show he was prejudiced where trial judge permitted a second prosecutor to conduct a voir dire examination of a witness when another prosecutor had begun the examination of that witness).

29.7 Defendant's Right to Testify or Not to Testify

A criminal defendant has the right to testify in his or her own defense. Although not recognized at common law or specifically enumerated in the U.S. Constitution, this right is now accepted to be an inherent part of the Due Process Clause of the Fourteenth Amendment and the Compulsory Process Clause of the Sixth Amendment to the U.S. Constitution. *See Rock v. Arkansas*, 483 U.S. 44 (1987); *State v. Colson*, 186 N.C. App. 281 (2007). Article I, section 23 of the N.C. Constitution also guarantees a criminal defendant the right to testify. *See State v. Murray*, 154 N.C. App. 631 (2002); *see also* G.S. 8-54 (providing that a criminal defendant is "at his own request, but not otherwise, a competent witness").

Likewise, a criminal defendant has a right to refuse to testify under the Fifth Amendment to the U.S. Constitution, as incorporated by the Fourteenth Amendment, and also under article I, section 23 of the N.C. Constitution. *Griffin v. California*, 380 U.S. 609 (1965); *State v. Mitchell*, 353 N.C. 309 (2001). G.S. 8-54 grants the defendant the right to testify, but the language of the statute makes it clear that nothing in it renders a criminal defendant "compellable to give evidence against himself."

For a more detailed discussion on the defendant's right to testify and right to refuse to testify, see *supra* § 21.3, Right to Testify.

29.8 Remote Testimony

"Remote testimony" refers to testimony given by a witness outside of the defendant's physical presence by way of a "live," closed-circuit television system. The system can be either "one-way" where the witness is not in the defendant's presence and cannot see the defendant but the defendant can see the witness, or "two-way" where the witness is not in the defendant's presence but the witness and defendant can see each other over video monitors.

The use of closed-circuit television systems is most often sought in cases involving child witnesses where the State asserts that the child would be traumatized if required to testify in the defendant's presence. If the State's motion to allow remote testimony is granted, the child is generally in a separate room and testifies by way of a one-way, closed-circuit television. The child cannot see the defendant during the testimony, but the defendant and the trier of fact can see the child and his or her demeanor while testifying.

A. Constitutional Implications

Exception for one-way, remote testimony for child witness. Although the defendant has the right to confront witnesses against him or her under the Sixth Amendment to the U.S. Constitution and under article I, section 23 of the N.C. Constitution, the right to confront a witness "face-to-face" may not be absolute when child witnesses are involved. In *Maryland v. Craig*, 497 U.S. 836 (1990), the U.S. Supreme Court found no Sixth Amendment violation where a child victim in a sexual abuse case was permitted, pursuant to a Maryland statute, to testify outside the defendant's presence via one-way, closed-circuit television. The statute allowed the witness, the prosecutor, and the defense attorney to withdraw to a separate room while the witness testified. The defendant, the judge, and the jury remained in the courtroom and watched the witness's testimony on a video monitor. The defendant could communicate electronically with his attorney, but the witness could not see the defendant.

The U.S. Supreme Court reviewed the arrangement used in *Craig* and found that a defendant's right to confrontation "may be satisfied absent a physical, face-to-face confrontation at trial" if the denial of confrontation "is necessary to further an important public policy" and "the reliability of the testimony is otherwise assured." *Id.* at 850. The finding of necessity must be made on a case-by-case basis. *Id.* at 855. A majority of the Court found that the State could show that the use of the special procedure was necessary to further its interest in protecting the physical and psychological well-being of child sexual abuse victims and that it could be sufficient to outweigh a defendant's right to face his or her accusers in court.

The Court stated that before this type of arrangement is allowed, the trial judge must:

- hold a hearing and take evidence to determine whether the use of the procedure is necessary to protect the welfare of the particular child witness;
- find that the child witness would be traumatized, not just by the courtroom generally, but by the defendant's presence; and
- find that the emotional distress suffered by the child witness in the defendant's presence is "more than *de minimis; i.e.*, more than 'mere nervousness or excitement or some reluctance to testify.'"

Id. at 855–56 (citation omitted). The majority held that the trial judge may rely solely on expert testimony in making his or her findings. The child need not attempt to testify in the defendant's presence to prove that he or she would be traumatized by doing so. *Id.* at 859–60.

The Court reasoned that even though there was no "face-to-face" confrontation, the reliability of the child witness's testimony was "otherwise assured" because the Maryland statute required the child to be competent as a witness and testify under oath, the defendant had the opportunity for contemporaneous cross-examination, and the defendant, judge, and jury all were able to view the demeanor and body of the child witness while he or she testified (albeit through the video monitor). *Id.* at 850–51; *see also In re Stradford*, 119 N.C. App. 654 (1995) (upholding the trial judge's authority to permit the remote testimony of a child witness on the facts of sexual abuse case and finding no state or federal constitutional violation).

Since the decision in *Craig*, "[t]he federal government and nearly all states have enacted statutes providing for alternatives to face-to-face confrontation when necessary to shield child witnesses or other sensitive witnesses." Hadley Perry, Note & Comment, *Virtually Face-to-Face: The Confrontation Clause and the Use of Two-Way Video Testimony*, 13 ROGER WILLIAMS U. L. REV. 565, 580 (2008). North Carolina statutes on remote testimony are discussed in subsections B. and C., below.

Questions remain, however, whether remote testimony by children or other witnesses satisfies the U.S. Supreme Court's revived approach to the Confrontation Clause in *Crawford v. Washington*, 541 U.S. 36 (2004). Although a majority of the Court in *Maryland v. Craig* approved remote testimony in that case, Justice Scalia dissented in typically strong language, arguing that the Confrontation Clause gives the defendant the right to cross-examine, face-to-face, witnesses against him or her and that remote testimony is not permissible under his reading of the Confrontation Clause. Justice Scalia later authored the *Crawford* decision, in which he led a majority of the Court in ruling that the Confrontation Clause restricts the introduction of out-of-court statements and in overruling the looser balancing test used in previous decisions. Cases challenging remote testimony are working their way through the appellate courts, but as yet neither the U.S. Supreme Court nor the N.C. Supreme Court have addressed the issue. *See* Jessica Smith, *Two-Way Remote Testimony: Will It Pass Muster? (Parts I, II, & III)*, N.C. CRIM. L., UNC SCH. OF GOV'T BLOG (Feb. 8–10, 2011), http://sogweb.sog.unc.edu/blogs/ncclaw/?p=1935 (and succeeding posts); *see also In re Court Rules*, 207 F.R.D. 89 (2002) (statement by Justice Scalia) (discussing proposed changes to Federal Rules of Criminal Procedure on remote testimony).

The N.C. Court of Appeals has addressed the permissibility of a child testifying remotely in light of *Crawford* in *State v. Jackson*, ___ N.C. App. ___, 717 S.E.2d 35 (2011). The court held that *Crawford* did not overrule earlier decisions holding that a child may testify remotely in a criminal case when the court finds a sufficient showing of need and uses appropriate procedures for taking the child's testimony. For a further discussion of *Jackson*, including the possibility of higher court review, see Jessica Smith, *N.C. App. Holds that Maryland v. Craig Survives Crawford*, N.C. CRIM. L., UNC SCH. OF GOV'T BLOG (Oct. 13, 2011), http://sogweb.sog.unc.edu/blogs/ncclaw/?p=2967.

Exceptions for adult witnesses. Should remote testimony in cases involving child witnesses survive scrutiny in light of *Crawford*, discussed above, it remains to be seen whether the U.S. Supreme Court or the N.C. appellate courts will extend *Craig* and allow the use of remote testimony for adult witnesses who are mentally retarded or developmentally disabled or for those who may be especially emotionally traumatized by the defendant's presence in court. Likewise, whether remote testimony will be allowed in cases where an elderly witness is physically unable to attend court, or in cases in which a witness is outside a party's subpoena power or is otherwise unable to be physically present, has not been determined yet in North Carolina or by the U.S. Supreme Court. *See generally Wrotten v. New York*, ___ U.S. ___, 130 S. Ct. 2520 (2010) (denying certiorari in an interlocutory case where the prosecuting witness was allowed to testify via two-way video due to his age and poor health; Justice Sotomayor noted in a statement filed with the denial that "[b]ecause the use of video testimony in this case arose in a strikingly different context than in *Craig*, it is not clear that the latter is controlling").

B. Statutory Authority for Remote Testimony of Child Witnesses

G.S. 15A-1225.1, effective December 1, 2009, authorizes a trial judge to permit the remote testimony of a minor who is under the age of sixteen at the time of his or her testimony if certain procedures are followed. The statute applies to criminal and juvenile delinquency proceedings. G.S. 15A-1225.1(a)(2). The statutory requirements are similar to those delineated by the U.S. Supreme Court in *Craig*, but in some respects the statute may exceed the constitutional limits described in *Craig*—for example, remote testimony is statutorily permissible in any criminal or juvenile delinquency case (assuming the various requirements are met), not just in a case involving particularly serious or sensitive allegations like the sexual abuse charges in *Craig*. The statute also would have to survive a general challenge under the Confrontation Clause analysis of *Crawford v. Washington*, discussed in subsection A., above.

For a further discussion of the statute, including ambiguities in the statute's provisions and potential constitutional issues, see John Rubin, *2009 Legislation Affecting Criminal Law and Procedure*, ADMINISTRATION OF JUSTICE BULLETIN No. 2009/09, at 23–26 (UNC School of Government, Dec. 2009), *available at* http://sogpubs.unc.edu/electronicversions/pdfs/aojb0909.pdf.

C. Statutory Authority for Remote Testimony of Developmentally Disabled or Mentally Retarded Witnesses

Under G.S. 15A-1225.2, effective December 1, 2009, a trial judge may permit the remote testimony of a developmentally disabled or mentally retarded witness (regardless of the witness's age) in a criminal or juvenile delinquency case if the judge finds by clear and convincing evidence that the witness would suffer serious emotional distress from testifying in the defendant's presence and that the ability of the witness to communicate with the trier of fact would be impaired by testifying in the defendant's presence. The hearing procedure, requirements for an order allowing the use of remote testimony, and authorized method of testimony are similar to those set out in G.S. 15A-1225.1 for child witnesses, discussed in subsection B., above, but there are differences.

This statute extends the category of witnesses permitted to give remote testimony beyond that authorized by *Craig*. To comply with the constitutional requirements of *Craig*, the State may need to show that the protection of this specific class of witnesses is necessary to further an important public policy; that the particular witness in question needs special protection; and that the methodology used does not offend the defendant's right to confront the witnesses against him or her. The statute also would have to survive a general challenge under the Confrontation Clause analysis of *Crawford v. Washington*, discussed in subsection A., above. For a further discussion of the statute, including ambiguities in the statute's provisions and potential constitutional issues, see John Rubin, *2009 Legislation Affecting Criminal Law and Procedure*, ADMINISTRATION OF JUSTICE BULLETIN No. 2009/09, at 26 (UNC School of Government, Dec. 2009), *available at* http://sogpubs.unc.edu/electronic versions/pdfs/aojb0909.pdf.

D. Additional Resources

For further discussion of remote witness testimony, see Annotation, *Closed-circuit Television Witness Examination*, 61 A.L.R.4th 1155 (1988 & Supp. 2010); Ralph H. Kohlmann, *The Presumption of Innocence: Patching the Tattered Cloak After* Maryland v. Craig, 27 ST. MARY'S L. J. 389 (1996) (discussing the importance of the right of confrontation with respect to defendant's presumption of innocence); Cathleen J. Cinella, Note, *Compromising the Sixth Amendment Right to Confrontation*—United States v. Gigante, 32 SUFFOLK U. L. REV. 135 (1998) (discussing compromise in the right of confrontation when adult witnesses are allowed to testify via closed-circuit television).

29.9 Oath or Affirmation

A. Applicable Statutes

Before testifying, each witness must declare by oath or affirmation that he or she will testify truthfully. The oath or affirmation must be "administered in a form calculated to awaken his conscience and impress his mind with his duty to do so." N.C. R. EVID. 603; *see also State v. James*, 322 N.C. 320 (1988). N.C. Rule of Evidence 603 "'is designed to afford the flexibility required in dealing with religious adults, atheists, conscientious objectors, mental defectives, and children. Affirmation is simply a solemn undertaking to tell the truth; no special verbal formula is required.'" N.C. R. EVID. 603 Official Commentary (quoting the Advisory Committee's Note to the virtually identical Fed. R. Evid. 603).

Solemnity required. An oath or an affirmation must be taken and administered "with the utmost solemnity." G.S. 11-1. The "solemnity" requirement applies both to the substance of the oath and to the form and manner of taking and administering it. *State v. Davis*, 69 N.C. 383 (1873).

Form of oath. When taking an oath, the witness is required to "lay his hand upon the Holy

Scriptures." G.S. 11-2. If a witness has a conscientious objection to laying his or her hand on the "Holy Gospel," the witness may stand with his or her "right hand lifted up towards heaven" while taking the oath in accordance with G.S. 11-3.

There has been some controversy about the meaning of the "Holy Scriptures" and whether G.S. 11-2 allows witnesses to swear on other religious texts. The issue has not been resolved definitively, but in an appropriate case the N.C. appellate courts may rule that a witness (or juror) has the right to swear on a religious text other than the Bible. In *ACLU of N.C., Inc. v. State*, 181 N.C. App. 430 (2007), the plaintiffs sought a declaratory judgment that the term "Holy Scriptures" in G.S. 11-2 referred not only to the Bible but also to other religious texts, including the Quran. In the alternative, plaintiffs sought a declaratory judgment that the statute was unconstitutional under the U.S. and N.C. Constitutions. The trial judge dismissed the plaintiffs' case for lack of a justiciable controversy, and the plaintiffs appealed. The Court of Appeals reversed the trial judge's dismissal and remanded, holding that the case was justiciable under the Declaratory Judgment Act and "allowing ACLU-NC to obtain from the court an interpretation of N.C.G.S. § 11-2 and the rights of its members under the statute." *Id.* at 435. On remand, the superior court judge declined to declare that the term "Holy Scriptures" in G.S. 11-2 included texts other than the Bible and also declined to find that G.S. 11-2 was unconstitutional. He did find, however. that under North Carolina's common law and precedent of the N.C. Supreme Court, oaths can be administered on sacred texts other than the Bible. *See ACLU of N.C., Inc. v. State*, No. 05 CVS 9872 (N.C. Super. Ct., Wake County, May 24, 2007), *available at* www.aclu.org/religion-belief/aclu-n-carolina-matten-v-north-carolina-order.

For further discussion of oaths to tell the truth, see Eugene R. Milhizer, *So Help Me Allah: An Historical and Prudential Analysis of Oaths as Applied to the Current Controversy of the Bible and Quran in Oath Practices in America*, 70 OHIO ST. L.J. 1 (2009).

Form of affirmation. A witness in a criminal case must swear that that he or she will tell "the truth, the whole truth, and nothing but the truth; so help [me] God." G.S. 11-11. If a witness has "conscientious scruples" against taking an oath with the "Holy Scriptures" or with his or her hand lifted up towards heaven, the witness may be "affirmed" instead. The witness will "affirm" instead of "swear" and the words "so help me God" will be deleted. G.S. 11-4.

B. Constitutional Implications

A defendant is entitled to have the testimony offered against him or her given under sanction of oath or affirmation as a part of his or her constitutional right of confrontation. *State v. Robinson*, 310 N.C. 530 (1984); *see also California v. Green*, 399 U.S. 149, 158 (1970) (the right to confront "insures that the witness will give his statements under oath—thus impressing him with the seriousness of the matter and guarding against the lie by the possibility of a penalty for perjury").

C. Interpreters

Interpreters are subject to the provisions of N.C. Rule of Evidence 603 and must make an oath or affirmation stating that they will make a true translation. N.C. R. EVID. 604; *see also* G.S. 8B-7 (specific oath for interpreters for deaf persons).

D. Preservation of Issue for Appeal

If a witness (or interpreter) offers testimony without being sworn or affirmed, a defendant must object or he or she waives the right to raise the issue on appeal. *State v. Robinson*, 310 N.C. 530 (1984); *see also State v. Beane*, 146 N.C. App. 220, 225 (2001) ("Despite the constitutional nature of the oath requirement, our appellate courts have consistently held that where the trial court fails to administer the oath to a witness, the defendant's failure to object waives appellate review of the court's error."). However, if the judge's decision not to administer an oath is deliberate, a defendant is not completely barred from raising the issue on appeal by failing to object. An objection under those circumstances would not have prompted the trial judge to take corrective action so plain error review is appropriate in that situation. *See Beane*, 146 N.C. App. 220.

E. Additional Resources

For additional discussion of oaths and affirmations, see 1 KENNETH S. BROUN, BRANDIS & BROUN ON NORTH CAROLINA EVIDENCE § 146 (oaths of witnesses), § 147 (interpreters) (7th ed. 2011), and WALKER JAMESON BLAKEY, DEAN P. LOVEN & GLEN WEISSENBERGER, NORTH CAROLINA EVIDENCE: 2011 COURTROOM MANUAL Ch. 603, at 179–80 (oath or affirmation), and Ch. 604, at 181–82 (interpreters) (2011).

Chapter 30
Motions to Dismiss Based on Insufficient Evidence

A motion to dismiss is the procedural device used to test the sufficiency of the evidence presented at trial to convict the defendant. The importance of making this motion at the appropriate times cannot be overestimated.

The scope of this chapter is limited to motions to dismiss based on the insufficiency of the evidence. Other types of motions to dismiss are covered elsewhere in this manual. These include:

- Motions to dismiss for pre-accusation delay or for violation of the right to a speedy trial. *See* 1 NORTH CAROLINA DEFENDER MANUAL Ch. 7 (Speedy Trial and Related Issues) (Nov. 2008).
- Motions to dismiss based on defective pleadings. *See* 1 NORTH CAROLINA DEFENDER MANUAL Ch. 8 (Criminal Pleadings) (July 2004).
- Motions to dismiss based on improper grand jury procedures. *See* 1 NORTH CAROLINA

DEFENDER MANUAL Ch. 9 (Grand Jury Proceedings) (Jan. 2009).

- Motions to dismiss based on lack of jurisdiction (other than lack of jurisdiction as a result of a defective pleading). *See* 1 NORTH CAROLINA DEFENDER MANUAL Ch. 10 (Jurisdiction) (Oct. 2010).
- Motions to dismiss based on improper venue. *See* 1 NORTH CAROLINA DEFENDER MANUAL Ch. 11 (Venue) (Nov. 2008).
- Motions to dismiss on double jeopardy grounds or for vindictive or selective prosecution. *See* 1 NORTH CAROLINA DEFENDER MANUAL Ch. 13 (Motions Practice) (Mar. 2009).

30.1 Legal Standard

A. Question Presented by Motion

State's burdens of proof. In all criminal cases, the State has two burdens of proof—a burden of persuasion and a burden of production. *See* 1 KENNETH S. BROUN, BRANDIS & BROUN ON NORTH CAROLINA EVIDENCE § 30, at 126 (7th ed. 2011) (defining the terms "burden of producing evidence" and "burden of persuasion"). To meet its burden of persuasion, the State must prove to the finder of fact, beyond a reasonable doubt, all facts necessary to establish the defendant's guilt of the charged offense. *See Mullaney v. Wilbur*, 421 U.S. 684 (1975); *In re Winship*, 397 U.S. 358 (1970). The State must meet a parallel burden of production to have the offense submitted to the finder of fact. Thus, the trial court must find that a rational finder of fact could accept the evidence as proof of the defendant's guilt beyond a reasonable doubt. *See Jackson v. Virginia*, 443 U.S. 307 (1979) (stating constitutional requirement, discussed further *infra* in § 30.2); 1 KENNETH S. BROUN, BRANDIS & BROUN ON NORTH CAROLINA EVIDENCE § 32, at 128 (7th ed. 2011) (burden of production is virtually always on State). A motion to dismiss for insufficiency of the evidence tests whether the State has met this burden of production.

Standard for determining whether to grant motion to dismiss. In ruling on a defendant's motion to dismiss, the question before the trial judge is whether the State has produced substantial evidence of (1) each essential element of the offense charged or of a lesser included offense and (2) defendant's being the perpetrator of the offense. *State v. Powell*, 299 N.C. 95, 98 (1980). This is a question of law for the trial judge to determine. *See State v. Cockerham*, 155 N.C. App. 729 (2003). The definition of "substantial evidence" is discussed further in subsection B., below.

The State is aided in meeting its burden by the principle that the evidence must be considered in the light most favorable to the State, with the State being entitled to every reasonable inference of fact arising from the evidence. *See State v. Brown*, 310 N.C. 563 (1984); *State v. Easterling*, 300 N.C. 594 (1980). This is true even if that same evidence also would support reasonable inferences of the defendant's innocence. *State v. Scott*, 356 N.C. 591 (2002). Discrepancies and contradictions, even in the State's evidence, are for the jury to resolve and do not warrant a dismissal. *State v. Henderson*, 276 N.C. 430, 438 (1970). The ultimate question for the trial judge is "whether a reasonable inference of defendant's guilt may be drawn from the circumstances." *State v. Lee*, 348 N.C. 474, 488

(1998); *see also infra* § 30.2, Due Process Requirements (noting that North Carolina courts have held that this standard is the same in substance as the federal due process standard).

Practice note: The courts have often said that in ruling on a motion to dismiss, the trial judge may consider all admitted evidence, whether competent or incompetent. The courts have reasoned that, if the trial judge had not allowed the incompetent evidence, the State might have offered other, admissible evidence. *See State v. Spencer*, 192 N.C. App. 143, 148 n.3 (2008). In light of this rationale, if you believe that the trial judge erroneously admitted certain evidence and that without that evidence the State's evidence is insufficient, ask the trial judge to reconsider his or her earlier ruling in addressing your motion to dismiss. At that stage of the proceedings, the trial judge can allow the State to reopen its case pursuant to section 15A-1226(b) of the North Carolina General Statutes (hereinafter G.S.), putting the State to the test of whether it actually has admissible evidence to offer in lieu of the incompetent evidence. *Cf. State v. Fleming*, 350 N.C. 109, 143 (1999) (appellate court did not address constitutionality of trial judge considering incompetent evidence on motion to dismiss for insufficient evidence; constitutional argument was not presented to trial judge).

B. Definition of Substantial Evidence

Substantial evidence has been defined as "such relevant evidence as a reasonable mind might accept as adequate to support a conclusion." *State v. Smith*, 300 N.C. 71, 78 (1980). "The substantial evidence test requires that the evidence must be existing and real, not just seeming and imaginary." *State v. Irwin*, 304 N.C. 93, 97–98 (1981). Evidence is not substantial if it arouses only a suspicion about the fact to be proved, even if the suspicion is strong. *State v. Malloy*, 309 N.C. 176 (1983).

C. Effect of the Defendant's Evidence

The courts have often stated that only evidence favorable to the State will be considered on a motion to dismiss for insufficient evidence. Accordingly, evidence offered by the defendant will generally not be considered if it relates to his or her defense or is in conflict with the State's evidence. *See State v. Earnhardt*, 307 N.C. 62 (1982); *State v. Henderson*, 276 N.C. 430 (1970). Nevertheless, if the defendant's evidence explains or clarifies the evidence offered by the State, the trial judge must consider it. The judge "must also consider the defendant's evidence which rebuts the inference of guilt when it is not inconsistent with the State's evidence." *State v. Bates*, 309 N.C. 528, 535 (1983).

D. Circumstantial Evidence

In ruling on a motion to dismiss, the trial judge may consider circumstantial as well as direct evidence. *State v. Salters*, 137 N.C. App. 553 (2000); *see also State v. Stone*, 323 N.C. 447, 452 (1988) ("Circumstantial evidence may withstand a motion to dismiss and support a conviction even when the evidence does not rule out every hypothesis of innocence."). The test for sufficiency is the same whether the evidence is circumstantial, direct, or a combination of the two. *State v. Jones*, 303 N.C. 500 (1981); 1 KENNETH S. BROUN, BRANDIS & BROUN ON NORTH CAROLINA EVIDENCE § 39, at 145 (7th ed. 2011).

Whether the evidence presented is direct or circumstantial, the trial judge must determine whether a reasonable inference of the defendant's guilt may be drawn from the evidence. *State v. Scott*, 356 N.C. 591 (2002). "[W]hile the State may base its case on circumstantial evidence requiring the jury to infer elements of the crime, that evidence must be real and substantial and not merely speculative." *State v. Reese*, 319 N.C. 110, 139 (1987). Once the judge decides that the circumstances give rise to a reasonable inference of the defendant's guilt, it is for the jury to decide whether the facts shown, taken singly or in combination, satisfy it beyond a reasonable doubt that the defendant is guilty. *See Scott*, 356 N.C. at 596; *see also State v. Irwin*, 304 N.C. 93 (1981).

E. Stacking of Inferences

Until the N.C. Supreme Court's ruling in *State v. Childress*, 321 N.C. 226 (1987), trial judges were not permitted to stack an inference on an inference in determining the sufficiency of the evidence in circumstantial evidence cases. *See, e.g., State v. Holland*, 318 N.C. 602 (1986); *State v. Byrd*, 309 N.C. 132 (1983); *State v. LeDuc*, 306 N.C. 62 (1982). In *Childress*, the court found no reason to prohibit consideration of an inference that naturally arises from a fact proven by circumstantial evidence and overruled its prior decisions.

F. Weight of the Evidence

When the trial judge considers a motion to dismiss, he or she is "concerned only with the legal sufficiency of the evidence to support a verdict, not its weight, which is a matter for the jury." *State v. Blake*, 319 N.C. 599, 604 (1987); *see also State v. Garcia*, 358 N.C. 382, 412 (2004) ("A 'substantial evidence' inquiry examines the sufficiency of the evidence presented but not its weight."). Evidentiary contradictions and discrepancies are for the jury to resolve and do not warrant dismissal. *State v. Holton*, 284 N.C. 391 (1973).

G. Credibility of the Witnesses

Ordinarily, the credibility of witnesses and the proper weight to be given their testimony is to be determined by the jury, not by the judge on a motion to dismiss. *State v. Miller*, 270 N.C. 726, 730 (1967). In rare instances, where the testimony presented is inherently incredible, the evidence may be found to be insufficient to withstand a defendant's motion to dismiss. *Id.* at 732 (evidence was insufficient to support conviction where sole identification of defendant came from a State's witness who was at least 286 feet from the perpetrator where "it is apparent that the distance was too great for an observer to note and store in memory features which would enable him, six hours later, to identify a complete stranger with the degree of certainty which would justify the submission of the guilt of such person to the jury"); *see also Jones v. Schaffer*, 252 N.C. 368, 378 (1960) ("'As a general rule, evidence which is inherently impossible or in conflict with indisputable physical facts or laws of nature is not sufficient to take the case to the jury, and in case of such inherently impossible evidence, the trial court has the duty of taking the case from the jury.'" (citations omitted)) .

30.2 Due Process Requirements

The federal constitutional right to due process of law requires that the State prove beyond a reasonable doubt every fact necessary for a criminal conviction. *In re Winship*, 397 U.S. 358 (1970). A conviction predicated on evidence insufficient to permit a reasonable juror to find that the State has proven beyond a reasonable doubt every element of the particular offense charged and that the defendant is the perpetrator of that offense violates the Fourteenth Amendment to the U.S. Constitution. *Jackson v. Virginia*, 443 U.S. 307 (1979).

The federal due process standard for sufficiency is "whether, after viewing the evidence in the light most favorable to the prosecution, *any* rational trier of fact could have found the essential elements of the crime beyond a reasonable doubt."*Jackson*, 443 U.S. at 319 (emphasis in original). The North Carolina courts have held that the state standard for determining the sufficiency of the evidence, discussed *supra* in § 30.1, is the same in substance as the federal due process standard set out in *Jackson*. *See State v. Jones*, 303 N.C. 500 (1981); *see also* 1 KENNETH S. BROUN, BRANDIS & BROUN ON NORTH CAROLINA EVIDENCE § 39, at 141–45 (7th ed. 2011) (discussing the sufficiency of evidence).

30.3 Procedural Requirements

A. In General

Motions to dismiss, motions for judgment as in case of nonsuit (that is, motions for nonsuit), and motions for a directed verdict of not guilty all have substantially the same legal effect. *See, e.g., State v. Bruce*, 315 N.C. 273 (1985); *State v. Mize*, 315 N.C. 285 (1985); *State v. Vietto*, 297 N.C. 8 (1979). Although a challenge to the sufficiency of the evidence is properly made by either a motion to dismiss or a motion for nonsuit (*see State v. Mendez*, 42 N.C. App. 141 (1979)), the modern approach is to denominate the procedural device as a "motion to dismiss for insufficient evidence."

Both G.S. 15-173 and G.S. 15A-1227 address motions to dismiss based on insufficient evidence. "The motion for dismissal referred to in G.S. 15A-1227 is the same motion for dismissal referred to in G.S. 15-173. Therefore, there is but one motion for dismissal for insufficiency of the evidence to sustain a conviction, and that motion is governed by the provisions of both G.S. 15-173 and G.S. 15A-1227." *Mendez*, 42 N.C. App. 141, 146. The statutes are identical in that "both statutes allow counsel to make a motion challenging the sufficiency of the evidence at the close of the State's evidence or at the close of all the evidence." *State v. Earnhardt*, 307 N.C. 62, 65 (1982). Since the statutes are identical in that respect, "cases dealing with the sufficiency of the evidence . . . under the older statute, G.S. 15-173, are applicable when ruling on motions made under the more recent statute, G.S. 15A-1227." *Id.* There are minor differences between the statutes, however, and each statute is reviewed separately below.

B. Provisions of G.S. 15-173

Motion at the close of the State's evidence. G.S. 15-173 is entitled "Demurrer to the evidence" and provides that in any criminal action in superior or district court, the defendant may move to dismiss the action, "or for judgment as in case of nonsuit," after the State has introduced its evidence and rested its case. If the trial judge allows the motion pursuant to the statute, a judgment dismissing the case shall be entered and that judgment has the force and effect of a "not guilty" verdict. *See also State v. Murrell*, 54 N.C. App. 342 (1981); N.C. R. APP. P. 10(a)(3). If the motion is denied, and the defendant does not put on evidence, he or she may raise the denial of the motion as grounds for reversal on appeal "without the necessity of the defendant's having taken exception to such denial," i.e., without taking further steps to preserve the issue. G.S. 15-173.

Introduction of defense evidence waives earlier motion. If the defendant introduces evidence, he or she waives the motion for dismissal made at the close of the State's evidence and cannot then raise the issue of sufficiency on appeal unless he or she renews the motion to dismiss at the close of all the evidence. G.S. 15-173; *see also State v. Bruce*, 315 N.C. 273 (1985) (because defendant offered evidence following the trial judge's denial of his motion for dismissal at the close of the State's evidence, the denial of that motion was not properly before the supreme court for review); *State v. Mendez*, 42 N.C. App. 141 (1979) (by presenting evidence, defendant waived his right to assert the denial of his motion to dismiss at the close of the State's evidence as a ground for appeal); N.C. R. APP. P. 10(a)(3).

Effect of introduction of evidence by co-defendant. Where defendants are tried jointly and one does not introduce evidence, the defendant who does not introduce evidence is entitled to have his or her motion to dismiss for insufficiency of the evidence considered on the basis of the facts in evidence when the State rested its case—that is, in resisting the moving defendant's motion, the State may not rely on any evidence introduced by the co-defendant. *See State v. Frazier*, 268 N.C. 249 (1966); *State v. Berryman*, 10 N.C. App. 649 (1971). This rule applies even if the attorney for the defendant who does not introduce evidence cross-examines the witnesses for the co-defendant (as long as the cross-examination does not constitute the "introduction" of evidence). *See State v. DiNunno*, 67 N.C. App. 316, 319 (1984) (defense counsel did not "introduce" evidence within the meaning of G.S. 15-173 when he cross-examined the co-defendant as to the events leading up to and surrounding the arrest where "he did not attempt to elicit substantive evidence beneficial to the defendant DiNunno"); *see also infra* § 33.5B, What Constitutes "Introduction" of Evidence (discussing what constitutes the "introduction" of evidence in determining whether the defendant has lost the right to last argument).

Motion at the close of all the evidence. The defendant may move to dismiss at the close of all the evidence regardless of whether he or she moved to dismiss at the close of the State's evidence. If the judge grants the motion at the close of all the evidence, a judgment dismissing the case shall be entered and that judgment has the force and effect of a "not guilty" verdict. If the motion is denied, the defendant may raise the denial of the motion as grounds for reversal on appeal without taking further steps to preserve the issue. G.S. 15-173; *see also* N.C. R. APP. P. 10(a)(3).

C. Provisions of G.S. 15A-1227

Timing of motion. G.S. 15A-1227 details additional times when a defendant may make a motion for dismissal for insufficiency of the evidence, but the requirements are essentially the same as under G.S. 15-173. Under G.S. 15A-1227(a), a motion to dismiss may be made:

- at the close of the State's evidence;
- at the close of all the evidence;
- after return of a verdict and before entry of judgment; and
- after discharge of the jury without a verdict and before the end of the session.

A motion to dismiss for insufficiency of the evidence may not be made any earlier than at the close of the State's evidence. *See State v. Seward*, 362 N.C. 210, 216 (2008) (once the grand jury has determined the sufficiency of evidence to support a charge, a trial judge "may not pass on the sufficiency of that evidence again until after the State has had an opportunity to present its case-in-chief").

If the defendant fails to make a motion to dismiss at the close of the State's evidence or after all the evidence, he or she may still make the motion for dismissal at the later times indicated in the statute. *See* G.S. 15A-1227(b).

Introduction of defense evidence waives earlier motion. Unlike G.S. 15-173, G.S. 15A-1227 does not have a specific provision stating that when a defendant introduces evidence, he or she waives any motion made at the close of the State's evidence and cannot thereafter raise that issue on appeal. Nevertheless, the courts have held that if a defendant introduces evidence, only his or her motion to dismiss made at the close of all the evidence will be considered on appeal. *See State v. Mendez*, 42 N.C. App. 141 (1979); *see also* N.C. R. APP. P. 10(a)(3).

Ruling on motion required. The trial judge must rule on a motion to dismiss for insufficient evidence before the trial may proceed further. G.S. 15A-1227(c). If he or she fails to rule on the motion in violation of this statute, the appellate courts will review the error to see if the defendant was prejudiced by the judge's failure to do so. *See State v. Hernandez*, 188 N.C. App. 193 (2008) (error, but not prejudicial, for judge to reserve ruling on defendants' motions to dismiss until after the jury returned its verdicts). If there is no reasonable possibility that the trial judge would have granted the defendant's motion to dismiss, then the error will not be found to be prejudicial. *Id.*; *see also State v. Garnett*, 4 N.C. App. 367, 371 (1969) (holding that judges should rule on every motion for nonsuit but the judge's failure to do so was not prejudicial error under the circumstances because "[t]here was ample evidence against this defendant to withstand the motion for judgment as of nonsuit and to require the submission of this case to the jury").

Motion required to preserve issue on appeal. G.S. 15A-1227(d) states that "[t]he sufficiency of all evidence introduced in a criminal case is reviewable on appeal without regard to whether a motion has been made during trial." G.S. 15A-1446(d)(5) likewise allows the sufficiency of the evidence to be reviewed on appeal "even though no objection, exception or motion has been made in the trial division." ***This is not correct!*** The N.C. Court of Appeals has held that the statutes conflict with N.C. Rule of Appellate Procedure 10(b)(3) [now, R. 10(a)(3)], which provided that a defendant had no right on appeal to raise the issue of the insufficiency of the evidence to prove the crime charged unless he or she moved to dismiss the action at trial. *See State v. O'Neal*, 77 N.C. App. 600 (1985). Likewise, the N.C. Supreme Court has held that "[t]o the extent that N.C.G.S. 15A-1446(d)(5) is inconsistent with N.C. R. App. P. 10(b)(3) [now, R. 10(a)(3)], the statute must fail." *State v. Stocks*, 319 N.C. 437, 439 (1987); *see also State v. Blackmon*, __ N.C. App. __, 702 S.E.2d 833, 836 n.1 (2010) ("The subsection of Rule 10 cited by the *Stocks* Court is now subsection (a)(3), pursuant to our revised Rules of Appellate Procedure that took effect on 1 October 2009.").

Accordingly, to preserve the issue for appeal, the defendant must make a motion to dismiss at the close of the State's evidence if the defendant does not introduce any evidence and a motion to dismiss at the close of all the evidence if he or she introduces evidence. As under G.S. 15-173, the defendant may make a motion to dismiss at the close of all the evidence without having made a motion to dismiss at the close of the State's evidence. *See* N.C. R. APP. P. 10(a)(3).

Uniform standard. Regardless of when it was made, a defendant's motion to dismiss under G.S. 15A-1227 is determined by the trial judge under a uniform standard. *See supra* § 30.1, Legal Standard (discussing the "substantial evidence" test). The same standard applies whether the motion to dismiss was made at the close of the State's evidence, at the close of all the evidence, after return of the verdict but before entry of judgment, or after discharge of the jury without a verdict and before the end of the session. *See State v. Scott*, 356 N.C. 591 (2002).

D. Motions to Dismiss after Verdict or to Set Aside Verdict under G.S. 15A-1414

Motion for appropriate relief based on insufficiency of the evidence. Under G.S. 15A-1414(b)(1)c., a defendant may file a motion for appropriate relief after return of the verdict asserting that "[t]he evidence, at the close of all the evidence, was insufficient to justify submission of the case to the jury." This ground may be asserted even if the defendant made no prior motion to dismiss based on insufficient evidence. *Id.* In reviewing the defendant's contention under this statute, the same "substantial evidence" test as set out *supra* in § 30.1 is used by the trial judge to determine whether the motion should be granted. *See State v. Acklin*, 71 N.C. App. 261 (1984) (citing *State v.*

Earnhardt, 307 N.C. 62 (1982)).

Motion to set aside the verdict as against the weight of the evidence. Under G.S. 15A-1414(b)(2), a defendant may file a motion for appropriate relief asserting that "[t]he verdict is contrary to the weight of the evidence." This motion is appropriately made when the State's evidence is legally sufficient to go to the jury but the evidence favorable to the defendant (whether offered by the defendant or the State) has greater probative force than the evidence introduced against him or her. *See Roberts v. Hill*, 240 N.C. 373 (1954). This type of motion requires the trial judge to appraise the testimony and exercise discretion in determining whether the verdict is contrary to the greater weight of the evidence. In ruling on the motion, the judge may consider "the number of witnesses, their intelligence, their opportunity of knowing the truth, their character, their behavior on the examination, and all the circumstances on both sides." *Id.* at 381 (citations omitted). Criminal appellate decisions in North Carolina have cited *Roberts*, a civil case, with approval. *See, e.g., State v. Puckett*, 46 N.C. App. 719 (1980).

Since this motion is addressed to the trial judge's discretion, the refusal to grant the motion will not be disturbed on appeal absent an abuse of that discretion. *See, e.g., State v. Acklin*, 71 N.C. App. 261 (1984) (comparing standards for motion for appropriate relief after verdict based on insufficiency of the evidence under G.S. 15A-1414(b)(1)c. and based on the verdict being against the weight of the evidence under G.S. 15A-1414(b)(2)); *State v. Cauthen*, 66 N.C. App. 630 (1984). Of course, if the evidence is sufficient to take the case to the jury, an appellate court is unlikely to find an abuse of discretion in the trial judge's refusal to find the verdict to be against the weight of the evidence. *See State v. Batts*, 303 N.C. 155 (1981) (finding no abuse of discretion in those circumstances); *Puckett*, 46 N.C. App. 719, 724 (finding no abuse of discretion in light of the victim's identification of defendant even though defendant presented alibi witnesses whose testimony led to the conclusion that it would have been "virtually impossible" for him to have robbed her). Likewise, the granting of such a motion will not be disturbed on appeal absent an abuse of discretion. *See State v. Surles*, 55 N.C. App. 179 (1981) (court upheld district court's decision to set aside its own verdict of guilty; however, appellate court remanded case for new trial, holding that district court could not enter verdict of not guilty after setting aside verdict on ground that it was against weight of evidence); *accord State v. Morgan*, 108 N.C. App. 673 (1993) (following *Surles* and also discussing court's authority to modify sentence after verdict).

Timing of motions. Motions made under G.S. 15A-1414 must be filed after the verdict but not more than ten days after entry of judgment. G.S. 15A-1414(a). Motions may be made and acted on by the trial judge even if notice of appeal has already been given. G.S. 15A-1414(c).

Practice note: ***Always*** move to dismiss ***all*** of the charges at the close of the State's evidence and again at the close of all the evidence if you have presented evidence even though you may not wish to be heard on all of the specific charges. (If you do not move to dismiss all of the charges for insufficient evidence and the client is convicted on charges not covered by your motion, the appellate lawyer is precluded from arguing insufficiency of the evidence with respect to those charges on appeal.) If the judge does not automatically send the jury out after the State or the defendant rests in order to give you an opportunity to make the motion, ask to be heard outside the presence of the jury before making your motion. If you forget to move to dismiss at the close of the State's evidence, you can always move to dismiss at the close of all the evidence. It is always preferable to move to dismiss before the return of the verdict, but if you fail to move to dismiss during the trial, be sure to make a motion to dismiss for insufficiency of the evidence after return of a verdict against the defendant. (A post-verdict ruling that the evidence was insufficient, however, would not bar the State from appealing and potentially having the conviction reinstated. *See infra* § 30.4B, State's Right to Appeal from Dismissal Based on Insufficient Evidence.) To preserve the denial of a motion to dismiss for appellate purposes, you must make sure that your motion and the trial judge's ruling are made on the record and not at an unrecorded bench conference or in chambers. *See* N.C. R. APP. P. 10.

30.4 Effect of Dismissal

A. Application of Double Jeopardy

If the trial judge grants a motion to dismiss based on the insufficiency of the evidence, double jeopardy precludes the State from trying the defendant again on the charge. *See Smalis v. Pennsylvania*, 476 U.S. 140, 142 (1986) ("[A] judgment that the evidence is legally insufficient to sustain a guilty verdict constitutes an acquittal for purposes of the Double Jeopardy Clause."); *State v. Ausley*, 78 N.C. App. 791 (1986); *State v. Murrell*, 54 N.C. App. 342 (1981); *see also* G.S. 15-173 (dismissal for insufficiency of evidence has force and effect of not guilty verdict). Retrial on the charge is barred because "the case was dismissed on the merits and did involve a determination of guilt or innocence." *See Murrell*, 54 N.C. App. 342, 345. Likewise, double jeopardy bars a retrial if the defendant's conviction is reversed by an appellate court because of insufficiency of the evidence. *Burks v. United States*, 437 U.S. 1 (1978); *State v. Mason*, 174 N.C. App. 206 (2005).

If the trial judge's dismissal was not based on grounds of factual guilt or innocence, the subsequent prosecution of a previously-dismissed charge does not violate double jeopardy (although it may be barred for other reasons). *State v. Priddy*, 115 N.C. App. 547 (1994); *see also United States v. Scott*, 437 U.S. 82 (1978) (prosecution's appeal from judgment dismissing defendant's charges was permitted since further prosecution did not violate double jeopardy because the dismissal was based on pre-indictment delay and did not amount to an acquittal on the merits).

B. State's Right to Appeal from Dismissals Based on Insufficient Evidence

Generally. There is no common law right providing for appeal by the State—the right is purely statutory. *State v. Harrell*, 279 N.C. 464 (1971). The State may not appeal a judgment in favor of a criminal defendant in the absence of a statute that clearly confers that right. *State v. Dobson*, 51 N.C. App. 445 (1981). Statutes granting the State a right to appeal in criminal cases are to be strictly construed. *State v. Elkerson*, 304 N.C. 658 (1982).

Applicable statutes. G.S. 15A-1432 addresses the State's right to appeal to superior court from dismissals in district court, and G.S. 15A-1445 addresses the State's right to appeal to the appellate courts from dismissals in superior court. As discussed in detail below, the State is precluded by each of these statutes from appealing from a judgment dismissing the charges for insufficient evidence *if reversal by the reviewing court would result in further prosecution. Cf. United States v. Scott*, 437 U.S. 82, 91 (1978) (in accordance with double jeopardy principles, "[a] judgment of acquittal, whether based on a jury verdict of not guilty or on a ruling by the court that the evidence is insufficient to convict, may not be appealed and terminates the prosecution when a second trial would be necessitated by a reversal"). This is true even if the judge's ruling was clearly erroneous. *See State v. Morgan*, 189 N.C. App. 716 (2008); *see also Smith v. Massachusetts*, 543 U.S. 462, 473 (2005) (acknowledging "the well-established rule" that the double jeopardy bar will attach to a pre-verdict acquittal even if it is "patently wrong in law").

No appeal from district to superior court of a dismissal based on insufficient evidence. G.S. 15A-1432(a)(1) provides that the State may appeal from district to superior court when there has been a decision or judgment dismissing criminal charges as to one or more counts "[u]nless the rule against double jeopardy prohibits further prosecution." In non-jury trials in district court, jeopardy attaches when the trial judge begins to hear evidence or testimony. *See State v. Brunson*, 327 N.C. 244 (1990); *see also State v. Fowler*, 197 N.C. App. 1, 17 (2009) ("'[U]ntil a defendant is "put to trial *before the trier of the facts*, whether the trier be a jury or a judge," jeopardy does not attach.'" (emphasis in original) (citations omitted)). The rationale behind this rule is that the potential for conviction exists only when evidence or testimony against a defendant is presented to and accepted by the court. *See State v. Ward*, 127 N.C. App. 115, 121 (1997).

Under North Carolina law, motions to dismiss based on insufficient evidence cannot be made pretrial because only those defenses, objections, or requests that are capable of being determined without the trial of the general issue (for example, a motion to dismiss for lack of jurisdiction or for a constitutional violation) may be resolved by pretrial motion, "and a court can *only* consider a motion to dismiss for insufficient evidence *after* the State has had an opportunity to present all of its evidence to the trier of fact *during* trial." *See Fowler*, 197 N.C. App. 1, 28 (emphases in original); *see also State v. Seward*, 362 N.C. 210, 216 (2008) (once the grand jury has determined the sufficiency of evidence to support a charge, a trial judge "may not pass on the sufficiency of that evidence again until after the State has had an opportunity to present its case-in-chief"). Accordingly, motions to dismiss on the grounds of insufficient evidence are made after the judge "begins to hear evidence or testimony," and jeopardy has attached by the time any ruling is made granting the motion to dismiss. Since a dismissal by a district court judge based on the insufficiency of the evidence has the effect of a not guilty verdict and constitutes an acquittal for double jeopardy purposes, the State may not appeal to the superior court from such a dismissal. *See Morgan*, 189 N.C. App. 716.

No appeal from superior court to the appellate division of a pre-verdict dismissal based on insufficient evidence. G.S. 15A-1445(a)(1) provides that the State may appeal from superior court to the appellate division from a decision or judgment dismissing criminal charges as to one or more counts "[u]nless the rule against double jeopardy prohibits further prosecution." Jeopardy attaches in superior court "when a defendant in a criminal prosecution is placed on trial: (1) on a valid indictment or information, (2) before a court of competent jurisdiction, (3) after arraignment, (4) after plea, and (5) when a competent jury has been empaneled and sworn." *See State v. Cutshall*, 278 N.C. 334, 344 (1971). Thus, the critical time for jeopardy purposes in a jury trial is the empanelment and swearing of the jury, not the taking of testimony of the first witness.

Double jeopardy will prohibit further prosecution in cases where the trial judge grants a defendant's motion to dismiss based on insufficient evidence *before the verdict* because "a reversal at the appellate level would result in a new trial—requiring defendant to once again defend himself, with all the emotional and monetary burdens associated therewith." *See State v. Scott*, 146 N.C. App. 283, 286 (2001), *reversed on other grounds*, 356 N.C. 591 (2002). Thus, as long as the motion to dismiss is granted after attachment of jeopardy and prior to a verdict being entered, the State is barred from appealing the decision.

Appeal permitted from superior court to the appellate division of a post-verdict dismissal based on insufficient evidence. If the trial judge grants a dismissal *after the verdict* is returned, the State is free to appeal and the conviction may be reinstated if the appellate court finds that the trial judge erroneously granted the motion. *See State v. Hernandez*, 188 N.C. App. 193 (2008). Double jeopardy does not prohibit an appeal in that instance because the jury has already rendered its verdict and, if the State is successful on appeal, the verdict could be reinstated without subjecting a defendant to retrial. *Id.*; *see also United States v. Jenkins*, 420 U.S. 358 (1975).

Additional resources. For further information on double jeopardy and the State's right to appeal, see Robert L. Farb, *Criminal Pleadings, State's Appeal from District Court, and Double Jeopardy Issues* (UNC School of Government, Feb. 1, 2010), www.sog.unc.edu/sites/www.sog.unc.edu/files/pleadjep.pdf, and Robert L. Farb, *Double Jeopardy, Ex Post Facto, and Related Issues* (UNC School of Government, Jan. 2007), www.sog.unc.edu/sites/www.sog.unc.edu/files/djoverview.pdf.

30.5 Fatal Variance

An objection to a variance between the indictment and proof at trial is properly raised by a motion to dismiss for insufficient evidence because there is not sufficient evidence to support the particular charge alleged in the indictment or other pleading. *See State v. Faircloth*, 297 N.C. 100 (1979); *State v. Bell*, 270 N.C. 25 (1967). Such a dismissal precludes the State from further prosecution of the offense charged in the indictment or other pleading because the charged offense has been dismissed for insufficient evidence (*see supra* § 30.4, Effect of Dismissal); but, it ordinarily does not preclude further prosecution of an offense that was not properly pled in the charging document. *See State v. Stinson*, 263 N.C. 283 (1965); *State v. Wall*, 96 N.C. App. 45 (1989); *State v. Johnson*, 9 N.C. App. 253 (1970); *cf. State v. Teeter*, 165 N.C. App. 680 (2004) (double jeopardy bars retrial if indictment would have supported conviction and judge incorrectly dismisses charge for fatal variance).

For further discussion on variances between pleading and proof, see 1 NORTH CAROLINA DEFENDER MANUAL Ch. 8 (Criminal Pleadings) (July 2004) and Jessica Smith, *The Criminal Indictment: Fatal Defect, Fatal Variance, and Amendment*, ADMINISTRATION OF JUSTICE BULLETIN No. 2008/03 (UNC School of Government, July 2008), *available at* http://sogpubs.unc.edu/electronicversions/pdfs/aojb0803.pdf.

Practice note: The N.C. Supreme Court has held that a defendant's motion to dismiss did not properly preserve a fatal variance issue for appellate review where the motion was based solely on insufficient evidence and the defense attorney did not specifically assert fatal variance. *See State v. Pickens*, 346 N.C. 628 (1997) (so holding but then addressing issue assuming arguendo that it had been preserved). Unpublished decisions by the N.C. Court of Appeals have ruled similarly, relying on N.C. Rule of Appellate Procedure 10(b)(1) [the predecessor to Rule 10(a)(1)], which requires a party to present a timely request, objection, or motion to the trial judge stating the specific grounds for the ruling sought if the specific grounds are not apparent from the context. This approach seems at odds with decisions holding that "a fatal variance between the indictment and proof is properly raised by a motion for judgment as of nonsuit or a motion to dismiss, since there is not sufficient evidence to support the charge laid in the indictment." *Faircloth*, 297 N.C. 100, 107. It also is difficult to reconcile with cases holding that a pleading that does not support the offense of conviction deprives the court of jurisdiction over that offense, which may not be waived even if no motion is made at the trial level. ***Nevertheless,*** in cases in which you believe there is a fatal variance, you should specifically state that the motion to dismiss for insufficient evidence is based on a fatal variance between the charges alleged in the indictment or other pleading and the evidence presented at trial.

Chapter 31
Mistrials

31.1 Purposes of Mistrial

A mistrial is a procedural device used by a judge to terminate a trial before the jury returns a verdict on the merits. *See State v. Diehl*, 137 N.C. App. 541 (2000), *rev'd on other grounds*, 353 N.C. 433 (2001). The courts have observed that the "purposes of mistrial are to prevent prejudice arising from conduct before the jury and to provide a remedy where the jury is unable to perform its function." *State v. O'Neal*, 67 N.C. App. 65, 69 (1984), *aff'd as modified*, 311 N.C. 747 (1984). They have also stated that although it is a "drastic remedy," a mistrial is appropriately granted when a party shows the occurrence of serious improprieties that render a fair and impartial verdict impossible. *See State v. Stocks*, 319 N.C. 437, 441 (1987); *see also State v. Taylor*, 362 N.C. 514 (2008).

Generally, the granting of a mistrial will not violate a defendant's right to be free from double jeopardy where a defendant's trial or sentencing hearing "ends with a mistrial declared for a manifest necessity or to serve the ends of public justice." *See State v. Sanders*, 347 N.C. 587, 599 (1998). A manifest necessity only exists when some event occurs at trial that creates "a situation where the defendant's right to have the trial continue to termination in a judgment is outweighed 'by the public's interest in fair trials designed to end in just judgments.'" *Id.* at 595 (quoting *Wade v. Hunter*, 336 U.S. 684, 689 (1949)); *see also State v. Lachat*, 317 N.C. 73, 82 (1986) (stating that the failure of a jury to reach a verdict due to deadlock is a manifest necessity justifying the declaration of a mistrial). The term "manifest necessity" is used throughout this chapter and is discussed further *infra* in § 31.9C, Mistrial Declared for Manifest Necessity.

The basic reasons for a mistrial can be categorized as follows. A mistrial may be granted if an event occurs during trial that:

- prejudices the defendant,
- prejudices the State, or
- prevents the trial from proceeding in conformity with the law.

Examples of events that commonly necessitate the granting of a mistrial include:

- hopeless deadlock by the jury,
- death or disability of a juror, or
- death or disability of the trial judge.

These types of mistrials and mistrials based on prejudice to the parties are discussed in this chapter as well as the practical effects of a mistrial, including the effect of a mistrial on a defendant's constitutional right to be free from double jeopardy.

31.2 Timing of Mistrial Order

An order granting a mistrial must be made before the jury renders a verdict. *See State v. O'Neal*, 67 N.C. App. 65 (1984), *aff'd as modified*, 311 N.C. 747 (1984). Once the jury has rendered a verdict and has been discharged, there is no purpose in ordering a mistrial because the proceedings may be determined by rulings of the court on matters of law, including motions for a new trial. *O'Neal*, 67 N.C. App. at 69. The prohibition on declaring a mistrial after verdict also may be viewed as protecting defendants. A retroactive declaration of a mistrial, if allowed, "would impermissibly place a defendant who made *any* mistrial motion at *any* time in peril, subject to the unlimited discretion of the trial court, of losing his constitutional right to not be twice put in jeopardy for the same offense." *Id.* (emphases in original) (trial judge had no authority to belatedly grant a motion for mistrial where five days had passed since the acceptance of the verdict and the discharge of the jury).

31.3 Standard of Review on Appeal

The decision to order a mistrial lies within the sound discretion of the trial judge and the decision will not be disturbed on appeal absent a showing of an abuse of that discretion. *State v. Upchurch*, 332 N.C. 439 (1992); *State v. Scott*, 150 N.C. App. 442 (2002); *see also Arizona v. Washington*, 434 U.S. 497 (1978). "An abuse of discretion occurs when a ruling is 'manifestly unsupported by reason, which is to say it is so arbitrary that it could not have been the result of a reasoned decision.'" *State v. Taylor*, 362 N.C. 514, 538 (2008) (citation omitted) (upholding denial of motion for mistrial). A trial judge's decision to grant a mistrial is given "great deference since he [or she] is in a far better position than an appellate court to determine the effect" of any error or impropriety on the jury. *State v. Thomas*, 350 N.C. 315, 341 (1999).

31.4 Mistrial Based on Prejudice to the Defendant

Sometimes misconduct, disruptive events, or improprieties occur during trial that prejudice the defendant in the eyes of the jury. A motion for mistrial may be the appropriate remedy if the prejudice cannot be cured in some less drastic manner, such as instructions to the jury or replacement of a juror with an alternate.

A. Statutory Authority for Mistrial

Section 15A-1061 of the North Carolina General Statutes (hereinafter G.S.) provides that "[u]pon motion of a defendant or with his concurrence the judge may declare a mistrial at any time during the trial." Pursuant to this statute, a defendant's motion for mistrial must be granted if, during the trial, an error or legal defect in the proceeding occurs or if conduct that results in "substantial and irreparable prejudice to the defendant's case" occurs inside or outside the courtroom.

Not every disruptive event or impropriety occurring during the trial will automatically require the judge to declare a mistrial. *State v. Newton*, 82 N.C. App. 555, 559 (1986). "'A mistrial should be granted only when there are improprieties in the trial so serious that they substantially and irreparably prejudice the defendant's case and make it impossible for the defendant to receive a fair and impartial verdict.'" *State v. Warren*, 327 N.C. 364, 376 (1990) (citation omitted).

B. Timing of Motion

The motion for mistrial must be made before the verdict. If made after the verdict, the motion would be for a new trial. *State v. Miller*, 271 N.C. 646 (1967). Additionally, if the motion for mistrial is not made in a timely manner, i.e., "at some time sufficiently close to the occurrence of the error to permit its correction," then denial of the motion may not be preserved for appellate review. *See* G.S. 15A-1446 Official Commentary; *see also State v. Summers*, 177 N.C. App. 691, 695 (2006) (court of appeals refused to review the denial of defendant's motion for mistrial based on improper photo identification testimony where defense counsel did not object to the testimony when it was offered but "waited until the testimony of an additional witness" before moving for mistrial); *State v. Smith*, 96 N.C. App. 352 (1989) (defendant waived appellate review where his motion for mistrial based on the prosecutor's alleged improper opening statement was not made until after the jury began deliberation); *see also* N.C. R. APP. P. 10 (requiring a timely objection or motion to preserve the error for appellate review).

C. Concurrence of the Defendant in Declaration of Mistrial

Even if the defendant does not move for mistrial under G.S. 15A-1061, the trial judge may nevertheless declare one pursuant to this statute if he or she believes that an error occurred resulting in substantial and irreparable prejudice to the defendant *and* the defendant concurs in the declaration of mistrial. The appellate courts might consider a defendant's failure to object to be a "concurrence." *See, e.g., State v. Cummings*, 169

N.C. App. 249 (2005) (finding that an order of mistrial was appropriate under G.S. 15A-1061 and double jeopardy did not bar retrial where the trial judge, after hearing the State's evidence and realizing that he had a personal familiarity with the case, rescheduled the case and the defendant made no objection).

In instances where a defendant does not move for mistrial or concur in the declaration of mistrial under G.S. 15A-1061, a trial judge may grant a mistrial pursuant to G.S. 15A-1063(1) if the error or defect made it "impossible for the trial to proceed in conformity with law." *See infra* § 31.6, Impossibility of Proceeding in Conformity with the Law.

Practice note: If you do not want a mistrial to be declared, you should expressly object to the order of mistrial on the record so that it will be clear on review that the defendant did not concur under G.S. 15A-1061. An objection is also necessary to preserve a double jeopardy issue for appellate review in non-capital cases. *See infra* § 31.9E, Preservation of Double Jeopardy Issue for Appellate Review When Mistrial is Granted on State's Motion or by Trial Judge Ex Mero Motu.

D. Co-Defendants

If two or more defendants are joined for trial, G.S. 15A-1061 provides that a mistrial may not be granted under that statute as to a defendant who did not make or join in a motion for mistrial.

E. Misconduct by the Defendant

When a defendant moves for a mistrial based on his or her own misconduct, the argument in support of mistrial will not be given great weight. *State v. Perkins*, 181 N.C. App. 209 (2007) (no abuse of discretion by trial judge in denying defendant's motion for mistrial based on the ground that she was prejudiced when a juror overheard defense counsel in a stairwell trying to convince defendant not to leave her own trial); *State v. Marino*, 96 N.C. App. 506, 507 (1989) (no error in the denial of defendant's motion for mistrial where any prejudice was a result of his own open-court "intemperate and profane outburst," the evidence of defendant's guilt was overwhelming, and it was unlikely that the outburst prevented defendant from receiving a fair and impartial verdict).

F. Misconduct by a Juror

A mistrial may be the appropriate remedy to seek when a juror has engaged in inappropriate conduct. For a detailed discussion of issues related to misconduct by a juror and the exposure of jurors to extraneous information, see *supra* Chapter 26, Jury Misconduct.

G. Selected Examples

The following cases contain examples of disruptive events or improprieties resulting in requests for mistrial by a defendant. In many of these cases, the appellate court found that there was no error by the trial judge in failing to grant a mistrial on the facts presented. Nevertheless, these cases represent various situations in which a mistrial motion may be appropriate.

- Emotional outbursts by a witness, a spectator, a co-defendant, a prosecutor, or the alleged victim. *See, e.g., State v. Moore*, 335 N.C. 567 (1994) (prosecutor); *State v. Blackstock*, 314 N.C. 232 (1985) (prosecuting witness); *State v. McGuire*, 297 N.C. 69 (1979) (co-defendant); *cf. State v. Turner*, 330 N.C. 249 (1991) (victim's family; no indication the defendant moved for a mistrial).
- Exposure of jurors to news reports or extraneous information about the case. *See, e.g., State v. Woods*, 293 N.C. 58 (1977); *State v. Hines*, 131 N.C. App. 457 (1998) (error to deny defendants' motion for mistrial).
- Improper contact with the jury by a third person. *See, e.g., State v. Wilson*, 314 N.C. 653 (1985) (error to deny defendant's motion for mistrial); *cf. State v. Lewis*, 188 N.C. App. 308 (2008) (finding abuse of discretion by trial judge's denial of defendant's motion for appropriate relief and granting new trial where lead detective made comments during break to deputy sheriff serving as juror that were intended to influence the verdict).
- Expressions of opinion or improper remarks by the trial judge in the jury's presence. *See, e.g., State v. Harris*, 308 N.C. 159 (1983).
- References to inadmissible evidence by a witness or prosecutor. *See, e.g., State v. Harris*, 323 N.C. 112 (1988); *State v. Moose*, 115 N.C. App. 707 (1994) (error to deny defendant's motion for mistrial); *cf. State v. Britt*, 288 N.C. 699 (1975) (prosecutor's improper cross-examination of defendant referencing that defendant had been on death row as a result of his prior conviction for the same murder was highly improper and incurably prejudicial).
- Misconduct by the prosecutor. *See, e.g., State v. Elliott*, 64 N.C. App. 525 (1983) (error to deny defendant's motion for mistrial).
- Appearance of the defendant in front of jurors while wearing some type of visible restraint. *See, e.g., State v. Montgomery*, 291 N.C. 235 (1976).
- Failure of the State to comply with discovery requirements. *See, e.g., State v. Walker*, 332 N.C. 520 (1992); *see also* G.S. 15A-910(a)(3a) (providing for mistrial as a possible remedy for discovery violations); Appendix A, *infra*, N.C. COMM'N ON INDIGENT DEFENSE SERVS., PERFORMANCE GUIDELINES FOR INDIGENT DEFENSE REPRESENTATION IN NON-CAPITAL CRIMINAL CASES AT THE TRIAL LEVEL, Guideline 7.5(g)(4) Confronting the Prosecution's Case (Nov. 2004) (recommending that counsel request appropriate relief, including mistrial, if the prosecutor failed to properly provide copies of all prior statements of prosecution witnesses as required by G.S. 15A-903(a)).
- Inappropriate remarks by a prosecutor during opening statement or closing argument. *See, e.g., State v. Dorton*, 172 N.C. App. 759 (2005); *State v. Jordan*, 149 N.C. App. 838 (2002) (error to deny defendant's motion for mistrial).

Practice note: When moving for a mistrial, assert not only the statutory basis for the motion but a constitutional basis as well. Argue that the legal defect or misconduct that occurred during trial violated your client's rights to a fair and impartial trial as guaranteed by the Fourteenth Amendment to the U.S. Constitution and article I, section 19 of the N.C. Constitution, and to a fair and impartial jury pursuant to the Sixth Amendment to the U.S. Constitution and article I, section 24 of the N.C. Constitution. *See State v. Garcell*, 363 N.C. 10 (2009) (the absence of a fair and impartial jury would violate the Sixth Amendment to the U.S. Constitution and article I, § 24 of the N.C. Constitution); *State v. Williams*, 330 N.C. 579, 583 (1992) ("[d]ue process requires that a defendant have 'a panel of impartial, 'indifferent' jurors'") (citations omitted); *State v. Tolley*, 290 N.C. 349, 364 (1976) ("[e]ssential to the concept of due process is the principle" that every person accused of a crime is entitled to a fair and impartial trial) (citations omitted); *State v. Mebane*, 106 N.C. App. 516 (1992) (individual's right to a fair trial by an impartial jury is guaranteed by the Sixth Amendment to the U.S. Constitution and by article I, § 24 of the N.C. Constitution).

31.5 Mistrial Based on Prejudice to the State

Sometimes misconduct, disruptive events, or improprieties occur during trial that prejudice the State in the eyes of the jury. A motion for mistrial may be the appropriate remedy if the prejudice cannot be cured in some less drastic manner, such as instructions to the jury or replacement of a juror with an alternate.

A. Statutory Authority

Generally. G.S. 15A-1062 provides that a judge may grant a motion for mistrial made by the State if there occurs during the trial, either inside or outside the courtroom, misconduct resulting in substantial and irreparable prejudice to the State's case and the misconduct was by

- a juror,
- the defendant,
- the defendant's lawyer, or
- someone acting at the behest of the defendant or his lawyer.

Interpretation of "someone acting at the behest" of defendant or lawyer. This part of the statute has been interpreted restrictively to mean that the trial judge can only grant the State's motion for mistrial if the defendant or his attorney engaged in "some sort of action or conduct" that induced or prompted the alleged misconduct. *See State v. Cooley*, 47 N.C. App. 376, 381 (1980). It is not sufficient that the defendant will benefit from the misconduct. The acts must have been done "at the behest of the defendant or his lawyer." *Id.* (finding that order for mistrial would not have been proper under G.S. 15A-1062 where there was no evidence that defendant or his attorney induced or prompted the alleged jury tampering activities; however, court found mistrial proper under G.S. 15A-1063, discussed *infra* in § 31.6, Impossibility of Proceeding in Conformity with the Law).

Juror misconduct. Under G.S. 15A-1062, the State may move for mistrial when conduct by a juror results in substantial prejudice to the State's case. This misconduct need not have occurred "at the behest of the defendant or his lawyer." *See, e.g., State v. Sanders*, 347 N.C. 587 (1998) (trial judge properly granted State's motion for mistrial pursuant to G.S. 15A-1062 based on juror misconduct not attributable to defendant). For a discussion of issues relating to juror misconduct, see *supra* Chapter 26, Jury Misconduct.

B. Co-Defendants

If two or more defendants are joined for trial, G.S. 15A-1062 provides that a mistrial may not be declared under that statute as to a defendant who does not join in the State's motion for mistrial if

- neither that defendant, his or her defense counsel, nor a person acting at that defendant's or defense counsel's behest participated in the misconduct; or
- the State's case was not substantially and irreparably prejudiced as to that defendant.

Practice note: Do not join in the State's motion for mistrial if you do not believe your client was prejudiced by a co-defendant's misconduct. If you join in the State's motion (or appear to consent), you will waive any future claim to dismissal based on double jeopardy. *See infra* § 31.9D, Mistrial Granted on Defendant's Motion or with Consent.

31.6 Impossibility of Proceeding in Conformity With the Law

Sometimes misconduct, disruptive events, or improprieties occur during trial that prohibit the trial from being fair and impartial and make it necessary for the judge to declare a mistrial. In that event, the mistrial may be granted at either party's request or on the judge's own motion.

A. Statutory Authority

G.S. 15A-1063(1) provides that "[u]pon motion of a party or upon his own motion, a judge may declare a mistrial if . . . [i]t is impossible for the trial to proceed in conformity with law." This statute "was intended to continue the North Carolina practice of allowing a mistrial when it becomes physically necessary to do so." *State v. Cooley*, 47 N.C. App. 376, 382 (1980).

The statute also allows a judge, even over a defendant's objection, to declare a mistrial for the necessity of doing justice and where he or she could reasonably conclude that the trial will not be fair and impartial. *Id.* (State's motion for mistrial pursuant to G.S. 15A-1063 was properly granted where the judge had reasonable grounds to believe that jury tampering had occurred); *see also State v. Malone*, 65 N.C. App. 782 (1984) (trial judge properly granted a mistrial on his own motion where one of the defendant's attorneys testified for the State).

B. Physical Impossibility

According to the Official Commentary, one of the reasons that G.S. 15A-1063(1) was enacted was to cover situations "in which it becomes physically impossible for the trial to proceed—such as may be caused by fire, flood, or other catastrophe." *Compare State v. Shoff*, 128 N.C. App. 432 (1998) (no abuse of discretion by trial judge in granting mistrial due to adverse weather conditions—three to six inches of snow—and the effect that these conditions had on both the jurors' and the defendant attorney's ability to physically get to court for the second day of trial), *with Whaley v. White Consol. Indus., Inc.*, 144 N.C. App. 88, 97 (2001) (trial judge did not abuse his discretion by refusing to declare a mistrial after the trial was interrupted by Hurricane Floyd flooding where record showed that the judge made inquiry as to the effect of the delay and reached a reasoned decision that the trial could continue based on the jurors' responses).

C. Physical Necessity

Death or disability of a juror. The Official Commentary to G.S. 15A-1063(1) states that one of the reasons the statute was enacted was to "cover[] the case in which a juror dies or becomes disabled to continue, and there is no alternate or else deliberations have already begun." *See also State v. Crocker*, 239 N.C. 446, 452 (1954) (a trial judge may order a mistrial if, during trial, a juror "is so incapacitated by reason of intoxicants or otherwise as to be incapable, physically or mentally, of functioning as a competent, qualified juror"); *State v. Beal*, 199 N.C. 278 (1930) (mistrial properly granted where juror became insane during trial); *State v. Ledbetter*, 4 N.C. App. 303 (1969) (no abuse of discretion by trial judge in granting a mistrial where a juror suddenly became ill and was taken to the hospital in serious condition).

If there is an alternate juror and deliberations have not yet begun when the original juror dies or becomes disabled, incapacitated, or disqualified, the trial judge is free to substitute the alternate and a mistrial would not be necessary. *See* G.S. 15A-1215(a) (substitution of alternate juror during trial); G.S. 15A-2000(a)(2) (substitution of alternate juror during a capital sentencing hearing).

Death or disability of the trial judge. If a trial judge becomes sick or disabled during a trial and is unable to continue presiding "without the necessity of a continuance," he or she may exercise discretion and order a mistrial. G.S. 15A-1224(a); *see also State v. Boykin*, 255 N.C. 432 (1961) (trial judge's declaration of mistrial from hospital bed was justified where the judge suffered a heart attack at the courthouse, kept the jury on call for three days hoping to return, and upon medical examination, it was determined he could not return).

A subsequent judge assigned to the case may also declare a mistrial because of the absence of the initial trial judge. *See* G.S. 15A-1224(b) ("If by reason of absence, death, sickness, or other disability, the judge before whom the defendant is being or has been tried is unable to perform the duties required of him before entry of judgment, and has not ordered a mistrial, any other judge assigned to the court may perform those duties, but if the other judge is satisfied that he cannot perform those duties because he did not preside at an earlier stage of the proceedings or for any other reason, he must order a mistrial.").

Death or disability of defense counsel. If the defense attorney suddenly dies or becomes ill during trial, a judge may grant a mistrial if it is "for 'necessity of doing justice.'" *See State v. Battle*, 267 N.C. 513, 518 (1966) (citation omitted) (trial judge properly granted a mistrial on his own motion in a non-capital case, over the four defendants' objections, where an attorney for one of the defendants suddenly became ill at the noon recess of the first day of trial).

31.7 Juror Deadlock

A. Statutory Authority

A jury's inability to reach a verdict due to deadlock justifies the declaration of a mistrial. *State v. Pakulski*, 319 N.C. 562, 570 (1987). Two statutes authorize a trial judge to declare a mistrial in the event that the jury becomes hopelessly deadlocked during deliberations. G.S. 15A-1063(2) states that "[u]pon motion of a party or upon his own motion, a judge may declare a mistrial if . . . [i]t appears there is no reasonable probability of the jury's agreement upon a verdict." *See also State v. O'Neal*, 67 N.C. App. 65 (1984) (noting judge's statutory authority to grant a mistrial, but finding that order for mistrial was not justified since the jury could and did reach a verdict in the case), *aff'd as modified*, 311 N.C. 747 (1984).

G.S. 15A-1235(d) also allows a judge to declare a mistrial on the same grounds as in G.S. 15A-1063(2), stating that "[i]f it appears that there is no reasonable possibility of agreement, the judge may declare a mistrial and discharge the jury." *See O'Neal*, 67 N.C. App. 65. The purpose behind the enactment of G.S. 15A-1235, which also prohibits the trial judge from requiring or threatening to require the jury to continue deliberating for an unreasonable length of time, was "to avoid coerced verdicts from jurors having a difficult time reaching a unanimous decision." *State v. Evans*, 346 N.C. 221, 227 (1997).

B. Capital Sentencing Hearings

If a jury becomes deadlocked during deliberations in a capital sentencing hearing, a mistrial and new sentencing hearing is not the appropriate remedy. Instead, G.S. 15A-2000(b) provides that "[i]f the jury cannot, within a reasonable time, unanimously agree to its sentence recommendation, the judge shall impose a sentence of life imprisonment; provided, however, that the judge shall in no instance impose the death penalty when the jury cannot agree unanimously to its sentence recommendation."

If misconduct occurs during jury deliberations at the sentencing phase, mistrial remains an appropriate remedy if there is a manifest necessity for its declaration. *See, e.g., State v. Sanders*, 347 N.C. 587 (1998) (record revealed "manifest necessity" based on misconduct by the jurors in failing to follow the judge's instructions concerning their duties and the law).

C. Retrial Permitted after Mistrial Based on Hung Jury

Generally. It has long been held that the prohibition against double jeopardy will not bar a retrial of a defendant whose previous trial ended in a deadlocked jury. *See State v. Odom*, 316 N.C. 306 (1986); *see also United States v. Perez*, 22 U.S. 579 (1824). "A 'hung' jury is a classic example of manifest necessity." *Odom*, 316 N.C. 306, 310 (citing *Arizona v. Washington*, 434 U.S. 497 (1978)); *see also State v. Simpson*, 303 N.C. 439 (1981).

Implied acquittal of offenses. In *Green v. United States*, 355 U.S. 184 (1957), the U.S. Supreme Court explained the doctrine of implied acquittal as follows: "when a jury convicts [a defendant] on a lesser alternate charge and fails to reach a verdict on the greater charge—without announcing any splits or divisions and having had a full and fair opportunity to do so—the jury's silence on the second charge is an implied acquittal." *Brazzel v. Washington*, 491 F.3d 976, 978 (9th Cir. 2007). "A verdict of implied acquittal is final and bars a subsequent prosecution for the same offense." *Id.* For example, when a defendant is tried for first degree murder on the theory of premeditation and deliberation and is found guilty of murder in the second degree, the jury has decided that there is not sufficient evidence to conclude beyond a reasonable doubt that defendant premeditated and deliberated the killing. The conviction of the lesser included offense of second-degree murder is an implied acquittal of the greater offense of first degree murder. *State v. Marley*, 321 N.C. 415, 424 (1988).

The North Carolina courts have held that if a mistrial is declared because the jury is deadlocked and unable to reach *any* verdict, the implied acquittal doctrine does not apply and the defendant is not entitled to the dismissal of the charge of the greater offense even if the jury indicated that it was deadlocked on a lesser-included offense. In the view of these cases, there must actually be a final verdict before there can be an implied acquittal in North Carolina. Since a deadlocked jury has been unable to reach any verdict, double jeopardy principles do not preclude a defendant from being tried again for the greater offense. *See State v. Booker*, 306 N.C. 302 (1982) (no double jeopardy bar to retrying defendant on a first-degree murder charge after a mistrial had been declared even though the jury at the first trial had sent a note to the trial judge stating that it was deadlocked seven to five in favor of a verdict of guilty of second-degree murder); *see also State v. Edwards*, 150 N.C. App. 544 (2002) (no implied acquittal of felony assault charge where mistrial was declared after jury indicated its deadlock on lesser included misdemeanor assault charge).

In *Booker*, the N.C. Supreme Court refused to adopt the rule announced by the Supreme Court of New Mexico in *State v. Castrillo*, 566 P.2d 1146 (N.M. 1977), that "'when a jury announces its inability to reach a verdict in a case involving included offenses, the trial court is required to submit verdict forms to the jury to determine if it has unanimously voted for acquittal on any of the included offenses, and the jury may then be polled with regard to any verdict thus returned.'" *Booker*, 306 N.C. 302, 306 (citation omitted). The N.C. Supreme Court agreed instead with the rationale espoused by other jurisdictions that a polling of the jury on the various possible verdicts that were submitted would amount to an "'unwarranted and unwise intrusion into the province of the jury.'" *Id.* (citation omitted).

In addition, when a trial judge elects not to submit lesser-included offenses of a greater charged offense, a defendant is not deemed to have been "acquitted" of those lesser charges if the trial results in a mistrial because of a hung jury. Thus, the defendant can be retried not only on the greater offense, but also on any lesser included offenses supported by the evidence at the second trial. *See State v. Hatcher*, 117 N.C. App. 78 (1994) (after mistrial was declared based on a hung jury, defendant could be retried on second-degree rape charge *and* any applicable lesser included offenses even though trial judge in first trial only charged on second-degree rape).

For additional information regarding double jeopardy in the context of mistrials, see *infra* § 31.9, Double Jeopardy and Mistrials. For a further discussion of the propriety of taking partial verdicts, see *infra* § 34.7F, Partial Verdicts.

D. Additional Resources

For further discussion of topics relevant to deadlock and jury deliberations, including lengthy deliberations, see *infra* Chapter 34, Deliberations and Verdict.

31.8 Findings of Fact

A. Statutory Requirement

Before granting a mistrial, G.S. 15A-1064 requires the trial judge to make findings of fact "with respect to the grounds for the mistrial and insert the findings in the record of the case." *See also State v. Jones*, 67 N.C. App. 377 (1984) (stating that a trial judge should exercise his or her power to grant a mistrial cautiously after a careful consideration of all available evidence and only after making the requisite findings of fact on the basis of evidence before the judge at the time the judicial inquiry is made). Before the enactment of this statute, the common law only required that judges in capital cases find facts and set them out in the record whenever he or she declared a mistrial due to a manifest necessity. *State v. Lachat*, 317 N.C. 73 (1986).

If the findings of fact are not supported by the evidence in the record, the order of mistrial cannot stand. *Id.* (defendant entitled to dismissal of capital murder charge based on former jeopardy where first trial judge failed to make both an inquiry and factual findings as to why he felt the jury was hopelessly deadlocked and the record did not indicate that there was a deadlock); *see also State v. Chriscoe*, 87 N.C. App. 404 (1987) (trial judge erred in granting State's motion for mistrial where the evidence did not support his finding that there was a manifest necessity for a mistrial).

B. Purpose of Requirement

The purpose of G.S. 15A-1064 is to protect a criminal defendant's "valued right" guaranteed by the constitutional prohibition of double jeopardy to have his or her trial completed before a particular tribunal by "ensur[ing] that mistrial is declared only where there exists real necessity for such an order." *State v. Jones*, 67 N.C. App. 377, 382 (1984); *see also* G.S. 15A-1064 Official Commentary (making of findings of fact is "important when the rule against prior jeopardy prohibits retrial unless the mistrial is upon certain recognized grounds or unless the defendant requests or acquiesces in the mistrial"; effect of request or acquiescence is discussed in subsection F., below). A secondary purpose is "to ensure that a full record is made." *Jones*, 67 N.C. App. 377, 385; *see also State v. Lachat*, 317 N.C. 73 (1986) (findings of fact are required so that the judge's conclusion as to the matter of law arising from the facts may be reviewed by the appellate courts).

C. Timing of Findings of Fact

To ensure full deliberation by the trial judge, the findings must be made *before* the mistrial is declared. To allow a judge to make retroactive findings in support of mistrial after it has already been granted would weaken the protections provided by G.S. 15A-1064. *State v. Jones*, 67 N.C. App. 377 (1984). *But see State v. Johnson*, 60 N.C. App. 369, 373 (1983) (noting that the reason for G.S. 15A-1064 was "valued highly by this Court" but finding that the declaration of mistrial before making findings of fact was harmless under the peculiar facts of the case where the trial judge had ordered the mistrial after experiencing chest pains during a heated trial of a drug case).

D. Failure to Make Findings

The requirements of G.S. 15A-1064 are mandatory and "'[e]ven the most exigent of circumstances do not justify circumvention of this rule.'" *State v. Jones*, 67 N.C. App. 377, 382 (1984) (citation omitted); *cf. Arizona v. Washington*, 434 U.S. 497 (1978) (while the U.S. Constitution does not require explicit findings supporting a manifest necessity before granting a mistrial, it does require that the record adequately disclose the necessity on which the order rests). The failure of the trial judge to make findings of fact is error. *See State v. Odom*, 316 N.C. 306 (1986); *see also State v. Lachat*, 317 N.C. 73 (1986). However, the failure to make findings, or the making of findings that do not comply with the statute, may be held harmless if the record shows ample factual support for the mistrial order. *See State v. Felton*, 330 N.C. 619 (1992); *State v. Pakulski*, 319 N.C. 562 (1987).

E. Necessity for Objection

In *non-capital* cases, the defendant must object to the trial judge's failure to make findings in support of a mistrial or the error is not subject to appellate review. *See State v. Pakulski*, 319 N.C. 562 (1987). The mandatory nature of G.S. 15A-1064 does not relieve a defendant of the duty to prevent avoidable errors and the resulting unnecessary appellate review by lodging an appropriate objection. *State* v. *Odom*, 316 N.C. 306, 311 (1986). In a *capital* case, the issue of the judge's failure to make findings of fact to support a mistrial will not be waived by the defendant's failure to object. *See Pakulski*, 319 N.C. 562; *State v. Lachat*, 317 N.C. 73 (1986); *see also infra* § 31.9E, Preservation of Double Jeopardy Issue for Appellate Review When Mistrial is Granted on State's Motion or by Trial Judge Ex Mero Motu (defendant's failure to object to declaration of mistrial waives later double jeopardy argument in noncapital case but not in capital case).

F. Motion Granted at Defendant's Request or with Defendant's Acquiescence

Generally, if a mistrial is granted based on a defendant's request, there can be no prejudice to the defendant resulting from a trial judge's failure to make findings of fact. *State v. White*, 85 N.C. App. 81 (1987), *aff'd*, 322 N.C. 506 (1988); *State v. Moses*, 52 N.C. App. 412 (1981). However, where the defendant's motion for mistrial was based on prosecutorial misconduct, findings of fact "may be as essential to adequate review of his double jeopardy claim as in a case in which mistrial is ordered over the defendant's objection." *White*, 85 N.C. App. 81, 85 (finding harmless error where trial judge made no findings of fact when granting defendant's motion for mistrial because grounds for the mistrial based on prosecutorial misconduct were clear from the record; however, prosecutorial misconduct in this case did not to bar retrial on double jeopardy grounds); *see also infra* § 31.9D, Mistrial Granted on Defendant's Motion or with Consent (discussing double jeopardy implications of mistrial granted on defendant's request).

Likewise, if the defendant acquiesces to a mistrial, a finding to that effect may cure the absence of other findings (subject to the above caveat about prosecutorial misconduct). *See* G.S. 15A-1064 Official Commentary ("If the defendant requests or acquiesces in the mistrial, that finding alone should suffice.").

Practice note: It is not clear what constitutes an acquiescence by the defendant to an order of mistrial. Obviously, if a defendant explicitly consents to the mistrial, he or she has acquiesced. *See, e.g., State v. Boykin*, 255 N.C. 432 (1961) (defendant and his attorney consented to the mistrial and signed the order). To properly preserve the defendant's rights in cases where you do not want a mistrial, always unequivocally object to the order of mistrial on the record. *See State v. Johnson*, 60 N.C. App. 369 (1983) (no discussion of particulars but finding that defendant did not acquiesce in declaration of mistrial).

31.9 Double Jeopardy and Mistrials

A. In General

The Double Jeopardy Clause of the Fifth Amendment to the U.S. Constitution precludes retrial of defendants in some instances where the proceedings are terminated before judgment. *State v. Cooley*, 47 N.C. App. 376, 384 (1980); *see also United States v. Dinitz*, 424 U.S. 600 (1976). This clause is applicable to the states through the Fourteenth

Amendment. *Benton v. Maryland*, 395 U.S. 784 (1969). The Law of the Land Clause, in article I, section 19 of the N.C. Constitution, may also prohibit a defendant from being tried again after an order of mistrial is declared. *See State v. Cameron*, 283 N.C. 191 (1973).

A defendant's right to have his or her trial completed before a particular tribunal has long been considered a "valued right" guaranteed by the constitutional prohibition of double jeopardy. *See, e.g., Wade v. Hunter*, 336 U.S. 684 (1949); *see also Cooley*, 47 N.C. App. 376, 384 ("The interest of the accused which is protected in such cases is his right to retain a given tribunal.").

> The reasons why this "valued right" merits constitutional protection are worthy of repetition. Even if the first trial is not completed, a second prosecution may be grossly unfair. It increases the financial and emotional burden on the accused, prolongs the period in which he is stigmatized by an unresolved accusation of wrongdoing, and may even enhance the risk that an innocent defendant may be convicted. The danger of such unfairness to the defendant exists whenever a trial is aborted before it is completed. Consequently, as a general rule, the prosecutor is entitled to one, and only one, opportunity to require an accused to stand trial.

Arizona v. Washington, 434 U.S. 497, 503–05 (1978) (footnotes omitted).

Whether a defendant's motion to dismiss based on double jeopardy should be granted depends on the validity of the order for mistrial. If the order for mistrial was valid, then a defendant's motion to dismiss will be denied. If the order for mistrial was improperly granted, then the defendant is entitled to dismissal based on former jeopardy. *See State v. Battle*, 267 N.C. 513 (1966).

B. When Jeopardy Attaches

In order for a defendant to move to dismiss a charge on double jeopardy grounds based on the declaration of a mistrial, jeopardy must have attached at the time the mistrial was ordered.

Superior court. Jeopardy attaches in superior court "when a defendant in a criminal prosecution is placed on trial: (1) on a valid indictment or information, (2) before a court of competent jurisdiction, (3) after arraignment, (4) after plea, and (5) when a competent jury has been empaneled and sworn." *State v. Cutshall*, 278 N.C. 334, 344 (1971). Thus, the critical time for jeopardy purposes in a jury trial is the empanelment and swearing of the jury.

District court. In non-jury trials in district court, jeopardy attaches when the trial judge begins to hear evidence or testimony. *State v. Brunson*, 327 N.C. 244 (1990); *see also State v. Fowler*, 197 N.C. App. 1, 17 (2009) ("'until a defendant is "put to trial *before the* *trier of the facts*, whether the trier be a jury or a judge," jeopardy does not attach'" (emphasis added by *Fowler* court) (citations omitted)). The rationale behind this rule is that the potential for conviction exists only when evidence or testimony against a defendant is presented to and accepted by the court. *See State v. Ward*, 127 N.C. App. 115, 121 (1997).

C. Mistrial Declared for a Manifest Necessity

Under the common law, a defendant's right to be free from double jeopardy will not be violated where a defendant's trial or sentencing hearing "ends with a mistrial declared for a manifest necessity or to serve the ends of public justice." *State v. Sanders*, 347 N.C. 587, 599 (1998). A manifest necessity only exists when some event occurs at trial that creates "a situation where the defendant's right to have the trial continue to termination in a judgment is outweighed 'by the public's interest in fair trials designed to end in just judgments.'" *Id.* at 595 (quoting *Wade v. Hunter*, 336 U.S. 684, 689 (1949)); *see also State v. Lachat*, 317 N.C. 73, 82 (1986) (stating that the failure of a jury to reach a verdict due to deadlock is a manifest necessity justifying the declaration of a mistrial).

What constitutes a "manifest necessity" depends on the circumstances of each case. The U.S. Supreme Court, in *Arizona v. Washington*, 434 U.S. 497, 506 (1978), explained that the "manifest necessity" standard is not one that "can be applied mechanically or without attention to the particular problem confronting the trial judge." In discussing "manifest necessity," the N.C. Supreme Court has stated:

> We think, that in all cases of this nature, the law has invested Courts of justice with the authority to discharge a jury from giving any verdict, whenever, in their opinion, taking all the circumstances into consideration, there is a manifest necessity for the act, or the ends of public justice would otherwise be defeated. They are to exercise a sound discretion on the subject; and it is impossible to define all the circumstances, which would render it proper to interfere. To be sure, the power ought to be used with the greatest caution, under urgent circumstances, and for very plain and obvious causes; and, in capital cases especially, Courts should be extremely careful how they interfere with any of the chances of life, in favour of the prisoner. But, after all, they have the right to order the discharge; and the security which the public have for the faithful, sound, and conscientious exercise of this discretion, rests, in this, as in other cases, upon the responsibility of the Judges, under their oaths of office. . . .

State v. Shuler, 293 N.C. 34, 43 (1977) (quoting *United States v. Perez*, 22 U.S. 579, 580 (1824)).

The Fourth Circuit Court of Appeals has addressed the "manifest necessity" standard as follows:

> While manifest necessity for a mistrial does not require that a mistrial be "necessary" in the strictest sense of the word, it does require a high degree of necessity. *See Arizona v. Washington*, 434 U.S. at 506. Perhaps the clearest example of a situation in which manifest necessity exists for a mistrial is when a jury is unable to reach a verdict. *See id.* at 509. At the other extreme are situations in which the prosecution seeks a mistrial in order to have additional time to marshal evidence to strengthen the case against the defendant. *See id.* at 508. Between these two extremes exists a spectrum of trial errors and other difficulties, some creating manifest necessity for a mistrial and others falling short of justifying a mistrial. In all cases, the determination of a trial court that a mistrial is manifestly necessary is entitled to great deference. *See id.* at 510. Nevertheless, "reviewing courts have an obligation to satisfy themselves that, in the words of Mr. Justice Story, the trial judge exercised 'sound discretion' in declaring a mistrial." *Id.* at 514. If the grant of a mistrial by the trial judge amounts to an irrational or irresponsible act, he must be found to have abused his discretion in finding that manifest necessity for the mistrial existed, for a trial judge "'must always temper the decision whether or not to abort the trial by considering the importance to the defendant of being able, once and for all, to conclude his confrontation with society through the verdict of a tribunal he might believe to be favorably disposed to his fate.'" *Id.* (quoting *United States v. Jorn*, 400 U.S. 470 (1971) (Harlan, J.) (plurality opinion)).

Sanders v. Easley, 230 F.3d 679, 685–87 (4th Cir. 2000) (finding that while none of the "numerous instances indicating that the jury deliberations had devolved into something much less than a reasoned, good faith attempt to reach a verdict . . . may have justified a mistrial if presented in isolation," the court could not say that the N.C. Supreme Court acted unreasonably in concluding that the incidents, taken together, created a manifest necessity for granting a mistrial).

D. Mistrial Granted on Defendant's Motion or with Consent

Generally. If a motion for mistrial is granted on a defendant's request or with his or her consent, the prohibition against double jeopardy will generally not bar reprosecution. *State v. White*, 322 N.C. 506 (1988); *see also Oregon v. Kennedy*, 456 U.S. 667 (1982); *United States v. Jorn*, 400 U.S. 470 (1971). "If a defendant moves for a mistrial, he or she normally should be held to have waived the right not to be tried a second time for the same offense." *White*, 322 N.C. 506, 511.

Motion based on prosecutorial misconduct. A narrow exception exists to the above general rule allowing retrial following the granting of a defendant's mistrial request. If the defendant's motion for mistrial is prompted by serious misconduct by the prosecutor *and* he or she can show that the prosecutor was motivated by the intent to provoke a mistrial, then double jeopardy will bar reprosecution. *White*, 322 N.C. 506, 510–11. The test is the same under the federal and state constitutions. *Id.* (adopting the test under the Fifth Amendment set out by the U.S. Supreme Court in *Oregon v. Kennedy*, 456 U.S. 667 (1982), as the appropriate standard under article I, section 19 of the N.C. Constitution). The U.S. Supreme Court has also stated that "the strictest scrutiny is appropriate when the basis for the mistrial is the unavailability of critical prosecution evidence, or when there is reason to believe that the prosecutor is using the superior resources of the State to harass or to achieve a tactical advantage over the accused." *Arizona v. Washington*, 434 U.S. 497, 508 (1978) (footnote omitted).

Motion based on judicial misconduct. Like prosecutors, judges also are prohibited from taking action intended to provoke requests for mistrial. *See Divans v. California*, 434 U.S. 1303, 1303 (1977) (to be entitled to relief under the Double Jeopardy Clause, the defendant must show error by the prosecution or by the court for the purpose of forcing the defendant to move for a mistrial). If the defendant can show that his or her motion for mistrial was prompted by bad-faith conduct by the judge that "threatens the '(h)arassment of an accused by successive prosecutions or declaration of a mistrial so as to afford the prosecution a more favorable opportunity to convict' the defendant[,]" double jeopardy will bar a retrial. *United States v. Dinitz*, 424 U.S. 600, 611 (1976) (citation omitted). *But cf. Oregon v. Kennedy*, 456 U.S. 667, 679 (1982) (reviewing case involving *prosecutorial* misconduct and noting that notwithstanding possibly broader language of *Dinitz* that applied to both prosecutorial and judicial misconduct, double jeopardy will only bar a retrial where "the conduct giving rise to the successful motion for a mistrial was intended to provoke the defendant into moving for a mistrial").

E. Preservation of Double Jeopardy Issue for Appellate Review When Mistrial is Granted on State's Motion or by Trial Judge Ex Mero Motu

Capital cases. The failure of the defendant in a capital case to object to the trial judge's declaration of mistrial will not bar the defendant from pleading former jeopardy and moving for a dismissal of the charge against him or her. *See State v. Lachat*, 317 N.C. 73 (1986). "To strictly require such objections to mistrials in capital cases would require payment of a price too high even for the commendable result of improved judicial efficiency." *Id.* at 85; *see also supra* § 31.8E, Necessity for Objection (defendant's failure to object to lack of findings of fact by trial court in declaring mistrial in capital case does not waive appellate review of issue).

Noncapital cases. Generally, to preserve a double jeopardy issue for review in noncapital cases, the defendant must lodge an objection to the declaration of mistrial at the time it is declared. If he or she fails to do so, the appellate court will find that the defendant waived the objection on appeal. *State v. Odom*, 316 N.C. 306 (1986). This rule is "a court made rule designed to prevent avoidable errors and the resulting unnecessary appeals." *Lachat*, 317 N.C. 73, 85. *But see supra* § 31.9D, Mistrial Granted on Defendant's Motion or with Consent (retrial following mistrial based on prosecutorial or judicial misconduct may not be permissible notwithstanding defendant's motion for or consent to mistrial).

F. No Set Limit on Number of Retrials

"[A]s a general rule, the prosecutor is entitled to one, and only one, opportunity to require an accused to stand trial." *Arizona v. Washington*, 434 U.S. 497, 505 (1978). This principle notwithstanding, there is no specific state or federal constitutional limit on how many times a defendant can be retried after a mistrial is granted. Instead, each double jeopardy claim must be examined individually and "considered in light of the particular facts of the case." *State v. Simpson*, 303 N.C. 439, 447 (1981) (no double jeopardy violation found in defendant's third trial for the same charges since there was no indication of harassment by the State or bad faith conduct by the trial judges in the prior trials, and it appeared that the previous juries were genuinely deadlocked and given every reasonable opportunity to reach a verdict); *State v. Williams*, 51 N.C. App. 613, 619 (1981) (finding that double jeopardy did not preclude a fourth retrial where the previous mistrials were properly ordered based on juror misconduct and juror deadlock with no objection by defendant, the State acted "expeditiously and fairly to achieve a final resolution, and all four trials took place in less than a year").

G. Other Double Jeopardy Issues

The above discussion has focused on the application of double jeopardy to mistrials. For a discussion of other double jeopardy issues, see 1 NORTH CAROLINA DEFENDER MANUAL § 13.4B (Motion to Dismiss on Double Jeopardy Grounds) (Mar. 2009); *see also* Robert L. Farb, *Double Jeopardy, Ex Post Facto, and Related Issues* (UNC School of Government, Jan. 2007), www.sog.unc.edu/sites/www.sog.unc.edu/files/djoverview.pdf.

31.10 Practical Effect of Mistrials

When a mistrial is properly granted, "in legal contemplation there has been no trial." *State v. Tyson*, 138 N.C. 627, 629 (1905). "Stated otherwise, a 'mistrial results in nullification of a pending jury trial.'" *Burchette v. Lynch*, 139 N.C. App. 756, 760 (2000) (citation omitted). The parties are returned to their original positions and, at a retrial, can introduce new evidence and assert new defenses that were not raised at the first trial. *United States v. Mischlich*, 310 F. Supp. 669, 672 (D.N.J. 1970), *aff'd sub nom. United States v. Pappas*, 445 F.2d 1194 (3d Cir. 1971). This principle applies to trials and sentencing hearings. *State v. Sanders*, 347 N.C. 587 (1998).

A. Procedure Following Mistrial

When a trial judge orders a mistrial, he or she must then "direct that the case be retained for trial or such other proceedings as may be proper." G.S. 15A-1065. According to the Official Commentary, the drafters did not address in this statute whether a defendant awaiting retrial should be held in custody or released on bail because it "thought the matter was already covered by Article 26, Bail." For a detailed discussion of pretrial release, see 1 NORTH CAROLINA DEFENDER MANUAL Ch. 1 (Pretrial Release) (Aug. 2010).

B. Rulings from Previous Trials

Evidentiary rulings. Rulings on the admissibility of evidence made by the trial judge in a previous trial are not binding on the judge when the defendant is subsequently tried again following a mistrial. "[N]either the doctrine of collateral estoppel nor the one judge overruling another rule can apply" to an evidentiary ruling made by the judge at a retrial since it was made after a mistrial was declared in the first trial. *State v. Harris*, 198 N.C. App. 371, 376 (2009) (holding that previous judge's ruling excluding evidence under N.C. Rule of Evidence 404(b) did not bind judge in later retrial because in legal contemplation, there had been no trial); *see also State v. Lawrence*, 179 N.C. App. 654 (2006) (unpublished) (trial judge on retrial could grant State's motion in limine to exclude evidence allegedly beneficial to the defendant that judge in first trial had denied); *Burchette v. Lynch*, 139 N.C. App. 756, 760 (2000) (if a defendant's trial results in a hung jury, the new trial is a trial de novo and is unaffected by rulings made during the original trial).

Pretrial non-evidentiary rulings. Pretrial non-evidentiary rulings are also not binding on the judge who presides over a retrial. *See Harris*, 198 N.C. App. 371 (holding that previous judge's ruling on defendant's motion for complete recordation did not bind judge in retrial).

Suppression rulings. Pretrial rulings on motions to suppress evidence made pursuant to Article 53 of Chapter 15A of the N.C. General Statutes are also unlikely to be binding on a subsequent judge at retrial. Motions made pursuant to this Article are a specific type of motion in limine and rulings on motions in limine are preliminary or interlocutory decisions that are subject to change if circumstances during trial make it necessary. *State v. McNeill*, 170 N.C. App. 574 (2005) (finding that even though the trial judge had granted defendant's pretrial motion to suppress based on Fourth Amendment grounds, the trial judge acted within his authority in reversing this ruling and subsequently admitting this evidence later during the same trial); *see also State v. Thomas*, 199 N.C. App. 319 (2009) (unpublished) (noting preliminary nature of motion to suppress).

Practice note: Always renew *all* of your motions at the retrial after a mistrial has been granted regardless of whether the motions were previously granted or denied. If your motions were originally denied, this is an opportunity to reargue them and obtain a different ruling. Although G.S. 15A-975(c) requires a showing of previously undiscovered facts before a defendant may renew a motion to suppress evidence, this statute likely does not apply at a retrial. As a practical matter, you should be prepared to persuade a second trial judge that the earlier ruling should be revisited.

You should also renew a motion to suppress even if it was originally granted at the first trial. However, you can assert to the judge at retrial that he or she is not required to rehear the motion but can instead adopt the previous ruling without hearing testimony or arguments. *See State v. Grogan*, 40 N.C. App. 371, 374 (1979) (after the first trial ended in a mistrial, defendant moved for a rehearing of his motion to suppress that had been previously denied but second trial judge refused to hear it—court of appeals noted that "nothing alleged by the defendant in his motion for rehearing and supporting affidavits required [the judge at retrial] to rehear the motion which had previously been finally denied").

Special verdicts. A party is precluded by the principles of res judicata and collateral estoppel from relitigating during a retrial an issue that was actually litigated and finally decided by special verdict during a previous trial that ended in mistrial. *See State v. Dial*, 122 N.C. App. 298 (1996) (defendant, at retrial, was precluded from relitigating jurisdiction issue where trial judge in first trial accepted jury's special verdict finding that North Carolina had jurisdiction but granted a mistrial due to the jury's deadlock on the issue of guilt or innocence).

C. Transcripts of Previous Trials

Determination of defendant's entitlement. The state must, as a matter of equal protection, provide an indigent defendant with a transcript of prior proceedings when that transcript is needed for an effective defense or appeal. *Britt v. North Carolina*, 404 U.S. 226, 227 (1971); *see also* G.S. 7A-450(b) (state must provide indigent defendant "with counsel and the other necessary expenses of representation"). However, under *Britt*, a free transcript need not always be provided. Upon a defendant's motion for transcript, the trial judge must determine:

- whether a transcript is necessary for preparing an effective defense; and
- whether there are alternative devices available to the defendant that are substantially equivalent to a transcript.

State v. Rankin, 306 N.C. 712, 716–17 (1982) (finding constitutional violation where the trial judge denied defendant's motion for transcript as untimely because the retrial had not yet been scheduled and the judge's offer to make the court reporter available to the defendant during retrial was clearly an insufficient alternative to the verbatim transcript). It is difficult to imagine a situation in which a defendant would not be entitled to the transcript of the prior trial under this standard.

Reimbursement may be required. A trial judge may order the defendant to reimburse the state for the cost of the transcript in the event that the defendant is convicted. *See State v. Harris*, 198 N.C. App. 371 (2009) (upholding trial judge's order requiring defendant, as a condition of post-release supervision, to reimburse the state for the cost of the transcript of defendant's previous trial); *see also* G.S. 7A-304(a), (c) (describing convicted defendant's obligation to repay costs); G.S. 7A-455(b) (same).

Chapter 32
Instructions to the Jury

The jury charge is a vital part of a criminal trial, and the content of the instructions can have a profound impact on the jury's determination of the defendant's guilt or innocence. Sections 15A-1231, 15A-1232, and 15A-1234 of the North Carolina General Statutes (hereinafter G.S.) contain the basic standards and procedures on instructions to the jury. This chapter addresses the general requirements relating to jury instructions as well as the duties of the trial judge, special requests for instructions by the defendant, and the preservation of issues for appeal.

32.1 General Requirements

In instructing the jury, "[i]t is well established that a judge must declare and explain the law arising upon the evidence." *State v. Little*, 163 N.C. App. 235, 240 (2004); *see also State v. McLean*, 74 N.C. App. 224 (1985); G.S. 15A-1232. The chief purposes of the charge to the jury are clarification of the issues, elimination of extraneous matters, and declaration and explanation of applicable law. *State v. Jackson*, 228 N.C. 656 (1948).

A trial judge is not required to follow any particular form in giving instructions and has wide discretion in presenting the issues to the jury. *State v. Harris*, 306 N.C. 724, 727–28 (1982). Still, the defendant always has the right to receive instructions on the substantial features of the case and is entitled to special instructions when requested and warranted by the evidence. *See infra* §§ 32.3B through D, Substantial Features of the Case, Subordinate Features of the Case, and Lesser Included Offenses, and § 32.4B, Requests for Special Instructions.

Before 1985, G.S. 15A-1232 required judges to summarize the evidence of both parties to the extent necessary to explain the application of the law to the evidence. This statute was amended in 1985 to remove that requirement, although the judge may still elect to do so. *See State v. Blue*, 356 N.C. 79 (2002); *State v. Taylor*, 80 N.C. App. 500 (1986); *see also* N.C. Pattern Jury Instruction—Crim. 100.00 (April 2005). If the judge does elect to summarize the evidence or explain the application of the law thereto, he or she "must be vigilant not to express an opinion as to the quality of the evidence or as to the credibility of a witness." *State v. Artis*, 325 N.C. 278, 309 (1989), *vacated on other grounds*, 494 U.S. 1023 (1990).

Practice note: You should consider asking the judge to specifically explain the application of the law to the evidence in cases where the jury, by its questions, indicates confusion or concern about how the law relates to the evidence in a particular case. *See, e.g., Blue*, 356 N.C. 79 (defendant argued that the trial judge erred in failing to specifically instruct the jury, in response to its question, that defendant had the same rights pertaining to self-defense and to the defense of habitation on his front porch as he did within his home); *State v. Moore*, 339 N.C. 456, 462 (1994) (defendant argued that the trial judge erred in failing to satisfy the jury's request for an explanation of the law on the felony-murder rule concerning the temporal link between the killing and the underlying felony of discharging a firearm into occupied property).

There are also mandatory and discretionary instructions about reaching a verdict, discussed *infra* Chapter 34, Deliberations and Verdict.

32.2 Charge Conference

Before closing arguments, a trial judge must conduct a conference to discuss proposed instructions out of the presence of the jury. G.S. 15A-1231(b); N.C. GEN. R. PRAC. SUPER. & DIST. CT. 21. Pursuant to G.S. 15A-1231(b), the charge conference must be recorded.

At the conference, the judge must inform the parties of the offenses, lesser included offenses, and affirmative defenses on which he or she will charge the jury. The parties must also be informed what, if any, parts of requested instructions will be given. On request, the judge must inform the parties whether he or she intends to include other particular instructions in the jury charge. G.S. 15A-1231(b).

The trial judge's failure to conduct a recorded charge conference in violation of G.S. 15A-1231(b) does not constitute grounds for appeal unless the judge's failure to comply was not corrected before the end of trial and it materially prejudiced the defendant's case. *See State v. Brunson*, 120 N.C. App. 571 (1995) (defendant unable to show material prejudice where trial judge held an informal, unrecorded charge conference).

Practice note: The charge conference is a significant stage of trial and counsel should prepare accordingly. Counsel should:

- file written requests for instructions as soon as possible so the trial judge will have time to read them before the charge conference;
- be prepared to argue in support of his or her tendered instructions and against detrimental ones submitted by the State or suggested by the trial judge;
- lodge specific objections to erroneous instructions at the charge conference;
- carefully listen to the instructions given during the jury charge and ask for corrections, additions, or modifications as necessary; and
- lodge or renew specific objections to erroneous instructions before the jury retires to deliberate.

32.3 Explanation of the Law

A. Pattern Jury Instructions

In instructing the jury, trial judges ordinarily use the North Carolina Pattern Jury Instructions for Criminal Cases, prepared by the North Carolina Conference of Superior Court Judges Committee on Pattern Jury Instructions. The Court of Appeals has stated generally that the use of the Pattern Jury Instructions is "the preferred method of jury instruction." *See Caudill v. Smith*, 117 N.C. App. 64, 70 (1994). The "Guide to the Use of this Book" that prefaces the Pattern Jury Instructions directs judges to review the pattern instructions and make adaptations as necessary before giving any instructions to the jury.

Practice note: The Pattern Jury Instructions are a good starting point in preparing instructions for the charge conference; however, counsel should always carefully review the pattern instructions to see if they need modification or clarification to fit the needs of the particular case. Do not rely on the judge to do it for you.

B. Substantial Features of the Case

The trial judge has considerable discretion in the manner in which the jury is charged, but he or she is always required to instruct the jury "on all substantial and essential features of the case embraced within the issue and arising on the evidence." *State v. Higginbottom*, 312 N.C. 760, 764 (1985); *State v. Young*, 16 N.C. App. 101 (1972). This is true regardless of requests by the parties. *State v. Harris*, 306 N.C. 724 (1982); *State v. McHone*, 174 N.C. App. 289 (2005). Under this principle, the trial judge must instruct not only on the crime charged in the indictment but also on lesser included offenses (discussed in subsection D., below), defenses (discussed in subsection E., below), and the identification of the defendant as the perpetrator when warranted by the evidence. *See State v. Shaw*, 322 N.C. 797, 803–04 (1988); *State v. Kinard*, 54 N.C. App. 443 (1981).

C. Subordinate Features of the Case

Instructions as to the significance of evidence not relating to the elements of the crime itself or to the defendant's criminal responsibility have been considered subordinate or nonessential features of the case. *State v. Hunt*, 283 N.C. 617 (1973). Absent a request by the defendant, the judge is not required to give instructions on these features. *State v. Lester*, 289 N.C. 239 (1976). However, when a defendant requests an instruction on a nonessential feature of a case and that instruction is correct in law and supported by the evidence, the judge must give the instruction in substance. *State v. Monk*, 291 N.C. 37, 54 (1976); *see also infra* § 32.4B, Requests for Special Instructions. A judge may elect to instruct on a subordinate feature even without a request by counsel. *Harris*, 306 N.C. 724, 727.

Examples. Some examples of subordinate features are:

- Alibi. *See State v. Hunt*, 283 N.C. 617 (1973); N.C. Pattern Jury Instruction—Crim. 301.10 (Mar. 2003); *see also infra* § 32.3E, Defenses (discussing practical considerations regarding alibi instruction and possible inconsistencies in case law).
- Accomplice testimony. *State v. Brinson*, 277 N.C. 286 (1970); N.C. Pattern Jury Instruction—Crim. 104.25 (June 2011).
- The absence of motive. *State v. Elliott*, 344 N.C. 242, 273 (1996); N.C. Pattern Jury Instruction—Crim. 104.10 (Apr. 2005).
- The credibility of an interested or biased witness. *State v. Dale*, 343 N.C. 71 (1996); N.C. Pattern Jury Instruction—Crim. 104.20 (June 2011).
- Evidence of the defendant's character for law-abidingness or other pertinent character trait. *See State v. Bogle*, 324 N.C. 190, 199–200 (1989); N.C. Pattern Jury Instruction—Crim. 105.30 (June 2011).
- Flight by the defendant. *State v. Lester*, 289 N.C. 239 (1976); N.C. Pattern Jury

Instruction—Crim. 104.35, 104.36 (Feb. 1994).

- Impeachment or corroboration of a witness by a prior statement. *State v. Detter*, 298 N.C. 604, 630–31 (1979); *State v. Borkar*, 173 N.C. App. 162 (2005); N.C. Pattern Jury Instruction—Crim. 105.20 (June 2011).
- The effect of the defendant's decision not to testify. *State v. Paige*, 272 N.C. 417 (1968); N.C. Pattern Jury Instruction—Crim. 101.30 (May 2005).
- Impeachment of defendant by evidence of prior convictions if elicited by the State. *State v. Jackson*, 161 N.C. App. 118 (2003) (defendant not entitled to limiting instruction where he voluntarily testified to prior convictions on direct examination); *State v. Gardner*, 68 N.C. App. 515 (1984), *aff'd*, 315 N.C. 444 (1986) (same); N.C. Pattern Jury Instruction—Crim. 105.40 (June 2011).

Reasonable doubt. Although "reasonable doubt" is not technically categorized as a subordinate feature of a criminal case, a trial judge need define it only if it is specifically requested by the defendant. *See infra* § 32.4B, Practice Note.

Practice note: Whether to request an instruction on a subordinate feature of the case is a tactical decision. Counsel should carefully consider the effect of the instruction on the jury since giving an instruction on a particular nonessential feature of the case may so concentrate attention on that subject "as to divert attention from unrelated weaknesses in the State's case." *Hunt*, 283 N.C. 617, 624. For example, if a prosecution witness has an emotional outburst during trial, counsel may decide not to request an instruction regarding the outburst because the instruction may further highlight the witness's emotional state. *See, e.g., State v. Blackstock*, 314 N.C. 232 (1985).

D. Lesser Included Offenses

Right to instruction. State and federal principles of due process require that a lesser included offense instruction be given when the evidence warrants such an instruction. *See Hopper v. Evans*, 456 U.S. 605 (1982); *State v. Arnold*, 329 N.C. 128 (1991); *State v. Ledwell*, 171 N.C. App. 328 (2005). The N.C. courts have often said that when the State's evidence is positive as to each and every element of the crime charged and there is no conflicting evidence relating to any element, submission of a lesser included offense is not required. *See, e.g., State v. Millsaps*, 356 N.C. 556 (2002); *State v. Harvey*, 281 N.C. 1 (1972). However, where there is some evidence of a lesser included offense, the trial judge *must* instruct the jury on it even in the absence of a special request for such instruction. *State v. Lawrence*, 352 N.C. 1, 19–20 (2000); *State v. Montgomery*, 341 N.C. 553 (1995); *State v. Bumgarner*, 147 N.C. App. 409 (2001); *see also* G.S. 15-170 (when a defendant is indicted for a criminal offense, he or she may be convicted of the charged offense or of a lesser included offense). This rule applies even when the defendant does not present any evidence but the State's evidence is conflicting. *State v. Smallwood*, 78 N.C. App. 365 (1985).

Trial strategy considerations. As a matter of trial strategy, a defendant may prefer that an instruction on a lesser included offense not be given and go for "all or nothing." However, it appears that under North Carolina law, the defendant has no right to preclude an instruction on a lesser included offense if the evidence warrants an instruction. *See State v. Jones*, 149

N.C. App. 977 (2002) (unpublished). Nor can the defendant preclude the giving of an instruction by not requesting it if there is evidence supporting the instruction. *State v. Harris*, 306 N.C. 724 (1982).

Waiver. To preserve the issue of the trial judge's failure to instruct on a lesser included offense that is supported by the evidence, a defendant must have requested such an instruction or he or she must have objected to the charge as given. *See State v. Collins*, 334 N.C. 54 (1993) (finding waiver under N.C. R. App. P. 10(b)(2) [now, N.C. R. App. P. 10(a)(2)] where defendant failed to object to trial judge's failure to instruct on lesser included offense of attempted murder); *see generally State v. Smith*, 311 N.C. 287 (1984) (because defendant's written request for instruction regarding the State's identification testimony had been previously denied, he did not have to repeat his objection to the jury instructions, after the fact, to preserve the issue for appellate review). Without proper preservation of the issue at trial, appellate counsel is limited to seeking review of the issue under the rigorous "plain error" standard of review. *State v. Thomas*, 350 N.C. 315, 348 (1999); *see also infra* § 32.9, Preservation of Issues for Appeal.

Invited error. A defendant may not decline an opportunity for an instruction on a lesser included offense and then claim on appeal that failure to instruct on the lesser included offense was error. *State v. Sierra*, 335 N.C. 753 (1994).

Practice note: Be sure to specifically constitutionalize your objection to the trial judge's instruction or omission of an instruction on a lesser included offense; otherwise, appellate counsel will be precluded from arguing a due process violation on appeal. *See infra* § 32.9A, Necessity of Specific Objection. State on the record that the giving (or omission) of the instruction violates the Fourteenth Amendment to the U.S. Constitution as well as article I, section 19 of the N.C. Constitution.

E. Defenses

Generally. Defenses raised by the evidence constitute substantial features of the case; thus, where the evidence, if accepted, discloses facts sufficient in law to constitute a defense to the crime for which the defendant is indicted, the judge is required to instruct the jury on the legal principles applicable to that defense. *State v. Fields*, 324 N.C. 204 (1989) (new trial granted where defendant's evidence merited an instruction on unconsciousness or automatism and trial judge failed to give the requested instruction); *State v. Deck*, 285 N.C. 209 (1974) (where the State's evidence was sufficient to require the trial judge to instruct on the law of self-defense, the trial judge's failure to so do constituted prejudicial error).

"What weight, if any, is to be given such evidence, is for determination by the jury." *Fields*, 324 N.C. 204, 210 (citations omitted). When determining whether the evidence is sufficient to entitle a defendant to jury instructions on a defense, the trial judge must consider the evidence in the light most favorable to the defendant. *State v. Oliver*, 334 N.C. 513, 520 (1993).

Practice note: While the judge has a duty, notwithstanding the absence of a request, to instruct on defenses that are supported by the evidence (*State v. Loftin*, 322 N.C. 375 (1988)), always file a written request when you want an instruction on an applicable defense. This will ensure that the issue is properly preserved for appeal in the event that the judge fails or refuses to instruct on the defense. *See State v. Smith*, 311 N.C. 287 (1984).

In some circumstances, the giving of an instruction on a defense when not supported by the evidence may warrant reversal of a conviction—for example, in cases in which the judge gives an instruction on a defense not raised by the evidence and the instruction conflicts with the defendant's theory of defense. *See, e.g., State v. Tillman*, 36 N.C. App. 141 (1978) (defendant did not rely on and presented no evidence of entrapment; instruction conflicted with defendant's theory of defense and required new trial); *State v. Ransom*, 2 N.C. App. 613 (1968) (to same effect); *cf. State v. Bland*, 19 N.C. App. 560 (1973) (trial judge instructed on entrapment although not requested by defendant; not error to give instruction in light of State's evidence and argument by defendant's counsel during trial).

Alibi. Although alibi is often referred to as a defense, this is "inexact." *State v. Hunt*, 283 N.C. 617, 624 (1973) (overruling cases that held that a defendant is entitled to an instruction on alibi if the evidence supported it even in the absence of a specific request). Unlike evidence of "true" defenses, evidence that the defendant was elsewhere when the crime was committed should be considered a subordinate feature of the case because it has "nothing to do with the elements of or criminal responsibility for the crime for which the defendant is indicted." *Id.* at 624. *But cf. State v. Alston*, 294 N.C. 577, 590 (1978) (stating in passing that the defendant's "alibi defense" was a "substantial feature[] of the case" [this general comment by court likely does not affect ruling in *Hunt*]). In crimes requiring a defendant's personal presence at the scene of its commission, alibi evidence is "simply evidence contradictory of the State's evidence that defendant committed the alleged crime." *Hunt*, 283 N.C. 617, 624. Since alibi evidence is a subordinate feature of the case, a trial judge is not required to instruct the jury on alibi unless the defendant specifically requests it. *See State v. Williams*, 355 N.C. 501, 582 (2002).

Practice note: Counsel should carefully consider whether to request a specific instruction on alibi or whether to just rely on the instructions of burden of proof and reasonable doubt. Use of the term "alibi" may harm a defendant's case, as the jury may view it not as a reason for finding that the defendant was not involved in the crime but rather as an artifice to conceal the defendant's alleged involvement.

Additional resources. For further information regarding select defenses and instructions thereon, see School of Government publications authored by John Rubin entitled:

- *The Voluntary Intoxication Defense*, ADMINISTRATION OF JUSTICE MEMORANDUM No. 93/01 (Apr. 1993), *available at* www.sog.unc.edu/sites/www.sog.unc.edu/files/aojm9301.pdf;
- *The Diminished Capacity Defense*, ADMINISTRATION OF JUSTICE MEMORANDUM No.

92/01 (Sept. 1992), *available at* www.sog.unc.edu/sites/www.sog.unc.edu/files/aojm9201.pdf;
- THE ENTRAPMENT DEFENSE IN NORTH CAROLINA (2001); and
- THE LAW OF SELF-DEFENSE IN NORTH CAROLINA (1996).

See also JESSICA SMITH, NORTH CAROLINA CRIMES: A GUIDEBOOK ON THE ELEMENTS OF CRIME 18–24 (UNC School of Government, 7th ed. 2012).

F. Words of Common Usage or Meaning

In the absence of a request for special instructions, it is not error for a trial judge to fail to define and explain words of common usage or meaning to the general public. This is true even if the word at issue is an essential element of the crime charged. *State v. Jones*, 300 N.C. 363 (1980) (finding no error in the trial judge's failure to define "intent" because the word is self-explanatory). However, if the meaning of the word is not clear, the judge must define it in order to give the jury proper guidance. *See State v. Patton*, 18 N.C. App. 266 (1973) (finding in a "public intoxication" case that the trial judge's failure to define the words "drunk" or "intoxicated" was error entitling defendant to a new trial).

32.4 Requests for Instructions

A. In General

Parties may submit proposed jury instructions at the close of the evidence or at an earlier time if directed by the judge. The instructions must be in writing, and parties must furnish copies to opposing counsel. G.S. 15A-1231(a).

B. Special Instructions

Form of request. A defendant may request special instructions on subordinate or nonessential features of a case that do not relate to the elements of the offense or to the defendant's criminal responsibility. *See supra* § 32.3C, Subordinate Features of the Case. These requests must be:

- in writing,
- entitled in the cause, and
- signed by counsel submitting them.

G.S. 1-181(a); *State v. Broome*, 268 N.C. 298 (1966) (per curiam). If a request for a special instruction does not meet these requirements, it is within the discretion of the trial judge whether to give or refuse the instruction. *State v. Harris*, 67 N.C. App. 97 (1984).

Timing of request. Requests for special instructions must be submitted to the judge before the judge begins to give the jury charge. G.S. 1-181(b); *see also* N.C. GEN. R. PRAC. SUPER. & DIST. CT. 21 (providing that "[i]f special instructions are desired, they should be submitted in writing to the trial judge at or before the jury instruction conference"); *State v. Long*, 20 N.C. App. 91 (1973) (holding that a request for special instruction is not timely if it is tendered after the jury retires to deliberate). However, the judge may, in his or her discretion, consider requests for special instructions regardless of the time they are made. G.S. 1-181(b).

Right to instruction. If a party requests a special instruction that is legally correct in itself and is pertinent to the evidence and the issues in the case, the judge must give the instruction at least in substance. *State v. Lamb*, 321 N.C. 633 (1988); *State v. Craig*, 167 N.C. App. 793 (2005). The judge need not give the instruction in the exact language of the request, but he or she may not change the sense of it or so qualify it as to weaken its force. *State v. Puckett*, 54 N.C. App. 576 (1981).

Practice note: If you would like an instruction defining reasonable doubt, you must specifically request it or the trial judge may not define the concept. *See State v. Miller*, 344 N.C. 658 (1996); *see also* N.C. Pattern Jury Instruction—Crim. 101.10 n.1 (June 2008), *citing State v. Shaw*, 284 N.C. 366, 374 (1973). For a discussion of other instructions that must be specifically requested, such as a defendant's decision not to testify, see *supra* § 32.3C, Subordinate Features of the Case.

32.5 Additional Instructions after Jury Retires

A. In General

After the jury has retired for deliberation, the trial judge may recall the jurors in order to give additional instructions to:

- respond to an inquiry of the jury made in open court; or
- correct or withdraw an erroneous instruction; or
- clarify an ambiguous instruction; or
- instruct on a point of law that should have been covered in the original instructions.

G.S. 15A-1234(a).

B. Repetition of Instructions

Whenever additional instructions are given, the judge may also give or repeat other instructions to avoid giving undue prominence to additional instructions. G.S. 15A-1234(b). The decision whether to repeat other instructions is within the trial judge's discretion. *State v. Prevette*, 317 N.C. 148 (1986). The trial judge is not required to repeat instructions that have been previously given absent an error in the charge. *State v. Hockett*, 309 N.C. 794 (1983). Courts have found needless repetition to be undesirable and have occasionally held it to be erroneous. *See State v. Dawson*, 278 N.C. 351 (1971).

C. Special Requirements

Notice requirement. Before giving additional instructions, the trial judge must inform the parties generally of the instructions he or she intends to give. The parties must be afforded an opportunity to be heard. G.S. 15A-1234(c). If a judge is merely repeating or clarifying an instruction at the jury's request, he or she does not have to give the parties an opportunity to be heard before reinstruction. *State v. Weathers*, 339 N.C. 441 (1994); *State v. Davidson*, 131 N.C. App. 276 (1998).

Right to additional arguments. If the additional instructions, by restriction or enlargement, change the permissible verdicts of the jury, the parties *must* be allowed additional jury arguments on request. Otherwise, whether to allow additional arguments by counsel is within the discretion of the trial judge. G.S. 15A-1234(c).

Procedural requirements. Under G.S. 15A-1234(d), all additional instructions must be given in open court and must be made a part of the record. The full jury must be returned to the courtroom when additional instructions are given under G.S. 15A-1234. *See State v. Tucker*, 91 N.C. App. 511 (1988) (finding that trial judge committed reversible error by summoning only the jury foreman to the courtroom and answering the jury's question regarding the law applicable to the case).

D. Instructions When Jury Indicates Deadlock

G.S. 15A-1235(c) provides that if the jury indicates a deadlock, the trial judge may give or repeat the instructions about reaching a verdict provided in G.S. 15A-1235(a) and (b). For discussion on further instructions to the jury when it has indicated its failure to reach a verdict, see *infra* § 34.5A, Deliberations and Verdict: Further Instructions.

32.6 Trial Judge's Authority to Provide Written Instructions to the Jury

The trial judge has the inherent authority to submit instructions to the jury in writing. This decision is a discretionary one and will not be reversed absent an abuse of that discretion. *See State v. McAvoy*, 331 N.C. 583, 591 (1992) (holding that trial judge erred in ruling as matter of law that he had no authority to give the jury written instructions, but finding no prejudicial error where trial judge orally repeated the requested instructions for the jury, thereby complying with the essence of the jury's request); *State v. Hester*, 111 N.C. App. 110 (1993) (holding that judge did not err in submitting written jury instructions to the jury and allowing them to take them into the jury room). The defendant's failure to object waives any alleged error on appeal. *State v. Bass*, 53 N.C. App. 40 (1981).

32.7 Disjunctive Jury Instructions

For a discussion on jury unanimity and the effect of disjunctive instructions thereon, see *supra* § 24.2D, Jury Unanimity.

32.8 IDS Performance Guidelines: Practical Considerations

Several considerations and recommendations with respect to reviewing, requesting, and objecting to jury instructions are contained *infra* in Appendix A, N.C. COMM'N ON INDIGENT DEFENSE SERVS., PERFORMANCE GUIDELINES FOR INDIGENT DEFENSE REPRESENTATION IN NON-CAPITAL CRIMINAL CASES AT THE TRIAL LEVEL (Nov. 2004). The pertinent guideline is reprinted below:

Guideline 7.8 Jury Instructions

(a) Counsel should be familiar with the law and the individual judge's practices concerning ruling on proposed instructions, charging the jury, use of pattern charges, and preserving objections to the instructions.

(b) Pursuant to G.S. 15A-1231, counsel should submit in writing proposed special instructions or modifications of the pattern jury instructions in light of the particular circumstances of the case, including the desirability of seeking a verdict on a lesser included offense. Where possible, counsel should provide case law in support of the proposed instructions. Counsel should try to ensure that all jury instruction discussions are on the record.

(c) Where appropriate, counsel should object to and argue against improper instructions proposed by the prosecution.

(d) If the court does not adopt instructions requested by counsel, or gives instructions over counsel's objection, counsel should take all steps necessary to preserve the record for appeal, including filing a copy of proposed instructions pursuant to G.S. 15A-1231.

(e) During delivery of the charge, counsel should be alert to any deviations from the judge's planned instructions, object to deviations unfavorable to the client, and, if necessary, request additional or curative instructions.

(f) If there are grounds for objecting to any jury instructions, counsel should object before the verdict form is submitted to the jury and the jury is allowed to begin deliberations.

(g) If the court proposes giving supplemental instructions to the jury, either upon request of the jurors or upon their failure to reach a verdict, counsel should ask the judge to state the proposed charge to counsel before it is delivered to the jury. Counsel should also try to ensure that any supplemental instructions are given to the entire jury in open court pursuant to G.S. 15A-1234(d).

32.9 Preservation of Issues for Appeal

A. Necessity of Specific Objection

N.C. Appellate Rule 10(a)(2) states that "[a] party may not make any portion of the jury charge or omission therefrom the basis of an issue presented on appeal unless the party objects thereto before the jury retires to consider its verdict . . . ." This rule also states that in order to properly preserve an objection to an instruction or to the omission of an instruction, trial counsel must state "distinctly that to which objection is made and the grounds of the objection . . . ." However, an objection is not required after the jury has been instructed if defense counsel, before jury arguments, submitted a written request for particular instructions and the trial judge denied this request. *See State v. Smith*, 311 N.C. 287 (1984) (holding that where the trial judge had denied defendant's written request for a proposed jury instruction regarding the State's identification testimony, neither N.C. R. App. P. 10(b)(2) [now, N.C. R. App. P. 10 (a)(2)] nor Rule 21 of the General Rules of Practice for the Superior and District Courts required defendant to repeat his objection to the jury instructions, after the fact, to preserve the issue for appellate review).

Caution: Under G.S. 15A-1231(d), all instructions given to the jury and all instructions tendered but refused become part of the record. This subsection also provides that the "failure to object to an erroneous instruction or to the erroneous failure to give an instruction does not constitute a waiver of the right to appeal on that error in accordance with G.S. 15A-1446(d)(13)." ***This is incorrect!*** G.S. 15A-1446(d)(13) has been ruled unconstitutional because it is in direct conflict with Appellate Rule 10(b)(2) [now, Rule 10(a)(2)] as promulgated by the N.C. Supreme Court pursuant to its exclusive authority under article IV, section 13(2) of the North Carolina Constitution. *See State v. Bennett*, 308 N.C. 530 (1983). Always object with specificity on the record to any errors committed by the trial judge in instructing the jury.

B. Opportunity to Object

Rule 21 of the General Rules of Practice for the Superior and District Courts requires the trial judge to give counsel an opportunity outside the hearing of the jury, or on request outside the presence of the jury, to object on the record to the jury charge or omission therefrom. Appellate Rule 10(a)(2) prohibits a party from making as the basis of an issue on appeal any instructional mistake absent a specific objection by trial counsel "provided that opportunity was given to the party to make the objection out of the hearing of the jury, and, on request of any party, out of the presence of the jury." The purpose of these rules is to allow the trial judge to correct any mistakes he or she made prior to deliberations. *State v. Maske*, 358 N.C. 40 (2004).

C. Plain Error Rule

To mitigate the potential harshness of Appellate Rule 10(b)(2) [now, R. 10(a)(2)], appellate courts will review an instructional error that was not preserved by trial counsel, but the error will be reviewed under the rigorous "plain error" standard of review. *See*

State v. Odom, 307 N.C. 655 (1983). The plain error rule is only applied where the error was sufficiently fundamental and prejudicial so as to amount to a miscarriage of justice or the denial of a fair trial, or where it can be fairly said that the instructional mistake had a probable impact on the jury's finding that the defendant was guilty. *State v. Harris*, 315 N.C. 556 (1986).

Chapter 33
Closing Arguments

Closing argument is a vital part of the adversarial process that forms the basis of our justice system and can be a critical part of winning a case. *State v. Jones*, 355 N.C. 117, 135 (2002). It is the "last clear chance" for the defense to persuade the trier of fact of the defendant's innocence or lesser culpability. *Herring v. New York*, 422 U.S. 853, 862 (1975). This chapter covers the procedural rules relating to closing arguments as well as the limitations on their scope.

The website of the Office of Indigent Defense Services has a collection of materials on Closing Arguments by various authors that may be accessed at www.ncids.org. Click on the "Training & Resources" link, then on "Training Materials", and then on "Training Materials—Indexed by Subject." The materials are located under the topic "Trial Practice." For additional considerations and recommendations on developing closing arguments, as well as objecting to improper arguments by prosecutors, see *infra* Appendix 33-1, Guideline 7.7 Closing Argument from N.C. COMM'N ON INDIGENT DEFENSE SERVS., PERFORMANCE GUIDELINES FOR INDIGENT DEFENSE REPRESENTATION IN NON-CAPITAL CRIMINAL CASES AT THE TRIAL LEVEL (Nov. 2004). For the complete guidelines, see *infra* Appendix A of this manual.

33.1 Right to Closing Argument

The defendant has a constitutional right under the Sixth Amendment to the U.S. Constitution to have his or her counsel make a closing argument. *Herring v. New York*, 422 U.S. 853 (1975). The trial judge cannot deny the defendant this right no matter how strong the prosecution's case may be. *Id.*; *see also State v. Eury*, 317 N.C. 511 (1986) (the right to make a closing argument is a substantial legal right of which the defendant cannot be deprived by the exercise of a trial judge's discretion).

33.2 Purpose and Scope of Closing Argument

A. In General

It has been observed that "[a] lawyer's function during closing argument is to provide the jury with a summation of the evidence, which in turn 'serves to sharpen and clarify the issues for resolution by the trier of fact' and should be limited to relevant legal issues." *State v. Jones*, 355 N.C. 117, 127 (2002) (citations omitted) (quoting *Herring v. New York*, 422 U.S. 853, 862 (1975)). "Closing argument is a 'reason offered in proof, to induce belief or convince the mind.'" *Jones*, 355 N.C. 117, 127 (citation omitted); *see also Sandoval v. Calderon*, 241 F.3d 765, 776 (9th Cir. 2000) (purpose of closing argument "is to explain to the jury what it has to decide and what evidence is relevant to its decision"); *United States v. Morris*, 568 F.2d 396, 401 (5th Cir. 1978) ("The purpose of summations is for the attorneys to assist the jury in analyzing, evaluating, and applying the evidence.").

During closing arguments, an attorney may, on the basis of his or her analysis of the evidence, argue any position or conclusion with respect to a matter in issue. N.C. GEN. STAT. § 15A-1230(a) (hereinafter G.S.). "[C]ounsel are given wide latitude in arguments to the jury and are permitted to argue the evidence that has been presented and all reasonable inferences that can be drawn from that evidence." *State v. Richardson*, 342 N.C. 772, 792–93 (1996).

Although counsel generally enjoys wide latitude in closing arguments, there are some boundaries and limitations. *See Jones*, 355 N.C. 117 (discussing the specific guidelines and parameters of closing argument); *see also* G.S. 15A-1230(a); N.C. GEN. R. PRAC. SUPER. & DIST. CT. 12; N.C. STATE BAR REV'D RULES OF PROF'L CONDUCT R. 3.4(e) (2006). Control of the argument is left largely in the trial judge's discretion and rulings thereon will not be disturbed on appeal in the absence of an abuse of that discretion. *Jones*, 355 N.C. 117.

Examples of permissible and impermissible arguments are collected below. The lists are not intended to be exhaustive. The information below applies to closing arguments by prosecutors and defense attorneys. Additional examples of restrictions on closing arguments by prosecutors are collected *infra* in § 33.7, Limitations on the Prosecution's Argument.

B. Permissible Content

During closing argument, counsel may:

- Argue any position or conclusion with respect to a matter in issue based on his or her analysis of the evidence. G.S. 15A-1230.
- Argue the evidence that has been presented and all reasonable inferences that can be drawn from that evidence. *State v. Forte*, 360 N.C. 427 (2006).
- State the law applicable to the case. G.S. 7A-97; *State v. Monk*, 286 N.C. 509 (1975); *see also infra* § 33.2E, Reading the Law.
- Comment on the demeanor of witnesses before the jury. *State v. Cummings*, 323 N.C. 181 (1988), *vacated on other grounds*, 494 U.S. 1021 (1990).
- Assert the guilt of another as long as there was evidence presented pointing directly to another's guilt. *State v. Bullock*, 154 N.C. App. 234 (2002); *see also Holmes v. South Carolina*, 547 U.S. 319 (2006) (unduly restricting evidence of another's guilt violates defendant's constitutional right to present a defense).
- Argue that a witness is credible or incredible. *See State v. Augustine*, 359 N.C. 709 (2005); *State v. Golphin*, 352 N.C. 364 (2000).
- Draw the jury's attention to the opposing party's failure to produce certain available witnesses (other than the defendant) or introduce particular evidence. *State v. Walters*, 357 N.C. 68 (2003) (prosecutor may comment on a defendant's failure to produce witnesses or exculpatory evidence to contradict or refute evidence presented by the State); *State v. Skeels*, 346 N.C. 147 (1997) (same); *see also State v. Snider*, 168 N.C. App. 701 (2005) (in response to defendant's argument that the State had failed to call two witnesses and the absence of that evidence was "very important," prosecutor properly argued that defense also failed to call those witnesses). *But cf. State v. Ratliff*, 341 N.C. 610 (1995) (in response to defendant's argument that the State failed to introduce a statement made by defendant after arrest, State improperly argued to

jury that defendant should have introduced it; State's argument misstated law because evidence rules precluded defendant from introducing his own statement in this case).

- Use illustrations and anecdotes. *State v. Maynor*, 272 N.C. 524 (1968).
- Make arguments based on common knowledge. *State v. Murillo*, 349 N.C. 573 (1998); *State v. Harris*, 338 N.C. 129 (1994).
- Display exhibits and use them in a proper manner as long as they were actually introduced into evidence. *State v. Call*, 349 N.C. 382 (1998) (prosecutor swinging objects through the air and dropping heavy items on counsel table found not to be improper); *see also State v. Oliver*, 309 N.C. 326 (1983) (prosecutor's use of photographs of victim during closing argument in the sentencing phase of a capital case was not improper); *State v. Torres*, 77 N.C. App. 345 (1985) (trial judge erred in allowing prosecutor to display pellet gun during closing argument because it had never been admitted into evidence). *But cf. State v. Golphin*, 352 N.C. 364 (2000) (stating that the court does not condone the pointing of weapons at the jury).
- Tell the jury that it may request review of the exhibits and testimony during their deliberations. *See* G.S. 15A-1233.
- Advise the jury to carefully scrutinize the testimony of a witness. *State v. Brown*, 327 N.C. 1 (1990).

C. Impermissible Content

Generally. During closing argument, counsel may not:

- Become abusive. G.S. 15A-1230(a); *State v. Jones*, 355 N.C. 117 (2002); *see also* N.C. GEN. R. PRAC. SUPER. & DIST. CT. 12 ("Counsel are at all times to conduct themselves with dignity and propriety.").
- Make uncomplimentary or derogatory comments about opposing counsel. *State v. Miller*, 271 N.C. 646 (1967); *State v. Jordan*, 149 N.C. App. 838 (2002); *see also* N.C. GEN. R. PRAC. SUPER. & DIST. CT. 12 ("All personalities between counsel should be avoided. The personal history or peculiarities of counsel on the opposing side should not be alluded to."); *State v. Sanderson*, 336 N.C. 1, 11 (1994) (prosecutor's entire course of conduct during capital trial, including abusive and persistent comments directed at opposing counsel, "may have undermined the ability of defense counsel to provide effective representation"). For cases in which the court found that the prosecutor made improper derogatory comments about the defendant's expert witnesses, see *infra* § 33.7C, Impermissible Content.
- Inject his or her personal experiences. G.S. 15A-1230(a); *State v. Simmons*, 205 N.C. App. 509 (2010).
- Express his or her personal belief as to the truth or falsity of the evidence. G.S. 15A-1230(a).
- State a personal opinion as to the credibility of a witness. *State v. Gladden*, 315 N.C. 398 (1986); *State v. Thompson*, 188 N.C. App. 102 (2008); N.C. STATE BAR REV'D RULES OF PROF'L CONDUCT R. 3.4(e) (2006).
- Express his or her personal belief as to the guilt or innocence of the defendant. G.S. 15A-1230(a); N.C. STATE BAR REV'D RULES OF PROF'L CONDUCT R. 3.4(e) (2006); *see also State v. Waring*, 364 N.C. 443 (2010); *State v. Britt*, 291 N.C. 528 (1977).

- Assert personal knowledge of facts in issue. *Sanderson*, 336 N.C. 1; *State v. Monk*, 286 N.C. 509 (1975); N.C. STATE BAR REV'D RULES OF PROF'L CONDUCT R. 3.4(e) (2006).
- Reveal legal rulings made by the trial judge outside the presence of the jury. *State v. Allen*, 353 N.C. 504 (2001).
- Engage in name-calling. *State v. Walters*, 357 N.C. 68 (2003); *State v. Jones*, 355 N.C. 117 (2002); *State v. Twitty*, ___ N.C. App. ___, 710 S.E.2d 421 (2011); *State v. Davis*, 45 N.C. App. 113 (1980).
- Assert that a witness is lying or call a witness a liar. *State v. Gell*, 351 N.C. 192, 210 (2000) (although prosecutor's argument that a defense witness was lying and a "convicted liar" was improper, it was not so grossly improper as to require the trial judge to intervene ex mero motu because the evidence supported this argument); *State v. McKenna*, 289 N.C. 668 (1976) (disapproving of language used by both defense counsel and prosecutor asserting that witnesses and defendant lied), *vacated in part on other grounds*, 429 U.S. 912 (1976). *But see State v. Brice*, 320 N.C. 119, 124 (1987) (trial judge did not abuse discretion in overruling defendant's objection to prosecutor's argument that a witness "did not tell you the truth" where the evidence supported this inference); *State v. Noell*, 284 N.C. 670, 696–97 (1974) (prosecutor's submission to the jury that defense witnesses "have lied to you" was a reasonable comment on the evidence), *vacated in part on other grounds*, 428 U.S. 902 (1976).
- Make arguments on the basis of matters outside the record except for matters concerning which the court may take judicial notice. G.S. 15A-1230(a); *see also Allen*, 353 N.C. 504; *State v. Cousins*, 289 N.C. 540 (1976); N.C. STATE BAR REV'D RULES OF PROF'L CONDUCT R. 3.4(e) (2006).
- Appeal to the jury's passion or prejudice. *Jones*, 355 N.C. 117.
- Make arguments calculated to mislead or prejudice the jury. *State v. Riddle*, 311 N.C. 734 (1984); *see also* N.C. GEN. R. PRAC. SUPER. & DIST. CT. 12 ("Counsel shall not knowingly misinterpret the contents of a paper, the testimony of a witness, the language or argument of opposite counsel or the language of a decision or other authority . . . .").
- Speculate about the outcome of a possible appeal, parole, executive commutation or pardon. *State v. McMorris*, 290 N.C. 286 (1976).
- Gratuitously interject race into a jury argument where race is otherwise irrelevant to the case being tried. *See State v. Diehl*, 353 N.C. 433 (2001) (no abuse of discretion in denial of defendant's motion for mistrial based on prosecutor's reference to the jury as "twelve white jurors in Randolph County" where defendant's objection to the reference had been sustained and race was an alleged secondary motivation for the crime); *State v. Moose*, 310 N.C. 482 (1984) (prosecutor's repeated references to the victim as an "old black gentleman" and a "black man" were not grossly improper where evidence supported an inference that the murder was, in part, racially motivated).

Capital cases. In addition to the above listed arguments, during the penalty phase of a capital trial, counsel may not:

- Argue the consequences of juror nonunanimity. *State v. Huff*, 325 N.C. 1 (1989), *vacated on other grounds*, 497 U.S. 1021 (1990).

- Argue that capital punishment does not have any deterrent effect. *See State v. Cherry*, 298 N.C. 86 (1979).
- Argue residual doubt as to the offense of first-degree murder or as to a basis underlying the first-degree murder conviction, such as premeditation and deliberation, because residual doubt is not a circumstance of the offense and, thus, is inappropriate. *State v. Fletcher*, 354 N.C. 455 (2001); *State v. Roseboro*, 351 N.C. 536 (2000).
- Describe the execution procedure because it is not based on the evidence presented. *State v. Holden*, 321 N.C. 125 (1987).

D. Informing Jury of Possible Punishment

Fair Sentencing. G.S. 7A-97 provides that "[i]n jury trials the whole case as well of law as of fact may be argued to the jury." In cases decided before structured sentencing took effect, this statute was interpreted by the N.C. Supreme Court to mean that it was permissible for counsel to inform the jury of the possible punishment the defendant faced if convicted of the crimes for which he or she was being tried. *See State v. McMorris*, 290 N.C. 286 (1976) (interpreting G.S. 84-14, the predecessor to G.S. 7A-97); *State v. Britt*, 285 N.C. 256 (1974) (same). The court stated that the purpose of informing the jury of the statutory punishment, at least in serious felony cases, was to impress on the jury the gravity of its duty. It was deemed proper for the defendant to advise the jury of "the possible consequence of imprisonment following conviction to encourage the jury to give the matter its close attention and to decide it only after due and careful consideration." *McMorris*, 290 N.C. 286, 288.

Structured Sentencing. Sentencing procedures changed with the imposition of structured sentencing in 1994. With the exception of Class A felonies and a few other offenses for which a particular punishment is set by statute, a defendant's sentencing range cannot be determined solely based on the statute that defines the offense.

In *State v. Lopez*, 363 N.C. 535 (2009), the N.C. Supreme Court addressed whether a prosecutor's argument about the sentence faced by the defendant was proper under structured sentencing. During the sentencing phase of that case in which the jury had to decide the aggravating factors alleged by the State, the prosecutor attempted to inform the jury of the amount of punishment that the jury's finding of an aggravating factor would empower the judge to impose. The court found the prosecutor's argument to be improper because it understated the potential sentence the defendant was facing. *Id.* at 538 (finding State's discussion of sentencing grids to be "inaccurate"). Specifically, the prosecutor informed the jury of the range of minimum sentences the defendant was facing and failed to inform the jury of the corresponding maximums (120% of the minimum at that time).

In addition, the court found that the State's argument was misleading because "it indicated potential specific sentencing ranges for defendant when defendant's sentencing range had not been, and in this case could not be, determined at the time the argument was made." *Id.* at 538. The court noted that a criminal sentence under structured sentencing is determined only after "numerous interlocking decisions and findings [are] made by the trial court after the jury has completed its work." *Id.* at 540. Therefore, jury arguments forecasting a defendant's sentence "are usually no better than educated estimates." *Id.* Still, the court concluded that "while attempts to forecast a sentence are fraught with risk," *id* at 541, it is permissible for the parties to explain the impact on the defendant's sentence of aggravating factors alleged by the State, which were the particular sentencing matter at issue in *Lopez.* Relying on G.S. 7A-97, the same statutory provision supporting a defendant's right to inform the jury of the defendant's potential sentence under Fair Sentencing, the court held that "a jury's understanding that its determination of the existence of any aggravating factors may have an effect on the sentence imposed is relevant to its role in a sentencing proceeding." *Id.*

The decision in *Lopez* leaves a number of questions unanswered about the appropriateness of arguments addressing a defendant's possible punishment under structured sentencing. *Lopez* appears to continue to allow the parties to inform the jury of the maximum possible sentence that the defendant is facing (based on the alleged offense, the defendant's prior record level, and any allegations of aggravating factors). It is less certain whether the parties would be able to inform the jury of the maximum aggravated sentence for the class of offense with which the defendant is charged if the defendant could not receive that sentence. When accepting a guilty plea, judges often inform the defendant of the maximum potential sentence that any defendant could receive for the charged offense. But, if that information does not reflect the sentence that the particular defendant could actually receive, it may not be considered sufficiently relevant for the jury's consideration after *Lopez.*

Regardless of the correct "maximum" that may be argued to the jury for an offense subject to structured sentencing, counsel should be able to argue the specific punishment faced by defendants charged with Class A offenses or offenses such as drug trafficking for which a particular punishment is fixed by statute. The maximum sentences for these offenses do not depend on the defendant's particular circumstances and therefore would be appropriate subjects of argument to the jury.

Practice note: If you plan to make a "numbers" argument for a case subject to structured sentencing, you may want to consider informing the judge ahead of time of your intended argument and be prepared to show him or her why your argument as to possible punishment is not misleading. For the judge to know the sentence you intend on arguing to the jury, you may have to stipulate ahead of time to your client's prior record level and also advise the judge whether you intend to ask for a mitigated sentence. You may want to clarify with the judge that the stipulated information is for the purpose of identifying the sentencing range to be described to the jury and is not itself admissible—that is, the jury should not be informed of any prior convictions unless your client testifies or the convictions are otherwise admissible. Because such a stipulation bears on your argument to the jury at the guilt-innocence phase, you may need to obtain your client's consent to the stipulation.

In determining the maximum potential sentence specific to your client, calculate the maximum sentence based on the highest minimum that could be imposed (120% of the minimum for Class F through I felonies, plus nine months, and 120% of the minimum plus nine months for Class A through E felonies, plus twelve months (or an additional sixty months for Class A through E felonies subject to sex offender registration), for offenses committed on or after December 1, 2011). Also consider any aggravating factors the State has alleged. If the trial is bifurcated, with the aggravating factors to be determined by the jury during a separate sentencing phase, you should be able to argue during the sentencing phase about the impact of the aggravators on your client's sentence (which was the situation in *Lopez*); but, the judge might not consider it appropriate for you to include those calculations in your sentencing argument at the trial of the underlying felony. *Cf. State v. Dammons*, 159 N.C. App. 284 (2003) (finding that the defendant was not entitled to inform the jury at the guilt-innocence phase of case of the potential maximum sentence should the jury later find the defendant to be a habitual felon).

Lopez also observed that in cases involving multiple charges, the judge has discretion to run sentences consecutively or concurrently (and, in a few cases, offenses may merge and require a single sentence); however, it is not clear from the decision that you must inform the jury of that possibility in addition to the potential sentence for each offense.

The decision in *Lopez* highlights that "numbers" arguments can be complicated and must be carefully crafted under structured sentencing. If the State attempts to make an argument as to the defendant's potential sentence as it did in *Lopez*, you should pay close attention and make objections as appropriate to limit the argument and ensure that any error will be preserved for appellate review.

Impermissible arguments. Although counsel may be able to inform the jury of the possible punishment in the case (as discussed above), counsel cannot:

- argue that because of the severity of the statutory punishment the jury ought to acquit or convict of a lesser offense;
- question the wisdom or appropriateness of the punishment; or
- state the punishment provision incorrectly.

State v. McMorris, 290 N.C. 286, 288 (1976).

Additionally, counsel may not:

- Attack the validity, constitutionality, or severity of the prescribed punishment for the crime or argue that the law ought to be otherwise. *State v. Britt*, 285 N.C. 256 (1974).
- Inform the jury, during the trial of the *principal felony*, of the possible maximum sentence that might be imposed upon an habitual felon adjudication. *State v. Dammons*, 159 N.C. App. 284 (2003); *State v. Wilson*, 139 N.C. App. 544 (2000). In light of these decisions, a trial judge may not have discretion to grant a defendant's request to inform the jury of the potential habitual felon sentence during trial of the principal felony.
- Inform a capital jury that the capital punishment statute authorizes the trial judge to

impose a life sentence if the jury is unable to return a unanimous verdict. *State v. Huff*, 325 N.C. 1 (1989), *vacated on other grounds*, 497 U.S. 1021 (1990).

Sentence in capital case. In *Simmons v. South Carolina*, 512 U.S. 154 (1994), the U.S. Supreme Court held that if a prosecutor argues "future dangerousness" of the defendant during a capital sentencing proceeding and the defendant's release on parole is prohibited by state law, due process requires the jury to be informed that if the defendant receives a life sentence, that sentence would be life imprisonment without parole. North Carolina law is broader in that G.S. 15A-2002 requires the judge in every capital case to instruct the jury "that a sentence of life imprisonment means a sentence of life without parole."

Before G.S. 15A-2002 was revised in 1994, there was no right to refer to parole eligibility during closing arguments in a capital sentencing hearing. *See State v. Parker*, 350 N.C. 411, 440 (1999); *State v. Miller*, 339 N.C. 663, 688 (1995). However, since G.S. 15A-2002 now requires instruction on the meaning of life imprisonment, counsel should be free to argue the law in this regard. *Cf. State v. Steen*, 352 N.C. 227, 276 (2000) (defendant's contention that the trial judge erroneously refused to allow him to argue that there would be no parole in this case was without merit since the record revealed that defense counsel did, in fact, assert "that life imprisonment did mean precisely life imprisonment without parole"); *see also infra* § 33.2E, Reading the Law (counsel may read or state to the jury a statute or other rule of law relevant to the case).

E. Reading the Law

Permissible arguments. G.S. 7A-97 states that "the whole case as well of law as of fact may be argued to the jury." This includes reading or stating to the jury a statute or other rule of law relevant to the case. *See State v. McMorris*, 290 N.C. 286 (1976) (interpreting G.S. 84-14, the predecessor to G.S. 7A-97); *State v. Britt*, 285 N.C. 256 (1974) (same); *see also supra* § 33.2D, Informing Jury of Possible Punishment.

Counsel also may read portions of reported cases that relate facts and state the law as long as those portions are relevant to the issues before the jury; however, counsel may not read the facts together with the result and imply that the jury should return a verdict favorable to his or her client. *See State v. Anthony*, 354 N.C. 372 (2001); *State v. Gardner*, 316 N.C. 605 (1986) (interpreting G.S. 84-14, the predecessor to G.S. 7A-97); *Wilcox v. Glover Motors, Inc.*, 269 N.C. 473 (1967) (same); *see also State v. Simmons*, 205 N.C. App. 509 (2010) (prejudicial error found where prosecutor injected his personal experience into closing argument by referring to a prior DWI case he had tried and then read the facts of that published opinion finding no reversible error to imply that the present jury should return the same verdict).

Impermissible arguments. In discussing the law, counsel may not:

- State the law incorrectly or read a statute that has been held unconstitutional. *Britt*, 285 N.C. 256.
- Read dictum. *State v. Austin*, 320 N.C. 276 (1987).

- Read from a dissenting opinion in a reported case unless it has later been adopted as the law of this state. *State v. Thomas*, 350 N.C. 315 (1999); *Gardner*, 316 N.C. 605.
- Read from treatises, medical books, or scientific writings (even if contained within a reported case) unless an expert has given an opinion and cited the treatise as his or her authority. *Austin*, 320 N.C. 276; *Gardner*, 316 N.C. 605.

F. Biblical References

Religious references discouraged. "Neither the 'law' nor the 'facts in evidence' include biblical passages, and, strictly speaking, it is improper for a party either to base or to color his arguments with such extraneous material." *State v. Artis*, 325 N.C. 278, 331 (1989), *vacated on other grounds*, 494 U.S. 1023 (1990). Even so, because counsel is given wide latitude in hotly contested cases, the N.C. Supreme Court has sometimes found biblical references to fall within permissible margins. *Id.*; *see, e.g.*, *State v. Gell*, 351 N.C. 192 (2000); *State v. Call*, 349 N.C. 382 (1998); *State v. Bond*, 345 N.C. 1 (1996); *State v. Walls*, 342 N.C. 1 (1995); *see also State v. Haselden*, 357 N.C. 1, 37 (2003) (Edmunds, J., dissenting) (arguing that "this Court has done a disservice to litigators and to itself by setting a standard of behavior while consistently excusing deviations from that standard").

The N.C. Supreme Court has, however, expressly discouraged prosecutors and defense attorneys from making arguments based on religion. The court has also strongly cautioned all attorneys to make their arguments based solely on the secular law and the facts. To base a jury argument on any of the world religions inevitably poses "a danger of distracting the jury from its sole and exclusive duty of applying secular law and unnecessarily risk[s] reversal of otherwise error-free trials." *State v. Williams*, 350 N.C. 1, 27 (1999) (so stating, but rejecting the defendant's argument that the prosecutor's use of biblical references during closing argument violated the First Amendment's principle of separation of church and state and the defendant's right to due process); *see also State v. Barden*, 356 N.C. 316 (2002) (again discouraging attorneys from making gratuitous biblical references and religious argument); *State v. Davis*, 349 N.C. 1 (1998) (urging caution in the use of biblical references).

Improper references by prosecutors. The N.C. Supreme Court has specifically expressed disapproval of certain types of prosecutorial arguments that make improper use of religious sentiment. *See, e.g.*, *State v. Moose*, 310 N.C. 482 (1984) (court cautioned prosecutor on resentencing not to argue that the powers of public officials, including the police, prosecutors, and judges, are ordained by God as his representatives on earth and that to resist those powers is to resist God himself); *State v. Oliver*, 309 N.C. 326 (1983) (indicating that prosecutorial arguments that the death penalty is divinely inspired are improper); *see also Haselden*, 357 N.C. 1, 34 (Brady, J., concurring) (biblical arguments fall within the parameters of the law "so long as prosecutors do not contend that the death penalty is divinely mandated" by God for a particular defendant).

Practice note: If the prosecutor's argument can be interpreted as encouraging the jury to base its verdict on biblical law, you should immediately object and argue that the comments are improper because they are based on matters outside the record and on law that is not applicable to the case. Also assert that the prosecutor's argument violates the defendant's state and federal constitutional rights under the Establishment Clause (separation of church and state) and under the Due Process Clause (right to a fair and impartial trial). If the prosecutor injects religion into his or her argument during the sentencing phase of a capital case, also assert that the argument violates the "Eighth Amendment principle that the death penalty may be constitutionally imposed only when the jury makes findings under a sentencing scheme that carefully focuses the jury on the specific factors it is to consider in reaching a verdict." *Sandoval v. Calderon*, 241 F.3d 765, 776 (9th Cir. 2000).

Invited response. In determining whether the prosecutor erred in referring to the Bible during closing argument, appellate courts will consider whether defense counsel also discussed passages from the Bible. If defense counsel made biblical references or even if it was reasonable for the prosecutor to anticipate that defense counsel would make religious references during closing argument, the court may find that the prosecutor's statements were not prejudicial error requiring reversal. *See, e.g., Haselden*, 357 N.C. 1, 24 (prosecutor's closing argument was not so grossly improper as to warrant a new sentencing proceeding because he "was addressing a potential defense argument that the death penalty is contrary to Christian doctrine"); *State v. Hunt*, 323 N.C. 407, 427 (1988) (prosecutor's biblical arguments were not grossly improper where he was "merely anticipating any possible reliance by the defense on the commandment 'Thou shalt not kill,' and arguing that the death penalty is not inconsistent with the Bible"), *vacated on other grounds*, 494 U.S. 1022 (1990); *Oliver*, 309 N.C. 326 (finding no reversible error where the prosecutor made biblical references during closing argument because defense counsel, as anticipated by the prosecutor, argued that the New Testament teaches forgiveness and mercy); *see also infra* § 33.7D, Invited Response (general discussion on invited responses).

Practice note: If you anticipate that the prosecutor will make arguments improperly based on religion, you should file a motion in limine before closing argument asking the judge to prohibit the prosecutor from making such arguments. If you do not plan to use religious arguments during your closing argument, you should assert that in the motion so that the State will be precluded from arguing on appeal that it reasonably made biblical references in anticipation of your argument. A sample "Motion to Restrict Prosecutor's Argument" is located on the website of the Office of Indigent Defense Services, www.ncids.org, under Training & Resources, then Capital Trial Motions (Penalty Phase Instructions Requests).

33.3 Time Limits

Misdemeanor and non-capital felony cases in superior court. Judges in superior court are authorized to limit the time of closing argument to "not less than one hour on each side" in misdemeanor cases, and "not less than two hours on each side" in non-capital felony cases. On motion of a party, the trial judge, in his or her discretion, may allow additional time if the interests of justice require it. G.S. 7A-97.

Capital cases. The trial judge may not limit the time of closing argument in capital cases "otherwise than by consent," but the judge may limit the number of attorneys who address the jury to three on each side. *Id.*

33.4 Number of Addresses

Misdemeanor and non-capital felony cases in superior court. G.S. 7A-97 (formerly G.S. 84-14) states that "[i]n all trials in the superior courts there shall be allowed two addresses to the jury for the State . . . and two for the defendant." If the defendant does not offer evidence, he or she is entitled to open and close the arguments to the jury. *See* N.C. GEN. R. PRAC. SUPER. & DIST. CT. 10; *see also State v. Eury*, 317 N.C. 511 (1986). If the defendant is represented by two attorneys, one may make the opening argument to the jury and the other the closing, or the defendant can waive opening argument and both attorneys can do a closing. *Eury*, 317 N.C. 511. However, if the defendant does offer evidence, he or she is only entitled to argue to the jury before the State argues. *See infra* § 33.5A, Right to Last Argument. If the defendant has two attorneys, both may address the jury during that closing argument as long as they stay within the time limits set out *supra* in § 33.3. *See Eury*, 317 N.C. 511 (discussing G.S. 84-14, the predecessor to G.S. 7A-27); *State v. Gladden*, 315 N.C. 398 (1986) (same); *State v. McCaskill*, 47 N.C. App. 289 (1980) (same).

Capital cases. There is no limit as to the number of addresses, but the judge may limit the number of attorneys who address the jury to three on each side. G.S. 7A-97. This statute (formerly G.S. 84-14) has been interpreted to mean that if the defendant offers evidence at the guilt-innocence phase, all of his or her addresses to the jury must be made before the State's closing argument. Up to three attorneys may address the jury during this argument, and each attorney may argue as often and for as long as he or she wishes. "Thus, for example, if one defense attorney grows weary of arguing, he may allow another defense attorney to address the jury and may, upon being refreshed, rise again to make another address during the defendant's time for argument." *Gladden*, 315 N.C. 398, 421.

If the defendant does not offer evidence at the guilt-innocence phase, he or she is entitled both to open and close the arguments to the jury, and the defendant's attorneys (up to three) may address the jury "as many times as they desire during the closing phase of the argument." *Eury*, 317 N.C. 511, 516–17. In *Eury*, the capital defendant did not present evidence, and her two attorneys sought permission for both to be allowed to address the jury after the State's closing argument. The trial judge denied this request and ruled that one of the defendant's attorneys could "open" argument, the State would argue, then the defendant's other attorney could make the final argument. The N.C. Supreme Court found that the trial judge erred in refusing the defendant's request and that the defendant was entitled to have both of his attorneys address the jury for as long as they wished after the State's closing argument. *See also State v. Mitchell*, 321 N.C. 650 (1988) (trial judge erred in refusing to permit both of defendant's attorneys to address the jury during final arguments of both phases of his capital trial).

A trial judge's refusal to permit up to three of the defendant's counsel to address the jury if they wish during the defendant's final arguments in both the guilt-innocence and sentencing phases constitutes prejudicial error per se. That error in the guilt-innocence phase entitles the defendant to a new trial as to the capital felony. Also, if a capital felony has been joined for trial with non-capital charges, the trial judge's failure to allow all of the defendant's counsel to make the closing argument is prejudicial error on the non-capital as well as the capital charges. *Mitchell*, 321 N.C. 650; *Eury*, 317 N.C. 511; *see also State v. Campbell*, 332 N.C. 116 (1992) (new trial granted where trial judge only allowed one of defendant's attorneys to address the jury during final argument in the guilt-innocence phase of his trial). If the error is made during the sentencing phase, the defendant is entitled to a new sentencing hearing. *See State v. Simpson*, 320 N.C. 313 (1987).

Practice note: If more than one attorney wishes to argue during final argument of a non-capital case or during either phase of a capital case, you should specifically announce this intention to the court and "request permission" to do so. Unless the record shows a clear refusal of the trial judge to permit more than one attorney to argue during final argument, the error may be waived for appellate purposes. *Compare State v. Williams*, 343 N.C. 345, 369 (1996) (overruling defendant's assignment of error because the court could not interpret the judge's ambiguous statements in the transcript as showing that he "refused to permit both of defendant's attorneys to argue after the State where they never specifically requested to do so and never objected"), *with State v. Barrow*, 350 N.C. 640, 644 (1999) (defense attorney's announcement in the guilt-innocence phase of a capital case in which defendant presented no evidence that the defense wished to make three closing arguments—one opening argument by one defense attorney and two final arguments, one by each of defendant's two attorneys, after the State's closing arguments—was a "clear request" and the trial judge's failure to allow the request was prejudicial error per se).

33.5 Order of Arguments

A. Right to Last Argument

Non-capital cases. A defendant who does not introduce evidence after the State has rested is entitled as a matter of right to open and close argument to the jury. *See* N.C. GEN. R. PRAC. SUPER. & DIST. CT. 10 ("[I]f no evidence is introduced by the defendant, the right to open and close the argument to the jury shall belong to him."). The right to final argument is a substantial legal right that cannot be taken away by an exercise of judicial discretion, and the erroneous denial of this critically important right entitles a defendant to a new trial. *State v. Raper*, 203 N.C. 489 (1932); *State v. English*, 194 N.C. App. 314 (2008); *State v. Hall*, 57 N.C. App. 561 (1982).

If the defendant introduces evidence within the meaning of Rule 10 of the N.C. General Rules of Practice for the Superior and District Courts, the State has the right to the opening and final closing arguments. *State v. Battle*, 322 N.C. 69 (1988); *State v. Gladden*, 315 N.C. 398 (1986); *State v. Pickard*, 107 N.C. App. 94 (1992); *State v. Curtis*, 18 N.C. App. 116 (1973). Eliciting evidence by the cross-examination of a State's witness is usually not considered the "introduction" of evidence by the defendant and does not deprive him or her of the right to last argument. *See Raper*, 203 N.C. 489; *see also infra* § 33.5B, What Constitutes "Introduction" of Evidence (discussing this issue in more detail).

Multiple defendants. In a case involving multiple defendants, the State is entitled to the final argument if any one of the defendants introduces evidence. N.C. GEN. R. PRAC. SUPER. & DIST. CT. 10; *see also State v. Taylor*, 289 N.C. 223 (1976); *State v. Diaz*, 155 N.C. App. 307 (2002).

Capital cases. If the defendant offers evidence, then all of his or her addresses to the jury during the *guilt-innocence* phase must be made before the prosecution's closing argument. *Gladden*, 315 N.C. 398. A defendant always has the right to the last argument in the *sentencing phase* of a capital case even if he or she has presented evidence during the sentencing phase. G.S. 15A-2000(a)(4); *State v. Barrow*, 350 N.C. 640 (1999). While G.S. 15A-2000(a)(4) grants a defendant the right to last argument in the sentencing phase, it does not give him or her the right to make both the first and last arguments. *State v. Wilson*, 313 N.C. 516 (1985).

B. What Constitutes "Introduction" of Evidence

Generally. A defendant clearly "introduces" evidence when he or she offers witness testimony or exhibits during the presentation of his or her case. However, even if a defendant does not formally offer testimony or other evidentiary matter during his or her case, the right to final argument may still be lost if the judge finds that the defendant "introduced" evidence, within the meaning Rule 10 of the N.C. General Rules of Practice for the Superior and District Courts, during the *cross-examination* of a State's witness. This can happen notwithstanding that (1) "any testimony elicited during cross-examination is 'considered as coming from the party calling the witness, even though its only relevance is its tendency to support the cross-examiner's case'"; and (2) the general rule is that there is no right to offer evidence during cross-examination of the other party's witness. *State v. Shuler*, 135 N.C. App. 449, 452–53 (1999) (quoting 1 KENNETH S. BROUN, BRANDIS & BROUN ON NORTH CAROLINA EVIDENCE § 170, at 559 (5th ed. 1998) [now, § 170 at 626 (7th ed. 2011)]. While there is generally no right to "offer" evidence during cross-examination, the trial judge, in his or her discretion, may vary the order of proof to allow the introduction of defense evidence during the State's case. *Shuler*, 135 N.C. App. 449, 452–53.

It is not always easy to determine what constitutes the "introduction" of evidence in North Carolina, but recent decisions recognize that cross-examination typically does not constitute the "introduction" of evidence.

The *Hall* test. The N.C. Court of Appeals first attempted to establish a test for determining when evidence has been introduced in *State v. Hall*, 57 N.C. App. 561 (1982). Defense counsel in *Hall* questioned a State's witness on cross-examination about the color of a sweatsuit allegedly worn by the defendant. In order to impeach the witness, defense counsel then showed the witness the sweatsuit and asked him to describe its colors (which were different than those earlier described by the witness). Although the sweatsuit was never formally offered into evidence and it was not given to the jury for examination, the trial judge held that the defendant had "introduced" the sweatsuit into evidence during his cross-examination and thereby lost the right to final argument.

The N.C. Court of Appeals reversed, finding that the trial judge erred in denying the defendant the right to final argument. The court stated that *"the proper test as to whether an object has been put in evidence is whether a party has offered it as substantive evidence or so that the jury may examine it and determine whether it illustrates, corroborates, or impeaches the testimony of a witness." Id.* at 564 (emphasis added). The sweatsuit in *Hall* was not offered into evidence because it was not given to the jury "for the purpose of their determination as to whether it impeached the witness." *Id.* The court further stated that if the party merely shows something to a witness in order to refresh his or her recollection, it has not been "offered" into evidence.

The N.C. Supreme Court relied on the *Hall* test in *State v. Macon*, 346 N.C. 109 (1997). In *Macon*, the defendant asked an officer on cross-examination about statements made by the defendant during an interview with that officer. The officer stated that another officer had made notes during that interview. Defense counsel then had the testifying officer read from the other officer's notes. The notes were marked as an exhibit but were not formally offered into evidence and were not published to the jury. The trial judge found that when defense counsel had the officer read the notes to the jury, the defendant had offered evidence and lost his right to open and close jury argument. The N.C. Supreme Court agreed, quoting the *Hall* test, but the court's reasoning was not entirely consistent with *Hall.* The court found that the contents of the notes were offered for substantive purposes, not impeachment or corroboration, suggesting that had the cross-examination been for impeachment or corroboration purposes, it would not have constituted the introduction of evidence. *Id.* at 114.

The *Shuler* test. In *State v. Shuler*, 135 N.C. App. 449 (1999), the N.C. Court of Appeals revisited the "introduction of evidence" issue. The defendant in *Shuler* was charged with multiple counts of embezzlement. One of the defendant's co-workers testified for the State about statements made by the defendant during an interview that both had attended. On cross-examination, defense counsel questioned the witness further about the interview and read portions of the transcript of the interviews to the witness to put the defendant's statements in context. Defense counsel also asked the witness about new matters and about the witness's accounting procedures. The trial judge ruled that the defendant had introduced evidence and had thereby lost the right to last argument.

In reviewing the trial judge's decision, the N.C. Court of Appeals stated that *evidence is "introduced" during cross-examination within the meaning of Rule 10 of the N.C.*

General Rules of Practice for the Superior and District Courts when (1) "it is 'offered' into evidence by the cross-examiner and accepted as such by the trial court"; or (2) "[a]lthough not formally offered and accepted into evidence, . . . new matter is presented to the jury during cross-examination and that matter is not *relevant to any issue in the case." Id.* at 452–53 (citations omitted and emphasis added). After reviewing the cross-examination testimony in *Shuler*, the court found that the trial judge had committed reversible error when he denied the defendant the right to final argument because the defendant had not "introduced" evidence and the matters that the defendant raised, although new, were relevant to testimony given during direct examination.

Subsequent cases. Cases decided by the N.C. Court of Appeals after *Hall* and *Shuler* have utilized either the *Shuler* or *Hall* test or both the *Hall* and *Shuler* tests. *See, e.g., State v. Hogan*, ___ N.C. App. ___, 720 S.E.2d 854 (2012) (defendant did not introduce evidence under Rule 10 when, during cross-examination of the prosecuting witness, defense counsel read and referenced the witness's police statement; court relied on a case that based its holding on *Shuler* and found that the statements used by defense counsel "were 'directly related to [the witness's] own testimony on direct examination.'") (citation omitted); *State v. Matthews*, ___ N.C. App. ___, 720 S.E.2d 829 (2012) (defendant questioned police officer on cross-examination and identified a report made by that officer in which another man was identified as a suspect; court, citing *Shuler*, granted a new trial and stated that it could not "say that the identification of other suspects by police constituted new evidence that was 'not relevant to any issue in the case.'"); *State v. English*, 194 N.C. App. 314 (2008) (after acknowledging the *Hall* test, the court found that defendant did not introduce evidence by eliciting detective's testimony about a statement taken during the investigation, contained in the detective's report, because the testimony related to evidence introduced on direct examination and could have been an attempt to impeach the co-defendant; it did not amount to "new matter" under *Shuler*); *State v. Hennis*, 184 N.C. App. 536 (2007) (defendant did not offer evidence under either the *Hall* or *Shuler* test when, on cross-examination, he had an officer draw a diagram of the arrest scene and questioned him about changes to an incident report that were added months after it was initially written); *State v. Bell*, 179 N.C. App. 430 (2006) (finding under the *Shuler* test that the defendant did not introduce evidence during his cross-examination of a drug chemist regarding the method and instruments she used to identify the substance seized from the defendant because the cross-examination was relevant and directly related to the chemist's testimony on direct); *State v. Wells*, 171 N.C. App. 136 (2005) (defendant did not introduce evidence under the *Shuler* test when he cross-examined a State's witness about his prior inconsistent statement because the statement directly related to the witness's testimony on direct examination). *But see State v. Wolfe*, 205 N.C. App. 324 (2010) (unpublished) (court cited both the *Hall* and *Shuler* tests, then upheld ruling by trial judge that defendant lost the last argument when he played a voice mail message during the cross-examination of a detective; following *Hall*, court found that the message was not introduced to illustrate the detective's testimony but was substantive evidence used to exculpate defendant).

Practice note: If you intend to cross-examine a State's witness about an object or document that has not been previously introduced by the State, be prepared to argue that you have not introduced evidence within the meaning of Rule 10 of the N.C. General Rules of Practice for the Superior and District Courts. If the facts permit, you should argue that you have not offered evidence under either the *Hall* test or the *Shuler* test and that the exhibit relates to the witness's testimony on direct examination or, at least, to other issues in the case.

Additional reference. For further discussion of the loss of the right to open and close arguments, see 1 KENNETH S. BROUN, BRANDIS & BROUN ON NORTH CAROLINA EVIDENCE § 166, at 597 n.517, and § 170, at 627 n.606 (7th ed. 2011).

33.6 Admissions of Guilt During Closing Argument

Before admitting the defendant's guilt to the crime charged or to a lesser included offense, counsel must obtain the defendant's express consent. *See State v. Berry*, 356 N.C. 490 (2002). This requirement applies to closing arguments during the guilt-innocence phase of the trial as well as to opening statements, discussed *supra* in § 28.6, Admissions of Guilt During Opening Statement.

A. Defendant's Consent Required Prior to Admission of Guilt

Generally, if counsel admits the defendant's guilt without first obtaining consent, it is per se ineffective assistance of counsel in violation of the Sixth Amendment to the U.S. Constitution and article I, sections 19 and 23 of the N.C. Constitution because counsel's admission deprives the defendant of the right to have his or her guilt or innocence determined by the jury. *State v. Harbison*, 315 N.C. 175 (1985).

In *Florida v. Nixon*, 543 U.S. 175, 192 (2004), the U.S. Supreme Court held on the facts of the case that, under the U.S. Constitution, counsel's admission during opening statement of the defendant's guilt without his express consent was not per se ineffective assistance of counsel but was subject to the prejudice analysis of *Strickland v. Washington*, 466 U.S. 668 (1984). The Court reasoned, "[I]n a capital case, counsel must consider in conjunction both the guilt and penalty phases in determining how best to proceed. When counsel informs the defendant of the strategy counsel believes to be in the defendant's best interest and the defendant is unresponsive, counsel's strategic choice is not impeded by any blanket rule demanding the defendant's explicit consent." *Nixon*, 543 U.S. 175, 192. Although the N.C. Supreme Court has had opportunities to do so, it has not disavowed the *Harbison* rule in light of the narrow ruling in *Nixon*. *See State v. Goss*, 361 N.C. 610 (2007); *State v. Campbell*, 359 N.C. 644 (2005); *see also State v. Maready*, 205 N.C. App. 1 (2010) (discussing *Nixon* and holding that North Carolina continues to adhere to the *Harbison* rule).

The rule prohibiting defense counsel from admitting a defendant's guilt to the jury without the defendant's consent applies only to the guilt-innocence phase of a trial. Our courts have stated that it does not apply to sentencing proceedings. *State v. Boyd*, 343 N.C. 699 (1996); *State v. Walls*, 342 N.C. 1 (1995).

Practice note: *Boyd* and *Walls*, cited above, were decided before the line of U.S. Supreme Court cases culminating in *Blakely v. Washington*, 542 U.S. 296 (2004), in which the Court recognized that circumstances that increase a defendant's sentence beyond the maximum authorized for an offense are the functional equivalent of an element of a greater offense. *See also Ring v. Arizona*, 536 U.S. 584 (2002) (holding that factors that authorize imposition of the death penalty are subject to the same analysis). The N.C. appellate courts have not specifically considered the impact of *Blakely* and like cases on the application of *Harbison* to what previously were characterized as purely sentencing matters, such as the determination of aggravating factors. *Cf. State v. Harris*, 175 N.C. App. 360 (2006) (observing that North Carolina cases finding that defense counsel's concession of aggravating factors were a sufficient admission by the defendant were not applicable after *Blakely*, which requires a valid waiver by the defendant of the right to a jury trial; the court cites *Harbison* in support of the requirement of a valid waiver), *vacated on other grounds*, 361 N.C. 154 (2006) (remanding for determination whether the failure to submit aggravating factors to the jury was harmless beyond a reasonable doubt). *But cf. State v. Womack*, ___ N.C. App. ___, 712 S.E.2d 193 (2011) (relying on prior cases and rejecting the argument that defense counsel violated *Harbison* by conceding the defendant's prior convictions at the habitual felon phase of the case without the defendant's consent because, among other things, *Harbison* does not apply to proceedings to determine whether the defendant's sentence should be enhanced). Regardless of how the N.C. appellate courts resolve this issue, as a practical matter defense counsel should ***not*** admit in jury argument a matter that increases the defendant's sentence beyond the statutory maximum for the underlying offense without the client's consent.

B. What Constitutes Admission of Guilt

Admission must be express. There must be an actual admission of guilt for error to occur. It is not impermissible under *Harbison* to argue that the defendant is not guilty, but if he or she is found guilty of any crime, it should be of a lesser included offense or of a lesser crime for which he or she has not been charged. *See State v. Gainey*, 355 N.C. 73, 93 (2002) (defense counsel did not admit guilt to murder but only that "if he's guilty of anything, he's guilty of accessory after the fact"); *State v. Greene*, 332 N.C. 565, 572 (1992) (no admission of guilt where defense counsel argued that the defendant was innocent of all charges, but if found guilty of any charge it should be of the lesser crime of involuntary manslaughter "because the evidence came closer to proving that crime than any of the other crimes charged"); *see also State v. Hinson*, 341 N.C. 66 (1995) (defense counsel's statements regarding the guilt of a co-defendant did not amount to an admission that the defendant himself had committed any crime).

Admissions of facts or elements. Merely admitting the existence of a fact or an element of an offense is not the equivalent of an admission of guilt. *See State v. Wiley*, 355 N.C. 592 (2002) (placed in context, defense counsel's remarks that there may be some physical evidence linking the defendant to the murder victim's car did not constitute an admission); *State v. Strickland*, 346 N.C. 443 (1997) (statements by defense counsel during jury voir dire that the uncontroverted evidence showed that the defendant was holding a gun when the victim was killed did not amount to a concession of guilt to which defendant had not agreed); *State v. Fisher*, 318 N.C. 512 (1986) (defense counsel's admission of the existence of malice was not an admission of guilt so it was not per se ineffective assistance of counsel); *State v. Maniego*, 163 N.C. App. 676 (2004) (defense counsel's admission of the fact that the defendant was present at the scene of the crime was not an admission of guilt and was consistent with the theory of defense).

Assertion of defense. Some defenses may constitute an admission of guilt, at least of a lesser offense, and require the defendant's consent. *See State v. Johnson*, 161 N.C. App. 68 (2003) (defense counsel in opening statement stated that defendant was unable to premeditate and deliberate killings because of his intoxication and jury should return verdict of lesser offense; trial judge's inquiry of defendant was adequate to show consent); *see also State v. Berry*, 356 N.C. 490 (2002) (trial judge conducted *Harbison* inquiry to determine whether defendant consented to insanity defense, which necessitated admission of critical aspects of charged offense).

C. Procedural Requirements

Although there is no particular procedure that the trial judge "must invariably follow when confronted with a defendant's concession" (*Berry*, 356 N.C. 490, 514), an on-the-record exchange between the trial judge and the defendant is the preferred method of determining whether the defendant knowingly and voluntarily consented to an admission of guilt. *See State v. McDowell*, 329 N.C. 363 (1991); *see also State v. Matthews*, 358 N.C. 102, 108 (2004) (holding that *Harbison* requires more than implicit consent based on an overall trial strategy and the defendant's intelligence). A clear record of consent is required, but the trial judge need not engage in the formal colloquy that is required for a guilty plea under G.S. 15A-1022(a). *State v. Perez*, 135 N.C. App. 543 (1999). Appellate courts will not presume the defendant's lack of consent from a silent record. *State v. Boyd*, 343 N.C. 699 (1996).

Practice note: If you decide that a concession of guilt is the best strategy in a particular case, it is imperative that you fully discuss the value of such a concession with the defendant. Before admitting guilt to the charge or to a lesser included offense during closing argument (or opening statement), present the defendant's written consent to the trial judge if you have obtained one or ask the judge to inquire of the defendant and obtain his or her express consent on the record. *See State v. House*, 340 N.C. 187, 197 (1995) (urging "both the bar and the trial bench to be diligent in making a full record of a defendant's consent when a *Harbison* issue arises at trial").

33.7 Limitations on the Prosecution's Argument

A. Duty of the Prosecutor

It is the duty of the prosecutor "to present the State's case with earnestness and vigor and to use every legitimate means to bring about a just conviction." *State v. Monk*, 286 N.C.

509, 515 (1975). In discharging this duty, he or she "should not be so restricted as to discourage a vigorous presentation of the State's case to the jury." *Id.*

However, it is as much the prosecutor's "duty to refrain from improper methods calculated to produce a wrongful conviction as it is to use every legitimate means to bring about a just one." *Berger v. United States*, 295 U.S. 78, 88 (1935). A prosecutor has a duty to the state that he or she represents and to the court as its officer to hold himself or herself "'under proper restraint and avoid violent partisanship, partiality, and misconduct'" that may tend to deprive the defendant of a fair trial. *State v. Britt*, 288 N.C. 699, 711 (1975) (citation omitted). "'When the prosecutor becomes abusive, injects his [or her] personal views and opinions into the argument before the jury,'" the rules of fair debate are violated and "'it becomes the duty of the trial judge to intervene to stop improper argument and to instruct the jury not to consider it.'" This is especially true in a capital case. *State v. Jones*, 355 N.C. 117, 130 (2002) (citation omitted).

Examples of permissible and impermissible arguments by prosecutors are collected below. The lists are not intended to be exhaustive.

B. Permissible Content

In addition to the permissible arguments set out *supra* in § 33.2B, courts have found that a prosecutor may engage in the following arguments or, at least, have found that the trial judge did not abuse his or her discretion in not intervening and limiting the prosecutor's argument. In some instances, the courts have drawn fine lines between permissible and impermissible arguments, illustrated by the contrasting cases cited below. Counsel therefore should continue to object to arguments in these contested areas (for example, arguments that appeal to the jury's relationship to the community).

Generally. The courts have permitted prosecutors to:

- Create scenarios of the crime or surrounding circumstances as long as they are based on reasonable inferences drawn from the facts. *See State v. Ingle*, 336 N.C. 617 (1994); *State v. Syriani*, 333 N.C. 350 (1993); *State v. Kirkley*, 308 N.C.196 (1983).
- Comment on the defendant's failure to produce exculpatory evidence or witnesses (other than the defendant) to corroborate the truth of an alibi or to contradict evidence presented by the State. *State v. Hester*, 343 N.C. 266 (1996); *State v. Hunt*, 339 N.C. 622 (1994); *State v. Brown*, 320 N.C. 179 (1987). However, if the prosecutor's comments could be construed as shifting the burden of proof to the defendant, the argument would be improper and counsel should immediately object. *See, e.g., United States v. Parker*, 903 F.2d 91, 98 (2d Cir. 1990) (while a prosecutor may comment on a defendant's failure to call witnesses to contradict the factual character of the government's case or to support the defendant's case, he or she may not "suggest that the defendant has any burden of proof or any obligation to adduce any evidence whatever"); *see also United States v. Mares*, 940 F.2d 455 (9th Cir. 1991) (prosecutor should not argue that the defendant's failure to adequately explain the weaknesses of his or her case requires a guilty verdict because this may

impermissibly shift the burden of proof to the defendant).

- Urge the jury "to act as the voice and conscience of the community." *State v. Gell*, 351 N.C. 192, 216 (2000) (although court disapproved of biblical references by prosecutor, his statement, "and let the people of Bertie County say amen," fell within "the permissible practice of 'urg[ing] the jury to act as the voice and conscience of the community'" (quoting *State v. Peterson*, 350 N.C. 518, 531 (1999)); *State v. Walls*, 342 N.C. 1, 62 (1995) (finding prosecutor's argument permissible because it merely reminded jury that its verdict would "send a message" to the people of the county and did not improperly relay to the jury that it should buckle under the pressure of the community). *But see State v. Golphin*, 352 N.C. 364, 471 (2000) (prosecutor cannot encourage the jury to "lend an ear to the community"); *State v. Boyd*, 311 N.C. 408, 418 (1984) (jury's decision cannot be based on "the jury's perceived accountability to the witnesses, to the victim, to the community, or to society in general").
- Comment on the defendant's demeanor in the courtroom, including his or her apparent lack of remorse. *Brown*, 320 N.C. 179; *State v. Myers*, 299 N.C. 671 (1980); *see also State v. Nicholson*, 355 N.C. 1 (2002) (prosecutor stated that defendant seemed bored), *vacated in part on other grounds sub nom. Nicholson v. Branker*, 739 F. Supp. 2d 839 (E.D.N.C. 2010); *State v. Flippen*, 349 N.C. 264 (1998) (prosecutor characterized defendant's demeanor at trial as sniveling). *But see infra* § 33.7C, Impermissible Content (citing cases disapproving of inappropriate characterizations of the defendant).
- Impeach the credibility of an expert witness hired by the defendant, including pointing out that the witness will be remunerated for his or her testimony. *Nicholson*, 355 N.C. 1; *State v. Norwood*, 344 N.C. 511 (1996).
- Use evidence of the defendant's prior convictions to impeach his or her credibility. *See State v. Tucker*, 317 N.C. 532, 543 (1986) (trial judge erred in allowing prosecutor, during closing argument, to use evidence of defendant's prior convictions as substantive evidence of guilt because impeachment "was the only legitimate purpose for which the evidence was admissible").
- Address the defendant's sexual orientation but only if it is relevant to the issues in the case. *See State v. Ross*, 100 N.C. App. 207 (1990) (permissible for State to argue that the defendant was a homosexual pedophile because it was a reasonable inference from the evidence and it supported the State's theory that the defendant killed the victims to keep his criminal activities from being exposed to the community), *aff'd on other grounds*, 329 N.C. 108 (1991).

Capital cases. "Prosecutors have a duty to advocate zealously that the facts in evidence warrant imposition of the death penalty, and they are permitted wide latitude in their arguments." *State v. Williams*, 350 N.C. 1, 25 (1999).

While wide latitude is allowed in closing arguments in both the guilt and sentencing phases of a trial, "the foci of the arguments in the two phases are significantly different." Thus, rhetoric that might be acceptable in the sentencing phase may be prejudicially improper in the guilt phase of a trial. *State v. Artis*, 325 N.C. 278, 324 (1989), *vacated on other grounds*, 494 U.S. 1023 (1990). "[T]he touchstone for propriety in sentencing arguments is whether the argument relates to the character of the [defendant] or the nature [or circumstances] of the crime." *Brown*, 320 N.C. 179, 203; *see also State v. Oliver*, 309 N.C. 326 (1983).

Prosecutors have been permitted during the sentencing phase of a capital case to:

- Argue that a death sentence should be imposed and that the jury should not sentence the defendant to life imprisonment. G.S. 15-176.1.
- Argue the possibility that the defendant could pose a future danger to prison staff and inmates if given a sentence of life imprisonment. *Nicholson*, 355 N.C. 1; *State v. Steen*, 352 N.C. 227 (2000).
- Encourage the jury to sentence the defendant to death to specifically deter that particular defendant from engaging in future murders (as opposed to making a general deterrence argument, which is impermissible). *State v. McNeil*, 350 N.C. 657 (1999); *State v. Syriani*, 333 N.C. 350 (1993).
- Urge the jurors to appreciate the circumstances of the crime. *State v. Gregory*, 340 N.C. 365, 425 (1995) (proper for prosecutor to detail the facts surrounding the murders and to state that "I don't believe any of us are capable of imagining the pure horror that was going on there" because the argument related to the nature of defendant's crimes); *Artis*, 325 N.C. 278, 324 (not improper for prosecutor to ask jurors to hold their breath for as long as they could over a four-minute period so they could "understand . . . the dynamics of manual strangulation").
- Argue to the sentencing jury that its decision should be based not on sympathy, mercy, or whether it wants to kill the defendant, but on the law. *State v. Rouse*, 339 N.C. 59 (1994).
- Legitimately deprecate the significance of the mitigating circumstances. *See State v. Haselden*, 357 N.C. 1 (2003); *State v. Billings*, 348 N.C. 169 (1998).
- Use victim impact statements regarding the specific harm caused by the murder of the victim and the impact of the murder on the victim's family as long as the victim impact evidence is not so unduly prejudicial that it renders the trial fundamentally unfair. *State v. Bishop*, 343 N.C. 518 (1996) (prosecutor's arguments about the victim and what she could have accomplished served to inform the jury about the specific harm caused by the crime and did not render the trial fundamentally unfair); *Gregory*, 340 N.C. 365 (prosecutor's argument that the deaths of the victims represented a unique loss to their families did not render defendant's trial fundamentally unfair); *see also* G.S. 15A-833 (specifically authorizing the introduction of victim impact evidence in criminal sentencing hearings); *Payne v. Tennessee*, 501 U.S. 808 (1991) (finding that the Eighth Amendment neither prohibits the introduction of victim impact evidence nor bars a prosecutor from arguing such evidence at the sentencing phase of a capital case).
- Ask the jury to imagine the emotions and fear of a victim (*State v. Wallace*, 351 N.C. 481 (2000); *State v. Bond*, 345 N.C. 1 (1996)), or what the victim was thinking at the time of death as long as the argument is fairly premised on evidence and testimony presented at trial. *See State v. Anthony*, 354 N.C. 372 (2001); *State v. Cummings*, 352 N.C. 600 (2000). *But see State v. McCollum*, 334 N.C. 208 (1993) (holding that prosecutor may not ask jurors to put themselves in place of victims and citing *United*

States v. Pichnarcik, 427 F.2d 1290 (9th Cir. 1970)).

- Call the jurors each by name and ask them to impose the death penalty as long as it is based on the law and not an attempt to persuade the jury to make a decision on an emotional basis. *See State v. Gell*, 351 N.C. 192 (2000) (no error in allowing prosecutor to address the jurors by name and inform them that it was time for them to impose the death penalty); *State v. Wynne*, 329 N.C. 507, 525 (1991) (no error where prosecutor called each juror by name and "merely asked the individual jurors to have no doubt, not to disregard their duty to deliberate together and reach a unanimous verdict"). *But cf. State v. Holden*, 321 N.C. 125, 163 (1987) (holding that *defense counsel's* argument in which he named each juror individually was improper because he asked them to spare the defendant's life "on an emotional basis . . . and in disregard of the jurors' duty to deliberate" together toward reaching a unanimous verdict).
- Argue that the defendant deserves the death penalty rather than a "comfortable life in prison." *State v. Forte*, 360 N.C. 427 (2006) (no error where evidence in record supported prosecutor's argument pointing out the amenities that defendant would have if sentenced to life in prison; no objection by defendant at trial); *State v. Alston*, 341 N.C. 198, 252 (1995) (prosecutor's argument "that it is hard to be penitent with televisions, basketball courts, and weight rooms emphasized the prosecution's position that life in prison was not an adequate punishment" for defendant's crime; defendant objected on grounds that this was an improper "general deterrent" argument but there was no specific objection that such argument was based on matters outside the record); *State v. Reeves*, 337 N.C. 700, 732 (1994) (no objection to prosecutor's comment that if sentenced to life, defendant would have a "cozy little prison cell . . . with [a] television set, air conditioning and three meals a day"; court held that the argument was not such an "egregious" use of hyperbole to describe prison life as to require the trial judge to intervene ex mero motu).

Practice note: The prison argument, discussed immediately above, is another example of a subject in which the courts have sometimes drawn fine lines between improper and proper closing arguments. Counsel therefore should object if the prosecutor argues about a "comfortable" prison life and lists all its amenities since this argument may involve matters outside the record, which are not based on common knowledge, and not all prisons have the same "amenities." *See State v. May*, 354 N.C. 172 (2001) (court acknowledged that prosecutor improperly argued facts not in the record when describing the life that defendant would have in prison (including card games, punching bags, snacks, television, radio, and candy), but held that the trial judge did not abuse his discretion by failing to intervene ex mero motu).

C. Impermissible Content

A prosecutor may argue vigorously, but he or she does not have free reign. In addition to the impermissible arguments discussed *supra* in § 33.2C, a prosecutor may not:

- Comment on the defendant's failure to testify. *See* U.S. CONST. amend. V; N.C. CONST. art. I, § 23; G.S. 8-54; *State v. Baymon*, 336 N.C. 748 (1994) (new trial granted where prosecutor's argument directly referred to defendant's failure to testify and was intended to disparage defendant in the eyes of the jury); *State v. Reid*, 334 N.C. 551 (1993) (new trial granted where prosecutor argued that defendant had not testified, that he had that right, and that the jury was not to hold it against him); *cf. State v. Bovender*, 233 N.C. 683, 689–90 (1951) (*defense counsel* may state the defendant's right not to testify but may not comment on or explain why the defendant did not testify because it "would open the door for the prosecution and create a situation the statute was intended to prevent"). [For a further discussion of commenting on the right not to testify, see *supra* § 21.3B, Right Not to Take the Stand.]

- Comment on the defendant's failure to talk to the police or silence during the investigation, subject to certain exceptions. *See State v. Ward*, 354 N.C. 231 (2001) (trial judge abused his discretion by failing to stop arguments by prosecutor regarding defendant's post-arrest silence where the arguments violated defendant's right to remain silent under the Fifth Amendment of the U.S. Constitution and under article I, section 23 of the N.C. Constitution); *State v. Boston*, 191 N.C. App. 637 (2008) (use of defendant's pre-arrest silence as substantive evidence of guilt violates the Fifth Amendment but if the defendant testifies, the State may use defendant's silence for impeachment purposes if it amounted to a prior inconsistent statement); *see also Doyle v. Ohio*, 426 U.S. 610 (1976) (use of a defendant's post-*Miranda* silence for impeachment purposes violates the Due Process Clause of the Fourteenth Amendment). *But see State v. Buckner*, 342 N.C. 198 (1995) (if *Miranda* warnings were not given, a defendant's post-arrest silence may be used to impeach a defendant without violating a defendant's constitutional rights as long as the evidence is admissible for impeachment purposes under the rules of evidence). For further discussion of the evidentiary use of a defendant's silence, see 2 KENNETH S. BROUN, BRANDIS & BROUN ON NORTH CAROLINA EVIDENCE § 211, at 827–29 (7th ed. 2011); ROBERT L. FARB, ARREST, SEARCH , AND INVESTIGATION IN NORTH CAROLINA, at 634–37 (4th ed. 2011).
- Assert that the defendant is "lying" or call him a "liar." *State v. Sexton*, 336 N.C. 321 (1994); *State v. Hunter*, ___ N.C. App. ___, 703 S.E.2d 776 (2010); *State v. Nance*, 157 N.C. App. 434 (2003). *But cf. State v. Brice*, 320 N.C. 119, 124 (1987) (trial judge did not abuse discretion in overruling defendant's objection to prosecutor's argument that a witness "did not tell you the truth" where the evidence supported this inference); *State v. Noell*, 284 N.C. 670, 696–97 (1974) (prosecutor's submission to the jury that defense witnesses "have lied to you" was a reasonable comment on the evidence), *vacated in part on other grounds*, 428 U.S. 902 (1976).
- Comment on the defendant's failure to call his or her spouse as a witness. G.S. 8-57 (spousal privilege); *State v. Thompson*, 290 N.C. 431 (1976); *State v. Martin*, 105 N.C. App. 182 (1992). *But see State v. Fearing*, 304 N.C. 471 (1981) (prosecutor properly argued that the State could not call defendant's wife, an occupant of the car, as a witness in response to defendant's argument that the State could have called the occupants of the car as witnesses but did not do so).
- Malign or belittle an expert's profession rather than arguing the law, the evidence, and its inferences. *State v. Smith*, 352 N.C. 531 (2000).
- Impute perjury to an expert witness solely on the basis that the witness had been or

will be compensated for his or her services. *State v. Rogers*, 355 N.C. 420 (2002).

- Ask the jurors to put themselves in the place of the victims. *State v. McCollum*, 334 N.C. 208, 224 (1993) (citing *United States v. Pichnarcik*, 427 F.2d 1290 (9th Cir. 1970)).
- Make reference to events and circumstances outside the evidence, such as the infamous acts of others, and make inappropriate comparisons or analogies, either directly or indirectly, to inflame the jury. *State v. Walters*, 357 N.C. 68 (2003) (prosecutor compared the defendant to Hitler in the context of being evil); *State v. Jones*, 355 N.C. 117 (2002) (prosecutor made comparative references to the Columbine school shooting and the Oklahoma City bombing).
- Degrade or compare criminal defendants to members of the animal kingdom. *State v. Roache*, 358 N.C. 243, 297 (2004) (characterizing defendants as a pack of wild dogs "high on the taste of blood and power over their victims"); *Jones*, 355 N.C. 117, 133 ("lower than the dirt on a snake's belly"); *State v. Richardson*, 342 N.C. 772, 792 (1996) ("animal"); *State v. Smith*, 279 N.C. 163, 165 (1971) ("lower than the bone belly of a cur dog"); *State v. Ballard*, 191 N.C. 122, 124 (1926) ("human hyena").
- Make unfair characterizations about the defendant. *See State v. Bowen*, 230 N.C. 710 (1949) (characterization is not argument and a prosecutor should not be permitted to characterize a defendant or his conduct by uncomplimentary terms that are not supported by the evidence); *State v. Correll*, 229 N.C. 640, 643 (1948) (trial judge "very properly sustained objection to the remarks of counsel characterizing defendant as 'a smalltime racketeering gangster'").
- Tell the jury that the community demands conviction and punishment of the defendant. *State v. Nicholson*, 355 N.C. 1 (2002), *vacated in part on other grounds sub nom. Nicholson v. Branker*, 739 F. Supp. 2d 839 (E.D.N.C. 2010); *State v. Erlewine*, 328 N.C. 626 (1991); *see also State v. Golphin*, 352 N.C. 364, 471 (2000) (prosecutor cannot encourage the jury to "lend an ear to the community"); *State v. Boyd*, 311 N.C. 408, 418 (1984) (jury's decision cannot be based on "the jury's perceived accountability to the witnesses, to the victim, to the community, or to society in general").
- Argue that evidence admissible only to impeach the defendant's credibility should be considered as substantive evidence. *State v. Tucker*, 317 N.C. 532 (1986).
- Assert that favorable rulings on the defendant's motions to exclude the admission of certain evidence are the result of "an effort on defendant's part to obscure the truth." *State v. Brown*, 327 N.C. 1, 19 (1990).

Capital cases. In the sentencing phase of a capital case, prosecutors are given more latitude to incorporate reasonable inferences and conclusions about the victim and the defendant as long as they are drawn from the evidence. However, mere conclusory arguments that are not reasonable (such as name-calling) or that are premised on matters outside the record (such as comparing the defendant's crimes to infamous acts) remain inappropriate. *See State v. Walters*, 357 N.C. 68 (2003).

During the sentencing phase of a capital case, prosecutors may not:

- Argue the general deterrent effect of the death penalty. *State v. Hill*, 311 N.C. 465

(1984); *State v. Kirkley*, 308 N.C. 196 (1983); *cf. State v. Cherry*, 298 N.C. 86 (1979) (criminal *defendants* may not offer evidence during the penalty phase to show that capital punishment does not have any deterrent effect).

- Make arguments that minimize the jury's sense of the importance of its role or lead the jury to believe that the responsibility for determining the appropriateness of the death penalty for the defendant rests elsewhere. *State v. Green*, 336 N.C. 142 (1994); *State v. Daniels*, 337 N.C. 243 (1994); *see also Caldwell v. Mississippi*, 472 U.S. 320 (1985).

Practice note: If you suspect that the prosecutor intends to make improper statements during closing argument (such as biblical references or fundamentally unfair victim impact assertions), you should consider filing a motion in limine before closing arguments asking the trial judge to preclude the prosecutor from making those arguments. If the motion is denied, you should also object to the prosecutor's statements *at the time they are made* to preserve the issue for appeal. *See infra* § 33.8, Preservation of Issues for Appellate Review. A sample "Motion to Restrict Prosecutor's Argument" is located on the website of the Office of Indigent Defense Services, www.ncids.org, under Training & Resources, Capital Trial Motions (Penalty Phase Instructions Requests).

D. Invited Response

Statements made by the prosecutor during closing argument are not viewed in "'an isolated vacuum'" on appeal. *State v. Elliott*, 344 N.C. 242, 283 (1996) (citation omitted). Appellate courts will give fair consideration "'to the context in which the remarks were made and to the overall factual circumstances to which they referred.'" *Id.* (citations omitted) (internal quotation marks omitted).

Appellate courts have occasionally found that counsel, in his or her closing argument to the jury, has invited responsive or retaliatory argument by opposing counsel. *See, e.g., Crutcher v. Noel*, 284 N.C. 568 (1974); *State v. Knotts*, 168 N.C. 173 (1914); *State v. Barber*, 93 N.C. App. 42 (1989); *see also State v. Trull*, 349 N.C. 428 (1998) (prosecutor may appropriately respond to defense counsel's closing arguments that are critical of the State's investigation and witnesses); *State v. Larrimore*, 340 N.C. 119 (1995) (prosecutor was allowed to respond to arguments made by defense counsel questioning the credibility of police detective); *State v. Oliver*, 309 N.C. 326 (1983) (finding no reversible error where the prosecutor made biblical references during closing argument because defense counsel, as anticipated by the prosecutor, argued that the New Testament teaches forgiveness and mercy); *State v. Cole*, 147 N.C. App. 637 (2001) (defendant's argument that the victim was a drug dealer and was killed by a disgruntled client invited prosecutor to argue that defendant was a drug dealer and the killing was drug-related); *see also supra* § 33.2F, Biblical References (discussing invited response specifically in relation to biblical references).

Practice note: In preparing your closing argument, you must carefully consider whether any of your statements "open the door" to what would otherwise be considered improper comments by the prosecutor. If any statements raise that possibility, consider removing them or be prepared to object to the prosecutor's response and to argue why the prosecutor's response is inappropriate.

33.8 Preservation of Issues for Appellate Review

A. Necessity for Objection

If the prosecutor makes improper and prejudicial statements during closing argument, defense counsel must object before the verdict in order to preserve the issue for appeal. "Upon objection, the trial court has the duty to censor remarks not warranted by the evidence or law. . . ." *State v. Anderson*, 322 N.C. 22, 37 (1998). Absent an objection, the trial judge only has a duty to intervene, ex mero motu, if the prosecutor's argument is grossly improper. *Id.*; *see also infra* § 33.8B, Waiver.

Generally, when a party objects to an improper argument of counsel, "it is not sufficient for the court merely to stop the argument without instructing the jury, either at the time or in the jury charge, to ignore the improper argument." *State v. Barber*, 93 N.C. App. 42, 48 (1989). However, when an objection to an improper argument is sustained, it is incumbent on the defendant to request a curative instruction. If he or she does not request a curative instruction, the judge does not err in failing to give one. *Id.*; *State v. Goblet*, 173 N.C. App. 112 (2005).

If a timely objection to an improper argument is made, the trial judge's error in failing to sustain the objection will be reviewed by the appellate court for an abuse of the trial judge's discretion. *See State v. Walters*, 357 N.C. 68 (2003); *State v. Jones*, 355 N.C. 117 (2002); *see also State v. Rashidi*, 172 N.C. App. 628 (2005) (to justify a new trial under the abuse of discretion standard of review, a prosecutor's improper remark during closing arguments must have been so grave that it prejudiced the result of the trial), *aff'd per curiam*, 360 N.C. 166 (2005).

Practice note: "It is not impolite to interrupt opposing counsel's summation—it is mandatory to preserve error and stop the prejudice." Ira Mickenberg, *Preserving the Record and Making Objections at Trial: A Win-Win Proposition for Client and Lawyer*, at 4 (North Carolina Defender Trial School, July 2011), *available at* www.ncids.org/Defender%20Training/2011DefenderTrialSchool/PreservingRecord%20_Mickenberg.pdf. Assert both statutory and constitutional grounds for the objection if applicable. State on the record that the improper argument violates the Sixth, Eighth, and Fourteenth Amendments to the U.S. Constitution, as well as article I, sections 19, 23, and 27 of the N.C. Constitution. If your objection is sustained, immediately ask the judge to instruct the jury to disregard the improper statements. You should also carefully consider whether further remedy is necessary or whether it would serve to draw further negative attention to the comments. If you decide that the prejudice resulting from a prosecutor's improper argument was severe and in need of further remedy, you may ask the judge to:

- admonish the prosecutor to refrain from that line of argument;

- require the prosecutor to retract the improper argument;
- repeat the curative instruction during the jury charge; or
- grant a mistrial.

See Jones, 355 N.C. 117, 129 (it is incumbent on trial judge to vigilantly monitor closing arguments, "to intervene as warranted, to entertain objections, and to impose any remedies pertaining to those objections"); *Wilcox v. Glover Motors, Inc.*, 269 N.C. 473 (1967) (listing several methods by which a trial judge, in his or her discretion, may correct an improper argument).

B. Waiver

Failure to timely object to the prosecutor's argument constitutes a waiver of the alleged error. In the absence of an objection, appellate courts will review the prosecutor's argument to determine "'whether it was so grossly improper that the trial court abused its discretion in failing to intervene *ex mero motu* to correct the error.'" *State v. Taylor*, 337 N.C. 597, 613 (1994) (quoting *State v. Allen*, 323 N.C. 208, 226 (1988), *vacated on other grounds*, 494 U.S. 1021 (1990)).

To establish an abuse of discretion in this context, the defendant must show that the prosecutor's comments "'so infected the trial with unfairness as to make the resulting conviction a denial of due process.'" *State v. Rose*, 339 N.C. 172, 202 (1994) (citations omitted) (internal quotation marks omitted). This is a much more stringent standard of review than is applied to preserved errors so it is critically important for appellate purposes to timely object to improper statements made by the prosecutor and to request curative instructions if the objection is sustained.

C. Complete Recordation

Requirement for and timing of motion. Pursuant to G.S. 15A-1241(a)(2), trial judges are not required to order the court reporter to record opening statements and closing arguments. However, on the motion of any party (or on the judge's own motion), these proceedings ***must*** be recorded. G.S. 15A-1241(b). "The motion for recordation of jury arguments must be made before the commencement of any argument and if one argument is recorded all must be." *Id.*

If a party suggests during an unrecorded argument that an improper statement has been made, the judge has the discretion to require that the rest of the argument be recorded. G.S. 15A-1241(b).

A sample Motion for Complete Recordation appears in the Non-Capital Trial Motions Bank, under Training & Resources, at www.ncids.org. This motion covers not only jury arguments but also pretrial hearings, jury selection in non-capital cases, motions hearings, and bench conferences since those proceedings are also exempt from mandatory recordation under G.S. 15A-1241(a).

Reconstruction of record. If an objection is made to an unrecorded statement or other conduct in the presence of the jury, on motion of either party the trial judge "must reconstruct for the record, as accurately as possible, the matter to which objection was made." G.S. 15A-1241(c). Where a defendant does not undertake the efforts necessary to reconstruct the record with regard to improper statements made by the prosecutor during closing argument, appellate courts will decline review. *See State v. Spellman*, 167 N.C. App. 374 (2004); *State v. Ussery*, 106 N.C. App. 371 (1992).

Practice note: The appellate courts have never held that it is ineffective assistance of counsel per se for defense counsel to fail to request complete recordation. *See, e.g., State v. Hardison*, 326 N.C. 646 (1990) (defendant cannot show ineffective assistance of counsel where there are no specific allegations of prejudice and no attempt to reconstruct the record); *State v. Verrier*, 173 N.C. App. 123, 130 (2005) (denying defendant's request to adopt "a per se rule granting a new trial where counsel neither requests nor the trial court requires that the entire trial, jury selection, arguments of counsel and bench conferences" be recorded). Still, ***there is no good reason not to make the request.*** Opening statements and closing arguments are often fertile ground for appellate issues. You must protect the rights of your client even if it means irritating the judge or court reporter, who may not feel that complete recordation is necessary. Complete recordation will obviate the need for reconstruction of the transcript in the event that improper statements are made and will greatly facilitate appellate review. It may also inhibit prosecutors from "push[ing] the envelope" during closing argument. *See State v. Jones*, 355 N.C. 117, 127 (2002). If, however, you have failed to request complete recordation and an issue arises regarding an improper statement made by the prosecutor, you must take steps to immediately ensure that the record is accurately reconstructed.

D. Absence of Trial Judge During Closing Argument

For a discussion addressing the absence of the trial judge during closing argument (and other parts of the trial, such as jury voir dire), see *supra* § 22.1D, Absence of Trial Judge During Proceedings.

E. Additional Resources

For a short, practical perspective on the topics covered in this section, see Staples Hughes, *Curbing Prosecutorial Misconduct and Preserving the Record in Closing Argument* (Public Defender Conference, Nov. 2008), *available at* www.ncids.org/Defender%20Training/2008%20Fall%20Conference/CurbingProsecutorialMisconduct.pdf.

Appendix 33-1
Guideline 7.7 Closing Argument*

(a) Counsel should be familiar with the substantive limits on both prosecution and defense summation, including the law governing closing arguments under G.S. 7A-97 and G.S. 15A-1230, Rule 10 of the General Rules of Practice for the Superior and District Courts, and North Carolina case law.

(b) In developing closing argument, counsel should review the proceedings to determine what aspects can be used in support of defense summation and, where appropriate, should consider:

(1) highlighting weaknesses in the prosecution's case;
(2) describing favorable inferences to be drawn from the evidence;
(3) incorporating into the argument:
 (A) the theory of the defense case;
 (B) helpful testimony from direct and cross-examinations;
 (C) verbatim instructions drawn from the expected jury charge;
 (D) responses to anticipated prosecution arguments; and
 (E) visual aids and exhibits; and
(4) the effects of the defense argument on the prosecution's rebuttal argument.

(c) Whenever the prosecutor exceeds the scope of permissible argument, counsel should consider objecting, seeking cautionary instructions, or requesting a mistrial unless sound tactical considerations suggest otherwise. Such tactical considerations may include, but are not limited to:

(1) the possibility that an objection or cautionary instruction might enhance the significance of the information in the jurors' minds;
(2) whether, with respect to a motion for mistrial, counsel believes that the case will result in a favorable verdict for the client; and
(3) the need to preserve the objection for appellate review.

---

*Reprinted from N.C. COMM'N ON INDIGENT DEFENSE SERVS., PERFORMANCE GUIDELINES FOR INDIGENT DEFENSE REPRESENTATION IN NON-CAPITAL CASES AT THE TRIAL LEVEL (Nov. 2004). For the complete guidelines, see *infra* Appendix A of this manual.

Chapter 34
Deliberations and Verdict

This chapter addresses two related topics. Sections 34.1 through 34.6 deal with issues surrounding jury deliberations leading up to the verdict, including instructions about reaching a verdict, juror requests, coercion, and deadlock. Section 34.7 addresses the return of the verdict, including the procedures and issues surrounding its return.

34.1 Instructions to the Jury about Reaching a Verdict

Section 15A-1235 of the North Carolina General Statutes (hereinafter G.S.) sets out mandatory and discretionary instructions to give to the jury on how to reach a verdict. The mandatory instruction is set out in G.S. 15A-1235(a), and it states: "Before the jury retires for deliberation, the judge must give an instruction which informs the jury that in order to return a verdict, all 12 jurors must agree to a verdict of guilty or not guilty."

G.S. 15A-1235(b) provides that before the jury retires to deliberate, the judge also may give an instruction that:

- jurors have a duty to consult with one another and to deliberate with a view to reaching an agreement, if it can be done without violence to individual judgment;
- each juror must decide the case for himself, but only after an impartial consideration of the evidence with his fellow jurors;
- in the course of deliberations, a juror should not hesitate to reexamine his own views and change his opinion if convinced it is erroneous; and
- no juror should surrender his or her honest conviction as to the weight or effect of the evidence solely because of the opinion of his fellow jurors or for the mere purpose of returning a verdict.

A trial judge is not required, even on request, to give the instructions set out in G.S. 15A-1235(b), but he or she may give them in his or her discretion. *See State v. Beasley*, 118 N.C. App. 508 (1995). However, if the judge decides to give the jury any of the instructions authorized by that subsection, whether given before the jury initially retires for deliberation or after the trial judge concludes that the jury is deadlocked, he or she must give all of them. *State v. Williams*, 315 N.C. 310 (1986). The judge does not have to read the statute verbatim as long as he or she gives the substance of the four instructions. *State v. Fernandez*, 346 N.C. 1 (1997).

Practice note: If the trial judge gives some, but not all, of the instructions found in G.S. 15A-1235(b), you must specifically object to preserve the issue for appeal. Otherwise, the appellate court will review the omission using the rigorous "plain error" standard of review.

For a further discussion of instructions to the jury, see *supra* Chapter 32, Instructions to the Jury.

34.2 Requests to Review Testimony and Exhibits During Deliberations

A. Review of Testimony and Exhibits in Open Court

During deliberations, juries will frequently send requests to the trial judge seeking a review of testimony or exhibits introduced at trial. Before hearing and ruling on such requests, the trial judge must summon all jurors to the courtroom. G.S. 15A-1233(a); *see also State v. Ashe*, 314 N.C. 28 (1985) (holding that under article I, section 24 of the N.C. Constitution, all the elements of a trial should be viewed and heard simultaneously by all twelve jurors).

Practice note: The lack of an objection to the trial judge's failure to return the jury to the courtroom after a jury request for review of evidence pursuant to G.S. 15A-1233(a) will not preclude the defendant from raising the issue on appeal. However, if you *consent* to a procedure that does not comply with the statutory mandate, it may be extremely difficult for the appellate attorney to show that the statutory violation prejudiced the defendant. *See State v. Nobles*, 350 N.C. 483, 506 (1999) (trial judge erred in failing to conduct the jury to the courtroom after jury requested to see evidence but defendant failed to show prejudice since (1) his counsel agreed "with the trial court when it erroneously thought it had discretion whether to bring the jury to the courtroom;" (2) there was unanimous agreement by all concerning the items requested by the jury; and (3) "the prosecution and the defense consented to permitting the jury to have those items"). The N.C. Court of Appeals later stated in *State v. Pointer*, 181 N.C. App. 93, 99 (2007), that "when a defendant's lawyer consents to the trial court's communication with the jury in a manner other than bringing the jury back into the courtroom, the defendant waives his right to assert a ground for appeal based on failure to bring the jury back to the courtroom." This holding appears to be inconsistent with *Nobles* because in that case the N.C. Supreme Court granted review of the issue even though the defendant consented to the procedure in that case. *See State v. Williams*, ___ N.C. App. ___, 715 S.E.2d 553, 560 (2011) ("consistent with *Nobles*," court of appeals addressed merits of defendant's argument and found error in trial judge's failure to return jury to courtroom to discuss exhibit request, but defendant failed to meet burden of showing prejudice where he consented to the jury's receiving the items and had no objection to submitting the items to the jury without bringing them to the courtroom); *accord State v. Harrison*, ___ N.C. App. ___, 721 S.E.2d 371 (2012) (to same effect).

G.S. 15A-1233(a) also requires the trial judge, after hearing the jury's request, to exercise his or her discretion in deciding whether or not to grant the request. *State v. Helms*, 93 N.C. App. 394 (1989); *see also Ashe*, 314 N.C. 28 (the statutory requirement that the trial judge exercise discretion in deciding whether to allow the jury's request to review evidence is a codification of the common law rule). After exercising discretion, and after giving notice to the prosecutor and to the defendant, the trial judge may direct that parts of the testimony be read to the jury and permit the jury to reexamine the requested materials. The reexamination of requested materials must take place in open court (unless the parties consent as discussed under subsection B., below). The judge, in his or her discretion, may also have the jury review other evidence that relates to the same factual issue so as not to give undue prominence to the evidence requested. G.S. 15A-1233(a).

When the trial judge fails to exercise his or her discretion under G.S. 15A-1233(a) under the erroneous belief that he or she has no power to grant the jury's request, error has been committed. *See State v. Johnson*, 346 N.C. 119 (1997); *see also State v. Long*, 196 N.C. App. 22 (2009). If the error is prejudicial to the defendant, he or she is entitled to a new trial. *See State v. Lang*, 301 N.C. 508 (1980); *see also Ashe*, 314 N.C. 28, 35 (finding reversible error where trial judge failed to exercise discretion in denying jury's request to review testimony; judge apparently felt he could not grant the request because he stated, "There is no transcript at this point. You and the other jurors will have to take your recollection of the evidence . . . .").

The trial judge has no authority to permit the jury to review exhibits or other materials if the requested items have not been received into evidence. *See State v. Bacon*, 326 N.C. 404 (1990) (trial judge correctly refused jury's request to see police report that was not introduced into evidence).

B. Review of Exhibits in the Jury Room

The trial judge may permit the jury to take requested exhibits into the jury room if all of the parties have consented. Whether jurors are allowed to take exhibits to the jury room is within the trial judge's discretion even if all the parties consent. If the judge permits the jury to take the requested exhibits or materials into the jury room, he or she may also have the jury take additional material or first review other evidence relating to the same factual issue so as not to give undue prominence to the evidence taken to the jury room. G.S. 15A-1233(b).

Unlike jury review of exhibits or testimony in open court, consent of all parties is required before the jury may take evidence into the jury room. G.S. 15A-1233(b); *see also State v. Barnett*, 307 N.C. 608 (1983). The rationale behind the rule against exhibits in the jury room without consent of all parties is that the jury should make its decision based on what was offered in open court, and not on comparisons or inferences made about the evidence in the jury room, "'because the opposite party ought to have an opportunity to reply to any suggestion of an inference contrary to what was made in open court.'" *See Doby v. Fowler*, 49 N.C. App. 162, 163 (1980) (quoting *Watson v. Davis*, 52 N.C. 178, 181 (1859)). Allowing the jury to view exhibits without the consent of all parties is not reversible error per se, and the party asserting the error on appeal must demonstrate that he or she was prejudiced thereby. *State v. Thomas*, 132 N.C. App. 515 (1999).

If the judge allows an exhibit to be taken to the jury room, he or she must, on request, instruct the jury not to conduct any experiments with the exhibit. G.S. 15A-1233(b).

Practice note: Before consenting to the jury taking an exhibit into the jury room, you should carefully consider how the jury may use the exhibit during its deliberations and whether it would be in the defendant's best interest to consent. If the trial judge, without obtaining consent from all parties, sends an exhibit to the jury room that you believe is harmful to the defendant's case, you should object on the record to ensure preservation of the issue on appeal. *See State v. Rogers*, 52 N.C. App. 676 (1981); *State v. Byrd*, 50 N.C. App. 736 (1981); *cf. State v. Locklear*, 349 N.C. 118, 151 (1999) (reviewing issue but finding that error, if any, was harmless in this instance).

34.3 Coercion of the Verdict by the Trial Judge

A. In General

Every person charged with a crime in North Carolina has an absolute right to a fair trial "before an impartial judge and an unprejudiced jury in an atmosphere of judicial calm." *State v. Carter*, 233 N.C. 581, 583 (1951). Article I, section 24 of the N.C. Constitution prohibits a trial judge from coercing a jury to return a verdict. *State v. Patterson*, 332 N.C. 409 (1992).

In an effort to avoid coerced verdicts from jurors who are having a difficult time reaching a decision, the General Assembly enacted G.S. 15A-1235. *State v. Evans*, 346 N.C. 221 (1997). The instructions contained in that statute are set out *supra* in § 34.1. G.S. 15A-1235 borrows from the standards approved by the American Bar Association and is the "proper reference for standards applicable to charges which may be given a jury that is apparently unable to agree upon a verdict." *State v. Easterling*, 300 N.C. 594, 608 (1980). The instructions given to a deadlocked jury must conform to those standards. *Id.*

Although *Easterling* held that a trial judge's instructions to a deadlocked jury must conform to those set out in G.S. 15A-1235, the mere failure by the trial judge to precisely follow those instructions is not itself reversible error. *State v. Peek*, 313 N.C. 266 (1985). In determining whether a judge has coerced a verdict, the appellate court must consider the totality of the circumstances under which the instructions were made and the probable impact of the instructions on the jury. *State v. Beaver*, 322 N.C. 462 (1988); *Peek*, 313 N.C. 266. If the circumstances suggest to a juror that he or she should surrender well-founded convictions conscientiously held or his or her own free will and judgment in deference to the views of the majority, then coercion has occurred. *See State v. Holcomb*, 295 N.C. 608 (1978); *State v. Roberts*, 270 N.C. 449 (1967).

Some of the factors to be considered in judging the totality of circumstances are whether the court

- conveyed an impression to the jury that it was irritated with them for not reaching a verdict;
- intimated to the jury that it would hold them until they reached a verdict; and
- told the jury a retrial would burden the court system if the jury did not reach a verdict.

Beaver, 322 N.C. 462, 464. If the judge's instructions merely served as a catalyst for further deliberations and did not encourage the jurors to concur in what is really a majority verdict rather than a unanimous verdict, then coercion has not occurred. *See Peek*, 313 N.C. 266; *State v. Dexter*, 151 N.C. App. 430 (2002), *aff'd per curiam*, 356 N.C. 604 (2002).

B. Inquiry into Numerical Split

A trial judge's inquiry as to the division of the jury, without asking which votes were for conviction or acquittal, is not inherently coercive and does not constitute a per se violation of the defendant's right to a jury trial as guaranteed by article I, section 24 of the N.C. Constitution. *State v. Fowler*, 312 N.C. 304 (1984). Likewise, such an inquiry does not violate a defendant's rights under the Due Process Clause or the Sixth Amendment to the U.S. Constitution. *Id.* (interpreting the decision in *Brasfield v. United States*, 272 U.S. 448 (1926), which found reversible error in a trial judge's inquiry into the numerical division of a jury deadlock, as based on the U.S. Supreme Court's supervisory power over the *federal* courts and not on the defendant's constitutional rights). The making of an inquiry into the numerical division of the jury lies within the sound discretion of the trial judge. *State v. Mann*, 317 N.C. 164 (1986).

C. Length of Deliberations

G.S. 15A-1235(c) states that the trial judge "may not require or threaten to require the jury to deliberate for an unreasonable length of time or for unreasonable intervals." There is no bright-line rule setting an outside time-limit on jury deliberations; nor is there a rule that deliberations for a certain length of time, in relation to the length of time spent by the State presenting its evidence, is too long. *State v. Baldwin*, 141 N.C. App. 596 (2000) (finding no coercion where the trial judge, after being informed that the jury was at an impasse after only two and one-half hours of deliberations, ordered the jury to continue deliberating, and the jury reached a verdict at 11:04 p.m. after about seven hours of deliberations).

A verdict is coerced if the trial judge's comments and actions, along with the length of deliberations, improperly influenced the jury to reach a decision. *See, e.g., State v. Dexter*, 151 N.C. App. 430 (2002) (holding that jury could have reasonably felt coerced where the jury had deliberated for three days and sent out three notes informing the judge it could not reach a verdict, and the judge did not respond in the presence of the jury to a juror's note asking for time off for his wife's surgery and only gave the instructions set out in G.S. 15A-1235 after the second note), *aff'd per curiam*, 356 N.C. 604 (2002); *State v. McEntire*, 71 N.C. App. 720 (1984) (finding jury coercion where, after five hours of deliberations and being told that the jury would probably not be able to agree, the judge instructed them to continue deliberating without giving the instructions set out in G.S. 15A-1235).

Practice note: Always request that the record reflect the exact amount of time spent by the jury in deliberations in the event that coercion becomes an issue on appeal. Court reporters do not always note this important information in the transcript.

D. Comment on the Inconvenience or Expense of Retrial

Due to the danger of coercion, a deadlocked jury may not be advised of the potential expense and inconvenience of retrying the case. *State v. Easterling*, 300 N.C. 594 (1980); *see also* G.S. 15A-1235 Official Commentary ("The Commission deleted from its draft a provision previously sanctioned under North Carolina case law which would have authorized the judge to inform the jurors that if they do not agree upon a verdict another jury may be called upon to try the case."); *State v. Buckom*, 111 N.C. App. 240 (1993) (trial judge committed prejudicial error by instructing the jury, as part of an anti-deadlock instruction, that the "main purpose" of trying to reconcile differences in further deliberations was to avoid an expensive retrial), *aff'd per curiam*, 335 N.C. 765 (1994); *State v. Johnson*, 80 N.C. App. 311 (1986) (finding prejudicial error where the judge knew the jury was deadlocked 11-1 and his instructions, inter alia, mentioned the potential inconvenience and use of the court's time). If the jury is not deadlocked, an isolated mention of the expense and inconvenience of retrying the case may be harmless error. *See State v. Mack*, 53 N.C. App. 127 (1981). However, once the trial judge knows that a jury is deadlocked, "the mention of inconvenience and additional expense may well be prejudicial and harmful to the defendant, and must be scrutinized with extraordinary care." *Id.* at 129.

Practice note: Be sure to object to any instructions by the trial judge that inform the jury of the expense or inconvenience of retrying a case should the jury fail to reach a verdict. If you fail to object, the appellate court will review the issue using the more stringent "plain error" standard of review. *See State v. Pate*, 187 N.C. App. 442, 445 (2007) (because defendant did not object to the judge's instructions to the deadlocked jury "that the parties had put a great deal of time and effort into the case, and if they failed to reach a unanimous verdict another jury could be brought in to decide the issues," the assignment of error would be analyzed under the plain error standard of review; court found that the judge's error in the instructions did not have "a probable impact on the jury's finding of guilt" under the facts of the case) (citation omitted).

34.4 Improper Expression of Opinion by Trial Judge

Comments and actions by the trial judge in the jury's presence, although not amounting to coercion of the jury as discussed in the preceding section, may constitute an improper expression of opinion as to the defendant's guilt and warrant relief. Questioning of witnesses by the judge, although permissible, may also indicate the judge's opinion as to the defendant's guilt and constitute an improper expression of opinion. For a discussion of these issues, see *supra* § 22.1B, Expression of Opinion Prohibited, and § 22.1C, Questioning of Witnesses Allowed, within Limits.

34.5 Deadlock

"In times long gone by, when a jury was unable to reach a verdict the trial court simply deprived the jurors of food, water, and fire until it reached a verdict. Today a more subtle approach is used to break a deadlocked jury." *State v. Lamb*, 44 N.C. App. 251, 253 (1979) (citations omitted).

A. Further Instructions

G.S. 15A-1235(c) provides that if the jury indicates a deadlock, the trial judge may give or repeat the instructions about reaching a verdict provided in G.S. 15A-1235(a) and (b). *See supra* § 34.1, Instructions to the Jury about Reaching a Verdict. The language of G.S. 15A-1235(c) is permissive rather than mandatory, and it is within the sound discretion of the trial judge whether to give those instructions. *State v. Williams*, 315 N.C. 310 (1986).

In lieu of the instructions set out in G.S. 15A-1235(b), the judge may give the pattern instruction entitled "Failure of Jury to Reach a Verdict," which is found in N.C. Pattern Jury Instruction—Crim.101.40 (June 2010). *See, e.g., State v. Walters*, ___ N.C. App. ___, 703 S.E.2d 493 (2011). This instruction is similar to the one found in G.S. 15A-1235(b). The instructions in both G.S. 15A-1235(b) and N.C. Pattern Jury Instruction—Crim. 101.40 are modified, weaker versions of the charge approved by the U.S. Supreme Court in *Allen v. United States*, 164 U.S. 492 (1896). Both are still sometimes referred to as an "*Allen*" or "dynamite" charge. *See State v. Fowler*, 312 N.C. 304, 306 (1984); *Lamb*, 44 N.C. App. 251, 253–54.

B. Mistrial

Grounds. If it appears that there is no reasonable possibility of the jury reaching a verdict, the judge may declare a mistrial and discharge the jury. G.S. 15A-1235(d). This statute allows a judge to declare a mistrial on the same grounds as in G.S. 15A-1063(2), which states that "[u]pon motion of a party or upon his own motion, a judge may declare a mistrial if . . . [i]t appears there is no reasonable probability of the jury's agreement upon a verdict." *State v. O'Neal*, 67 N.C. App. 65 (1984) (noting judge's authority to grant a mistrial under G.S. 15A-1063(2), but order for mistrial not justified since the jury could and did reach a verdict in the case), *aff'd in pertinent part*, 311 N.C. 747 (1984). The jury's inability to reach a verdict due to deadlock constitutes "manifest necessity," justifying the declaration of a mistrial. *State v. Pakulski*, 319 N.C. 562, 570 (1987). Whether to grant a motion for a mistrial is a matter that lies within the sound discretion of the trial judge, and that ruling will not be disturbed on appeal unless it was so clearly erroneous that it amounted to an abuse of discretion. *State v. McCarver*, 341 N.C. 364, 383 (1995).

Findings of fact. Pursuant to G.S. 15A-1064, "[b]efore granting a mistrial, the judge must make finding of facts with respect to the grounds for the mistrial and insert the findings in the record of the case." In non-capital cases, a trial judge's failure to make findings in support of a mistrial is not subject to appellate review unless timely objected to by defense counsel. "However, in a *capital* case, the failure to object to a mistrial declaration will not prevent a defendant from assigning the declaration of mistrial as error on appeal." *Pakulski*, 319 N.C. 562, 569 (emphasis in original).

For further discussion of mistrials after a jury has become deadlocked, see *supra* § 31.7, Juror Deadlock.

34.6 Use of Juror Notes During Deliberations

Jurors are permitted to use their trial notes during deliberations unless otherwise directed by the trial judge. G.S. 15A-1228; *see supra* § 27.1, Note Taking by the Jury.

34.7 Verdicts

"A verdict is the unanimous decision made by the jury and reported to the court." *State v. Hemphill*, 273 N.C. 388, 389 (1968). A verdict in a criminal action should be "clear and free from ambiguity or uncertainty." The "enforcement of the criminal law and the liberty of the citizen" demand "exactitude." *State v. Jones*, 227 N.C. 47, 49–50 (1946).

A. Basic Requirements

Pursuant to G.S. 15A-1237(a) and (b), a verdict must be:

- in writing;
- signed by the foreman;
- made a part of the record of the case;
- unanimous; and
- returned by the jury in open court.

According to the Official Commentary to G.S. 15A-1237, the purpose of enacting a statute that requires a verdict to be in writing was to "cure a great many defects that occur when the [foreperson] of the jury inadvertently omits some essential element of a verdict in stating it orally." *See also State v. Goodman*, 298 N.C. 1, 15–16 (1979).

This statute does not require that a written verdict contain each element of the offense to which it refers. It is sufficient if it provides the judge "a proper basis upon which to pass judgment and sentence the defendant appropriately." *State v. Sanderson*, 62 N.C. App. 520, 524 (1983); *see also State v. Collins*, 50 N.C. App. 155, 160 (1980) (although G.S. 15A-1237(a) specifically states that the verdict must be signed by the foreman, court found no error by the trial judge in receiving and recording unsigned verdict because the written verdict form "properly set forth, without any possibility of ambiguity or confusion, the essential elements of the verdicts that could be returned"); *see also State v. Wiggins,* 161 N.C. App. 583 (2003).

Practice note: Always place objections to the contents of the verdict sheet on the record in order to preserve the issue for appellate review. If you fail to object to the error at trial, the error will be reviewed under the stricter "plain error" standard of review. *State v. Gilbert*, 139 N.C. App. 657 (2000) (applying plain error analysis where jury returned a verdict on a verdict sheet captioned in the name of a different defendant and there was no timely objection by trial counsel); *see also State v. Wiggins*, 161 N.C. App. 583 (2003).

B. Types of Verdicts

General and special verdicts distinguished. Verdicts in criminal cases may be either general or special. A general verdict is rendered where jurors take the law as given by the trial judge, apply it to the facts as they find them to be, and reach a general conclusion, usually "guilty" or "not guilty." *State v. Ellis*, 262 N.C. 446, 449 (1964). "A special verdict is a common law procedural device by which the jury may answer specific questions posed by the trial judge that are separate and distinct from the general verdict." *State v. Blackwell*, 361 N.C. 41, 46–47 (2006).

The right to have the jury make the ultimate determination of guilt is guaranteed by the Due Process Clause of the Fifth Amendment and by the Sixth Amendment right to a jury trial. *See United States v. Gaudin*, 515 U.S. 506 (1995); *Blackwell*, 361 N.C. 41; *see also* N.C. Const. art. I, § 24 ("No person shall be convicted of any crime but by the unanimous verdict of a jury in open court."). Special verdicts in criminal cases do not replace general verdicts but instead are commonly used to supply information *in addition to* the general verdict. *See* Kate H. Nepveu, *Beyond "Guilty" or "Not Guilty": Giving Special Verdicts in Criminal Jury Trials*, 21 YALE L. & POLICY REV. 263 (2003). To avoid any possible constitutional violations, trial judges "using special verdicts in criminal cases must require juries to apply [the] law to the facts they find, in some cases 'straddl[ing] the line between facts and law' as a 'mini-verdict' of sorts." *Blackwell*, 361 N.C. 41, 47 (citing Nepveu, 21 YALE L. & POL'Y REV. 276).

Limitations of special verdicts. Special verdicts are subject to two limitations: (1) the jury must use the "beyond a reasonable doubt" standard in reaching the special verdict; and (2) the jury must apply the law to the facts—that is, the jury cannot simply make findings on the factual components of the essential elements alone and leave the final judgment to the court. *State v. Wilson*, 181 N.C. App. 540 (2007).

Examples of special verdicts. Special verdicts in North Carolina are commonly submitted to juries in order to determine:

- The theory or theories of first degree murder on which the defendant is found guilty. *See State v. Lewis*, 321 N.C. 42 (1987).
- Whether a defendant was found not guilty by reason of insanity. *See infra* § 34.7H, Insanity.
- Jurisdiction where the defendant has challenged the State's ability to prove beyond a reasonable doubt that the crime occurred within North Carolina. *See State v. Batdorf*, 293 N.C. 486 (1977).
- The existence of aggravating factors. *See Blackwell*, 361 N.C. 41, 49.
- Whether the defendant fathered an illegitimate child and whether he then willfully neglected or refused to support the child in violation of G.S. 49-2. *See State v. Ellis*, 262 N.C. 446 (1964); *State v. Hobson*, 70 N.C. App. 619 (1984).
- The constitutionality of an ordinance or statute in a criminal proceeding on grounds that do not appear on the face of the record. *See State v. Underwood*, 283 N.C. 154 (1973) (where defendants, convenience store employees, moved to quash the warrants

charging them with violations of a Sunday closing ordinance on the ground that the ordinance was unconstitutional, the trial judge exceeded his jurisdiction in finding facts relating to whether items sold by defendants overlapped with those sold by newsstands, filling stations, and other businesses permitted to stay open all day because those facts were determinative and could only have been found by a jury in a special verdict).
- Whether or not a defendant has attained the status of habitual felon. *See State v. Sullivan*, 110 N.C. App. 779 (1993).

C. Acceptance of Verdict by Judge

A verdict is a substantial right of the defendant. Although not complete until the trial judge accepts it, a trial judge does not have unrestrained discretion to accept or reject a verdict. *State v. Rhinehart*, 267 N.C. 470 (1966). "The trial judge should examine a verdict with respect to its form and substance to prevent a doubtful or insufficient verdict from becoming the record of the court . . . ." *Id.* at 481. However, "only when a verdict is not responsive to the indictment or . . . is incomplete, insensible or repugnant," may a judge decline to accept it and order "the jury to retire and bring in a proper verdict." *State v. Hampton*, 294 N.C. 242, 247–48 (1978); *see also State v. Abraham*, 338 N.C. 315 (1994) (trial judge properly declined verdict and ordered further deliberations where jury's original verdict incorrectly found defendant guilty of both first-degree murder and second-degree murder for the same homicide).

If the issues are substantially answered by the verdict so as to allow the trial judge to pass judgment in accordance with the manifest intention of the jury, the verdict should be received and recorded. *State v. Smith*, 299 N.C. 533 (1980). A verdict is considered sufficient if it "can be properly understood by reference to the indictment, evidence and jury instructions." *State v. Connard*, 81 N.C. App. 327, 336 (1986), *aff'd per curiam*, 319 N.C. 392 (1987).

D. Unanimity

G.S. 15A-1237(b) and article I, section 24 of the N.C. Constitution require that the verdict be unanimous. For a more detailed discussion on unanimity, see *supra* § 24.2D, Jury Unanimity.

E. Inconsistent Verdicts

Generally. Consistency between verdicts is generally not required in North Carolina. *See, e.g., State v. Reid*, 335 N.C. 647 (1994); *see also Dunn v. United States*, 284 U.S. 390, 393 (1932) ("Consistency in the verdict is not necessary."). However, North Carolina jurisprudence recognizes a difference between verdicts that are "merely inconsistent" and verdicts that are "legally inconsistent *and* contradictory." *State v. Mumford*, 364 N.C. 394, 398 (2010).

> According to our Supreme Court, inconsistent verdicts fall into one of two categories. First, some verdicts are inconsistent only. These verdicts "represent[] an apparent flaw in the jury's logic[,]" such as in the *Mumford* case when "presumably, a finding of guilt in the greater offense would establish guilt in the lesser offense." *Id.* at 400, 699 S.E.2d at 915. The second category consists of verdicts that are inconsistent because they are mutually exclusive in that "a verdict purports to establish that the [defendant] is guilty of two separate and distinct criminal offenses, the nature of which is such that guilt of one necessarily excludes guilt of the other." *Id.* (citation and internal quotation marks omitted) (alteration in original).

State v. Blackmon, ___ N.C. App. ___, 702 S.E.2d 833, 838 (2010).

"Merely inconsistent" verdicts. Verdicts rendered by the jury in the same trial against the same defendant or as between co-defendants that are "merely inconsistent" will ordinarily not be disturbed. *See, e.g., Mumford*, 364 N.C. 394, 401 (upholding verdicts acquitting defendant of driving while impaired but convicting him of felony serious injury by vehicle, which includes as an element that the defendant was driving while under the influence of an impairing substance; verdicts were "certainly inconsistent" but not "mutually exclusive"); *State v. Reid*, 335 N.C. 647 (1994) (allowing conviction of defendant for acting in concert with a co-defendant even though jury acquitted co-defendant of committing the offense); *Blackmon*, ___ N.C. App. ___, 702 S.E.2d 833 (jury deadlocked on the charge of felony breaking and entering but found the defendant guilty of felony larceny premised on the breaking and entering; result was merely inconsistent, not mutually exclusive); *State v. Cole*, 199 N.C. App. 151, 160 (2009) (no error by trial judge in accepting "the seemingly inconsistent verdicts" of guilty of assault with a deadly weapon and not guilty of possession of a firearm by a felon); *State v. Shaffer*, 193 N.C. App. 172 (2008) (although difficult to rationally reconcile the jury's verdicts, no error where defendant was convicted of first-degree sexual offense for anal intercourse and crime against nature for forced fellatio and the State's evidence also would have supported guilty verdicts of first-degree rape and the greater offense of first-degree sexual offense for the forced fellatio); *State v. Bagnard*, 24 N.C. App. 54 (1974) (no error in defendant's conviction for possession with intent to distribute marijuana where co-defendant was convicted only of possession of the same marijuana).

Verdicts also will not be disturbed in cases where the jury returns a verdict of guilty to a lesser degree of a crime and all the evidence points to the more serious crime or in cases where the defendant is charged with separate offenses resulting from the same act and the jury returns a verdict of guilty on one count and not guilty on the other. *See, e.g., State v. Bullard*, 82 N.C. App. 718 (1986) (finding no merit in defendant's argument that the trial judge erred in allowing a verdict of guilty to second-degree rape when all the evidence indicated guilt of first-degree rape or not guilty); *State v. Rosser*, 54 N.C. App. 660 (1981) (finding that consistency between verdicts was not required where jury found defendant guilty of manufacturing marijuana but not guilty of possession of the same marijuana).

The rationale behind upholding "merely inconsistent" verdicts embodies the acknowledgment of several factors. *See State v. Reid*, 335 N.C. 647 (1994). "The acquittal may represent the mistake of the jury due to 'compromise[] or lenity.' If this is true, 'the Government has no recourse if it wishes to correct the jury's error; the Government is precluded from appealing or otherwise upsetting such an acquittal by the Constitution's Double Jeopardy Clause.'" *Id.* at 659 (citation omitted) (quoting *United States v. Powell*, 469 U.S. 57, 65 (1984)). The rule against permitting a criminal defendant to upset an inconsistent verdict also acknowledges that he or she has already been "'afforded protection against jury irrationality or error by the independent review of the sufficiency of the evidence undertaken by the trial and appellate courts.'" *Id.* (quoting *Powell*, 469 U.S. 57, 67 (citation omitted)). "The fact that the inconsistency may be the result of lenity, coupled with the Government's inability to invoke review, suggests that inconsistent verdicts should not be reviewable." *Id.* (quoting *Powell*, 469 U.S. 57, 66).

Mutual exclusivity. While a "mere inconsistency" will not invalidate the verdicts, verdicts that are inconsistent *and* contradictory— i.e., mutually exclusive—will entitle a defendant to relief. *State v. Mumford*, 364 N.C. 394 (2010); *see also State v. Meshaw*, 246 N.C. 205 (1957) (new trial granted where defendant was convicted of the mutually exclusive offenses of larceny and receiving stolen goods); *State v. Hames*, 170 N.C. App. 312 (2005) (offenses of assault with a deadly weapon inflicting serious injury and attempted voluntary manslaughter were mutually exclusive since defendant either did or did not have the intent to kill; new trial granted where trial judge permitted jury to convict defendant of both offenses and imposed the same sentence for each and ran them concurrently).

If the offenses are mutually exclusive and they are properly joined for trial, the trial judge may submit both offenses to the jury but the jury must be instructed that it may convict the defendant of only one of the offenses. *See, e.g., State v. Speckman*, 326 N.C. 576 (1990) (defendant could be tried but not convicted for both embezzlement and obtaining property by false pretenses; the charges are mutually exclusive because embezzlement requires that property be obtained lawfully and then wrongfully converted while obtaining by false pretenses requires that property be obtained unlawfully at the outset); *see also* 1 NORTH CAROLINA DEFENDER MANUAL § 6.1B (Standard for Joinder of Offenses) (Dec. 2008) (discussing joinder of mutually exclusive offenses).

Practice note: If your client is being tried for mutually exclusive offenses, you must request at the charge conference that the trial judge give the *Speckman* instruction informing the jury that it may convict your client of only one of the offenses, if any. If you fail to make such a request, the appellate court will review the instructional error under the more stringent "plain error" standard of review. *See State v. Melvin*, 364 N.C. 589 (2010) (although defendant was convicted of the mutually exclusive offenses of first-degree murder and accessory after the fact to murder, no plain error was found in trial judge's failure to give a *Speckman* instruction where he arrested judgment on accessory after the fact and sentenced defendant to life without parole for first degree murder and the evidence supported that conviction).

F. Partial Verdicts

Generally. In *State v. Sargeant*, 206 N.C. App. 1 (2010), *aff'd as modified on other grounds*, 365 N.C. 58 (2011), our appellate courts addressed, in part, the propriety of taking partial verdicts. In *Sargeant*, the defendant was charged with first-degree murder based on premeditation and deliberation, felony murder, and lying in wait. He also was charged with armed robbery, kidnapping, and burning personal property. At the end of a full day of deliberations, the trial judge directed the jury to return verdicts on those charges on which it had agreed. The jury returned verdict sheets finding the defendant guilty of all charges except first-degree murder based on premeditation and deliberation. The following day the jury continued deliberating and found the defendant guilty of premeditated and deliberate murder.

Focusing on the taking of verdicts on two of the theories of first-degree murder while the jury was still deliberating on the third theory, the defendant argued that the trial judge's action violated his constitutional right to a unanimous jury. The court of appeals, affirmed by the supreme court, agreed, holding that the trial judge's action erroneously locked the jury in on two theories of first-degree murder before it had unanimously agreed on a final verdict. The court of appeals observed that this procedure "may have 'cut short [the jury's] opportunity to fully consider the evidence . . . [or] deprive[d] the defendant of the very real benefit of reconsideration and change of mind or heart.'" 206 N.C. App. 1, 14 (alterations in original) (citation omitted). The court also observed that the State's argument concerning the limited impact of a verdict on the premeditation theory once the jury rendered its decision on the two other theories "disregards the importance of the potential of juror compromises during the jury's deliberations." *Id.* at 12.

Practice note: The appellate courts in *Sargeant* did not address the taking of verdicts on the non-homicide charges in the case (e.g., the kidnapping and armed robbery charges) while the jury was still deliberating on the homicide charge since the issue was not raised on appeal. The court of appeals stated, "Even assuming, without deciding, that partial verdicts as to multiple charges are permissible in North Carolina, we hold that a trial court may not take partial verdicts as to theories of a crime." 206 N.C. App. at 11. No other cases in North Carolina appear to have considered the issue, but the reasoning of *Sargeant* may apply in other contexts. In addition to the bar on partial verdicts on theories of an offense, *Sargeant* may bar partial verdicts when the offenses are legally interrelated. For example, in a case involving felony breaking and entering and larceny where larceny is the crime that the defendant allegedly intended to commit, it may be inappropriate for the judge to take a verdict on one charge while the jury is still deliberating on the other. Likewise, it may be inappropriate in a felony murder case predicated on a particular felony to split up the jury's deliberations on the murder charge and the underlying felony. (In *Sargeant*, the jury did not return a partial verdict on felony murder and the underlying felonies, as it returned a verdict at the same time on felony murder, armed robbery, and kidnapping.) Whether or not legally interrelated, *Sargeant* may weigh against the taking of a partial verdict in any case in which multiple offenses are joined for trial because a requirement for joinder is that the offenses be factually interrelated.

This discussion does *not* apply in cases in which the jury deadlocks on some offenses and reaches a verdict on others. In that instance, the jury has completed its deliberations on all offenses, and the judge may take a verdict on the offenses on which the jury has unanimously agreed and declare a mistrial on the offenses on which the jury has deadlocked. For a discussion of mistrials based on a jury deadlock, see *supra* § 31.7, Juror Deadlock.

Verdict following deadlock on lesser offense. In *Sargeant*, the court of appeals analogized the taking of a partial verdict with determining the jury's verdict on greater offenses when it has deadlocked on a lesser offense, a procedure discussed in *State v. Booker*, 306 N.C. 302 (1982). In *Booker*, at the defendant's first trial on first-degree murder, the trial judge declared a mistrial. The defendant asserted that during the first trial the jury sent a note to the judge stating that the jury was deadlocked on second-degree murder. At his second trial, the defendant argued that double jeopardy barred retrial on first-degree murder because the jury implicitly acquitted him of that offense when it deadlocked on second-degree murder. The court rejected the defendant's argument, finding that the jury did not reach a final verdict.

The *Booker* court also rejected the defendant's request to adopt the rule, announced by the Supreme Court of New Mexico in *State v. Castrillo*, 566 P.2d 1146 (N.M. 1977), that "'when a jury announces its inability to reach a verdict in a case involving included offenses, the trial court is required to submit verdict forms to the jury to determine if it has unanimously voted for acquittal on any of the included offenses, and the jury may then be polled with regard to any verdict thus returned.'" *Booker*, 306 N.C. 302, 306 (citation omitted). Discussing this part of the *Booker* case, the court of appeals in *Sargeant* stated that such a procedure, if followed with respect to greater or lesser offenses, would amount to an attempt "to establish unanimity on aspects of a charged crime in advance of a final verdict on the charged crime," a form of partial verdict. 206 N.C. App. 1, 11. Determining the jury's position on greater offenses after it has deadlocked on a lesser offense does not appear to involve true partial verdicts, however. Such a procedure would not require the jury to return a verdict on one charge while it is still deliberating on other charges; rather, the procedure would only come into play when the judge determines that the jury is deadlocked and has completed its deliberations.

For a more detailed discussion of the double jeopardy implications of a deadlocked jury, see *supra* § 31.7, Juror Deadlock.

G. Co-defendants

Where a defendant is tried jointly with one or more co-defendants, the jury must return a separate verdict with respect to each defendant. "If the jury agrees upon a verdict for one defendant but not another, it must return that verdict upon which it agrees." G.S. 15A-1237(d).

H. Insanity

G.S. 15A-1237(c) provides that "[i]f the jurors find the defendant not guilty on the ground that he was insane at the time of the commission of the offense charged, their verdict must so state."

The N.C. Supreme Court has suggested different procedures for the judge to follow for instructing the jury and preparing verdict sheets where insanity is at issue. In *State v. Linville*, 300 N.C. 135 (1980), the court suggested that the trial judge should first submit the issues of guilt or innocence in the normal fashion. After those issues have been submitted, a special issue should be submitted, which states:

> *Special Issue*: Did you find defendant not guilty because you were satisfied that he was insane?

The court also stated that the jury should be instructed that it is not to consider the special issue *unless* it has returned a general verdict of not guilty. If a general verdict of not guilty is returned, to comply with G.S. 15A-1237(c) "the jury must clarify for the record whether its general verdict of not guilty was or was not based upon its satisfaction that defendant was insane." *Id.* at 142. If the reason for a not guilty verdict is not based on a finding of insanity, then the reason need not be specified. *Id.*

In other opinions, the N.C. Supreme Court has suggested that the jury may first determine the issue of insanity and then address the issue of guilt or innocence. *See State v. Cooper*, 286 N.C. 549 (1975) (holding that the "better procedure" would be to instruct the jury to consider the insanity issue first, and if answered negatively, then to proceed to determine defendant's guilt or innocence of the offense charged). Whether to order the instructions in this way is in the trial judge's discretion. *See State v. Hudson*, 331 N.C. 122 (1992) (although *Cooper* stated the "better procedure," it is "merely advisory"); *State v. Mancuso*, 321 N.C. 464 (1988) (order in which the insanity issue is submitted should be left to the discretion of the trial judge).

N.C. Pattern Jury Instruction—Crim. 304.10 (June 2009) also addresses the insanity defense and advises the judge to give the insanity instruction just before the mandate of the instruction on the offense charged. This pattern instruction states that a jury should consider evidence of insanity "only if . . . the State has proved beyond a reasonable doubt" each of the elements of the offense charged. *See also State v. Mize*, 315 N.C. 285 (1985) (jury should first decide whether State has met its burden of proof on the offense charged and then reach the insanity question only if it finds defendant guilty). The instruction also directs the judge to add the *Linville* Special Issue at the end of the verdict form.

Practice note: Although it is permissible for the trial judge to instruct the jury to decide first whether or not the State has met its burden of proof on the elements of the offense before considering the insanity issue, this order of the issues may reduce the jury's willingness to consider insanity because it will already have found the defendant guilty before considering the issue. Pursuant to *Cooper* and *Hudson*, counsel can argue that the jury should first determine the issue of insanity before deciding guilt or innocence.

I. Judicial Comment on the Verdict

A trial judge is prohibited from commenting on the verdict in criminal cases in open court in the presence or hearing of any member of the jury panel. If he or she comments on the verdict, or praises or criticizes the jury on account of its verdict, any defendant whose case is calendared for that session of court is entitled to a continuance of his or her case to a time when all members of the jury panel are no longer serving. *See* G.S. 15A-1239; G.S. 1-180.1. The right to a continuance is waived by failing to move to continue before trial. *State v. Neal*, 60 N.C. App. 350 (1983). Under the provisions of G.S. 15A-1239 and G.S. 1-180.1, a continuance is the only remedy for a judicial comment on the verdict. *Id.*

J. Polling of the Jury

For a discussion on the right to poll the jury in criminal cases, see *supra* § 27.6, Polling of the Jury.

K. Impeachment of the Verdict

As a general rule, once a verdict is rendered, it may not be impeached—that is, a juror may not testify nor may evidence be received as to matters occurring during deliberations or calling into question the reasons on which the verdict was based. *See State v. Cherry*, 298 N.C. 86 (1979). There are limited exceptions to this rule. For a detailed discussion of the anti-impeachment rule and its exceptions, see *supra* § 26.2B, Exposure to Extraneous Information: Discovered After Verdict.

Chapter 35
Appeals, Post-Conviction Litigation, and Writs

This chapter primarily discusses litigation after a defendant has been convicted. The topics include the procedures for appealing from district and superior courts, motions for appropriate relief, a trial judge's authority to modify or correct judgments, and resentencings after a successful appellate or post-conviction attack.

The topics also include the writ of habeas corpus and other types of extraordinary writs, which the defendant may be able to seek before or after conviction, and the procedures before the N.C. Innocence Inquiry Commission.

Appeals in juvenile delinquency cases are discussed in Chapter 16 of the Juvenile Defender Manual, and appeals in involuntary commitments cases are discussed in Chapter 2 of the Civil Commitment Manual, both available on the Office of Indigent Defense Services website, www.ncids.org, under Training & Resources and then Reference Manuals.

This chapter does not discuss sentencing or probation except with respect to appeals from those matters. It also does not address post-release supervision or parole. Those topics would take up their own book and are beyond the scope of this manual.

35.1 Appeals by the Defendant

A. In General

After a defendant has been found guilty or has pled guilty or no contest, a trial judge has the power to do one of three things:

1. pronounce judgment and place it into immediate effect;
2. pronounce judgment and suspend or stay its execution; or
3. enter a prayer for judgment continued.

State v. Griffin, 246 N.C. 680 (1957). A defendant in North Carolina has the right to appeal from a district or superior court judgment but not necessarily from a prayer for judgment continued (discussed *infra* in § 35.1L). In cases decided in superior court, the types of issues that may be appealed following judgment depend on whether the defendant pled guilty or was found guilty and on the type of sentence that was imposed (discussed *infra* in § 35.1C and D).

Basis of right to appellate review. A defendant's right to appeal from a criminal conviction in North Carolina is afforded by statute. *State v. Berryman*, 360 N.C. 209 (2006); *see also State v. Shoff*, 118 N.C. App. 724 (1995) (noting that G.S. 15A-1444(d) provides the exclusive statutory authority for appeals in criminal cases), *aff'd per curiam*, 342 N.C. 638 (1996).

There is no federal constitutional right to appeal to the appellate division in criminal cases. *See Abney v. United States*, 431 U.S. 651 (1977); *see also Halbert v. Michigan*, 545 U.S. 605 (2005); *State v. Pimental*, 153 N.C. App. 69 (2002). Likewise, the N.C. Constitution does not mandate appellate review of criminal convictions. *Berryman*, 360 N.C. 209, 213–14. However, if a state provides an appeal of right, as North Carolina has done, the procedures utilized in deciding the appeal must comply with the demands of the Due Process and Equal Protection Clauses of the U.S. Constitution. *Evitts v. Lucey*, 469 U.S. 387 (1985); *Berryman*, 360 N.C. 209.

Other methods of obtaining review. The following discussion addresses the right to appeal from a trial court's judgment. Other methods for obtaining review may exist apart from whether a defendant has a right to appeal and are discussed later in this chapter under the headings applicable to that method of review.

Practice note: For a discussion of district court trial counsel's obligations to file and pursue an appeal for a trial de novo following a district court conviction, see *infra* "District court counsel's obligations regarding defendant's right to appeal and to continue representation for trial de novo" in § 35.1B, Defendant's Right to Appeal from District Court Judgment. For a discussion of superior court trial counsel's obligations regarding the filing of appeal to the appellate division following a superior court conviction, see *infra* subsection O. of § 35.1, Trial Counsel's Obligations regarding Defendant's Right to Appeal after Superior Court Conviction.

B. Defendant's Right to Appeal from District Court Judgment

Right to appeal to superior court. A defendant has the right to appeal a district court conviction to superior court for a trial de novo before a jury. N.C. CONST. art. I, § 24; N.C. GEN. STAT. § 15A-1431(b) (hereinafter G.S.); *see also* G.S. 7A-196(b); G.S. 7A-271(b); G.S. 7A-290. This is true even if the district court trial was free from error (*State v. Spencer*, 276 N.C. 535 (1970)) or the defendant pled guilty in district court. *State v. Fox*, 34 N.C. App. 576 (1977).

Practice note: A district court may take a guilty plea to (but not try) a Class H or I felony under G.S. 7A-272(c). If the defendant pleads guilty to a Class H or I felony in district court, the defendant does *not* have the right to appeal to superior court for a trial de novo. The defendant's appeal is to the appellate division. G.S. 7A-272(d); *see also State v. Goforth*, 130 N.C. App. 603 (1998) (finding that attorney erroneously advised defendant that she could appeal sentence to superior court after felony guilty plea in district court but that defendant was not prejudiced). For a discussion of the right to appeal a probation revocation decision in a case involving a felony guilty plea taken in district court, see *infra* "Appeal from a finding of violation of probation" in this subsection B.

Constitutionality of two-tier system. The U.S. Supreme Court has held that due process is not violated by a two-tier system in which a defendant convicted in an inferior court has an absolute right to a trial de novo in a court of general criminal jurisdiction because such a system does not penalize a defendant for seeking a new trial. *See Colten v. Kentucky*, 407 U.S. 104 (1972).

Article I, section 24 [formerly article I, section 13] of the N.C. Constitution authorizes a two-tier trial de novo system. It states: "No person shall be convicted of any crime but by the unanimous verdict of a jury in open court. The General Assembly may, however, provide for other means of trial for misdemeanors, with the right of appeal for trial de novo." A defendant's constitutional right to a jury trial is not abridged by first having to submit to a trial without a jury in district court if the defendant has the "unfettered" right to appeal to superior court for a jury trial. *See Spencer*, 276 N.C. 535, 545; *accord State v.*

Pulliam, 184 N.C. 681 (1922); *State v. Sherron*, 4 N.C. App. 386 (1969). *But cf. infra* "Appeals in implied-consent cases" in this subsection B (discussing limits enacted by General Assembly on right to appeal in certain cases).

Form of notice of appeal. A defendant may give oral notice of appeal in open court or file a written notice of appeal with the clerk within ten days of the entry of the district court judgment. G.S. 7A-290; G.S. 15A-1431(c). Judgment is entered when the sentence is pronounced. G.S. 15A-101(4a).

Effect of notice of appeal. Criminal district courts are not "courts of record" (*State v. Gurganus*, 71 N.C. App. 95, 99 (1984)), and a trial de novo is not an "appeal on the record." *State v. Brooks*, 287 N.C. 392 (1975). An appeal from the district court judgment wipes the slate clean, and the trial in superior court is a new trial from beginning to end on both the law and the facts. *See Spencer*, 276 N.C. 535 (holding that once a defendant appeals from district court to superior court, the plea, trial, and verdict entered in district court are completely disregarded). The district court record is not before the superior court and is totally irrelevant to its proceedings. *Brooks*, 287 N.C. 392 (citing *Colten*, 407 U.S. 104).

Scope of jurisdiction on appeal. If notice of appeal is given and not withdrawn within the ten-day period, the clerk must transfer the case to the superior court docket. G.S. 7A-290; G.S. 15A-1431(c). Once an appeal is docketed, the superior court has the same jurisdiction over the charges for which the defendant was convicted as the district court had.

Ordinarily, offenses for which the defendant was charged but not convicted in district court (e.g., charges that were dismissed or for which the defendant was found not guilty) are not within the superior court's jurisdiction on the defendant's appeal of other charges. However, any charges that were dismissed, reduced, or modified pursuant to a plea arrangement in district court are reinstated if the defendant appeals. G.S. 7A-271(b); G.S. 15A-1431(b); *see also State v. Fox*, 34 N.C. App. 576 (1977) (the State is not bound by a plea agreement if the defendant elects to appeal and invoke the right to a trial de novo).

For further discussion of the scope of superior court jurisdiction on appeal from district court, including limitations on the bringing of new charges in superior court based on the same conduct, see 1 NORTH CAROLINA DEFENDER MANUAL § 10.7B (Misdemeanor Appeals from District Court) (Oct. 2010).

Sentencing following appeal. A defendant may receive a lighter or a heavier sentence in superior court than he or she received in district court. The imposition of a more severe sentence does not violate a defendant's statutory rights or his or her federal or state constitutional rights to due process or to a trial by jury. *See Spencer*, 276 N.C. 535; *State v. Sparrow*, 276 N.C. 499 (1970). A defendant's right to be free from double jeopardy is likewise not violated by the imposition of a more severe sentence in superior court. *See Colten*, 407 U.S. 104.

Release pending appeal. Unless modified, the original bail remains in effect during appeal to superior court. G.S. 7A-290; G.S. 15A-1431(e). The statutes conflict on the authority of a district court judge, as opposed to a superior court judge, to modify a defendant's bond after he or she appeals for a trial de novo. G.S. 15A-534(e)(1) indicates that a district court judge may not modify pretrial release conditions after the "noting of an appeal," while G.S. 7A-290 and G.S. 15A-1431(c) suggest that a district court judge has ten days from the date of judgment to modify pretrial release conditions because the statutes state that at the expiration of ten days the clerk transfers the case to superior court. For a thorough discussion of the applicable statutes, the limits on a district court judge's authority to modify bond after the giving of notice of appeal, and practical considerations for defense counsel in giving notice of appeal, see 1 NORTH CAROLINA DEFENDER MANUAL § 1.10A (Appeal from District Court Conviction) (Aug. 2010).

Once the case is in superior court, a superior court judge has the authority to modify the conditions of pretrial release. G.S. 15A-534(e). Before or after appeal to superior court, a defendant may apply to the superior court to modify a bond set by or allowed to stand by the district court judge. *See* G.S. 15A-538; *see also* G.S. 15A-547 (recognizing defendant's right to habeas corpus).

District court judgment stayed. Entry of notice of appeal stays the execution of all portions of the district court judgment including:

- payment of costs;
- payment of a fine;
- probation or special probation (i.e., split sentences under G.S. 15A-1351); and
- active punishment.

G.S. 15A-1431(f1).

Compliance does not bar appeal. A defendant who has complied with a district court judgment is not barred from appealing from that judgment. However, notice of appeal after compliance must be made by the defendant in person to the judge who heard the case. G.S. 15A-1431(d). If that judge is not available, then the notice must be given in an open session of district court in the applicable district. G.S. 15A-1431(d)(2).

G.S. 15A-1431(d) directs the district court judge to review the case and set appropriate conditions of pretrial release. *Cf.* 1 NORTH CAROLINA DEFENDER MANUAL § 1.10A (Appeal from District Court Conviction) (Aug. 2010) (discussing district court's authority to modify bond after giving of notice of appeal). Any fine or costs paid by the defendant must be remitted to him or her unless the judge orders the remission delayed pending the determination of the appeal. G.S. 15A-1431(d).

Withdrawal of appeal in cases not involving an implied-consent offense. Within ten days of entry of judgment for an offense that is not an implied-consent offense, a defendant may withdraw his or her appeal and comply with the judgment. G.S. 15A-1431(c). No costs will be taxed to the defendant if he or she withdraws the appeal within this time period. G.S. 7A-304(b). At the end of this ten-day period, superior court costs will attach. *See id.*; *see also* G.S. 15A-1431 Official Commentary. These costs may be remitted by the superior court trial judge.

If a defendant withdraws his or her appeal after the ten-day period but before the case has been calendared in superior court, the case is automatically remanded to the district court for the execution of judgment. G.S. 15A-1431(g). If the case has already been calendared, a defendant may only withdraw his or her appeal with the superior court's consent. If consent to withdraw the appeal is granted, the defendant will be taxed with court costs unless remitted by the court. The court then may order the case remanded to the district court for the execution of the judgment with any additional court costs that have attached and have not been remitted. G.S. 15A-1431(h).

A form for the remand of a case involving a non-implied-consent offense after it has been calendared in superior court can be found on the Administrative Office of the Courts website. *See* AOC Form AOC-CR-321, "Order of Remand in Non-Implied-Consent Offense Cases" (Dec. 2008), *available at* www.nccourts.org/Forms/Documents/1106.pdf.

Appeals in implied-consent cases. Appeals from convictions in implied-consent cases (as defined in G.S. 20-16.2(a1)) are treated somewhat differently than appeals from other types of offenses. As soon as notice of appeal to superior court is given from a district court conviction for an implied-consent offense, the district court sentence is vacated. After expiration of the ten-day period in which notice of appeal can be given (and withdrawn), the case may be remanded to district court only if both the prosecutor and the superior court consent. When an appeal is noted and then withdrawn within ten days of the entry of judgment, or when a case is remanded to district court after that period, a new sentencing hearing must be held and the district court judge must consider any new convictions. *See* G.S. 20-38.7(c); G.S 20-179(c).

Practice note: Before advising a client who has been convicted of any implied-consent offense in district court regarding the advantages and disadvantages of exercising his or her right to appeal the conviction to superior court, you should carefully review G.S. 20-38.7(c) and G.S. 20-179(c). While the appeal is pending, the defendant will not have an implied-consent conviction that could be used as a grossly aggravating factor (pursuant to G.S. 20-179(c)(1)c.) if the defendant is convicted of a second implied-consent offense. Unlike in other misdemeanor cases, however, a new sentencing hearing is required to be conducted in every case returned to district court after a withdrawal of the notice of appeal or after a remand. If the client is convicted of a second driving while impaired charge (or other implied-consent offense) before the new sentencing hearing, that second implied-consent offense conviction will be a grossly aggravating factor that must be considered by the district court judge at the new sentencing hearing on the first conviction.

G.S. 20-38.7(d) addresses a defendant's right to appeal following a new sentencing hearing in an implied-consent case after notice of appeal has been withdrawn or after a remand. It provides that a defendant has a right to appeal to the superior court only if:

1. the sentence is based on additional facts considered by the district court that were not considered in the previously vacated sentence; and

2. the defendant would be entitled to a jury determination of those facts pursuant to G.S. 20-179.

The above language may have a number of adverse effects on a defendant. First, although the General Assembly's apparent aim was for the court to take account of new convictions, as reflected in the requirement in G.S. 20-38.7(c) that the district court judge at resentencing "shall consider any new convictions," the language of G.S. 20-38.7(d) suggests that a district court judge may change a sentence based on facts other than a new conviction. Second, G.S. 20-38.7(d) may not afford a defendant the right to appeal if the district court increases a sentence in reliance on matters that would not be subject to a jury determination under G.S. 20-179. Third, in cases that are appealable under the statute, the language of G.S. 20-38.7(d) suggests that the defendant has a right to a de novo trial on the resentencing determination only, not on the entire case.

Practice note: No appellate cases appear to have considered the district court judge's sentencing authority following remand and the defendant's rights should the judge impose a greater sentence. This practice note addresses one scenario that has come to the authors' attention and suggests a possible response—that is, if on remand a district court judge imposes a longer sentence even though the defendant has had no intervening impaired driving convictions. Such an increase not only may exceed the authority the General Assembly intended to give the district court, but it also may violate *North Carolina v. Pearce*, 395 U.S. 711 (1969), in which the U.S. Supreme Court held that an increased sentence on remand may only be based on *identifiable matters*, shown in the record, *that occurred after* the initial sentencing determination to ensure that vindictiveness played no part in the increased sentence. *See infra* § 35.5A, Resentencing after Successful Appellate or Post-Conviction Review: In General (discussing constitutional restrictions on resentencing under *Pearce*). In such a case, counsel should consider the following approach. First, regardless whether the statute specifically gives the defendant the right to appeal, counsel still should consider filing a notice of appeal to superior court. Counsel should be prepared to argue that denial of the right to appeal would violate the constitutional requirements for a two-tiered trial de novo system. *See supra* "Constitutionality of two-tier system" in this subsection B. Second, if the appeal is dismissed, counsel should consider filing a motion for appropriate relief with the district court under G.S. 15A-1415. Constitutional grounds may include the lack of the right of appeal as well as the imposition of a presumptively vindictive sentence. If the district court denies the motion for appropriate relief, the defendant may petition the superior court for certiorari review. *See infra* § 35.7D, Certiorari of Trial Court Orders and Judgments.

If the defendant appeals following a new sentencing hearing and subsequently withdraws the notice of appeal, the sentence will be imposed by the district court as a final judgment not subject to further appeal. G.S. 20-38.7(d).

A form for the withdrawal of an appeal from a conviction of an implied-consent offense can be found on the Administrative Office of the Courts website. *See* AOC Form AOC-CR-321, Side Two, "Withdrawal of Appeal Order of Remand Implied-Consent Offenses" (Dec. 2008), *available at* www.nccourts.org/Forms/Documents/1106.pdf.

Appeal from a finding of violation of probation. A defendant may appeal to superior court for a de novo revocation hearing if a district court judge finds a violation of probation and activates the defendant's suspended sentence or imposes a condition of special probation (split sentence). If at the de novo hearing the superior court judge finds a violation of probation and activates a defendant's sentence or imposes special probation, the defendant may appeal to the appellate division pursuant to G.S. 7A-27. G.S. 15A-1347 (detailing authority of superior court to hear appeals). G.S. 15A-1347 does not specifically address whether a defendant has the right to appeal confinement in response to a violation under G.S. 15A-1344(b2), which can be as long as ninety days, a part of probation changes made in 2011 by the General Assembly in the Justice Reinvestment Act. *See* Jamie Markham, *Confinement in Response to Violations (CRV) and Limits on Probation Revocation Authority*, N.C. CRIM. L., UNC SCH. OF GOV'T BLOG (Oct. 25, 2011), http://sogweb.sog.unc.edu/blogs/ncclaw/?p=2994.

If the defendant pleads guilty to a felony in district court pursuant to G.S. 7A-272, is placed on probation, and has his or her probation revoked by the district court, the defendant has the right to appeal for a de novo revocation hearing in superior court. *State v. Hooper*, 358 N.C. 122 (2004). After the issuance of *Hooper*, the General Assembly added G.S. 7A-271(e) to limit the right to a de novo revocation hearing. That statute provides that the superior court has exclusive jurisdiction to hold probation revocation hearings on felony guilty pleas taken in district court unless the State and the defendant agree to have the revocation hearing in district court. If the revocation hearing is in district court, the defendant has the right to appeal for a de novo hearing in superior court as described in *Hooper*. If, however, the initial revocation hearing is in superior court, the defendant's appeal is to the appellate division as in other revocation cases heard in superior court. *See infra* § 35.1E, Appeal from a Finding of Violation of Probation in Superior Court.

District court counsel's obligations regarding defendant's right to appeal and to continue representation for trial de novo. After a conviction in district court, trial counsel should advise the client of his or her right to appeal for a trial de novo with a jury in superior court. *See infra* Appendix A, N.C. COMM'N ON INDIGENT DEFENSE SERVS., PERFORMANCE GUIDELINES FOR INDIGENT DEFENSE REPRESENTATION IN NON-CAPITAL CRIMINAL CASES AT THE TRIAL LEVEL, Guideline 9.1(a) Appeal of Misdemeanor Conviction for Trial *de Novo* in Superior Court (Nov. 2004). "Counsel should also advise the client of the potential advantages and disadvantages of exercising that right." *Id.* If the client wishes to appeal, counsel must give notice of appeal on the client's behalf. N.C. Commission on Indigent Defense Services Rule 1.7(a) (June 2011), *available at* www.ncids.org/Rules%20&%20Procedures/IDS%20Rules/IDS%20Rules%20Part%201.pdf.

If the client wants to appeal for a trial de novo, counsel is obligated to represent him or her until entry of final judgment in superior court unless relieved by the court. *See* G.S. 15A-143 (providing that counsel who makes a general appearance in a criminal proceeding undertakes to represent the defendant until entry of final judgment at the trial stage); N.C. Commission on Indigent Defense Services Rule 1.7(a) (June 2011), *available at* www.ncids.org/Rules%20&%20Procedures/IDS%20Rules/IDS%20Rules

%20Part%201.pdf (recognizing counsel's obligation to continue representation). Local appointment plans in a few districts may provide for substitution of district court counsel if a defendant appeals for a jury trial in superior court, but counsel who represented the defendant in district court presumably would have to obtain the court's permission to withdraw. Counsel from the district court proceedings remains obligated to advise the defendant of the right to appeal and enter notice of appeal at the client's request even if counsel intends to move to withdraw thereafter.

C. Defendant's Right to Appeal from Conviction after Jury Trial in Superior Court

Statutory right to appeal. A defendant who pleads not guilty and is found guilty by a jury may appeal from the final judgment as a matter of right. G.S. 15A-1444(a); *see also State v. Brown*, 170 N.C. App. 601 (2005). Judgment is entered when the sentence is pronounced. G.S. 15A-101(4a).

Appellate jurisdiction. A defendant's appeal from a judgment of a superior court, other than a judgment imposing the death penalty, lies of right to the N.C. Court of Appeals. G.S. 7A-27(b); *see also* N.C. R. APP. P. 4(d). If the defendant is convicted of first-degree murder and sentenced to death, the appeal lies of right to the N.C. Supreme Court. G.S. 7A-27(a); N.C. R. APP. P. 4(d).

Exclusion of right to appeal presumptive sentence. Defendants who are found guilty by a jury and are sentenced in the presumptive range have no right to appeal the issue of whether their sentences are supported by the evidence presented at trial or at the sentencing hearing. G.S. 15A-1444(a1); *see also State v. Hill*, 179 N.C. App. 1 (2006) (defendant sentenced in the presumptive range had no statutory right to appeal his sentence; court would not review whether the trial judge erred in failing to sentence defendant in the mitigated range when he presented evidence of mitigating factors and the State offered no evidence of aggravating factors). A presumptive sentence may be subject to appeal for other reasons, however. *See State v. Fuller*, 179 N.C. App. 61 (2006) (remanding for new sentencing hearing because trial judge imposed maximum presumptive sentence based, in part, on defendant's exercise of the right to a jury trial); *see also infra* "Limited right of appeal" in § 35.1D, Defendant's Right to Appeal from Guilty Plea in Superior Court (discussing right to appeal various sentencing errors, such as the miscalculation of the defendant's prior record level; the discussion concerns appeals after a guilty plea, but a defendant also would have the right to appeal these errors after a guilty verdict by a jury).

Requirements and procedures for giving notice of appeal. The procedural requirements for giving notice of appeal after a conviction by a jury are discussed *infra* in § 35.1F, Procedural Requirements for Appealing from Superior Court.

Correction of errors. The appellate division may correct the following errors:

1. lack of jurisdiction over the offense or the person;
2. failure of the criminal pleading to charge a crime;
3. insufficiency of the evidence as a matter of law;

4. prejudicial procedural errors, including the erroneous
   - denial of a pretrial, trial, or post-trial motion or other relief,
   - admission or exclusion of evidence, or
   - instructions to the jury;
5. state or federal constitutional violations resulting in an invalid conviction;
6. insufficiency of the evidence introduced at the trial and sentencing hearing to support the sentence imposed (if the defendant is sentenced outside the presumptive range as described in G.S. 15A-1444(a1));
7. violations of structured sentencing, including
   - the improper calculation of the defendant's prior record level,
   - an unauthorized sentence disposition, or
   - an unauthorized minimum or maximum term of imprisonment; and
8. any other prejudicial error of law committed by the trial judge.

G.S. 15A-1442. Unless the error is one that is preserved automatically for appellate review by rule or law, a defendant must have made a timely motion or objection at the trial level. *See* G.S. 15A-1446; N.C. R. APP. P. 10; *see also State v. Wilson*, 363 N.C. 478 (2009). The preservation of errors for appellate review is discussed in detail *infra* in Appendix B, Preserving the Record on Appeal.

D. Defendant's Right to Appeal from Guilty Plea in Superior Court

Limited right of appeal. If a defendant pleads guilty or no contest to a misdemeanor or a felony in superior court, he or she has a very limited right to appeal. A defendant who has entered a plea of guilty or no contest is not entitled to appellate review as a matter of right unless he or she is appealing the following issues:

1. Whether the prior record level was properly calculated. G.S. 15A-1444(a2)(1).
2. Whether the sentence disposition was a type that was authorized for the defendant's class of offense and prior record level (e.g., the defendant received an active or intermediate sentence when only an intermediate or community sentence was authorized). G.S. 15A-1444(a2)(2).
3. Whether the lengths of the minimum and maximum sentences are outside those set by statute for the defendant's class of offense and prior record level. G.S. 15A-1444(a2)(3).
4. If the defendant was sentenced outside of the presumptive range, whether there were improper findings of aggravating circumstances or improper failures to find mitigating circumstances. *See* G.S. 15A-1444(a1); *see also State v. Davis*, ___ N.C. App. ___, 696 S.E.2d 917 (2010); *State v. Rogers*, 157 N.C. App. 127 (2003). The N.C. Court of Appeals has interpreted the governing statutory provision to mean that a defendant is entitled to an appeal when his or her sentence falls within the aggravated range *or* within the mitigated range. *See State v. Mabry*, ___ N.C. App. ___, 720 S.E.2d 697 (2011) (holding that "a defendant receiving a mitigated sentence must, under the plain language of the statute, have a right to appeal the sufficiency of the evidence supporting his or her sentence").
5. Whether a motion to withdraw the plea of guilty or no contest was improperly denied. G.S. 15A-1444(e); *see also State v. Handy*, 326 N.C. 532 (1990) (defendant entitled to

an appeal as of right after the trial judge denied his motion to withdraw his plea of guilty; death sentence vacated because denial of the presentence motion was improper).

6. Whether there were evidentiary and procedural issues in a sentencing hearing before a jury on the existence of aggravating circumstances or sentence enhancements. *See, e.g., State v. Hurt*, 361 N.C. 325 (2007) (granting new sentencing hearing where trial judge's *Blakely* error in failing to submit an aggravating factor to the jury was not harmless beyond a reasonable doubt).
7. Whether a motion to suppress evidence based on constitutional grounds or on a substantial violation of Chapter 15A was improperly denied. G.S. 15A-979(b); G.S. 15A-1444(e); *see also State v. Smith*, 193 N.C. App. 739 (2008).

Practice note: To preserve the right to appeal the denial of a motion to suppress when your client pleads guilty, you must notify the State and the trial judge ***before*** entering the guilty plea of your intention to appeal the denial of the motion or the right to do so is waived by the guilty plea. Giving notice of appeal ***after*** the plea has been entered will not suffice. *See State v. Tew*, 326 N.C. 732 (1990); *State v. Brown*, 142 N.C. App. 491 (2001); *State v. McBride*, 120 N.C. App. 623 (1995), *aff'd per curiam*, 344 N.C. 623 (1996). Additionally, a stipulation in the appellate record that the defendant intended to appeal the denial of a suppression motion is not sufficient to preserve the issue—the trial record itself must demonstrate the defendant's intention to appeal before entry of the plea. *See Brown*, 142 N.C. App. 491. The best way to proceed is to advise the State during plea negotiations of your intent to appeal and file a written "notice of intent to appeal" before entry of the plea. The written transcript of plea and the record from the in-court plea colloquy also should include a statement that the defendant intends to appeal the denial of a suppression motion under G.S. 15A-979.

The last step is to enter an oral or written "notice of appeal" from the judgment itself (not from the denial of the motion to suppress) ***after*** entry of final judgment in order to confer jurisdiction on the appellate court. *See State v. Miller*, 205 N.C. App. 724 (2010); N.C. R. APP. P. 4; *see also* 1 NORTH CAROLINA DEFENDER MANUAL § 14.7 (Appeal of Suppression Motions) (July 2002).

The issues set out above are the only issues that may be appealed after the entry of a guilty or no contest plea. No other issue can be raised on appeal as a matter of right. *See, e.g., State v. Rinehart*, 195 N.C. App. 774 (2009) (because defendant pled guilty, he had no right to appeal the denial of his motions to dismiss based on double jeopardy and violation of his right to a speedy trial); *State v. Smith*, 193 N.C. App. 739 (2008) (finding that the defendant, after pleading guilty, did not have the right to appeal the denial of his motion to dismiss his habitual felon indictment and the court did not have the authority to grant certiorari review under Appellate Rule 21); *State v. Jeffery*, 167 N.C. App. 575 (2004) (because the defendant pled guilty, he had no right to appeal (1) whether the bills of information were unconstitutionally vague and therefore violated the right against double jeopardy; and (2) whether the factual basis for the plea supported the bills of indictment); *State v. Bivens*, 155 N.C. App. 645 (2002) (after pleading guilty, defendant could not appeal as of right from the denial of his motion to continue); *State v. Pimental*, 153 N.C. App. 69 (2002) (defendant had no statutory right to appellate review of multiple issues at his trial before the entry of his guilty plea; defendant did have an appeal of right as to a sentencing issue); *see also* 1 NORTH CAROLINA DEFENDER MANUAL § 13.4B (Motion to Dismiss on Double Jeopardy Grounds) (Mar. 2009) (discussing difficulty of obtaining appellate review of double jeopardy issue after entry of guilty plea). Possible alternative remedies—writs of certiorari and motions for appropriate relief—are discussed below.

Practice note: If your client is considering pleading guilty or no contest in superior court, you should advise him or her about the consequences of the plea, including that the right to appeal is extremely limited. *See infra* Appendix A, N.C. COMM'N ON INDIGENT DEFENSE SERVS., PERFORMANCE GUIDELINES FOR INDIGENT DEFENSE REPRESENTATION IN NON-CAPITAL CRIMINAL CASES AT THE TRIAL LEVEL, Guideline 6.1(c) The Plea Negotiation Process and the Duties of Counsel (Nov. 2004). If your client wants to appeal from a ruling on a pretrial motion other than a motion to suppress as discussed above, you will have to try the case to completion to preserve that right. (The grounds for a writ of certiorari or motion for appropriate relief, discussed below in this subsection D., also are limited after a guilty plea.) Even a stipulation in a plea arrangement that allows for an appeal of the denial of a pretrial motion is not valid and will not confer jurisdiction on the appellate court. *See Rinehart*, 195 N.C. App. 774; *Smith*, 193 N.C. App. 739. An invalid stipulation assuring the right to appeal may give a defendant a basis for withdrawing a guilty plea because he or she cannot get the benefit of his or her bargain, but in some circumstances the defendant may have to proceed by motion for appropriate relief and not by appeal to obtain that relief. *Compare State v. White*, ___ N.C. ___, 711 S.E.2d 862 (2011) (where appellate court had jurisdiction over the case based on defendant's proper appeal from a denial of a motion to suppress, it could vacate the judgment and allow defendant on remand to withdraw a guilty plea that was given with the intent to preserve an appeal from the denial of defendant's pretrial motion to suppress *and* pretrial motion to dismiss), and *Smith*, 193 N.C. App. 739 (to same effect), *with Rinehart*, 195 N.C. App. 774 (distinguishing *Smith* and other decisions, in which it had vacated a guilty plea based on a plea agreement that included a reservation of the right to appeal that was ineffective, and holding that the defendant's recourse was to file a motion for appropriate relief where only issue he raised (denial of pretrial motion to dismiss) was not appealable).

Appellate jurisdiction ordinarily in N.C. Court of Appeals. If the defendant has the right to appeal from a plea of guilty (or no contest) taken in superior court, the appeal lies of right to the N.C. Court of Appeals unless the defendant received a sentence of death. If the defendant received the death penalty, the appeal lies of right to the N.C. Supreme Court. *See* G.S. 7A-27 (a), (b); N.C. R. APP. P. 4(d).

Requirements and procedures for giving notice of appeal. The procedural requirements for giving notice of appeal from a judgment after a guilty plea are the same as those after a conviction by a jury and are discussed *infra* in § 35.1F.

Writ of certiorari. Although a defendant may not be entitled to an appeal of right after pleading guilty, G.S. 15A-1444 states that he or she may petition the appellate division for review by writ of certiorari. *See* G.S. 15A-1444(e), (g). However, writs of certiorari to review trial court orders and judgments are allowed by the N.C. Rules of Appellate

Procedure in three instances only:

1. where the party lost the right to appeal by failing to take timely action;
2. where the order appealed from is interlocutory and there is no right of appeal; or
3. to review a trial judge's denial of a motion for appropriate relief.

See N.C. R. APP. P. 21(a)(1).

Faced with these conflicting provisions, the N.C. appellate courts have reached the conclusion that, other than in the three instances set out above and the one exception discussed below, they have no authority to issue a writ of certiorari. *See State v. Pimental*, 153 N.C. App. 69 (2002) (although G.S. 15A-1444(e) allows a defendant to petition for a writ of certiorari after pleading guilty, the appellate court is still limited to granting certiorari under the three circumstances set out in Appellate Rule 21; appellate rules prevail over the general statutes when there is a conflict).

Because of the limitations of Appellate Rule 21, a writ of certiorari generally will not be granted to review the denial of pretrial motions in cases in which the defendant pled guilty. *See, e.g., State v. Rinehart*, 195 N.C. App. 774 (2009) (court found that it did not have the authority to issue a writ of certiorari to review double jeopardy and speedy trial issues raised by defendant before pleading guilty); *State v. Jamerson*, 161 N.C. App. 527 (2003) (where defendant pled guilty, the court held it was without authority under Rule 21 to review the denial of defendant's motion to dismiss the habitual felon indictment or his assertion that the judgment was unconstitutional); *State v. Pimental*, 153 N.C. App. 69 (2002) (court found that it did not have the authority to issue a writ of certiorari to review multiple issues raised by defendant before his guilty plea).

There is one additional exception to Appellate Rule 21 permitting a defendant who has pled guilty to obtain review by writ of certiorari. N.C. appellate courts may grant a petition for writ of certiorari after a defendant pleads guilty to review challenges to the procedures employed by the trial judge in accepting the defendant's plea. *See State v. Bolinger*, 320 N.C. 596 (1987) (reviewing the defendant's assertion that the trial judge erred in accepting his guilty plea because the judge failed to determine whether the plea was entered knowingly and did not inquire whether defendant was in fact guilty; court did not specifically address the applicability of Rule 21); *State v. Ahearn*, 307 N.C. 584 (1983) (treating defendant's appeal from a guilty plea as a petition for writ of certiorari and reviewing whether there was a factual basis for the plea); *see also State v. Demaio*, ___ N.C. App. ___, 716 S.E.2d 863 (2011) (defendant sought review of his contention that his plea was uninformed because he entered it under the erroneous impression that he was preserving the right to appeal from the denial of his pretrial motion to dismiss and motion in limine; court recognized that *Bolinger* did not specifically address Rule 21 but held that the Court of Appeals could not overrule *Bolinger* and the court had the authority to grant certiorari to review the issue); *State v. Santos*, ___ N.C. App. ___, 708 S.E.2d 208 (2011) ("given defendant's lengthy sentences," court elected to treat defendant's purported appeal from a guilty plea as a petition for writ of certiorari and found the plea to have been knowingly and voluntarily made); *State v. Flint*, 199 N.C. App. 709 (2009) (allowing certiorari to review whether there was a sufficient factual basis for defendant's plea); *State v. Carriker*, 180 N.C. App. 470 (2006) (allowing a writ of certiorari and holding that trial judge should have informed defendant of her right to withdraw her guilty plea after the judge decided to impose a sentence other than the one set out in the plea arrangement); *State v. Poore*, 172 N.C. App. 839 (2005) (granting a writ of certiorari and addressing defendant's argument that there was an insufficient factual basis supporting the entry of his plea); *State v. Rhodes*, 163 N.C. App. 191 (2004) (writ of certiorari allowed to address defendant's challenge to the procedures employed in accepting his guilty plea); *State v. Carter*, 167 N.C. App. 582 (2004) (following *Bolinger* and granting review of defendant's assertion that the trial judge failed to determine that defendant's guilty plea was made knowingly and voluntarily). *But see State v. Nance*, 155 N.C. App. 773 (2003) (holding that court was without authority under Rule 21 to allow defendant's petition for writ of certiorari to review the issue of whether his guilty plea was made knowingly and voluntarily).

For a further discussion of writs of certiorari, see *infra* § 35.7D, Certiorari of Trial Court Orders and Judgments.

Motion for appropriate relief. Although a defendant may not be entitled to an appeal of right after pleading guilty, he or she may be able to pursue a motion for appropriate relief under G.S. 15A-1414 and 15A-1415. *See infra* § 35.3, Motions for Appropriate Relief. Generally, a defendant who enters a guilty plea waives all errors in the proceeding, including constitutional violations that occurred before entry of the plea. One exception to this rule is that the defendant may challenge the power of the state to bring him or her into court. *See Blackledge v. Perry*, 417 U.S. 21, 30–31 (1974); *State v. Reynolds*, 298 N.C. 380 (1979) (discussing *Blackledge*). For example, a defendant who pled guilty may use a motion for appropriate relief to challenge a conviction based on a fatally defective indictment, which constitutes a jurisdictional defect under North Carolina law. A defendant also may challenge whether his or her guilty plea was voluntary and intelligent and whether he received effective assistance of counsel in entering the plea. *See State v. Mercer*, 84 N.C. App. 623 (1987); *see also Blackledge v. Allison*, 431 U.S. 63 (1977). Additionally, a defendant may file a motion for appropriate relief seeking relief from a guilty plea if it was entered under the mistaken impression that he or she could preserve the right to appeal from the denial of pretrial motions (other than a motion to suppress from which there is a right to appeal). *See State v. Rinehart*, 195 N.C. App. 774, 777 (2009) (dismissing defendant's appeal for lack of appellate jurisdiction "without prejudice to defendant's right to file a motion for appropriate relief . . . .").

For a further discussion of possible grounds for motions for appropriate relief after a guilty plea, see Jessica Smith, *Two Issues in MAR Procedure: Hearings and Showing Required to Succeed on a MAR*, ADMINISTRATION OF JUSTICE BULLETIN No. 2001/04 (UNC School of Government, Oct. 2001), *available at* www.sog.unc.edu/sites/www.sog.unc.edu/files/aoj200104.pdf.

E. Appeal from a Finding of Violation of Probation in Superior Court

A defendant may appeal under G.S. 7A-27 to the N.C. Court of Appeals from a superior court's finding of a violation of probation if the judge either activated the defendant's suspended sentence or imposed a condition of special probation (split sentence). G.S. 15A-1347. If the judge finds a violation but continues a defendant on probation or modifies the terms of probation without imposing a condition of special probation, there is no right to appeal that ruling under G.S. 15A-1347. *See State v. Edgerson*, 164 N.C. App. 712 (2004) (although trial judge found a violation of probation and modified defendant's probation to add four more conditions of probation, defendant had no right to appeal; court also found it was without authority to grant certiorari to review the trial judge's modifications under Appellate Rule 21). G.S. 15A-1347 does not specifically address whether a defendant has the right to appeal confinement in response to a violation under G.S. 15A-1344(b2), which can be as long as ninety days, a part of probation changes made in 2011 by the General Assembly in the Justice Reinvestment Act. *See* Jamie Markham, *Confinement in Response to Violations (CRV) and Limits on Probation Revocation Authority*, N.C. CRIM. L., UNC SCH. OF GOV'T BLOG (Oct. 25, 2011), http://sogweb.sog.unc.edu/blogs/ncclaw/?p=2994.

F. Procedural Requirements for Appealing from Superior Court

Manner and time. Notice of appeal may be given orally at trial, or it may be filed in written form with the clerk of superior court. The written notice must be filed within fourteen days of the entry of judgment, and copies of the notice must be served on all adverse parties. N.C. R. APP. P. 4(a); *see also* G.S. 15A-1448(b) ("Notice of appeal shall be given within the time, in the manner and with the effect provided in the rules of appellate procedure."). Judgment is entered when the sentence is pronounced. *See* G.S. 15A-101(4a).

Contents of written notice of appeal. If written notice of appeal is given, the notice must

- specify the party taking the appeal;
- designate the judgment or order from which appeal is taken;
- designate the court to which the appeal is taken; and
- be signed by counsel of record or by the defendant if not represented by counsel.

N.C. R. APP. P. 4(b).

Manner of giving of appeal of satellite monitoring determination. Because the North Carolina appellate courts consider the imposition of satellite based monitoring for a sex offender to be a civil matter, they have held that oral notice of appeal is not sufficient to confer jurisdiction on the appellate court. The defendant must file written notice of appeal within thirty days pursuant to Rule 3 of the N.C. Rules of Appellate Procedure as required in civil cases. *State v. Brooks*, 204 N.C. App. 193 (2010); *see also State v. Clayton*, 206 N.C. App. 300 (2010) (treating improperly noticed appeal as petition for writ of certiorari because the defendant's satellite-based monitoring hearing at which he gave oral notice of appeal predated appellate decisions holding that satellite-based monitoring is a civil matter and that oral notice of appeal is insufficient). The content of the written notice of appeal is identical to the content of the written notice of appeal for criminal cases discussed above. *See* N.C. R. APP. P. 3(d).

Divestiture of jurisdiction. Once notice of appeal is given and the time for giving notice of appeal has expired, the superior court no longer has jurisdiction over the case. G.S. 15A-1448(a)(3). The superior court retains authority over the case to determine limited matters, such as indigency and whether and on what conditions a defendant may be granted post-trial release. *Id.*; G.S. 15A-1453; *see also infra* § 35.1J, Release Pending Appeal from Superior Court Judgment; § 35.3B, Types of Motions for Appropriate Relief by Defendant; § 35.6, Trial Judges' Authority to Correct, Modify, or Amend Judgments.

Practice note: The form used by superior court judges to note a defendant's appeal, set conditions of release if any, order the transcript, and appoint appellate counsel can be found on the Administrative Office of the Courts website. *See* AOC Form AOC-CR-350, "Appellate Entries" (June 2011), *available at* www.nccourts.org/Forms/Documents/133.pdf. The completion of this form by the clerk, even though it states that the defendant has given notice of appeal, does ***not*** fulfill the defendant's requirement to file a written notice of appeal under Rule 4 of the N.C. Rules of Appellate Procedure. *See State v. Hughes*, ___ N.C. App. ___, 707 S.E.2d 777 (2011); *State v. Blue*, 115 N.C. App. 108 (1994). For a discussion of steps trial counsel should take to perfect a client's appeal, see *infra* subsection O. of § 35.1, Trial Counsel's Obligations regarding Defendant's Right to Appeal after Superior Court Conviction.

G. Stay of Superior Court Sentence

When a defendant gives notice of appeal from a superior court judgment,

- payment of costs is stayed;
- payment of any fine is stayed;
- confinement is stayed if the defendant is released pursuant to post-trial terms of release set by the judge (discussed *infra* in § 35.1J); and
- probation and special probation (i.e., split sentences under G.S. 15A-1351) are stayed.

G.S. 15A-1451(a); *see also* N.C. R. APP. P. 8(b) (when a defendant gives notice of appeal in a criminal case, the portion of the sentence that imposes fines or costs is automatically stayed pursuant to G.S. 15A-1451).

Sentence of imprisonment. The entry of notice of appeal does not automatically stay a sentence of imprisonment. A stay of imprisonment or a stay of the execution of a death sentence must be sought under G.S. 15A-536 (release after conviction in superior court, discussed *infra* in § 35.1J) or Rule 23 of the N.C. Rules of Appellate Procedure (supersedeas).

Probationary sentences. Under G.S. 15A-1451(a)(4), probation is automatically stayed by the entry of notice of appeal. This includes any split sentence imposed as a condition of special probation. Although probation is stayed, the superior court retains the authority to impose conditions of release under G.S. 15A-536 pending the defendant's appeal. *See State v. Howell*, 166 N.C. App. 751 (2004) (after defendant gave notice of appeal from a probationary sentence, trial judge had authority to impose a new bond and set conditions, including the condition that defendant not possess a computer or reside in or visit any home where a computer was present); *see also infra* § 35.1J, Release Pending Appeal from Superior Court Judgment.

Practice note: Occasionally, the Division of Community Corrections (that is, the probation department) will mistakenly try to supervise a defendant who received a probationary sentence and entered notice of appeal. If your client receives a probationary sentence, you should stress to him or her that probation is stayed and that he or she is not required to comply with the conditions of probation (although he or she is required to comply with any conditions of release). If a probation officer tells your client that he or she has to comply with the conditions of probation during the pendency of the appeal, you should contact the officer (or his or her supervisor if the officer is uncooperative) and point out that G.S. 15A-1451(a)(4) automatically stays probation.

Release during State's appeal. If the State appeals from a dismissal of charges against the defendant, the effect of the dismissal is not stayed and the defendant is free from such charges unless they are reinstated after an appellate determination. G.S. 15A-1451(b).

H. Withdrawal of Notice of Appeal from Superior Court Judgment

Procedural requirements. A defendant who has entered notice of appeal may choose to withdraw his or her appeal at any time before a decision by the appellate court. To withdraw an appeal, the defendant must file a written withdrawal with the clerk of superior court where the notice of appeal was filed. The notice of withdrawal must be signed by the defendant and, if represented, by his or her current attorney. The clerk will forward a copy of the withdrawal to the appellate court where the case is pending. G.S. 15A-1450.

Withdrawal after record on appeal filed. If the record on appeal has already been filed in the appellate court, the defendant also must file a written notice of the withdrawal with the clerk of the appropriate appellate court. N.C. R. APP. P. 37(d). If the defendant withdraws his or her appeal after the record on appeal has been filed, he or she may be taxed with costs of the appeal. *See* G.S. 15A-1450; *see also* N.C. R. APP. P. Appendix F ("Court costs on appeal total $9.00 . . . and are imposed when a notice of appeal is withdrawn or dismissed . . . .").

Stay lifted on withdrawal. Any stay of costs, fines, confinement, or probation pursuant to G.S 15A-1451 will be terminated once the appeal is withdrawn. *See* G.S. 15A-1450 Official Commentary.

Reentry of notice of appeal. A defendant does not lose the right to appeal when he or she withdraws an appeal as long as notice of appeal is reentered within the fourteen-day period for taking an appeal from superior court. *See* G.S. 15A-1448(a)(5); *see also* N.C. R. APP. P. 4(a)(2). According to the Official Commentary to G.S. 15A-1448, a defendant "has free choice" within the time period for taking an appeal to enter and withdraw an appeal and then enter it again.

I. Compliance with Superior Court Judgment

If a defendant complies with all or a portion of a judgment imposed in superior court, he or she does not waive the right to appeal. If the defendant complies and then decides to enter notice of appeal, the superior court judge may enter an order remitting any fines or costs that have been paid by the defendant or the remission may be delayed until the appeal has been finally determined. G.S. 15A-1448(a)(6). According to the Official Commentary to G.S. 15A-1448, the judge has the discretion to delay the repayment of the fines or costs in order to simplify the collection and remission procedures.

J. Release Pending Appeal from Superior Court Judgment

Statutory authorization. A defendant who has been convicted in superior court and who has entered notice of appeal may be released pending appeal on appropriate conditions set by a superior court judge. *See* G.S. 15A-536(a). If the judge decides to release a defendant pending the resolution of his or her appeal, the judge must impose conditions that will reasonably assure the defendant's presence when required and that will adequately protect persons and the community. G.S. 15A-536(b).

The judge may impose the same conditions allowed for pretrial release in G.S. 15A-534(a). These conditions include

- releasing the defendant on his or her written promise to appear;
- releasing the defendant if he or she executes an unsecured appearance bond in the amount set by the judge;
- placing the defendant in the custody of a designated person or organization;
- requiring the defendant to post an appearance bond in an amount set by the judge;
- ordering the defendant to be placed under house arrest with electronic monitoring; and
- placing restrictions on the defendant's travel, associations, conduct, or abode.

See G.S. 15A-534(a); G.S. 15A-536(b). The judge must take into account all reliable evidence available to him or her in deciding on the conditions to impose. The judge is not strictly bound by the rules of evidence in making the determination. G.S. 15A-536(f).

Procedural requirements. If post-trial release is granted, the trial judge must file an order with the clerk of court

- stating the conditions imposed, if any;
- informing the defendant of the penalties that will result from non-compliance; and
- advising the defendant that he or she will be arrested immediately if he or she violates the conditions.

A copy of the order must be served on the defendant. G.S. 15A-536(d).

Modifications and revocations. The release order may be modified or revoked. If a defendant is arrested based on a revocation or modification of a release order, he or she is entitled to an immediate hearing to determine whether he or she is entitled to release and, if so, on what conditions. G.S. 15A-536(e).

No constitutional right to post-trial release. The right to release pending appeal is statutory and does not arise from any provision in the state or federal constitution. *See State v. Parker*, 220 N.C. 416 (1941); *see also Reddy v. Snepp*, 357 F. Supp. 999 (W.D.N.C. 1973). The decision whether to grant or deny a post-trial bond and, if granted, in what amount are within the trial judge's discretion and will not be disturbed on appeal in the absence of a showing of an abuse of that discretion. *See State v. Sparks*, 297 N.C. 314 (1979); *State v. Keaton*, 61 N.C. App. 279 (1983); *In re Reddy*, 16 N.C. App. 520 (1972).

Release pending appeal from probationary sentence. Even though probationary sentences are automatically stayed when a defendant gives notice of appeal (*see* G.S. 15A-1451(a)(4)), trial judges still may set conditions of post-trial release under G.S. 15A-536 for defendants who receive probation. *State v. Howell*, 166 N.C. App. 751, 754 (2004) (to interpret G.S. 15A-536 as applying only to defendants who are in custody or who are facing custody "would lead to the absurd result that the court would have no oversight over defendants with probationary sentences on appeal"; legislative intent was "to address possible flight by the defendant and/or danger to the community").

K. Interlocutory Appeals to Appellate Division

Generally. As a general rule, appeals from interlocutory orders may not be taken in criminal cases. *See State v. Henry*, 318 N.C. 408 (1986); *see also* G.S. 7A-27 and G.S. 15A-1444(a) (providing for appellate review of final judgments only). The courts have observed that to allow appeals from every interlocutory order entered in the course of a criminal prosecution "would lead to interminable delay and render the enforcement of the criminal law well-nigh impossible." *State v. Howard*, 70 N.C. App. 487, 488 (1984) (quoting *State v. Webb*, 155 N.C. 426, 430 (1911)).

An exception to the general rule prohibiting appeals of interlocutory orders in criminal cases is found in G.S. 15A-1432(d). This statute allows a defendant to maintain an interlocutory appeal of a superior court's reversal of a district court's dismissal of criminal charges. *See State v. Joseph*, 92 N.C. App. 203 (1988); *see also infra* § 35.2A, State's Right to Appeal from District Court Judgment.

Although G.S. 1-277(a) permits appeals to be taken from interlocutory orders that affect a substantial right, this statute does not apply in criminal cases. *See Joseph*, 92 N.C. App. 203, 206 (the enactment of G.S. 15A-1444 as the exclusive authority for criminal appeals "precludes [a] defendant's resort to any 'substantial right' analysis" under G.S. 1-277); *see also State v. Shoff*, 118 N.C. App. 724 (1995), *aff'd*, 342 N.C. 638 (1996).

Writs of certiorari. Although a criminal defendant may not be entitled to an appeal of right from an interlocutory order, he or she may petition the appellate division for review by writ of certiorari. *See* G.S. 15A-1444(g). Writs of certiorari are allowed by the N.C. Rules of Appellate Procedure "when no right of appeal from an interlocutory order exists." N.C. R.

APP. P. 21(a)(1); *see also* G.S. 7A-32(b) (supreme court has jurisdiction to issue a writ of certiorari "in exercise of its general power to supervise and control the proceedings" of any of the lower courts); G.S. 7A-32(c) (court of appeals has jurisdiction to issue writ of certiorari "to supervise and control the proceedings of any of the trial courts").

The application for the writ of certiorari is addressed to the court of the appellate division to which appeal of right might lie if there was a final judgment in the case. N.C. R. APP. P. 21(b). For further discussion of the writ of certiorari, see *infra* § 35.7D, Certiorari of Trial Court Orders and Judgments.

L. Appeals from Prayers for Judgment Continued

Generally. Since a defendant may only appeal from a final judgment, whether he or she has a right to appeal when a district court or superior court judge has entered a prayer for judgment continued (PJC) depends on whether the judge's order is in the nature of a "final judgment." The general rule is that there is no right to appeal because "'there is no judgment—only a motion or prayer by the prosecuting officer for judgment.'" *See State v. Popp*, 197 N.C. App. 226, 228 (2009) (quoting *State v. Griffin*, 246 N.C. 680, 683 (1957)).

However, if the "judge imposes conditions 'amounting to punishment' on the continuation of the entry of judgment, the judgment loses its character as a PJC and becomes a final judgment." *State v. Brown*, 110 N.C. App. 658, 659 (1993) (quoting *Griffin*, 246 N.C. 680, 683). The defendant may then have the right to appeal pursuant to G.S. 15A-1444 and G.S. 7A-27 (authorizing appeals from final judgments).

What constitutes "punishment." "Prayer for judgment continued upon payment of costs, without more, does not constitute the entry of judgment." G.S. 15A-101(4a); *see also Brown*, 110 N.C. App. 658. Imposing a condition that the defendant must obey the law likewise does not constitute the entry of judgment. *See State v. Cheek*, 31 N.C. App. 379 (1976) (requirements that defendant not escape from prison and not break the law did not transform the prayer for judgment continued into a final judgment).

The appellate courts have found that the imposition of the following conditions "amounted to punishment"; therefore, the order lost its character as a prayer for judgment continued and became an appealable final judgment:

- Payment of a fine. *Griffin*, 246 N.C. 680.
- Imprisonment. *Id.*
- Continuation of mental health treatment. *Brown*, 110 N.C. App. 658 (court did not reach the question of whether the order that defendant not contact his ex-wife, the prosecuting witness, was punishment).
- Completion of a high school education. *Popp*, 197 N.C. App. 226.
- Enrollment in an institution of higher education or enlistment in the armed forces. *Id.*
- Compliance with a curfew. *Id.*
- Submission to monthly drug testing. *Id.*

- Performance of community service and payment of a community service fee. *Id.*
- Preparation of a letter of apology. *Id.*
- Continued employment. *Id.*

Additional resources. For additional discussion of this topic, see Jessica Smith, *Prayer for Judgment Continued* (May 2009), *in* THE SURVIVAL GUIDE: SUPERIOR COURT JUDGES' BENCHBOOK, www.sog.unc.edu/node/2155. *See also* Jamie Markham, *The Unwelcome Prayer for Judgment Continued*, N.C. CRIM. L., UNC SCH. OF GOV'T BLOG (Sept. 18. 2009) (discussing possible remedies when a defendant does not want a PJC), http://sogweb.sog.unc.edu/blogs/ncclaw/?p=717.

M. Death of Defendant While Appeal Is Pending

If a defendant dies while his or her North Carolina state criminal conviction is on appeal, the action is abated and the appeal will be dismissed. *See State v. Dixon*, 265 N.C. 561 (1965); *State v. Young*, 27 N.C. App. 308 (1975); *State v. Boyette*, 24 N.C. App. 587 (1975). North Carolina appears to have adopted the doctrine of abatement ab initio. *See Alaska v. Carlin*, 249 P.3d 752 (Ak. 2011) (asserting that North Carolina is among the nineteen states that strictly apply the doctrine of abatement ab initio); *People v. Robinson*, 699 N.E.2d 1086 (Ill. App. Ct. 1998) (listing North Carolina as a jurisdiction that abates a deceased defendant's appeal ab initio and citing *Dixon*, 265 N.C. 561), *vacated on other grounds*, 719 N.E.2d 662 (Ill. 1999). Under that doctrine, when a criminal defendant dies, not only is his or her appeal dismissed, but the conviction is also vacated and the indictment is dismissed because the appeal had not been, and now can never be, resolved. Abatement ab initio acts to restore the pre-indictment presumption of innocence to the defendant. *See* Rosanna Cavallaro, *Better Off Dead: Abatement, Innocence, and the Evolving Right of Appeal*, 73 U. COLO. L. REV. 943 (2002).

N. Right to Appeal from Denial of Defendant's Post-Conviction Motion for DNA Testing

Right to appeal from denial of request to test. Pursuant to G.S. 15A-269, a defendant who has been convicted may request that DNA testing be performed. If the motion for testing is denied, the defendant may appeal the order and is entitled to the appointment of counsel for the appeal if indigent. G.S 15A-270.1. Although the statute does not specify the time period for taking the appeal, in order to avoid the potential for dismissal of the appeal, the notice of appeal should comply with Rule 4 of the N.C. Rules of Appellate Procedure and be given in open court or filed within fourteen days of the denial of the defendant's motion.

No right to appeal from denial of relief after testing. If the defendant's motion for DNA testing is granted, the trial judge must hold a hearing once the testing results are received in order to determine whether the results are favorable or unfavorable to the defendant. G.S. 15A-270. If the trial judge determines that the results are unfavorable and denies the defendant any relief, the defendant does not have the right to appeal from this ruling. *See State v. Norman*, 202 N.C. App. 329, 333 (2010) (stating that "'[t]he General Assembly simply has not provided for appeals from [a court's ruling under § 15A-270] and under those circumstances, harsh as the result may seem, we must hold that [this Court is] without subject matter jurisdiction to entertain [Defendant's] appeal.'") (quoting *Palmer v. Wilkins*, 73 N.C. App. 171, 173 (1985)).

Additional resources. For further discussion of post-conviction motions for DNA testing, *see* Jessica Smith, *Post-Conviction: Motions for DNA Testing and Early Disposal of Biological Evidence* (Feb. 2010), *in* THE SURVIVAL GUIDE: SUPERIOR COURT JUDGES' BENCHBOOK, www.sog.unc.edu/node/2168.

O. Trial Counsel's Obligations regarding Defendant's Right to Appeal after Superior Court Conviction

After a conviction in superior court, trial counsel's duties are not quite over. Counsel must complete the following duties before his or her representation is over.

1. Counsel should inform the client of his or her right to appeal and advise him or her of the consequences of appealing. *See* N.C. Commission on Indigent Defense Services Rule 1.7(a) (June 2011), *available at* www.ncids.org/Rules%20&%20Procedures/IDS%20Rules/IDS%20Rules%20Part%201.pdf; *see also infra* Appendix A, N.C. COMM'N ON INDIGENT DEFENSE SERVS., PERFORMANCE GUIDELINES FOR INDIGENT DEFENSE REPRESENTATION IN NON-CAPITAL CRIMINAL CASES AT THE TRIAL LEVEL, Guideline 9.3 Right to Appeal to the Appellate Division (Nov. 2004).

2. If the client wants to appeal, counsel must take the necessary steps to give proper notice of appeal. *See* N.C. Commission on Indigent Defense Services Rule 1.7(a) (June 2011), *available at* www.ncids.org/Rules%20&%20Procedures/IDS%20Rules/IDS%20Rules%20Part%201.pdf. By entering notice of appeal on the client's behalf, trial counsel is not obligating himself or herself to represent the client in the appellate division. *See* G.S. 15A-143 (an attorney who represents a defendant in a criminal action without limiting his or her appearance represents the defendant at all stages of the case until entry of final judgment at the trial stage); N.C. Commission on Indigent Defense Services Rule 1.7(a) (June 2011), *available at* www.ncids.org/Rules%20&%20Procedures/IDS%20Rules/IDS%20Rules%20Part%201.pdf ("Unless otherwise provided by law, [appointed counsel] is required to continue with the representation through judgment at the trial level, discussion with the client about his or her right to appeal, and entry of notice of appeal or expiration of the time for giving notice of appeal.").

3. If you give notice of appeal orally in open court at trial, you should request that the judge determine the indigency of your client at that time so that, if the client is indigent, the Office of the Appellate Defender can be appointed and the transcript can be ordered at state expense. *See* N.C. Commission on Indigent Defense Services Rule 3.2(b) (May 2010), *available at* www.ncids.org/Rules%20&%20Procedures/IDS%20Rules/IDS%20Rules%20Part%203.pdf. You also should request that the trial judge set an appeal bond or other conditions of post-trial release under G.S. 15A-536 so that your client can be released pending the determination of the appeal. *See supra* § 35.1J, Release Pending Appeal from Superior Court Judgment; *see also infra* Appendix A, N.C. COMM'N ON INDIGENT DEFENSE SERVS., PERFORMANCE GUIDELINES FOR INDIGENT DEFENSE REPRESENTATION IN NON-

CAPITAL CRIMINAL CASES AT THE TRIAL LEVEL, Guideline 9.4 Bail Pending Appeal (Nov. 2004). If you file written notice of appeal, you should make sure that the case is added back on the docket in superior court in order to have the trial judge address the issues discussed above.

4. It is extremely helpful to appellate counsel for you to make sure when you enter notice of appeal in open court (or at a subsequent hearing, discussed in 3. above, if written notice of appeal was filed) that the clerk notes all the pretrial hearing dates in the order requiring transcription. This order is part of the Appellate Entries form filled out by the clerk when notice of appeal is entered, available on the Administrative Office of the Courts website. *See* AOC Form AOC-CR-350, "Appellate Entries" (June 2011), *available at* www.nccourts.org/Forms/Documents/133.pdf. If all the pertinent dates are not included in the transcript order, the appeal may be delayed many months while appellate counsel tracks down dates and court reporters and gets additional transcript orders signed.

5. If the client does not have a right to appeal but counsel believes that he or she has a meritorious issue that can be raised by a petition for writ of certiorari, counsel should advise the client of this opinion and counsel should consult with the Office of the Appellate Defender about the appropriate procedure. *See infra* Appendix A, N.C. COMM'N ON INDIGENT DEFENSE SERVS., PERFORMANCE GUIDELINES FOR INDIGENT DEFENSE REPRESENTATION IN NON-CAPITAL CRIMINAL CASES AT THE TRIAL LEVEL, Guideline 9.3(c) Right to Appeal to the Appellate Division (Nov. 2004). Counsel also should consult with the Office of the Appellate Defender if the trial judge denies appointment of counsel on appeal or denies indigency status for purposes of appeal. *See infra* Appendix A, Guideline 9.3(d) Right to Appeal to the Appellate Division.

6. Once notice of appeal is perfected and appellate counsel is appointed, trial counsel should cooperate in providing information to the client's appellate attorney concerning the trial court proceedings. *See infra* Appendix A, N.C. COMM'N ON INDIGENT DEFENSE SERVS., PERFORMANCE GUIDELINES FOR INDIGENT DEFENSE REPRESENTATION IN NON-CAPITAL CRIMINAL CASES AT THE TRIAL LEVEL, Guideline 9.3(e) Right to Appeal to the Appellate Division (Nov. 2004). This includes filling out a questionnaire seeking information about the case that is sent to the trial attorney by the Office of the Appellate Defender once it receives the appointment.

35.2 Appeals by the State

There is no common law right providing for appeal by the State—the right is purely statutory. *State v. Harrell*, 279 N.C. 464 (1971). The State may not appeal a judgment in favor of a criminal defendant in the absence of a statute that clearly confers that right. *State v. Dobson*, 51 N.C. App. 445 (1981). Statutes granting the State a right to appeal in criminal cases are to be strictly construed. *State v. Elkerson*, 304 N.C. 658 (1982).

A. State's Right to Appeal from District Court Judgment

Statutory right to appeal. G.S. 15A-1432 addresses the State's right to appeal to superior court from dismissals or rulings entered by the district court. Unless the rule against double jeopardy prohibits further prosecution, the State may appeal from district court to the superior court in two instances:

1. when there has been a decision or judgment dismissing criminal charges as to one or more counts; or
2. when a motion for a new trial has been granted on the grounds of newly discovered or newly available evidence but only on questions of law.

G.S. 15A-1432(a); *see also infra* § 35.2B, State's Right to Appeal from a District Court's "Preliminary Determination" in Implied-Consent Cases.

When double jeopardy attaches. The State is precluded from appealing from a judgment dismissing the charges for insufficient evidence *if reversal by the reviewing court would result in further prosecution. See supra* § 30.4, Effect of Dismissal; *cf. United States v. Scott*, 437 U.S. 82, 91 (1978) (in accordance with double jeopardy principles, "[a] judgment of acquittal, whether based on a jury verdict of not guilty or on a ruling by the court that the evidence is insufficient to convict, may not be appealed and terminates the prosecution when a second trial would be necessitated by a reversal"). This is true even if the judge's ruling was clearly erroneous. *See State v. Morgan*, 189 N.C. App. 716 (2008); *see also Smith v. Massachusetts*, 543 U.S. 462, 473 (2005) (acknowledging "the well-established rule" that the double jeopardy bar will attach to a pre-verdict acquittal even if it is "patently wrong in law"). Thus, the State cannot appeal from district to superior court when the defendant's motion to dismiss for insufficient evidence is granted in a misdemeanor case. *See State v. Harrell*, 279 N.C. 464 (1971); *State v. Fowler*, 197 N.C. App. 1 (2009).

Since criminal trials in district court are non-jury trials, jeopardy attaches when the trial judge begins to hear evidence or testimony. *See State v. Brunson*, 327 N.C. 244 (1990); *see also Fowler*, 197 N.C. App. 1, 17 ("'until a defendant is "put to trial *before the trier of the facts*, whether the trier be a jury or a judge," jeopardy does not attach'" (emphasis added by *Fowler* court) (citations omitted)). The rationale behind this rule is that the potential for conviction exists only when evidence or testimony against a defendant is presented to and accepted by the court. *See State v. Ward*, 127 N.C. App. 115, 121 (1997).

If a dismissal is granted based on a pretrial motion of the defendant and evidence has not been accepted by the district court for an adjudication of the defendant's guilt, the State is free to appeal to superior court. *See, e.g., id.* (jeopardy had not attached and State properly appealed to superior court where district court dismissed charges before trial based on prosecutorial misconduct).

Procedural requirements. When appealing pursuant to G.S. 15A-1432(a), the State must file a written motion specifying the basis of the appeal. G.S. 15A-1432(b); *see also State v. Hinchman*, 192 N.C. App. 657, 661–62 (2008) (State properly asserted the legal basis of appeal in its motion for appeal, which asserted that "no competent evidence was presented to support the [defendant's] motion and order to dismiss" and the "[d]ismissal of the charges was contrary to law"). The motion must be filed with the clerk and served on the defendant within ten days after entry of the district court judgment. G.S. 15A-1432(b).

Minor inadequacies in the State's "motion of appeal" will not be fatal to the superior court's jurisdiction unless the defendant can show prejudice. *See Hinchman*, 192 N.C. App. 657 (defendant showed no prejudice resulting from the State's mistake in captioning its motion to appeal as having been filed in the district court division instead of superior court); *Ward*, 127 N.C. App. 115 (State's appeal designated as "Notice of Appeal" and setting forth the legal bases on which it sought review was sufficient to vest the superior court with jurisdiction even though the document was not labeled a "motion" as required by G.S. 15A-1432(b)).

The State and the defendant are entitled to file briefs addressing the motion and to adequate time for their preparation, "consonant with the expeditious handling of the appeal." G.S. 15A-1432(c).

Scope of review. The superior court must conduct a de novo review of the district court's decision. Since district courts are not courts of record, there would be no way for the superior court to exercise appellate-like jurisdiction to determine whether the district court's findings of fact and conclusions of law were sufficient. In many instances, the only way for a superior court judge to determine whether the district court's order should be affirmed or reversed will be to hold a full evidentiary hearing. *See Ward*, 127 N.C. App. 115; *State v. Gurganus*, 71 N.C. App. 95 (1984).

De novo review in this context does not mean that the State has the opportunity for a new trial on the merits, as when a defendant appeals for a trial de novo in superior court. The hearing in superior court on the State's appeal is limited to a de novo review of the district court's order dismissing criminal charges against a defendant or granting a motion for a new trial based on newly discovered evidence. *Gurganus*, 71 N.C. App. 95 (State was only entitled to a hearing de novo on the issue of whether the second prosecution of the charges by the State was barred by double jeopardy).

Disposition by superior court. If the superior court finds that the district court's decision was erroneous, it must reinstate the charges and remand the case to district court for further proceedings. The defendant may appeal from this order to the appellate division "as in the case of other orders of the superior court." This is true even though the appeal is interlocutory if the defendant, or his or her attorney, certifies to the superior court judge "that the appeal is not taken for the purpose of delay" and "the judge finds the cause is appropriately justiciable in the appellate division as an interlocutory matter." G.S. 15A-1432(d).

If the superior court finds that the district court's decision was correct, it must enter an order affirming the district court judgment. The State may appeal from this order to the appellate division if the district attorney certifies to the ruling judge that the appeal is not taken for the purpose of delay. G.S. 15A-1432(e).

Additional resources. For further information on double jeopardy and the State's right to appeal, see Robert L. Farb, *Criminal Pleadings, State's Appeal from District Court, and Double Jeopardy Issues*, UNC SCH. OF GOV'T (Feb. 1, 2010), www.sog.unc.edu/sites/www.sog.unc.edu/files/pleadjep.pdf, and Robert L. Farb, *Double Jeopardy, Ex Post Facto, and Related Issues*, UNC SCH. OF GOV'T (Jan. 2007), www.sog.unc.edu/sites/www.sog.unc.edu/files/djoverview.pdf.

B. State's Right to Appeal from a District Court's "Preliminary Determination" in Implied-Consent Cases

The Motor Vehicle Driver Protection Act of 2006 set forth specific procedures that must be followed for implied-consent offenses committed on or after December 1, 2006. When a district court judge determines that a defendant's pretrial motion to suppress or dismiss made pursuant to G.S. 20-38.6(a) should be granted, he or she must issue a written "preliminary determination" setting forth findings of fact and conclusions of law. G.S. 20-38.6(f). The State may appeal from that "preliminary determination" to superior court. If there is a dispute about the findings of fact, the superior court is not bound by the district court's findings and must determine the matter de novo. G.S. 20-38.7(a). The superior court will determine the merits of the defendant's motion and remand to district court for the entry of final judgment.

If the judge affirms the district court's "preliminary determination" granting the defendant's motion to suppress or dismiss and remands for the entry of final judgment, the State has no statutory right to appeal but may petition the N.C. Court of Appeals for a writ of certiorari. *See State v. Fowler*, 197 N.C. App. 1 (2009); *State v. Palmer*, 197 N.C. App. 201 (2009).

The defendant may not appeal from a district court judge's determination that his or her pretrial motion to suppress or dismiss made pursuant to G.S. 20-38.6(a) should be denied. He or she must wait and appeal for a trial de novo if convicted of the offense. *See* G.S. 20-38.7(b).

Additional resources. For a detailed discussion of the procedures applicable to and issues surrounding appeals from a district court's "preliminary determination," see Shea Riggsbee Denning, *Motions Procedures in Implied Consent Cases after* State v. Fowler *and* State v. Palmer, ADMINISTRATION OF JUSTICE BULLETIN No. 2009/06 (UNC School of Government, Dec. 2009), *available at* http://sogpubs.unc.edu/electronicversions/pdfs/aojb0906.pdf, and John K. Fanney, *Pretrial Motions and Hot Topics in DWI Cases* (North Carolina Public Defender Attorney and Investigator Conference, Spring 2008), *available at* www.ncids.org/Defender%20Training/2008%20Spring%20Conference/HotTopicsinDWIMS.pdf.

C. State's Right to Appeal from Superior Court Judgment

Statutory right to appeal. Unless the rule against double jeopardy prohibits further prosecution, the State may appeal from superior court to the appellate courts in the following instances:

1. when there has been a decision or judgment dismissing criminal charges as to one or more counts;
2. after a motion for a new trial on the ground of newly discovered or newly available evidence is granted but only on questions of law;
3. when the State alleges that the sentence imposed
   - results from an incorrect determination of the defendant's prior record level or the defendant's prior conviction level,
   - contains a type of sentence disposition that is not authorized by statute for the defendant's class of offense and prior record or conviction level,
   - contains a term of imprisonment that is for a duration not authorized by statute for the defendant's class of offense and prior record or conviction level, or
   - imposes an intermediate punishment pursuant to G.S. 15A-1340.13(g) based on findings of extraordinary mitigating circumstances that are not supported by evidence or are insufficient as a matter of law to support the dispositional deviation.

G.S. 15A-1445(a).

Appeals from the granting of a defendant's motion to suppress. The State also may appeal from an order by the superior court granting a defendant's motion to suppress before trial pursuant to G.S. 15A-979. *See* G.S. 15A-1445(b). The prosecutor must certify to the trial judge who granted the motion that the appeal is not taken for the purpose of delay and that the evidence is essential to the case. G.S. 15A-979(c). The appeal is directed to the appellate court that would have jurisdiction if the defendant were found guilty of the charge and received the maximum punishment. If the order suppressing the evidence affects multiple charges, the State's appeal is to the court with jurisdiction over the offense carrying the highest punishment. *Id.*

When double jeopardy attaches. The State is precluded from appealing from a judgment dismissing the charges for insufficient evidence *if reversal by the reviewing court would result in further prosecution. See supra* § 30.4, Effect of Dismissal; *cf. United States v. Scott*, 437 U.S. 82, 91 (1978) (in accordance with double jeopardy principles, "[a] judgment of acquittal, whether based on a jury verdict of not guilty or on a ruling by the court that the evidence is insufficient to convict, may not be appealed and terminates the prosecution when a second trial would be necessitated by a reversal"). This is true even if the judge's ruling was clearly erroneous. *See State v. Morgan*, 189 N.C. App. 716 (2008); *see also Smith v. Massachusetts*, 543 U.S. 462, 473 (2005) (acknowledging "the well-established rule" that the double jeopardy bar will attach to a pre-verdict acquittal even if it is "patently wrong in law"). Thus, the State cannot appeal from the superior court to the appellate division when the defendant's motion to dismiss for insufficient evidence is granted. *See State v. Ausley*, 78 N.C. App. 791 (1986); *State v. Murrell*, 54 N.C. App. 342 (1981).

Jeopardy attaches in superior court "when a defendant in a criminal prosecution is placed on trial: (1) on a valid indictment or information, (2) before a court of competent jurisdiction, (3) after arraignment, (4) after plea, and (5) when a competent jury has been empaneled and sworn." *See State v. Cutshall*, 278 N.C. 334, 344 (1971). Thus, the critical time for jeopardy purposes in a jury trial is the empanelment and swearing of the jury, not the taking of testimony of the first witness.

Double jeopardy will prohibit further prosecution in cases where the trial judge grants a defendant's motion to dismiss based on insufficient evidence *before the verdict* because "a reversal at the appellate level would result in a new trial—requiring defendant to once again defend himself, with all the emotional and monetary burdens associated therewith." *See State v. Scott*, 146 N.C. App. 283, 286 (2001), *rev'd on other grounds*, 356 N.C. 591 (2002); *see also United States v. Scott*, 437 U.S. 82, 91 (1978) ("A judgment of acquittal . . . based . . . on a ruling by the court that the evidence is insufficient to convict, may not be appealed and terminates the prosecution when a second trial would be necessitated by a reversal."). As long as the motion to dismiss is granted after the jury has been empaneled but has not yet rendered a verdict, the State is barred from appealing the decision.

If the trial judge grants a dismissal *after the verdict* is returned, the State is free to appeal and the conviction may be reinstated if the appellate court finds that the trial judge erroneously granted the motion. Double jeopardy does not prohibit an appeal in that instance because the jury already has rendered its verdict and, if the State is successful on appeal, the verdict can be reinstated without subjecting a defendant to retrial. *See State v. Hernandez*, 188 N.C. App. 193 (2008).

Additional resources. For further information on double jeopardy and the State's right to appeal, see Robert L. Farb, *Double Jeopardy, Ex Post Facto, and Related Issues*, UNC SCH. OF GOV'T (Jan. 2007), www.sog.unc.edu/sites/www.sog.unc.edu/files/djoverview.pdf.

35.3 Motions for Appropriate Relief

A. In General

A motion for appropriate relief (MAR) is a motion made after verdict (or after sentencing if the defendant pled guilty and there was no verdict) to correct any error occurring before, during, or after a criminal trial or proceeding. *State v. Handy*, 326 N.C. 532 (1990). Article 89 of Chapter 15A addresses motions for appropriate relief and was enacted to provide "a single, unified procedure for raising at the trial level errors which are asserted to have been made during" a defendant's criminal trial. Ch. 15A, art. 89 Official Commentary. The MAR provided for in Article 89 was intended by the General Assembly "to replace motions in arrest of judgment, motions to set aside the verdict, motions for new trial, post-conviction proceedings, *coram nobis* and all other post-trial motions, but was not intended as a bar to relief by writ of habeas corpus." *State v. Bush*, 307 N.C. 152, 165–66 (1982) (citing G.S. 15A-1411(c)).

The procedures required by Article 89 are quite detailed and somewhat complicated. A failure to comply with the statutory requirements may result in the dismissal of the motion or the denial of relief. *See, e.g., State v. Jones*, 317 N.C. 487 (1986) (MAR after ten-day time limit for that type of MAR was properly denied by superior court judge on the ground that the superior court no longer had jurisdiction); *State v. Moore*, 185 N.C. App. 257 (2007) (defendant failed to properly present a Sixth Amendment argument to the trial judge in accordance with the rules governing MARs where he filed neither a new MAR nor a written amendment adding this argument either before or after the hearing on his original MAR); *see also State v. Riley*, 137 N.C. App. 403 (2000) (denying defendant's MAR because, among other things, he was in a position to have raised the issue on a previous appeal and failed to do so).

B. Types of Motions for Appropriate Relief by Defendant

MAR within ten days of judgment. Article 89 provides for two types of MARs. The first is governed by G.S. 15A-1414. Under this statute, a defendant may seek relief for any error that occurred before or during trial. The MAR must be filed within ten days after entry of judgment and may be acted on by the trial court even if notice of appeal has already been given. G.S. 15A-1414(a), (c). The errors that may be asserted under this statute include but are not limited to the following:

- the trial judge erroneously failed to dismiss the charge before trial pursuant to G.S. 15A-954;
- the trial judge ruled contrary to law with regard to motions made before and during trial or with regard to the admission or exclusion of evidence;
- at the close of all the evidence, the trial judge erroneously failed to dismiss the charges based on insufficiency of the evidence (whether or not a motion to dismiss was made before the verdict was rendered);
- the trial judge gave erroneous jury instructions;
- the verdict was contrary to the weight of the evidence (this ground is discussed in more detail *supra* in § 30.3D);
- the sentence imposed was not supported by the evidence introduced at trial and at the sentencing hearing; and
- for any other cause the defendant did not receive a fair and impartial trial.

G.S. 15A-1414(b).

MAR at any time after judgment. The second type of MAR is governed by G.S. 15A-1415 and may be filed by a defendant at any time after verdict in non-capital cases. Capital cases have an outer time limit, and MARs in those cases must be filed in accordance with the requirements of G.S. 15A-1415(a). The defendant may raise the following grounds for relief under G.S. 15A-1415(b):

- at the time the defendant committed the acts charged, they did not amount to a violation of criminal law;
- the trial court did not have personal jurisdiction over the defendant or subject matter jurisdiction;
- the conviction was obtained in violation of the state or federal constitution;
- the statute under which the defendant was convicted or sentenced violated the state or

federal constitution;

- the conduct for which the defendant was prosecuted was protected by the state or federal constitution;
- there has been a significant change in law, either substantive or procedural, applied in the proceedings leading to the defendant's conviction or sentence, and retroactive application of the changed legal standard is required;
- the sentence imposed was unauthorized at the time imposed, contained a type of sentence disposition or a term of imprisonment not authorized for the particular class of offense and prior record or conviction level, was illegally imposed, or is otherwise invalid as a matter of law; and
- the defendant is entitled to be released from confinement because his or her sentence has been fully served.

A defendant also may file a MAR alleging newly discovered evidence under this statute; however, this type of motion must be filed "within a reasonable time of its discovery." G.S. 15A-1415(c).

Note: The State has a limited right to make a motion for appropriate relief as described in G.S. 15A-1416.

C. Additional Resources

For a resource on the requirements and procedures for making motions for appropriate relief in North Carolina, see Jessica Smith, *Motions for Appropriate Relief*, ADMINISTRATION OF JUSTICE BULLETIN No. 2010/03 (June 2010), *available at* http://sogpubs.unc.edu/electronicversions/pdfs/aojb1003.pdf. For a condensed version, see Jessica Smith, *Motions for Appropriate Relief* (July 2010), *in* THE SURVIVAL GUIDE: SUPERIOR COURT JUDGES' BENCHBOOK, www.sog.unc.edu/node/2167.

35.4 State Habeas Corpus

A. In General

A defendant who is imprisoned in North Carolina for any criminal or supposed criminal matter may challenge the lawfulness of his or her custody by applying for a writ of habeas corpus (ad subjiciendum). *See* G.S. 17-3. This writ was known as the "great Writ of Right." *See State v. Herndon*, 107 N.C. 934, 936 (1890); *see also In re Holley*, 154 N.C. 163, 168 (1910) (the writ of habeas corpus is "the most important, perhaps, in our system of government, having its origin long prior to Magna Charta"). The purpose of this ancient writ "'is to give a person restrained of his liberty an immediate hearing so that the legality of his detention may be inquired into and determined.'" *State v. Lewis*, 274 N.C. 438, 441 (1968) (citation omitted). It is not the purpose of the writ of habeas corpus to determine the guilt or innocence of a prisoner. 39 AM. JUR. 2D *Habeas Corpus and Postconviction Remedies* § 1 (2008).

Habeas corpus is a collateral attack on a judgment of imprisonment and is not a substitute for appeal. *In re Palmer*, 265 N.C. 485 (1965); *In re Burton*, 257 N.C. 534 (1962). A court in a habeas corpus proceeding is not allowed to act as an appeals court and review a conviction for errors—its function is solely to determine whether the applicant is being held unlawfully. *See State v. Cannon*, 244 N.C. 399 (1956). If the defendant is seeking review of errors occurring at trial or sentencing, he or she should appeal the judgment directly, file a petition for a writ of certiorari, or file a motion for appropriate relief. *See, e.g., State v. Hamrick*, 2 N.C. App. 227 (1968) (although defendant entitled his petition "Application for Writ of Habeas Corpus," it was in substance a motion for appropriate relief since it alleged trial error, and the trial judge should have handled it in that manner).

B. Authority and Procedures for Writ

The writ of habeas corpus is guaranteed by article I, section 21 of the N.C. Constitution [previously article I, sections 18 and 21]. Chapter 17 of the N.C. General Statutes implements the right to habeas corpus, setting out the procedural requirements for the application and enforcement of the writ.

The application for the writ must be made in writing and signed by the applicant. It may be demanded of any one of the justices or judges of the appellate division or of any superior court judge whether or not court is in session. G.S. 17-6; *see also* 1 NORTH CAROLINA DEFENDER MANUAL § 10.8H (Writ of Habeas Corpus) (Oct. 2010) (discussing authority of individual judges to hear writ). Additional materials on applying for a habeas corpus writ, including form applications and orders, can be found on the website of the N.C. Office of Indigent Defense Services, www.ncids.org. Highlight Training & Resources, click on Training Materials and then Training Materials—Indexed by Subject, and scroll down to Habeas Corpus.

For special procedures pertaining to habeas corpus applications in capital cases, see Rule 25 of the General Rules of Practice for the Superior and District Courts.

C. Scope of Writ

Traditionally, at common law an applicant in a habeas corpus proceeding could be released from imprisonment only if the record disclosed that the court that imprisoned him or her did not have jurisdiction of the offense or of the person of the defendant, or that the judgment was void because it was not authorized by law. *See, e.g., In re Burton*, 257 N.C. 534, 540 (1962) ("The only questions open to inquiry [in a habeas corpus proceeding] are whether on the record the court which imposed the sentence had jurisdiction of the matter or had exceeded its powers."). However, the scope of the court's habeas corpus jurisdiction has been expanded and is now much broader. *See Hoffman v. Edwards*, 48 N.C. App. 559 (1980) (noting that G.S. 17-33(2) broadened the scope of habeas corpus to allow a party to be discharged from custody even though the original imprisonment was lawful where some act, omission, or event that took place afterwards causes the party to be entitled to release); *see also In re Imprisonment of Stevens*, 28 N.C. App. 471 (1976) (same).

Pursuant to G.S. 17-33, an applicant must be released from custody if no legal cause is found for the imprisonment or restraint. Additionally, if it appears that the applicant is in custody by process issued by a legally constituted court or by an officer in the course of judicial proceedings authorized by law, he or she may be discharged if:

- the jurisdiction of such court or officer was exceeded, either as to matter, place, sum, or person;
- the original imprisonment was lawful but some subsequent act, omission, or event has caused the applicant to become entitled to be discharged;
- the process was defective causing it to be void;
- the process, although in proper form, was issued in a case not allowed by law;
- the person having custody of the applicant under such process is not the person empowered by law to detain him or her; or
- the process was not authorized by any judgment, order, or decree of any court, nor by any provision of law.

G.S. 17-33(1)–(6).

D. Selected Examples

Reported cases indicate that defendants have applied for writs of habeas corpus in the following circumstances. The list does not exhaust the possible uses of the writ, however. Defendants have applied for habeas corpus writs to:

- Challenge the defendant's continued imprisonment because the life sentence imposed on him for first-degree murder committed in 1975 was defined by statute as a term of eighty years and the defendant alleged that he had earned sufficient credits to have completed the sentence. *Jones v. Keller*, 364 N.C. 249 (2010).
- Inquire into the legality of the defendant's continued imprisonment beyond the maximum term set for committed youthful offenders. *State v. Niccum*, 293 N.C. 276 (1977).
- Seek immediate release from custody on the basis that the defendant was not the individual who was indicted for the crime. *State v. Lewis*, 274 N.C. 438 (1968).
- Test the legality of an attorney's imprisonment where a judge found the attorney to be in contempt of court and imprisoned him for ten days. *In re Burton*, 257 N.C. 534 (1962).
- Procure immediate release where the defendant's sentence of imprisonment was for a term in excess of that allowed by law and the defendant had already served the maximum sentence authorized by law. *State v. Austin*, 241 N.C. 548 (1955).
- Contest the defendant's restraint where he was imprisoned for allegedly violating the conditions of a suspended judgment without the opportunity for a hearing on the alleged violation. *State v. Phillips*, 185 N.C. 614 (1923).

See also 1 NORTH CAROLINA DEFENDER MANUAL § 1.8A (Who Hears the Motion) (Aug. 2010) (noting possibility of habeas corpus review of district court pretrial release determination); 1 NORTH CAROLINA DEFENDER MANUAL § 3.2C (Scheduling Requirements) (Nov. 2008) (discussing use of writ to challenge defendant's continued detention in cases in which a probable cause hearing has not been held within statutory time limits).

E. Appeal from Adverse Ruling

The applicant does not have an appeal of right from an order denying a writ of habeas corpus but may petition the appropriate appellate court for a writ of certiorari. *See State v. Niccum*, 293 N.C. 276 (1977); *State v. Wambach*, 136 N.C. App. 842 (2000). *But cf.* N.C. R. APP. P. 21(a) (authorizing appellate courts to grant a writ of certiorari only in the following three situations: (1) where the party lost the right to appeal by failing to take timely action; (2) where the order appealed from is interlocutory and there is no right of appeal; or (3) to review a trial judge's denial of a motion for appropriate relief).

F. Additional Resources

For a further discussion of the law related to state habeas corpus writs, see Jessica Smith *Habeas Corpus* (Jan. 2010), *in* THE SURVIVAL GUIDE: SUPERIOR COURT JUDGES' BENCHBOOK, www.sog.unc.edu/node/2166.

35.5 Resentencing after Successful Appellate or Post-Conviction Review

A. In General

Federal constitutional requirements. At a resentencing hearing, due process of law "requires that vindictiveness against a defendant for having successfully attacked his first conviction must play no part in the sentence he receives after a new trial." *North Carolina v. Pearce*, 395 U.S. 711, 725 (1969). "[D]ue process also requires that a defendant be freed of apprehension of . . . a retaliatory motivation on the part of the sentencing judge" at resentencing; otherwise, "the fear of such vindictiveness may unconstitutionally deter a defendant's exercise of the right to appeal or collaterally attack his [or her] first conviction." *Id.*

In *Pearce*, the U.S. Supreme Court held that whenever a harsher sentence is imposed at resentencing, the record must affirmatively show the existence of factors that would justify a more severe sentence. The reasons for the increased sentence "must be based upon objective information concerning identifiable conduct on the part of the defendant occurring after the time of the original sentencing proceeding." *Id.* at 726. If the reasons do not appear in the record, the harsher sentence will be presumed to be retaliatory and in violation of the Due Process Clause. Additionally, the defendant must be given credit for the time he or she spent in custody before resentencing.

Although a more severe punishment may violate the Due Process Clause, "neither the double jeopardy provision nor the Equal Protection Clause imposes an absolute bar to a more severe sentence upon reconviction." *Id.* at 723. A judge at resentencing "is not constitutionally precluded . . . from imposing a new sentence, whether greater or less than the original sentence, in light of events subsequent to the first trial that may have thrown new light upon the defendant's 'life, health, habits, conduct, and mental and moral propensities.'" *Id.* (citation omitted); *see also Alabama v. Smith*, 490 U.S. 794 (1989) (holding that presumption of vindictiveness does not apply if defendant successfully appeals a guilty plea and then goes to trial and receives harsher sentence because of the additional information the trial judge obtains from a trial; placing burden on defendant in these circumstances to show actual vindictiveness in violation of due process).

Broader protection of state statute. In 1977, the General Assembly codified and expanded the rule established in *Pearce.* G.S. 15A-1335 provides a broad rule that whenever a superior court judgment has been set aside on direct review or collateral attack, the resentencing judge may not impose a new sentence for the same offense, or for a different offense based on the same conduct, that is more severe than the original sentence less the portion of the original sentence that the defendant has previously served. *See also* G.S. 15A-1335 Official Commentary (stating that "[t]his section embodies generally the rule of *North Carolina v. Pearce* . . . but does not allow a more severe sentence even if intervening factors would argue for a more severe sentence, as the *Pearce* decision permits"). While this statute provides defendants with greater protection against retaliation or vindictiveness for exercising the right to appeal or collaterally attack a judgment, the statute may have some surprising exceptions, discussed in B., below, of which counsel must be aware in advising clients.

B. Applicability of G.S. 15A-1335

Unlike the rule applicable in federal courts, G.S. 15A-1335 applies to resentencings held after a successful attack on a superior court judgment regardless of whether the original conviction was the result of a jury trial or a guilty plea. *Compare State v. Wagner*, 356 N.C. 599, 602 (2002) (finding that for the purposes of G.S. 15A-1335, "the fact that defendant's original conviction resulted from a negotiated plea bargain rather than a finding of guilty by a jury is of no consequence"), *with Alabama v. Smith*, 490 U.S. 794 (1989) (holding that no presumption of vindictiveness under the U.S. Constitution arises when a defendant's original sentence was based on a guilty plea and the subsequent sentence follows a trial). Per *Wagner*, the statute appears to preclude a court from imposing a more severe sentence for a conviction that has been set aside regardless of whether the original sentence resulted from a negotiated plea or an open plea and regardless of whether the defendant, after vacation of the original sentence, reenters a guilty plea or is found guilty after a jury trial. *See also State v. Dunston*, 193 N.C. App. 247 (2008) (unpublished) (applying rule in case involving jury trial after negotiated guilty plea was set aside); *State v. Burton*, 187 N.C. App. 510 (2007) (unpublished) (applying rule in case involving negotiated guilty plea after earlier negotiated guilty plea was set aside).

Exceptions to G.S. 15A-1335 exist, however. The statute does not:

- Apply to de novo appeals from district court to superior court. *State v. Burbank*, 59 N.C. App. 543, 547 (1982) ("the possibility of a more severe sentence being imposed is a risk inherent to this type of review"). *But cf.* 1 NORTH CAROLINA DEFENDER MANUAL § 10.7B (Misdemeanor Appeals from District Court) (Oct. 2010) (discussing limits on filing of more serious charges on appeal for a trial de novo).

- Bar a more severe sentence when that sentence is statutorily mandated by the General Assembly. *See State v. Kirkpatrick*, 89 N.C. App. 353 (1988) (judge was required to increase defendant's sentence from three to fifteen years on resentencing because the habitual felon statute required it); *State v. Williams*, 74 N.C. App. 728 (1985) (imposition of fourteen-year sentence for armed robbery was proper even though it was two years more than defendant had originally received because the judge imposed the statutory mandatory sentence and had no discretion to impose a lesser sentence).
- Prohibit a resentencing judge from consolidating the convictions in a manner different from the original judge so long as the total sentence is not greater than the original sentence. *State v. Moffitt*, 185 N.C. App. 308 (2007).
- Apply to sentences imposed after the State properly prays judgment on previously arrested convictions. *State v. Pakulski*, 106 N.C. App. 444, 452 (1992) (where first-degree felony murder conviction was overturned on appeal, trial judge could impose life sentence for armed robbery conviction that was predicate felony for murder and originally had been arrested; sentence did "not constitute a resentencing within the meaning of G.S. 15A-1335").
- Prohibit a resentencing judge from changing concurrent sentences to consecutive sentences "provided neither the individual sentences, nor the aggregate sentence, exceeds that imposed at the original sentencing hearing." *State v. Oliver*, 155 N.C. App. 209, 211 (2002); *see also State v. Ransom*, 80 N.C. App. 711 (1986).
- Prevent a resentencing judge from finding new or different aggravating or mitigating factors so long as the sentence is not more severe than the original sentence. *State v. Hemby*, 333 N.C. 331 (1993).

The following two circumstances may constitute significant additional exceptions to the bar in G.S. 15A-1335, but the law is unsettled.

Reinstatement of charges previously dismissed pursuant to a plea agreement. If the defendant is successful in having his or her guilty plea vacated on appeal or by collateral attack, any charges that had been dismissed by the State as part of a negotiated plea agreement could be reinstated. The Court of Appeals has held (albeit in an opinion without precedential value) that G.S. 15A-1335 does not bar the imposition of a sentence on those reinstated charges since that statute only applies to "conviction[s] or sentence[s] imposed in superior court [that] ha[ve] been set aside on direct review or collateral attack." *See State v. Williams*, 180 N.C. App. 477 (2006) (unpublished) (defendant improperly given a more severe sentence on a charge he had originally pled to but properly given a consecutive sentence on a charge that had been dismissed under the original plea agreement for which he was subsequently convicted). *But cf.* G.S. 15A-1335 (bar on greater sentence applies to the same offense or "a different offense based on the same conduct").

Reinstatement of and sentencing on greater offense following vacation of negotiated plea to lesser offense. It is unsettled what the result would be under G.S. 15A-1335 if a defendant successfully obtains vacation of his or her guilty plea to a lesser included offense and then is convicted of the original greater offense. The language of the statute would appear to prohibit the imposition of a harsher sentence since it applies to a resentencing for "a different offense based on the same conduct." The issue, however, has not been squarely decided by the North Carolina appellate courts.

The N.C. Court of Appeals directly ruled on the issue in *State v. Rico*, No. COA10-1536 (Dec. 6, 2011), but the case was withdrawn one week later. In *Rico*, the defendant and the State had entered into a plea agreement whereby the defendant would plead guilty to voluntary manslaughter and admit the existence of the aggravating factor that he used a deadly weapon at the time of the alleged crime in exchange for the State's dismissal of the first degree murder charge. Under the plea agreement, the defendant was to receive a specified active sentence in the aggravated range. Almost a year after the defendant pled guilty, he filed a motion for appropriate relief seeking relief from the judgment. The judge hearing the MAR amended the original judgment in an attempt to correct procedural errors and ultimately denied the remainder of the allegations. [The specific allegations and rulings on procedural errors are not detailed here since they are not relevant to this discussion.] The Court of Appeals found, among other things, that the defendant's plea agreement had to be set aside, holding that it was improper under the facts of the case to use the aggravating factor that "defendant used a deadly weapon at the time of the crime" to elevate the defendant's sentence because it also was an element of the offense of voluntary manslaughter. Concerned that a post-conviction motion could be made and ruled on years after a conviction, thereby possibly depriving the State of evidence or witnesses, the court held that the State, on remand, could choose to (1) re-indict the defendant on the greater offense that had been dismissed in exchange for his plea to a lesser offense and to an aggravated sentence; or (2) have the defendant resentenced on his guilty plea to the lesser offense. The court noted that regardless of which choice the State elected to make, G.S. 15A-1335 would apply to prohibit a more severe sentence on remand.

The Court of Appeals filed its new opinion in the case the following month. *State v. Rico*, ___ N.C. App. ___, 720 S.E.2d 801 (2012), *writ of supersedeas and motion for temporary stay allowed*, ___ N.C. ___, 721 S.E.2d 229 (2012). In that opinion, the court removed the language from its earlier decision finding that the plea agreement must be set aside as well as the language dealing with the consequences that would have ensued in that event. The court instead found that there was a mistake in a material portion of the plea agreement because the agreement erroneously required the defendant to admit to the existence of the aggravating factor that was an element of the offense. The court held the plea agreement should not be set aside because the defendant had fully performed his part under the plea agreement and it would be inequitable to release the State from its obligations under the agreement. According to the court, the State bears a higher degree of responsibility for the contents of a plea agreement since it should be well cognizant of the law. The court then vacated the judgment and the order denying the defendant's motion for appropriate relief and remanded the case for resentencing on the defendant's guilty plea to voluntary manslaughter.

The N.C. Supreme Court has granted the State's petition for writ of supersedeas pending its review of the N.C. Court of Appeals' decision. Thus, it remains an open question for the time being as to how G.S. 15A-1335 will be interpreted with regard to the imposition of a more severe sentence based on a greater offense after a defendant has successfully attacked a guilty plea to a lesser included offense.

Practice note: Great care must be taken when advising a client who is considering an attack on a guilty plea to a lesser included offense, as the law remains unsettled. If the N.C. appellate courts ultimately conclude that G.S. 15A-1335 is inapplicable, a defendant who pleads guilty to a lesser included offense and then seeks to have it vacated may be subjecting himself or herself to re-prosecution on the greater offense and imposition of a more severe sentence. As a matter of federal constitutional law, if a defendant undoes the plea, no presumption of vindictiveness applies to protect against a harsher sentence. *See Alabama v. Smith*, 490 U.S. 794 (1989). Counsel therefore should very explicitly explain the risks to a client who is seeking to undo a plea to a lesser charge.

For an annotation collecting and analyzing state and federal cases discussing whether a defendant may properly be tried on a greater charge after a successful attack on his or her guilty plea to a lesser charge, see Michael A. DiSabatino, Annotation, *Retrial on Greater Offense Following Reversal of Plea-based Conviction of Lesser Offense*, 14 A.L.R.4th 970 (2008).

C. Additional Resources

For further discussion of the topic covered in this section, see Jessica Smith, *Limitations on a Judge's Authority to Impose a More Severe Sentence after a Defendant's Successful Appeal or Collateral Attack*, ADMINISTRATION OF JUSTICE BULLETIN No. 2003/03 (UNC School of Government, July 2003), *available at* www.sog.unc.edu/sites/www.sog.unc.edu/files/aoj200303.pdf.

35.6 Trial Judges' Authority to Correct, Modify, or Amend Judgments

When errors in a judgment are discovered after the sentence has been pronounced, a party or the judge, sua sponte, may seek to correct them. Whether or not the trial judge may correct the error or modify, amend, or vacate the judgment depends on several variables, discussed below.

A. Changes to Judgment Made During Same Session of Court

Generally. A trial judge has the discretion to modify, amend, or set aside his or her judgment during the same session of court. *State v. Mead*, 184 N.C. App. 306 (2007), *aff'd*, 362 N.C. 218 (2008); *see also State v. Sammartino*, 120 N.C. App. 597, 600 (1995) (trial judge had authority to modify judgments to increase defendants' sentences because the original judgments and modified judgments were entered during the week of court assigned to the trial judge and "there had been no adjournment *sine die*"). This is true even if notice of appeal has been given. *State v. Davis*, 58 N.C. App. 330 (1982); *In re Tuttle*, 36 N.C. App. 222 (1978). During this time period the judgment is said to be in fieri, i.e., incomplete, not final. *See State v. Garris*, 191 N.C. App. 276 (2008).

Definition of "session." A "session of court" in superior court has been defined "as the time during which a court sits for business and refers to a typical one-week assignment of court." *Sammartino*, 120 N.C. App. 597, 599.

A district court session typically lasts one day. *See* Michael Crowell, *Out-of-Term, Out-of-Session, Out-of-County*, ADMINISTRATION OF JUSTICE BULLETIN No. 2008/05 (UNC School of Government, Nov. 2008), *available at* http://sogpubs.unc.edu/electronicversions/pdfs/aojb0805.pdf; *see also* Alyson Grine, *District Court is in Session . . . But for How Long?*, N.C. CRIM. L., UNC SCH. OF GOV'T BLOG (Nov. 20, 2009) (discussing multiday sessions in district court), http://sogweb.sog.unc.edu/blogs/ncclaw/?p=876.

A session of court may be extended by the trial judge if a trial is not completed by the close of that session of court. For further discussion of the extension of a session of court to complete a trial and to enter orders after session, see 1 NORTH CAROLINA DEFENDER MANUAL § 10.8D (Extending Session to Complete Trial) (Oct. 2010).

B. Changes to Judgment Made After Expiration of Court Session

Clerical errors. A trial judge may correct a clerical mistake regardless of whether the session of court has expired in order to make the record "speak the truth." *See, e.g., State v. Dixon*, 139 N.C. App. 332 (2000); *State v. Davis*, 123 N.C. App. 240 (1996). "Clerical error" has been defined as "'[a]n error resulting from a minor mistake or inadvertence, esp. in writing or copying something on the record, and not from judicial reasoning or determination.'" *State v. Jarman*, 140 N.C. App. 198, 202 (2000) (quoting BLACK'S LAW DICTIONARY 563 (7th ed. 1999), but not adopting the dictionary's definition). Although a judge is authorized to make the record correspond to the actual facts, he or she "cannot, under the guise of an amendment of its records, correct a judicial error [discussed below] or incorporate anything in the minutes except a recital of what actually occurred." *State v. Cannon*, 244 N.C. 399, 404 (1956).

If notice of appeal has been given, the trial judge may continue to correct clerical errors until the time that the record on appeal is filed in the appellate court. Once the record on appeal has been filed, the trial judge may only amend or correct its judgment if so directed by the appellate court. *Dixon*, 139 N.C. App. 332.

Non-clerical errors. A judge's authority to modify a judgment to correct a non-clerical, or "judicial error," is limited. After the session has concluded, a trial judge may make changes to his or her judgment and sentence within ten days if a proper motion for appropriate relief is made by the defendant pursuant to G.S. 15A-1414 or by the State pursuant to G.S. 15A-1416. After ten days, a judgment may be modified if a proper motion for appropriate relief is made by the defendant pursuant to G.S. 15A-1415. A trial judge, on his or her own motion, also may grant relief *to the defendant* if at any time the defendant would be entitled to relief by way of a MAR. *See* G.S. 15A-1420(d). A judge also may vacate a judgment on a defendant's application for habeas corpus. *See supra* § 35.4, State Habeas Corpus.

Illegal sentences. Although the general rule is that after a session of court has concluded a trial judge may not make modifications or changes to a judgment other than to correct clerical errors (absent authority conferred by the post-conviction MAR statutes or by way of a petition for habeas corpus), it appears that a judge has the authority to correct a judicial error when the error resulted in an illegal sentence. *See State v. Branch*, 134 N.C. App. 637 (1999) (trial judge, after notification by the Department of Correction that defendant's sentence was illegal as a matter of law, had the authority to correct an illegal judgment even though the session of court had ended and no motion for appropriate relief had been filed to correct the sentence); *State v. Bonds*, 45 N.C. App. 62, 64 (1980) (stating that after a session expires, North Carolina courts "have always had the authority" after a session expires to vacate judgments that are invalid as a matter of law "pursuant to petition for writ of habeas corpus and, more recently, by way of post conviction proceedings").

Additional resources. For further discussion of a trial judge's authority to modify a judgment to correct clerical and non-clerical errors, see Jessica Smith, *Trial Judge's Authority to* Sua Sponte *Correct Errors After Entry of Judgment in a Criminal Case*, ADMINISTRATION OF JUSTICE BULLETIN No. 2003/02 (UNC School of Government, May 2003), *available at* www.sog.unc.edu/sites/www.sog.unc.edu/files/aoj200302.pdf.

35.7 Extraordinary Writs

A. Mandamus

Generally. "A writ of mandamus is an extraordinary court order to 'a board, corporation, inferior court, officer or person commanding the performance of a specified official duty imposed by law.'" *In re T.H.T.*, 362 N.C. 446, 453 (2008) (citation omitted). The literal translation of the word "mandamus" is "We command." *Id.* (citing BLACK'S LAW DICTIONARY 980 (8th ed. 2004)).

Mandamus is a civil action and is the proper remedy when a trial judge fails or refuses to perform a particular duty that is required by law. *See* 52 AM. JUR. 2D *Mandamus* §1 (2000). Mandamus may be issued only to enforce established rights, not to create new ones. If there is another legally adequate remedy, such as an appeal, mandamus will not lie. *In re T.H.T.*, 362 N.C. 446.

The writ will be granted "only in case of necessity" and "will not issue to compel the performance of an act which a defendant shows a willingness to perform without coercion." *Sutton v. Figgatt*, 280 N.C. 89, 93 (1971) (writ of mandamus would not issue ordering a magistrate to examine plaintiffs under oath about their complaints that deputies had assaulted them because the magistrate announced in open court his readiness to perform this duty and waited several hours but plaintiffs never availed themselves of the opportunity).

Required elements. The following elements must be shown for a writ of mandamus to be issued:

1. The petitioner must demonstrate a clear legal right to the act requested.

2. The respondent must have a clear legal duty to perform the act requested and the duty must exist both at the time of application for the writ and at the time the court issues the writ.
3. The performance of the duty-bound act must be ministerial in nature and cannot involve the exercise of discretion. However, a court may issue a writ of mandamus to a public official compelling the official to make a discretionary decision as long as the court does not require a particular result.
4. The respondent must have failed or refused to perform the act requested, and the time for the performance of the act must have expired. Mandamus is not appropriate to reprimand an official, to redress a past wrong, or to prevent a future legal injury.
5. There must be no alternative, legally adequate remedy.

In re T.H.T., 362 N.C. 446, 453–54. If a petitioner shows all these elements, the court cannot refuse to issue a writ of mandamus. *Id.*

Who can issue. The N.C. Supreme Court and the N.C. Court of Appeals have jurisdiction, exercisable by one or more judges or justices, to issue a writ of mandamus "to supervise and control the proceedings" of inferior courts. G.S. 7A-32(b), (c). A superior court judge has no authority or jurisdiction to issue a writ of mandamus to a district court judge. *In re Redwine*, 312 N.C. 482 (1984). That power is reserved to the appellate courts. *Id.*; *see* N.C. CONST. art. IV, § 12(1), (2); G.S. 7A-32.

A petition for the writ should be directed to the appellate court to which an appeal of right might lie from a final judgment entered in the cause. N.C. R. APP. P. 22(a).

Procedural requirements. The procedures for filing a petition for writ of mandamus are set out in Rule 22 of the N.C. Rules of Appellate Procedure.

Selected examples. Mandamus has been found to be the proper remedy in the following instances:

- Where a trial judge refused to hold voluntary admissions hearings for juveniles residing in a state mental treatment facility. *State ex rel. Goff v. Wilkinson*, 302 N.C. 393 (1981).
- Where a trial judge failed to enter a timely order. *See In re T.H.T.*, 362 N.C. 446 (2008) (trial judge failed to adhere to the statutory time limit set in the Juvenile Code for entering a written order in an abuse and neglect case brought by the department of social services); *Stevens v. Guzman*, 140 N.C. App. 780 (2000) (trial judge failed to enter a written order denying the plaintiff's motions for a judgment notwithstanding the verdict and a new trial).

B. Prohibition

Generally. A writ of prohibition is a discretionary writ that issues to a lower court from a higher court having supervision and control to prevent the lower court from proceeding further in a pending matter. It is the opposite of a writ of mandamus. As its name indicates, it prohibits action instead of compelling action. *State v. Whitaker*, 114 N.C. 818 (1894).

The writ has been commonly defined as one that prevents a tribunal possessing judicial or quasi-judicial powers from exercising jurisdiction over matters that are not within its jurisdiction or from exceeding its legitimate powers. *See* 63C AM. JUR. 2D *Prohibition* §§ 1, 3 (2009). It is the proper remedy to seek when the jurisdiction of the trial court depends on a legal question rather than a factual question. 63C AM. JUR. 2D *Prohibition* § 3 (2009).

Like mandamus, prohibition will be denied if there is another remedy, such as appeal or certiorari. *See Whitaker*, 114 N.C. 818 (writ would not issue to prohibit mayor's court from hearing matter without a jury because the defendants had a right to appeal to superior court in the event they were convicted); *see also State v. Inman*, 224 N.C. 531 (1944); *Perry v. Shepherd*, 78 N.C. 83 (1878).

Required elements. The requirements that must be shown by a petitioner before a writ of prohibition will be issued are generally stated as follows:

1. that some judge, officer, or person is about to exercise judicial or quasi-judicial power;
2. that the power about to be exercised is unauthorized by law; and
3. if the power is exercised, it will result in an injury for which there is no other adequate remedy.

63C AM. JUR. 2D *Prohibition* § 8 (2009).

Who can issue. The N.C. Supreme Court and the N.C. Court of Appeals have jurisdiction, exercisable by one or more judges or justices, to issue a writ of prohibition "to supervise and control the proceedings" of inferior courts. G.S. 7A-32(b), (c). A superior court judge has no authority or jurisdiction to issue a writ of prohibition to a district court judge. *See Perry*, 78 N.C. 83. That power is reserved to the appellate courts. *See* N.C. CONST. art. IV, § 12(1), (2); G.S. 7A-32.

The petition for the writ should be directed to the appellate court to which an appeal of right might lie from a final judgment entered in the cause. N.C. R. APP. P. 22(a).

Procedural requirements. The procedures for filing a petition for writ of prohibition are set out in Rule 22 of the N.C. Rules of Appellate Procedure.

Selected examples. Prohibition has been found to be the proper remedy in the following instances:

- where a court, without any legal authority for doing so, granted a new trial at a subsequent term after the defendant was convicted of a felony;
- to prevent a lower court from exceeding its jurisdiction by attempting to execute a judgment when an appeal from that judgment had been noted to the superior court; and
- to preclude a probate court from exercising jurisdiction over a deceased person's estate when it could not do so lawfully.

See State v. Whitaker, 114 N.C. 818 (1894).

C. Supersedeas Pending Review of Decisions of the Trial Court

Generally. A writ of supersedeas is an extraordinary writ that issues from an appellate court to a lower court "to preserve the status quo pending the exercise of the appellate court's jurisdiction." *City of New Bern v. Walker*, 255 N.C. 355, 356 (1961). Supersedeas suspends the power of the lower court to issue an execution on the judgment or decree appealed from. 5 AM. JUR. 2D *Appellate Review* § 398 (2007).

The writ "is issued only to hold the matter in abeyance pending review, and may be issued only by the court in which an appeal is pending." *Walker*, 255 N.C. 355, 356; *see also* N.C. R. APP. P. 23(a) (an appeal or a petition for mandamus, prohibition, or certiorari must be pending in the appellate court where the application for writ of supersedeas is filed); *Craver v. Craver*, 298 N.C. 231, 237–38 (1979) ("The writ of supersedeas may issue only in the exercise of, and as ancillary to, the revising power of an appellate court . . . .").

Who can issue. The N.C. Supreme Court and the N.C. Court of Appeals have jurisdiction, exercisable by one or more judges or justices, to issue a writ of supersedeas "to supervise and control the proceedings" of inferior courts. G.S. 7A-32(b), (c); *see also* N.C. CONST. art. IV, § 12(1), (2). A petition for the writ should be made in the N.C. Court of Appeals in all cases except those originally docketed in the N.C. Supreme Court. N.C. R. APP. P. 23(a)(2).

Temporary stays. If a petition for supersedeas is filed, the applicant also may apply to the appellate court for an order temporarily staying the enforcement or execution of a trial court's judgment or order pending the appellate court's decision on the petition for supersedeas. N.C. R. APP. P. 23(e).

Procedural requirements. The procedures for filing a petition for writ of mandamus and motion for temporary stay are set out in Rule 23 of the N.C. Rules of Appellate Procedure.

Practice note: An application for writ of supersedeas would be appropriate if you want to stay the enforcement of any part of a trial court's judgment that is not automatically stayed pursuant to G.S. 15A-1451(a) after a defendant enters of notice of appeal (*see supra* § 35.1G, Stay of Superior Court Sentence), or to stay enforcement of a judgment while a petition for writ of certiorari is pending. A motion for temporary stay must be filed in the appellate court in order to stay the effect of a judgment immediately while the appellate court makes its decision on whether to grant the writ of supersedeas. When considering whether to file a petition for writ of supersedeas and motion for temporary stay, counsel should consult with the Office of the Appellate Defender on how to proceed and whether appellate counsel should be appointed to file the petition and motion.

D. Certiorari of Trial Court Orders and Judgments

Generally. A writ of certiorari is "an extraordinary remedial writ to correct errors of law." *State v. Simmington*, 235 N.C. 612, 613 (1952). It issues from a higher court to a lower court, and it lies only to review judicial or quasi-judicial action to determine the action's validity and to correct errors therein. *State v. Roux*, 263 N.C. 149, 153 (1964).

A petition for writ of certiorari must show merit or that error was probably committed below. The writ is discretionary and will issue only if the petitioner can show good and sufficient cause. *State v. Grundler*, 251 N.C. 177, 189 (1959).

Who can issue. The N.C. Supreme Court and the N.C. Court of Appeals have jurisdiction, exercisable by one or more judges or justices, to issue a writ of certiorari "to supervise and control the proceedings" of inferior courts. G.S. 7A-32(b), (c); *see also* N.C. CONST. art. IV, § 12(1), (2). A petition for the writ should be filed in the court to which an appeal of right might lie from a final judgment in the cause. N.C. R. APP. P. 21(b).

The superior court also has jurisdiction to issue a writ of certiorari to review district court proceedings pursuant to Rule 19 of the General Rules of Practice for the Superior and District Courts. The authority of a superior court to grant a writ of certiorari under Practice Rule 19 is analogous to the power of the appellate court to issue a writ of certiorari pursuant to Rule 21 of the N.C. Rules of Appellate Procedure. *State v. Hamrick*, 110 N.C. App. 60 (1993).

When authorized. Rule 21 of the N.C. Rules of Appellate Procedure authorizes a writ of certiorari to be issued by the appellate division in appropriate circumstances to review judgments and orders of trial tribunals in three situations only:

1. where the right to appeal has been lost by the failure to take timely action;
2. when no right to appeal from an interlocutory order exists; or
3. to review a trial judge's denial of a motion for appropriate relief under G.S. 15A-1422(c)(3).

See N.C. R. APP. P. 21(a)(1).

G.S. 15A-1444(e) purports to allow a defendant to petition for a writ of certiorari after pleading guilty; however, the N.C. appellate courts have held that they are limited to granting certiorari in the three circumstances set out above in Appellate Rule 21 (and the additional circumstance described below). *See State v. Pimental*, 153 N.C. App. 69 (2002) (holding that the court did not have the authority to issue a writ of certiorari to review defendant's arguments because he had no right to appeal and his case did not fall into one of the categories listed in Appellate Rule 21; court stated that appellate rules prevail over the general statutes when there is a conflict); *see also State v. Smith*, 193 N.C. App. 739 (2008) (finding that the defendant, after pleading guilty, did not have the right to appeal the denial of his motion to dismiss his habitual felon indictment and the court did not have the authority to grant certiorari review under Appellate Rule 21).

The N.C. Supreme Court also has recognized a fourth instance in which a defendant may petition for a writ of certiorari—when challenging guilty plea procedures. For a discussion of that topic, *see supra* § 35.1D, Defendant's Right to Appeal from Guilty Plea in Superior Court: Writ of Certiorari.

It is not clear whether the limits applicable to writs of certiorari in the appellate division would apply to writs of certiorari by the superior court to review district court judgments and orders, which are governed by Rule 19 of the General Rules of Practice for the Superior and District Courts. Rule 19 does not specify such limits, and they may or may not apply by analogy. *See generally State v. Hamrick*, 110 N.C. App. 60 (1993) (finding that superior court properly granted State's petition for writ of certiorari to review a district court judge's order dismissing the defendant's case based on double jeopardy where State had lost its right to appeal under G.S. 15A-1432 through its failure to file notice of appeal in a proper manner).

Procedural requirements. The procedures for filing a petition for writ of certiorari in the appellate courts are set out in Rule 21 of the N.C. Rules of Appellate Procedure. The procedures for filing a petition for writ of certiorari in the superior court are set out in Rule 19 of the General Rules of Practice for the Superior and District Courts.

35.8 Innocence Inquiry Commission

A. In General

In 2006, the General Assembly added Article 92 to Chapter 15A, creating the North Carolina Innocence Inquiry Commission and establishing "an extraordinary procedure to investigate and determine credible claims of factual innocence." G.S. 15A-1461. North Carolina is the first state in the nation to create this type of commission.

According to its website, www.innocencecommission-nc.gov/about.html, the Commission "is charged with providing an independent and balanced truth-seeking forum for credible post-conviction claims of innocence in North Carolina." In essence, Article 92 authorizes the Commission to investigate claims of innocence and refer meritorious cases to a special three-judge panel appointed by the Chief Justice of the N.C. Supreme Court. G.S. 15A-1469(a). If, after an evidentiary hearing, the panel unanimously finds that the convicted person has proved by clear and convincing evidence that he or she is innocent of the charges, it is required to dismiss the charges. G.S. 15A-1469(h). Its decision is final and is not subject to any further review. G.S. 15A-1470(a); *see also About Us*, NORTH CAROLINA INNOCENCE INQUIRY COMMISSION, www.innocencecommission-nc.gov/about.html (last visited Dec. 15, 2011) ("A person exonerated by the Commission process is declared innocent and cannot be retried for the same crime."). The Commission is to give priority to cases in which the convicted person is currently incarcerated solely for the crime for which he or she has filed a claim of innocence. G.S. 15A-1466(2).

B. Structure of the Innocence Commission

The North Carolina Innocence Inquiry Commission is an independent commission within the Judicial Department and receives administrative support from the Administrative Office of the Courts. G.S. 15A-1462. It consists of eight members—a superior court judge, who serves as chair; a prosecutor; a victim advocate; a criminal defense attorney; a public member who is neither an attorney nor an employee of the Judicial Department; a sheriff currently holding office at the time of appointment; and two members whose vocations are within the discretion of the Chief Justice of the N.C. Supreme Court. The Chief Justice appoints five members as specified in the act, and the Chief Judge of the N.C. Court of Appeals appoints three members. G.S. 15A-1463(a). The Director of the Commission must be a North Carolina attorney, and he or she may hire staff with the approval of the Commission Chair. G.S. 15A-1465. For more details regarding the method of appointment of Commission members, their terms, and the duties of the director, see G.S. 15A-1463 through 15A-1465.

C. Meaning of "Claim of Factual Innocence"

The Commission is authorized to consider "claims of factual innocence," as defined in G.S. 15A-1460(1). To qualify, a claim must be

- on behalf of a living person
- convicted of a felony in the North Carolina trial courts
- asserting complete innocence for the felony for which the person was convicted and for any reduced level of criminal responsibility relating to the crime
- for which there is some credible, verifiable evidence of innocence
- that has not been presented at trial or considered at a hearing granted through post-conviction relief.

The last element of the definition requires that evidence supporting the claim be "new" in a limited sense. Thus, it requires that "some" evidence be submitted in support of the claim that was not previously presented, but all of the evidence need not meet this requirement. *See also* Superior Court Judge Calvin E. Murphy, *Innocence Inquiry Commission Update* 3 (N.C. Superior Court Judges' Conference, June 2010) ("The 'new evidence' standard is merely a threshold that, once crossed, allows the panel to hear all relevant evidence of the Claimant's actual innocence."), *available at* www.sog.unc.edu/sites/www.sog.unc.edu/files/Murphy_InnocenceInquiryCommissionUpdate.pdf. The definition does not require the claimant to have been unaware of the evidence or to have been unable to obtain the evidence at the time of trial; it only requires that the evidence not have been presented at a trial or at a hearing granted through post-conviction relief. Evidence is not considered to have been previously presented in post-conviction proceedings if it was presented in support of a post-conviction request for which a hearing was not granted. *See* John Rubin, *2006 Legislation Affecting Criminal Law and Procedure*, ADMINISTRATION OF JUSTICE BULLETIN No. 2007/03, at 10 (UNC School of Government, Jan. 2007) (so interpreting last element of definition of claim of factual innocence, which provides that evidence must not have been "considered at a hearing granted through postconviction relief"), *available at* http://sogpubs.unc.edu/electronicversions/pdfs/aojb0703.pdf.

D. Submission of Claim and Waiver of Rights

Any person, court, or agency may submit a claim of innocence to the Commission on behalf of a convicted person. The Commission may informally screen and dismiss a case summarily or undertake a formal inquiry. G.S. 15A-1467(a). Before the Commission begins a formal inquiry, the convicted person must execute an agreement waiving his or her procedural safeguards and privileges and agreeing to provide full disclosure to the Commission on matters related to his or her claim of innocence. The waiver does not apply to matters unrelated to the claim. G.S. 15A-1467(b). However, evidence of criminal acts, professional misconduct, or other wrongdoing disclosed during the formal inquiry or later Commission proceedings are referred to the appropriate authority. Evidence favorable to the convicted person disclosed through the formal inquiry or later Commission proceedings also must be disclosed to the convicted person and his or her counsel. G.S. 15A-1468(d). If at any point during the inquiry, the convicted person refuses to comply with the Commission's requests or is otherwise deemed to be uncooperative, the Commission may discontinue the inquiry. G.S. 15A-1467(g).

E. Right to Counsel

The convicted person has the right to advice of counsel before executing a waiver of rights and, if a formal inquiry is conducted, throughout the formal inquiry. If the convicted person does not have counsel, the Commission Chair must determine whether the person is indigent and, if appropriate, enter an order for the appointment of counsel. G.S. 15A-1467(b); *see also* G.S. 15A-1469(e) (indigent person has right to appointed counsel in proceedings before three-judge panel).

For a discussion of appointed counsel's role, see memoranda prepared by the Office of Indigent Defense Services (IDS) and the North Carolina Center on Actual Innocence (a different organization than the Innocence Commission), a part of a collection of materials compiled by IDS. *See* INNOCENCE INQUIRY PROCEEDINGS MANUAL, www.ncids.org/Other%20Manuals/Innocence%20Inquiry/Innocence%20Inquiry%20Links.htm.

F. Notice to Victim

If the Commission proceeds with a formal inquiry, the Director must use due diligence to notify the victim in the case and explain the process. The victim has the right to present his or her views and concerns throughout the Commission's investigation. G.S. 15A-1467(c). The victim also has the right to notice of any proceedings before the full Commission, discussed below, and to attend Commission proceedings subject to limitations imposed by the Commission. G.S. 15A-1468(b); *see also* G.S. 15A-1469(f) (victim receives notice of hearing before three-judge panel).

G. Access to Evidence

The Commission has the power to issue process to compel the attendance of witnesses and production of evidence, administer oaths, and petition the superior court of Wake County or of the original jurisdiction for enforcement of process or other relief. G.S. 15A-1467(d), (e). In addition, all state discovery and disclosure statutes in effect at the time of the inquiry are enforceable as if the convicted person were being tried for the charge being investigated by the Commission. G.S. 15A-1467(f).

Practice note: In 2009, the General Assembly added an immunity provision for witnesses who provide information in proceedings before the Commission. *See* G.S. 15A-1468(a1). Counsel representing a witness in Commission proceedings should be aware that the immunity afforded by this provision is limited and may not fully protect a witness from criminal prosecution for information he or she provides. Counsel should so advise the witness and, if the Commission directs the witness to provide information that could be self-incriminating, should take appropriate steps to protect the witness. *See* John Rubin, *2009 Legislation Affecting Criminal Law and Procedure*, ADMINISTRATION OF JUSTICE BULLETIN No. 2009/09, at 39–40 (UNC School of Government, Dec. 2009) (discussing alternatives that counsel for a witness may take to ensure that the witness has adequate immunity from future prosecution), *available at* http://sogpubs.unc.edu/electronicversions/pdfs/aojb0909.pdf.

H. Commission Proceedings

G.S. 15A-1468 details the procedures before the Commission once the formal inquiry is completed. All relevant evidence from the inquiry must be presented to the full Commission, which may hold a public hearing or keep the proceedings closed. G.S. 15A-1468(a). After reviewing the evidence, the Commission votes on whether to refer the case for review by a three-judge panel. In cases in which the convicted person did not plead guilty, five or more Commission members must find sufficient evidence of innocence for the case to be referred for judicial review. In cases in which the convicted person pled guilty, all eight Commission members must find sufficient evidence of innocence. G.S. 15A-1468(c). The Commission must issue an opinion, whether it finds sufficient or insufficient evidence of innocence. If a case is referred to a three-judge panel, all of the records in support of the Commission's conclusion, including a transcript of the hearing before the Commission, become public; if the case is not referred for judicial review, the files remain confidential except as the statute otherwise provides. G.S. 15A-1468(e).

I. Review by Three-Judge Panel

G.S. 15A-1469 details the procedures before the three-judge panel. If the Commission concludes that there is sufficient evidence of innocence to merit judicial review, the Chief Justice appoints a three-judge panel to conduct an evidentiary hearing. The panel may not include any trial judge who has had substantial previous involvement in the case. Following an order setting a date for a hearing, the State has ninety days to file a response to the Commission's opinion. The district attorney of the district of conviction, or his or her designee, represents the State at the hearing. The panel may compel the testimony of any witness, including the convicted person. The convicted person has the right to be present but may not assert any privilege or prevent any witness from testifying. If the three-judge panel unanimously finds by clear and convincing evidence that the convicted person is innocent of the charges, it enters a dismissal of the charges. If the vote is not unanimous, the panel denies relief.

J. Finality of Proceedings and Availability of Other Relief

The decisions of the Commission and the three-judge panel are final and are not subject to review. G.S. 15A-1470(a). Submission of a claim to the Commission does not adversely affect the right to other post-conviction relief. G.S. 15A-1470(b); G.S. 15A-1411(d) (claim to Commission does not constitute motion for appropriate relief and does not affect right to relief under post-conviction statutes). G.S. 15A-1417(a) provides that a court may, in ruling on a motion for appropriate relief, refer a claim of factual innocence to the Commission; but, the statute does not permit the court to defer claims to the Commission based on other grounds for post-conviction relief, such as a constitutional violation.

K. Additional Resources

For additional information about Innocence Commission proceedings, see

- North Carolina Innocence Inquiry Commission website, www.innocencecommission-nc.gov, which includes the Commission's rules, a case flowchart, and other resources.
- INNOCENCE INQUIRY PROCEEDINGS MANUAL, www.ncids.org/Other%20Manuals/Innocence%20Inquiry/Innocence%20Inquiry%20Links.htm, which includes memoranda on counsel's responsibilities in Commission proceedings and other resources.
- John Rubin, *2006 Legislation Affecting Criminal Law and Procedure*, ADMINISTRATION OF JUSTICE BULLETIN No. 2007/03, at 10–11 (UNC School of Government, Jan. 2007) (summarizing the legislation that created the Innocence Commission), *available at* http://sogpubs.unc.edu/electronicversions/pdfs/aojb0703.pdf.
- John Rubin, *2009 Legislation Affecting Criminal Law and Procedure*, ADMINISTRATION OF JUSTICE BULLETIN No. 2009/09, at 39–40 (UNC School of Government, Dec. 2009) (summarizing amendments to the Innocence Commission statutes that create limited immunity for witnesses), *available at* http://sogpubs.unc.edu/electronicversions/pdfs/aojb0909.pdf.

North Carolina Commission on Indigent Defense Services

Performance Guidelines for Indigent Defense Representation in Non-Capital Criminal Cases at the Trial Level

Adopted November 12, 2004

North Carolina Commission on Indigent Defense Services

Performance Guidelines for Indigent Defense Representation in Non-Capital Criminal Cases at the Trial Level

Preface

The primary goal of the Commission on Indigent Defense Services ("IDS Commission") is to ensure that indigent defendants in North Carolina are afforded high quality legal representation. *See* G.S. 7A-498.1(2). To further that goal, the Indigent Defense Services Act of 2000 directs the Commission to establish "[s]tandards for the performance of public defenders and appointed counsel." G.S. 7A-498.5(c)(4).

These performance guidelines are based largely on the "Performance Guidelines for Criminal Defense Representation" that have been promulgated by the National Legal Aid and Defender Association, as well as a review of standards and guidelines in several other jurisdictions, including Connecticut, Kansas, Massachusetts, New Mexico, New York City, Oregon, and Washington. Over a period of several months, a Committee of the IDS Commission reviewed a draft of these guidelines and revised them to fit the nuances of North Carolina law and practice. Initial proposed guidelines were then sent to 70 public and private defense attorneys around the state, with a request that they provide feedback. Based on the comments that were received, the Committee made a number of changes to that earlier draft. In August 2004, the revised guidelines were mailed to all public defenders and assistant public defenders, more than 2,000 private defense attorneys, all active district and superior court judges, and all elected district attorneys for comments. Again, based on the comments that were received, the Committee made a number of improvements to the guidelines. The full IDS Commission then adopted the attached performance guidelines on November 12, 2004.

These performance guidelines cover all indigent adult non-capital criminal cases in district and superior court. The guidelines are intended to identify issues that may arise at each stage of a criminal proceeding, and to recommend effective approaches to resolving those issues. Because all provisions will not be applicable in all cases, the guidelines direct counsel to use his or her best professional judgment in determining what steps to undertake in specific cases. The Commission hopes these guidelines will be useful as a training tool and resource for new and experienced defense attorneys, as well as a tool for potential systemic reform in some areas. The guidelines are not intended to serve as a benchmark for ineffective assistance of counsel claims or attorney disciplinary proceedings.

The IDS Commission believes that providing high quality criminal defense representation is a difficult and challenging endeavor, which requires great skill and dedication. That skill and dedication is demonstrated by defense counsel across North Carolina on a daily basis, and the Commission commends those counsel. The Commission recognizes that the goals embodied in these guidelines will not be attainable without sufficient funding and resources, and hopes the North Carolina General Assembly will continue its support of quality indigent defense services.

The IDS Commission thanks all of the defense attorneys who zealously represent indigent defendants across the state. In addition, the Commission thanks everyone who worked on the drafting of these performance guidelines and who offered comments. The Commission plans to review and revise the guidelines on a regular basis to ensure that they continue to comply with North Carolina law and reflect quality performance, and invites ongoing feedback from the defense bar and criminal justice community.

North Carolina Commission on Indigent Defense Services

Performance Guidelines for Indigent Defense Representation in Non-Capital Criminal Cases at the Trial Level

SECTION 1:

Guideline 1.1 Function of Performance Guidelines

(a) The Commission on Indigent Defense Services hereby adopts these performance guidelines to promote one of the purposes of the Indigent Defense Services Act of 2000—improving the quality of indigent defense representation in North Carolina—and pursuant to G.S. 7A-498.5(c)(4).

(b) These guidelines are intended to serve as a guide for attorney performance in non-capital criminal cases at the trial level, and contain a set of considerations and recommendations to assist counsel in providing quality representation for indigent criminal defendants. The guidelines also may be used as a training tool.

(c) These are performance guidelines, not standards. The steps covered in these guidelines are not to be undertaken automatically in every case. Instead, the steps actually taken should be tailored to the requirements of a particular case. In deciding what steps are appropriate, counsel should use his or her best professional judgment.

Guideline 1.2 Role of Defense Counsel

(a) The paramount obligations of criminal defense counsel are to provide zealous and quality representation to their clients at all stages of the criminal process, and to preserve, protect, and promote their clients' rights and interests throughout the criminal proceedings. Attorneys also have an obligation to conduct themselves professionally, abide by the Revised Rules of Professional Conduct of the North Carolina State Bar and other ethical norms, and act in accordance with all rules of court.

(b) Defense counsel are the professional representatives of their clients. Counsel should candidly advise clients regarding the probable success and consequences of adopting any posture in the proceedings, and provide clients with all information necessary to make informed decisions. Counsel does not have an obligation to execute any directive of a client that does not comport with law or standards of ethics or professional conduct.

Guideline 1.3 Education, Training and Experience of Defense Counsel

(a) To provide quality representation, counsel must be familiar with the substantive criminal law and the law of criminal procedure and its application in North Carolina. Counsel should also be informed of any applicable local rules, including those set forth in the district's case docketing plan, as well as the practices of the specific judge before whom a case is pending.

(b) Counsel has an ongoing obligation to stay abreast of changes and developments in criminal law and procedure, and to continue his or her legal education, skills training, and professional development.

(c) Prior to accepting appointment to an indigent criminal matter, counsel should have sufficient experience, skills, training, and supervision to provide quality representation. Where appropriate to provide competent representation, counsel should consult with more experienced attorneys to acquire necessary knowledge and information, including information about the practices of judges, prosecutors, and other court personnel.

Guideline 1.4 General Duties of Defense Counsel

(a) Before accepting appointment to an indigent criminal case, an attorney has an obligation to ensure that he or she has available sufficient time, resources, knowledge, and experience to afford quality representation to a defendant in a particular matter. If it later appears that counsel is unable to afford quality representation in the case, counsel should move to withdraw. If counsel is allowed to withdraw, he or she should cooperate with new counsel to the extent that such cooperation is in the best interests of the client and in accord with the Revised Rules of Professional Conduct.

(b) Counsel must be alert to all actual and potential conflicts of interest that would impair their ability to represent a client. If counsel identifies an actual conflict of interest, counsel should immediately move to withdraw. If counsel identifies a potential conflict of interest, counsel should fully disclose the conflict to all affected clients and, if appropriate, obtain informed consent to proceed on behalf of those clients. Where appropriate, counsel may seek an advisory opinion on any potential conflicts from the North Carolina State Bar. Mere tactical disagreements between counsel and a client ordinarily do not justify withdrawal from a case. If it is necessary for counsel to withdraw, counsel should do so in a way that protects the client's rights and interests, and does not violate counsel's ethical duties to the client.

(c) Counsel has an obligation to maintain regular contact with the client and keep the client informed of the progress of the case. Counsel should promptly comply with a client's reasonable requests for information, and reply to client correspondence and telephone calls.

(d) Counsel should appear on time for all scheduled court hearings in a client's case. If scheduling conflicts arise, counsel should resolve them in accordance with Rule 3.1 of the General Rules of Practice.

(e) Counsel should never give preference to retained clients over appointed clients, or suggest that retained clients should or would receive preference.

SECTION 2:

Guideline 2.1 General Obligations of Counsel Regarding Pretrial Release

Where appropriate, counsel has an obligation to attempt to secure the prompt pretrial release of the client under the conditions most favorable to the client.

Guideline 2.2 Initial Interview

(a) Counsel shall arrange for an initial interview with the client as soon as practicable after being assigned to the client's case. Absent exceptional circumstances, if the client is in custody, the initial interview should take place within three business days after counsel receives notice of assignment to the client's case. If necessary, counsel may arrange for a designee to conduct the initial interview.

(b) *Preparation:*

Prior to conducting the initial interview, the attorney should, where possible:

(1) be familiar with the charges against the client, as well as the elements and potential punishment of each charged offense;

(2) obtain copies of any relevant documents that are available, including copies of any charging documents, recommendations and reports made by pretrial service or detention agencies concerning pretrial release, and law enforcement reports;

(3) be familiar with the legal criteria for determining pretrial release conditions and the procedures that will be followed in setting those conditions;

(4) be familiar with the different types of pretrial release conditions the court may set, as well as any written policies of the judicial district, and whether any pretrial service or other agencies are available to act as a custodian for the client's release; and

(5) be familiar with any procedures available for reviewing the trial judge's setting of bail.

(c) *The Interview:*

(1) The purpose of the initial interview is to acquire information from the client concerning pretrial release and, where appropriate, the facts of the case, and to provide the client with information concerning the case. Counsel should try to ensure at this and all successive interviews and proceedings that barriers to communication, such as differences in language or literacy, be overcome. If appropriate, counsel should file a motion to have a foreign language or sign language interpreter appointed by the court and present at the initial interview.

(2) Information that should be acquired during the initial interview includes, but is not limited to:

(A) the client's ties to the community, including the length of time he or she has lived at the current and former addresses, family relationships, employment record and history, and immigration status (if applicable);

(B) the client's physical and mental health, including any impairing conditions such as substance abuse or learning disabilities, and educational and armed services history;

(C) the client's immediate medical and/or mental health needs;

(D) the client's past criminal history, if any, including arrests and convictions for adult and juvenile offenses and prior history of court appearances or failure to appear in court;

(E) the existence of any other pending charges against the client and the identity of any other appointed or retained counsel;

(F) whether the client is on probation or parole, and the client's past or present performance under supervision;

(G) the ability of the client to meet any financial conditions of release; and

(H) the names of individuals or other sources that counsel can contact to verify the information provided by the client, and the permission of the client to contact those individuals.

(3) Information to be provided to the client during the initial interview includes, but is not limited to:

(A) an explanation of the procedures that will be followed in setting the conditions of pretrial release;

(B) an explanation of the type of information that will be requested in any interview that may be conducted by a pretrial release agency, and an explanation that the client is not required to and should not make statements concerning the offense;

(C) an explanation of the attorney-client privilege and instructions not to talk to anyone about the facts of the case without first consulting the attorney;

(D) the nature of the charges and potential penalties;

(E) a general procedural overview of the progression of the case, where possible;

(F) how counsel can be reached and when counsel plans to have contact with the client next;

(G) realistic answers, where possible, to the client's most urgent questions; and

(H) what arrangements will be made or attempted for the satisfaction of the client's most pressing needs, such as medical or mental health attention, and contact with family members.

(4) Where appropriate, counsel should be prepared at the initial interview to ask the client to sign a release authorizing counsel to access confidential information.

(d) *Additional Information*

Whenever possible, counsel should use the initial interview to gather additional information relevant to preparation of the defense. Such information may include, but is not limited to:

(1) the facts surrounding the charges against the client and the client's view of any potential defenses;

(2) any evidence of improper police investigative practices or prosecutorial conduct that may affect the client's rights;

(3) any possible witnesses who should be located;

(4) any evidence that should be preserved; and

(5) where appropriate, evidence of the client's competence to stand trial and/or mental state at the time of the offense.

Guideline 2.3 Pretrial Release Proceedings in Misdemeanor and Felony Cases

(a) As soon as possible after appointment, where the client has not been able to obtain pretrial release, counsel should consider filing a motion to reduce bond or otherwise modify any pretrial release conditions that were set by the magistrate or other judicial official at the client's initial appearance.

(b) Counsel should be prepared to present to the appropriate judicial official a statement of the factual circumstances and the legal criteria supporting release and, where appropriate, to make a proposal concerning conditions of release. Counsel should consider the potential consequences of allowing the client to make statements at any bond reduction hearing.

(c) In counties with a pretrial service program, counsel should consider utilizing the services of that program where it would be likely to benefit the client.

(d) Counsel should fully inform the client of his or her conditions of release after such conditions have been set by the court.

(e) If the court sets conditions of release that require the posting of a monetary bond or the posting of real property as collateral for release, counsel should be familiar with and explain to the client the available options and the procedures that must be followed in posting such assets. Where appropriate, counsel should advise the client and others acting in his or her behalf how properly to post such assets.

(f) Where the client is incarcerated and unable to obtain pretrial release, counsel should alert the jail, and if appropriate the court, to any special medical or psychiatric and security needs of the client that are known to counsel.

Guideline 2.4 Probable Cause Hearing in Felony Cases

(a) Counsel should discuss with the client the meaning of probable cause and the procedural aspects surrounding a probable cause determination, and should consider the tactical advantages and disadvantages of having a probable cause hearing. Counsel should consider any concessions the prosecution might make if the defendant waives, or does not oppose a continuance of, a probable cause hearing. Before waiving a probable cause hearing, counsel should consider the possible benefits of a hearing, including the potential for discovery and the development of impeachment evidence. Counsel also should be aware of all consequences if the client waives a probable cause hearing, including the effect of waiver on the statutory deadline for requesting voluntary discovery under G.S. 15A-902(d).

(b) In preparing for a probable cause hearing, counsel should consider:

(1) the elements of each of the offenses alleged;

(2) the law for establishing probable cause;

(3) factual information that is available concerning the existence or lack of probable cause;

(4) the tactics of full or partial cross-examination;

(5) additional factual information and impeachment evidence that could be discovered by counsel during the hearing; and

(6) any continuing need to pursue modification of the conditions of release if the client is in custody.

Counsel ordinarily should not call the client or defense witnesses to testify at the probable cause hearing unless there are sound tactical reasons for doing so.

Guideline 2.5 Charging Language in Criminal Pleadings

(a) Counsel should review the criminal pleadings in all cases and, unless there are sound tactical reasons for not doing so, move to dismiss the pleading if there are defects in the charging language, including but not limited to:

(1) the pleading does not list all of the essential elements of the charged offense; and

(2) the pleading contains more than one charge in a single count.

(b) Even if the pleading adequately charges a crime, counsel should be sufficiently familiar with the language of the pleading to recognize a fatal variance at trial and move to dismiss the charge if the evidence is insufficient to support the charge as pled.

(c) Counsel should be aware of all time limits applicable to challenges to defects in the charging language of a criminal pleading. Counsel also should be aware of the potential consequences of alerting the prosecution to defects in the charging language.

Guideline 2.6 Indictments and Bills of Information in Felony Cases

(a) Upon return of a bill of indictment, unless there are sound tactical reasons for not doing so, counsel should consider any potential grounds for quashing the indictment or challenges to the grand jury proceedings, including, but not limited to:

(1) improper composition of the grand jury as a whole, including any systematic exclusion of qualified persons either in the drawing of the list of potential grand jurors or the selecting of grand jurors from the list;

(2) the inclusion of a grand juror who does not meet the requirements of G.S. 9-3;

(3) the bill of indictment lacks the signatures and markings required by G.S. 15A-644;

(4) the bill of indictment was not found to be true by at least twelve grand jurors and/or was not returned in open court; and

(5) the bill of indictment was based entirely on the testimony of witnesses who were disqualified or evidence that is incompetent.

(b) Counsel should be aware of all time limits applicable to motions to quash the indictment or challenges to the grand jury proceedings.

(c) Where applicable, counsel should consider, and inform the client of, the advantages and disadvantages of waiving a bill of indictment and consenting to a bill of information pursuant to G.S. 15A-642 and G.S. 15A-923.

Guideline 2.7 Arraignment in Felony Cases

Counsel should consider whether to request arraignment under G.S. 15A-941(d). Counsel should be aware that some pretrial motions may be waived if they are not filed at or before arraignment (or within the time limit prescribed by G.S. 15A-952 if arraignment is waived), including a motion to continue, motion challenging venue or for change of venue, motion to join or sever offenses, motion challenging grand jury composition, motion for a bill of particulars, and motion challenging non-jurisdictional pleading defects. Counsel should also consult local calendaring rules to determine whether they establish different deadlines for pretrial motions.

SECTION 3:

Guideline 3.1 Search Warrants and Prosecution Requests for Non-Testimonial Evidence

(a) Counsel should be familiar with the law governing search warrants under G.S. 15A-241 *et seq.* and applicable case law, including, but not limited to, the requirements for a search warrant application, the basis for issuing a search warrant, the required form and content of a search warrant, the execution and service of a search warrant, and the permissible scope of the search.

(b) Counsel should be familiar with the law governing the prosecution's power to require a defendant to provide non-testimonial evidence (such as participation in an in-person lineup, handwriting exemplars, and physical specimens), the potential consequences if a defendant refuses to comply with a non-testimonial identification order issued pursuant to G.S. 15A-271 *et seq.*, and the extent to which counsel may participate in or observe the proceedings.

Guideline 3.2 Client's Competence and Capacity to Proceed

(a) When defense counsel has a good faith doubt as to the client's capacity to proceed in a criminal case, counsel may:

(1) file an *ex parte* motion to obtain the services of a mental health expert and thereby determine whether to raise the client's competency before the court; or

(2) file a motion questioning the client's competence to stand trial or enter a plea under G.S. 15A-1001(a) and applicable case law, in which case the court may order a mental health examination at a state mental health facility or by the appropriate local forensic examiner.

(b) While the client's wishes ordinarily control, counsel may question competency without the client's assent or over the client's objection if necessary.

(c) After counsel receives and reviews the report from any court-ordered competency examination, counsel should consider whether to file a motion requesting a formal hearing on the client's capacity to proceed.

(d) Whenever competency is at issue, counsel still has a continuing duty to prepare the case for all anticipated court proceedings.

(e) If the court enters an order finding the client incompetent and orders involuntary commitment proceedings to be initiated, defense counsel ordinarily will not represent the client at those proceedings, but should cooperate with the commitment attorney upon request.

SECTION 4:

Guideline 4.1 Case Review, Investigation, and Preparation

(a) Counsel has a duty to conduct an independent case review and investigation. The client's admissions or statements to counsel of facts constituting guilt do not necessarily obviate the need for such independent review and investigation. The review and investigation should be conducted as promptly as possible.

(b) Sources of review and investigative information may include the following:

(1) *Charging Documents, Statutes, and Case Law*

Copies of all charging documents in the case should be obtained and examined to determine the specific charges that have been brought against the client. The relevant statutes and precedents should be examined to identify:

(A) the elements of the offense(s) with which the client is charged;

(B) the defenses, ordinary and affirmative, that may be available, as well as the proper manner and timeline for asserting any available defenses; and

(C) any defects in the charging documents, constitutional or otherwise, such as statute of limitations, double jeopardy, or irregularities in the grand jury proceedings.

(2) *The Client*

An in-depth interview or interviews of the client should be used to:

(A) seek information concerning the incident or events giving rise to the charge(s);

(B) elicit information concerning possible improper police investigative practices or prosecutorial conduct that may affect the client's rights;

(C) explore the existence of other potential sources of information relating to the offense or client, including school, work, jail, probation, and prison records;

(D) collect information relevant to sentencing; and

(E) continue to assess the client's medical and/or mental health needs.

(3) *Potential Witnesses*

Counsel should consider whether to interview the potential witnesses, including any complaining witnesses and others adverse to the client. If the attorney conducts such interviews of potential witnesses, he or she should attempt to do so in the presence of a third person who will be available, if necessary, to testify as a defense witness at trial. Alternatively, counsel should have an investigator conduct such interviews.

(4) *The Police and Prosecution*

Counsel should utilize available discovery procedures to secure information in the possession of the prosecution or law enforcement authorities, including police reports, unless a sound tactical reason exists for not doing so (*e.g.*, defense obligations under G.S. 15A-905).

(5) *The Courts*

If possible, counsel should request and review any tapes or transcripts from previous hearings in the case. Counsel should also review the client's prior court file(s) where appropriate.

(6) *Information in the Possession of Third Parties*

Where appropriate, counsel should seek a release or court order to obtain necessary confidential information about the client, co-defendant(s), witness(es), or victim(s) that is in the possession of third parties. Counsel should be aware of privacy laws and other requirements governing disclosure of the type of confidential information being sought.

(7) *Physical Evidence*

Where appropriate, counsel should make a prompt request to the police or investigative agency for any physical evidence or expert reports relevant to the offense or sentencing. Counsel should view the physical evidence consistent with case needs.

(8) *The Scene*

Where appropriate, counsel or an investigator should view the scene of the alleged offense. This should be done under circumstances as similar as possible to those existing at the time of the alleged incident (*e.g.*, weather, time of day, lighting conditions, and seasonal changes). Counsel should consider the taking of photographs and the creation of diagrams or charts of the actual scene of the alleged offense.

(9) *Assistance from Experts, Investigators, and Interpreters*

Counsel should consider whether expert or investigative assistance, including consultation and testimony, is necessary or appropriate to:

(A) prepare a defense;

(B) adequately understand the prosecution's case;

(C) rebut the prosecution's case; and/or

(D) investigate the client's competence to proceed, mental state at the time of the offense, and/or capacity to make a knowing and intelligent waiver of constitutional rights.

If counsel determines that expert or investigative assistance is necessary and appropriate, counsel should file an *ex parte* motion setting forth the particularized showing of necessity required by *Ake v. Oklahoma*, *State v. Ballard*, and their progeny. If appropriate, counsel should file a motion to have a foreign language or sign language interpreter appointed by the court. Counsel should take all necessary steps to preserve for appeal any denial of expert, investigative, or interpreter funding.

(c) During case preparation and throughout trial, counsel should identify potential legal issues and the corresponding objections. Counsel should consider the tactics of when and how to raise those objections. Counsel should also consider how best to respond to objections that could be raised by the prosecution.

Guideline 4.2 Discovery in Cases Within the Original Jurisdiction of the Superior Court

(a) Counsel has a duty to pursue discovery procedures provided by the applicable rules of criminal procedure within the time periods prescribed by G.S. 15A-902, and to pursue such informal discovery methods as may be available to supplement the factual investigation of the case.

(b) Prior to filing a formal motion with the court, counsel must first serve the prosecutor with a written request for voluntary discovery unless counsel and the prosecutor agree in writing to comply voluntarily with G.S. 15A-901 *et seq.* Counsel must file a motion to compel discovery if the prosecution's response is unsatisfactory or delayed. Regardless of the prosecution's response, counsel should file a motion to compel discovery if the case is proceeding to trial.

(c) In exceptional cases, counsel should consider not making a discovery request or signing a written agreement under G.S. 15A-902(a), on the ground that it will trigger a defense obligation to disclose evidence under G.S. 15A-905.

(d) Unless there is a sound tactical reason for not requesting discovery or signing a written agreement under G.S. 15A-902(a) (*e.g.*, defense obligations under G.S. 15A-905), counsel should seek discovery to the broadest extent permitted under federal and state law, including but not limited to, the following items:

(1) all information to which the defendant is entitled under G.S. 15A-903;

(2) all potential exculpatory information and evidence to which the defense is entitled under *Brady v. Maryland* and its progeny, including but not limited to:

(A) impeachment evidence, such as a witness' prior convictions or other misconduct; bias of a witness; a witness' capacity to observe, perceive, or recollect; and psychiatric evaluations of a witness;

(B) evidence discrediting police investigation and credibility;

(C) evidence undermining the identification of the client;

(D) evidence tending to show the guilt of another;

(E) the identity of favorable witnesses; and

(F) exculpatory physical evidence; and

(3) to the extent not provided under statutory discovery, any other information necessary to the defense of the case, including but not limited to:

(A) the names, addresses, and availability of state witnesses;

(B) the details of the circumstances under which any oral or written statements by the accused or a co-defendant were made;

(C) any evidence of prior bad acts that the prosecution may intend to use against the client;

(D) the data underlying any expert reports; and

(E) any evidence necessary to enable counsel to determine whether to file a motion to suppress evidence under G.S. 15A-971 *et seq.*

(e) Counsel should seek the timely production and preservation of discoverable evidence. If the prosecution fails to disclose or belatedly discloses discoverable evidence, counsel should consider requesting one or more of the sanctions provided by G.S. 15A-910.

(f) If counsel believes the state may destroy or consume in testing evidence that is significant to the case (*e.g.*, rough notes of law enforcement interviews, 911 tapes, drugs, or blood samples), counsel should also file a motion to preserve the evidence in the event that it is discoverable.

(g) Counsel should timely comply with all of the requirements in G.S. 15A-905 governing disclosure of evidence by the defendant and notice of defenses and expert witnesses. Counsel also should be aware of the possible sanctions for failure to comply with those requirements under G.S. 15A-910.

Guideline 4.3 Theory of the Case

During case review, investigation, and trial preparation, counsel should develop and continually reassess a theory of the case. A theory of the case is one central theory that organizes the facts, emotions, and legal basis for the client's acquittal or conviction of a lesser offense, while also telling the defense story of innocence, reduced culpability, or unfairness. The theory of the case furnishes the basic position from which counsel determines all actions in a case.

SECTION 5:

Guideline 5.1 The Decision to File Pretrial Motions

(a) Counsel should consider filing appropriate pretrial motions whenever there exists a good-faith reason to believe that the applicable law may entitle the client to relief which the court has authority to grant.

(b) The decision to file pretrial motions should be made after thorough investigation and after considering the applicable law in light of the circumstances of each case, as well as the need to preserve issues for appellate review. Among the issues that counsel should consider addressing in pretrial motions are:

(1) the pretrial custody of the client and a motion to review conditions of release;

(2) the constitutionality of the implicated statute or statutes;

(3) any potential defects in the grand jury composition or charging process;

(4) the sufficiency of the charging document under all applicable statutory and constitutional provisions;

(5) the dismissal of a charge on double jeopardy grounds;

(6) the need for a bill of particulars;

(7) the propriety and prejudice of any joinder or severance of charges or defendants;

(8) the statutory and constitutional discovery obligations of the prosecution;

(9) the suppression of evidence gathered as the result of violations of the North Carolina Constitution and the United States Constitution, including:

(A) the fruits of illegal searches or seizures;

(B) involuntary statements or confessions;

(C) statements or confessions obtained in violation of the client's right to counsel, or privilege against self-incrimination; and

(D) unreliable identification evidence that would give rise to a substantial likelihood of irreparable misidentification;

(10) the suppression of evidence gathered in violation of any right, duty, or privilege arising out of North Carolina law;

(11) access to necessary support or investigative resources or experts;

(12) the need for a change of venue;

(13) the defendant's speedy trial rights and/or calendaring rights under G.S. 7A-49.4;

(14) the defendant's right to a continuance in order adequately to prepare his or her case;

(15) matters of trial evidence that may be appropriately litigated by means of a pretrial motion in *limine*;

(16) the suppression of a prior conviction obtained in violation of the defendant's right to counsel;

(17) the recusal of the trial judge;

(18) the full recordation of all proceedings pursuant to G.S. 15A-1241;

(19) matters of trial or courtroom procedure; and

(20) notice of affirmative defenses if required by G.S. 15A-905(c) and G.S. 15A-959.

(c) Counsel should be aware of all time limits on the filing of pretrial motions, and should know whether a motion must or may be accompanied by a factual affidavit.

(d) Unless there are sound tactical reasons for not doing so, counsel should request that the court rule on all previously filed defense motions.

Guideline 5.2 Filing and Arguing Pretrial Motions

(a) Motions should be filed in a timely manner, should comport with the formal requirements of statute and court rules, and should succinctly inform the court of the authority relied upon.

(b) When a hearing on a motion requires the taking of evidence, counsel's preparation for the evidentiary hearing should include:

(1) investigation, discovery, and research relevant to the claim(s) advanced;

(2) the subpoenaing of all helpful evidence, and the subpoenaing and preparation of all helpful witnesses;

(3) full understanding of the burdens of proof, evidentiary principles and procedures applying to the hearing, including the benefits and costs of having the client and other defense witnesses testify;

(4) obtaining the assistance of an expert witness where appropriate and necessary; and

(5) preparation and submission of a memorandum of law where appropriate.

(c) If a hearing on a pretrial motion is held in advance of trial, counsel should attempt to obtain the transcript of the hearing for use at trial where appropriate.

Guideline 5.3 Subsequent Filing and Renewal of Pretrial Motions

Counsel should be prepared to raise during the subsequent proceedings any issue that is appropriately raised pretrial, but could not have been so raised because the facts supporting the motion were unknown or not reasonably available. Further, counsel should be prepared to renew pretrial motions or file additional motions at any subsequent stage of the proceedings if new supporting information is later disclosed or made available. Counsel should also renew pretrial motions and object to the admission of challenged evidence at trial as necessary to preserve the motions and objections for appellate review.

SECTION 6:

Guideline 6.1 The Plea Negotiation Process and the Duties of Counsel

(a) After appropriate investigation and case review, counsel should explore with the client the possibility and desirability of reaching a negotiated disposition of the charges rather than proceeding to trial. In doing so, counsel should fully explain to the client the rights that would be waived by a decision to enter a plea and not proceed to trial.

(b) Counsel should keep the client fully informed of any plea discussions and negotiations, and convey to the client any offers made by the prosecution for a negotiated settlement. Counsel may not accept any plea agreement without the client's express authorization.

(c) Counsel should explain to the client those decisions that ultimately must be made by the client, as well as the advantages and disadvantages inherent in those choices. The decisions that must be made by the client after full consultation with counsel include whether to plead guilty or not guilty, whether to accept a plea agreement, and whether to testify at the plea hearing. Counsel should also explain to the client the impact of the decision to enter a guilty plea on the client's right to appeal. Although the decision to enter a plea of guilty ultimately rests with the client, if counsel believes the client's decisions are not in his or her best interest, counsel should attempt to persuade the client to change his or her position.

(d) Notwithstanding the existence of ongoing tentative plea negotiations with the prosecution, counsel should continue to prepare and investigate the case to the extent necessary to protect the client's rights and interests in the event that plea negotiations fail.

(e) Counsel should not allow a client to plead guilty based on oral conditions that are not disclosed to the court. Counsel should ensure that all conditions and promises comprising a plea arrangement between the prosecution and defense are included in writing in the transcript of plea.

Guideline 6.2 The Contents of the Negotiations

(a) In conducting plea negotiations, counsel should attempt to become familiar with any practices and policies of the particular district, judge, and prosecuting attorney that may affect the content and likely results of a negotiated plea bargain.

(b) To develop an overall negotiation plan, counsel should be fully aware of, and fully advise the client of:

(1) the maximum term of imprisonment that may be ordered under the applicable sentencing laws, including any habitual offender statutes, sentencing enhancements, mandatory minimum sentence requirements, and mandatory consecutive sentence requirements;

(2) the possibility of forfeiture of assets seized in connection with the case;

(3) any registration requirements, including sex offender registration;

(4) the likelihood that a conviction could be used for sentence enhancement in the event of future criminal cases, such as sentencing in the aggravated range, habitual offender status, or felon in possession of a firearm;

(5) the possibility of earned-time credits;

(6) the availability of appropriate diversion or rehabilitation programs;

(7) the likelihood of the court imposing financial obligations on the client, including the payment of attorney fees, court costs, fines, and restitution; and

(8) the effect on the client's appellate rights.

Counsel should also discuss with the client that there may be other potential collateral consequences of entering a plea, such as deportation or other effects on immigration status; motor vehicle or other licensing; parental rights; possession of firearms; voting rights; employment, military, and government service considerations; and the potential exposure to or impact on any federal charges.

(c) In developing a negotiation strategy, counsel should be completely familiar with:

(1) concessions that the client might offer the prosecution as part of a negotiated settlement, including but not limited to:

(A) declining to assert the right to proceed to trial on the merits of the charges;

(B) refraining from asserting or litigating any particular pretrial motion(s);

(C) agreeing to fulfill specified restitution conditions and/or participation in community work or service programs, or in rehabilitation or other programs;

(D) providing the prosecution with assistance in prosecuting or investigating the present case or other alleged criminal activity;

(E) waiving challenges to validity or proof of prior convictions; and

(F) waiving the right to indictment and consenting to a bill of information on a related but unindicted offense;

(2) benefits the client might obtain from a negotiated settlement, including but not limited to, an agreement:

(A) that the prosecution will not oppose the client's release on bail pending sentencing or appeal;

(B) that the client may enter a conditional plea to preserve the right to litigate and contest the denial of a suppression motion;

(C) to dismiss or reduce one or more of the charged offenses either immediately, or upon completion of a deferred prosecution agreement;

(D) that the client will not be subject to further investigation or prosecution for uncharged alleged criminal conduct;

(E) that the client will receive, with the agreement of the court, a specified sentence or sanction or a sentence or sanction within a specified range;

(F) that at the time of sentencing and/or in communications with the preparer of a sentencing services plan or presentence report, the prosecution will take, or refrain from taking, a specified position with respect to the sanction to be imposed on the client by the court; and

(G) that at the time of sentencing and/or in communications with the preparer of a sentencing services plan or presentence report, the prosecution will not present certain information;

(3) information favorable to the client concerning such matters as the offense, mitigating factors and relative culpability, prior offenses, personal background, employment record and opportunities, educational background, and family and financial status;

(4) information that would support a sentencing disposition other than incarceration, such as the potential for rehabilitation or the nonviolent nature of the crime; and

(5) information concerning the availability of treatment programs, community treatment facilities, and community service work opportunities.

(d) In conducting plea negotiations, counsel should be familiar with:

(1) the various types of pleas that may be agreed to, including a plea of guilty, a plea of *nolo contendere*, a conditional plea of guilty in which the defendant retains the right to appeal the denial of a suppression motion, and a plea in which the defendant is not required to personally acknowledge his or her guilt (*Alford* plea);

(2) the advantages and disadvantages of each available plea according to the circumstances of the case; and

(3) whether the plea agreement is binding on the court and prison authorities.

Guideline 6.3 The Decision to Enter a Plea of Guilty

(a) Counsel shall inform the client of any tentative negotiated agreement reached with the prosecution, and explain to the client the full content of the agreement, including its advantages, disadvantages, and potential consequences.

(b) When counsel reasonably believes that acceptance of a plea offer is in the client's best interests, counsel should attempt to persuade the client to accept the plea offer. However, the decision to enter a plea of guilty ultimately rests with the client.

Guideline 6.4 Entry of the Plea before the Court

(a) Prior to the entry of a plea, counsel should:

(1) fully explain to the client the rights he or she will waive by entering the plea;

(2) fully explain to the client the conditions and limits of the plea agreement and the maximum punishment, sanctions, and other consequences the client will be exposed to by entering a plea; and

(3) fully explain to the client the nature of the plea hearing and prepare the client for the role he or she may play in the hearing, including answering questions of the judge and providing a statement concerning the offense.

(b) When entering the plea, counsel should ensure that the full content and conditions of the plea agreement between the prosecution and defense are made part of the transcript of plea.

(c) Subsequent to the acceptance of a plea, counsel should review and explain the plea proceedings to the client, and respond to any client questions and concerns.

<u>**SECTION 7:**</u>

Guideline 7.1 General Trial Preparation

(a) Throughout preparation and trial, counsel should consider the theory of the defense and ensure that counsel's decisions and actions are consistent with that theory.

(b) The decision to proceed to trial rests solely with the client. Counsel should discuss with the client the relevant strategic considerations of this decision. When appropriate, counsel should also explain to the client that decisions concerning trial strategy are ordinarily to be made by counsel, after consultation with the client and investigation of the applicable facts and law. However, counsel should be aware that, under North Carolina law, if counsel and a fully informed competent client reach an absolute impasse as to tactical decisions, the client's wishes may control.

(c) In advance of trial, counsel should take all steps necessary to complete thorough investigation, discovery, and research. Among the steps counsel should consider in preparation are:

(1) interviewing and subpoenaing all potentially helpful witnesses;

(2) examining and subpoenaing all potentially helpful physical or documentary evidence;

(3) obtaining funds for defense investigators and experts, and arranging for defense experts to consult and/or testify on issues that are potentially helpful;

(4) obtaining and reading transcripts of any prior proceedings in the case or related proceedings; and

(5) obtaining photographs or preparing charts, maps, diagrams, or other visual aids of all scenes, persons, objects, or information that may aid the fact finder in understanding the defense case.

(d) Where appropriate, counsel should have the following information and materials available at the time of trial:

(1) copies of all relevant documents filed in the case;

(2) relevant documents prepared by investigators;

(3) reports, test results, and other materials disclosed by the prosecution pursuant to G.S. 15A-901 *et seq.*;

(4) *voir dire* topics, plans, or questions;

(5) a plan, outline, or draft of opening statement;

(6) cross-examination plans for all possible prosecution witnesses;

(7) direct-examination plans for all prospective defense witnesses;

(8) copies of defense subpoenas;

(9) prior statements of all prosecution witnesses (*e.g.*, transcripts, police reports);

(10) prior statements of all defense witnesses;

(11) reports from defense experts;

(12) a list of all defense exhibits, and the witnesses through whom they will be introduced;

(13) originals and copies of all documentary exhibits;

(14) proposed jury instructions with supporting case citations;

(15) copies of critical statutes and cases; and

(16) a plan, outline, or draft of closing argument.

(e) Counsel should be fully informed as to the rules of evidence and the law relating to all stages of the trial process, and should be familiar with legal and evidentiary issues that reasonably can be anticipated to arise in the trial.

(f) Counsel should be familiar with case law concerning making admissions of guilt to the jury without the client's consent.

(g) Counsel should decide if it is beneficial to secure an advance ruling on issues likely to arise at trial (*e.g.*, use of prior convictions to impeach the defendant) and, where appropriate, should prepare motions and memoranda for such advance rulings.

(h) Where appropriate, counsel should advise the client as to suitable courtroom dress and demeanor. If the client is incarcerated, counsel should try to ensure that the client does not appear before the jury in jail or other inappropriate clothing, or in shackles or handcuffs. If an incarcerated client is brought before the jury in jail clothing, shackles, or handcuffs, counsel should object and seek appropriate relief from the court.

(i) Counsel should plan with the client, court personnel, and/or sheriff's office for the most convenient system for conferring throughout the trial.

(j) Throughout preparation and trial, counsel should consider the potential effects that particular actions may have upon sentencing if there is a finding of guilt.

Guideline 7.2 Preserving the Record on Appeal

Counsel should establish a proper record for appellate review throughout the trial process, including requesting recordation of all significant portions of the trial under G.S. 15A-1241(b). If something non-verbal transpires during trial that is relevant and important, counsel should ask to have the record reflect what happened.

Guideline 7.3 *Voir Dire* and Jury Selection

(a) *Preparation*

(1) Counsel should be familiar with the procedures by which a jury panel is selected, and should be alert to any potential legal challenges to the composition or selection of the panel.

(2) Counsel should be familiar with the local practices and the individual trial judge's procedures for selecting a jury from the panel, and should be alert to any potential legal challenges to those procedures.

(3) Prior to jury selection, counsel should seek to obtain a prospective juror list where feasible, and should develop a method for tracking juror selection and seating.

(4) Counsel should be familiar with any juror questionnaire that may be used by the court or prosecution and, where appropriate, should develop a defense questionnaire and file a pretrial motion to authorize its use.

(5) In advance of trial, counsel should develop *voir dire* topics, plans, or questions that are tailored to the specific case. Among the purposes *voir dire* questions should be designed to serve are:

(A) to elicit information about the attitudes of individual jurors, which will inform the use of peremptory strikes and challenges for cause;

(B) to determine the jurors' attitudes toward legal principles that are critical to the defense case, including, where appropriate, the client's decision not to testify; and

(C) to present the client, preview the defense case, and assess the impact of damaging information on the jurors' ability to fairly consider the case.

In conducting *voir dire*, counsel should be aware that jurors may develop impressions of counsel and the defendant, and should recognize the importance of establishing a relationship of credibility.

(6) Counsel should be familiar with the law concerning mandatory and discretionary *voir dire* inquiries so as to be able to defend any request to ask particular questions of prospective jurors.

(7) Counsel should be familiar with the law concerning challenges for cause and peremptory strikes. Counsel also should be aware of the statutory and case law directing that peremptory challenges need to be exhausted in order to preserve for appeal the denial of any challenges for cause.

(b) *Examining the Prospective Jurors*

(1) Counsel should personally conduct the *voir dire* examination of the panel.

(2) If the court denies counsel's request to ask questions during *voir dire* that are significant or necessary to the defense of the case, counsel should take all steps necessary to protect the *voir dire* record for appeal, including filing a written motion listing the proposed *voir dire* questions or otherwise making proposed questions part of the record.

(3) If the *voir dire* questions may elicit sensitive answers or where otherwise appropriate, counsel should request individual *voir dire*.

(c) *Challenges and Objections*

(1) Counsel should consider challenging for cause all persons who are subject to challenge under G.S. 15A-1212, including all persons about whom a legitimate argument can be made for actual prejudice or bias relevant to the case, when it is likely to benefit the client.

(2) When a challenge for cause is denied, counsel should consider exercising a peremptory challenge to remove the juror. Counsel should be aware of the requirements in G.S. 15A-1214(h) for preserving the denial of a challenge for cause for appellate review.

(3) In exercising challenges for cause and peremptory strikes, counsel should consider both the panelists who may replace a person who is removed and the total number of peremptory challenges available.

(4) Counsel should object to and preserve for appellate review all issues relating to the unconstitutional exclusion of jurors by the prosecution or court.

Guideline 7.4 Opening Statement

(a) Prior to delivering an opening statement, counsel should consider whether to ask for sequestration of witnesses.

(b) Counsel should be familiar with North Carolina law and the individual trial judge's practices regarding the permissible content of an opening statement. Counsel should consider the need to, and if appropriate, ask the court to instruct the prosecution not to mention in opening statement contested evidence for which the court has not determined admissibility.

(c) Counsel should consider the strategic advantages and disadvantages of disclosure of particular information during opening statement.

(d) Counsel's objectives in making an opening statement may include the following:

(1) to introduce the theory of the defense case;

(2) to provide an overview of the defense case;

(3) to identify the weaknesses of the prosecution's case;

(4) to emphasize the prosecution's burden of proof;

(5) to summarize the anticipated testimony of witnesses, and the role of each in relationship to the entire case;

(6) to describe the exhibits that will be introduced and the role of each in relationship to the entire case;

(7) to clarify the jurors' responsibilities;

(8) to state the ultimate inferences counsel wants the jury to draw;

(9) to personalize the client and counsel for the jury; and

(10) to prepare the jury for the client's testimony or decision not to testify.

(e) Counsel should consider incorporating the promises of proof the prosecutor makes to the jury during opening statement into the defense opening statement and summation.

(f) Whenever the prosecutor oversteps the bounds of a proper opening statement, counsel should consider objecting, requesting a mistrial, or seeking cautionary instructions, unless sound tactical considerations weigh against any such objections or requests. Such tactical considerations may include, but are not limited to:

(1) the significance of the prosecutor's error; and

(2) the possibility that an objection might enhance the significance of the information in the jurors' minds, or otherwise negatively affect the jury.

Guideline 7.5 Confronting the Prosecution's Case

(a) Counsel should anticipate weaknesses in the prosecution's proof, and research and prepare to argue corresponding motions for judgment of dismissal or nonsuit.

(b) Counsel should consider the advantages and disadvantages of entering into stipulations concerning the prosecution's case.

(c) Unless sound tactical reasons exist for not doing so, counsel should make timely objections and motions to strike improper state evidence, and assert all possible statutory and constitutional grounds for exclusion of the evidence. If evidence is admissible only for a limited purpose, counsel should consider requesting an appropriate limiting instruction.

(d) In preparing for cross-examination, counsel should be familiar with North Carolina law and procedures concerning cross-examination and impeachment of witnesses. Counsel should be prepared to question witnesses as to the existence and content of prior statements.

(e) In preparing for cross-examination, counsel should:

(1) consider the need to integrate cross-examination, the theory of the defense, and closing argument;

(2) consider whether cross-examination of each individual witness is likely to generate helpful information, and avoid asking questions that are unnecessary or might elicit responses harmful to the defense case;

(3) anticipate those witnesses the prosecution might call in its case-in-chief or in rebuttal, and consider a cross-examination plan for each of the anticipated witnesses;

(4) be alert to inconsistencies, variations, and contradictions within each witness' testimony;

(5) be alert to inconsistencies, variations, and contradictions between different witnesses' testimony;

(6) if applicable, review all prior statements of the witnesses and any prior relevant testimony of the prospective witnesses;

(7) where appropriate, review relevant statutes and local police regulations for possible use in cross-examining police witnesses;

(8) be alert to issues relating to witness credibility, including bias and motive for testifying; and

(9) be fully familiar with North Carolina statutory and case law on objections, motions to strike, offers of proof, and preserving the record on appeal.

(f) Counsel should consider conducting a *voir dire* examination of potential prosecution witnesses who may not be competent to give particular testimony, including expert witnesses whom the prosecutor may call. Counsel should be aware of the law concerning competency of witnesses in general, and admission of expert testimony in particular, to be able to raise appropriate objections.

(g) Before beginning cross-examination, counsel should ascertain whether the prosecutor provided copies of all prior statements of prosecution witnesses as required by G.S. 15A-903(a). If disclosure was not properly made, counsel should request relief as appropriate under G.S. 15A-910, including:

(1) a cautionary instruction;

(2) adequate time to review the documents or investigate and prepare further before commencing cross-examination, including a continuance or recess if necessary;

(3) exclusion of the witness' testimony and all evidence affected by that testimony;

(4) a mistrial;

(5) dismissal of the case; and/or

(6) any other sanctions counsel believes would remedy the violation.

(h) At the close of the prosecution's case and out of the presence of the jury, counsel should move for a judgment of dismissal or nonsuit on each count charged. Where appropriate, counsel should be prepared with supporting case law.

Guideline 7.6 Presenting the Defense Case

(a) Counsel should develop, in consultation with the client, an overall defense strategy. In deciding on defense strategy, counsel should consider whether the client's interests are best served by not presenting defense evidence, and instead relying on the evidence and inferences, or lack thereof, from the prosecution's case.

(b) Counsel should discuss with the client all of the considerations relevant to the client's decision to testify, including but not limited to, the likelihood of cross-examination and impeachment concerning prior convictions and prior bad acts that affect credibility.

(c) Counsel should be aware of the elements of any affirmative defense(s) and know whether the defense bears a burden of persuasion or production. Counsel should be familiar with the notice requirements for affirmative defenses and introduction of expert testimony that are imposed by G.S. 15A-905(c), G.S. 15A-959, and North Carolina case law.

(d) In preparing for presentation of a defense case, counsel should, where appropriate:

(1) develop a plan for direct examination of each potential defense witness;

(2) determine the implications that the order of witnesses may have on the defense case;

(3) consider the possible use of character witnesses and any negative consequences that may flow from such testimony;

(4) consider the need for expert witnesses;

(5) consider the use of demonstrative evidence and the order of exhibits; and

(6) be fully familiar with North Carolina statutory and case law on objections, motions to strike, offers of proof, and preserving the record on appeal.

(e) In developing and presenting the defense case, counsel should consider the implications it may have for rebuttal by the prosecution.

(f) Counsel should prepare all defense witnesses for direct examination and possible cross-examination. Where appropriate, counsel should also advise witnesses and the defendant of suitable courtroom dress and demeanor.

(g) If a prosecution objection is sustained or defense evidence is improperly excluded, counsel should make appropriate efforts to rephrase the question(s) and/or make an offer of proof.

(h) Counsel should conduct redirect examination as appropriate.

(i) At the close of all of the evidence, counsel should renew the motion for judgment of dismissal or nonsuit on each charged count.

Guideline 7.7 Closing Argument

(a) Counsel should be familiar with the substantive limits on both prosecution and defense summation, including the law governing closing arguments under G.S. 7A-97 and G.S. 15A-1230, Rule 10 of the General Rules of Practice for the Superior and District Courts, and North Carolina case law.

(b) In developing closing argument, counsel should review the proceedings to determine what aspects can be used in support of defense summation and, where appropriate, should consider:

(1) highlighting weaknesses in the prosecution's case;

(2) describing favorable inferences to be drawn from the evidence;

(3) incorporating into the argument:

(A) the theory of the defense case;

(B) helpful testimony from direct and cross-examinations;

(C) verbatim instructions drawn from the expected jury charge;

(D) responses to anticipated prosecution arguments; and

(E) visual aids and exhibits; and

(4) the effects of the defense argument on the prosecution's rebuttal argument.

(c) Whenever the prosecutor exceeds the scope of permissible argument, counsel should consider objecting, seeking cautionary instructions, or requesting a mistrial unless sound tactical considerations suggest otherwise. Such tactical considerations may include, but are not limited to:

(1) the possibility that an objection or cautionary instruction might enhance the significance of the information in the jurors' minds;

(2) whether, with respect to a motion for mistrial, counsel believes that the case will result in a favorable verdict for the client; and

(3) the need to preserve the objection for appellate review.

Guideline 7.8 Jury Instructions

(a) Counsel should be familiar with the law and the individual judge's practices concerning ruling on proposed instructions, charging the jury, use of pattern charges, and preserving objections to the instructions.

(b) Pursuant to G.S. 15A-1231, counsel should submit in writing proposed special instructions or modifications of the pattern jury instructions in light of the particular circumstances of the case, including the desirability of seeking a verdict on a lesser included offense. Where possible, counsel should provide case law in support of the proposed instructions. Counsel should try to ensure that all jury instruction discussions are on the record.

(c) Where appropriate, counsel should object to and argue against improper instructions proposed by the prosecution.

(d) If the court does not adopt instructions requested by counsel, or gives instructions over counsel's objection, counsel should take all steps necessary to preserve the record for appeal, including filing a copy of proposed instructions pursuant to G.S. 15A-1231.

(e) During delivery of the charge, counsel should be alert to any deviations from the judge's planned instructions, object to deviations unfavorable to the client, and, if necessary, request additional or curative instructions.

(f) If there are grounds for objecting to any jury instructions, counsel should object before the verdict form is submitted to the jury and the jury is allowed to begin deliberations.

(g) If the court proposes giving supplemental instructions to the jury, either upon request of the jurors or upon their failure to reach a verdict, counsel should ask the judge to state the proposed charge to counsel before it is delivered to the jury. Counsel should also try to ensure that any supplemental instructions are given to the entire jury in open court pursuant to G.S. 15A-1234(d).

SECTION 8:

Guideline 8.1 Obligations of Counsel in Sentencing

Counsel's obligations in the sentencing process include:

(a) where a defendant chooses not to proceed to trial, to attempt to negotiate a plea agreement with consideration of the sentencing, correctional, and financial implications;

(b) to try to ensure the client is not harmed by inaccurate information or information that is not properly before the court in determining the sentence to be imposed;

(c) to ensure that all reasonably available mitigating and favorable evidence, which is likely to benefit the client, is presented to the court;

(d) to develop a plan that seeks to achieve the sentencing alternative most favorable to the client, and that reasonably can be obtained based on the facts and circumstances of the offense, the defendant's background, the applicable sentencing provisions, and other information pertinent to the sentencing decision;

(e) to try to ensure that all information presented to the court which may harm the client, if inaccurate, untruthful, or otherwise improper, is stricken from the text of any sentencing services plan or presentence report;

(f) to consider the need for and availability of sentencing specialists, or mental health or mental retardation professionals; and

(g) to identify and preserve potential issues for appeal.

Guideline 8.2 Sentencing Options, Consequences, and Procedures

(a) Counsel should be familiar with and advise the client of the sentencing provisions and options applicable to the case, including:

(1) the applicable sentencing laws, including any habitual offender statutes, sentencing enhancements, mandatory minimum sentence requirements, mandatory consecutive sentence requirements, and constitutional limits on sentences;

(2) deferred prosecution, prayer for judgment continued, probation without a conviction, and diversionary programs;

(3) probation or suspension of sentence, and mandatory and permissible conditions of probation;

(4) confinement in a mental institution;

(5) forfeiture of assets seized in connection with the case;

(6) any mandatory registration requirements, including sex offender registration, or mandatory DNA testing; and

(7) the possibility of expungement and sealing of records.

(b) Counsel should be familiar with and advise the client of the direct and collateral consequences of the judgment and sentence, including:

(1) credit for pretrial detention;

(2) the likelihood that the conviction could be used for sentence enhancement in the event of future criminal cases, such as sentencing in the aggravated range, habitual offender status, or felon in possession of a firearm;

(3) the possibility of earned-time credits;

(4) the availability of correctional programs and work release;

(5) the availability of drug rehabilitation programs, psychiatric treatment, and health care; and

(6) the likelihood of the court imposing financial obligations on the client, including the payment of attorney fees, court costs, fines, and restitution.

Counsel should also discuss with the client that there may be other potential collateral consequences of the judgment and sentence, such as deportation or other effects on immigration status; motor vehicle or other licensing; parental rights; possession of firearms; voting rights; employment, military, and government service considerations; and the potential exposure to or impact on any federal charges.

(c) Counsel should be familiar with the sentencing procedures, including:

(1) the effect that plea negotiations may have upon the sentencing discretion of the court;

(2) the procedural operation of the applicable sentencing system, including concurrent and consecutive sentencing;

(3) the practices of those who prepare the sentencing services plan or presentence report, and the defendant's rights in that process;

(4) access to the sentencing services plan or presentence report by counsel and the defendant;

(5) the defense sentencing presentation and/or sentencing memorandum;

(6) the opportunity to challenge information presented to the court for sentencing purposes;

(7) the availability of an evidentiary hearing to challenge information, and the applicable rules of evidence and burdens of proof at such a hearing; and

(8) the participation that victims and prosecution or defense witnesses may have in the sentencing proceedings.

Guideline 8.3 Preparation for Sentencing

In preparing for sentencing, counsel should consider the need to:

(a) inform the client of the applicable sentencing requirements, options, and alternatives, and the sentencing judge's practices and procedures if known;

(b) maintain regular contact with the client prior to the sentencing hearing, and inform the client of the steps being taken in preparation for sentencing;

(c) obtain from the client relevant information concerning such subjects as his or her background and personal history, prior criminal record, employment history and skills, education, medical and mental health history and condition, and financial status, and obtain from the client sources through which the information provided can be corroborated;

(d) inform the client of his or her right to speak at the sentencing proceeding and assist the client in preparing the statement, if any, to be made to the court, after considering the possible consequences that any admission of guilt may have on an appeal, subsequent retrial, or trial on other offenses;

(e) inform the client of the effects that admissions and other statements may have on an appeal, retrial, or other judicial proceedings, such as collateral or restitution proceedings;

(f) inform the client if counsel will ask the court to consider a particular sentence or range of sentences; and

(g) collect and present documents and affidavits to support the defense position and, where relevant, prepare and present witnesses to testify at the sentencing hearing.

Guideline 8.4 The Sentencing Services Plan or Presentence Report

(a) Counsel should be familiar with the procedures concerning the preparation and submission of a sentencing services plan or presentence report, and should consider the tactical implications of requesting that a plan be prepared.

(b) If a plan is prepared, counsel should:

(1) provide to the official preparing the plan relevant information favorable to the client, including, where appropriate, the client's version of the offense;

(2) prepare the client to be interviewed by the person preparing the plan;

(3) review the completed plan and discuss it with the client;

(4) try to ensure the client has adequate time to examine the completed plan; and

(5) take appropriate steps to ensure that erroneous or misleading information that may harm the client is challenged or deleted from the plan.

Guideline 8.5 The Prosecution's Sentencing Position

Unless there is a sound tactical reason for not doing so, counsel should attempt to determine whether the prosecution will advocate that a particular type or length of sentence be imposed, including the factual basis for any sentence in the aggravated range.

Guideline 8.6 The Defense Sentencing Theory

Counsel should prepare a defense sentencing presentation and, where appropriate, a defense sentencing memorandum. Among the topics counsel may wish to include in the sentencing presentation or memorandum are:

(a) information favorable to the defendant concerning such matters as the offense, mitigating factors and relative culpability, prior offenses, personal background, employment record and opportunities, educational background, and family and financial status;

(b) information that would support a sentencing disposition other than incarceration, such as the potential for rehabilitation or the nonviolent nature of the crime;

(c) information concerning the availability of treatment programs, community treatment facilities, and community service work opportunities;

(d) challenges to incorrect or incomplete information, and inappropriate inferences and characterizations that are before the court; and

(e) a defense sentencing proposal.

Guideline 8.7 The Sentencing Process

(a) Counsel should be prepared at the sentencing proceeding to take the steps necessary to advocate fully for the requested sentence and to protect the client's legal rights and interests.

(b) Where appropriate, counsel should be prepared to present supporting evidence, including testimony of witnesses, affidavits, letters, and public records, to establish the facts favorable to the defendant.

(c) Where the court has the authority to do so, counsel should request specific orders or recommendations from the court concerning the place of confinement and psychiatric treatment or drug rehabilitation, and against deportation or exclusion of the defendant.

(d) Where appropriate, counsel should prepare the client to personally address the court. In addition, counsel should prepare any expert and other witnesses to address the court.

(e) After the sentencing hearing is complete, counsel should fully explain to the client the terms of the sentence, including any conditions of probation.

SECTION 9:

Guideline 9.1 Appeal of Misdemeanor Conviction for Trial *de Novo* in Superior Court

(a) When a defendant has been convicted of a misdemeanor in district court, except where the defendant explicitly waives his or her right to appeal as part of a plea agreement, counsel should advise the client of the right to appeal for trial *de novo* with a jury in superior court. Counsel should also advise the client of the potential advantages and disadvantages of exercising that right.

(b) Counsel should be aware of, and advise the client of, the time limit for *de novo* appeal set forth in G.S. 15A-1431(c).

Guideline 9.2 Motion for Appropriate Relief in the Trial Division

(a) Counsel should be familiar with the procedures available under G.S. 15A-1411 *et seq.* to seek a new trial, dismissal of charges, or other relief. Counsel should be aware of the grounds for relief that must be asserted within 10 days after entry of judgment, and the grounds that may be asserted more than 10 days after entry of judgment.

(b) When a judgment has been entered against the defendant after trial, counsel should consider whether it is appropriate to file a motion for appropriate relief with the trial court pursuant to G.S. 15A-1414. In deciding whether to file such a motion, the factors counsel should consider include:

(1) the likelihood of success of the motion, given the nature of the error or errors that can be raised; and

(2) the effect that such a motion might have on the client's appellate rights, including whether the filing of such a motion will assist in preserving the defendant's right to raise on appeal the issues that might be raised in the motion for appropriate relief.

Guideline 9.3 Right to Appeal to the Appellate Division

(a) Counsel should inform the defendant of his or her right to appeal the judgment of the court to the appellate division and the action that must be taken to perfect an appeal.

(b) If the defendant has a right to appeal and wants to file an appeal, the attorney shall preserve the defendant's right to do so by entering notice of appeal in accordance with the procedures and timelines set forth in G.S. 15A-1448 and the Rules of Appellate Procedure. Pursuant to Rule 33(a) of the North Carolina Rules of Appellate Procedure and Rules 1.7(a) and 3.2(a) of the Rules of the Commission on Indigent Defense Services, the entry of notice of appeal does not constitute a general appearance as counsel of record in the appellate division.

(c) If the defendant does not have a right to appeal and counsel believes there is a meritorious issue in the case that might be raised in the appellate division by means of a petition for writ of *certiorari*, counsel should inform the defendant of his or her opinion and consult with the Office of the Appellate Defender about the appropriate procedure.

(d) If counsel believes the defendant has a right to appeal and continues to be indigent, but the trial court denies appointed appellate counsel or denies indigency status for purposes of appeal, trial counsel should consult with the Office of the Appellate Defender about the defendant's options and inform the defendant of those options.

(e) Where the client takes an appeal, trial counsel should cooperate in providing information to appellate counsel concerning the proceedings in the trial court, and should timely respond to reasonable requests from appellate counsel for additional information about the case.

Guideline 9.4 Bail Pending Appeal

(a) Where a client indicates a desire to appeal the judgment and/or sentence of the court, counsel should inform the client of any right that may exist under G.S. 15A-536 to be released on bail pending the disposition of the appeal and, prior to the appointment of appellate counsel, make such a motion where appropriate.

(b) Where an appeal is taken and after appellate counsel is appointed, trial counsel should cooperate with appellate counsel in providing information if appellate counsel pursues a request for bail.

Guideline 9.5 Post-Disposition Obligations

Even after counsel's representation in a case is complete, counsel should comply with a client's reasonable requests for information and materials that are part of counsel's file. Counsel should also take reasonable steps to correct clerical or other errors in court documents, including jail credit calculations.

PRESERVING THE RECORD ON APPEAL

These training materials were originally written by Danielle M. Carman, Assistant Director and General Counsel, Office of Indigent Defense Services, and updated by Anne M. Gomez, Assistant Appellate Defender, Office of the Appellate Defender, and Julie R. Lewis, Assistant Public Defender, Mecklenburg County

Last updated June 2011 by
Julie R. Lewis

I. INTRODUCTION:

- Our appellate courts are increasingly using "waiver" to avoid reaching the merits of defense challenges in criminal cases.
- While appellate attorneys can and do fail to preserve appellate issues, "waiver" most often begins at the trial level . . . .

II. BASIC PRESERVATION PRINCIPLES:

- **Express disagreement with what the trial court did (or did not do) and the complete grounds for that disagreement by objection, motion, request, or otherwise.**
- Assert your position in a timely fashion.
- Assert your position in the form required by the applicable rule or statute.
- **Constitutionalize your position whenever possible by explicitly asserting both Federal and State constitutional grounds.**
- Reassert your position every time the same or a substantially similar issue arises.
- Obtain a ruling on your request, motion, or objection. If the judge says he or she will rule "later," make sure that he or she does so.
- Make an offer of proof if your evidence is wrongly excluded.
- Case Note: In *State v. Canady*, 355 N.C. 242 (2002), the trial attorneys preserved a number of statutory and constitutional errors. While the individual errors may not have warranted a new trial, the N.C. Supreme Court held that, when "taken as a whole," the cumulative preserved errors "deprived defendant of his due process right to a fair trial." *Id.* at 254. The Court's opinion in *Canady* demonstrates the benefit of lodging timely, specific, and frequent objections.

For a further discussion of how preserving the record not only protects a later appeal but also supports the defense at trial, see Ira Mickenberg, *Preserving the Record and Making Objections at Trial: A Win-Win Proposition for Client and Lawyer* (North Carolina Defender Trial School, July 2011), *available at* www.ncids.org/Defender%20Training/2011DefenderTrialSchool/PreservingRecord%20_Mickenberg.pdf.

III. PRETRIAL:

A. Short-Form Indictments:

- G.S. 15-144, 15-144.1, and 15-144.2 permit short-form indictments in first-degree murder, first-degree rape, and first-degree sexual offense cases. In all cases utilizing such a short-form indictment, as well as any cases where the indictment does not in fact set forth all elements of the offense, you should move to dismiss the indictment on the ground that it violates the Fifth, Sixth, and Fourteenth Amendments to the United States Constitution. *See Jones v. United States*, 526 U.S. 227 (1999), and *Apprendi v. New Jersey*, 530 U.S. 466 (2000). In capital cases, you should move to strike the death penalty from consideration because no aggravating factors are alleged in the indictment. *See Ring v. Arizona*, 536 U.S. 584 (2002) (aggravating factors are elements of a capital offense and must be found by the jury).
- Make a motion for a bill of particulars asking the State to identify the degrees of the offense (e.g., first-degree vs. second-degree) and the theories (e.g., premeditation and deliberation vs. felony murder). If the judge denies the motion, the State cannot then argue on appeal that the defense attorney waived any opportunity to obtain adequate notice of the charge.
- In numerous cases, the Supreme Court of North Carolina has rejected the argument that short-form first-degree murder indictments that do not allege premeditation and deliberation violate *Apprendi*. *See, e.g.*, *State v. Braxton*, 352 N.C. 158 (2000); *see also Allen v. Lee*, 366 F.3d 319 (4th Cir. 2004) (en banc) (finding N.C.'s use of the short-form indictment alleging the elements of "common law" murder to be sufficient to inform the defendant of the charge against him or her, thus satisfying the requirements of the Sixth and Fourteenth Amendments). The N.C. Supreme Court has also rejected a challenge to the failure of an indictment to allege aggravating factors in a capital case. *See State v. Hunt*, 357 N.C. 257 (2003). Regardless of the above decisions, you should still preserve the issue for federal review.
- For preservation purposes, you should also move to dismiss under article I, sections 22 and 23 of the N.C. Constitution. Argue two bases for the motion: (1) that the indictment does not give the trial court jurisdiction to try the defendant or to enter a judgment; and (2) that the indictment does not give the defendant adequate notice of the charge.

B. Miscellaneous:

- If your ex parte motion for expert assistance is denied, make sure you get the substance of your motion and the trial judge's order on the record.
- If you believe that your client's right to presence has been violated by an ex parte contact, find a way to have the record reflect that the contact occurred.

IV. GUILTY PLEAS:

- **The ONLY pretrial motion that you can preserve for appeal after a guilty plea is the denial of a motion to suppress.** G.S. 15A-979(b); *State v. Smith*, 193 N.C. App. 739, 742 (2008). **To preserve this error, you must notify the State and the trial court before entering the plea of your intention to appeal the denial of the motion, or the right to do so is waived by the guilty plea.** *State v. Tew*, 326 N.C. 732, 735 (1990); *State v. Brown*, 142 N.C. App. 491, 492 (2001). The best way to proceed is to advise the State during plea negotiations of your intent to appeal and put in writing a "Notice of Intent to Appeal" and file it with the court before entry of the plea. After the plea is entered, you must give notice of appeal from the judgment itself (not from the denial of the motion to suppress) in order to confer jurisdiction on the appellate courts. *State v. Miller*, 205 N.C. App. 724 (2010).

V. COMPLETE RECORDATION:

- In criminal cases, the trial judge must require the court reporter to record all proceedings *except* non-capital jury selection, opening and closing statements to the jury, and legal arguments of the attorneys. *See* G.S. 15A-1241(a).
- However, **you should move to have *everything* recorded under G.S. 15A-1241(b)!!** Upon motion, the court reporter "must" record all proceedings. You should also ensure that the court reporter is actually present and recording at all stages of trial.
- If a bench conference is not recorded, ask the trial judge to reproduce it for the record and ensure that all of your objections are in the record.
- If something "non-verbal" happens at trial, ask to have the record reflect what happened.
  - ✓ *e.g.*: In *State v. Golphin*, 352 N.C. 364, 452–54 (2000), the trial attorneys should have asked to have the record reflect that the prosecutor pointed a gun at the only African American juror during closing arguments.
  - ✓ *e.g.*: If your client is shackled without the necessary hearing and factual findings required by G.S. 15A-1031, and the jury saw the shackles, ask to have the record reflect that fact. Also describe for the record what type of restraint was being used.

VI. JURY SELECTION:

A. Preserving Your Right to Ask a Question on *Voir Dire*:

- *e.g.*: In a case involving an interracial crime, you want to ask prospective jurors questions about their views on interracial dating. However, the trial court sustains the State's objections to your questions.
- G.S. 15A-1212(9) provides that "[a] challenge for cause to an individual juror may be made by any party on the ground that the juror . . . [f]or any other cause is unable to

render a fair and impartial verdict." This section allows a statutory challenge for cause based on juror bias and, thus, should give a defendant a statutory right to explore possible sources of bias.

- In addition, you should try to constitutionalize your right to ask the question. *See, e.g.*, *Turner v. Murray*, 476 U.S. 28 (1986) (right to impartial jury under the Fifth, Sixth, and Fourteenth Amendments guarantees a capital defendant accused of interracial crime the right to question prospective jurors about racial bias; violation of right requires death sentence to be vacated).
- To fully preserve any error based on curtailed defense questioning during voir dire, you should submit a written motion listing the questions you want to ask and obtain a ruling on the record. You also need to exhaust your peremptory challenges. *See State v. Fullwood*, 343 N.C. 725, 734–35 (1996).

B. Preserving Your Denied Motion to Excuse for Cause:

- State clearly and completely the grounds for your challenge for cause. If the trial court denies your challenge, you *must* use a peremptory to excuse that juror unless you have already exhausted all peremptories.
- In addition, G.S. 15A-1214(h) and (i) require that you then: **(1) exhaust all peremptories; (2) renew your challenge for cause; and (3) have your renewed challenge denied.** *See State v. Cunningham*, 333 N.C. 744 (1993) (ordering a new trial where defendant satisfied requirements of G.S. 15A-1214(h)); *State v. Hightower*, 331 N.C. 636 (1992) (same). This procedure is mandatory and must be precisely followed or the error is waived on appeal. *State v. Garcell,* 363 N.C. 10 (2009).

C. *Batson* Error:

- **Establish the races of all prospective jurors for the record**: File a pretrial motion asking the trial court to ensure that the races of prospective jurors are recorded by (1) the judge inquiring and making findings for the record, or (2) the judge requiring the parties to stipulate to jurors' races as selection proceeds. If the court will not permit any other way, ask each juror to put his or her race on the record orally or by questionnaire.
- **If you use juror questionnaires, move to have them admitted into evidence and made part of the record.** If the questionnaires are left in your possession, save them for the appellate attorney.
- Object every time the prosecutor excuses a juror for even arguably racial reasons. *See State v. Smith*, 351 N.C. 251 (2000). If you are prepared to make a prima facie showing, ask the trial court for an opportunity to present evidence. The court is required to honor this request. *See State v. Green*, 324 N.C. 238 (1989).
- If the trial court declines to find a prima facie case, object. If the court asks the prosecutor to offer race-neutral reasons, ask for an opportunity to rebut the prosecutor's showing.
- Remember that *Batson* applies to gender-based challenges as well!

VII. Evidentiary Rulings:

- If you do not make timely and proper objections at trial, erroneous evidentiary rulings will only be reviewed for "plain error"—an extremely difficult standard to meet. On appeal, the defendant will have to show the error was so fundamental that it denied him a fair trial or had a probable impact on the jury's verdict. *See State v. Odom*, 307 N.C. 655, 660 (1983).

A. Objecting to the State's Evidence:

- Make timely objections. *See* G.S. 15A-1446(a); N.C. R. Evid. 103(a)(1); N.C. R. App. P. 10(a)(1). If the prosecutor asks a question that you think is improper or may elicit improper testimony, enter a quick *general* objection. If the trial court invites you to argue the objection or rules against you, you should follow up by stating the *basis* for your objection.
  - ✓ **A defendant's general objection to the State's evidence is ineffective unless there is *no* proper purpose for which the evidence is admissible.** *See State v. Moseley*, 338 N.C. 1, 32 (1994) (burden on defendant to show no proper purpose).
  - ✓ **If evidence is objectionable on more than one ground, *every* ground must be asserted at the trial level. Failure to assert a specific ground waives that ground on appeal.** *See State v. Moore*, 316 N.C. 328, 334 (1986); N.C. R. App. P. 10(a)(1).
- If evidence is admissible for a limited purpose, object to its use for all other improper purposes and request a limiting instruction. *See State v. Stager*, 329 N.C. 278, 309–10 (1991). Upon request, the trial court is required to restrict such evidence to its proper scope and to instruct the jury accordingly. *See* N.C. R. Evid. 105.
  - ✓ *e.g.*: If the trial court rules that hearsay statements are admissible for corroboration, ask the trial court to instruct the jury about the permissible uses of that evidence.
  - ✓ If there are portions of the statements that are non-corroborative, specify those portions and ask to have them excised.
  - ✓ If there are portions of the statements that are objectionable on other grounds (e.g., inadmissible "other crimes" evidence), specify those portions and ask to have them excised.
- **When appropriate, constitutionalize your objections.** If a defendant wishes to claim error on appeal under the state or federal constitution as well as statutory law, the defendant must have raised the constitutional claim when the error occurred at trial. *See State v. Rose*, 339 N.C. 172, 192 (1994); *State v. Skipper*, 337 N.C. 1, 56 (1994).
  - ✓ *e.g.*: If the trial court excludes your proffered evidence, do not object solely on state law relevance grounds. You should also cite your client's constitutional due process right to present evidence in his or her defense.
  - ✓ *e.g.*: If the State offers hearsay evidence, do not object solely on state law hearsay

grounds. You should also cite the Confrontation Clause.

- ❖ Object to any attempts by the prosecutor to admit substantive or impeachment evidence about your client's post-*Miranda* exercise of his or her constitutional rights to remain silent and have an attorney present. *See Doyle v. Ohio*, 426 U.S. 610 (1976).
  - ✓ *e.g.*: If the State offers police testimony that your client refused to talk and asked for his or her attorney, object.
  - ✓ *e.g.*: If the State tries to cross-examine your client about his or her failure to tell certain facts to the police, object.

B. Moving to Strike the State's Evidence:

- ❖ If the prosecutor's question was not objectionable (or if your objection to a question is overruled and it later becomes apparent that the testimony is inadmissible) but the witness's *answer* was improper in form or substance, you must make a timely motion to strike that answer. *See State v. Grace*, 287 N.C. 243 (1975); *State v. Marine*, 135 N.C. App. 279, 285 (1999).
- ❖ Similarly, if the trial judge sustains your objection but the witness answers anyway, you must make a timely motion to strike the answer. *See State v. Barton*, 335 N.C. 696, 709 (1994); *State v. McAbee*, 120 N.C. App. 674, 685 (1995).

C. Waiving Prior Objections:

- ❖ **If you make a motion in limine to exclude certain evidence but then fail to object when the evidence is actually offered and admitted at trial, the issue is *not* preserved for appeal.** *See State v. Hayes*, 350 N.C. 79, 80 (1999) (per curiam); *State v. Wynne*, 329 N.C. 507, 515–16 (1991). Similarly, if your suppression motion is denied, you must renew that motion or object to the evidence when it is introduced at trial to preserve the error. *See State v. Golphin*, 352 N.C. 364, 463 (2000). **You must do this even if the trial judge specifically says you don't have to.** *See State v. Goodman*, 149 N.C. App. 57, 66–67 (2002), *rev'd in part on other grounds*, 357 N.C. 43 (2003).
- ❖ **Do NOT rely on N.C. Evidence Rule 103(a)(2) to preserve the issue!!!** Although the N.C. General Assembly attempted to make things easier by amending Evidence Rule 103(a)(2) in 2003 to add a second sentence that states that once the trial court makes a definitive ruling admitting or excluding evidence, either at or before trial, there is no need to later renew the objection, do not rely on this rule. Rule 103(a)(2) has been held to be invalid because it conflicts with N.C. Appellate Rule 10(b)(1) [now, Appellate Rule 10(a)(1)], which has been consistently interpreted to provide that an evidentiary ruling on a pretrial motion is not sufficient to preserve the issue for appeal unless the defendant renews the objection during trial. *See State v. Oglesby*, 361 N.C. 550 (2007).
- ❖ **If you initially object but then allow the same or similar evidence to be admitted later without objection, the issue is not preserved for appeal.** *See State v. Jolly*, 332 N.C. 351, 361 (1992). Likewise, you waive appellate review if you fail to object at the time the testimony is first admitted, even if you object when the same or similar evidence is later admitted. *See State v. Davis*, 353 N.C. 1, 19 (2000). **Bottom line:** You must

object each and every time the evidence is admitted.

- One way to deal with this problem is to enter a standing line objection to the evidence when it is offered at trial. *See* G.S. 15A-1446(d)(9) & (d)(10); *see also* 1 KENNETH S. BROUN, BRANDIS & BROUN ON NORTH CAROLINA EVIDENCE § 22 (7th ed. 2011) (discussing waiver and the status of line objections in North Carolina).
    - ✓ To preserve a line objection, you must ask the trial court's permission to have a standing objection to a particular line of questions. *See, e.g.*, *State v. Crawford*, 344 N.C. 65, 76 (1996). In addition, you should clearly state your grounds for the standing objection. If the court denies your request, object to every question that is asked.
    - ✓ **You cannot make a line objection at the time you lose your motion to suppress or your motion in limine; you must object to the evidence at the time it is offered.** *See State v. Gray*, 137 N.C. App. 345, 348 (2000).
    - ✓ If there are additional grounds for objection to a specific question within that line, you must interpose an objection on the additional ground.
        - *e.g.*: If you have a standing line objection based on relevance and a specific question in that line calls for hearsay, you need to interpose an additional hearsay objection.

D. Making an Offer of Proof:

- N.C. Evidence Rule 103(a)(2) provides that "[e]rror may not be predicated upon a ruling which . . . excludes evidence unless . . . the substance of the evidence was made known to the court by offer or was apparent from the context within which questions were asked." G.S. 15A-1446(a) provides that "when evidence is excluded a record must be made . . . in order to assert upon appeal error in the exclusion of that evidence."
- Thus, **if the trial court sustains the prosecutor's objection and precludes you from presenting evidence, making an argument, or asking a question, you must make an offer of proof.** For further discussion of this topic, see 1 KENNETH S. BROUN, BRANDIS & BROUN ON NORTH CAROLINA EVIDENCE § 18 (7th ed. 2011).
- **You should make your offer of proof by actually filing the documentary exhibit or by eliciting testimony from the witness outside the presence of the jury.** It is not enough to rely on the context surrounding the question. *See State v. Williams*, 355 N.C. 501, 534 (2002). Summarizing what the witness would have said also may not be sufficient. *See State v. Long*, 113 N.C. App. 765, 768–69 (1994).
- If the court does not allow you to make an offer of proof, state: "Defendant wants the record to reflect that we have tried to make an offer of proof." Also state that the trial court's failure to allow you to do so violates the defendant's constitutional rights to confrontation, to present a defense, and, if applicable, to compulsory process. It is error for the court to prohibit you from making an offer of proof. *State v. Silva*, 304 N.C. 122, 134–36 (1981).
- If the court tells you to make your offer "later," the burden is on you to remember and to make sure that the offer is made.

VIII. Motions to Dismiss Based on Insufficient Evidence:

- Always move to dismiss all charges at the close of the State's case. *See* G.S. 15-173; G.S. 15A-1227.
- **Always renew your motion to dismiss all charges at the close of all the evidence (even if you only introduce exhibits and even if you do not wish to be heard on all charges)**. The defendant is barred from raising insufficiency of the evidence on appeal if you fail to do so. *See* N.C. R. App. P. 10(a)(3); *see also State v. Stocks*, 319 N.C. 437 (1987) (appellate rule abrogates the contrary provision in G.S. 15A-1446(d)(5)). Furthermore, the appellate courts will not review the error using the "plain error" standard of review if the motion is not renewed. *See State v. Freeman*, 164 N.C. App. 673 (2004) (plain error analysis only applies to jury instructions and evidentiary matters in criminal cases).
- **If your motion to dismiss is denied, assert that defendant's rights to due process under the Fifth and Fourteenth Amendments to the United States Constitution and under article I, section 19 of the North Carolina Constitution have been violated.**
- If you forget to renew your motion to dismiss at the close of all the evidence, you should move to dismiss based on the insufficiency of the evidence after the verdict and before entry of judgment. G.S. 15A-1227(a). You can also move to dismiss after the jury is discharged without a verdict and before the end of the session. *Id.* G.S. 15A-1414(b)(1)c. also allows a defendant to file a motion for appropriate relief after return of the verdict asserting that "[t]he evidence, at the close of all the evidence, was insufficient to justify submission of the case to the jury . . . ." This ground may be asserted even if the defendant made no prior motion to dismiss based on insufficient evidence. *Id.* In reviewing the defendant's contention under this statute, the judge will use the same "substantial evidence" test that would have been used by the judge if the motion to dismiss had been made during trial. *See State v. Acklin*, 71 N.C. App. 261 (1984).
- After a guilty verdict is rendered, you may file a motion for appropriate relief under G.S. 15A-1414(b)(2) asserting that "[t]he verdict is contrary to the weight of the evidence." This motion is appropriately made when the State's evidence is legally sufficient to go to the jury but the evidence favorable to the defendant (whether offered by the defendant or the State) has greater probative force than the evidence introduced against him or her. *See Roberts v. Hill*, 240 N.C. 373 (1954). This type of motion is addressed to the discretion of the trial court and is reviewable on appeal under an abuse of discretion standard. *See State v. Batts*, 303 N.C. 155 (1981).

IX. Closing Arguments:

- Always object to improper arguments. Failure to timely object to the prosecutor's argument constitutes a waiver of the alleged error. In the absence of an objection, appellate courts will review the prosecutor's argument to determine "whether it was so grossly improper that the trial court abused its discretion in failing to intervene *ex mero motu* to correct the error." *State v. Taylor*, 337 N.C. 597, 613 (1994) (citation omitted). This is a much more stringent standard of review than is applied to preserved errors so it is critically important for appellate purposes to timely object to improper statements made by the prosecutor and to request curative instructions if the objection is sustained.

- ❖ If your objection is sustained, immediately ask the judge to instruct the jury to disregard the improper statements. You should also carefully consider whether further remedy is necessary or whether it would serve to draw further negative attention to the comments. If you decide that the prejudice resulting from a prosecutor's improper argument was severe and in need of further remedy, you may ask the judge to:
  - admonish the prosecutor to refrain from that line of argument;
  - require the prosecutor to retract the improper argument;
  - repeat the curative instruction during the jury charge; or
  - grant a mistrial.

  See State v. Jones, 355 N.C. 117, 129 (2002) (explaining that it is incumbent on trial judge to vigilantly monitor closing arguments, "to intervene as warranted, to entertain objections, and to impose any remedies pertaining to those objections"); *Wilcox v. Glover Motors, Inc.*, 269 N.C. 473 (1967) (listing several methods by which a trial judge, in his or her discretion, may correct an improper argument).
- ❖ The filing of a motion in limine regarding closing arguments is not sufficient, by itself, to preserve closing argument error. N.C. Appellate Rule 10(a)(1) requires that you actually obtain a ruling on the motion from the trial judge. *See State v. Daniels*, 337 N.C. 243, 275–76 n.1 (1994). In addition, you should renew the motion or object during the prosecutor's closing argument.
- ❖ Object to any attempts by the prosecutor to argue in closing that your client's post-*Miranda* exercise of his or her constitutional rights to silence and counsel support an inference of guilt. *See Doyle v. Ohio*, 426 U.S. 610 (1976).
- ❖ The Supreme Court of North Carolina has displayed an increasing willingness to find reversible error due to improper closing arguments by prosecutors. Be vigilant to improper arguments and object!

X. JURY INSTRUCTIONS:

- ❖ Clearly and specifically object to erroneous jury instructions before the jury retires to deliberate. *See* N.C. R. APP. P. 10(a)(2); *see also State v. Bennett*, 308 N.C. 530, 535 (1983) (appellate rule abrogates the contrary provision in G.S. 15A-1231(d) and 15A-1446(d)(13)). If you do not object at trial, instructional errors will only be reviewed for plain error—an extremely difficult standard to meet. *See State v. Odom*, 307 N.C. 655, 660 (1983).
- ❖ **Submit all of your proposed jury instructions—especially special instructions—*in writing*.** *See* G.S. 1-181; G.S. 15A-1231(a). Requested instructions that are refused then become a part of the record on appeal by statute. G.S. 15A-1231(d). Then follow along on your copy as the judge instructs the jury. Judges very often make unintentional

mistakes while instructing the jury.

- **Submit your proposed jury instructions as early as possible so the judge will have a chance to review them and make a ruling.** Parties may submit proposed jury instructions at the close of the evidence or at an earlier time if directed by the judge. G.S. 15A-1231(a). Requests for special instructions must be submitted to the judge before the judge begins to give the jury charge. G.S. 1-181(b); *see also* N.C. GEN. R. PRAC. SUPER. & DIST. CT. 21 (providing that "[i]f special instructions are desired, they should be submitted in writing to the trial judge at or before the jury instruction conference"); *State v. Long*, 20 N.C. App. 91, 96 (1973) (holding that a request for special instruction is not timely if it is tendered after the jury retires to deliberate). However, the judge may, in his or her discretion, consider requests for special instructions regardless of the time they are made. G.S. 1-181(b).

XI. JURY DELIBERATIONS:

- Before consenting to the jury's request to take an exhibit into the jury room pursuant to G.S. 15A-1233(b), carefully consider how the jury may use the exhibit during its deliberations and decide whether it would be in the defendant's best interest to consent. If the trial judge, without obtaining consent from all parties, sends an exhibit to the jury room that you believe is harmful to the defendant's case, object on the record in order to ensure preservation of the issue on appeal.
- Make sure that the timing of jury deliberations is made a part of the record. Lengthy or troubled jury deliberations are an extremely helpful way to show prejudice on appeal.
- Make sure that all jury notes and other communications between the judge and jury are made a part of the record.

XII. SENTENCING:

- **Do not stipulate as a matter of course to the prior record level worksheet or to the defendant's prior convictions, especially if they are out-of-state convictions.** The burden is on the prosecution to prove that the defendant's prior convictions exist. G.S. 15A-1340.14(f). If they are out-of-state convictions, the State must prove they are substantially similar to North Carolina convictions or else they must be classified at the lowest punishment level (Class I for felonies, Class 3 for misdemeanors). G.S. 15A-1340.14(e). If you stipulate (or fail to object when asked or agree in any way), the State does not have to prove anything. *See State v. Alexander*, 359 N.C. 824 (2005). The issue will most likely be preserved if you "take no position" but the safer position is to object (even if you do not wish to be heard).
- Errors that occur during sentencing are supposed to be automatically preserved for review. *See* G.S. 15A-1446(d)(18); *State v. Canady*, 330 N.C. 398 (1991); *State v. McQueen*, 181 N.C. App. 417 (2007). However, the N.C. Court of Appeals has also repeatedly found that a defendant waives appellate review of a sentencing error when he

or she fails to object. *See, e.g.*, *State v. Black*, 197 N.C. App. 731 (2009) (right to appellate review of constitutional issue was waived because defendant failed to raise it at the sentencing hearing); *State v. Kimble*, 141 N.C. App. 144 (2000) (issue regarding sufficiency of the evidence to support the finding of aggravating factors was not properly before the court because defendant did not object during the sentencing hearing). To be safe, always object to errors that occur during the sentencing hearing.

- In response to the United States Supreme Court decision in *Blakely v. Washington*, 542 U.S. 296 (2004), the N.C. General Assembly substantially amended the Structured Sentencing Act. Session Law 2005-145, referred to as the *Blakely* bill, went into effect on June 30, 2005, and applies to prosecutions for all offenses committed on or after that date. It is prudent to preserve all *Blakely* issues just as you would preserve other issues during a trial. This includes motions to dismiss for failure to prove an aggravating factor beyond a reasonable doubt, objections to evidence, and objections to erroneous jury instructions.

- Present evidence to support mitigating factors if the evidence was not presented at trial. *E.g.*, Have your client's mom testify about his or her support system in the community. If the mitigating factors are supported by documentary evidence, ask that the documents be entered into evidence.

www.ingramcontent.com/pod-product-compliance
Lightning Source LLC
LaVergne TN
LVHW080010210926
848481LV00011B/2980